MICROSOFT
.NET
MY SERVICES
SPECIFICATION

Microsoft
.net

Based on Beta Code

PUBLISHED BY
Microsoft Press
A Division of Microsoft Corporation
One Microsoft Way
Redmond, Washington 98052-6399

Library of Congress Cataloging-in-Publication Data

    Microsoft® .NET My Services Specification / Microsoft Corporation.
        p. cm.
     Includes index.
     ISBN 0-7356-1556-X
     1. XML (Document markup language)   2. Microsoft software.   I. Microsoft
Corporation.

    QA76.76.H94 M53   2001
    005.7'2--dc21   2001044828

Printed and bound in the United States of America.

2 3 4 5 6 7 8 9   QWE   6 5 4 3 2 1

Distributed in Canada by Penguin Books Canada Limited.

A CIP catalogue record for this book is available from the British Library.

Microsoft Press books are available through booksellers and distributors worldwide. For further information about international editions, contact your local Microsoft Corporation office or contact Microsoft Press International directly at fax (425) 936-7329. Visit our Web site at www.microsoft.com/mspress. Send comments to *mspinput@microsoft.com*.

Acquisitions Editor: Juliana Aldous Atkinson
Project Editor: Rebecca McKay

Body Part No. X08-52432

Contents

Foreword

Why would developers be interested in Microsoft .NET My Services? First of all, .NET My Services was developed with the end user in mind. It was built so that the end user's information could be decoupled from applications, allowing them to have the benefit of that information wherever they go. Information provided through .NET My Services is available to the user anytime, anyplace, and from any device or application. .NET My Services turns the traditional information access model inside out. Instead of thinking of information as owned and managed by a single application, the information is owned and managed by the end user, and the end user is free to access the information from any .NET My Services-aware application. The end user is also free to easily share the information with any user or application he or she chooses to share it with. Think of how things work today… If I want to buy tickets to a baseball game, I go to the Seattle Mariners' Web site and view the game schedule in one window, and in another window, I view my calendar, mentally mapping my free days to days with games. Add in my family, and I have to mentally map the family calendar as well. With .NET My Services, all I do is tell the Mariners' Web site to overlay my calendar and my family's calendar with the team calendar. This is very simple to any developer capable of basic XML processing. Enabling this scenario in today's world is virtually impossible. All calendar information is locked up inside applications with no standard schema, no standard access or sharing mechanisms, no standard extensibility mechanism… In .NET My Services, the end user information is the first-class object. The information is accessed through a uniform set of XML Web services and is available to any application running on any platform and on any device. With .NET My Services, the ability for developers to innovate and create real end user value is immense. Developers are limited only by their imagination and creativity. As you read through this book, carefully look through the various XML fragments that represent an XML skeleton view of our service schemas. All of this information is available to you, assuming the end user you are providing value to is willing to share. Think outside the box. Read our schemas and understand that this is a baseline for you to build upon. Anywhere you see **{any}**, read this as a location where you can extend the schema with your own freeform, namespace-qualified XML. You can choose to publish your namespace and schema so that others can understand and build upon your schema additions, or you can choose to hold these additions as proprietary information that only your software can act upon.

.NET My Services is a great opportunity for all of you. Who is going to write the software for the Mariners' Web site to aggregate calendar information in a useful, end-user beneficial way? Who is going to write the software that provides advanced call management, with which your friends can interrupt you at mealtime, but your family cannot? Who is going to write the software that reads your e-mail to you on your car's navigation system? Who is going to extend this software to display your calendar, to-do list, grocery list, and more? .NET My Services is designed so that you can have fun doing your job and have fun pleasing your customers and providing them with value.

The value of the XMI (XML Message Interface) architectural specification contained in this book is to get developers to start appreciating how much information the .NET My Services services are designed to expose, how they can innovate on top of those services, and what the SOAP-based interfaces that interact with the information exposed by the services look like. The developers can take a look at the .NET contacts service and think about how to put it to use. Maybe one developer works on a shipping component for an e-commerce package. To him, the .NET contacts service or the .NET profile service provides him with easy access to address information. Maybe he gets creative and decides to sign the address as one that he trusts, and uses the .NET My Services {any} extension mechanism to put his mark on an address. Even if developers don't plan to write anything today, they can start planning future projects.

What can developers look forward to? If I were an independent developer that got a chance to use this stuff, I would be thinking: How can I add convenience and value to regular people's lives? If I develop software for the cell phone industry, maybe I would write the software that makes a user's .NET My Services-based address book available on her cell phone. Maybe I would extend this to let her block or allow calls from people in her address book. Maybe I would tie this to her calendar, or maybe that's a V2 feature. If I worked at a consumer electronics firm, maybe I would write the software to automatically record favorite TV shows that my user is going to miss because I noticed, from interacting with his .NET calendar service, that he is out of town this Thursday. Maybe I noticed that from his past viewing habits and his .NET favorite Web sites information that he is an F1 fan, so I will record the season for him even if he forgot to do it himself. The possibilities are endless, and they are there for you to exploit.

The beauty of the XMI reference is that it is as easy to use for object-oriented programmers as it is for XSL wizards. It is pretty easy to look at the XMI reference and see how these services could work for you.

Look to .NET My Services because of the opportunities it presents to you. You all are part of an amazing industry and you should be having fun and changing people's lives in a positive way every day you go to work. .NET My Services is designed for you. Get wild, innovate like crazy. .NET My Services is your opportunity to get in touch with your end user customers and deliver compelling value any time, any place, and from any device or application.

*Mark Lucovsky, Distinguished Engineer and Chief Software Architect of
.NET My Services*

C H A P T E R   1

Introducing .NET My Services

This book is a preview of Microsoft's new platform for building user-centric applications, Microsoft .NET My Services.[1] .NET My Services is implemented as a set of XML-based Web services that are accessed over the Internet. The bulk of this early book, which is intended for a developer audience, is the .NET My Services XML Messaging Interface (XMI) Architectural reference. The XMI is the XML services equivalent of an application programming interface (API). This book assumes you have working knowledge of Internet technologies such as Extensible Markup Language (XML) and Simple Object Access Protocol (SOAP). For more up-to-date and detailed information on the rapidly developing .NET My Services technologies, see the forthcoming book *Introduction to .NET My Services* from Microsoft Press, which will be in stores in the spring of 2002.

This introductory chapter is intended merely to give you a preliminary overview of .NET My Services and to help you start thinking about how you could use it. This chapter includes a brief explain of what .NET My Services is, why you would be interested in using it, and how to get on the road to .NET My Services implementation. The next chapter introduces the concepts and technologies behind the XMI reference, including a detailed discussion of HSDL to help the developer learn how to use the HSDL/XMI syntax against .NET My Services.

What is .NET My Services?

.NET My Services is a set of user-focused XML Web services offered by Microsoft to create new opportunities for the industry. It will allow you, the developer, to use the data-centered nature of XML Web services to build user-oriented Internet applications, including those used by Web sites, Web services, applications, and devices. If you know how to use XML to create SOAP messages to send over HTTP or DIME protocols, you can build XML Web services that take advantage of .NET My Services.

---

[1] Note and disclaimer: This information is based on the pre-beta information available at the time that this went to print. Details are subject to change as the technology develops.

The following graphic represents how .NET My Services extends user data by exposing various services provided by the .NET My Services service fabric.

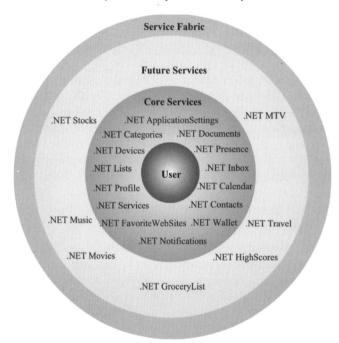

Because .NET My Services will expose your end user's data for use by the consuming applications and services, the following sections describe .NET My Services from the perspective of both the end user and the developer.

Perspectives on .NET My Services

.NET My Services was built with the end user in mind. Instead of end-user data being stored in many separate applications that cannot communicate with each other, which would limit the way end users can utilize their information, .NET My Services is data-centric and was purposefully designed that way so that end user data would not be gated by applications.

This provides a great opportunity for developers to build exciting services and applications on top of .NET My Services. Think about the possibilities at your disposal to provide your end users with new and exciting services that were previously impossible.

For the End User: What is .NET My Services?

.NET My Services will enable the end user to gain access to key information and receive alerts about important events anywhere, on any device, at any time. This technology will put users in total control of their data and make them more productive. .NET My Services connects Internet applications, devices, and services, and then transforms them into a user's personal network, a network that works on behalf of the user and with the user's permission. This is very powerful because it "connects the dots" of the user experience. No longer will a user be required to log on to one service to check e-mail; use another application to check a work calendar, and use yet another to check personal calendar entries; start a browser to check favorite Web sites; enter passwords, addresses, and other personal information in the fifty different consumer Web sites they visit; and so on. With .NET My Services, users don't have to worry about re-entering their data on many different devices, and they don't have to be concerned about which e-commerce site has their most current information.

.NET My Services gives the end user a "digital safe-deposit box" for placing their personal information. Microsoft makes sure that it is private, secure, and available. By default, only end users have access to their information, which they can access via mobile devices while online and via mobile-device synchronization for access while offline. Their lives are made easier because they have access to their inbox, calendar, contacts, and other key information. Additionally, the end users can choose, with a fine granularity of control, to grant access to pieces of their personal data to various entities, such as friends, family, groups they are affiliated with, and businesses. End users can change their address data in one place and then give their updated addresses to others by using their .NET My Services "digital safe-deposit box." They can make their calendars available to help coordinate their schedules with the schedules of others. End users will not have to re-enter their information multiple times in multiple places. They can rely on their .NET My Services "digital safe-deposit box" to save them time, help them harness the power of the Internet, and increase the benefits of owning and using mobile devices.

In addition to single end user scenarios, one of the strengths of .NET My Services is the natural extension of these services to groups and organizations. By assigning users to groups or organizations, you can effectively extend the .NET My Services services to include tasks such as broadcasting e-mail messages to an entire group or aggregating contact and calendar information for an organization. For instance, a soccer group could grant access to its calendar to make it easy for parents to enroll their children. They could notify parents of important events that require immediate attention, and they could receive e-mail in the soccer group's inbox. Similarly, corporations could use .NET My Services to better serve their customers and to coordinate with their partners.

The following graphic represents how .NET My Services provides access to user-centric services from mobile devices using XML, SOAP and Microsoft .NET Passport authentication.

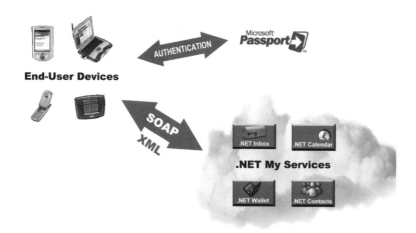

Unlike architectures of the past, .NET My Services has been developed to be as user-centric as possible. This means that the focus is on user data, not on specific applications, platforms, or devices. .NET My Services will deliver user data by using XML Web services, and it will leave the interpretation and rendering of tasks to the platform-specific and device-specific consuming applications. As part of this user focus, .NET My Services will employ the strong security and privacy provided by the .NET Passport service. .NET My Services will also require end users to explicitly grant permissions for access to their data before the data can be used by any client application using XML Web services.

Core Services

The .NET My Services services are designed around the specific needs of the end user. To meet those needs, the following core services will be included with .NET My Services for the beta release:

- **.NET presence service**—Contains the user's electronic presence information to establish where the user wants to receive alerts. For example, users can set their presence to Online/Offline/Busy/Away, On-Phone/Off-Phone, and so on.
- **.NET services service**—Keeps track of the services that a user has signed up for.
- **.NET notifications service**—Allows applications, Web sites, and XML Web services to send a notification about an important event to a person on any device, anytime, anywhere.

- **.NET calendar service**—Stores all of a user's calendar information in one place so that work, family, and personal information can be accessed by the user from any device at any time. The user can choose to share part or all of their calendar with others—for instance, a spouse might have full access, a boss might have access to work meeting information, and a ticket-purchasing site might only have access to the user's free/busy data so that it knows if the user would be interested in purchasing tickets for certain dates and times.

- **.NET contacts service**—Similar to the well-known buddy list, lets users store contact information from their personal and professional lives and enables them to access that information whenever and wherever they like. They can also share this information. For example, if parents are going out of town, they might share their emergency contact information with the caretaker for the length of time that they will be away.

- **.NET inbox service**—Gives users access to their e-mail from any device. This means that users can check e-mail from Microsoft Hotmail or other e-mail services on any computer or device from which they sign in to .NET My Services.

- **.NET documents service**—Provides users with secure storage for personal and professional documents and enables them to access those files from any computer or device.

- **.NET wallet service**—Allows the user to store information used for purchasing items online. One advantage of this service is that it frees the user from the tiresome task of re-entering credit card and shipping information every time such data is required. By default, this information is only accessible to the end user. If the end user wants to make a purchase, he or she can identify a credit card, a ship to address, and a bill to address and .NET My Services will send just that information to the e-commerce Web site, saving the end user from having to enter the information manually.

- **.NET application settings service**—Stores user information, such as toolbars, icons, and screensavers, so that any device the user signs in to automatically adjusts itself to those settings.

- **.NET profile service**—Allows the user to store personal information such as addresses, birthdays, and so on.

- **.NET favorite web sites service**—Gives users access to their favorite Web sites from any of their devices and from any application or browser.

- **.NET devices service**—Allows users to set up the devices (including PDAs, pagers, or cellular phones) on which they want to be contacted or use to access their .NET My Services information. Device characteristics could be set here—for example, the screen dimensions of a handheld PDA or bandwidth limitations.

- **.NET lists service**—Allows users to store any kind of list they want, for instance, grocery lists, wish lists, or to do lists.

- **.NET categories service**—Contains a standardized list of categories that are available across all of the user's services. Categories are used to group data documents together. The user could group contacts to form a buddy list or group calendar events to reflect a holiday.

As with any beta release, this list of services is subject to change, and Microsoft is likely to extend the available services in the future.

For the Developer: What is .NET My Services?

From the developer's perspective, .NET My Services is a set of XML Web services, accessed by sending and receiving SOAP messages sent though the HTTP or DIME protocols and using the .NET Passport system for authentication. XML Web services are all about allowing applications to share data. Prior to XML Web services, transferring data between applications required writing custom code to handle incoming data streams of various formats on varying platforms. In contrast, XML Web services can be implemented on any platform that adheres to public standards organizations, such as the World Wide Web Consortium (W3C).

But how exactly does it work? .NET My Services consists of three things:

- Authentication, which will be provided by .NET Passport when .NET My Services goes live in 2002
- SOAP, the communication protocol
- XML, following the rules and schemas set out in the XMI Reference, which provides the data formatting and organization information

Authentication

Authentication for the .NET My Services services will be provided by .NET Passport. This Microsoft service will implement the Kerberos-distributed security protocol for the .NET My Services services. Kerberos is a proven industry standard security protocol that is used by the Microsoft Windows 2000 and Microsoft Windows XP operating systems for user authentication. In the simplest sense, Kerberos is responsible for authenticating client requests based on centralized security information and distributing tickets, which are temporary encryption keys that clients use to access specific services.

The following list explains how .NET My Services authenticates users:

1. The user clicks the .NET Passport sign-in link, which is displayed on a Web page of a Passport-participating Web site or on the user interface (UI) of a client application.
2. The user then enters his or her .NET Passport sign-in name and password.
3. This sign-in process initiates a request from the client application or Web site to .NET Passport for a ticket-granting-ticket (TGT).
4. Once .NET Passport verifies the user's credentials, it grants the TGT, indicating that the user has successfully signed in. This TGT can be cached for later access to the service, as specified by security constraints.
5. The client or Web site then presents the TGT back to .NET Passport, which is now acting as the ticket granting server (TGS), and requests a session ticket for the .NET My Services service.

6. .NET Passport uses the TGT to authenticate the client and to verify that the ticket has not expired. .NET Passport then returns a session ticket to the requested .NET My Services service along with a session key. The session key is used for encryption between the client and the service that the client is accessing. All user data is encrypted with this key for greater protection.

7. The client or Web site presents this session ticket to the .NET My Services service, which verifies it and then grants access to the service at a level appropriate for that particular user.

SOAP

This new Internet protocol known as SOAP is an XML-based protocol that drives the .NET My Services XML Web services. A SOAP message is comprised of:

- An envelope that defines a framework for describing what is in the message and how to process it
- A set of rules for how to handle different data types
- A convention for representing remote procedure calls and responses

By using XML Web services implemented by SOAP, not only can applications share data, but they can also invoke the methods and properties of other remote applications without any knowledge of the other application's architecture. This enables applications to communicate directly, without the need for custom binaries, run-time libraries, or other platform-specific information that has plagued cross-platform data transfer in the past. .NET My Services uses SOAP messages to access the services by means of the XMI.

XML Using the XMI

At the core of .NET My Services is the XML, a plain text markup language based on Standard Generalized Markup Language (SGML). The beauty of XML is that it is a self-describing, data-centric format. This means that all of the information that an application needs to utilize the data in an XML document is supplied by the XML. As a result, an XML data stream can be easily interpreted and rendered appropriately, regardless of the specific client device that is gaining access to the information. For example, when an incoming XML document contains data for an e-mail message, that XML can be parsed, rendered, and formatted either for display as an HTML page or for a handheld device, such as a personal digital assistant (PDA) or cellular phone. Also, because of the nature of XML, XML-based Web services are easily transmitted through firewalls using HTTP and DIME protocols.

.NET My Services uses elements of the XMI bound to a .NET Passport Unique ID (PUID)—a number used for identification of a user or group of users. XMI elements are easy to access because the architecture is centered on XML documents, facilitating easy data communication and manipulation. All the services can be accessed by sending SOAP messages containing the XML data through the HTTP or DIME protocols.

Example .NET My Services Message

To illustrate how you will use a SOAP message to access .NET My Services, the following is example code from a SOAP packet that contains the request to return user data from the .NET profile service.

```xml
<?xml version='1.0'?>
<s:Envelope xmlns:s="http://schemas.xmlsoap.org/soap/envelope/"
            xmlns:x="http://schemas.xmlsoap.org/rp"
            xmlns:h="http://schemas.microsoft.com/hs/2001/10/core"
            xmlns:ss="http://schemas.xmlsoap.org/soap/security/2000-12">

<s:Header>
    <x:path>
        <x:action>http://schemas.microsoft.com/hs/2001/10/core#request</x:action>
<x:rev><x:via /></x:rev>
        <x:to>http://species8472</x:to>
        <x:id>35b4474a-a7d9-11d5-bf0e-00b0d0ccc121</x:id>
    </x:path>
    <ss:licenses>
        <h:identity mustUnderstand="1">
            <h:kerberos>1</h:kerberos>
        </h:identity>
    </ss:licenses>
    <h:request mustUnderstand="1" service="myServices" document="content"
method="query" genResponse="always">
        <h:key instance="0" cluster="0" puid="3066" />
    </h:request>
</s:Header>
<s:Body>
<queryRequest xmlns:mp = "http://schemas.microsoft.com/hs/2001/10/myProfile"
    xmlns:ms = "http://schemas.microsoft.com/hs/2001/10/myServices">
<xpQuery opId="1" select="/ms:myServices/ms:service
                [@name='myProfile']"/>
    </queryRequest>
</s:Body>
</s:Envelope>
```

This sample SOAP packet contains:

- Soap envelope encoding information
- Header information detailing the requested service and passing the Passport PUID
- Body element containing the .NET My Services **queryRequest** call to the **.NET profile** service

The queryRequest call in the previous example (in bold) is essentially a select of the root /*myProfile* against the *myProfile* service document. This will return all of the child elements of the *myProfile* document, or in essence, the user's entire profile.

The following diagram illustrates how a client application gains access to a .NET My Services service.

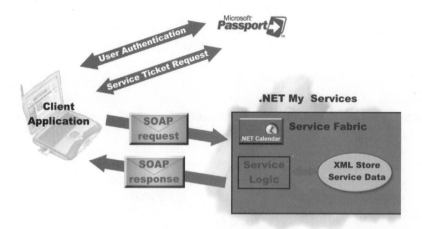

A Quick Discussion of the Service Fabric

If you have looked at a few white papers and graphics about .NET My Services, you keep coming across references to the .NET My Services service fabric. Just what does this refer to? The service fabric refers to the infrastructure of the .NET My Services services—the common way they are built and the common set of interfaces for them. The next chapter will have a more in depth discussion of the service fabric.

There are also some real value-adds that the flexibility of .NET My Services provides. The .NET My Services schemas that describe the .NET My Services services are often extendable, meaning there are places that you can extend the schema if you are willing to create your own namespace and schema. Another huge bonus is the fact that the XMI that you will read later in this book is fairly easy to read and understand for developers, whether they are experts in object-oriented programming or Web wizards with years of XSL experience. This is not some obscure technology that only the elite can read and understand. Developers will be limited only by their imaginations and creativity.

Can .NET My Services Live Up to Its Own Hype?

Okay—I know you are dying to ask—does .NET My Services live up to all the promises you've heard? Will it really be accessible from any device or platform? Can Microsoft keep the user data secure? What about privacy concerns? What about availability?

Open Access

Can you really use any language to access .NET My Services services? Yes. The services are accessed using SOAP and XML, as well as other protocols, such as HTTP and DIME. Here is a quick picture of how you will interact with .NET My Services:

- You can use a socket connection, a formulated SOAP message, and the ability to understand the data that is in the returned SOAP message.
- You do not need to be running a Windows operating system to access .NET My Services—you can use a Macintosh, a UNIX or Linux system, a handheld device, or even a cellular phone.

Security

Microsoft has pledged to use state-of-the-art security technologies because one of the main services it provides with .NET My Services is the idea of a "digital safe-deposit box" for user data. Microsoft knows that it needs to do the utmost to keep this data secure. The database servers that will store this data will not be accessible from the Internet or by anyone within Microsoft except certified personnel. Sensitive data will of course be encrypted using the most sophisticated and tested encryption technology available, both in the database and on any backup drives.

.NET My Services uses XML encryption standards and Microsoft has the ability to alter the encryption algorithms and the scope of the encryption so they are fairly flexible.

Privacy

As an industry-wide leader in privacy protection, Microsoft has promised that it will make no secondary use of any .NET My Services data. This means Microsoft will not mine, sell, rent, or publish this data in any way. Users will control who has access to their information; Microsoft will only have access to data if the user gives permission to one of our Microsoft MSN Web properties. Even then, users can choose to share only some of their data with the MSN site and keep the rest of their data private within their .NET My Services "digital safe-deposit box."

Microsoft will continue to adhere to its documented Fair Information Practices[2] that are based on the principles of notice, choice, access, security, and enforcement. In addition, Safe Harbor, a controlling body of the European Union, will be auditing Microsoft on a regular basis to ensure that it is following the strictest privacy processes.

In some ways, .NET My Services is the most privacy-enhancing Web system available. What other system allows users to give or deny access to their information to specific Web sites or Internet users? The fact that .NET My Services is user-centric and allows the user to turn on and off access to personal data according to how much the user trusts that site or person is truly unique.

---

2 Microsoft's privacy policy is available online at http://www.microsoft.com/MISC/privacy.htm.

So, Will All Our Users' Data Belong to Microsoft?

No. .NET My Services has been built so that the user is the only one who can give access to their data to others. The data is stored in a person's "digital safe-deposit box." This technology is like a bank that provides its customers with safe-deposit boxes: If the bank were stealing from its customers' boxes, would the customers continue to use that bank's services? Of course not.

This business simply does not work if the privacy and security of those "digital safe-deposit boxes" cannot be guaranteed. Microsoft will take all measures available to ensure that no one, inside or outside of Microsoft, gains illegal or inappropriate access to its customers' data.

In addition, Microsoft plans to allow trusted third parties to host the .NET My Services services so that users will have a choice of where their data is stored. From the beginning, Microsoft decided that although it is the one who rolls out the Web services, it will partner with other companies with different customer segments in all kinds of industries to help host the services. As Mark Lucovsky, Distinguished Engineer and Chief Software Architect of .NET My Services, says, "We [Microsoft] have no desire to be the big disk drive in the sky."

Stability

Microsoft has been making great strides in operation excellence in the last year. Microsoft's first XML Web service, .NET Passport, has had a history of high availability. Microsoft realizes that the availability of .NET My Services is a key success factor for Microsoft and its partners and is committed to doing the work and making the necessary investments in this area.

Will Running .NET My Services Require Managed Code?

.NET My Services does not require any managed code to access services. As long as you have access to a sockets library and can grab a Kerberos library from somewhere, you can play (in any language). Microsoft is also working hard to support the Microsoft Visual Studio .NET users who use managed code so that they can make calling .NET My Services services easier for developers.

Why Should I Care About .NET My Services? What's In It for Me?

If you don't immediately see how this set of services can benefit you, think about this: How much does your company spend on keeping track of user data? On authentication of users? How much trouble did you have building an in-house system secure and stable enough to handle your user capacity? And can users access their data on any device, anywhere?

Another question: How many times have you asked yourself, "How do we make purchasing something from our site easier for our users? How do we lower the 'abandonment' rate caused by people getting frustrated with registering over and over again or updating their address and credit card information yet another time?"

Scenarios and Business Model

So you think it sounds great. Now you want to see an example of how .NET My Services would work in the real world for an end-user, a developer, and a business.

Sample Scenario: Jane Gets Concert Tickets

Now let's look at a fairly simple e-commerce scenario of Jane buying concert tickets using the .NET notifications service, .NET wallet service, .NET calendar service, .NET music service,[3] and .NET My Services services. We will walk through the scenario from the perspective of the end user, the developer, and the business.

End User Perspective

In this scenario, Jane is sitting at her computer doing homework. She has signed in to .NET Passport. She gets an alert from the Web site of a local concert venue. Jane had previously granted this site access to her music preferences using her .NET music service, and now the site is using her .NET notifications service to invite her to buy tickets for a concert featuring one of her favorite artists. Because she asked their system to alert her when the tickets for her favorite artists went on sale, she gets the first chance to buy those tickets. Jane calls up her .NET wallet service to automatically send the necessary information to the Web site to purchase the tickets. Based on the data stored in her .NET wallet service, she does not have to enter any additional credit card information. After the transaction, the site enters the date of the event into Jane's online calendar using the .NET calendar service so that she will not forget to go.

Developer Perspective

From a developer's point of view, let's walk through the previous transaction step-by-step at a conceptual level.

---

[3] The .NET music service does not exist at this time and will not be included in the .NET My Services core services; however, it is a possible future service that would have great value to the end user.

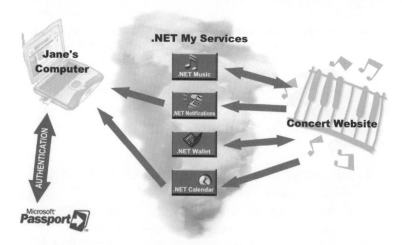

1. **.NET Passport authentication.** At some point, Jane logs on to .NET Passport by supplying her sign-in name and password. .NET Passport returns Jane's uniquely encrypted PUID. This TGT can now be used to request .NET Passport authentication to .NET My Services services.

2. **Retrieving music preferences.** When Jane previously visited the concert site, she gave authorization for the site to both access her music preferences using the .NET music service and to send her notifications of upcoming events by using the .NET notifications service. After being granted authorization, the site sent a SOAP message requesting that the service return a SOAP message containing all of Jane's music entries. The site then loaded this information into its database.

3. **Notification of ticket sale**. At some point in time, an event is scheduled at the concert site server that sends a SOAP message containing the information regarding the ticket sale to Jane's .NET notifications service. Upon receiving the message, the .NET notifications service sends a SOAP message containing the alert, along with additional information about the sale to Jane's client application.

4. **Purchasing the tickets.** Jane responds affirmatively to buying the tickets, so the site sends a SOAP message to her .NET wallet service requesting an authorization for billing Jane's credit card. With Jane's permission, her .NET wallet service sends the encrypted data to the site for payment.

5. **Updating Jane's calendar.** After receiving payment for the tickets, the site sends a SOAP message to Jane's .NET calendar service to update her calendar with the date and time of the concert.

Business Perspective

In the end user scenario presented above, the key .NET My Services services for businesses were the .NET wallet service and the .NET notifications service. The business value of these services is discussed in the following section:

.NET wallet service

This service allows users to make online purchases using personal information stored securely in .NET My Services.

The following lists some of the key benefits of this service:

- **Increase revenues**—With the .NET wallet service, it was easy and painless for Jane to purchase the set of tickets to the concert.
- **Reduce abandoned shopping carts**—With the .NET wallet service, Jane didn't have to re-enter all of her sensitive credit card information. This leads to a more secure transaction that is easier to use. Users get frustrated re-entering their information over and over again, and the .NET wallet service makes the transaction quick and easy for the buyer.
- **Supply the freshest data available**—Because .NET My Services provides users with centralized data storage for personal information, it is more likely to be kept current than if users have to try and maintain a separate profile on every Web site. So if a user changes a shipping address, they will be sure to update the data in .NET My Services first, and you won't accidentally ship the purchase to an old address.

.NET notifications service

This service allows you to notify your users of important events, if, for example, the user has been outbid on an online auction, gone over his or her credit card or checking account limit, or if the user's flight has been delayed. Because users can configure the device on which they receive these notifications, you can be sure that you can reach your end users in the best way possible—be it by cellular phone, by pager, or on their work or home computers. In this case, the notification of the concert tickets going on sale was a key component in Jane's purchase.

Microsoft Business Model for .NET My Services[4]

The .NET My Services business model will be in line with the new .NET strategy in that it will be mostly end user subscription based, service-oriented, and user-centric. In general, Microsoft does not view .NET My Services developers and service operators— a service operator being any company that runs a Web site, Internet service, wireless service, or other application that uses the .NET My Services services—as the primary means to drive revenue or profits. Several Microsoft product divisions will create targeted end user subscriptions enabled by .NET My Services. So the plan for now is as follows:

- End users will be charged subscription and/or premium fees for Web services and applications that utilize .NET My Services services.

- Some .NET My Services services may have usage-sensitive charges, for example, charging more for extra storage space for the .NET documents service.

- Service operators will be charged a reasonable, flat annual fee including a base-level SLA and service usage; additional charges may apply for premium SLAs and exceptional volume usage.

- .NET My Services code and test tools will be broadly available through Microsoft MSDN and other channels at no charge to encourage adoption. Developers might be assessed a nominal pre-production test environment access fee for each Web service or application that calls .NET My Services services.

Because at the time of this printing the business model was not completely finalized, the information here is subject to change. Microsoft plans to publish more specific business models at the Professional Developers Conference (PDC) in Los Angeles, California on October 22–26, 2001. Please go to www.microsoft.com/myservices for the latest business information about .NET My Services.

So, How Do I Start Using It? Can I Implement .NET My Services Today?

An early version of the .NET My Services Beta will be released at the October 2001 PDC in Los Angeles, California. .NET My Services will have a full beta version available to developers in the spring of 2002, utilizing .NET Passport authentication technology and a full working set of services. Availability of the .NET My Services production service will occur in 2002, as soon as the service is deemed ready to perform its functions with the reliability that its users demand.

---

4 The information contained in this document represents the current view of Microsoft Corporation on the issues discussed as of the date of publication. Because Microsoft must respond to changing market conditions, it should not be interpreted as a commitment on the part of Microsoft, and Microsoft cannot guarantee the accuracy of any information presented after the date of publication.

For more updated and complete information, please go to MSDN at http://www.msdn.microsoft.com and Microsoft's Web site http://www.microsoft.com/myservices. The information on those sites is continually updated as .NET My Services progresses.

The .NET My Services release at the PDC will not include live services; instead, it will be a version of "Microsoft® .NET Service Services-in-a-box" that you will be able to run on your local LAN. It will use early bits of a future version of .NET Passport for authentication and will include a subset of the .NET My Services services including: .NET services service, .NET profile service, .NET contacts service, .NET notifications service, .NET presence service, .NET calendar service, .NET wallet service, .NET devices service, .NET lists service, .NET categories service, and .NET favorite web sites service. The complete beta version in the spring of 2002 will include more live services and will utilize .NET Passport 3.0, and the version of ".NET My Services Services-in-a-box" will include all fourteen core services at that time.

So what can you do today? Is there any way to get your Web site ready for enabled .NET My Services services?

The Road to .NET My Services

The main authentication service that .NET My Services will use is available today and implementation is available today for .NET Passport. Implementing .NET Passport today is the best way for you and your company to get on track for .NET My Services.

Implementing the existing Microsoft .NET Alerts and the Microsoft MSN Messenger services, which will become the .NET notifications service, will also be useful because it will allow your users to send and receive alerts and see the benefits before .NET My Services becomes available.

.NET Passport

Right now, there are over 165 million .NET Passport accounts. .NET Passport allows you to offload the expense of building and using your own proprietary authentication mechanism and leave that part of the work to Microsoft. It allows customers "single sign in" convenience, meaning they have to put their user name and password in only one time to access all of the sites that use .NET Passport. By using secure socket layer (SSL) security today, and with .NET Passport 3.0 implementing the Kerberos security protocols discussed earlier, .NET Passport does the often-difficult authentication work for you..NET Passport performs up to two billion authentications a month. Currently, .NET Passport supports only PIN/password credentials, but eventually, it will be able to use credentials as sophisticated as smart cards and biometrics. Microsoft does not allow .NET Passport partners to gain access to user data without explicit user permission, Microsoft will not sell any user data, and Microsoft will ensure that all .NET Passport and .NET My Services partners adhere to strict privacy policy standards.

For more information, go to http://www.passport.com.

.NET Alerts

The .NET Alerts service provides a simple and effective way for content and service providers to send instant notifications to their users. Alerts are routed according to user preference and can be delivered to Windows desktops, mobile devices, and any e-mail address. For example, a subscriber can specify that alerts are to be delivered to the Microsoft Windows Messenger client when online and forwarded to a mobile device when away from the computer.

The following graphic shows how an incoming alert could be displayed on a graphics-capable device.

Microsoft .NET Alerts is an "opt-in" service—users subscribe only to the alerts they want. They never receive alerts they did not subscribe to and can unsubscribe at any time.

MSN Messenger and Windows Messenger

In addition to messaging, the MSN Messenger and Windows Messenger clients can be used for file transfer, video conferencing, and shared white boards. MSN Messenger and Windows Messenger are convenient and easy to access for developers.

The following screens show how an incoming alert is displayed and accessed by Windows Messenger.

Visual Studio .NET

Getting up to speed on Visual Studio .NET will put you a step ahead in terms of developing Web services against the .NET platform. As mentioned before, the .NET My Services team is working hard to make creating the .NET My Services Web services as easy as possible for developers who use Visual Studio .NET.

The Future of .NET My Services

As you can probably tell, the exciting thing about .NET My Services is that the future is wide open for developers who want to create exciting services and applications by using .NET My Services. Just think what your users could do with portable high scores to their favorite games or a portable music download center. Service opportunities might include things like .NET high scores service, .NET music service, .NET TV, .NET movies service, .NET grocery list service, and .NET portfolio service. The list is limited only by your imagination. Depending on your business goals and your customer needs, you can extend and build on .NET My Services services until you have created something your customers have never seen before and never knew they always wanted.

For the latest and most up-to-date information on .NET My Services, go to www.microsoft.com/net.

CHAPTER 2

Understanding the .NET Data Manipulation Language and XMI

Microsoft .NET My Services is a data service and as such provides access to user data as well as services surrounding that data, collectively known as the service fabric. In addition to providing XML-based access to your data, .NET My Services provides facilities for protecting and securing your information and for authenticating individuals and applications that want to gain access to your data. Beyond these features, the service fabric allows you to tailor how your .NET My Services messages are transported, by allowing for the creation of synchronization points. The service fabric also provides an infrastructure for you, as a developer, to extend your Web offerings to your users.

Included in the service fabric are the fundamental application programming interface (API) and transport features. To use .NET My Services, you have to speak XML and do so with SOAP. Fortunately, SOAP and XML are available just about everywhere. Although .NET My Services might use SOAP as a protocol, and .NET My Services might allow for Web service connectivity via WSDL and object proxies in Microsoft Visual Studio .NET, all .NET My Services interaction comes down to some simple XML commands. These commands, known as HSDL, drive interaction with the Web services. HSDL allows for queries, updates, inserts, and other actions as well as allowing their payloads to interact with .NET My Services services. HSDL is itself carried inside a SOAP envelope. In this chapter, we will examine .NET My Services's XML data manipulation language called HSDL, and we will look at the exposed features of the different XML-based service documents known as the XML Message Interface (XMI).

HSDL and XMI make up a large portion of a developer's interaction with .NET My Services. The XMI is a series of exposed XML-based interfaces that support service interaction for .NET My Services. HSDL is the name for the XML elements used while interacting with the service.

HSDL Basics

HSDL is the command interface for .NET My Services. Six core commands are used in the course of interaction with the various services, along with specific methods designed for common tasks in particular services. HSDL is primarily focused on transporting data in and out of .NET My Services service documents, but its design and syntax reflect two other underpinnings of .NET My Services: security and data structure.

Security

Each .NET My Services service supports the six primary commands but allows fine-tuning of the commands depending on who is gaining access to the service on your behalf. For example, you might want an airline to have access to your calendar but not to your list of contacts. Each service contains a wealth of attributes that you can use to tailor the visibility and privacy of your .NET My Services data. .NET My Services will enforce a role map against both users and applications that attempt to gain access to this data.

Security is a part of every .NET My Services request. From the SOAP headers that include Kerberos information to the service's inspection of the packet and enforcement of roles and ACLs, security plays a big part in how a service operates. In this chapter, however, we focus primarily on the nature of an HSDL message and not so much on its security information.

Service Structure

Apart from security, each .NET My Services service is made up of key XML nodes that hold more relevance than others. HSDL has established two main types of nodes. The first type is referred to as *blue* in the XMI Manual (included with the .NET My Services SDK) and represents primary data elements of any given .NET My Services service. Every immediate child of any service root element (such as *<myProfiles>* or *<myContacts>*) is a *blue*, or primary, element. The second type of XML node that HSDL is concerned with reflects .NET My Services's extensive utilization of XPath in HSDL. XPath is a part of every HSDL command because XPath is used to target a specific element or portion of a service document. XPath uses the concept of a predicate to DEFINITION. In HSDL, *red* nodes represent attributes and elements that you can use as part of an XPath predicate when selecting nodes in HSDL. In other words, consider the following service document fragment:

```
<myContacts>
   <contact id="some_guid">
```

Both *myContacts* and the contact element are *blue* types, as they are primary elements in the service definition. The *id* attribute is defined as a *red* element within the service, which opens the door for its use in an XPath statement as a predicate:

```
/myContacts/contact[id='some_guid']
```

The above XPath would select a specific contact element that contained a child *id* attribute with the value of *some_guid*.

In addition to these primary and secondary (*blue* and *red*) elements, some sections of service data cannot be directly manipulated with HSDL. For example:

```
<contact>
    <name>
        <firstName>Christopher</firstName>
        <middleName>A.</middleName>
        <lastName>Jones</lastName>
    </name>
</contact>
```

In the above contact entry within the .NET contacts service, you could not write an HSDL statement that attempts to select (again, via XPath syntax) */contact/name[middleName="A."]*. The service would not let you predicate against this generic element of the service document because it is neither the *blue* nor *red* type. As we dive into some specific HSDL commands, you will better understand the role that XPath plays.

HSDL Commands

Regardless of security or roles, .NET My Services offers six fundamental commands to interact with the various .NET My Services service documents.

insert

The insert command allows a .NET My Services client to insert a new primary element (*blue*) into the user's service document or to insert a secondary element or attribute (*red*) into a primary (*blue*) element. The SOAP response of an insert request indicates the node count of the request's select attribute, as well as the unique, .NET My Services-created IDs for each of the new nodes created.

update

The update command allows a client to combine a series of insert, delete, and replace requests into one bulk request. This allows the combination of actions to be treated as a single atomic command in terms of success or failure.

query

The query request command allows for basic data retrieval functionality. As with all the others, an XPath statement rides in a *select* attribute telling .NET My Services which XML nodes within the service document you wish to see.

replace

The replace message command allows the client to target a specific primary element within the service document and replace its contents with the contents supplied in the current replace request. The targeted element is replaced in its entirety.

delete

The delete request command is a simple element with a select attribute indicating (again with XPath) the targeted element to delete from the service document.

subscriptionResponse

The subscriptionResponse command is used to request a subscription to certain .NET My Services information and be notified when that information has changed.

XPath and HSDL

XPath plays a major role in the six .NET My Services commands discussed earlier. Since all .NET My Services data is maintained in XML, it is critical to understand exactly how you target specific information both for retrieval and for manipulation. All HSDL commands utilize a select attribute at some point in their structure. This select attribute targets an XML node or nodeset within the document. For example, consider the following document:

```
<myContacts>
 <contact visibility="public" changeNumber="1"
  id="7c77a388-934a-11d5-a972-00b0d0f1dea5">
  <name changeNumber="1"
   id="7c77a389-934a-11d5-a972-00b0d0f1dea5">
   <title>Mr.</title>
   <firstName>Christopher</firstName>
   <lastName>Jones</lastName>
  </name>
  <notes/>
  <emailAddress
   id="7c77a38a-934a-11d5-a972-00b0d0f1dea5" changeNumber="1">
   <address>chrisaj@microsoft.com</address>
  </emailAddress>
  <emailAddress
   id="9f6cb21d-934a-11d5-a972-00b0d0f1dea5" changeNumber="1">
   <address>ca_jones23@hotmail.com</address>
  </emailAddress>
```

```
  <workInformation
   id="7c77a38b-934a-11d5-a972-00b0d0f1dea5"
   changeNumber="1">
   <profession>Maybe</profession>
   <company>
    <name>Microsoft</name>
   </company>
   <jobTitle>Programmer/Writer</jobTitle>
  </workInformation>
 </contact>
</myContacts>
```

In this document, a single contact element contains information about an individual contact. If you wanted to retrieve this contact and all other contact elements within the service document, your HSDL insert request would appear as:

```
<queryRequest><xpQuery select="//contact"/></queryRequest>
```

This query request contains an XPath query (*xpQuery*) that selects all contact elements beneath the root node in standard XPath syntax (the // is XPath for select all). The response to this message would be a collection of contact elements and all of their content.

If you just wanted to select the e-mail addresses of this contact (or all of your contacts), you could tailor your query differently:

```
<queryRequest>
  <xpQuery select="//emailAddress"/>
</queryRequest>
```

This example selects all *emailAddress* elements within the service document. The response would be all of the *emailAddress* elements. The earlier document contains a contact with multiple e-mail addresses. Performing the preceding *queryRequest* against it would generate a response looking something like this:

```
<queryResponse>
 <xpQueryResponse status="success">
  <emailAddress
   id="7c77a38a-934a-11d5-a972-00b0d0f1dea5" changeNumber="1">
   <address>someone@microsoft.com</address>
  </emailAddress>
  <emailAddress
   id="9f6cb21d-934a-11d5-a972-00b0d0f1dea5" changeNumber="1">
   <address>ca_jones23@hotmail.com</address>
  </emailAddress>
 </xpQueryResponse>
</queryResponse>
```

You can use XPath predicates against secondary (*red*) elements and attributes to further tailor your queries. For example, if you wanted a contact with a specific name element, in this case containing a specific first name such as Christopher, you could use a predicate to pull the right contact element for you:

```
<queryRequest>
  <xpQuery select="/myContacts/contact[name/firstName='Christopher']"/>
</queryRequest>
```

The XPath selects a contact element but only a *contact* element with a child *name* element that contains a *firstName* element with the text "Christopher."

Actual HSDL Examples

To really understand HSDL, you have to use it. The last section shows how XPath is used in conjunction with a *queryRequest* to extract information. In this section, we'll look at some of the other HSDL commands. You can start by populating a service document using the hspost utility provided with the .NET My Services SDK. Within the *bin* directory of your SDK CD, there are two command line tools: *hsprov* and *hspost*. If you read the installation instructions and set up the server, you most likely have provisioned yourself for a particular service. If not, the syntax is quite simple:

```
C:\> hsprov -l http://yourServer -o username -s myProfile
```

Of course, you'll need to replace *yourServer* with the name of your machine running ".NET My Services Services-in-a-Box" and replace *username* with your log in name.

An insert Example

Once provisioned, you can begin inserting data into the service. To populate your profile with some bare minimum information, you can start with the following document fragment, substituting values for your own:

```
<myName visibility="public">
  <title>Mr.</title>
  <firstName>Christopher</firstName>
  <middleName>A.</middleName>
  <lastName>Jones</lastName>
</myName>
<picture visibility="public">
  <url>http://www.zeropath.com</url>
</picture>
```

To deliver this payload and insert it, you'll need to wrap it with a proper HSDL *insertRequest* command and select the appropriate place within the service document to insert the new content:

```
<insertRequest select="/myProfile">
 <myName visibility="public">
  <title>Mr.</title>
  <firstName>Christopher</firstName>
  <middleName>A.</middleName>
  <lastName>Jones</lastName>
 </myName>
 <picture visibility="public">
  <url>http://www.zeropath.com</url>
 </picture>
</insertRequest>
```

At this point, you can use hspost.exe to submit the data to .NET My Services and gauge the success of your action by the response that is returned. When you run hspost.exe, it will return the complete SOAP envelope returned by .NET My Services to you.

```
G:\bin\sdk\bin>hspost -d content -s myProfile -f insertProfEx.xml
<?xml version='1.0'?>
<s:Envelope xmlns:s="http://schemas.xmlsoap.org/soap/envelope/"
xmlns:h="http://schemas.microsoft.com/hs/2001/10/core">
<s:Header>
<m:path xmlns:m="http://schemas.xmlsoap.org/srp"
s:mustUnderstand="1"
s:actor="http://schemas.xmlsoap.org/soap/actor/next">
<m:action>http://schemas.microsoft.com/hs/2001/10/core#response</m:action>
<m:from>http://ozmatron</m:from>
<m:rev></m:rev>
<m:id>29e9cad4-9368-11d5-a972-00b0d0f1dea5</m:id>
<m:relatesTo>29dac581-9368-11d5-a2d1-00b0d0e9071d</m:relatesTo>
</m:path>
<h:response s:mustUnderstand="1"></h:response>
</s:Header>
<s:Body>
<responseBody>
<insertResponse status="success" selectedNodeCount="1"
newChangeNumber="450">
<newBlueId id="29e9cad2-9368-11d5-a972-00b0d0f1dea5"/>
<newBlueId id="29e9cad3-9368-11d5-a972-00b0d0f1dea5"/>
</insertResponse>
</responseBody>
</s:Body>
</s:Envelope>
```

The .NET My Services response shows the new primary elements that were created, specifically your *myName* element and your *picture* element. They have been given IDs and change numbers as well. Both items play an important role in synchronizing and caching. The IDs also give you the ability to insert duplicate elements into the service document. When a seemingly identical contact element is placed within *myContacts*, for example, perhaps content within a descendent element is different, it is given a unique ID to ensure that there is no confusion with another element.

A delete Example

The task of deleting a single .NET My Services element or collection of elements requires significantly less XML than inserting data does (for obvious reasons). A single *deleteRequest* element with an accompanying *select* attribute is all that is required to delete an XML node within a service document.

To delete a specific element, you would use a specific XPath expression coupled perhaps with an ID predicate:

```
<deleteRequest
select="/myProfile/picture[@id='29e9cad3-9368-11d5-a972-00b0d0f1dea5']"/>
```

This action would delete the picture element created in the insert example. The ID predicate is retrievable in the response of the *insertRequest*. The *insertRequest* response contained *newBlueId* elements that contained the ID value of the freshly created elements.

To delete your profile in its entirety, you can use a more generic XPath expression that will remove everything below the root node:

```
<deleteRequest select="/myProfile/*"/>
```

This *deleteRequest* would wipe out all the elements appearing beneath *myProfile*.

A replace Example

Replacing an element is a good choice when you are changing information within the document, such as your e-mail address or name. In the *myProfile* document I created earlier, I used *title*, *firstName*, *middleName*, and *lastName* elements. That's a little too formal for me, so I can replace the *myName* element with abbreviated content:

```
<replaceRequest
 select="/myProfile/myName[@id='63e63000-936e-11d5-a972-00b0d0f1dea5']">
  <myName visibility="public">
    <firstName>Chris</firstName>
    <lastName>Jones</lastName>
  </myName>
</replaceRequest>
```

Now the *myName* element is replaced with one that does not contain a *title* or *middleName* element. The *replaceRequest* XPath expression looks for a *myName* element with a specific ID. After deleting myProfile earlier and then recreating it, I was able to track the *newBlueId* used for the *myName* element. I used that ID here in my XPath to select and replace the correct *myName* element.

As you can see, many of the HSDL commands work in a similar fashion and they all depend on XPath. The XMI Manual that ships with the .NET My Services SDK provides a comprehensive reference on HSDL syntax.

HSDL and SOAP

In the last section, you used hspost.exe from the .NET My Services SDK to send your HSDL requests to the .NET My Services server. The server responded with a SOAP packet, which hspost.exe dumped to standard output for you to see. In this section, we'll look at the SOAP packet a little more closely.

A .NET My Services SOAP packet is a straightforward envelope that carries the HSDL payload (or response) in the SOAP envelope. .NET My Services makes extensive use of the SOAP header element, placing within it the elements and attributes relevant to security and the current transaction and requesting application. For example, consider the following HSDL *queryRequest*:

```
<queryRequest>
  <xpQuery select="/myProfile"/>
</queryRequest>
```

The SOAP packet generated by hspost.exe to send this queryRequest illustrated earlier in the chapter appears as the following:

```
<?xml version='1.0'?>
<s:Envelope xmlns:s="http://schemas.xmlsoap.org/soap/envelope/"
            xmlns:x="http://schemas.xmlsoap.org/rp"
            xmlns:h="http://schemas.microsoft.com/hs/2001/10/core"
            xmlns:ss="http://schemas.xmlsoap.org/soap/security/2000-12">

<s:Header>
    <x:path>
        <x:action>http://schemas.microsoft.com/hs/2001/10/core#request</x:action>
      <x:rev><x:via /></x:rev>
       <x:to>http://species8472</x:to>
       <x:id>34ef9bf1-a942-11d5-bf0e-00b0d0ccc121</x:id>
    </x:path>
    <ss:licenses>
        <h:identity mustUnderstand="1">
            <h:kerberos>1</h:kerberos>
```

(continued)

(continued)

```
        </h:identity>
    </ss:licenses>
    <h:request mustUnderstand="1" service="myServices" document="content"
method="query" genResponse="always">
        <h:key instance="0" cluster="0" puid="3066" />
    </h:request>
</s:Header>

<s:Body>
    <queryRequest
            xmlns:mp = "http://schemas.microsoft.com/hs/2001/10/myProfile"
            xmlns:ms = "http://schemas.microsoft.com/hs/2001/10/myServices">
            <xpQuery opId="1"
select="/ms:myServices/ms:service[@name='myProfile']"/>
        </queryRequest>
</s:Body>
</s:Envelope>
```

As you can see, the simple HSDL request is wrapped in a significant amount of SOAP. The SOAP header's *path* element contains information about the forward path of the message and may optionally contain information about the reverse path as well. While it is probably best to think in terms of a client device querying .NET My Services for its user's information, in production deployment, it is likely that any number of Web servers or applications may end up requesting .NET My Services on a user's behalf and may want fine grained control over the message pathway.

The SOAP header also contains an interesting *licenses* element. As of this writing, .NET My Services is not yet using Kerberos and Passport. The structure of this SOAP header is not likely to change too greatly, but the contents certainly will. This header will include the security information for any given .NET My Services SOAP packet.

The *request* element within the SOAP header contains several practical pieces of information related directly to the request at hand. The *service* attribute defines the particular service targeted. The *document* method indicates whether or not this request is intended for administrative purposes ("admin") or data-related purposes ("content"). The *method* attribute indicates the type of request being performed—the HSDL command. As of this writing, this corresponds to the first word of the request element. For example, a <queryRequest> requires a *method* attribute with the value "query". An <insertRequest> requires an "insert" *method*.

The SOAP body is probably the simplest aspect of a .NET My Services request, as that is where the HSDL resides. In this case, the *Body* element simply contains the request:

```
<s:Body>
  <queryRequest>
    <xpQuery opId="1"
     select="/myServices/service[@name='myProfile']"/>
  </queryRequest>
</s:Body>
```

As .NET My Services evolves, different APIs and run time services may help you avoid writing SOAP packets by hand. As of this writing, service integration with Visual Studio .NET is planned, allowing you to treat .NET My Services as any other Web service using Visual Studio, including the use of simple proxy objects. Likewise, a client run time is in development that will help the developer in securing Kerberos information, defining a service end point, and delivering the SOAP packet. Fundamentally, though, .NET My Services's philosophy is that if you can speak SOAP and can access a Kerberos library, you can talk to .NET My Services from any platform, in any language, and on any device.

.NET My Services Service Structure

Now that you have a greater understanding of how SOAP and HSDL interact with .NET My Services services, it may help to look more closely at a particular service.

In this section, we'll examine a brief portion of the .NET contacts service to understand what elements you can manipulate, which nodes are accessible via your XPath queries, and what elements are required of the .NET contacts service and a contact entry. When you come to understand the basics of how a service is constructed, the .NET My Services XMI Manual becomes an extremely valuable resource as you perform more complex service operations. For the walk-through in this section, we'll use the following abbreviated XML *contact* element that you might place in your .NET contacts service:

```
<myContacts >
    <contact visibility="...">
        <name visibility="...">
            <title></title>
            <firstName></firstName>
            <middleName></middleName>
            <lastName></lastName>
            <suffix></suffix>
            <fileAsName></fileAsName>
        </name>
        <address visibility="...">
            <officialAddressLine ></officialAddressLine>
```

(continued)

(continued)

```
        <internalAddressLine ></internalAddressLine>
        <primaryCity ></primaryCity>
        <secondaryCity ></secondaryCity>
        <subdivision ></subdivision>
        <postalCode></postalCode>
        <countryCode></countryCode>
    </address>
    <emailAddress visibility="...">
        <address></address>
        <friendlyName ></friendlyName>
    </emailAddress>
</contact>
</myContacts>
```

In this XML example, there are three primary elements (*blue*) within the particular unpopulated contact example. They are *name*, *address*, and *emailAddress*. With each of these elements, there are different requirements and options for predication in your XPath queries.

The name Element

For the *name* element, there are no required child elements. However, if present, you can use the elements *firstName*, *lastName*, and *fileAsName* (and their textual content) as predicates in your XPath queries. That is, if you have a contact fragment such as:

```
<contact>
  <name>
<firstName>Christopher</firstName>
</name>
</contact>
```

You can select this particular *contact* element using XPath:

```
<xpQuery select='/myProfile/contact[name/firstName="Christopher"]'/>
```

You select the *contact* element, but you use the *firstName* element as a predicate. In a .NET My Services service, not every XML node is addressable within an XPath query. That is, you may want to search your contacts by *middleName*, but .NET My Services will not allow you to create a predicate based on *middleName*.

The address Element

As for the *address* element, it is intended to represent a geographical address and not an electronic address (see *emailAddress* later). The *address* element also contains no required descendent elements. The *address* element allows for predication upon the *changeNumber* and *creator* attributes—both supplied by .NET My Services. In other words, you can't necessarily build an XPath query that selects *address* elements based on postal code. (Note: .NET My Services supports an extended set of XPath functionality detailed in the SDK documentation, including *reshapers*, which give you added support for sorting and ordering node sets.)

The emailAddress Element

The *emailAddress* element also allows you to predicate upon *changeNumber* and *creator*, but in addition, it allows you to predicate upon its child *address* element and *friendlyName* elements. If you had a contact fragment such as:

```
<contact>
  <emailAddress>
    <address>chrisaj@microsoft.com</address>
  </emailAddress>
</contact>
```

With the above XML, you could write an XPath query that selects a contact based on the e-mail address:

```
select="/myContacts/contact[emailAddress/address='chrisaj@microsoft.com']"
```

It's important to remember which element constitutes the selected one and which elements are part of the predicate. In this case, the contact element would be returned.

Service Specific Methods

In addition to the six fundamental commands supported by .NET My Services services, some services offer specific methods that are unique to their functionality. In this section, we'll examine a couple of these and understand the reason for their existence.

.NET calendar service

The .NET calendar service (which as of this writing is still in development) utilizes several service-specific methods to facilitate using the service. These methods are meant to reduce the amount of code that clients on any platform would need to write. For example, if you wanted to find days on someone's calendar when they were available, you would potentially have to query a great chunk of the XML and manipulate it accordingly to determine free days and busy days.

The *getFreeBusyDays* method allows you to query someone's calendar (provided you have been granted access by the user) for blocks of free time and busy time. For example, blocks of time may come back indicating things such as:

- Busy from 12pm to 3pm
- Free from 3pm to 6pm

Additional methods are in development, including:

- *getCalendarDays*—This method returns the calendar appointments and events between the supplied dates.
- *getQuickView*—This method is intended to communicate, within a given range of dates, the days that have more than one appointment and the days that have no appointments.
- *setCalendarAttachment*—This method allows you to store an attachment within the myCalendar service.
- *getCalendarAttachment*—This method allows you to retrieve an attachment that has previously been stored in the .NET calendar service.
- *meetingUpdate*—This method allows you to invite attendees to an event.

The .NET calendar service is still in development, and this is by no means a comprehensive list of its exposed methods. Additionally, many other .NET My Services services feature service-specific methods as well. These are detailed in the XMI Manual.

The XMI Manual

The XMI Manual is the definitive reference for HSDL, service schemas, and particular service-specific methods. A current snapshot of the XMI Manual makes up the rest of this book. When developing your applications with the .NET My Services SDK, you can refer to the XMI Manual to better understand the XML required within a particular service document or to learn how to fine tune your HSDL commands across all services.

This chapter is provided in this book in preliminary form. When published in the forthcoming title (Spring/Summer 2002), the maturity of .NET My Services will have increased and this chapter will contain more detailed information.

CHAPTER 3

Introduction

Microsoft .NET My Services is a set of XML Message Interfaces (XMI) delivered as part of the Microsoft .NET initiative.

.NET My Services is implemented as a set of Web services bound to a .NET Identity, called a Microsoft Passport Unique ID (PUID). Each service presents itself as a set of XML documents that can be manipulated using a set of standard methods and domain-specific methods. The effect is that each identity has tied to it a set of services that are partitioned along schema boundaries and across different identities. The XML document-centric architecture of .NET My Services is a unique model for manipulating and communicating service states. To programmers unaccustomed to XML and loose binding to data, this approach will feel very foreign. However, anyone familiar with XML processing, node selection, and node manipulations will find this model very natural to work with. In a world of XML Web services, and taking into account the services we are promoting through .NET My Services, we feel that by taking this XML document-centric approach and by encouraging loose binding to the data exposed by the services, we will enable a very exciting class of applications.

A .NET Identity is an identifier assigned to an individual, a group of individuals, or some form of organization or project. Using this identifier as a steering mechanism, .NET My Services services that are bound to that identity can be located and manipulated.

.NET My Services is designed to present these services using a uniform and consistent service and method within a service naming model, a uniform and consistent data access and manipulation model, and a uniform and consistent security authorization model.

.NET My Services is based upon open Internet standards. All services are accessed by means of SOAP messages containing an XML payload. All service input and output is expressed as XML document fragments. Each of these document fragments must conform to an XML schema document, the content is available from the interaction with the .NET My Services service endpoint.

Access to .NET My Services services is accomplished using SOAP messages formatted with .NET My Services-specific header and body content. All .NET My Services services will accept these messages by means of an HTTP POST operation, and all services will generate a response by "piggy-backing" on the HTTP Response, or by issuing an HTTP POST to a .NET My Services response-processing endpoint. In addition to HTTP as the message transfer protocol, .NET My Services services will support raw SOAP over TCP, a transfer protocol known as Direct Internet Message Encapsulation (DIME).

Because .NET My Services services are naturally accessed by protocol, Microsoft-implemented client-side binding code, object models, API layers, or equivalents are optional. Microsoft is actively designing and building .NET My Services binding mechanisms, and is releasing .NET My Services with full support for WSDL. It is not mandatory that applications wishing to interact with .NET My Services make use of the Microsoft bindings, and these bindings are not part of this document. This document is described in terms of the messages that flow between requestors of a particular service and the service endpoints. In order to interact with .NET My Services, a service must simply be able to format a .NET My Services message and deliver that message to a .NET My Services service endpoint. In order to format a message, the client must be able to manipulate XML document fragments, and perform some simple, public-domain cryptographic operations on portions of the message.

Each .NET My Services service presents three logical XML documents. These documents are addressable using the .NET My Services message headers. These documents are manipulated using standard .NET My Services methods. In addition to these common methods, each service may include additional domain-specific methods. For example, the .NET calendar service might choose to expose a "getFreeBusy" method rather than expose free/busy as writeable fragments in the content document.

The .NET My Services documents are:

content
   This is the main, service-specific document. The schema for this document is a function of the class of service. In the case of the .NET calendar service, the content document presents data in the shape dictated by the .NET My Services .NET calendar service schema. In the case of the .NET favorite web sites service, the content document presents data in the shape dictated by the .NET My Services .NET favorite web sites service schema.

roleList
   This document contains roleList information, information that governs access to the data, and methods exported by the service. It is manipulated using the .NET My Services standard data manipulation mechanisms. The shape of this document is governed by the .NET My Services core schema's roleListType XML data type.

system

This document contains service-specific system data like the roleMap, schemMap, messageMap, version information, and service-specific global data. The document is manipulated using the standard .NET My Services data manipulation mechanism, but modifications are limited in a way that allows only the service itself to modify the document. The shape of this document is governed by the system document schema for the service in question (each service extends a base system document type with service- specific information).

The rest of this XMI Manual is organized into major sections covering .NET My Services messaging, data manipulation, security, error reporting, and an architectural overview. In addition to these infrastructure components, this manual includes a chapter for each .NET My Services service. This document is not intended to act as a complete programming guide. Its purpose is more as a working design document used to communicate the .NET My Services model and service schemas.

CHAPTER 4

provisioning/Introduction

Before a user can start using a Microsoft .NET My Services service, the user must be provisioned for the service. The provisioning functionality of the admin API enables an application to provision a user for a particular service and also gives the application a chance to insert initial startup data.

The simplest form of provisioning is to simply add a user to a service. This action requires the provisioning application to create a document in the service database and another one in the related security database to give this user proper identification and a role to enable their to use of the service.

Similar to the creation of the accounts, if and when the user needs to be removed, these documents need to be removed from the related security and service data, databases. Removal is also accomplished using provisioning methods.

provisioning/createDocument Method

The "createDocument" method is designed to create a document for the user of the service that is called. The body of the message for this method contains one or more hsdl createDocumentRequest entries. Each hsdl:createDocumentRequest entry can point to a different document. Valid document values are:

- content
- acl

If the document type selected in the hsdl:createDocumentRequest element is the content document, then the contents of that element are validated using the schema for the service that this request is being made. The service name is in the adminRequest header. If the document type is acl document, then the contents of hsdl:createDocumentRequest element are validated against the security database schema.

provisioning/createDocumentRequest

This method is accessed using an adminRequest message, and in response may generate an adminResponse message or a SOAP Fault message. The following sample document fragments illustrate the structure and meaning of the elements and attributes in the request and response messages.

provisioning/Example/createDocumentRequest - single document

```
<hsadmin:createDocumentRequest>
    <hsdl:createDocumentRequest hsadmin:document="acl">
        <acl changeNumber="7" id="6334">


            <!--
            //
            // myGuys localGroup
            //
            -->
            <localGroup name="myGuys" changeNumber="7" id="567">
                <puid>puid-of:cisco</puid>
                <puid>puid-of:sean</puid>
            </localGroup>

            <localGroup name="myGals" changeNumber="4" id="863">
                <puid>puid-of:jen</puid>
                <puid>puid-of:stef</puid>
                <puid>puid-of:maddie</puid>
            </localGroup>

            <role name="owner" changeNumber="7" id="324">

                <!--
                //
                // This subject is a specific puid that must carry a credential
strength >= 4
                // and must be coming from a platform whose credential strength
is >= 8
                //
                -->
                <subject>
                    <userId credStrength="4" type="puid">puid-of:markl</userId>
                    <platformId credStrength="8"/>
                </subject>
```

```
            </role>

            <role name="friend" changeNumber="5" id="323">

                <!--
                //
                // This subject matches any id in the localGroup named myGuys
                // The subject is considered valid until 5/11/2001 at 11:15am pst
                //
                -->
                <subject>
                    <userId type="localGroup">myGuys</userId>
                    <expiresAt>2001-05-11T11:15:00-08:00</expiresAt>
                </subject>

            </role>
        </acl>
    </hsdl:createDocumentRequest>
</hsadmin:createDocumentRequest>
```

provisioning/Example/createDocumentRequest - multiple documents

```
<hsadmin:createDocumentRequest>
    <hsdl:createDocumentRequest hsadmin:document="acl">
        <acl changeNumber="9" id="6335">
            <role name="owner" changeNumber="7" id="324">
                <!--
                //
                // This subject is a specific puid that must carry a credential
strength >= 4
                // and must be coming from a platform whose credential strength
is >= 8
                //
                -->
                <subject>
                    <userId credStrength="4" type="puid">puid-of:markl</userId>
                    <platformId credStrength="8"/>
                </subject>
            </role>
        </acl>
    </hsdl:createDocumentRequest>
```

(continued)

(continued)

```
<hsdl:createDocumentRequest hsadmin:document="content">
    <myAddress>
        <!--
        //
        // You could have valid .NET address service data here to be
inserted...
        //
        -->
    </myAddress>
</hsdl:createDocumentRequest>
</hsadmin:createDocumentRequest>
```

CHAPTER 5

The .NET messages service/Introduction

As stated in the introduction, Microsoft .NET My Services is a set of services whose functionality is accessed by means of SOAP messages. A .NET My Services message always refers to a SOAP message carrying .NET My Services parameters and all methods within a service present themselves using a request/response message-exchange model. The .NET My Services request/response semantics are expressed directly within each .NET My Services message so that it is clear whether a .NET My Services message is a .NET My Services request or a .NET My Services response, regardless of how the message is exchanged. This allows .NET My Services to support asynchronous messaging easily, even when messages are being delivered on a request/response message transfer protocol like HTTP.

Decoupling the .NET My Services request/response model from the message-transfer mechanism opens up the possibility to transmit .NET My Services messages over a variety of protocols and delivery mechanisms, including HTTP, DIME, SMTP and others. The expectation is, however, that the majority of .NET My Services messages at least initially will be transferred over HTTP, which is the message-transfer protocol that all .NET My Services services must support.

Because asynchronous messaging in a request/response protocol is sometimes difficult for novices to program to, and is usually difficult to bind a higher level language to, .NET My Services easily supports HTTP where the request is carried inside of an HTTP POST, and the response is "piggy-backed" inside the corresponding HTTP response. However, it is important to note that .NET My Services can be used in many ways that may or may not involve HTTP at all.

In addition to the request/response semantics being expressed within each .NET My Services message, .NET My Services defines the notion of a message path that specifies how a message is intended to travel from the initial sender to the ultimate destination and whether there are intermediaries along the way.

The .NET My Services message path can be illustrated as follows: A .NET My Services request flows along the forward message path from the initial sender (the end-client) through zero or more intermediaries to the ultimate destination (the end-server). An intermediary is an application that is both a .NET My Services client and a .NET My Services server. The purpose of an intermediary can be, for example, to route a .NET My Services message from an HTTP environment to a DIME environment or to pass a .NET My Services message through a proxy. A .NET My Services response (if any) flows from the end-server through zero or more intermediaries to the end-client. The response may follow a reverse message path defined by the .NET My Services request, or it may use a message path that is completely independent of the request message path. If the underlying protocol supports a request/response style message exchange, a .NET My Services response may be piggy-backed onto the response of the underlying protocol. However, a .NET My Services response may also be exchanged independently of any response provided by the underlying protocol.

.NET My Services can be used in combination with a variety of underlying protocols including HTTP, SMTP, DIME, and others (initially, .NET My Services servers only support HTTP and DIME). As an example, it is possible to send a .NET My Services request using HTTP and later receive a response over DIME. It is also possible to change the underlying protocol for a message as it flows along the message path. For example, the first part of the message path may be using DIME and the latter part may be using HTTP for transferring the same .NET My Services message from the end-client to the end-server.

Note that the terms "end-client", "intermediary", and "end-server" are similar to the terms defined by HTTP: "user-agent", "intermediary" and "origin server"; but because .NET My Services is not fundamentally tied to HTTP, the .NET My Services terms do not imply use of HTTP in any way.

.NET My Services messaging supports the following features, which are expressed using the various SOAP headers:

Message Identity
> Each .NET My Services message contains a UUID which uniquely identifies the message to both the .NET My Services service software and the application software. Applications may use this message id to correlate a request with its matching response.

Message Sender Identity License
> Each .NET My Services message contains an identity license that identifies to the intended recipient of the message the licensed software stack and the user on whose behalf the message is being sent. In a request message, the license identifies the requester of the .NET My Services service, and in response messages it represents the .NET My Services service software that is providing the response. This license conforms to the license guidelines defined by the SOAP-SEC initiative.

Message Integrity
> Each .NET My Services message contains an integrity header that is an XML Digital Signature covering large portions of the .NET My Services message. This header is part of the SOAP-SEC initiative.

Rich Echo Back Context
> Each .NET My Services message may include a free-form echoBack header that is opaque to .NET My Services but is faithfully transmitted from the service request to the recipient of the service response. This may be used to pass out-of-band, free-form XML used for richer correlation, or any other application-specific use.

Management of Request/Response Modes
> While .NET My Services is typically thought of as a request/response message protocol, support for fire-and-forget semantics, and rich control of the request/response flow, are part of the message protocol. This control allows the following options:

- Request that no .NET My Services response be generated upon successful or fault conditions.
- Request a .NET My Services response piggy-backed in the underlying protocol response, if applicable.
- Request a .NET My Services response piggy-backed in the underlying protocol response, if applicable, but ONLY if the response represents a "fault" condition.
- Request a .NET My Services response directed to an arbitrary URI.
- Request a .NET My Services response directed to an arbitrary URI, but only if the response represents a "fault" condition.

The basic structure of a .NET My Services message is a SOAP Envelope with a single SOAP Header containing .NET My Services header elements, and a SOAP Body containing .NET My Services request or response elements.

A sample request message might look like the document illustrated below.

```
<s:Envelope xmlns:s="http://schemas.xmlsoap.org/soap/envelope/"
            xmlns:srp="http://schemas.xmlsoap.org/rp"
            xmlns:m="http://schemas.microsoft.com/hs/2001/10/myProfile"
            xmlns:hs="http://schemas.microsoft.com/hs/2001/10/core"
            xmlns:ss="http://schemas.xmlsoap.org/soap/security/2000-12"
            >
    <s:Header>
        <srp:path>
```

(continued)

(continued)

```
<srp:action>http://schemas.microsoft.com/hs/2001/10/core#request</srp:action>
          <srp:to>http://vbe1.vfd1.myProfile.msn.com/chloe@msn.com/</srp:to>
          <srp:rev>
            <srp:via/>
          </srp:rev>
          <srp:id>uuid:76343E4501</srp:id>
       </srp:path>
       <ss:licenses>
          <hs:identity>
             <hs:kerberos>865E1DB32AC3</hs:kerberos>
          </hs:identity>
       </ss:licenses>
       <hs:request service="myprofile" document="content" method="update"
genResponse="always">
          <hs:key puid="e09fB22233334444" instance="chloe@msn.com"
cluster="vbe1.vfe1"/>
       </hs:request>
    </s:Header>
    <s:Body>
       <hs:insertRequest select="/hs:myProfile">
          <m:address>
             <m:cat @ref="system/home"/>
             <m:officialAddressLine xml:lang="en">1236 Lisa
Lane</m:officialAddressLine>
             <m:primaryCity xml:lang="en">Los Altos</m:primaryCity>
          </m:address>
       </hs:insertRequest>
    </s:Body>
</s:Envelope>
```

A sample response message might look like the document illustrated below.

```
<s:Envelope xmlns:s="http://schemas.xmlsoap.org/soap/envelope/"
           xmlns:srp="http://schemas.xmlsoap.org/srp"
           xmlns:m="http://schemas.microsoft.com/hs/2001/10/myProfile"
           xmlns:hs="http://schemas.microsoft.com//hs/2001/10/core"
           xmlns:ss="http://schemas.xmlsoap.org/soap/security/2000-12"
           >
    <s:Header>
       <srp:path>

<srp:action>http://schemas.microsoft.com/hs/2001/10/core#response</srp:action>
```

```
            <srp:id>uuid:76343E4502</srp:id>
            <srp:relatesTo>uuid:76343E4501</srp:relatesTo>
        </srp:path>
        <ss:licenses>
            <hs:identity>
                <hs:kerberos>348738472</hs:kerberos>
            </hs:identity>
            <hs:authorizedRole>7tE345qq</hs:authorizedRole>
        </ss:licenses>
        <hs:response role="rt0"/>
    </s:Header>
    <s:Body>
        <hs:insertResponse status="success"/>
            <hs:newBlueId id="44542239"/>
        </hs:insertResponse/>
    </s:Body>
</s:Envelope>
```

The .NET messages service/path

The path header is part of the SOAP-RP initiative and is used to specify the ultimate
destination of the message along with any intermediaries that it has to go through while
traversing the message path. The path header is a mandatory part of every .NET My
Services message regardless of whether it is a request or a response message. For
.NET My Services requests, the path header describes how the request is to be
transferred from the end-client to the end-server and whether there are potential
intermediaries along the way. For responses, the path header describes how the
response is to be transferred from the end-server to the end-client and again, whether
there are intermediaries along the way.

```
<srp:path
    xmlns:srp="http://schemas.xmlsoap.org/rp">_{1..1}
    <srp:action>_{1..1}</srp:action>
    <srp:to>_{0..1}</srp:to>
    <srp:fwd>_{0..1}
        <srp:via vid="...">_{0..unbounded}</srp:via>
    </srp:fwd>
    <srp:rev>_{0..1}
        <srp:via vid="...">_{0..unbounded}</srp:via>
    </srp:rev>
    <srp:id>_{1..1}</srp:id>
    <srp:relatesTo>_{0..1}</srp:relatesTo>
</srp:path>
```

The meaning of the attributes and elements shown in the preceding sample document fragment are listed in the following section.

/path (minOccurs=1 maxOccurs=1)

This element specifies how a message is to be transferred along the forward message path. In addition, an optional reverse path can be built to provide a mechanism for returning a response (if any). The path element is required in every message regardless of whether it is a request or a response.

/path/action (anyURI minOccurs=1 maxOccurs=1)

The action element is used to indicate the intent of the message in a manner similar to the SOAPAction HTTP header field defined for the SOAP HTTP binding. The value is an absolute URI and similar to the HTTP SOAPAction header field. There are currently four valid values for this field for .NET My Services messages:

http://schemas.microsoft.com/hs/2001/10/core#request

This action URI specifies that the message is a .NET My Services request message. Detailed routing information for the request is located in the request header element. When the request is transmitted by HTTP, the SOAPAction HTTP header field MUST contain this URI.

http://schemas.microsoft.com/hs/2001/10/core#response

This action URI specifies that the message is a .NET My Services response message.

http://schemas.microsoft.com/hs/2001/10/core#notification

This action URI specifies that the message is a .NET My Services notification message.

http://schemas.microsoft.com/hs/2001/10/core#fault

This action URI specifies that the message is a .NET My Services fault message.

/path/to (anyURI minOccurs=0 maxOccurs=1)

The to element contains the ultimate destination of a message in the form of an absolute URI. The .NET services service is responsible for providing the value of this element to the initial sender. This element MUST be present in all .NET My Services request messages. In this sense, it is similar to the HTTP Request-URI in that it designates where the message is going. However, the to element MAY also be present in .NET My Services response messages allowing .NET My Services to send responses to end-clients that have a name in their own right. This can be used, for example, to indicate the destination of a response in case it was directed to an arbitrary URI. The value of the to element is an absolute URI and MUST be determined by the initial sender and MUST NOT be modified along the message path.

.NET My Services requires that the to element must contain the following pieces of information using a format dictated by the scheme of the URI:

protocol://[*cluster*.]*service*.*domain*/[*instance*]

An example would be:

http://vbe1.vfe2.profile.msn.com/2376187213

where:

protocol - http
> This component specifies the message transfer protocol carrying the message that contains this path element.

cluster - vbe1.vfe2
> This optional component specifies the virtual front end (vfe2) and virtual back end (vbe1) addresses for the cluster hosting this .NET My Services service. This information is useful for routing the .NET My Services message to its ultimate destination, as well as for providing an input to the partitioning system used to locate the .NET My Services data within the service endpoint.

service - myProfile
> This component specifies the .NET profile service.

domain - msn.com
> This component specifies the domain hosting the service.

instance - 2376187213
> This optional component specifies the instance of the service. In some services this will be a unique number, and in others, a unique name.

/path/fwd (minOccurs=0 maxOccurs=1)
> The optional fwd element contains an ordered list of intermediaries that the message must pass through along the forward message path. Like the ultimate destination, intermediaries are identified by an absolute URI carried within the fwd/via element, listed in the top-down order in which they are to be contacted.

/path/fwd/via (anyURI minOccurs=0 maxOccurs=unbounded)
> The via element is used to indicate that a message is to go through the intermediary identified by the value of the via element. The value of a via element can be either empty or an absolute URI. A non-empty value indicates the explicit endpoint of the intermediary that is to receive the message at a given point in the forward or reverse message path. An empty value (normally only occurring in a rev/via construct) indicates an implicit endpoint provided by the underlying protocol binding typically as a result of a previous message having built a reverse message path using that underlying communication channel. For example, an empty value used in a .NET My Services request carried in an HTTP request message would indicate that the reverse path for the .NET My Services response (if any) is the corresponding HTTP response.

/path/fwd/via/@vid (anyURI minOccurs=0 maxOccurs=1)
> This optional attribute may be used within empty via elements to allow an intermediary to identify implicit path elements and to correlate this implicit path with a path addressable only to that intermediary.

/path/rev (minOccurs=0 maxOccurs=1)

The rev element is used to indicate a reverse path for returning a potential .NET My Services response to the initial sender. The rev element describes the reverse path that the response must follow in the same manner as the fwd element describes the forward path. Each party in the reverse message path, including the initial sender, is listed in a top-down order using the via element.

/path/rev/via (anyURI minOccurs=0 maxOccurs=unbounded)

The via element is used to indicate that a message is to go through the intermediary identified by the value of the via element. The value of a via element can be either empty or an absolute URI. A non-empty value indicates the explicit endpoint of the intermediary that is to receive the message at a given point in the forward or reverse message path. An empty value (normally only occuring in a rev/via construct) indicates an implicit endpoint provided by the underlying protocol binding typically as a result of a previous message having built a reverse message path using that underlying communication channel. For example, an empty value used in a .NET My Services request carried in an HTTP request message would indicate that the reverse path for the .NET My Services response (if any) is the corresponding HTTP response.

/path/rev/via/@vid (anyURI minOccurs=0 maxOccurs=1)

This optional attribute may be used within empty via elements to allow an intermediary to identify implicit path elements and to correlate this implicit path with a path addressable only to that intermediary.

/path/id (anyURI minOccurs=1 maxOccurs=1)

This element specifies the message id that uniquely identifies THIS .NET My Services message over time and space. The id element enables .NET My Services applications to keep track of messages, and together with the relatesTo element, allows for simple request/response correlation. The id element must be present in all .NET My Services messages and must be generated by the initial sender. The value of the id element is a globally unique, absolute URI. The uniqueness of this URI is guaranteed by the initial sender. It is strongly recommended that the URI be a Universally Unique Identifier (UUID) or be generated from message content using cryptographic hash algorithms such as MD5. The value must not be reused in any other message and in particular must not be shared between requests and responses.

/path/relatesTo (anyURI minOccurs=0 maxOccurs=1)

The relatesTo element is used to indicate that one .NET My Services message is related to another .NET My Services message in some way. The relatesTo element must be present in all .NET My Services responses providing a simple request/response correlation mechanism independent of the message path used for the request and response. The relatesTo element in a .NET My Services response must be generated by the end-server and the value must be the exact value of the corresponding "id" element in the .NET My Services request for which the message is a response. The relatesTo element may be used in .NET My Services requests but in this case its meaning is not defined by .NET My Services. Note that the id element must be present regardless of whether a relatesTo element is present or not.

messages/Example/path - no response

In this example, we demonstrate a sample use of the path element to send a request and ask that no response be generated (lack of rev element).

```
<srp:path xmlns:srp="http://schemas.xmlsoap.org/rp">
    <srp:action>http://schemas.microsoft.com/hs/2001/10/core#request</srp:action>
    <srp:to>http://vbe2.vfe4.myProfile.msn.com/656277/</srp:to>
    <srp:id>uuid:987654321</srp:id>
</srp:path>
```

messages/Example/path - piggy-backed response

In this example, we demonstrate a sample use of the path element to send a request and ask that the response be piggy-backed on the original channel that delivered the request message. The response is carried in the response to the original HTTP POST request. This is the most common way to issue a synchronous .NET My Services request.

```
<srp:path xmlns:srp="http://schemas.xmlsoap.org/rp">
    <srp:action>http://schemas.microsoft.com/hs/2001/10/core#request</srp:action>
    <srp:to>http://vbe2.vfe4.myProfile.msn.com/656277/</srp:to>
    <srp:rev>
        <srp:via/>
    </srp:rev>
    <srp:id>uuid:987654321</srp:id>
</srp:path>
```

messages/Example/path - directed response

In this example, we demonstrate a sample use of the path element to send a request and ask that the response be directed to a specific address.

```
<srp:path xmlns:srp="http://schemas.xmlsoap.org/rp">
    <srp:action>http://schemas.microsoft.com/hs/2001/10/core#request</srp:action>
    <srp:to>http://vbe2.vfe4.myProfile.msn.com/656277/</srp:to>
    <srp:rev>
        <srp:via>http://response.xyz.com</srp:via>
    </srp:rev>
    <srp:id>uuid:987654321</srp:id>
</srp:path>
```

messages/Example/path - proxy traverse

In this example, we demonstrate a sample use of the path element to send a request, but instead of going directly from the client to the server, we send the message "via" a .NET My Services (actually SOAP-RP)-aware proxy.

```
<srp:path xmlns:srp="http://schemas.xmlsoap.org/rp">
    <srp:action>http://schemas.microsoft.com/hs/2001/10/core#request</srp:action>
    <srp:to>http://vbe2.vfe4.myProfile.msn.com/656277/</srp:to>
    <fwd>
        <srp:via>http://itgproxy:80</srp:via>
    </fwd>
    <srp:rev>
        <srp:via/>
    </srp:rev>
    <srp:id>uuid:987654321</srp:id>
</srp:path>
```

messages/Example/path - proxy traverse

In this example, we demonstrate a sample use of the path element to send a request, but instead of going directly from the client to the server, we send the message "via" a .NET My Services (actually SOAP-RP) aware proxy. The request passes through this stateful proxy in both directions using both the fwd/via and rev/via components. Note that in the fwd direction, the internal name of the proxy is used. In the reverse direction, a publicly visible name is used. The proxy would typically insert these components as it passes the message on to the ultimate destination.

```
<srp:path xmlns:srp="http://schemas.xmlsoap.org/rp">
    <srp:action>http://schemas.microsoft.com/hs/2001/10/core#request</srp:action>
    <srp:to>http://vbe2.vfe4.myProfile.msn.com/656277/</srp:to>
    <fwd>
        <srp:via>http://itgproxy:80</srp:via>
    </fwd>
    <srp:rev>
        <srp:via>http://hsresponse.itgproxy.xyzcorp.com</srp:via>
        <via vid="uuid:3746347FE65ADB832"/>
    </srp:rev>
    <srp:id>uuid:987654321</srp:id>
</srp:path>
```

The .NET messages service/licenses

The "licenses" header is used to specify licenses being transmitted in the .NET My Services message. Licenses are described more fully in the SOAP-SEC specification. For the purposes of .NET My Services, this header may encapsulate the identity license, and possibly an authorizedRole license.

The licenses header is a mandatory part of every .NET My Services message and must always carry a well-formed and valid identity license that describes the identity of the sender to the message recipient.

```
<ss:licenses {any}="..."
    xmlns:ss="http://schemas.xmlsoap.org/soap/security/2000-12"
    xmlns:hs="http://schemas.microsoft.com/hs/2001/10/core"
    xmlns:ds="http://www.w3.org/2000/09/xmldsig"
    xmlns:enc="http://www.w3.org/2001/04/xmlenc">1..1 {any}</ss:licenses>
```

The meaning of the attributes and elements shown in the preceding sample document fragment are listed in the following section.

/licenses (minOccurs=1 maxOccurs=1)

This element defines the SOAP-SEC licenses header. Its purpose is to encapsulate free-form XML licenses that are agreed to between the SOAP producer and consumer. Licenses have additional properties which are defined in the SOAP-SEC specification.

This header is designed to allow all valid SOAP attributes as well as other namespace qualified attributes that are appropriate in the context with which this is used.

/licenses/@{any} (minOccurs=0 maxOccurs=1)

This placeholder is designed to indicate that in addition to SOAP mustUnderstand and actor attributes, other reasonable attributes may be specified.

/licenses/{any} (minOccurs=0 maxOccurs=unbounded)

This element is a placeholder that indicates where the license(s) contained in the SOAP-SEC licenses tag belong.

The .NET messages service/licenses/identity

The identity license is used to specify to the .NET My Services service, or to the recipient of a .NET My Services response, the identity of the original sender of the message. This license is always carried within a SOAP-SEC licenses element.

The precise format of this element is in active development (encoding format as well as encryption format). The identity license is expressed in terms of passport style identifiers. These identifiers are carried within a Kerberos AP request. The .NET My Services architecture is extensible. An identity license may be extended to include a variety of license encodings and formats. As currently defined, an identity license takes the form of a base85 encoded Kerberos AP request.

The major pieces of information that go into this request are shown below. The astute reader will note that not ALL pieces of information are shown. This is done on purpose to simplify the documentation. In reality, all required, standard Kerberos information is in the "AP request"; it is just not fully documented here.

{servicePrincipalName, [{Uk, Kx3, {A/Y, g}}Kh]Kp , {T}Kx3, otherKerberosStuff }

Where the expression above means:

servicePrincipalName
> This value comes from the spn element of the .NET services service. This value includes the service class and the DNS name of the service.

Uk
> This value specifies the PUID of the user on whose behalf the message is being sent. This value is also known as the value of the <userId> element seen in the roleList document.

Kx3
> This value specifies the session key used for encrypting and integrity-checking the messages involved in this transaction.

A
> This value specifies the PUID of the application sending the message. This value is a portion of the <appAndPlatformId> element seen in the roleList document.

Y
> This value specifies the PUID of the platform hosting the application that is sending the message. This value is a portion of the <appAndPlatformId> element seen in the roleList document.

g
> This value is reserved and will be used in the future for passing group membership information in the service ticket.

Kh
> This value is the key to the .NET My Services service shared with the .NET My Services domain authority controlling the realm of the addressed service.

Kp
> This value is the key to the .NET My Services domain authority controlling the realm of the addressed service.

T
> This value specifies the current time.

otherKerberosStuff
> This value represents the other pieces of a standard Kerberos "AP request" that are not documented above.

The notation in the expression above can be decoded as follows:

{a,b,...,z}
  represents the concatenation of the byte strings a, b,...,z

HMAC(Ki,m)
  is the HMAC of the byte string m with key Ki.

[m]Ki
  is the byte string {m,HMAC(Ki,m}}--that is, a message with an integrity check added.
  An example of this from the expression above is:

  [{Uk, Kx3, {A/Y, g}}Kh]Kp

{ m }Ke
  is the encryption of the byte string m with the key Ke. Examples of this from the
  expression above include:

  {Uk, Kx3, {A/Y, g}}Kh

  {T}Kx3

As you can see from the expressions and definitions given previously, the identity
license contains three pieces of information used by the .NET My Services security
system. This information is presented to the recipient of a message using Kerberos. The
three primary pieces of information transmitted are:

- userId - Uk

- appId - A

- platformId - Y

```
<hs:identity
    xmlns:hs="http://schemas.microsoft.com/hs/2001/10/core">1..1
    <hs:kerberos>1..1</hs:kerberos>
</hs:identity>
```

The meaning of the attributes and elements shown in the preceding sample document
fragment are listed in the following section.

/identity (minOccurs=1 maxOccurs=1)
  This element is a SOAP-SEC compliant license that identifies the sender of this
  message to the recipient. The contents are encoded and encrypted using algorithms
  demonstrated and documented in the .NET My Services client access runtime. This
  license includes all elements needed to identify the sender of the .NET My Services
  message. An identity license must be present in all .NET My Services service
  requests and is always contained within a SOAP-SEC licenses tag.

/identity/kerberos (hexBinary minOccurs=1 maxOccurs=1)

This element specifies the identity of the sender of the message in the form of a Kerberos AP request:

{servicePrincipalName, [{Uk, Kx3, {A/Y, g}}Kh]Kp , {T}Kx3, otherKerberosStuff }

which is easily transformed into:

userId

The user on whose behalf this message is being sent. The user can be an actual user, or an identity representing an arbitrary user account. This value is extractable as a Passport Unique ID (PUID).

appAndPlatformId

The PUIDs that represents the licenses granted to an application, and a platform on which the application runs.

The .NET messages service/authorizedRole

The authorizedRole license is a license transmitted within a SOAP-SEC licenses element. The license is typically issued by a .NET My Services service and contains the authorizedRole for a given request message. The .NET My Services service may choose to honor this license if it feels that it is valid and this allows the .NET My Services service to bypass an role evaluation. The typical usage pattern is that a client application issues a .NET My Services service request without an authorizedRole license, or with an invalid authorizedRole license. .NET My Services will then validate that the client application has access to the service, and if so, will issue an authorizedRole license. If this license is used in a subsequent .NET My Services request by the same client, then .NET My Services may more efficiently determine that the request should proceed, process the request, and issue another authorizedRole license. The authorizedRole license is a one-time use license. This license is always carried within a SOAP-SEC licenses element.

The precise format of this license is visible only to .NET My Services services and its encoding, encryption algorithms, encryption keys, and its content is opaque to the recipient.

```
<hs:authorizedRole

xmlns:hs="http://schemas.microsoft.com/hs/2001/10/core">1..1</hs:authorizedRole>
```

The meaning of the attributes and elements shown in the preceding sample document fragment are listed in the following section.

/authorizedRole (string minOccurs=1 maxOccurs=1)

This element is a SOAP-SEC compliant license that does two things:

- When presented to a .NET My Services service in a SOAP-SEC licenses tag during a .NET My Services request message, it specifies to the .NET My Services service the authorized role of the sender of the message. The .NET My Services service is free to accept this license when it feels that the license is valid. If .NET My Services does not believe the license, it is free to ignore the license, perform its own role evaluation and possibly issue a new license in a response header.

  .NET My Services services are the grantors of this type of license and the content is totally opaque to the sender.

- When this license appears in a SOAP-SEC licenses tag during a .NET My Services response message, this license is considered issued to the recipient for an undetermined amount of time. On a subsequent request, this license may be presented and may allow accelerated processing of the request.

The .NET messages service/integrity

The integrity header is a SOAP-SEC message integrity header and is simply an element designed to accept SOAP mustUnderstand and actor attributes, and to wrap the Signature element specified by the XML Digital Signature initiative.

```
<ss:integrity {any}="..."
    xmlns:ss="http://schemas.xmlsoap.org/soap/security/2000-12"
    xmlns:hs="http://schemas.microsoft.com/hs/2001/10/core"
    xmlns:ds="http://www.w3.org/2000/09/xmldsig"
    xmlns:enc="http://www.w3.org/2001/04/xmlenc">...{any}</ss:integrity>
```

The meaning of the attributes and elements shown in the preceding sample document fragment are listed in the following section.

/integrity (minOccurs=1 maxOccurs=1)

This element defines the SOAP-SEC integrity header. Its purpose is to encapsulate the XML Digital Signature of the SOAP message that contains this header.

This header is designed to allow all valid SOAP attributes as well as other namespace qualified attributes that are appropriate in the context with which this is used.

/integrity/@ {any} (minOccurs=0 maxOccurs=1)

This placeholder is designed to indicate that in addition to SOAP mustUnderstand and actor attributes, other reasonable attributes may be specified.

/integrity/{any} (minOccurs=0 maxOccurs=unbounded)

This free-form extension may include additional, namespace qualified XML.

The .NET messages service/confidentiality

The confidentiality header is a SOAP-SEC message header and is simply an element designed to accept SOAP mustUnderstand and actor attributes, and to wrap the EncryptedData element specified by the XML Encryption initiative.

```
<ss:confidentiality {any}="..."
    xmlns:ss="http://schemas.xmlsoap.org/soap/security/2000-12"
    xmlns:hs="http://schemas.microsoft.com/hs/2001/10/core"
    xmlns:ds="http://www.w3.org/2000/09/xmldsig"
    xmlns:enc="http://www.w3.org/2001/04/xmlenc">1..1 {any}</ss:confidentiality>
```

The meaning of the attributes and elements shown in the preceding sample document fragment are listed in the following section.

/confidentiality (minOccurs=1 maxOccurs=1)

This element defines the SOAP-SEC confidentiality header. Its purpose is to encapsulate the XML EncryptedData element which defines encrypted portions of this SOAP message.

This header is designed to allow all valid SOAP attributes as well as other namespace qualified attributes that are appropriate in the context with which this is used.

/confidentiality/@ {any} (minOccurs=0 maxOccurs=1)

This placeholder is designed to indicate that in addition to SOAP mustUnderstand and actor attributes, other reasonable attributes may be specified.

/confidentiality/{any} (minOccurs=0 maxOccurs=unbounded)

This free-form extension may include additional, namespace qualified XML.

The .NET messages service/request

The request header is used to specify .NET My Services-specific request information including which document is being addressed, which method is being addressed, what sort of response should be generated, what keys (puid, instance id) should be used to locate the document, and what partition key should be used to locate the document within a cluster. In a typical call-frame based environment, this information would normally be passed as procedure call arguments. In .NET My Services, the SOAP envelope defines the calling convention so these arguments become header elements.

```
<hs:request service="..." document="..." method="..." genResponse="..."
    xmlns:hs="http://schemas.microsoft.com/hs/2001/10/core">1..1
    <hs:key puid="..." instance="..." cluster="...">1..100</hs:key>
</hs:request>
```

The meaning of the attributes and elements shown in the preceding sample document fragment are listed in the following section.

/request (minOccurs=1 maxOccurs=1)

The request header is used to specify request-specific arguments including the service being addressed, the method being accessed, the document being manipulated, how the response should be processed, key information used to locate the document including the PUID that owns the document, the document instance, and the cluster. The request header MUST occur in each request message.

/request/@service (string minOccurs=0 maxOccurs=1)

This element contains the name of the service being accessed by this request message.

/request/@document (string minOccurs=0 maxOccurs=1)

This element specifies the document class being accessed by this message. Valid values include:

- content - the main content document
- roleList - the authorization list document
- system - the global system document
- policy - TBD

/request/@method (string minOccurs=0 maxOccurs=1)

This element specifies the method being accessed within the service. For instance, to access one of the standard methods, valid values would include:

- insertRequest
- deleteRequest
- replaceRequest
- updateRequest
- queryRequest

/request/@genResponse (string minOccurs=0 maxOccurs=1)

This element, coupled with rev/via, controls how a response to this request is generated and delivered. Valid values include:

always

Always generate a response message and deliver to rev/via.

never

Never generate a response message.

faultOnly

Generate a response message, but only if the request message results in a fault message.

/request/key (minOccurs=1 maxOccurs=100)

This element specifies key information used to zoom in on the document being manipulated. This information includes the PUID that owns the document, the instance id of the document, and the cluster or partition key used to locate the machine resources that hold the document.

In certain situations, a client will want to send the same message to a number a instances of a particular service. In order to accomplish this, the client may repeat this element multiple times. The cluster attributes in all elements must match each other, but the PUID and instance attributes may differ. A unique response message is generated for each key specified.

The entire contents of this element comes from the ,NET services service.

/request/key/@puid (string minOccurs=0 maxOccurs=1)

This element specifies the PUID of the entity that "owns" the service being accessed.

/request/key/@instance (string minOccurs=0 maxOccurs=1)

This element specifies the particular instance of the service for this id being accessed. For instance, if a given id is provisioned with multiple .NET calendar service documents on the same cluster and in the same data center, the documents would differ only by this value.

/request/key/@cluster (string minOccurs=0 maxOccurs=1)

This element specifies information used by the .NET My Services system to locate the document on a particular back-end server or database. It is used as the virtual partition key for the document being addressed. This technique is preferable to computing this partition key based on some hash of the PUID/instance.

messages/Example/request - single

The following example illustrates a simple, single-operation request header. In this header, we are addressing the content document for the .NET profile service, for a user whose Passport ID is e09fB22233334444. We are addressing this document instance 77, which is visible through cluster vbe1.vfe1, and we are always supposed to generate a response message.

```
<hs:request service="myProfile" document="content" method="update"
genResponse="always" >
    <hs:key puid="e09fB22233334444" instance="77" cluster="vbe1.vfe1"/>
</hs:request>
```

messages/Example/request - multiple

The following example illustrates a slightly more complex request header where we are performing the same addNotification operation on a number of users. This is a common scenario that would occur to send a notification to a small subscription list, add a calendar event to a number of calendars, and so on. Each key element marks a logically unique request operation for which a unique response may be generated. In this operation, the caller is requesting that a response be generated only in the case of a fault/message failure. There is a practical limit to the number of key elements allowed in a message. Currently this limit is 100, and is noted in the schema. Note that in order to use multiple keys in a message, the cluster value for each key must match.

```
<hs:request service="myNotifications" document="content" method="addNotification"
genResponse="faultOnly" >
    <hs:key puid="e09fB22233334444" instance="77" cluster="vbe1.vfe1"/>
    <hs:key puid="e09fB22233334445" instance="34" cluster="vbe2.vfe1"/>
    <hs:key puid="e09fB22233334446" instance="22" cluster="vbe2.vfe1"/>
    <hs:key puid="e09fB22233334447" instance="12" cluster="vbe1.vfe1"/>
    <hs:key puid="e09fB22233334448" instance="14" cluster="vbe1.vfe1"/>
    <hs:key puid="e09fB22233334449" instance="67" cluster="vbe2.vfe1"/>
    <hs:key puid="e09fB2223333444a" instance="90" cluster="vbe2.vfe1"/>
    <hs:key puid="e09fB2223333444b" instance="17" cluster="vbe1.vfe1"/>
    <hs:key puid="e09fB2223333444c" instance="64" cluster="vbe2.vfe1"/>
    <hs:key puid="e09fB2223333444d" instance="32" cluster="vbe2.vfe1"/>
</hs:request>
```

The .NET messages service/response

The response header is used to carry response information to the intended recipient of the response. It does not carry data requested in the request message, but instead carries bookkeeping information, such as the role the sender evaluated to.

```
<hs:response role="..."
    xmlns:hs="http://schemas.microsoft.com/hs/2001/10/core">1..1</hs:response>
```

The meaning of the attributes and elements shown in the preceding sample document fragment are listed in the following section.

/response (minOccurs=1 maxOccurs=1)

This element contains information related to the response message. In current implementations, this information is limited to the role that was computed for the sender assuming the original request was formed well enough to progress this far through the .NET My Services message-processing system. This header element must be present in all response messages.

/response/@role (string minOccurs=0 maxOccurs=1)

This optional attribute contains the role that was computed for the sender. If the original request message was malformed in such a way as not to make it far enough through the message processor to compute a value for this element, the role attribute will be missing from the response header. This situation typically occurs whenever the identity header is so malformed that the basic set of sender identity PUIDs can not be extracted from the service ticket.

The .NET messages service/echoBack

The echoBack header is a header element that applications may use to pass additional correlation data or "out-of-band" data between the request and the response recipients. It is considered bad form to use this header during synchronous, piggy-backed responses. In that situation, the call stack should be all that is required to keep sufficient context, during cases where responses are not generated, or are only generated during fault conditions. If the UUIDs in the path/id and path/relatesTo are insufficient to provide correlation data, the echoBack header may be used to pass arbitrarily structured XML between the service requestor and the recipient of the associated .NET My Services response.

.NET My Services services make no attempt to process or inspect the contents of this header. They simply transmit the header from the request message to the response message and treat it as an opaque body of XML.

```
<hs:echoBack
    xmlns:hs="http://schemas.microsoft.com/hs/2001/10/core">1..1
{any}</hs:echoBack>
```

The meaning of the attributes and elements shown in the preceding sample document fragment are listed in the following section.

/echoBack (minOccurs=1 maxOccurs=1)

The echoBack header is a header element that applications may use to pass additional correlation data or out-of-band data between the request and the response recipients. It is considered bad form to use this header during synchronous, piggy-backed responses, because in that situation, the call stack should be all that is required to keep sufficient context, or during cases where responses are not generated, or only generated during fault conditions. If the UUIDs in the path/id, and path/relatesTo are insufficient to provide correlation data, then the echoBack header may be used to pass arbitrarily structured XML between the service requester and the recipient of the associated .NET My Services response.

.NET My Services services make no attempt to process or inspect the contents of this header. They simply transmit the header from the request message to the response message and treat it as an opaque body of XML.

/echoBack/{any} (minOccurs=0 maxOccurs=unbounded)

messages/Example/echoBack sample

In this header, the application is passing the "applicationContext" node from the request message to the response message. The contents and structure of this node are not understood or interpreted by .NET My Services.

```
<hs:echoBack xmlns:ebc="http://schemas.xyzcorp.net/hs/ebc/">
    <ebc:applicationContext>
        <ebc:applicationTag1>31</ebc:applicationTag1>
        <ebc:applicationTag2>31Fe4</ebc:applicationTag2>
    </ebc:applicationContext>
</hs:echoBack>
```

The .NET messages service/adminRequest

The "adminRequest" header is used to specify .NET My Services-specific adminRequest information including which method is being addressed, what sort of response should be generated, what keys (puid, instance id) should be used to locate the document, and what partition key should be used to locate the document within a cluster. In a typical call-frame based environment, this information would normally be passed as procedure call arguments. In .NET My Services, the SOAP envelope defines the calling convention so these arguments become header elements.

Admin requests can target three different documents:

- content
- roleList
- server

content and *roleList* documents are only accessed through the "createDocument" method. *server* document is accessed through other HSDL methods (*query, insert, update, replace, delete, changeNotify*).

Contents of the request is validated against the schema of the document that is pointed out by the adminHeader/@document attribute.

document	schema
content	my* service schema
roleList	roleList document schema
server	server status document schema

```
<hsa:adminRequest service="..." method="..." document="..." genResponse="..."
    xmlns:hsa="urn:schemas-microsoft-com:hsadmin"
    xmlns:hs="http://schemas.microsoft.com/hs/2001/10/core">₁..₁
    <hsa:key puid="..." instance="..." cluster="...">₁..₁₀₀</hsa:key>
</hsa:adminRequest>
```

The meaning of the attributes and elements shown in the preceding sample document fragment are listed in the following section.

/adminRequest (minOccurs=1 maxOccurs=1)

The adminRequest header is used to specify request-specific arguments including the service being addressed, the method being accessed, the type of the admin request being sent, how the response should be processed, key information used to locate documents in adminRequest types where a document needs to be manipulated. The adminRequest header MUST occur in each admin request message.

/adminRequest/@service (string minOccurs=0 maxOccurs=1)

This element contains the name of the service being accessed by this admin request message.

/adminRequest/@method (string minOccurs=0 maxOccurs=1)

This element specifies the admin method being called with this request. Method name has to map into a different set of methods for different admin request types. For instance, in an admin request that has the type 'query', the method can only be 'query'.

/adminRequest/@document (string minOccurs=0 maxOccurs=1)

This element specifies the document class being accessed by this message. Valid values include:

- content—the main content document
- acl—the access control list document
- server—the server status and administration document

/adminRequest/@genResponse (string minOccurs=0 maxOccurs=1)

This element, coupled with rev/via, controls how a response to this request is generated and delivered. Valid values include:

always

Always generate a response message and deliver to rev/via.

never

Never generate a response message.

faultOnly

Generate a response message, but only if the request message results in a fault message.

/adminRequest/key (minOccurs=1 maxOccurs=100)

> This element specifies key information used to zoom in on the document being manipulated. This information includes the PUID that owns the document, the instance id of the document, and the cluster or partition key used to locate the machine resources that hold the document.
>
> In an adminRequest, this element is only used when the requestType attribute is "provisioning". In other cases, this element is ignored.
>
> In certain situations, a client will want to send the same message to a number a instances of a particular service. In order to accomplish this, the client may repeat this element multiple times. The cluster attributes in all elements must match each other, but the PUID and instance attributes may differ. A unique response message is generated for each key specified.
>
> The entire contents of this element comes from the .NET services service.

/adminRequest/key/@puid (string minOccurs=0 maxOccurs=1)

> This element specifies the PUID of the entity that "owns" the service being accessed.

/adminRequest/key/@instance (string minOccurs=0 maxOccurs=1)

> This element specifies the particular instance of the service for this id being accessed. For instance, if a given id is provisioned with multiple .NET calendar documents on the same cluster and in the same data center, the documents would differ only by this value.

/adminRequest/key/@cluster (string minOccurs=0 maxOccurs=1)

> This element specifies information used by the .NET My Services system to locate the document on a particular back-end server or database. It is used as the virtual partition key for the document being addressed. This technique is preferable to computing this partition key based on some hash of the PUID/instance.

messages/Example/adminRequest - single

The following example illustrates the adminRequest header of a createDocument request made to a .NET contacts service.

```
<hs:adminRequest service="myProfile" document="content" method="createDocument"
            genResponse="faultOnly" >
   <hs:key puid="e09fB22233334447" instance="324" cluster="vbe1.vfe3" />
</hs:adminRequest>
```

messages/Example/adminRequest - multiple

The following example illustrates the adminRequest header of a createDocument request for the .NET profile service. The request is made for more than one user, which is a scenario that could occur to setup and provision multiple users.

```
<hs:adminRequest service="myProfile" document="content" method="createDocument"
            genResponse="faultOnly" >
  <hs:key puid="e09fB22233334444" instance="77" cluster="vbe1.vfe1"/>
  <hs:key puid="e09fB22233334445" instance="34" cluster="vbe2.vfe1"/>
  <hs:key puid="e09fB22233334446" instance="22" cluster="vbe2.vfe1"/>
  <hs:key puid="e09fB22233334447" instance="12" cluster="vbe1.vfe1"/>
  <hs:key puid="e09fB22233334448" instance="14" cluster="vbe1.vfe1"/>
  <hs:key puid="e09fB22233334449" instance="67" cluster="vbe2.vfe1"/>
  <hs:key puid="e09fB2223333444a" instance="90" cluster="vbe2.vfe1"/>
  <hs:key puid="e09fB2223333444b" instance="17" cluster="vbe1.vfe1"/>
  <hs:key puid="e09fB2223333444c" instance="64" cluster="vbe2.vfe1"/>
  <hs:key puid="e09fB2223333444d" instance="32" cluster="vbe2.vfe1"/>
</hs:adminRequest>
```

The .NET messages service/adminResponse

```
<hsa:adminResponse
    xmlns:hsa="urn:schemas-microsoft-com:hsadmin"

xmlns:hs="http://schemas.microsoft.com/hs/2001/10/core">1...1</hsa:adminResponse>
```

The meaning of the attributes and elements shown in the preceding sample document fragment are listed in the following section.

/adminResponse (minOccurs=1 maxOccurs=1)

This element contains information related to the response message. Depending on the adminRequest message that was received the information within this element may vary. Refer to individual method implementations for the responses they return. This header element MUST be present in all response messages.

C H A P T E R   6

hsdl/Introduction

HSDL is the core data-manipulation language implemented by all Microsoft .NET My Services services. Before going into detail on the data manipulation language, we begin by describing some fundamental constructs that all .NET My Services data adheres to.

All .NET My Services data is defined using heavily annotated XSD schema files. The XSD files accurately type the data, but since XSD is a verbose and complex language, it is not always an efficient way to convey structure and meaning. For this reason, our documentation is done in terms of schema fragments and element/attribute descriptions. Links to the actual schema files are included in this document, but document structure is easier to comprehend using document skeletons.

The following section demonstrates a document skeleton, a construct you will find throughout this document.

```
<myAddress changeNumber="..." instanceId="...">
    <address  changeNumber="..." id="...">
        <cat ref="..."></cat>
        <officialAddressLine xml:lang="..."></officialAddressLine>
        <internalAddressLine xml:lang="..."></internalAddressLine>
        <primaryCity xml:lang="..."></primaryCity>
        <secondaryCity xml:lang="..."></secondaryCity>
        <subdivision xml:lang="..."></subdivision>
        <postalCode></postalCode>
        <countryOrRegion xml:lang="..."></countryOrRegion>
        <geoLocation>
            <latitude></latitude>
            <longitude></longitude>
            <elevation></elevation>
        </geoLocation>
        {any}
    </address>
    <webSite changeNumber="..." id="...">
        <cat ref="..."></cat>
        <url></url>
        {any}
    </webSite>
    <emailAddress changeNumber="..." id="...">
        <cat ref="..."></cat>
```

(continued)

(continued)

```
        <address></address>
        <friendlyName xml:lang="..."></friendlyName>
        {any}
    </emailAddress>
    <telephoneNumber changeNumber="..." id="...">
        <cat ref="..."></cat>
        <countryCode></countryCode>
        <nationalCode></nationalCode>
        <number></number>
        <numberExtension></numberExtension>
        <pin></pin>
        {any}
    </telephoneNumber>
</myAddress>
```

These document skeletons are produced by running some XSL transformations on our source schema documents. They accurately show the structure of the data contained within a service (but obviously do not show many other necessary document attributes like types, minOccurs/maxOccurs, and so on). When viewing the document online, or when you print it print in color, you will notice that items contained within the document are colored **bold blue**, <u>underlined red</u>, or black.

The colorization is very significant to the data model and to the data-manipulation language. Looking closely at the document fragment listed above, you can see very clearly some of the patterns that occur in the .NET My Services data model.

- Each document contains a root element whose element name matches the name of the service. In this case the sample skeleton is a portion of the .NET address service, so the element name is *myAddress*.

  The .NET My Services name for this item is the **root**.

- Documents contain elements that look like first-class top-level objects. In the skeleton above, these first-class, top-level objects are:
  - **<address/>**
  - **<webSite/>**
  - **<emailAddress/>**
  - **<telephoneNumber/>**
  - **<myAddress/>**

  These items are always colored **bold blue**, and are marked in the schema files using the **<xdb:blue/>** tag.

  The xdb:blue items define major blocks of data within a service. These node sets are directly addressable through the data manipulation language and are the basic unit that enables caching. The xdb:blue items are always uniquely identified by an @id attribute and their change status is tracked through the @changeNumber attribute.

- Each xdb:blue root contains one or more <u>underlined red</u> elements and attributes. These items are marked in the schema files using the <u><xdb:red/></u> tag. These items are special in that they may be used within predicates to aid in xdb:blue selection. These items are also directly addressable and may be manipulated directly by the hsdl primitives. In the skeleton listed above, the <u><xdb:red/></u> items are:
  - **myAddress[<u>@changeNumber</u>]**
  - **address[<u>@changeNumber</u>]**
  - **address[<u>@id</u>]**
  - **address**[cat/<u>@ref</u>]
  - **address[<u>any</u>]**
  - **webSite[<u>@changeNumber</u>]**
  - **webSite[<u>@id</u>]**
  - **webSite**[cat/<u>@ref</u>]
  - **webSite[<u>any</u>]**
  - **emailAddress[<u>@changeNumber</u>]**
  - **emailAddress[<u>@id</u>]**
  - **emailAddress**[cat/<u>@ref</u>]
  - **emailAddress[<u>any</u>]**
  - **telephoneNumber[<u>@changeNumber</u>]**
  - **telephoneNumber[<u>@id</u>]**
  - **telephoneNumber**[cat/<u>@ref</u>]
  - **telephoneNumber[<u>any</u>]**

- Each xdb:blue root contains one or more elements and attributes that are neither red or blue. These are perfectly valid and semantically meaningful XML items in the service document. They are, however, completely opaque to .NET My Services' data-manipulation language. These elements and attributes may not be directly addressed, may not be selected in a node selection operation, and may not be used in a predicate node test. If one of these items is in the path to a red item, it may be used in a location step to the red item, but may not be used as the selected node. Note that being opaque does not mean that the item is not considered during schema validation. It simply means that the item may not be used in a predicate and may not be directly addressed.

A basic understanding of XPath-style navigation and node selection in an XML document is enough for many to appreciate the implications of the red/blue approach outlined above. What .NET My Services is doing is limiting the granularity of access to nodes within the service document. Only xdb:blue and xdb:red marked items are directly addressable. Only those elements and attributes tagged with the xdb:red annotation may be used in predicates to influence the node selection. Using this technique, the .NET My Services storage system can efficiently manage indexes, increase the performance of node selection, partially shred the document data, and in general (because the node selections are well defined) fine-tune the node selection logic on a per-xdb:blue basis. The primary purpose of the xdb:blue is to define a base-level XML object that is designed to be operated on as a unit. The primary purpose of the xdb:red items is to aid in the selection of xdb:blues. The xdb:red items may be changed by the hsdl primitives so some level of fine-grained manipulation of the data is available, but only in very limited ways.

The rest of this document focuses on the .NET My Services data manipulation language (HSDL). This language defines the core messages used to manipulate .NET My Services data. This includes node selection, insertion, deletion, and so on. As you read, you will see the relationship to blue/red items.

HSDL is implemented as a set of request and response messages sent to the various .NET My Services services. It includes the following basic messages:

insert

This message allows the sender to insert a xdb:blue XML item into the specified service at the specified document location. This message also allows the insertion of an xdb:red item into the selected xdb:blue. When inserting an xdb:blue, an xdb:blue must be selected. When inserting an xdb:red, an xdb:blue must be selected.

delete

This message allows the sender to delete the specified xdb:blues from the specified document. This message also allows the deletion of an xdb:red item from the selected xdb:blues. In all cases, the item being selected is deleted, and the selection must always specify either an xdb:red or an xdb:blue.

replace

This message allows the sender to replace the content of the specified xdb:blue or xdb:red with the content supplied in the replaceRequest message. Content includes all attributes and descendent elements of the specified item.

update

This message allows the sender to chain together a series of insert, delete, and replace messages into a single combination message allowing the sender to update the specified document efficiently.

query

This message allows the sender to issue a query against the specified document, returning either 1) the specified xdb:blue items, or 2) a set of instructions telling the sender whether his cached information is invalid and if so, how to correct it.

subscriptionResponse

This message is generated in response to a subscription firing within a service. A subscription is registered by inserting a subscription element into a content document.

All messages operate on data relative to the "current context". For all messages except update, the "current context" is "/", which specifies the root of the specified document. This point is not very interesting when looking at the standalone messages (insert, delete, replace), but when viewed in the context of update, it becomes significant.

In this chapter and others that follow, in addition to the red/blue convention, there are a few basic constructs in our schemas that all readers should understand:

hsdl:attribute element

> This element may appear multiple times in the content of an insertRequest and in the content of a replaceRequest. Its purpose is to specify a single attribute to be inserted into or replaced into the set of selected nodes. When encountered in one of these messages, .NET My Services searches the selected node for a matching attribute and updates it with the new value.

> Note that this construct is typically most meaningful when inserting a new xdb:red into an existing xdb:blue.

any element

> All .NET My Services services have some level of extension capability. The extensions are locations built into the service schemas where free-form XML extensions may be added into the service data. The construct {any} is the notation used in the outline view schema fragments to note that free-form XML extensions are permitted at the given location. .NET My Services expects that free-form extensions are always properly namespace qualified.

> This same convention is used in this chapter to mark content that is to be inserted or replaced into the service. When this element is used in this mode, the schema for the content is not understood by the .NET My Services Data Manipulation layer. It is, however, understood and schema-validated by the service layer as long as the content is service data falling within the namespace of the service as opposed to free-form XML being added to the service that falls outside of this namespace.

> Free-form XML extensions are semi-opaque to .NET My Services. The name of the element and all attributes are automatically considered as xdb:red, and all element/text content is treated us non-colorized opaque information. What this means is that visibility to the extension in predicates and in other data manipulations is limited to the name of the outer element that defines the extension, and in the attributes attached to this element. Therefore, in a free-form extension of <xyz:foo xyz:name="fred"><xyz:bar x="7"/></xyz:foo>, the data-manipulation language may use xyz:foo, and xyz:fred/@xyz:name in predicates and in navigation, but xyz:fred/xyz:bar is invisible. In red/blue terms, the element name and all of its attributes are considered red.

id attribute on a xdb:blue elements

In .NET My Services schemas, ALL xdb:blue (blue items) contain the attribute "id", and the id is of type "hc:idType". The id is a universally unique id normally assigned by .NET My Services (clients may request on some hsdl operations that .NET My Services not generate the id value, and instead use a client-supplied id). The id attributes are read only, and if client software attempts to write these attributes, the writes are silently ignored. Elements that contain this sort of attribute are very efficiently addressed using a **select="//*[@id='*id-value*']"** construct.

These elements are special elements for a number of reasons:

- In cache-related operations, elements of this type mark the boundary of cacheable information. When anything changes within this element and client software asks for a change summary, the entire tree (with xdb:blue granularity) under this element is returned. Elements tagged with the xdb:blue annotation can be considered as cache blocks.

- When issuing a changeQuery request, client software must anchor the query by specifying (in its node selection) an xdb:blue (which always contains an id attribute and a changeNumber attribute). The response contains the child xdb:blues that have changed with respect to the synchronization base. The change granularity is the xdb:blue.

- When client software "subscribes", the nodes being watched must be anchored in the same way as described above.

changeNumber element

.NET My Services is designed to efficiently support client software that wants to maintain either a read-only or a write-through cache of .NET My Services data. In order to do this, client software must be able to ask whether its cache is out of sync, and if so, what operations it can perform on its cache to get it in sync. The changeNumber attribute (type="hc:changeNumber") is the central attribute involved in these questions. The changeNumber attribute is used to indicate a synchronization base value that is exposed through various portions of the tree. At any point in the tree, client software can ask the question, "Is my tree in sync relative to the changeNumber I possess in my cache?" When this question is asked, .NET My Services computes the state of the .NET My Services data with respect to the changeNumber specified by the client, and returns to the client a set of processing instructions (in the form of an updateRequest) that, if applied the client's cache, will bring that cache in sync. The changeNumber attribute is threaded throughout the entire document, but is only exposed on xdb:blue items.

Examples below will illustrate how changeNumbers nest and interact with one and other.

The .NET My Services team is investigating the feasibility of extending this model to include client-generated version history at xdb:blue granularity, which will enable multi-master replication. This is currently in the design stage.

.NET My Services data access is based on selection using a subset of XPath. The subset of XPath implemented by .NET My Services is defined in the .NET My Services XPath Language section.

What follows below is a brief example of all six hsdl primitives. After each message description we show a set of example messages and what their impact is on a sample document fragment.

hsdl/insert Method

The insert message is designed to insert an xdb:blue into the selected xdb:blue, or to insert an xdb:red value into the selected xdb:blue. A single insert operation may add the same XML fragment in multiple locations of the document. This is a function of the XPath expression used to the specify the node-set.

The operation allows the programmer to specify a minimum and maximum set of matching nodes; if the set of nodes matched by the select attribute is outside of those ranges, an error occurs.

The select attribute on the insert request must specify an existing xdb:blue.

hsdl/insertRequest

This method is accessed using a request message, and in response may generate a response message or a SOAP Fault message. The following sample document fragments illustrate the structure and meaning of the elements and attributes in the request and response messages.

The following section describes the request message for this method.

The format of the insertRequest message is shown below.

```
<hs:insertRequest select="..." useClientIds="..." minOccurs="..." maxOccurs="..."
    xmlns:hs="http://schemas.microsoft.com/hs/2001/10/core">₁.₁
    <hs:options>₀.₁ {any}</hs:options>
    <hs:attribute name="..." value="...">₀..unbounded</hs:attribute>
    {any}
</hs:insertRequest>
```

The meaning of the attributes and elements shown in the preceding sample document fragment are listed in the following section.

/insertRequest (minOccurs=1 maxOccurs=1)

This element indicates a request to insert an xdb:blue or xdb:red into the specified xdb:blue. The select attribute must always select an xdb:blue. This element selects a node-set within the specified document relative to the externally established current context.

/insertRequest/@select (string minOccurs=0 maxOccurs=1)
:   This attribute MUST always select an xdb:blue.

/insertRequest/@useClientIds (string minOccurs=0 maxOccurs=1)
:   This attribute specifies that if an xdb:blue item is created during an insert or replace operation, and an id would normally be generated, the id specified in the request content should be used instead of having .NET My Services generate an id. Applications using this option must ensure that they are properly generating unique id's in the form of a UUID. They must ensure that they do not assign the same ID to multiple xdb:blue items; this can happen if the insert select attribute selects multiple nodes.

/insertRequest/@minOccurs (int minOccurs=0 maxOccurs=1)
:   This optional attribute specifies the minimum number of nodes that must be selected by the select operation in order for this operation to be successfully attempted. The default value is 0, meaning that if no nodes are selected, the operation silently succeeds as a NOP. A value of one means that a minimum of one node must be selected. In this case, if no nodes are selected, the operation fails with an error.

/insertRequest/@maxOccurs (int minOccurs=0 maxOccurs=1)
:   This optional attribute specifies the maximum number of nodes that may be selected by the select operation in order for this operation to be successfully attempted. The default value is unbounded. If the number of nodes selected by the select attribute is greater than this value, an error condition occurs.

/insertRequest/options (minOccurs=0 maxOccurs=1)
:   TBD

/insertRequest/options/**{any}** (minOccurs=0 maxOccurs=unbounded)

/insertRequest/attribute (minOccurs=0 maxOccurs=unbounded)
:   This element is used to specify a single attribute to be manipulated by the .NET My Services data-manipulation primitives. For example, when used in an insertRequest, this element specifies an attribute to be inserted at the specified node.

/insertRequest/attribute/@name (string minOccurs=0 maxOccurs=1)
:   This element is used to specify the name of the attribute being operated on.

/insertRequest/attribute/@value (string minOccurs=0 maxOccurs=1)
:   This element is used to specify the value of the attribute being operated on.

/insertRequest/**{any}** (minOccurs=0 maxOccurs=unbounded)
:   This element is a placeholder that indicates where the content being inserted is to be specified.

hsdl/Example/insert xdb:blue

This example illustrates a successful insert of an xdb:blue.

```
<!--
//
// document skeleton
//
-->
<myA id="" changeNumber="">
    <b id="" changeNumber=""/>
    <c id="" changeNumber="">
        <z/>
        <d/>
        <e/>
    </c>
</myA>
<!--
//
// insertRequest
//
-->
<insertRequest select="/myA[@id='1']">
    <b/>
</insertRequest>
<!--                                    <!--
//                                      //
// Before                               // After
//                                      //
-->                                     -->
<myA id="1" changeNumber="1">           <myA id="1" changeNumber="2">
</myA>                                       <b id="2" changeNumber="2"/>
                                        </myA>

<!--
//
// Response
//
-->
<insertResponse newChangeNumber="2" selectedNodeCount="1" status="success">
    <newBlueId id="2"/>
</insertResponse>
```

hsdl/Example/insert xdb:blue, useClientlds

This example illustrates a successful insert of an xdb:blue where the client has specified the useClientIds attribute. So instead of .NET My Services generating an id for the inserted xdb:blue, it will use the client-generated id instead.

```
<!--
//
// document skeleton
//
-->
<myA id="" changeNumber="">
    <b id="" changeNumber=""/>
    <c id="" changeNumber="">
        <z/>
        <d/>
        <e/>
    </c>
</myA>
<!--
//
// insertRequest
//
-->
<insertRequest select="/myA[@id='1']" useClientIds="true">
    <b id="234432"/>
</insertRequest>
<!--                            <!--
//                             //
// Before                      // After
//                             //
-->                            -->
<myA id="1" changeNumber="1">   <myA id="1" changeNumber="2">
</myA>                              <b id="234432" changeNumber="2"/>
                               </myA>
<!--
//
// Response
//
-->
<insertResponse newChangeNumber="2" selectedNodeCount="1" status="success"/>
```

hsdl/Example/insert multiple xdb:blues

This example illustrates a successful insert of multiple xdb:blues.

```
<!--
//
// document skeleton
//
-->
<myA id="" changeNumber="">
    <b id="" changeNumber=""/>
    <c id="" changeNumber="">
        <z/>
        <d/>
        <e/>
    </c>
</myA>
<!--
//
// insertRequest
//
-->
<insertRequest select="/myA[@id='1']">
    <b/>
    <c>
        <z/>
        <d/>
        <e/>
    </c>
    <c>
        <z/>
        <d/>
        <e/>
    </c>
</insertRequest>
```

(continued)

(continued)

```
<!--                             <!--
//                               //
// Before                        // After (note system generated id's)
//                               //
-->                              -->
<myA id="1" changeNumber="1">    <myA id="1" changeNumber="2">
    <b id="20" changeNumber="1"/>    <b id="20" changeNumber="1"/>
</myA>                               <b id="123433432" changeNumber="2"/>
                                     <c id="126764545" changeNumber="2">
                                         <z/>
                                         <d/>
                                         <e/>
                                     </c>
                                     <c id="474354211" changeNumber="2">
                                         <z/>
                                         <d/>
                                         <e/>
                                     </c>
                                 </myA>

<!--
//
// Response
//
-->
<insertResponse newChangeNumber="2" selectedNodeCount="1" status="success">
    <newBlueId id="123433432"/>
    <newBlueId id="126764545"/>
    <newBlueId id="474354211"/>
</insertResponse>
```

hsdl/Example/insert xdb:red

This example illustrates a successful insert of an xdb:red. Note that no newBlueId element is returned because this is a red insert, not an id-generating insert.

```
<!--
//
// document skeleton
//
-->
<myA id="" changeNumber="">
    <b id="" changeNumber=""/>
    <c id="" changeNumber="">
        <z/>
        <d/>
        <e/>
    </c>
</myA>
<!--
//
// insertRequest
//
-->
<insertRequest select="//c[id='3']">
    <z/>
</insertRequest>
<!--                              <!--
//                                //
// Before                         // After
//                                //
-->                               -->
<myA id="1" changeNumber="1">     <myA id="1" changeNumber="2">
    <c id="3" changeNumber="1">       <c id="3" changeNumber="2">
        <e/>                              <z/>
    </c>                                  <e/>
</myA>                                </c>
                                  </myA>

<!--
//
// Response
//
-->
<insertResponse newChangeNumber="2" selectedNodeCount="1" status="success"/>
```

hsdl/Example/insert failure (non-colorized)

This example illustrates a failure on an attempt to insert a non-colorized item into an xdb:blue.

```
<!--
//
// document skeleton
//
-->
<myA id="" changeNumber="">
    <b id="" changeNumber=""/>
    <c id="" changeNumber="">
        <z/>
        <d/>
        <e/>
    </c>
</myA>
<!--
//
// insertRequest
//
-->
<insertRequest select="//c[id='3']">
    <d/>
</insertRequest>
<!--                                    <!--
//                                      //
// Before                               // After
//                                      //
-->                                     -->
<myA id="1" changeNumber="1">           <myA id="1" changeNumber="1">
    <c id="3" changeNumber="1">             <c id="3" changeNumber="1">
        <e/>                                    <e/>
    </c>                                    </c>
</myA>                                   </myA>
<!--
//
// Response
//
-->
<insertResponse newChangeNumber="1" selectedNodeCount="1" status="failure"/>
```

hsdl/Example/insert failure maxOccurs violation

This example illustrates the use of maxOccurs to generate a failure if the select attribute selects more than one node. A failure here would tell the application software to further qualify the select attribute to identify the desired node more accurately.

```
<!--
//
// document skeleton
//
-->
<myA id="" changeNumber="">
    <b id="" changeNumber=""/>
    <c id="" changeNumber="">
        <z/>
        <d/>
        <e/>
    </c>
</myA>
<!--
//
// insertRequest
//
-->
<insertRequest select="//c" maxOccurs="1">
    <z/>
</insertRequest>
<!--                                    <!--
//                                      //
// Before                               // After
//                                      //
-->                                     -->
<myA id="1" changeNumber="1">           <myA id="1" changeNumber="1">
    <c id="3" changeNumber="1">             <c id="3" changeNumber="1">
        <e/>                                    <e/>
    </c>                                    </c>
    <c id="4" changeNumber="1">             <c id="4" changeNumber="1">
        <d/>                                    <d/>
    </c>                                    </c>
</myA>                                   </myA>
<!--
//
// Response
//
-->
<insertResponse newChangeNumber="1" selectedNodeCount="2" status="failure"/>
```

hsdl/insertResponse

Upon successful completion of this method, a response message is generated. The format of the response message is described below.

The insertResponse message may occur in either a SOAP Body element (in the case of a non-fault response) or in a SOAP Fault element (in the case of a fault). The format of the response is shown below. The important thing to note in the response message is that the .NET My Services server will generate id's, and that each insert of an xdb:blue has the potential to cause the generation of an id. The response message includes a newBlueId item for each id generated by .NET My Services. It is up to application software to relate this id to the blue items that it inserted. Clients keeping a client-side cache should not have a problem with this because their cache must map onto the document and, assuming the client understands the shape of the .NET My Services data, the elements inserted have deterministic location and numbers. Note that when clients use the useClientIds attribute to prevent .NET My Services from generating an id, the associated newBlueId element is NOT returned.

```
<hs:insertResponse newChangeNumber="..." selectedNodeCount="..." status="..."
    xmlns:hs="http://schemas.microsoft.com/hs/2001/10/core">₁..₁
    <hs:newBlueId id="...">₀..unbounded</hs:newBlueId>
</hs:insertResponse>
```

The meaning of the attributes and elements shown in the preceding sample document fragment are listed in the following section.

/insertResponse (minOccurs=1 maxOccurs=1)
    This element specifies the response to the insertRequest.

/insertResponse/@newChangeNumber (minOccurs=0 maxOccurs=1)
    This attribute returns the changeNumber resulting from the insert operation. This attribute is not returned when contained within an updateResponse because in that message, the root contains the changeNumber.

/insertResponse/@selectedNodeCount (int minOccurs=0 maxOccurs=1)
    This attribute is used to return the number of selected nodes, selected by the corresponding hsdl operation.

/insertResponse/@status (string minOccurs=0 maxOccurs=1)
    This attribute indicates the status of the matching operation. The status can be one of the following:

success
    The corresponding operation was completed successfully. Note that a match of 0 nodes, coupled with minOccurs="0", is considered successful.

failure
    The corresponding operation was not completed successfully.

notAttempted
    The corresponding operation was not attempted.

/insertResponse/newBlueId (minOccurs=0 maxOccurs=unbounded)
    This element exists once for each xdb:blue item that was successfully inserted.

/insertResponse/newBlueId/@id (minOccurs=0 maxOccurs=1)
    This attribute specifies the id of the deleted item.

hsdl/delete Method

The delete message is designed to delete a set of xdb:blues or xdb:reds from the specified .NET My Services document at the selected location. A single delete operation may delete multiple matching nodes. This is a function of the XPath expression used to the specify the node-set. The select attribute MUST select either an xdb:blue or an xdb:red.

The operation allows the programmer to specify a minimum and maximum set of matching nodes and, if the set of nodes matched by the select attribute is outside of those ranges, an error occurs.

hsdl/deleteRequest

This method is accessed using a request message, and in response may generate a response message or a SOAP Fault message. The following sample document fragments illustrate the structure and meaning of the elements and attributes in the request and response messages.

The following section describes the request message for this method.

The format of the deleteRequest message is shown below.

```
<hs:deleteRequest select="..." minOccurs="..." maxOccurs="..."
    xmlns:hs="http://schemas.microsoft.com/hs/2001/10/core">₁..₁
    <hs:options>₀..₁ {any}</hs:options>
</hs:deleteRequest>
```

The meaning of the attributes and elements shown in the preceding sample document fragment are listed in the following section.

/deleteRequest (minOccurs=1 maxOccurs=1)
    This element indicates a request to delete the selected xdb:blue or xdb:red items from the specified XML document. This element selects a node-set within the specified document relative to the externally established current context.

/deleteRequest/@select (string minOccurs=0 maxOccurs=1)
> This attribute MUST always select an xdb:blue or an xdb:red.

/deleteRequest/@minOccurs (int minOccurs=0 maxOccurs=1)
> This optional attribute specifies the minimum number of nodes that must be selected by the select operation in order for this operation to be successfully attempted. The default value is 0, meaning that if no nodes are selected, the operation silently succeeds as a NOP. A value of one means that a minimum of one node must be selected. In this case, if no nodes are selected, the operation fails with an error.

/deleteRequest/@maxOccurs (int minOccurs=0 maxOccurs=1)
> This optional attribute specifies the maximum number of nodes that may be selected by the select operation in order for this operation to be successfully attempted. The default value is unbounded. If the number of nodes selected by the select attribute is greater than this value, an error condition occurs.

/deleteRequest/options (minOccurs=0 maxOccurs=1)
> TBD

/deleteRequest/options/*{any}* (minOccurs=0 maxOccurs=unbounded)

hsdl/Example/delete multiple xdb:blue

This example illustrates a successful delete of an xdb:blue.

```
<!--
//
// document skeleton
//
-->
<myA id="" changeNumber="">
    <b id="" changeNumber=""/>
    <c id="" changeNumber="">
        <z/>
        <d/>
        <e/>
    </c>
</myA>
<!--
//
// deleteRequest
//
-->
<deleteRequest select="//b"/>
```

```
<!--
//
// Before
//
-->
<myA id="1" changeNumber="1">
    <b id="20" changeNumber="1"/>
    <b id="2" changeNumber="1"/>
    <c id="3" changeNumber="1">
        <z/>
        <d/>
        <e/>
    </c>
    <c id="4" changeNumber="1">
        <z/>
        <d/>
        <e/>
    </c>
</myA>
<!--
//
// Response
//
-->
<deleteResponse newChangeNumber="2" selectedNodeCount="2" status="success"/>
```

```
<!--
//
// After
//
-->
<myA id="1" changeNumber="2">
    <c id="3" changeNumber="1">
        <z/>
        <d/>
        <e/>
    </c>
    <c id="4" changeNumber="1">
        <z/>
        <d/>
        <e/>
    </c>
</myA>
```

hsdl/Example/delete xdb:red

This example illustrates a successful delete of an xdb:red.

```
<!--
//
// document skeleton
//
-->
<myA id="" changeNumber="">
    <b id="" changeNumber=""/>
    <c id="" changeNumber="">
        <z/>
        <d/>
        <e/>
    </c>
</myA>
```

(continued)

(continued)

```
<!--
//
// deleteRequest
//
-->
<deleteRequest select="//c[id='4']/z"/>
<!--                                        <!--
//                                          //
// Before                                   // After
//                                          //
-->                                         -->
<myA id="1" changeNumber="1">               <myA id="1" changeNumber="2">
    <b id="20" changeNumber="1"/>               <b id="20" changeNumber="1"/>
    <b id="2" changeNumber="1"/>                <b id="2" changeNumber="1"/>
    <c id="3" changeNumber="1">                 <c id="3" changeNumber="1">
        <z/>                                        <z/>
        <d/>                                        <d/>
        <e/>                                        <e/>
    </c>                                        </c>
    <c id="4" changeNumber="1">                 <c id="4" changeNumber="2">
        <z/>                                        <d/>
        <d/>                                        <e/>
        <e/>                                    </c>
    </c>                                    </myA>
</myA>
<!--
//
// Response
//
-->
<deleteResponse newChangeNumber="2" selectedNodeCount="1" status="success"/>
```

hsdl/Example/delete failure (non-colorized)

This example illustrates the failure to delete due to a selection of a non-colorized node.

```
<!--
//
// document skeleton
//
-->
<myA id="" changeNumber="">
    <b id="" changeNumber=""/>
    <c id="" changeNumber="">
        <z/>
        <d/>
        <e/>
    </c>
</myA>
<!--
//
// deleteRequest
//
-->
<deleteRequest select="//c[id='4']/d"/>
<!--                                    <!--
//                                      //
// Before                               // After
//                                      //
-->                                     -->
<myA id="1" changeNumber="1">           <myA id="1" changeNumber="1">
    <b id="20" changeNumber="1"/>           <b id="20" changeNumber="1"/>
    <b id="2" changeNumber="1"/>            <b id="2" changeNumber="1"/>
    <c id="3" changeNumber="1">             <c id="3" changeNumber="1">
        <z/>                                    <z/>
        <d/>                                    <d/>
        <e/>                                    <e/>
    </c>                                    </c>
    <c id="4" changeNumber="1">             <c id="4" changeNumber="1">
        <z/>                                    <z/>
        <d/>                                    <d/>
        <e/>                                    <e/>
    </c>                                    </c>
</myA>                                   </myA>
```

(continued)

(continued)

```
<!--
//
// Response
//
-->
<deleteResponse newChangeNumber="1" selectedNodeCount="0" status="failure"/>
```

hsdl/Example/delete failure (maxOccurs violation)

This example illustrates the failure to delete due to a maxOccurs violation.

```
<!--
//
// document skeleton
//
-->
<myA id="" changeNumber="">
    <b id="" changeNumber=""/>
    <c id="" changeNumber="">
        <z/>
        <d/>
        <e/>
    </c>
</myA>
<!--
//
// deleteRequest
//
-->
<deleteRequest select="//c" maxOccurs="1"/>
```

```
<!--                                    <!--
//                                      //
// Before                               // After
//                                      //
-->                                     -->
<myA id="1" changeNumber="1">           <myA id="1" changeNumber="1">
    <b id="20" changeNumber="1"/>           <b id="20" changeNumber="1"/>
    <b id="2" changeNumber="1"/>            <b id="2" changeNumber="1"/>
    <c id="3" changeNumber="1">             <c id="3" changeNumber="1">
        <z/>                                    <z/>
        <d/>                                    <d/>
        <e/>                                    <e/>
    </c>                                    </c>
```

```
        <c id="4" changeNumber="1">            <c id="4" changeNumber="1">
            <z/>                                    <z/>
            <d/>                                    <d/>
            <e/>                                    <e/>
        </c>                                    </c>
</myA>                                  </myA>
<!--
//
// Response
//
-->
<deleteResponse newChangeNumber="1" selectedNodeCount="2" status="failure"/>
```

hsdl/Example/delete xdb:red attribute

This example illustrates the deletion of an xdb:red attribute.

```
<!--
//
// document skeleton
//
-->
<myA id="" changeNumber="">
    <b id="" changeNumber=""/>
    <c id="" changeNumber="" name="">
        <z/>
        <d/>
        <e/>
    </c>
</myA>
<!--
//
// deleteRequest
//
-->
<deleteRequest select="//c[@id='3']/@name"/>
```

```
<!--
//
// Before
//
-->
<myA id="1" changeNumber="1">
    <b id="20" changeNumber="1"/>
    <b id="2" changeNumber="1"/>
    <c id="3" name="fred"
changeNumber="1">
        <z/>
        <d/>
        <e/>
    </c>
    <c id="4" name="barney"
changeNumber="1">
        <z/>
        <d/>
        <e/>
    </c>
</myA>
<!--
//
// Response
//
-->
<deleteResponse newChangeNumber="2" selectedNodeCount="1" status="success"/>
```

```
<!--
//
// After
//
-->
<myA id="1" changeNumber="2">
    <b id="20" changeNumber="1"/>
    <b id="2" changeNumber="1"/>
    <c id="3" changeNumber="2">
        <z/>
        <d/>
        <e/>
    </c>
    <c id="4" name="barney"
changeNumber="1">
        <z/>
        <d/>
        <e/>
    </c>
</myA>
```

hsdl/deleteResponse

Upon successful completion of this method, a response message is generated. The format of the response message is described below.

The deleteResponse message may occur in either a SOAP Body element (in the case of a non-fault response) or in a SOAP Fault element (in the case of a fault). The format of the response is shown below.

```
<hs:deleteResponse newChangeNumber="..." selectedNodeCount="..." status="..."
    xmlns:hs="http://schemas.microsoft.com/hs/2001/10/core">...</hs:deleteResponse>
```

The meaning of the attributes and elements shown in the preceding sample document fragment are listed in the following section.

/deleteResponse (minOccurs=1 maxOccurs=1)

This element specifies the response to the deleteRequest.

/deleteResponse/@newChangeNumber (minOccurs=0 maxOccurs=1)

This attribute returns the changeNumber resulting from the delete operation. This attribute is not returned when contained within an updateResponse, because in that message, the root contains the changeNumber.

/deleteResponse/@selectedNodeCount (int minOccurs=0 maxOccurs=1)

This attribute is used to return the number of selected nodes, selected by the corresponding hsdl operation.

/deleteResponse/@status (string minOccurs=0 maxOccurs=1)

This attribute indicates the status of the matching operation. The status can be one of the following:

success

The corresponding operation was completed successfully. Note that a match of 0 nodes, coupled with minOccurs="0", is considered successful.

failure

The corresponding operation was not completed successfully.

notAttempted

The corresponding operation was not attempted.

hsdl/replace Method

The replace message is designed to replace the specified xdb:blue(s) or xdb:red(s) with the specified new content for the selected node. One way to think of this operation is as an atomic delete of the content of the selected node, followed by an insert. All of the content in the selected node is replaced with the new item specified in this message. It is important to note that content includes the attributes of the selected node as well as all descendant nodes. When the selected node is an xdb:blue, the existing replaced item's id attribute is preserved, and if this message contains an id attribute, it is ignored. The node type of the selected node and of the replacement node MUST be the same. The select attribute MUST specify either an xdb:blue or an xdb:red. A single replace operation may affect multiple nodes. This is a function of the XPath expression used to specify the node-set.

The operation allows the programmer to specify a minimum and maximum set of matching nodes, and if the set of nodes matched by the select attribute is outside of those ranges, an error occurs.

hsdl/replaceRequest

This method is accessed using a request message, and in response may generate a response message or a SOAP Fault message. The following sample document fragments illustrate the structure and meaning of the elements and attributes in the request and response messages.

The following section describes the request message for this method.

The format of the replaceRequest message is shown below.

```
<hs:replaceRequest select="..." useClientIds="..." minOccurs="..."
maxOccurs="..."
    xmlns:hs="http://schemas.microsoft.com/hs/2001/10/core">₁..₁
    <hs:options>₀..₁ {any}</hs:options>
    <hs:attribute name="..." value="...">₀..unbounded</hs:attribute>
    {any}
</hs:replaceRequest>
```

The meaning of the attributes and elements shown in the preceding sample document fragment are listed in the following section.

/replaceRequest (minOccurs=1 maxOccurs=1)

This element indicates a request to replace an existing xdb:blue or xdb:red with the XML document fragment contained within this message. This element selects a node-set within the specified document relative to the externally established current context. The selected node MUST be an xdb:blue or an xdb:red.

The message first selects a node set, and then for each node, replaces the selected node with the content of this message. For xdb:blue nodes, the node's id is preserved.

/replaceRequest/@select (string minOccurs=0 maxOccurs=1)

This attribute MUST always select an xdb:blue or an xdb:red.

/replaceRequest/@useClientIds (string minOccurs=0 maxOccurs=1)

This attribute specifies that if an xdb:blue item is created during an insert or replace operation, and an id would normally be generated, the id specified in the request content should be used instead of having .NET My Services generate an id. Applications using this option must ensure that they are properly generating unique id's in the form of a UUID. They must ensure that they do not assign the same ID to multiple xdb:blue items; this can happen if the insert select attribute selects multiple nodes.

/replaceRequest/@minOccurs (int minOccurs=0 maxOccurs=1)

This optional attribute specifies the minimum number of nodes that must be selected by the select operation in order for this operation to be successfully attempted. The default value is 0, meaning that if no nodes are selected, the operation silently succeeds as a NOP. A value of one means that a minimum of one node must be selected. In this case, if no nodes are selected, the operation fails with an error.

/replaceRequest/@maxOccurs (int minOccurs=0 maxOccurs=1)
> This optional attribute specifies the maximum number of nodes that may be selected by the select operation in order for this operation to be successfully attempted. The default value is unbounded. If the number of nodes selected by the select attribute is greater than this value, an error condition occurs.

/replaceRequest/options (minOccurs=0 maxOccurs=1)
> TBD

/replaceRequest/options/*{any}* (minOccurs=0 maxOccurs=unbounded)
/replaceRequest/attribute (minOccurs=0 maxOccurs=unbounded)
> This element is used to specify a single attribute to be manipulated by the .NET My Services data-manipulation primitives. For example, when used in an insertRequest, this element specifies an attribute to be inserted at the specified node.

/replaceRequest/attribute/@name (string minOccurs=0 maxOccurs=1)
> This element is used to specify the name of the attribute being operated on.

/replaceRequest/attribute/@value (string minOccurs=0 maxOccurs=1)
> This element is used to specify the value of the attribute being operated on.

/replaceRequest/*{any}* (minOccurs=0 maxOccurs=unbounded)
> This element is a placeholder that indicates where the content of the item being replaced is to be specified.

hsdl/Example/replace xdb:blue

This example illustrates the use of replaceRequest to replace an existing xdb:blue. Note that the content of the replaceRequest is the content for the xdb:blue, not a new skeleton. Also note that the id attribute is supplied, but silently ignored.

```
<!--
//
// document skeleton
//
-->
<myA id="" changeNumber="">
    <b id="" changeNumber=""/>
    <c id="" changeNumber="" name="">
        <z/>
        <d/>
        <e/>
    </c>
</myA>
```

```
<!--
//
// replaceRequest
//
--->
<replaceRequest select="//c[@id='3']">
    <c name="mark">
        <z/>
        <d/>
    </c>
</replaceRequest>
<!--                                          <!--
//                                            //
// Before                                     // After
//                                            //
-->                                           -->
<myA id="1" changeNumber="1">                 <myA id="1" changeNumber="2">
    <b id="20" changeNumber="1"/>                 <b id="20" changeNumber="1"/>
    <b id="2" changeNumber="1"/>                  <b id="2" changeNumber="1"/>
    <c id="3" name="fred"                         <c id="3" name="mark"
changeNumber="1">                             changeNumber="2">
        <z/>                                          <z/>
        <d/>                                          <d/>
        <e/>                                      </c>
    </c>                                          <c id="4" name="barney"
    <c id="4" name="barney"                   changeNumber="1">
changeNumber="1">                                     <z/>
        <z/>                                          <d/>
        <d/>                                          <e/>
        <e/>                                      </c>
    </c>                                      </myA>
</myA>
<!--
//
// Response
//
-->
<replaceResponse newChangeNumber="2" selectedNodeCount="1" status="success"/>
```

hsdl/Example/replace xdb:red

This example illustrates the use of replaceRequest to replace an existing xdb:red. Note that the content of the replaceRequest is the content for the xdb:red, not a new skeleton.

```
<!--
//
// document skeleton
//
-->
<myA id="" changeNumber="">
    <b id="" changeNumber=""/>
    <c id="" changeNumber="" name="">
        <z/>
        <d/>
        <e/>
    </c>
</myA>
<!--
//
// replaceRequest
//
-->
<replaceRequest select="//c[@id='3']/@name">
    <hsdl:attribute name="name" value="sally"/>
</replaceRequest>
<!--                                        <!--
//                                          //
// Before                                   // After
//                                          //
-->                                         -->
<myA id="1" changeNumber="1">               <myA id="1" changeNumber="2">
    <b id="20" changeNumber="1"/>               <b id="20" changeNumber="1"/>
    <b id="2" changeNumber="1"/>                <b id="2" changeNumber="1"/>
    <c id="3" name="fred"                       <c id="3" name="sally"
changeNumber="1">                           changeNumber="2">
        <z/>                                        <z/>
        <d/>                                        <d/>
        <e/>                                        <e/>
    </c>                                        </c>
    <c id="4" name="barney"                     <c id="4" name="barney"
changeNumber="1">                           changeNumber="1">
        <z/>                                        <z/>
        <d/>                                        <d/>
        <e/>                                        <e/>
```

(continued)

(continued)

```
    </c>                                      </c>
</myA>                                    </myA>
<!--
//
// Response
//
-->
<replaceResponse newChangeNumber="2" selectedNodeCount="1" status="success"/>
```

hsdl/Example/replace failure (non-colorized)

This example illustrates a failure in replace when the node selection does not specify an xdb:blue or an xdb:red.

```
<!--
//
// document skeleton
//
-->
<myA id="" changeNumber="">
    <b id="" changeNumber=""/>
    <c id="" changeNumber="" name="">
        <z/>
        <d/>
        <e/>
    </c>
</myA>
<!--
//
// replaceRequest
//
-->
<replaceRequest select="//c[@id='3']/d">
    goodbye
</replaceRequest>
<!--                                      <!--
//                                        //
// Before                                 // After
//                                        //
-->                                       -->
<myA id="1" changeNumber="1">             <myA id="1" changeNumber="1">
    <b id="20" changeNumber="1"/>             <b id="20" changeNumber="1"/>
    <b id="2" changeNumber="1"/>              <b id="2" changeNumber="1"/>
    <c id="3" name="fred"                     <c id="3" name="fred"
changeNumber="1">                         changeNumber="1">
```

```
            <z/>                              <z/>
            <d>hello</d>                     <d>hello</d>
            <e/>                              <e/>
        </c>                              </c>
        <c id="4" name="barney"          <c id="4" name="barney"
changeNumber="1">                    changeNumber="1">
            <z/>                              <z/>
            <d/>                              <d/>
            <e/>                              <e/>
        </c>                              </c>
</myA>                               </myA>
<!--
//
// Response
//
-->
<replaceResponse newChangeNumber="1" selectedNodeCount="0" status="failure"/>
```

hsdl/Example/replace failure (minOccurs violation)

This example illustrates a failure in replace when there is a minOccurs violation.

```
<!--
//
// document skeleton
//
-->
<myA id="" changeNumber="">
    <b id="" changeNumber=""/>
    <c id="" changeNumber="" name="">
        <z/>
        <d/>
        <e/>
    </c>
</myA>
<!--
//
// replaceRequest
//
-->
<replaceRequest select="//c[@id='33']" minOccurs="1">
    <c name="mark">
        <z/>
        <d>frog</d>
    </>
```

(continued)

(continued)

```
</replaceRequest>
<!--                              <!--
//                                //
// Before                        // After
//                                //
-->                               -->
<myA id="1" changeNumber="1">     <myA id="1" changeNumber="1">
    <b id="20" changeNumber="1"/>     <b id="20" changeNumber="1"/>
    <b id="2" changeNumber="1"/>      <b id="2" changeNumber="1"/>
    <c id="3" name="fred"             <c id="3" name="fred"
changeNumber="1">                 changeNumber="1">
        <z/>                              <z/>
        <d>hello</d>                      <d>hello</d>
        <e/>                              <e/>
    </c>                              </c>
    <c id="4" name="barney"           <c id="4" name="barney"
changeNumber="1">                 changeNumber="1">
        <z/>                              <z/>
        <d/>                              <d/>
        <e/>                              <e/>
    </c>                              </c>
</myA>                            </myA>
<!--
//
// Response
//
-->
<replaceResponse newChangeNumber="1" selectedNodeCount="0" status="failure"/>
```

hsdl/replaceResponse

Upon successful completion of this method, a response message is generated. The format of the response message is described below.

The replaceResponse message may occur in either a SOAP Body element (in the case of a non-fault response) or in a SOAP Fault element (in the case of a fault). The format of the response is shown below.

```
<hs:replaceResponse newChangeNumber="..." selectedNodeCount="..." status="..."
    xmlns:hs="http://schemas.microsoft.com/hs/2001/10/core">1...1
    <hs:newBlueId id="...">0..unbounded</hs:newBlueId>
</hs:replaceResponse>
```

The meaning of the attributes and elements shown in the preceding sample document fragment are listed in the following section.

/replaceResponse (minOccurs=1 maxOccurs=1)
> This element specifies the response to the replaceRequest.

/replaceResponse/@newChangeNumber (minOccurs=0 maxOccurs=1)
> This attribute returns the changeNumber resulting from the replace operation. This attribute is not returned when contained within an updateResponse, because in that message, the root contains the changeNumber.

/replaceResponse/@selectedNodeCount (int minOccurs=0 maxOccurs=1)
> This attribute is used to return the number of selected nodes, selected by the corresponding hsdl operation.

/replaceResponse/@status (string minOccurs=0 maxOccurs=1)
> This attribute indicates the status of the matching operation. The status can be one of the following:

> success
>> The corresponding operation was completed successfully. Note that a match of 0 nodes, coupled with minOccurs="0", is considered success.

> failure
>> The corresponding operation was not completed successfully.

> notAttempted
>> The corresponding operation was not attempted.

/replaceResponse/newBlueId (minOccurs=0 maxOccurs=unbounded)
> This element exists once for each xdb:blue item that was successfully inserted.

/replaceResponse/newBlueId/@id (minOccurs=0 maxOccurs=1)
> This attribute specifies the id of the deleted item.

hsdl/update Method

The update message is designed to group multiple insert, replace, and delete operations efficiently in a single message, providing application software with an easy way to apply a set of changes to the specified document. The message allows the application to group operations relative to a specific node set in the document, and provides rich control over the failure modes relative to that node set. The most efficient way to use this message is to bundle document changes by xdb:blues that are as close as possible to the nodes that are to be manipulated.

This message uses the updateBlock element to mark transaction boundaries in the message. Each updateBlock defines an xdb:blue element whose path is the relative path for all of the updateBlock's child elements. Each update block determines for itself how error conditions within the block are handled. An update block is able to specify that upon error, its operations are to be rolled back to their original state. Once rolled back, the updateRequest can continue or generate a failure. The updateBlock can also specify that errors are to be ignored.

The update message generates an updateResponse designed to help applications that are maintaining caches to update their caches with the new changeNumbers, id's, and deletions. In order to push changeNumbers properly back into your client-side cache, the first updateBlock should select context that includes the outermost changeNumber that the client wishes to treat as its cache.

hsdl/updateRequest

This method is accessed using a request message, and in response may generate a response message or a SOAP Fault message. The following sample document fragments illustrate the structure and meaning of the elements and attributes in the request and response messages.

The following section describes the request message for this method.

The format of the updateRequest message is shown below.

```
<hs:updateRequest
    xmlns:hs="http://schemas.microsoft.com/hs/2001/10/core">1..1
    <hs:updateBlock select="..." onError="...">1..unbounded
        <hs:insertRequest select="..." useClientIds="..." minOccurs="..."
maxOccurs="...">0..unbounded
            <hs:options>0..1 {any}</hs:options>
            <hs:attribute name="..." value="...">0..unbounded</hs:attribute>
            {any}
        </hs:insertRequest>
        <hs:deleteRequest select="..." minOccurs="..." maxOccurs="...">0..unbounded
            <hs:options>0..1 {any}</hs:options>
        </hs:deleteRequest>
        <hs:replaceRequest select="..." useClientIds="..." minOccurs="..."
maxOccurs="...">0..unbounded
            <hs:options>0..1 {any}</hs:options>
            <hs:attribute name="..." value="...">0..unbounded</hs:attribute>
            {any}
        </hs:replaceRequest>
    </hs:updateBlock>
</hs:updateRequest>
```

The meaning of the attributes and elements shown in the preceding sample document fragment are listed in the following section.

/updateRequest (minOccurs=1 maxOccurs=1)

The update request is designed to take a set of individual insert, replace, and delete requests and apply them to the specified document. The message is designed to contain a series of updateBlocks that share a common document context and that share common failure semantics.

/updateRequest/updateBlock (minOccurs=1 maxOccurs=unbounded)

A sequence of operations grouped by a common context in the XML document sharing the same failure semantics.

/updateRequest/updateBlock/@select (string minOccurs=0 maxOccurs=1)

This item specifies an XPath expression that establishes global context for this updateBlock. The selection MUST specify an xdb:blue. With this context established, the enclosed operation's select attributes select nodes within this global context. It is not an error to match 0 nodes with this select attribute. The empty node set is simply the context for the enclosed operations, and their minOccurs and maxOccurs attributes dictate success or failure.

/updateRequest/updateBlock/@onError (string minOccurs=0 maxOccurs=1)

This attribute controls how error conditions raised by individual operations within an updateBlock affect the entire updateRequest message. Error conditions can trigger one of the following actions:

rollbackBlockAndFail

If any operation within the updateBlock fails, all enclosed operations are rolled back to their initial state and the updateRequest ends in a failure condition.

rollbackBlockAndContinue

If any operation within the updateBlock fails, all enclosed operations are rolled back to their initial state and execution proceeds to the next updateBlock.

ignore

Failures within an individual updateBlock do not trigger a rollback or a failure in the updateRequest. A failure simply terminates execution of the updateBlock. Successful operations are tagged in the updateResponse. Execution continues at the next updateBlock.

/updateRequest/updateBlock/insertRequest (minOccurs=0 maxOccurs=unbounded)

This element indicates a request to insert an xdb:blue or xdb:red into the specified xdb:blue. The select attribute must always select an xdb:blue. This element selects a node-set within the specified document relative to the externally established current context.

/updateRequest/updateBlock/insertRequest/@select (string minOccurs=0 maxOccurs=1)

This attribute MUST always select an xdb:blue.

/updateRequest/updateBlock/insertRequest/@useClientIds (string minOccurs=0 maxOccurs=1)

This attribute specifies that if an xdb:blue item is created during an insert or replace operation, and an id would normally be generated, the id specified in the request content should be used instead of having .NET My Services generate an id. Applications using this option must ensure that they are properly generating unique id's in the form of a UUID. They must ensure that they do not assign the same id to multiple xdb:blue items; this can happen if the insert select attribute selects multiple nodes.

/updateRequest/updateBlock/insertRequest/@minOccurs (int minOccurs=0 maxOccurs=1)

This optional attribute specifies the minimum number of nodes that must be selected by the select operation in order for this operation to be successfully attempted. The default value is 0, meaning that if no nodes are selected, the operation silently succeeds as a NOP. A value of one means that a minimum of one node must be selected. In this case, if no nodes are selected, the operation fails with an error.

/updateRequest/updateBlock/insertRequest/@maxOccurs (int minOccurs=0 maxOccurs=1)

This optional attribute specifies the maximum number of nodes that may be selected by the select operation in order for this operation to be successfully attempted. The default value is unbounded. If the number of nodes selected by the select attribute is greater than this value, an error condition occurs.

/updateRequest/updateBlock/insertRequest/attribute (minOccurs=0 maxOccurs=unbounded)

This element is used to specify a single attribute to be manipulated by the .NET My Services data-manipulation primitives. For example, when used in an insertRequest, this element specifies an attribute to be inserted at the specified node.

/updateRequest/updateBlock/insertRequest/attribute/@name (string minOccurs=0 maxOccurs=1)

This element is used to specify the name of the attribute being operated on.

/updateRequest/updateBlock/insertRequest/attribute/@value (string minOccurs=0 maxOccurs=1)

This element is used to specify the value of the attribute being operated on.

/updateRequest/updateBlock/insertRequest/*{any}* (minOccurs=0 maxOccurs=unbounded)

This element is a placeholder that indicates where the content being inserted is to be specified.

/updateRequest/updateBlock/deleteRequest (minOccurs=0 maxOccurs=unbounded)

This element indicates a request to delete the selected xdb:blue or xdb:red items from the specified XML document. This element selects a node-set within the specified document relative to the externally established current context.

/updateRequest/updateBlock/deleteRequest/@select (string minOccurs=0 maxOccurs=1)

This attribute MUST always select an xdb:blue or an xdb:red.

/updateRequest/updateBlock/deleteRequest/@minOccurs (int minOccurs=0 maxOccurs=1)

This optional attribute specifies the minimum number of nodes that must be selected by the select operation in order for this operation to be successfully attempted. The default value is 0, meaning that if no nodes are selected, the operation silently succeeds as a NOP. A value of one means that a minimum of one node must be selected. In this case, if no nodes are selected, the operation fails with an error.

/updateRequest/updateBlock/deleteRequest/@maxOccurs (int minOccurs=0 maxOccurs=1)

This optional attribute specifies the maximum number of nodes that may be selected by the select operation in order for this operation to be successfully attempted. The default value is unbounded. If the number of nodes selected by the select attribute is greater than this value, an error condition occurs.

/updateRequest/updateBlock/replaceRequest (minOccurs=0 maxOccurs=unbounded)

This element indicates a request to replace an existing xdb:blue or xdb:red with the XML document fragment contained within this message. This element selects a node-set within the specified document relative to the externally established current context. The selected node MUST be an xdb:blue or an xdb:red.

The message first selects a node set, and then for each node, replaces the selected node with the content of this message. For xdb:blue nodes, the node's id is preserved.

/updateRequest/updateBlock/replaceRequest/@select (string minOccurs=0 maxOccurs=1)

This attribute must always select an xdb:blue or an xdb:red.

/updateRequest/updateBlock/replaceRequest/@useClientIds (string minOccurs=0 maxOccurs=1)

This attribute specifies that if an xdb:blue item is created during an insert or replace operation, and an id would normally be generated, the id specified in the request content should be used instead of having .NET My Services generate an id. Applications using this option must ensure that they are properly generating unique id's in the form of a UUID. They must ensure that they do not assign the same ID to multiple xdb:blue items; this can happen if the insert select attribute selects multiple nodes.

/updateRequest/updateBlock/replaceRequest/@minOccurs (int minOccurs=0 maxOccurs=1)

This optional attribute specifies the minimum number of nodes that must be selected by the select operation in order for this operation to be successfully attempted. The default value is 0, meaning that if no nodes are selected, the operation silently succeeds as a NOP. A value of one means that a minimum of one node must be selected. In this case, if no nodes are selected, the operation fails with an error.

/updateRequest/updateBlock/replaceRequest/@maxOccurs (int minOccurs=0 maxOccurs=1)

This optional attribute specifies the maximum number of nodes that may be selected by the select operation in order for this operation to be successfully attempted. The default value is unbounded. If the number of nodes selected by the select attribute is greater than this value, an error condition occurs.

/updateRequest/updateBlock/replaceRequest/options/*{any}* (minOccurs=0
maxOccurs=unbounded)
/updateRequest/updateBlock/replaceRequest/attribute (minOccurs=0
maxOccurs=unbounded)

> This element is used to specify a single attribute to be manipulated by the .NET My
> Services data-manipulation primitives. For example, when used in an insertRequest,
> this element specifies an attribute to be inserted at the specified node.

/updateRequest/updateBlock/replaceRequest/attribute/@name (string minOccurs=0
maxOccurs=1)

> This element is used to specify the name of the attribute being operated on.

/updateRequest/updateBlock/replaceRequest/attribute/@value (string minOccurs=0
maxOccurs=1)

> This element is used to specify the value of the attribute being operated on.

/updateRequest/updateBlock/replaceRequest/*{any}* (minOccurs=0
maxOccurs=unbounded)

> This element is a placeholder that indicates where the content of the item being
> replaced is to be specified.

hsdl/Example/update single updateBlock

In this example we illustrate an updateRequest with a single updateBlock containing
both replace and delete operations. The updateBlock is marked as
onError="rollbackAndFail". This means that if any operation within the updateBlock fails
(due to minOccurs or maxOccurs constraints or due to data validity), the entire
updateBlock fails and all operations within the block that were completed are rolled back.

```
<!--
//
// document skeleton
//
-->
<myA id="" changeNumber="">
    <b id="" changeNumber=""/>
    <c id="" changeNumber="" name="">
        <z/>
        <d/>
        <e/>
    </c>
</myA>
```

```
<!--
//
// updateRequest
//
-->
<updateRequest>
    <updateBlock select="/myY[@changeNumber='5']/c" onError="rollbackAndFail">
        <replaceRequest select="./[@id='3']" maxOccurs="1">
            <c>
                <d>foo</d>
            </c>
        </replaceRequest>
        <replaceRequest select="./[@id='4']/@name" maxOccurs="1">
            <hsdl:attribute name="name" value="betty"/>
        </replaceRequest>
        <deleteRequest select="./[@id='5']" maxOccurs="1"/>
    </updateBlock>
</updateRequest>
```

```
<!--                                          <!--
//                                            //
// Before                                     // After
//                                            //
-->                                           -->
<myA id="1" changeNumber="5">                 <myA id="1" changeNumber="6">
    <b id="20" changeNumber="5"/>                 <b id="20" changeNumber="5"/>
    <b id="2" changeNumber="5"/>                  <b id="2" changeNumber="5"/>
    <c id="3" changeNumber="4"                    <c id="3" changeNumber="6">
name="fred">                                          <d>foo</d>
        <z/>                                      </c>
        <d>hello</d>                              <c id="4" changeNumber="6"
        <e/>                                  name="betty">
    </c>                                              <z/>
    <c id="4" changeNumber="4"                        <d/>
name="barney">                                        <e/>
        <z/>                                      </c>
        <d/>                                  </myA>
        <e/>
    </c>
    <c id="5" changeNumber="5"
name="wilma">
        <d/>
        <e/>
    </c>
</myA>
```

(continued)

(continued)

```
<!--
//
// Response
//
-->
<updateResponse newChangeNumber="6">
    <updateBlockStatus selectedNodeCount="3" status="success">
        <replaceResponse selectedNodeCount="1" status="success"/>
        <replaceResponse selectedNodeCount="1" status="success"/>
        <replaceResponse selectedNodeCount="1" status="success"/>
    </updateBlockStatus>
</updateResponse>
```

hsdl/Example/update multi-updateBlock

In this example we illustrate an updateRequest with two updateBlocks. This example is meant to illustrate how different updateBlocks are used when the node set context for the updateBlocks are different. The updateBlocks are marked as rollbackAndFail. This means that if any operation within the updateBlocks fails (due to minOccurs or maxOccurs constraints or due to data validity), the entire updateBlock fails and all operations within the block that were completed are rolled back. In this example, both updateBlocks succeed.

```
<!--
//
// document skeleton
//
-->
<myA id="" changeNumber="">
    <b id="" changeNumber=""/>
    <c id="" changeNumber="" name="">
        <z/>
        <d/>
        <e/>
    </c>
</myA>
<!--
//
// updateRequest
//
-->
<updateRequest>
    <updateBlock select="/myA[@changeNumber='5']/c"
```

```
onError="rollbackAndContinue">
        <replaceRequest select="./[@id='3']" maxOccurs="1">
            <c>
                <d>foo</d>
            </c>
        </replaceRequest>
        <deleteRequest select="./[@name='barney']" maxOccurs="1"/>
    </updateBlock>
    <updateBlock select="/myA[@changeNumber='5']/b" onError="rollbackAndFail">
        <deleteRequest select="./[@id='20']" maxOccurs="1"/>
    </updateBlock>
</updateRequest>
<!--                                            <!--
//                                              //
// Before                                       // After
//                                              //
-->                                             -->
<myA id="1" changeNumber="5">                   <myA id="1" changeNumber="6">
    <b id="20" changeNumber="5"/>                   <b id="2" changeNumber="5"/>
    <b id="2" changeNumber="5"/>                    <c id="3" changeNumber="6">
    <c id="3" changeNumber="4"                          <d>foo</d>
name="fred">                                        </c>
        <z/>                                        <c id="5" changeNumber="5"
        <d>hello</d>                            name="wilma">
        <e/>                                            <d/>
    </c>                                                <e/>
    <c id="4" changeNumber="4"                      </c>
name="barney">                                  </myA>
        <z/>
        <d/>
        <e/>
    </c>
    <c id="5" changeNumber="5"
name="wilma">
        <d/>
        <e/>
    </c>
</myA>
<!--
//
// Response
//
-->
<updateResponse newChangeNumber="6">
    <updateBlockStatus selectedNodeCount="3" status="success">
```

(continued)

(continued)

```
        <replaceResponse selectedNodesStatus="1" status="success"/>
        <deleteResponse selectedNodesStatus="1" status="success"/>
    </updateBlockStatus>
    <updateBlockStatus selectedNodeCount="2" status="success">
        <deleteResponse selectedNodesStatus="1" status="success"/>
    </updateBlockStatus>
</updateResponse>
```

hsdl/Example/update multi-updateBlock, 1st update block fails

In this example we illustrate an updateRequest with two updateBlocks. The first one contains multiple operations and is marked rollbackAndContinue. The delete operation is designed to fail, so the entire updateBlock fails and is rolled back. The second updateBlock succeeds.

```
<!--
//
// document skeleton
//
-->
<myA id="" changeNumber="">
    <b id="" changeNumber=""/>
    <c id="" changeNumber="" name="">
        <z/>
        <d/>
        <e/>
    </c>
</myA>
<!--
//
// updateRequest
//
-->
<updateRequest>

    <!--
    //
    // establish a global context for this block.
    // all "c" nodes are part of this context
    //
    -->
    <updateBlock select="/myA[@changeNumber='5']/c"
onError="rollbackAndContinue">
```

```
            <replaceRequest select="./[@id='3']" maxOccurs="1">
                <c>
                    <d>foo</d>
                </c>
            </replaceRequest>
            <deleteRequest select="./[@name='winston']" maxOccurs="1"/>
        </updateBlock>
        <updateBlock select="/myA[@changeNumber='5']/b" onError="rollbackAndFail">
            <deleteRequest select="./[@id='20']" maxOccurs="1"/>
        </updateBlock>
    </updateRequest>
<!--                                    <!--
//                                      //
// Before                               // After
//                                      //
-->                                     -->
<myA id="1" changeNumber="5">           <myA id="1" changeNumber="6">
    <b id="20" changeNumber="5"/>           <b id="2" changeNumber="5"/>
    <b id="2" changeNumber="5"/>            <c id="3" changeNumber="4"
    <c id="3" changeNumber="4"          name="fred">
name="fred">                                    <z/>
        <z/>                                    <d>hello</d>
        <d>hello</d>                            <e/>
        <e/>                                </c>
    </c>                                    <c id="4" changeNumber="4"
    <c id="4" changeNumber="4"          name="barney">
name="barney">                                  <z/>
        <z/>                                    <d/>
        <d/>                                    <e/>
        <e/>                                </c>
    </c>                                    <c id="5" changeNumber="5"
    <c id="5" changeNumber="5"          name="wilma">
name="wilma">                                   <d/>
        <d/>                                    <e/>
        <e/>                                </c>
    </c>                                </myA>
</myA>
<!--
//
// Response
//
-->
<updateResponse newChangeNumber="6">
    <updateBlockStatus selectedNodeCount="3" status="rollback">
```

(continued)

(continued)

```
        <replaceResponse selectedNodeCount="1" status="success"/>
        <deleteResponse selectedNodeCount="1" status="failure"/>
    </updateBlockStatus>
    <updateBlockStatus selectedNodeCount="2" status="status">
        <deleteResponse selectedNodeCount="1" status="success"/>
    </updateBlockStatus>
</updateResponse>
```

hsdl/updateResponse

Upon successful completion of this method, a response message is generated. The format of the response message is described below.

The updateResponse message is designed to inform the caller of the status of each updateBlock and of each operation within that updateBlock. Like the other hsdl operations that modify data, the updateResponse includes changeItem and deletedItem tags to help client software maintain id's and changeNumbers in their caches. These summaries are not a replacement for the client issuing changeSummary queries at appropriate times. They are done because our expectation is that client applications will use the updateRequest message to synchronize their client-side caches, will write through their caches and then issue an updateRequest, and will then need to make their changeNumbers match the .NET My Services state of the changeNumber tree.

```
<hs:updateResponse newChangeNumber="..."
    xmlns:hs="http://schemas.microsoft.com/hs/2001/10/core">1..1
    <hs:updateBlockStatus selectedNodeCount="..." status="...">0..unbounded
        <hs:insertResponse newChangeNumber="..." selectedNodeCount="..."
status="...">0..unbounded
            <hs:newBlueId id="...">0..unbounded</hs:newBlueId>
        </hs:insertResponse>
        <hs:deleteResponse newChangeNumber="..." selectedNodeCount="..."
status="...">0..unbounded</hs:deleteResponse>
        <hs:replaceResponse newChangeNumber="..." selectedNodeCount="..."
status="...">0..unbounded
            <hs:newBlueId id="...">0..unbounded</hs:newBlueId>
        </hs:replaceResponse>
    </hs:updateBlockStatus>
</hs:updateResponse>
```

The meaning of the attributes and elements shown in the preceding sample document fragment are listed in the following section.

/updateResponse (minOccurs=1 maxOccurs=1)

This message contains the results of an updateRequest message. It may appear as a response to an updateRequest, or, in the case of a fault during the processing of an updateRequest, may appear in a SOAP Fault element.

The updateResponse message contains multiple updateBlockStatus elements. One of these elements exists for each updateBlock in the updateRequest message. Each of these contains an updateOperationStatus element for each operation in the updateBlock. Additionally, if the changes alter an ancestor changeNumber, a changeNumberSummary element is present so clients may bring their caches up to date.

/updateResponse/@newChangeNumber (minOccurs=0 maxOccurs=1)

This attribute returns the changeNumber resulting from the entire updateRequest. A given updateRequest only changes a single changeNumber value and the application must update affected nodes in its own cache.

/updateResponse/updateBlockStatus (minOccurs=0 maxOccurs=unbounded)

This element contains status information for the updateBlock whose operation id in the updateRequest matches this element's operation id attribute. This element indicates the status of the entire updateBlock status. It can be one of the following: success, failure, rollback, or notAttempted.

If the status is rollback or notAttempted, the .NET My Services service data was not affected by the corresponding updateBlock. A value of success means that the updateBlock did the specified work, which may or may not have side effects. A value of failure means that the updateBlock was partially executed and the updateOperationStatus elements have additional information.

/updateResponse/updateBlockStatus/@selectedNodeCount (int minOccurs=0 maxOccurs=1)

This attribute is used to return the number of selected nodes, selected by the corresponding hsdl operation.

/updateResponse/updateBlockStatus/@status (string minOccurs=0 maxOccurs=1)

This attribute indicates the status of the corresponding updateBlock and may take on one of the following values:

success

The corresponding updateBlock was completed successfully.

failure

The corresponding updateBlock was not completed successfully. Any side effect of the operation is left present in the service.

rollback

The corresponding updateBlock failed, but was rolled back to its pre-updateBlock status.

notAttempted
>   The corresponding updateBlock was not attempted. This occurs when a previous operation failed.

/updateResponse/updateBlockStatus/insertResponse (minOccurs=0 maxOccurs=unbounded)
>   This element specifies the response to the insertRequest.

/updateResponse/updateBlockStatus/insertResponse/@newChangeNumber (minOccurs=0 maxOccurs=1)
>   This attribute returns the changeNumber resulting from the insert operation. This attribute is not returned when contained within an updateResponse because in that message, the root contains the changeNumber.

/updateResponse/updateBlockStatus/insertResponse/@selectedNodeCount (int minOccurs=0 maxOccurs=1)
>   This attribute is used to return the number of selected nodes, selected by the corresponding hsdl operation.

/updateResponse/updateBlockStatus/insertResponse/@status (string minOccurs=0 maxOccurs=1)
>   This attribute indicates the status of the matching operation. The status can be one of the following:

success
>   The corresponding operation was completed successfully. Note that a match of 0 nodes, coupled with minOccurs="0", is considered success.

failure
>   The corresponding operation was not completed successfully.

notAttempted
>   The corresponding operation was not attempted.

/updateResponse/updateBlockStatus/insertResponse/newBlueId (minOccurs=0 maxOccurs=unbounded)
>   This element exists once for each xdb:blue item that was successfully inserted.

/updateResponse/updateBlockStatus/insertResponse/newBlueId/@id (minOccurs=0 maxOccurs=1)
>   This attribute specifies the id of the deleted item.

/updateResponse/updateBlockStatus/deleteResponse (minOccurs=0 maxOccurs=unbounded)
>   This element specifies the response to the deleteRequest.

/updateResponse/updateBlockStatus/deleteResponse/@newChangeNumber (minOccurs=0 maxOccurs=1)
>   This attribute returns the changeNumber resulting from the delete operation. This attribute is not returned when contained within an updateResponse, because in that message, the root contains the changeNumber.

/updateResponse/updateBlockStatus/deleteResponse/@selectedNodeCount (int minOccurs=0 maxOccurs=1)

>   This attribute is used to return the number of selected nodes, selected by the corresponding hsdl operation.

/updateResponse/updateBlockStatus/deleteResponse/@status (string minOccurs=0 maxOccurs=1)

>   This attribute indicates the status of the matching operation. The status can be one of the following:

>   success

>>   The corresponding operation was completed successfully. Note that a match of 0 nodes, coupled with minOccurs="0", is considered success.

>   failure

>>   The corresponding operation was not completed successfully.

>   notAttempted

>>   The corresponding operation was not attempted.

/updateResponse/updateBlockStatus/replaceResponse (minOccurs=0 maxOccurs=unbounded)

>   This element specifies the response to the replaceRequest.

/updateResponse/updateBlockStatus/replaceResponse/@newChangeNumber (minOccurs=0 maxOccurs=1)

>   This attribute returns the changeNumber resulting from the replace operation. This attribute is not returned when contained within an updateResponse, because in that message, the root contains the changeNumber.

/updateResponse/updateBlockStatus/replaceResponse/@selectedNodeCount (int minOccurs=0 maxOccurs=1)

>   This attribute is used to return the number of selected nodes, selected by the corresponding hsdl operation.

/updateResponse/updateBlockStatus/replaceResponse/@status (string minOccurs=0 maxOccurs=1)

>   This attribute indicates the status of the matching operation. The status can be one of the following:

>   success

>>   The corresponding operation was completed successfully. Note that a match of 0 nodes, coupled with minOccurs="0", is considered success.

>   failure

>>   The corresponding operation was not completed successfully.

>   notAttempted

>>   The corresponding operation was not attempted.

/updateResponse/updateBlockStatus/replaceResponse/newBlueId (minOccurs=0 maxOccurs=unbounded)

This element exists once for each xdb:blue item that was successfully inserted.

/updateResponse/updateBlockStatus/replaceResponse/newBlueId/@id (minOccurs=0 maxOccurs=1)

This attribute specifies the id of the deleted item.

hsdl/query Method

The query request message is designed to return a selected node-set to the client software that sends this message, or to return a set of changes relative to a client-side cache's synchronization base changes that should bring the client-side cache into sync with the .NET My Services data.

As shown below, the queryRequest is a multi-part operation containing both content queries and change summary queries. Content queries are specified by using the xpQuery (xpath query) and xmQuery (XML Query) elements. The xmQuery element is not described in this document yet. Change summary queries are specified using the changeQuery element.

Content queries are relatively simple. The content query message selects a node-set and those nodes are returned in the query response message. Change queries are a little more complex and require that the client software select a node-set whose root element contains both an id attribute and a changeNumber attribute, and in addition, specify a changeNumber that describes the changeNumber found in its client-side cache at the same location. With this information, .NET My Services is able to compute a change summary in the form of an update request message that the client software may process and play back into its cache, bringing it up to date. When this set of updates can not be computed efficiently, .NET My Services will indicate this through the status attribute of the change summary response, which a client application can use as an instruction to resynchronize its cache.

hsdl/queryRequest

This method is accessed using a request message, and in response may generate a response message or a SOAP Fault message. The following sample document fragments illustrate the structure and meaning of the elements and attributes in the request and response messages.

The following section describes the request message for this method.

The format of the queryRequest message is shown below.

```
<hs:queryRequest
    xmlns:hs="http://schemas.microsoft.com/hs/2001/10/core">₁..₁
    <hs:xpQuery select="..." minOccurs="..." maxOccurs="...">₀..unbounded
        <hs:options>₀..₁
            <hs:sort direction="..." key="...">₀..unbounded</hs:sort>
            <hs:range first="..." count="...">₀..unbounded</hs:range>
            <hs:shape base="...">₀..₁
                <hs:include select="...">₁..unbounded</hs:include>
                <hs:exclude select="...">₀..unbounded</hs:exclude>
            </hs:shape>
            {any}
        </hs:options>
    </hs:xpQuery>
    <hs:changeQuery select="..." baseChangeNumber="...">₀..unbounded
        <hs:options>₀..₁
            <hs:sort direction="..." key="...">₀..unbounded</hs:sort>
            <hs:range first="..." count="...">₀..unbounded</hs:range>
            <hs:shape base="...">₀..₁
                <hs:include select="...">₁..unbounded</hs:include>
                <hs:exclude select="...">₀..unbounded</hs:exclude>
            </hs:shape>
            {any}
        </hs:options>
    </hs:changeQuery>
</hs:queryRequest>
```

The meaning of the attributes and elements shown in the preceding sample document fragment are listed in the following section.

/queryRequest (minOccurs=1 maxOccurs=1)

The purpose of the queryRequest message is to return, in the queryResponse message, information from the specified document. The message is designed to carry multiple query operations in a single request message. This allows applications to specify efficient queries and address different pieces of the document in a single message transmission.

The queryRequest message may contain zero or more xpQuery elements. These elements specify data queries on the specified document. They contain an xpath expression that selects a set of nodes, and by using minOccurs and maxOccurs, they can control how many nodes are returned in a given operation.

The queryRequest message may contain zero or more changeQuery elements. The purpose of this element is to aid client software in building caches populated with .NET My Services data. These elements are designed to issue a query relative to a changeNumber, and instead of simply returning content, they return a summary of changed or deleted blue items.

The .NET My Services effort will likely evolve to include support for XML Query. In anticipation of this, our plans include support for zero or more xmQuery elements that will be used to encapsulate the XML Query language.

/queryRequest/xpQuery (minOccurs=0 maxOccurs=unbounded)
This element specifies an XPath query against the data contained within the specified document. The element is tagged with a client-computed operation id, an XPath expression that selects the nodes the client needs to extract from .NET My Services, and constraints on how many nodes the selection must match.

/queryRequest/xpQuery/@select (string minOccurs=0 maxOccurs=1)
This item specifies an XPath expression that specifies the nodes that are to be selected and returned in the response for this operation. The selected nodes are encapsulated in the xqQueryResponse element whose operation id attribute matched the operation id attribute of this element.

/queryRequest/xpQuery/@minOccurs (int minOccurs=0 maxOccurs=1)
This optional attribute specifies the minimum number of nodes that must be selected by the select operation in order for this operation to be successfully attempted. The default value is 0, meaning that if no nodes are selected, the operation silently succeeds as a NOP. A value of 1 means that a minimum of one node must be selected. In this case, if no nodes are selected, the operation fails with an error.

/queryRequest/xpQuery/@maxOccurs (int minOccurs=0 maxOccurs=1)
This optional attribute specifies the maximum number of nodes that may be selected by the select operation in order for this operation to be successfully attempted. The default value is unbounded. If the number of nodes selected by the select attribute is greater than this value, an error condition occurs.

/queryRequest/xpQuery/options (minOccurs=0 maxOccurs=1)
TBD

/queryRequest/xpQuery/options/sort (minOccurs=0 maxOccurs=unbounded)
TBD

/queryRequest/xpQuery/options/sort/@direction (string minOccurs=0 maxOccurs=1)
TBD: Direction of sorting (ascending or descending).

/queryRequest/xpQuery/options/sort/@key (string minOccurs=0 maxOccurs=1)
TBD: Sort key (e.g. subject or @size).

/queryRequest/xpQuery/options/range (minOccurs=0 maxOccurs=unbounded)
TBD

/queryRequest/xpQuery/options/range/@first (string minOccurs=0 maxOccurs=1)
TBD: Position of element which will be first element in resulting node-set (like '1', 'count()' or 'position-of(.[@id='93247519328475']). Note: Only subsets of XPath will work here.

/queryRequest/xpQuery/options/range/@count (int minOccurs=0 maxOccurs=1)
TBD: Positive number of elements.

/queryRequest/xpQuery/options/shape (minOccurs=0 maxOccurs=1)
TBD

/queryRequest/xpQuery/options/shape/@base (string minOccurs=0 maxOccurs=1)
This attribute specifies the initial set of nodes visible through the shape.

A value of t indicates that the shape is initialized to include all possible nodes relative to the shape that is currently in effect. For instance, each role defines a scope containing a shape. When defining a shape for a role, the value t indicates all possible nodes available in the specified document for this role. When defining a shape in an ACL entry, a value of t means all of the nodes visible in the shape for the computed role. When using a shape in an hsdl operation, a value of t indicates all of the possible nodes selected by the hsdl operation (relative to the ACL shape which itself is relative to the role's shape).

The value nil indicates the opposite of t, which is the empty node set. Nodes from this set may then be included in the shape.

/queryRequest/xpQuery/options/shape/include (minOccurs=1 maxOccurs=unbounded)
This element specifies the set of nodes that should be included into the shape relative to the possible set of nodes indicated by the base attribute.

/queryRequest/xpQuery/options/shape/include/@select (string minOccurs=0 maxOccurs=1)
This item specifies an XPath expression that selects a set of nodes relative to the externally established context. The expression can never travel outside the node-set established by this externally established current context. The expression may match 0 or more nodes, and the operation manipulates all selected nodes. The minOccurs and maxOccurs attributes are optional and place restrictions and limitations on the number of nodes selected.

/queryRequest/xpQuery/options/shape/exclude (minOccurs=0 maxOccurs=unbounded)
This element specifies the set of nodes that should be excluded from the shape relative to the possible set of nodes indicated by the base attribute.

/queryRequest/xpQuery/options/shape/exclude/@select (string minOccurs=0 maxOccurs=1)
This item specifies an XPath expression that selects a set of nodes relative to the externally established context. The expression can never travel outside the node-set established by this externally established current context. The expression may match 0 or more nodes, and the operation manipulates all selected nodes. The minOccurs and maxOccurs attributes are optional and place restrictions and limitations on the number of nodes selected.

/queryRequest/xpQuery/options/*{any}* (minOccurs=0 maxOccurs=unbounded)

/queryRequest/changeQuery (minOccurs=0 maxOccurs=unbounded)

This element is used to request a list of updates relative to a single selected node and a changeNumber value on that node. It is designed specifically to support client-side caching of .NET My Services content. Any xdb:blue node may be selected with the select attribute. It is an error condition to select more than a single node. While this element does not support minOccurs/maxOccurs, it is as if minOccurs=0 and maxOccurs=1. The response to this message is an updateRequest message that contains the insert, replace, and delete operations that should be processed by the client software to bring its cache up to date with respect to the change number specified in this element.

There will be times when the .NET My Services system will be unable to return a changeQueryResponse that is complete enough to process in a way that will bring a clients cache in sync. This can occur when the client is way out of date and numerous deletes have occurred. In these situations, a changeQuery will simply fail with a fault condition and in response to this message, the client should throw away and rebuild its cache.

/queryRequest/changeQuery/@select (string minOccurs=0 maxOccurs=1)

This attribute specifies an XPath expression that specifies the single node that the change query is relative to. This node, in conjunction with the specified changeNumber attribute, controls the change computation. The selected node is located, and all nodes containing id attributes (of type idType) are examined. Any of these nodes that have changed relative to the specified changeNumber are returned in the updateRequest.

/queryRequest/changeQuery/@baseChangeNumber (minOccurs=0 maxOccurs=1)

This attribute specifies the changeNumber value that the client has in its cache for the node specified by the select attribute. As explained above, this value establishes the synchronization base used to compute the changes underneath this node.

/queryRequest/changeQuery/options (minOccurs=0 maxOccurs=1)

TBD

/queryRequest/changeQuery/options/sort (minOccurs=0 maxOccurs=unbounded)

TBD

/queryRequest/changeQuery/options/sort/@direction (string minOccurs=0 maxOccurs=1)

TBD: Direction of sorting (ascending or descending).

/queryRequest/changeQuery/options/sort/@key (string minOccurs=0 maxOccurs=1)

TBD: Sort key (e.g. subject or @size).

/queryRequest/changeQuery/options/range (minOccurs=0 maxOccurs=unbounded)

TBD

/queryRequest/changeQuery/options/range/@first (string minOccurs=0 maxOccurs=1)

TBD: Position of element which will be first element in resulting node-set (like '1', 'count()' or 'position-of(.[@id='93247519328475']). Note: Only subsets of XPath will work here.

/queryRequest/changeQuery/options/range/@count (int minOccurs=0 maxOccurs=1)
TBD: Positive number of elements.

/queryRequest/changeQuery/options/shape (minOccurs=0 maxOccurs=1)
TBD

/queryRequest/changeQuery/options/shape/@base (string minOccurs=0 maxOccurs=1)
This attribute specifies the initial set of nodes visible through the shape.

A value of t indicates that the shape is initialized to include all possible nodes relative to the shape that is currently in effect. For instance, each role defines a scope containing a shape. When defining a shape for a role, the value t indicates all possible nodes available in the specified document for this role. When defining a shape in an ACL entry, a value of t means all of the nodes visible in the shape for the computed role. When using a shape in an hsdl operation, a value of t indicates all of the possible nodes selected by the hsdl operation (relative to the ACL shape which itself is relative to the role's shape).

The value nil indicates the opposite of t, which is the empty node set. Nodes from this set may then be included into the shape.

/queryRequest/changeQuery/options/shape/include (minOccurs=1 maxOccurs=unbounded)
This element specifies the set of nodes that should be included into the shape relative to the possible set of nodes indicated by the base attribute.

/queryRequest/changeQuery/options/shape/include/@select (string minOccurs=0 maxOccurs=1)
This item specifies an XPath expression that selects a set of nodes relative to the externally established context. The expression can never travel outside the node-set established by this externally established current context. The expression may match 0 or more nodes, and the operation manipulates all selected nodes. The minOccurs and maxOccurs attributes are optional and place restrictions and limitations on the number of nodes selected.

/queryRequest/changeQuery/options/shape/exclude (minOccurs=0 maxOccurs=unbounded)
This element specifies the set of nodes that should be excluded from the shape relative to the possible set of nodes indicated by the base attribute.

/queryRequest/changeQuery/options/shape/exclude/@select (string minOccurs=0 maxOccurs=1)
This item specifies an XPath expression that selects a set of nodes relative to the externally established context. The expression can never travel outside the node-set established by this externally established current context. The expression may match 0 or more nodes, and the operation manipulates all selected nodes. The minOccurs and maxOccurs attributes are optional and place restrictions and limitations on the number of nodes selected.

/queryRequest/changeQuery/options/*{any}* (minOccurs=0 maxOccurs=unbounded)

hsdl/queryResponse

Upon successful completion of this method, a response message is generated. The format of the response message is described below.

The format of the queryResponse message is shown below.

```
<hs:queryResponse
    xmlns:hs="http://schemas.microsoft.com/hs/2001/10/core">1..1
    <hs:xpQueryResponse status="...">0..unbounded {any}</hs:xpQueryResponse>
    <hs:changeQueryResponse baseChangeNumber="..." status="...">0..unbounded
        <hs:changedBlue>0..1 {any}</hs:changedBlue>
        <hs:deletedBlue id="...">0..1</hs:deletedBlue>
    </hs:changeQueryResponse>
</hs:queryResponse>
```

The meaning of the attributes and elements shown in the preceding sample document fragment are listed in the following section.

/queryResponse (minOccurs=1 maxOccurs=1)
> The queryResponse element contains the response data for a given queryRequest. This element contains both xpQueryResponse elements and changeQueryResponse elements. These elements contain operation id attributes that correlate to the matching xpQuery and changeQuery elements in the queryRequest message.

/queryResponse/xpQueryResponse (minOccurs=0 maxOccurs=unbounded)
> This element contains the node set selected by the matching xpQuery. If the selected node set matches zero nodes, and minOccurs was 0, this element will still be present but will contain empty content indicating that there were no matching nodes.

/queryResponse/xpQueryResponse/@status (string minOccurs=0 maxOccurs=1)
> This attribute indicates the status of the matching operation. The status can be one of:

success
> The corresponding operation was completed successfully. Note that a match of 0 nodes is considered successful.

failure
> The corresponding operation was not completed successfully.

/queryResponse/xpQueryResponse/*{any}* (minOccurs=0 maxOccurs=unbounded)
> This element is a placeholder that indicates where the content of the item being queried is returned.

/queryResponse/changeQueryResponse (minOccurs=0 maxOccurs=unbounded)
> This element contains the response to the associated changeQuery. The content of this element is a single, optional changeSummary element in the form of an updateRequest that describes the changes for the selected node set, relative to the synchronization base specified by the changeNumber attribute. The client software maintaining a cache of .NET My Services data should process this updateRequest into its own cache, bringing that cache up to date.

/queryResponse/changeQueryResponse/@baseChangeNumber (minOccurs=0 maxOccurs=1)

> This element contains the base change number for this changeQuery. On request, the baseChangeNumber is supplied and is associated with a subtree in the document. This attribute returns the new value for the change number in that subtree. It is assumed that the client software will easily know where to place this.

/queryResponse/changeQueryResponse/@status (string minOccurs=0 maxOccurs=1)

> This attribute indicates the status of the matching operation. The status can be one of:

> success

>> The corresponding operation was completed successfully. Note that a match of 0 nodes is considered successful.

> failure

>> The corresponding operation was not completed successfully.

> refresh

>> The corresponding operation requested a changeSummary that could not be computed efficiently. The client software should refresh its cache.

/queryResponse/changeQueryResponse/changedBlue (minOccurs=0 maxOccurs=1)

> This element is typically found in the body of an hsdl response message. It indicates a changed item (insert, replace) and supplies the server-generated id, the related localTag, and the change number. The granularity of this element is an xdb:blue item. When used in a changeQuery, this element returns the content of the specified id.

/queryResponse/changeQueryResponse/changedBlue/*{any}* (minOccurs=0 maxOccurs=unbounded)

> This element is a placeholder that indicates where the content of the changed node xdb:blue item is returned.

/queryResponse/changeQueryResponse/deletedBlue (minOccurs=0 maxOccurs=1)

> This element is typically found in the body of an hsdl response message. It indicates a deleted item and supplies the server-generated id of the deleted item. The granularity of this element is an xdb:blue item.

/queryResponse/changeQueryResponse/deletedBlue/@id (minOccurs=0 maxOccurs=1)

> This attribute specifies the id of the deleted item.

hsdl/Example/xpQuery xdb:blue

This simple query demonstrates a query against an xdb:blue item without using a predicate.

```
<!--
//
// document skeleton
//
-->
<myA id="" changeNumber="">
    <b id="" changeNumber=""/>
```

(continued)

(continued)

```
    <c id="" changeNumber="" name="">
        <z/>
        <d/>
        <e/>
    </c>
</myA>
<!--
//
// queryRequest
//
-->
<queryRequest>
    <xpQuery select="/myA/b"/>
</queryRequest>
<!--
//
// Current .NET My Services Data
//
-->
<myA id="1" changeNumber="2">
    <b id="2" changeNumber="2"/>
    <c id="3" changeNumber="2" name="emily">
        <d name="fred"/>
        <e/>
    </c>
    <c id="4" changeNumber="2" name="sally">
        <d/>
        <e/>
    </c>
    <c id="5" changeNumber="2" name="betty">
        <z/>
        <e/>
    </c>
</myA>
<!--
//
// Response
//
-->
<queryResponse>
    <xpQueryResponse status="success">
        <b id="2" changeNumber="2"/>
    </xpQueryResponse>
</queryResponse>
```

hsdl/Example/xpQuery using xdb:red predicate

This simple query demonstrates a query for a blue item using a red predicate.

```
<!--
//
// document skeleton
//
-->
<myA id="" changeNumber="">
    <b id="" changeNumber=""/>
    <c id="" changeNumber="" name="">
        <z/>
        <d/>
        <e/>
    </c>
</myA>
<!--
//
// queryRequest
//
-->
<queryRequest>
    <xpQuery select="/myA/c[@id='4']"/>
</queryRequest>
<!--
//
// Current .NET My Services Data
//
-->
<myA id="1" changeNumber="2">
    <b id="2" changeNumber="2"/>
    <c id="3" changeNumber="2" name="emily">
        <d name="fred"/>
        <e/>
    </c>
    <c id="4" changeNumber="2" name="sally">
        <d/>
        <e/>
    </c>
    <c id="5" changeNumber="2" name="betty">
        <z/>
        <e/>
    </c>
```

(continued)

(continued)

```
</myA>
<!--
//
// Response
//
-->
<queryResponse>
    <xpQueryResponse status="success">
        <c id="4" changeNumber="2" name="sally">
            <d/>
            <e/>
        </c>
    </xpQueryResponse>
</queryResponse>
```

hsdl/Example/xpQuery using xdb:red predicate with sorted results

This simple query demonstrates a query for a blue item, reshaping the resulting node-set with a sort.

```
<!--
//
// document skeleton
//
-->
<myA id="" changeNumber="">
    <b id="" changeNumber=""/>
    <c id="" changeNumber="" name="">
        <z/>
        <d/>
        <e/>
    </c>
</myA>
<!--
//
// queryRequest
//
-->
<queryRequest>
    <xpQuery select="/myA/c{sort-by-ascending(@id='4')}"/>
</queryRequest>
<!--
```

```
//
// Current .NET My Services Data
//
-->
<myA id="1" changeNumber="2">
    <b id="2" changeNumber="2"/>
    <c id="3" changeNumber="2" name="emily">
        <d name="fred"/>
        <e/>
    </c>
    <c id="4" changeNumber="2" name="sally">
        <d/>
        <e/>
    </c>
    <c id="5" changeNumber="2" name="betty">
        <z/>
        <e/>
    </c>
</myA>
<!--
//
// Response
//
-->
<queryResponse>
    <xpQueryResponse status="success">
        <c id="5" changeNumber="2" name="betty">
            <z/>
            <e/>
        </c>
        <c id="3" changeNumber="2" name="emily">
            <d name="fred"/>
            <e/>
        </c>
        <c id="4" changeNumber="2" name="sally">
            <d/>
            <e/>
        </c>
    </xpQueryResponse>
</queryResponse>
```

hsdl/Example/xpQuery multi-part

This simple query demonstrates a multi-part or batch query.

```
<!--
//
// document skeleton
//     .
-->
<myA id="" changeNumber="">
    <b id="" changeNumber=""/>
    <c id="" changeNumber="" name="">
        <z/>
        <d/>
        <e/>
    </c>
</myA>
<!--
//
// queryRequest
//
-->
<queryRequest>
    <xpQuery select="/myA/c{sort-by-ascending(@id='4')}{range(2,2)}"/>
    <xpQuery select="/myA/b"/>
</queryRequest>
<!--
//
// Current .NET My Services Data
//
-->
<myA id="1" changeNumber="2">
    <b id="2" changeNumber="2"/>
    <c id="3" changeNumber="2" name="emily">
        <d name="fred"/>
        <e/>
    </c>
    <c id="4" changeNumber="2" name="sally">
        <d/>
        <e/>
    </c>
    <c id="5" changeNumber="2" name="betty">
        <z/>
        <e/>
    </c>
```

```
</myA>
<!--
//
// Response
//
-->
<queryResponse>
    <xpQueryResponse status="success">
        <c id="3" changeNumber="2" name="emily">
            <d name="fred"/>
            <e/>
        </c>
        <c id="4" changeNumber="2" name="sally">
            <d/>
            <e/>
        </c>
    </xpQueryResponse>
    <xpQueryResponse status="success">
        <b id="2" changeNumber="2"/>
    </xpQueryResponse>
</queryResponse>
```

hsdl/Example/xpQuery multi-part, one failure

This simple query demonstrates a multi-part or batch query where the first query fails because of an attempt to predicate on a black item.

```
<!--
//
// document skeleton
//
-->
<myA id="" changeNumber="">
    <b id="" changeNumber=""/>
    <c id="" changeNumber="" name="">
        <z/>
        <d/>
        <e/>
    </c>
</myA>
<!--
//
// queryRequest
//
-->
```

(continued)

(continued)

```
<queryRequest>
    <xpQuery select="/myA/c[d='foo']"/>
    <xpQuery select="/myA/b"/>
</queryRequest>
<!--
//
// Current .NET My Services Data
//
-->
<myA id="1" changeNumber="2">
    <b id="2" changeNumber="2"/>
    <c id="3" changeNumber="2" name="emily">
        <d name="fred"/>
        <e/>
    </c>
    <c id="4" changeNumber="2" name="sally">
        <d/>
        <e/>
    </c>
    <c id="5" changeNumber="2" name="betty">
        <z/>
        <e/>
    </c>
</myA>
<!--
//
// Response
//
-->
<queryResponse>
    <xpQueryResponse status="failure"/>
    <xpQueryResponse status="success">
        <b id="2" changeNumber="2"/>
    </xpQueryResponse>
</queryResponse>
```

hsdl/Example/simple changeQuery

This simple changeQuery shows the results of a changeQuery when the client's cache is slightly out of sync.

```
<!--
//
// document skeleton
//
-->
<myA id="" changeNumber="">
    <b id="" changeNumber=""/>
    <c id="" changeNumber="" name="">
        <z/>
        <d/>
        <e/>
    </c>
</myA>
<!--
//
// queryRequest
//
-->
<queryRequest>
    <changeQuery select="/myA" baseChangeNumber='1'/>
</queryRequest>
```

```
<!--                                <!--
//                                  //
// Current Client Data              // Current .NET My Services Data
//                                  //
-->                                 -->
<myA id="1" changeNumber="1">       <myA id="1" changeNumber="2">
    <c id="3" changeNumber="1"          <b id="2" changeNumber="2"/>
name="fred">                            <c id="3" changeNumber="1"
        <d/>                        name="fred">
        <e/>                                <d/>
    </c>                                    <e/>
    <c id="4" changeNumber="1"          </c>
name="barney">                          <c id="4"changeNumber="1"
        <d/>                        name="barney">
        <e/>                                <d/>
    </c>                                    <e/>
    <c id="5"changeNumber="1"           </c>
name="betty">                           <c id="5" changeNumber="1"
```

(continued)

(continued)

```
        <d/>                              name="betty">
        <e/>                                  <d/>
    </c>                                      <e/>
</myA>                                    </c>
                                        </myA>

<!--
//
// Response
//
-->
<queryResponse>
    <changeQueryResponse baseChangeNumber="2" status="success">
        <changedBlue>
            <b id="2" changeNumber="2"/>
        </changeBlue>
    </changeQueryResponse>
</queryResponse>
```

hsdl/Example/changeQuery with deleted nodes

This simple changeQuery shows the results of a changeQuery when the client's cache is slightly out of sync and when items have been deleted from the .NET My Services data.

```
<!--
//
// document skeleton
//
-->
<myA id="" changeNumber="">
    <b id="" changeNumber=""/>
    <c id="" changeNumber="" name="">
        <z/>
        <d/>
        <e/>
    </c>
</myA>
<!--
//
// queryRequest
//
-->
```

```
<queryRequest>
    <changeQuery select="/myA" baseChangeNumber='1'/>
</queryRequest>
<!--                                        <!--
//                                          //
// Current Client Data                      // Current .NET My Services Data
//                                          //
-->                                         -->
<myA id="1" changeNumber="1">               <myA id="1" changeNumber="2">
    <c id="3" changeNumber="1"                  <b id="2" changeNumber="2"/>
name="fred">                                    <c id="4"changeNumber="1"
        <d/>                                name="barney">
        <e/>                                        <d/>
    </c>                                            <e/>
    <c id="4" changeNumber="1"                  </c>
name="barney">                                  <c id="5" changeNumber="1"
        <d/>                                name="betty">
        <e/>                                        <d/>
    </c>                                            <e/>
    <c id="5"changeNumber="1"                   </c>
name="betty">                               </myA>
        <d/>
        <e/>
    </c>
</myA>
<!--
//
// Response
//
-->
<queryResponse>
    <changeQueryResponse baseChangeNumber="2" status="success">
        <deletedBlue id="3"/>
        <changedBlue>
            <b id="2" changeNumber="2"/>
        </changeBlue>
    </changeQueryResponse>
</queryResponse>
```

hsdl/Example/changeQuery with filtering of what you want reported

This simple changeQuery shows the results of a changeQuery when the client's cache is slightly out of sync in a number of areas, and the client has requested some filtering.

```
<!--
//
// document skeleton
//
-->
<myA id="" changeNumber="">
    <b id="" changeNumber=""/>
    <c id="" changeNumber="" name="">
        <z/>
        <d/>
        <e/>
    </c>
</myA>
<!--
//
// queryRequest
//
-->
<queryRequest>
    <changeQuery select="/myA/b" baseChangeNumber='1'/>
</queryRequest>
<!--                                          <!--
//                                            //
// Current Client Data                        // Current .NET My Services Data
//                                            //
-->                                           -->
<myA id="1" changeNumber="1">                 <myA id="1" changeNumber="5">
    <b id="98"changeNumber="1"/>                  <b id="2" changeNumber="2"/>
    <c id="3" changeNumber="1"                    <b id="66" changeNumber="3"/>
name="fred">                                      <b id="67" changeNumber="4"/>
        <d/>                                      <b id="77" changeNumber="5"/>
        <e/>                                      <c id="4"changeNumber="1"
    </c>                                      name="barney">
    <c id="4" changeNumber="1"                        <d/>
name="barney">                                        <e/>
        <d/>                                      </c>
        <e/>                                      <c id="5" changeNumber="1"
    </c>                                      name="betty">
```

```
      <c id="5"changeNumber="1"                    <d/>
name="betty">                                       <e/>
        <d/>                                      </c>
        <e/>                                      <c id="55" changeNumber="4"
    </c>                                  name="betty">
</myA>                                              <d/>
                                                    <e/>
                                                  </c>
                                                </myA>

<!--
//
// Response
//
// Note that c node changes or deletes are not reported
-->
<queryResponse>
    <changeQueryResponse baseChangeNumber="5" status="success">
        <deletedBlue id="98"/>
        <changedBlue>
            <b id="2" changeNumber="2"/>
        </changeBlue>
        <changedBlue>
            <b id="66" changeNumber="3"/>
        </changeBlue>
        <changedBlue>
            <b id="67" changeNumber="4"/>
        </changeBlue>
        <changedBlue>
            <b id="77" changeNumber="5"/>
        </changeBlue>
    </changeQueryResponse>
</queryResponse>
```

hsdl/Example/changeQuery that is way out of date

This simple changeQuery illustrates the response when the client is way out of date and simply needs to refresh its cache.

```
<!--
//
// document skeleton
//
-->
<myA id="" changeNumber="">
    <b id="" changeNumber=""/>
```

(continued)

(continued)

```
    <c id="" changeNumber="" name="">
        <z/>
        <d/>
        <e/>
    </c>
</myA>
<!--
//
// queryRequest
//
-->
<queryRequest>
    <changeQuery select="/myA" baseChangeNumber='1'/>
</queryRequest>
<!--                                      <!--
//                                        //
// Current Client Data                    // Current .NET My Services Data
//                                        //
-->                                       -->
<myA id="1" changeNumber="1">             <myA id="1" changeNumber="234">
    <c id="3" changeNumber="1"                <b id="12761726"
name="fred">                              changeNumber="212"/>
        <d/>                                  <b id="16781726"
        <e/>                              changeNumber="135"/>
    </c>                                      <b id="10098726"
    <c id="4" changeNumber="1"            changeNumber="230"/>
name="barney">                                <b id="12761342"
        <d/>                              changeNumber="234"/>
        <e/>                                  <c id="454"changeNumber="1"
    </c>                                  name="yellow">
    <c id="5"changeNumber="1"                     <d>foo</d>
name="betty">                                 </c>
        <d/>                              </myA>
        <e/>
    </c>
</myA>
<!--
//
// Response
//
-->
<queryResponse>
    <changeQueryResponse baseChangeNumber="234" status="refresh"/>
</queryResponse>
```

hsdl/Example/changeQuery with deleted nodes

This simple changeQuery shows the results of a changeQuery when the client's cache is slightly out of sync and when items have been deleted from the .NET My Services data.

```
<!--
//
// document skeleton
//
-->
<myA id="" changeNumber="">
    <b id="" changeNumber=""/>
    <c id="" changeNumber="" name="">
        <z/>
        <d/>
        <e/>
    </c>
</myA>
<!--
//
// queryRequest
//
-->
<queryRequest>
    <changeQuery select="/myA" baseChangeNumber='1'/>
</queryRequest>
```

```
<!--                                    <!--
//                                      //
// Current Client Data                  // Current .NET My Services Data
//                                      //
-->                                     -->
<myA id="1" changeNumber="1">           <myA id="1" changeNumber="2">
    <c id="3" changeNumber="1"              <b id="2" changeNumber="2"/>
name="fred">                                <c id="4"changeNumber="1"
        <d/>                            name="barney">
        <e/>                                    <d/>
    </c>                                        <e/>
    <c id="4" changeNumber="1"              </c>
name="barney">                              <c id="5" changeNumber="1"
        <d/>                            name="betty">
        <e/>                                    <d/>
    </c>                                        <e/>
    <c id="5"changeNumber="1"              </c>
name="betty">                           </myA>
        <d/>
```

(continued)

(continued)

```
        <e/>
    </c>
</myA><!--
//
// Response
//
-->
<queryResponse>
    <changeQueryResponse baseChangeNumber="2" status="success">
        <deletedBlue id="3"/>
        <changedBlue>
            <b id="2" changeNumber="2"/>
        </changeBlue>
    </changeQueryResponse>
</queryResponse>
```

hsdl/subscription

Subscriptions are a mechanism through which applications can request the notification of changes to information within a document. Subscriptions to information are requested by writing a subscription element into the document in question (normally the content document), whose trigger specifies a node selection. When information covered by the trigger changes, those changes are bundled up as a subscriptionResponse message and are delivered to the subscriber by way of the specified <to/> element. Note that this element may specify an arbitrary .NET My Services listener endpoint capable of receiving subscription notifications whose domain is contained within the subscribers domain, or it may specify the .NET notifications service for the creator.

The reporting latency is controlled by the service being subscribed to and as of this writing is not controllable through software.

Subscriptions may contain an expiration time. When the current time is greater than the subscription's expiration time, the service may remove the subscription element from the document and is no longer required to send subscription response messages. The latency of this operation is determined by the subscribed to service and at the time of this writing, is not controllable through software.

Each subscription element contains an address that the subscription response messages are sent to. If persistent delivery errors occur on a subscription, a service is free to delete the subscription element.

The format of the subscription element is shown below. A subscription element is added to a document using the insertRequest message or by using the replaceRequest. Subscriptions are "canceled" by using the deleteRequest message. Subscriptions may be automatically canceled when their expiration time is reached. They may also be automatically canceled if persistent delivery errors occur.

```
<hs:subscription changeNumber="..." id="..." creator="..."
    xmlns:hs="http://schemas.microsoft.com/hs/2001/10/core">1..1
    <hs:trigger select="..." mode="..." baseChangeNumber="...">1..1</hs:trigger>
    <hs:expiresAt>0..1</hs:expiresAt>
    <hs:context uri="...">1..1 {any}</hs:context>
    <hs:to>1..1</hs:to>
</hs:subscription>
```

The meaning of the attributes and elements shown in the preceding sample document fragment are listed in the following section.

/subscription (minOccurs=1 maxOccurs=1)

This element defines a subscription node that is designed to be an xdb:blue node which when placed in a content document causes a subscription to be registered. A subscription contains a trigger element that selects a scope of coverage. When items that are under this scope of coverage change, a subscriptionResponse message is generated and sent to the specified destination address.

/subscription/@changeNumber (minOccurs=0 maxOccurs=1)

The changeNumber attribute is designed to facilitate caching of the element and its descendants. This attribute is assigned to this element by the .NET My Services system. The attribute is read-only to applications. Attempts to write this attribute are silently ignored.

/subscription/@id (minOccurs=0 maxOccurs=1)

This attribute is a globally unique ID assigned to this element by .NET My Services. Normally, .NET My Services will generate and assign this ID during an insertRequest operation, or possibly during a replaceRequest. Application software can override this ID generation by specifying the useClientIds attribute in the request message. Once an ID is assigned, the attribute is read-only and attempts to write it are silently ignored.

/subscription/@creator (string minOccurs=0 maxOccurs=1)

This attribute identifies the creator in terms of userId, appId, and platformId of the node.

/subscription/trigger (minOccurs=1 maxOccurs=1)
/subscription/trigger/@select (string minOccurs=0 maxOccurs=1)

This item specifies an XPath expression that specifies the nodes that are to be selected and watched for changes. The selection may only select xdb:blue nodes. As changes in this node set occur, they trigger the generation of a subscription message. These messages are then sent to the SOAP receiver listed in the "to" element.

/subscription/trigger/@mode (string minOccurs=0 maxOccurs=1)

This attribute specifies whether or not the content of the changes that triggered the subscription are delivered in the subscription message, or if the message simply indicates that something changed under the trigger. The attribute may be:

includeData

The data that changed, causing the subscription to trigger is included in the subscription message. Note that deleted nodes are specified by their id, not by value.

excludeData

The data that changed, causing the subscription to trigger is NOT included in the subscription message.

/subscription/trigger/@baseChangeNumber (minOccurs=0 maxOccurs=1)

This attribute specifies the changeNumber value that the trigger is relative to. All changes between the specified change number and the current state of the document relative to the selection are transmitted as subscription messages. This allows a client application to establish a subscription relative to some baseline. As in changeQuery, if the baseChangeNumber is way out of date relative to the current state of the document, and the service cannot supply the changes in the subscription message, the subscription insert is rejected. A value of 0 means that the current values of the selected nodes are transmitted in the subscription message.

/subscription/expiresAt (dateTime minOccurs=0 maxOccurs=1)

This optional element specifies an absolute time after which the subscription is no longer active. The subscription node is automatically removed when the subscription expires. If this element is missing, the subscription does not expire.

/subscription/context (minOccurs=1 maxOccurs=1)

This element returns the context element from the original subscription. Applications should use this element and only this element to correlate the subscription response with one of their subscriptions.

/subscription/context/@uri (anyURI minOccurs=0 maxOccurs=1)

This attribute specifies the URI value chosen by the subscriber that is associated with this subscription.

/subscription/context/*{any}* (minOccurs=0 maxOccurs=unbounded)

/subscription/to (anyURI minOccurs=1 maxOccurs=1)

This attribute specifies the location that is to receive the subscription message. The value of this element may be one of the following forms:

- *hs:myNotifications* - this URI indicates that generated subscription messages are to be delivered inside the body of a notification and delivered to the default .NET notifications service of the creator.

- *protocol://service* - this URI indicates that generated subscription messages are delivered to the specified service at the domain of the creator's platformId. For instance, a platformId indicating someDomain.com and a value in this element of http://subscriptionResponse would cause delivery of the subscription message to http://subscriptionResponse.someDomain.com.

If this value is not specified, then the subscription message is delivered as a notification to the "creator's" .NET notifications service.

hsdl/subscriptionResponse

When the data covered by a subscription changes, a subscription response message is delivered to the subscriber. Like all asynchronous .NET My Services response messages, this message may be delivered as a notification to the creator's .NET notifications service. This is requested in the subscription element by specifying the following <to>hs:myNotifications</to>. The subscriptionResponse message may also be directed to an addressable .NET My Services message processor that is in the same domain as the platform Id of the creator. This is accomplished by specifying the URI of the listener.

```
<hs:subscriptionResponse
    xmlns:hs="http://schemas.microsoft.com/hs/2001/10/core">1..1
    <hs:triggerData>0..1
        <hs:changedBlue>0..1 {any}</hs:changedBlue>
        <hs:deletedBlue id="...">0..1</hs:deletedBlue>
    </hs:triggerData>
    <hs:context uri="...">1..1 {any}</hs:context>
</hs:subscriptionResponse>
```

The meaning of the attributes and elements shown in the preceding sample document fragment are listed in the following section.

/subscriptionResponse (minOccurs=1 maxOccurs=1)
> This element defines the format of subscription response message. The message is delivered when a subscription's trigger fires.

/subscriptionResponse/triggerData (minOccurs=0 maxOccurs=1)
> This element contains the data in the form of changedBlue nodes and in the form of deletedBlue nodes for the data that has changed relative to the trigger.

/subscriptionResponse/triggerData/changedBlue (minOccurs=0 maxOccurs=1)
> This element is typically found in the body of an hsdl response message. It indicates a changed item (insert, replace) and supplies the server-generated id, the related localTag, and the change number. The granularity of this element is an xdb:blue item. When used in a changeQuery, this element returns the content of the specified id.

/subscriptionResponse/triggerData/changedBlue/{any} (minOccurs=0 maxOccurs=unbounded)
> This element is a placeholder that indicates where the content of the changed node xdb:blue item is returned.

/subscriptionResponse/triggerData/deletedBlue (minOccurs=0 maxOccurs=1)
> This element is typically found in the body of an hsdl response message. It indicates a deleted item and supplies the server-generated id of the deleted item. The granularity of this element is an xdb:blue item.

/subscriptionResponse/triggerData/deletedBlue/@id (minOccurs=0 maxOccurs=1)
   This attribute specifies the id of the deleted item.

/subscriptionResponse/context (minOccurs=1 maxOccurs=1)
   This element returns the contains the context element from the original subscription.
   Applications should use this element, AND ONLY this element to correlate the
   subscription response with one of their subscriptions.

/subscriptionResponse/context/@uri (anyURI minOccurs=0 maxOccurs=1)
   This attribute specifies the URI value chosen by the subscriber that is associated with
   this subscription.

/subscriptionResponse/context/*{any}* (minOccurs=0 maxOccurs=unbounded)

hsdl/Example/simple subscription

This example demonstrates the use of the subscription element and shows the
subscriptionResponse message generated when something changes that is covered by
the subscription's trigger.

```
<!--
//
// subscription element
//
-->
<subscription
        changeNumber="3"
        id="17"
        creator="532656235265"
        >
    <trigger
        select="/myA"
        mode="includeData"
        baseChangeNumber='1'
        />
    <context uri="uuid:32328738787"/>
    <to>hs:myNotifications</to>
</subscription>
<!--                                       <!--
//                                         //
// Initial .NET My Services Data           // Current .NET My Services Data
//                                         //
-->                                        -->
<myA id="1" changeNumber="4">              <myA id="1" changeNumber="6">
    <c id="3" changeNumber="1"                  <b id="2" changeNumber="6"/>
```

```
name="fred">                                      <c id="4"changeNumber="2"
        <d/>                              name="barney">
        <e/>                                      <d/>
    </c>                                          <e/>
    <c id="4" changeNumber="2"                </c>
name="barney">                                    <c id="5" changeNumber="3"
        <d/>                              name="betty">
        <e/>                                      <d/>
    </c>                                          <e/>
    <c id="5"changeNumber="3"                 </c>
name="betty">                                     <subscription
        <d/>                                      changeNumber="4"
        <e/>                                      id="17"
    </c>                                          creator="532656235265"
    <subscription                                 >
        changeNumber="4"                          <trigger
        id="17"                                       select="/myA"
        creator="532656235265"                        mode="includeData"
        >                                             baseChangeNumber='1'
        <trigger                                      />
            select="/myA"                         <context
            mode="includeData"           uri="uuid:32328738787"/>
            baseChangeNumber='1'                  <to>hs:myNotifications</to>
            />                                </subscription>
        <context uri="uuid:32328738787"/></myA>
        <to>hs:myNotifications</to>
    </subscription>
</myA>
<!--
//
// subscriptionResponse
//
-->
<subscriptionResponse>
    <triggerData>
        <deletedBlue id="3"/>
        <changedBlue>
            <b id="2" changeNumber="6"/>
        </changeBlue>
    </triggerData>
    <context uri="uuid:32328738787"/>
</subscriptionResponse>
```

CHAPTER 7

The .NET security service/Introduction

Microsoft .NET My Services is designed to facilitate the sharing of information across a wide range of applications. .NET My Services is based on an affirmative consent model for sharing—nothing is shared unless the owner of the information consents to share the information.

Because nothing is shared unless .NET My Services is told to share, .NET My Services must be informed that sharing is desired. .NET My Services must be told the following items:

1. Who to share information with
2. What information to share
3. How to share that information

The .NET My Services security authorization system is designed to act on these three inputs and facilitate the sharing of information. The goals of the system are very simply to facilitate the sharing of information that the owner has expressed a desire to share. Accomplishing this goal is a challenge. We must be sensitive to the fact that an overly complex set of inputs will result in users mis-configuring the system and in effect sharing more information with the wrong people, sharing the intended information with the wrong applications, sharing the correct information in the wrong way. Obviously there are many combinations that all result in the wrong type of sharing.

In order to accomplish this, we translated the sharing concepts into a set of implementation level goals:

- Build a system where the authorization and authorization enforcement system was standalone and as de-coupled as possible from the backend service logic. We wanted to ensure that authors of services DID NOT have to implement authorization and authorization enforcement. All services benefit from a single instance and implementation of this critical logic so that cut and paste errors are eliminated, and incorrect or immature code sequences developed early in the product life cycles are not cloned throughout the system.

- We wanted to provide relatively coarse grained sharing so that people could more successfully share information with others and have a higher degree of confidence, knowing that what they intended to share was what was actually shared.

- We wanted a model where given a fragment of information you wanted to share, you could share the information in a way that allowed some users to see the information in one way, and another set of users would see it a different way. Examples of this would be sharing your address in full fidelity with a shipper, but only the zip code component with another entity. Sharing equity names from your portfolio with a stock ticker application, while sharing holding information with your broker and accountant.

As pointed out previously, .NET My Services needs to know who to share with, what to share, and how to share. .NET My Services models who, what, and how in the authorization data structures as:

Who
> Who is embodied in a subject element of a role, and specifies the user and the application that is requesting service from .NET My Services.

What
> What is specified using the scope element of a roleTemplate or role and is used to specify which fragments of XML data are made available to the subject. Choices include the ability to expose all information defined by the service to the subject, or any proper subset with pre-configured scopes, and per-subject scopes.

How
> How is specified by indicating which methods a subject is able to request from the .NET My Services service.

The .NET My Services authorization system is based on the following XML data structures:

scope
> Each .NET My Services service defines a set of XML information in the form of an XML Schema. The service makes this information available to authorized users through a set of methods. Scopes, are used to define which XML node sets are visible to each authorized user. For example, a scope can define a node set that includes all information exposed by the service, only information that is considered "public", all information except for node sets that are marked "top-secret", just the postalCode from an address record. Scopes may be combined for very fine grained views of the data exposed by a service.

roleTemplate and roleMap
> Each service defines a static, per-service roleMap which is is used to describe what information is to be shared, and how sharing is to occur. The roleMap contains a set of scope elements that define what information to share, and a set of roleTemplate elements that define how the information is to be shared.

A roleTemplate element has a name and the set of methods allowed by that roleTemplate and the scope for that method. A roleTemplate therefore defines the set of methods allowed by the roleTemplate, and the scope of data made visible to that method. This allows the service author to design a roleTemplate that allows all methods to interact with all data, and another roleTemplate that allows read-only access to just a small subset of information. .NET My Services services are typically defined with a very small number of roleTemplates (3–5) that are virtually identical across all services.

roleList and role entries

Each user has a content document which contains the content data for the service, and each user has a roleList document which contains the users that are authorized to access the content document. The roleList is designed to describe who the user is willing to share information with, and by binding this to information in the roleMap, it is able to describe who to share with, how to share it, and what to share.

The roleList contains role elements which contain a subject, a roleTemplate reference for that subject, and an optional scope which further scopes the information available to the user relative to the scope for the roleTemplate. The best way to understand this double scoping is to consider that the roleTemplate makes a set of nodes available to the user through its associated scope. The optional scopeReference for the role may further reduce the available node set.

The following documents illustrate an XML fragment which is a roleMap and a sample roleList for a sample service. This information is exposed early in the document just to get the reader some hands on familiarity with the concepts that will be explored later in this chapter. Note that namespace qualification and un-necessary attributes are not shown. The fragments are not meant to be schema valid. Also, note that puid-of:frank is meant to be a placeholder for the passport id (puid) of frank.

```
<roleMap>

    <!--
    //
    // all data scope
    //
    -->
    <scope id="1">
        <shape base="t"/>
    </scope>

    <!--
    //
    // only public items scope
    //
    -->
```

(continued)

(continued)

```
    <scope id="2">
        <shape base="nil">
            <include select="/*[cat/@ref="public"]/>
        </shape>
    </scope>

    <!--
    //
    // full access (all methods), all information
    //
    -->
    <roleTemplate name="rt0">
        <method name="query" scopeRef="1"/>
        <method name="insert" scopeRef="1"/>
        <method name="replace" scopeRef="1"/>
        <method name="delete" scopeRef="1"/>
        <method name="update" scopeRef="1"/>
    </roleTemplate>

    <!--
    //
    // read-only (query method), all information
    //
    -->
    <roleTemplate name="rt1">
        <method name="query" scopeRef="1"/>
    </roleTemplate>

    <!--
    //
    // read-only (query method), limited information
    //
    -->
    <roleTemplate name="rt1">
        <method name="query" scopeRef="2"/>
    </roleTemplate>

    <!--
    //
    // no access
    //
    -->
    <roleTemplate name="rt99"/>
</roleMap>
```

This roleMap is very simple and is actually very typical of a standard, .NET My Services roleMap. This roleMap means the following:

- Callers mapping to rt0 may call all methods and have access to all information.
- Callers mapping to rt1 may call only the query method, and when they do, they have access to all information.
- Callers mapping to rt2 may call only the query method, and when they do, they have access to only those nodes that are categorized as "public" (<cat ref="public"/>.
- Callers mapping to rt99 have no access to any information in the service.

```
<roleList>
    <!--
    //
    // only golf related stuff
    //
    -->
    <scope id="1">
        <shape base="nil">
            <include select="/*[cat/@ref="golf"]/>
        </shape>
    </scope>

    <role roleTemplateRef="rt0">
        <subject userId="puid-of:fred" appAndPlatformId="puid-
of:calendar@microsoft.com"/>
    </role>

    <role roleTemplateRef="rt1">
        <subject userId="puid-of:fred" appAndPlatformId="puid-
of:calendar@msn.com"/>
    </role>

    <role scopeRef="1" roleTemplateRef="rt2">
        <subject userId="puid-of:barry"/>
    </role>

    <role roleTemplateRef="rt99">
        <subject userId="ALL_USERS" appAndPlatformId="puid-
of:someApp@someDomain.com"/>
    </role>
</roleList>
```

Again, we have a very simple and intuitive roleList which means:

- Fred, running calendar@microsoft.com, can access all information, through all methods.
- Fred, running calendar@microsoft.com, only has read-only access to all information.
- Barry, running any application, has read-only access to public information, but only those pieces of public information that are categorized as golf related.
- Any and all users running the someApplication@someDomain.com application have no access to any information held within this service.

These example XML fragments are designed to illustrate the simplicity of the .NET My Services authorization system.

At a very high level, the .NET My Services authorization system flow of control is as follows:

1. Determine the userId, appAndPlatformId, and credential type from the incoming message (this information is contained within a .NET My Services identity license).
2. Locate the matching role element from the user's roleList using the match algorithm defined in sections to follow.
3. If a matching role element is not found, fail the message with an authorization fault.
4. If the matching role element contains an <expiresAt/> element, determine if the role element has expired, and if so fail the message with an authorization fault.
5. Locate the roleTemplate element from the roleMap which is referenced by the role element. From this template, determine if the method requested is allowed by the template. If it is not allowed, then fail the message with an authorization fault.
6. Using the scope from the roleMap (referenced by the roleTemplate), combined with the optional scope referenced by the role element, compute the node set visible to this message.
7. Perform the requested operation ensuring that the user has no access to information outside the scope computed above.

From the flow algorithm above, it should be clear that the bulk of the .NET My Services authorization work can occur in the message flow and in a service neutral algorithm. The only touch point into the service is the scope computation and since all of our services are based on schema, even scope computation is isolated from service logic (scope computation impacts the execution plan that drives data access, but service specific logic does not need to know or understand that scope computation affected an execution plan).

The authorization algorithm uses the data structures mentioned above (roleList/* and roleTemplate/*) as well as portions of headers carried inside the .NET My Services message. The header elements used by the authorization system are fully specified in the messages chapter. In this section we simply call out the components used to perform authorization:

licenses

The licenses header is used by the authorization system to compute the userId, the appAndPlatformId, and the credential type used to make authorization decisions. This information is contained within the SOAP-SEC compliant, ".NET My Services Identity License" <hs:identity/> element. The .NET My Services Identity License is a kerberos AP request ticket, which when broken apart into it's component pieces contains the following pieces of information used by the authorization system:

1. The account id (userId) associated with the account transmitting the message. In the case of delegation where user A is representing user B, this account id designates user A. The delegation chain, (A on behalf of B is part of the the license, but this fact is not used to make authorization decisions). The account id typically represents an actual user, but may also represent a virtual user or machine account.

   Associated with this id is the credential type (credType) used to authenticate this user. Authorization decisions can therefore distinguish between a user authenticated with a four digit PIN, from users authenticated with a smart card, from users authenticated with some form of bio-metric device.

2. The account id associated with an application, and the account id of the platform the application is licensed to run on. In this document, and many other .NET My Services documents, we treat this combination as a single unit and usually represent it as *application*@**platform**. For instance:

   • calendar@msn.com means the calendar application licensed to run on the msn.com platform

   • office@windows means the office application (or suite of applications covered by the office account id) licensed to run on the windows platform.

   The two account id's are treated as a single appAndPlatformId when performing authorization actions.

request

The request header is used to identify the method being accessed, whose service is being accessed, and which document within the service is being accessed. The following portions of the request element contain this information.

1. The request/@method attribute determines the type of access being requested (query, insert, delete, etc.).

2. The request/key/@puid and @instance specifies which users information is being accessed, and which instance of that information is being accessed for users having multiple instances in a single location.

3. The request/@service attribute specifies which service (the .NET profile service, the .NET inbox service, etc.) is being accessed.

4. The request/@document attribute specifies which document (content, roleList, system, etc.) is being accessed.

integrity

The integrity header is a SOAP-SEC compliant header designed to contain the digital signature of message being transmitted. While not used specifically by the authorization header, this header is processed prior to authorization to guarantee to the rest of the code in the message processing flow that the message has not been tampered with in flight, and that the message is as constructed by the original sender.

confidentiality

The confidentiality header is a SOAP-SEC compliant header designed to communication portions of the message that happen to be encrypted. Note that this header is most useful when describing portions of the message that are not part of the soap envelope, or encryption that spans portions of the envelope. For instance, the contents of the soap Body element are encrypted, but this is not expressed using this header and is instead expressed using soap-enc directly inline with the body content.

The .NET security service/roleList

The roleList is similar to the content document for each user's instance of a service, there is a roleList document that is addressable through the document attribute in the request. The roleList contains a set of scope elements, and a set of role elements. The purpose of the role elements is to define which users have access rights into the service's content document. The purpose of the scope elements are to provide finer grained per-user or per-group-of-users data fidelity control. The simplest way to think of this is that the content document is defined by a full fidelity view of the schema that defines the content document. A scope from the roleMap uses this view as a base line and may eliminate portions of the document using the capabilities of the shape element. The result of this is a scoped baseline that is equal to or less than the original. A scope element in the roleList uses this scoped baseline as it's base, and may further reduce from there. The scope elements that we define in the roleMap for a service are very broad/generic scopes. For example, we will define scopes that include all of the information, all of the information created by the sender of a message, and all information categorized as public. A roleList scope will typically reduce this set to a specific set of items that should be made visible to a particular user. For example, a scope in a roleList might use the "only public data" scope as a baseline and further reduce this to only allow items categorized as having something to do with golf.

The roleList is a critical data structure for computing authorization. Before a message can be authorized to proceed, a role element must exist in the roleList that maps the sender of a message to a roleTemplate in the service's roleMap. If there is no matching role element, the message is terminated with an authorization fault. Once a role element is located, a check is made to see if it has expired, and if it's still valid, the referenced roleTemplate is located and processed to see if the message should proceed or be turned around with an authorization fault.

```
<hs:roleList changeNumber="..." instanceId="..."
    xmlns:hs="http://schemas.microsoft.com/hs/2001/10/core">1..1
    <hs:scope changeNumber="..." id="..." creator="...">0..unbounded
        <hs:shape base="...">1..1
            <hs:include select="...">1..unbounded</hs:include>
            <hs:exclude select="...">0..unbounded</hs:exclude>
        </hs:shape>
    </hs:scope>
    <hs:role scopeRef="..." roleTemplateRef="..." changeNumber="..." id="..."
creator="...">0..unbounded
        <hs:cat ref="...">0..unbounded</hs:cat>
        <hs:notes xml:lang="...">0..unbounded</hs:notes>
        <hs:subject userId="..." credType="..."
appAndPlatformId="...">1..1</hs:subject>
        <hs:expiresAt>0..1</hs:expiresAt>
        {any}
    </hs:role>
</hs:roleList>
```

The meaning of the attributes and elements shown in the preceding sample document fragment are listed in the following section.

/roleList (minOccurs=1 maxOccurs=1)

This element encapsulates a roleList for the identity. This is a first class root document type which specifies the sharing that is allowed over the content document.

/roleList/@changeNumber (minOccurs=0 maxOccurs=1)

The changeNumber attribute is designed to facilitate caching of the element and its descendants. This attribute is assigned to this element by the .NET My Services system. The attribute is read-only to applications. Attempts to write this attribute are silently ignored.

/roleList/@instanceId (string minOccurs=0 maxOccurs=1)

This attribute is a unique identifier typically assigned to the root element of a service. It is a read-only element and assigned by the .NET My Services system when a user is provisioned for a particular service.

/roleList/scope (minOccurs=0 maxOccurs=unbounded)

A scope contains a shape element designed to restrict the information visible to the user of the scope. When used within a roleMap, the scope's shape defines the data shape that is visible to all members of the role. When used within an ACL, the scope's shape defines the data shape that is visible for the acl entry relative to the shape for the role.

/roleList/scope/@changeNumber (minOccurs=0 maxOccurs=1)

The changeNumber attribute is designed to facilitate caching of the element and its descendants. This attribute is assigned to this element by the .NET My Services system. The attribute is read-only to applications. Attempts to write this attribute are silently ignored.

/roleList/scope/@id (minOccurs=0 maxOccurs=1)

This attribute is a globally unique ID assigned to this element by .NET My Services. Normally, .NET My Services will generate and assign this ID during an insertRequest operation, or possibly during a replaceRequest. Application software can override this ID generation by specifying the useClientIds attribute in the request message. Once an ID is assigned, the attribute is read-only and attempts to write it are silently ignored.

/roleList/scope/@creator (string minOccurs=0 maxOccurs=1)

This attribute identifies the creator in terms of userId, appId, and platformId of the node.

/roleList/scope/shape (minOccurs=1 maxOccurs=1)

A shape defines the node set visible through the document when operating through this shape element.

/roleList/scope/shape/@base (string minOccurs=0 maxOccurs=1)

This attribute specifies the initial set of nodes visible through the shape.

A value of t indicates that the shape is initialized to include all possible nodes relative to the shape that is currently in effect. For instance, each role defines a scope containing a shape. When defining a shape for a role, the value t indicates all possible nodes available in the specified document for this role. When defining a shape in an ACL entry, a value of t means all of the nodes visible in the shape for the computed role. When using a shape in an hsdl operation, a value of t indicates all of the possible nodes selected by the hsdl operation (relative to the ACL shape which itself is relative to the role's shape).

The value nil indicates the opposite of t, which is the empty node set. Nodes from this set may then be included into the shape.

/roleList/scope/shape/include (minOccurs=1 maxOccurs=unbounded)

This element specifies the set of nodes that should be included into the shape relative to the possible set of nodes indicated by the base attribute.

/roleList/scope/shape/include/@select (string minOccurs=0 maxOccurs=1)

This item specifies an XPATH expression that selects a set of nodes relative to the externally established context. The expression can never travel outside the node-set established by this externally established current context. The expression may match 0 or more nodes, and the operation manipulates all selected nodes. The minOccurs and maxOccurs attributes are optional and place restrictions and limitations on the number of nodes selected.

/roleList/scope/shape/exclude (minOccurs=0 maxOccurs=unbounded)

This element specifies the set of nodes that should be excluded from the shape relative to the possible set of nodes indicated by the base attribute.

/roleList/scope/shape/exclude/@select (string minOccurs=0 maxOccurs=1)
    This item specifies an XPATH expression that selects a set of nodes relative to the
    externally established context. The expression can never travel outside the node-set
    established by this externally established current context. The expression may match
    0 or more nodes, and the operation manipulates all selected nodes. The minOccurs
    and maxOccurs attributes are optional and place restrictions and limitations on the
    number of nodes selected.

/roleList/role (minOccurs=0 maxOccurs=unbounded)
    This type defines an role record which defines a matching subject, an optional scope
    reference, the roleTemplate for this entry, and some maintenance information.

/roleList/role/@scopeRef (string minOccurs=0 maxOccurs=1)
    This attribute specifies the scope within this document that is in effect for this
    matching authorizationEntry.

/roleList/role/@roleTemplateRef (string minOccurs=0 maxOccurs=1)
    This item specifies the name of the roleTemplate in the service's roleMap that this role
    is bound to.

/roleList/role/@changeNumber (minOccurs=0 maxOccurs=1)
    The changeNumber attribute is designed to facilitate caching of the element and its
    descendants. This attribute is assigned to this element by the .NET My Services
    system. The attribute is read-only to applications. Attempts to write this attribute are
    silently ignored.

/roleList/role/@id (minOccurs=0 maxOccurs=1)
    This attribute is a globally unique ID assigned to this element by .NET My Services.
    Normally, .NET My Services will generate and assign this ID during an insertRequest
    operation, or possibly during a replaceRequest. Application software can override this
    ID generation by specifying the useClientIds attribute in the request message. Once
    an ID is assigned, the attribute is read-only and attempts to write it are silently
    ignored.

/roleList/role/@creator (string minOccurs=0 maxOccurs=1)
    This attribute identifies the creator in terms of userId, appId, and platformId of the
    node.

/roleList/role/cat (minOccurs=0 maxOccurs=unbounded)
    This element is used to categorize the element that contains it by referencing a global
    category definition in either the /NET categories service system document or an
    external resource containing category definitions, or by referencing an identity centric
    category definition in the content document of the .NET categories service for a
    particular puid.

/roleList/role/cat/@ref (anyURI minOccurs=0 maxOccurs=1)
    This attribute references a category definition (<catDef/>) element using the rules
    outlined in the .NET categories XMI manual.

/roleList/role/notes (string minOccurs=0 maxOccurs=unbounded)
    This element specifies optional notes that may be used to specify reasoning behind
    adding this role to the roleList.

/roleList/role/notes/@xml:lang (minOccurs=1 maxOccurs=1)

This required attribute is used to specify an ISO 639 language code or an ISO 3166 country code as described in RFC 1766. The value of this attribute indicates the language type of the content within this element.

/roleList/role/subject (minOccurs=1 maxOccurs=1)

This element encapsulates a subject that includes a userId, and a combined application and platformId. The subject element is matched against the incoming message to determine which role if any is to be used to authorize and scope continued message processing. The match algorithm is very simple. The userId in the message chooses the set of matching subjects. Once this set of subjects is identified, a test for subjects containing credType attributes is done relative to the credType passed in the license. Matching subject entries remain. If no subjects match, then all subjects containing credType are discarded keeping only those subjects that do not contain credType. Then the combined platform id and application id select a matching subject. Matching subject entries remain. If no subjects match, then all subjects containing appAndPlatformId attributes are discarded keeping only those subjects that do not contain this attribute. These remaining subjects are considered to represent the set of possible roles to use for the request. The referenced roleDefinitions are extracted from the roleMap and sorted keeping only the highest priority roleDefinition.

/roleList/role/subject/@userId (string minOccurs=0 maxOccurs=1)

This id represents an authenticated userId. It must always be specified.

/roleList/role/subject/@credType (string minOccurs=0 maxOccurs=1)

This optional attribute specifies a credential type value which represents the type of credential used to authenticate the userId. During a match operation, this value may be used to further qualify the set of subjects that match in the userId dimension.

/roleList/role/subject/@appAndPlatformId (string minOccurs=0 maxOccurs=1)

This optional attribute specifies the authenticated id of an application-platform combination. For instance, the puid of calendar@msn.com represents the calendar application at msn. The puid of office@windows represents the office application running on the windows platform.

/roleList/role/expiresAt (dateTime minOccurs=0 maxOccurs=1)

This optional element specifies a time after which the subject entry is no longer considered valid for matching purposes. If this element is missing, the subject entry does not expire.

/roleList/role/*{any}* (minOccurs=0 maxOccurs=unbounded)

The .NET security service/roleMap

The purpose of this document is to define, for each role (from the roleList), what the allowable methods are, and what scope of data is visible while using this method. The role map is the same for all instances of a particular service, and is authored by the implementer of the service. The goal of the role map is to simplify the security authorization layer as it appears to the end user. It does this by specifying the fixed set of access patterns that occur on a given service. The end user, or agents acting on the end user's behalf, now have the relatively simple job of deciding which users map to which roles. They don't have to specify what a role means.

```
<hs:roleMap changeNumber="..." id="..." creator="..."
    xmlns:hs="http://schemas.microsoft.com/hs/2001/10/core">1..1
    <hs:scope id="...">0..unbounded
        <hs:shape base="...">1..1
            <hs:include select="...">1..unbounded</hs:include>
            <hs:exclude select="...">0..unbounded</hs:exclude>
        </hs:shape>
    </hs:scope>
    <hs:roleTemplate name="..." priority="...">0..unbounded
        <hs:fullDescription xml:lang="...">0..1</hs:fullDescription>
        <hs:method name="..." scopeRef="...">0..unbounded</hs:method>
    </hs:roleTemplate>
</hs:roleMap>
```

The meaning of the attributes and elements shown in the preceding sample document fragment are listed in the following section.

/roleMap (minOccurs=1 maxOccurs=1)

This element encapsulates all the elements that make up a roleMap, which include document class relative roleTemplate, priority, name, method, and per-method scope. An individual roleTemplate defines the maximum scope of information, and the allowable methods used to access that information for each request mapped into the template.

/roleMap/@changeNumber (minOccurs=0 maxOccurs=1)

The changeNumber attribute is designed to facilitate caching of the element and its descendants. This attribute is assigned to this element by the .NET My Services system. The attribute is read-only to applications. Attempts to write this attribute are silently ignored.

/roleMap/@id (minOccurs=0 maxOccurs=1)

This attribute is a globally unique ID assigned to this element by .NET My Services. Normally, .NET My Services will generate and assign this ID during an insertRequest operation, or possibly during a replaceRequest. Application software can override this ID generation by specifying the useClientIds attribute in the request message. Once an ID is assigned, the attribute is read-only and attempts to write it are silently ignored.

/roleMap/@creator (string minOccurs=0 maxOccurs=1)

This attribute identifies the creator in terms of userId, appId, and platformId of the node.

/roleMap/scope (minOccurs=0 maxOccurs=unbounded)

This element defines a scope which may be referred to by roles within this roleMap to indicate what portions of the document are visible to this role for the specified method.

/roleMap/scope/@id (minOccurs=0 maxOccurs=1)

This attribute is a globally unique ID assigned to this element by .NET My Services. Normally, .NET My Services will generate and assign this ID during an insertRequest operation, or possibly during a replaceRequest. Application software can override this ID generation by specifying the useClientIds attribute in the request message. Once an ID is assigned, the attribute is read-only and attempts to write it are silently ignored.

/roleMap/scope/shape (minOccurs=1 maxOccurs=1)

A shape defines the node set visible through the document when operating through this shape element.

/roleMap/scope/shape/@base (string minOccurs=0 maxOccurs=1)

This attribute specifies the initial set of nodes visible through the shape.

A value of t indicates that the shape is initialized to include all possible nodes relative to the shape that is currently in effect. For instance, each role defines a scope containing a shape. When defining a shape for a role, the value t indicates all possible nodes available in the specified document for this role. When defining a shape in an ACL entry, a value of t means all of the nodes visible in the shape for the computed role. When using a shape in an hsdl operation, a value of t indicates all of the possible nodes selected by the hsdl operation (relative to the ACL shape which itself is relative to the role's shape).

The value nil indicates the opposite of t, which is the empty node set. Nodes from this set may then be included into the shape.

/roleMap/scope/shape/include (minOccurs=1 maxOccurs=unbounded)

This element specifies the set of nodes that should be included into the shape relative to the possible set of nodes indicated by the base attribute.

/roleMap/scope/shape/include/@select (string minOccurs=0 maxOccurs=1)

This item specifies an XPATH expression that selects a set of nodes relative to the externally established context. The expression can never travel outside the node-set established by this externally established current context. The expression may match 0 or more nodes, and the operation manipulates all selected nodes. The minOccurs and maxOccurs attributes are optional and place restrictions and limitations on the number of nodes selected.

/roleMap/scope/shape/exclude (minOccurs=0 maxOccurs=unbounded)

This element specifies the set of nodes that should be excluded from the shape relative to the possible set of nodes indicated by the base attribute.

/roleMap/scope/shape/exclude/@select (string minOccurs=0 maxOccurs=1)

This item specifies an XPATH expression that selects a set of nodes relative to the externally established context. The expression can never travel outside the node-set established by this externally established current context. The expression may match 0 or more nodes, and the operation manipulates all selected nodes. The minOccurs and maxOccurs attributes are optional and place restrictions and limitations on the number of nodes selected.

/roleMap/roleTemplate (minOccurs=0 maxOccurs=unbounded)

This element encapsulates the definition of a role. The attribute set for this element includes the document class that this roleTemplate refers to, the name of the roleTemplate, and the priority of the roleTemplate.

/roleMap/roleTemplate/@name (string minOccurs=0 maxOccurs=1)

This element specifies the name of the role.

/roleMap/roleTemplate/@priority (int minOccurs=0 maxOccurs=1)

This element specifies the priority of the roleTemplate which is used to select that actual roleTemplate when the role evaluation determines that the subject maps to multiple roleTemplates.

/roleMap/roleTemplate/fullDescription (string minOccurs=0 maxOccurs=1)

This element contains a description of this role template which specifies the capabilities a caller will have when accessing information through this role.

/roleMap/roleTemplate/fullDescription/@xml:lang (minOccurs=1 maxOccurs=1)

This required attribute is used to specify an ISO 639 language code or an ISO 3166 country code as described in RFC 1766. The value of this attribute indicates the language type of the content within this element.

/roleMap/roleTemplate/method (minOccurs=0 maxOccurs=unbounded)

This element specifies the methods available within this roleTemplate by name, and by scope. When a subject maps to a roleTemplate, the method in the request must match one of these elements for the message to continue to flow. If the method exists, the data available to the method is a function of the scope referenced by this method combined with an optional scope referenced by the role defined in the roleList.

/roleMap/roleTemplate/method/@name (string minOccurs=0 maxOccurs=1)

This element specifies the name of the method.

/roleMap/roleTemplate/method/@scopeRef (string minOccurs=0 maxOccurs=1)

This attribute specifies the scope within this document that is in effect for this method.

The .NET security service/standardRoleTemplates

This section describes the standard roleTemplate elements that will exist in all .NET My Services services. This establishes a uniform baseline sharing model that all .NET My Services services can build on. The following list enumerates these baseline roleTemplates. It is important to note that services will extend the templates at times to accommodate the inclusion of domain specific custom methods. This standard template should be viewed as a baseline that the services will build on.

1. rt0—The purpose of this roleTemplate is to provide full access to all information.
2. rt1—The purpose of this roleTemplate is to provide full ability to read information with minimal ability to write. The caller can add information to the service, and can only delete information that it inserted or replaced.
3. rt2—read-only: query/subscribe, all information.
4. rt3—read-only: query/subscribe, public information only.
5. rt99—no access.

security/Example/rt0

```
<scope id="1">
    <shape base="t"/>
</scope>
<roleTemplate name="rt0">
    <method name="query" scopeRef="1"/>
    <method name="insert" scopeRef="1"/>
    <method name="replace" scopeRef="1"/>
    <method name="delete" scopeRef="1"/>
    <method name="update" scopeRef="1"/>
</roleTemplate>
```

security/Example/rt1

```
<scope id="1">
    <shape base="t"/>
</scope>
<scope id="2">
    <shape base="nil">
        <include select="//*[@creator='$callerId']/>
    </shape>
</scope>
<roleTemplate name="rt1">
    <method name="query" scopeRef="1"/>
    <method name="insert" scopeRef="2"/>
    <method name="replace" scopeRef="2"/>
    <method name="delete" scopeRef="2"/>
</roleTemplate>
```

security/Example/rt2

```
<scope id="1">
    <shape base="t"/>
</scope>
<scope id="3">
    <shape base="nil">
        <include select="//subscription[@creator='$callerId']/>
    </shape>
</scope>
<roleTemplate name="rt2">
    <method name="query" scopeRef="1"/>
    <method name="insert" scopeRef="3"/>
    <method name="replace" scopeRef="3"/>
    <method name="delete" scopeRef="3"/>
</roleTemplate>
```

security/Example/rt3

```
<scope id="1">
    <shape base="t"/>
</scope>
<scope id="4">
    <shape base="nil">
        <include select="//*[cat/@ref='hs:public']/>
        <include select="//subscription[@creator='$callerId']/>
    </shape>
</scope>
<roleTemplate name="rt3">
    <method name="query" scopeRef="1"/>
    <method name="insert" scopeRef="4"/>
    <method name="replace" scopeRef="4"/>
    <method name="delete" scopeRef="4"/>
</roleTemplate>
```

CHAPTER 8

system/Introduction

This section defines the structure of the system document, a document that is addressable using normal Microsoft .NET My Services messages by specifying request/@document="system".

The system document is shared by all PUIDs assigned to this service instance and is read-only to all.

system/.

This schema fragment illustrates the base schema of the .NET address service.

```
<sys:system changeNumber="..." instanceId="..."
    xmlns:hs="http://schemas.microsoft.com/hs/2001/10/core"
    xmlns:sys="http://schemas.microsoft.com/hs/2001/10/myLists/system">1..1
    <hs:roleMap changeNumber="..." id="..." creator="...">1..1
        <hs:scope id="...">0..unbounded
            <hs:shape base="...">1..1
                <hs:include select="...">1..unbounded</hs:include>
                <hs:exclude select="...">0..unbounded</hs:exclude>
            </hs:shape>
        </hs:scope>
        <hs:roleTemplate name="..." priority="...">0..unbounded
            <hs:fullDescription xml:lang="...">0..1</hs:fullDescription>
            <hs:method name="..." scopeRef="...">0..unbounded</hs:method>
        </hs:roleTemplate>
    </hs:roleMap>
    <hs:methodMap changeNumber="..." id="..." creator="...">1..1
        <hs:method name="...">0..unbounded {any}</hs:method>
    </hs:methodMap>
    <hs:schemaMap changeNumber="..." id="..." creator="...">1..1
        <hs:schema namespace="..." schemaLocation="..." alias="...">0..unbounded
{any}</hs:schema>
    </hs:schemaMap>
    <hs:wsdlMap changeNumber="..." id="..." creator="...">1..1
        <hs:wsdl wsdlLocation="...">0..unbounded {any}</hs:wsdl>
        <hs:disco discoLocation="...">0..unbounded {any}</hs:disco>
    </hs:wsdlMap>
    {any}
</sys:system>
```

The meaning of the attributes and elements shown in the preceding sample document fragment are listed in the following section.

/system (minOccurs=1 maxOccurs=1)
This element encapsulates the system document for the .NET lists service.

/system/@changeNumber (minOccurs=0 maxOccurs=1)
The changeNumber attribute is designed to facilitate caching of the element and its descendants. This attribute is assigned to this element by the .NET My Services system. The attribute is read-only to applications. Attempts to write this attribute are silently ignored.

/system/@instanceId (string minOccurs=0 maxOccurs=1)
This attribute is a unique identifier typically assigned to the root element of a service. It is a read-only element and assigned by the .NET My Services system when a user is provisioned for a particular service.

/system/roleMap (minOccurs=1 maxOccurs=1)
This element encapsulates all the elements that make up a roleMap, which include document class relative roleTemplate, priority, name, method, and per-method scope. An individual roleTemplate defines the maximum scope of information, and the allowable methods used to access that information for each request mapped into the template.

/system/roleMap/@changeNumber (minOccurs=0 maxOccurs=1)
The changeNumber attribute is designed to facilitate caching of the element and its descendants. This attribute is assigned to this element by the .NET My Services system. The attribute is read-only to applications. Attempts to write this attribute are silently ignored.

/system/roleMap/@id (minOccurs=0 maxOccurs=1)
This attribute is a globally unique ID assigned to this element by .NET My Services. Normally, .NET My Services will generate and assign this ID during an insertRequest operation, or possibly during a replaceRequest. Application software can override this ID generation by specifying the useClientIds attribute in the request message. Once an ID is assigned, the attribute is read-only and attempts to write it are silently ignored.

/system/roleMap/@creator (string minOccurs=0 maxOccurs=1)
This attribute identifies the creator in terms of userId, appId, and platformId of the node.

/system/roleMap/scope (minOccurs=0 maxOccurs=unbounded)
This element defines a scope that may be referred to by roles within this roleMap to indicate what portions of the document are visible to this role for the specified method.

/system/roleMap/scope/@id (minOccurs=0 maxOccurs=1)

> This attribute is a globally unique ID assigned to this element by .NET My Services. Normally, .NET My Services will generate and assign this ID during an insertRequest operation, or possibly during a replaceRequest. Application software can override this ID generation by specifying the useClientIds attribute in the request message. Once an ID is assigned, the attribute is read-only and attempts to write it are silently ignored.

/system/roleMap/scope/shape (minOccurs=1 maxOccurs=1)

> A shape defines the node set visible through the document when operating through this shape element.

/system/roleMap/scope/shape/@base (string minOccurs=0 maxOccurs=1)

> This attribute specifies the initial set of nodes visible through the shape.

> A value of t indicates that the shape is initialized to include all possible nodes relative to the shape that is currently in effect. For instance, each role defines a scope containing a shape. When defining a shape for a role, the value t indicates all possible nodes available in the specified document for this role. When defining a shape in an ACL entry, a value of t means all of the nodes visible in the shape for the computed role. When using a shape in an hsdl operation, a value of t indicates all of the possible nodes selected by the hsdl operation (relative to the ACL shape which itself is relative to the role's shape).

> The value nil indicates the opposite of t, which is the empty node set. Nodes from this set may then be included in the shape.

/system/roleMap/scope/shape/include (minOccurs=1 maxOccurs=unbounded)

> This element specifies the set of nodes that should be included in the shape relative to the possible set of nodes indicated by the base attribute.

/system/roleMap/scope/shape/include/@select (string minOccurs=0 maxOccurs=1)

> This item specifies an XPATH expression that selects a set of nodes relative to the externally established context. The expression can never travel outside the node-set established by this externally established current context. The expression may match 0 or more nodes, and the operation manipulates all selected nodes. The minOccurs and maxOccurs attributes are optional and place restrictions and limitations on the number of nodes selected.

/system/roleMap/scope/shape/exclude (minOccurs=0 maxOccurs=unbounded)

> This element specifies the set of nodes that should be excluded from the shape relative to the possible set of nodes indicated by the base attribute.

/system/roleMap/scope/shape/exclude/@select (string minOccurs=0 maxOccurs=1)

> This item specifies an XPATH expression that selects a set of nodes relative to the externally established context. The expression can never travel outside the node-set established by this externally established current context. The expression may match 0 or more nodes, and the operation manipulates all selected nodes. The minOccurs and maxOccurs attributes are optional and place restrictions and limitations on the number of nodes selected.

/system/roleMap/roleTemplate (minOccurs=0 maxOccurs=unbounded)
This element encapsulates the definition of a role. The attribute set for this element includes the document class that this roleTemplate refers to, the name of the roleTemplate, and the priority of the roleTemplate.

/system/roleMap/roleTemplate/@name (string minOccurs=0 maxOccurs=1)
This element specifies the name of the role.

/system/roleMap/roleTemplate/@priority (int minOccurs=0 maxOccurs=1)
This element specifies the priority of the roleTemplate that is used to select that actual roleTemplate when the role evaluation determines that the subject maps to multiple roleTemplates.

/system/roleMap/roleTemplate/fullDescription (string minOccurs=0 maxOccurs=1)
This element contains a description of this role template that specifies the capabilities a caller will have when accessing information through this role.

/system/roleMap/roleTemplate/fullDescription/@xml:lang (minOccurs=1 maxOccurs=1)
This required attribute is used to specify an ISO 639 language code or an ISO 3166 country code as described in RFC 1766. The value of this attribute indicates the language type of the content within this element.

/system/roleMap/roleTemplate/method (minOccurs=0 maxOccurs=unbounded)
This element specifies the methods available within this roleTemplate by name and by scope. When a subject maps to a roleTemplate, the method in the request must match one of these elements for the message to continue to flow. If the method exists, the data available to the method is a function of the scope referenced by this method combined with an optional scope referenced by the role defined in the roleList.

/system/roleMap/roleTemplate/method/@name (string minOccurs=0 maxOccurs=1)
This element specifies the name of the method.

/system/roleMap/roleTemplate/method/@scopeRef (string minOccurs=0 maxOccurs=1)
This attribute specifies the scope within this document that is in effect for this method.

/system/methodMap (minOccurs=1 maxOccurs=1)
This element defines the methodMap. While it is true that in most cases the roleMap section contains a definitive list of methods, these methods are likely to be scattered about the roleMap in various templates. This section contains the definitive non-duplicated list of methods available within the service.

/system/methodMap/@changeNumber (minOccurs=0 maxOccurs=1)
The changeNumber attribute is designed to facilitate caching of the element and its descendants. This attribute is assigned to this element by the .NET My Services system. The attribute is read-only to applications. Attempts to write this attribute are silently ignored.

/system/methodMap/@id (minOccurs=0 maxOccurs=1)

This attribute is a globally unique ID assigned to this element by .NET My Services. Normally, .NET My Services will generate and assign this ID during an insertRequest operation, or possibly during a replaceRequest. Application software can override this ID generation by specifying the useClientIds attribute in the request message. Once an ID is assigned, the attribute is read-only and attempts to write it are silently ignored.

/system/methodMap/@creator (string minOccurs=0 maxOccurs=1)

This attribute identifies the creator in terms of userId, appId, and platformId of the node.

/system/methodMap/method (minOccurs=0 maxOccurs=unbounded)

This element defines a method that is available within this service.

/system/methodMap/method/@name (string minOccurs=0 maxOccurs=1)

This attribute specifies the name of a method available within the service.

/system/methodMap/method/*{any}* (minOccurs=0 maxOccurs=unbounded)

/system/schemaMap (minOccurs=1 maxOccurs=1)

This element defines the various schemas that define the data structures and shape of information managed by this service. Each schema is defined by its namespace URI, its location, and a preferred namespace alias.

/system/schemaMap/@changeNumber (minOccurs=0 maxOccurs=1)

The changeNumber attribute is designed to facilitate caching of the element and its descendants. This attribute is assigned to this element by the .NET My Services system. The attribute is read-only to applications. Attempts to write this attribute are silently ignored.

/system/schemaMap/@id (minOccurs=0 maxOccurs=1)

This attribute is a globally unique ID assigned to this element by .NET My Services. Normally, .NET My Services will generate and assign this ID during an insertRequest operation, or possibly during a replaceRequest. Application software can override this ID generation by specifying the useClientIds attribute in the request message. Once an ID is assigned, the attribute is read-only and attempts to write it are silently ignored.

/system/schemaMap/@creator (string minOccurs=0 maxOccurs=1)

This attribute identifies the creator in terms of userId, appId, and platformId of the node.

/system/schemaMap/schema (minOccurs=0 maxOccurs=unbounded)

This element defines a schema that defines data-structures and the shape of information managed by this service. Multiple schema elements exist for each service, once for each logical grouping of information exposed by the service.

/system/schemaMap/schema/@namespace (anyURI minOccurs=0 maxOccurs=1)

This attribute specifies the namespace URI of this schema.

/system/schemaMap/schema/@schemaLocation (anyURI minOccurs=0 maxOccurs=1)
> This attribute specifies the location (in the form of a URI) of the resource containing schema. When a schema is reachable through a variety of URIs, one schema element will exist for each location.

/system/schemaMap/schema/@alias (string minOccurs=0 maxOccurs=1)
> This attribute specifies the preferred alias that should be used if possible when manipulating information covered by this schema in the context of this service.

/system/schemaMap/schema/*{any}* (minOccurs=0 maxOccurs=unbounded)

/system/wsdlMap (minOccurs=1 maxOccurs=1)
> This element defines the wsdlMap for this service. This map includes the location of WSDL documents, DISCO documents, and WISL documents for this Web service. These documents are used by applications to understand the format of messages that may be sent to the various services.

/system/wsdlMap/@changeNumber (minOccurs=0 maxOccurs=1)
> The changeNumber attribute is designed to facilitate caching of the element and its descendants. This attribute is assigned to this element by the .NET My Services system. The attribute is read-only to applications. Attempts to write this attribute are silently ignored.

/system/wsdlMap/@id (minOccurs=0 maxOccurs=1)
> This attribute is a globally unique ID assigned to this element by .NET My Services. Normally, .NET My Services will generate and assign this ID during an insertRequest operation, or possibly during a replaceRequest. Application software can override this ID generation by specifying the useClientIds attribute in the request message. Once an ID is assigned, the attribute is read-only and attempts to write it are silently ignored.

/system/wsdlMap/@creator (string minOccurs=0 maxOccurs=1)
> This attribute identifies the creator in terms of userId, appId, and platformId of the node.

/system/wsdlMap/wsdl (minOccurs=0 maxOccurs=unbounded)
> This element is used to specify the location of a WSDL file for this service. Multiple entries may exist pointing to the same file hosted in multiple locations, or to variations on the content within the WSDL files.

/system/wsdlMap/wsdl/@wsdlLocation (anyURI minOccurs=0 maxOccurs=1)
> This attribute is a URI that specifies the location of the WSDL file.

/system/wsdlMap/wsdl/*{any}* (minOccurs=0 maxOccurs=unbounded)

/system/wsdlMap/disco (minOccurs=0 maxOccurs=unbounded)
> This element is used to specify the location of a DISCO file for this service. Multiple entries may exist pointing to the same file hosted in multiple locations, or to variations on the content within the DISCO files.

/system/wsdlMap/disco/@discoLocation (anyURI minOccurs=0 maxOccurs=1)
> This attribute is a URI that specifies the location of the DISCO file.

/system/wsdlMap/disco/*{any}* (minOccurs=0 maxOccurs=unbounded)

/system/*{any}* (minOccurs=0 maxOccurs=unbounded)

CHAPTER 9

admin/Introduction

This section defines the structure of adminRequest and adminResponse messages. These messages can target the following document types:

- content
- acl
- server

content and **acl** documents can only be targeted when the method being called is a provisioning method. In other words, provisioning methods can only operate on **content** or **acl** document. **server** document is an XML document that represents the current state of the Microsoft .NET My Services front-end server. This document can be accessed using the standard HSDL methods to query for data and also add/remove certain records from the sections of this document where these actions are allowed.

The query method is used for status checks where insert/update/replace/delete are used to add/remove virtual filters and timers alike. changeNotify is specifically used to place alarms. Not all parts of the server document are read/write.

Admin Request Types and Methods

1. provisioning
2. server

CHAPTER 10

The .NET Application Settings Service/Introduction

This is the specification for the Microsoft .NET application settings service.

The .NET Application Settings Service/Roles

The .NET application settings service controls access by using the following roleTemplates:

- rt0
- rt1
- rt2
- rt3
- rt99

The .NET application settings service uses the following scopes:

- **scope id 1**

```
<hs:scope id=1>

    <hs:shape base=t>

    </hs:shape>

</hs:scope>
```

- **scope id 2**

```
<hs:scope id=2>

    <hs:shape base=nil>

        <hs:include select=//*[@creator='$callerId']/>

    </hs:shape>

</hs:scope>
```

- **scope id 3**

```
<hs:scope id=3>

    <hs:shape base=nil>

        <hs:include select=//subscription[@creator='$callerId']/>

    </hs:shape>

</hs:scope>
```

- **scope id 4**

```
<hs:scope id=4>

    <hs:shape base=nil>

        <hs:include select=//*[cat/@ref='hs:public']/>

        <hs:include select=//subscription[@creator='$callerId']/>

    </hs:shape>

</hs:scope>
```

The .NET application settings service roleTemplate rt0

The purpose of this role is to give complete read/write access to all information within the content document of the service being protected through this roleTemplate.

The following table illustrates the available methods and the scope in effect when accessing the .NET application settings service through that method while mapped to this roleTemplate.

method	scopeRef
query	scopeRef=1
insert	scopeRef=1
replace	scopeRef=1
delete	scopeRef=1
update	scopeRef=1

The .NET application settings service roleTemplate rt1

The purpose of this role is to give complete read access to all information within the content document of the service being protected through this roleTemplate. Applications mapping to this role also have a limited ability to write to information in the content document. They may create nodes in any location, but may only change/replace, or delete nodes that they created.

The following table illustrates the available methods and the scope in effect when accessing the .NET application settings service through that method while mapped to this roleTemplate.

method	scopeRef
query	scopeRef=1
insert	scopeRef=2
replace	scopeRef=2
delete	scopeRef=2

The .NET application settings service roleTemplate rt2

The purpose of this role is to give complete read access to all information within the content document of the service being protected through this roleTemplate. Applications mapping to this role have very limited write access and are only able to create and manipulate their own subscription nodes.

The following table illustrates the available methods and the scope in effect when accessing the .NET application settings service through that method while mapped to this roleTemplate.

method	scopeRef
query	scopeRef=1
insert	scopeRef=3
replace	scopeRef=3
delete	scopeRef=3

The .NET application settings service roleTemplate rt3

The purpose of this role is to give limited read access to information within the content document that is categorized as "public."

The following table illustrates the available methods and the scope in effect when accessing the .NET application settings service through that method while mapped to this roleTemplate.

method	scopeRef
query	scopeRef=4

The .NET application settings service roleTemplate rt99

The purpose of this role is to block all access to the content document. Note that lack of a role in the roleList has the same effect as assigning someone to rt99.

The .NET Application Settings Service/Content

The content document is an identity-centric document. Its content and meaning is a function of the Microsoft .NET Passport Unique ID (PUID) used to address the service. Accessing the document is controlled by the associated roleList document.

This schema outline illustrates the layout and meaning of the information found in the content document for the .NET application settings service.

```
<m:myApplicationSettings changeNumber="..." instanceId="..."
    xmlns:m="http://schemas.microsoft.com/hs/2001/10/myApplicationSettings"
    xmlns:hs="http://schemas.microsoft.com/hs/2001/10/core">1..1
    <m:application changeNumber="..." id="...">0..unbounded
        <m:cat ref="...">0..unbounded</m:cat>
        <m:name xml:lang="...">1..unbounded</m:name>
        {any}
    </m:application>
    {any}
</m:myApplicationSettings>
```

The meaning of the attributes and elements shown in the preceding sample document fragment are listed in the following section.

/myApplicationSettings (minOccurs=1 maxOccurs=1)
This element encapsulates the content document for the service. The cache scope for this document is the entire content document—that is, there is a single changeNumber attribute, and it occurs at the root element. Any change to the document changes this attribute.

/myApplicationSettings/@changeNumber (minOccurs=0 maxOccurs=1)
The changeNumber attribute is designed to facilitate caching of the element and its descendants. This attribute is assigned to this element by the Microsoft .NET My Services system. The attribute is read-only to applications. Attempts to write this attribute are silently ignored.

/myApplicationSettings/@instanceId (string minOccurs=0 maxOccurs=1)
This attribute is a unique identifier typically assigned to the root element of a service. It is a read-only element and assigned by the .NET My Services system when a user is provisioned for a particular service.

/myApplicationSettings/application (minOccurs=0 maxOccurs=unbounded)
This element defines the basic application type.

/myApplicationSettings/application/@changeNumber (minOccurs=0 maxOccurs=1)
> The changeNumber attribute is designed to facilitate caching of the element and its descendants. This attribute is assigned to this element by the .NET My Services system. The attribute is read-only to applications. Attempts to write this attribute are silently ignored.

/*myApplicationSettings*/application/@id (minOccurs=0 maxOccurs=1)
> This attribute is a globally unique ID assigned to this element by .NET My Services. Normally, .NET My Services will generate and assign this ID during an insertRequest operation, or possibly during a replaceRequest. Application software can override this ID generation by specifying the useClientIds attribute in the request message. Once an ID is assigned, the attribute is read-only and attempts to write it are silently ignored.

/myApplicationSettings/application/cat (minOccurs=0 maxOccurs=unbounded)
> This element is used to categorize the element that contains it by referencing a global category definition in either the .NET categories service system document or an external resource containing category definitions, or by referencing an identity centric category definition in the content document of the >net categories service for a particular PUID.

/myApplicationSettings/application/cat/@ref (anyURI minOccurs=0 maxOccurs=1)
> This attribute references a category definition (<catDef/>) element using the rules outlined in the .NET categories service section of the *XMI Manual*.

/myApplicationSettings/application/name (string minOccurs=1 maxOccurs=unbounded)
> The name of the application.

/myApplicationSettings/application/name/@xml:lang (minOccurs=1 maxOccurs=1)
> This required attribute is used to specify an ISO 639 language code or an ISO 3166 country code as described in RFC 1766. The value of this attribute indicates the language type of the content within this element.

/myApplicationSettings/application/*{any}* (minOccurs=0 maxOccurs=unbounded)
/myApplicationSettings/*{any}* (minOccurs=0 maxOccurs=unbounded)

The .NET Application Settings Service/System

The system document is a global document for the service. Its content and meaning is independent of the PUID used to address the service, and the document is read-only to all users. The system document contains a set of base items common to all .NET My Services services, and is optionally extended by each service to include service-specific global information.

This schema outline illustrates the layout and meaning of the information found in the system document for the .NET application settings service.

```
<sys:system changeNumber="..." instanceId="..."
    xmlns:hs="http://schemas.microsoft.com/hs/2001/10/core"

xmlns:sys="http://schemas.microsoft.com/hs/2001/10/myApplicationSettings/system">₁
...₁
     <hs:roleMap changeNumber="..." id="..." creator="...">₁..₁
        <hs:scope id="...">₀..unbounded
           <hs:shape base="...">₁..₁
              <hs:include select="...">₁..unbounded</hs:include>
              <hs:exclude select="...">₀..unbounded</hs:exclude>
           </hs:shape>
        </hs:scope>
        <hs:roleTemplate name="..." priority="...">₀..unbounded
           <hs:fullDescription xml:lang="...">₀..₁</hs:fullDescription>
           <hs:method name="..." scopeRef="...">₀..unbounded</hs:method>
        </hs:roleTemplate>
     </hs:roleMap>
     <hs:methodMap changeNumber="..." id="..." creator="...">₁..₁
        <hs:method name="...">₀..unbounded {any}</hs:method>
     </hs:methodMap>
     <hs:schemaMap changeNumber="..." id="..." creator="...">₁..₁
        <hs:schema namespace="..." schemaLocation="..." alias="...">₀..unbounded
{any}</hs:schema>
     </hs:schemaMap>
     <hs:wsdlMap changeNumber="..." id="..." creator="...">₁..₁
        <hs:wsdl wsdlLocation="...">₀..unbounded {any}</hs:wsdl>
        <hs:disco discoLocation="...">₀..unbounded {any}</hs:disco>
     </hs:wsdlMap>
     {any}
</sys:system>
```

The meaning of the attributes and elements shown in the preceding sample document fragment are listed in the following section.

/system (minOccurs=1 maxOccurs=1)

This element encapsulates the system document for the *myApplicationsSettings* service.

/system/@changeNumber (minOccurs=0 maxOccurs=1)

The changeNumber attribute is designed to facilitate caching of the element and its descendants. This attribute is assigned to this element by the .NET My Services system. The attribute is read-only to applications. Attempts to write this attribute are silently ignored.

/system/@instanceId (string minOccurs=0 maxOccurs=1)

This attribute is a unique identifier typically assigned to the root element of a service. It is a read-only element and assigned by the .NET My Services system when a user is provisioned for a particular service.

/system/roleMap (minOccurs=1 maxOccurs=1)

This element encapsulates all the elements that make up a roleMap, which include document class relative roleTemplate, priority, name, method, and per-method scope. An individual roleTemplate defines the maximum scope of information, and the allowable methods used to access that information for each request mapped into the template.

/system/roleMap/@changeNumber (minOccurs=0 maxOccurs=1)

The changeNumber attribute is designed to facilitate caching of the element and its descendants. This attribute is assigned to this element by the .NET My Services system. The attribute is read-only to applications. Attempts to write this attribute are silently ignored.

/system/roleMap/@id (minOccurs=0 maxOccurs=1)

This attribute is a globally unique ID assigned to this element by .NET My Services. Normally, .NET My Services will generate and assign this ID during an insertRequest operation, or possibly during a replaceRequest. Application software can override this ID generation by specifying the useClientIds attribute in the request message. Once an ID is assigned, the attribute is read-only and attempts to write it are silently ignored.

/system/roleMap/@creator (string minOccurs=0 maxOccurs=1)

This attribute identifies the creator in terms of userId, appId, and platformId of the node.

/system/roleMap/scope (minOccurs=0 maxOccurs=unbounded)

This element defines a scope which may be referred to by roles within this roleMap to indicate what portions of the document are visible to this role for the specified method.

/system/roleMap/scope/@id (minOccurs=0 maxOccurs=1)

This attribute is a globally unique ID assigned to this element by .NET My Services. Normally, .NET My Services will generate and assign this ID during an insertRequest operation, or possibly during a replaceRequest. Application software can override this ID generation by specifying the useClientIds attribute in the request message. Once an ID is assigned, the attribute is read-only and attempts to write it are silently ignored.

/system/roleMap/scope/shape (minOccurs=1 maxOccurs=1)

A shape defines the node set visible through the document when operating through this shape element.

/system/roleMap/scope/shape/@base (string minOccurs=0 maxOccurs=1)

This attribute specifies the initial set of nodes visible through the shape.

A value of t indicates that the shape is initialized to include all possible nodes relative to the shape that is currently in effect. For instance, each role defines a scope containing a shape. When defining a shape for a role, the value t indicates all possible nodes available in the specified document for this role. When defining a shape in an ACL entry, a value of t means all of the nodes visible in the shape for the computed role. When using a shape in an hsdl operation, a value of t indicates all of the possible nodes selected by the hsdl operation (relative to the ACL shape which itself is relative to the role's shape).

The value nil indicates the opposite of t, which is the empty node set. Nodes from this set may then be included into the shape.

/system/roleMap/scope/shape/include (minOccurs=1 maxOccurs=unbounded)
This element specifies the set of nodes that should be included into the shape relative to the possible set of nodes indicated by the base attribute.

/system/roleMap/scope/shape/include/@select (string minOccurs=0 maxOccurs=1)
This item specifies an XPath expression that selects a set of nodes relative to the externally established context. The expression can never travel outside the node-set established by this externally established current context. The expression may match 0 or more nodes, and the operation manipulates all selected nodes. The minOccurs and maxOccurs attributes are optional and place restrictions and limitations on the number of nodes selected.

/system/roleMap/scope/shape/exclude (minOccurs=0 maxOccurs=unbounded)
This element specifies the set of nodes that should be excluded from the shape relative to the possible set of nodes indicated by the base attribute.

/system/roleMap/scope/shape/exclude/@select (string minOccurs=0 maxOccurs=1)
This item specifies an XPath expression that selects a set of nodes relative to the externally established context. The expression can never travel outside the node-set established by this externally established current context. The expression may match 0 or more nodes, and the operation manipulates all selected nodes. The minOccurs and maxOccurs attributes are optional and place restrictions and limitations on the number of nodes selected.

/system/roleMap/roleTemplate (minOccurs=0 maxOccurs=unbounded)
This element encapsulates the definition of a role. The attribute set for this element includes the document class that this roleTemplate refers to, the name of the roleTemplate, and the priority of the roleTemplate.

/system/roleMap/roleTemplate/@name (string minOccurs=0 maxOccurs=1)
This element specifies the name of the role.

/system/roleMap/roleTemplate/@priority (int minOccurs=0 maxOccurs=1)
This element specifies the priority of the roleTemplate which is used to select that actual roleTemplate when the role evaluation determines that the subject maps to multiple roleTemplates.

/system/roleMap/roleTemplate/fullDescription (string minOccurs=0 maxOccurs=1)
This element contains a description of this role template which specifies the capabilities a caller will have when accessing information through this role.

/system/roleMap/roleTemplate/fullDescription/@xml:lang (minOccurs=1 maxOccurs=1)
This required attribute is used to specify an ISO 639 language code or an ISO 3166 country code as described in RFC 1766. The value of this attribute indicates the language type of the content within this element.

/system/roleMap/roleTemplate/method (minOccurs=0 maxOccurs=unbounded)
This element specifies the methods available within this roleTemplate by name, and by scope. When a subject maps to a roleTemplate, the method in the request must match one of these elements for the message to continue to flow. If the method exists, the data available to the method is a function of the scope referenced by this method combined with an optional scope referenced by the role defined in the roleList.

/system/roleMap/roleTemplate/method/@name (string minOccurs=0 maxOccurs=1)
This element specifies the name of the method.

/system/roleMap/roleTemplate/method/@scopeRef (string minOccurs=0 maxOccurs=1)
This attribute specifies the scope within this document that is in effect for this method.

/system/methodMap (minOccurs=1 maxOccurs=1)
This element defines the methodMap. While it is true that in most cases, the roleMap section contains a definitive list of methods, these methods are likely to be scattered about the roleMap in various templates. This section contains the definitive non-duplicated list of methods available within the service.

/system/methodMap/@changeNumber (minOccurs=0 maxOccurs=1)
The changeNumber attribute is designed to facilitate caching of the element and its descendants. This attribute is assigned to this element by the .NET My Services system. The attribute is read-only to applications. Attempts to write this attribute are silently ignored.

/system/methodMap/@id (minOccurs=0 maxOccurs=1)
This attribute is a globally unique ID assigned to this element by .NET My Services. Normally, .NET My Services will generate and assign this ID during an insertRequest operation, or possibly during a replaceRequest. Application software can override this ID generation by specifying the useClientIds attribute in the request message. Once an ID is assigned, the attribute is read-only and attempts to write it are silently ignored.

/system/methodMap/@creator (string minOccurs=0 maxOccurs=1)
This attribute identifies the creator in terms of userId, appId, and platformId of the node.

/system/methodMap/method (minOccurs=0 maxOccurs=unbounded)
This element defines a method that is available within this service.

/system/methodMap/method/@name (string minOccurs=0 maxOccurs=1)
This attribute specifies the name of a method available within the service.

/system/methodMap/method/*{any}* (minOccurs=0 maxOccurs=unbounded)
/system/schemaMap (minOccurs=1 maxOccurs=1)
This element defines the various schema's that define the data structures and shape of information managed by this service. Each schema is defined by its namespace URI, its location, and a preferred namespace alias.

/system/schemaMap/@changeNumber (minOccurs=0 maxOccurs=1)

The changeNumber attribute is designed to facilitate caching of the element and its descendants. This attribute is assigned to this element by the .NET My Services system. The attribute is read-only to applications. Attempts to write this attribute are silently ignored.

/system/schemaMap/@id (minOccurs=0 maxOccurs=1)

This attribute is a globally unique ID assigned to this element by .NET My Services. Normally, .NET My Services will generate and assign this ID during an insertRequest operation, or possibly during a replaceRequest. Application software can override this ID generation by specifying the useClientIds attribute in the request message. Once an ID is assigned, the attribute is read-only and attempts to write it are silently ignored.

/system/schemaMap/@creator (string minOccurs=0 maxOccurs=1)

This attribute identifies the creator in terms of userId, appId, and platformId of the node.

/system/schemaMap/schema (minOccurs=0 maxOccurs=unbounded)

This element defines a schema which defines data-structures and the shape of information managed by this service. Multiple schema elements exist for each service, once for each logical grouping of information exposed by the service.

/system/schemaMap/schema/@namespace (anyURI minOccurs=0 maxOccurs=1)

This attribute specifies the namespace URI of this schema.

/system/schemaMap/schema/@schemaLocation (anyURI minOccurs=0 maxOccurs=1)

This attribute specifies the location (in the form of a URI) of the resource containing schema. When a schema is reachable through a variety of URIs, one schema element will exist for each location.

/system/schemaMap/schema/@alias (string minOccurs=0 maxOccurs=1)

This attribute specifies the preferred alias that should be used if possible when manipulating information covered by this schema in the context of this service.

/system/schemaMap/schema/*{any}* (minOccurs=0 maxOccurs=unbounded)

/system/wsdlMap (minOccurs=1 maxOccurs=1)

This element defines the wsdlMap for this service. This map includes the location of WSDL documents, DISCO documents, and WISL documents for this Web service. These documents are used by applications to understand the format of messages that may be sent to the various services.

/system/wsdlMap/@changeNumber (minOccurs=0 maxOccurs=1)

The changeNumber attribute is designed to facilitate caching of the element and its descendants. This attribute is assigned to this element by the .NET My Services system. The attribute is read-only to applications. Attempts to write this attribute are silently ignored.

/system/wsdlMap/@id (minOccurs=0 maxOccurs=1)

    This attribute is a globally unique ID assigned to this element by .NET My Services. Normally, .NET My Services will generate and assign this ID during an insertRequest operation, or possibly during a replaceRequest. Application software can override this ID generation by specifying the useClientIds attribute in the request message. Once an ID is assigned, the attribute is read-only and attempts to write it are silently ignored.

/system/wsdlMap/@creator (string minOccurs=0 maxOccurs=1)

    This attribute identifies the creator in terms of userId, appId, and platformId of the node.

/system/wsdlMap/wsdl (minOccurs=0 maxOccurs=unbounded)

    This element is used to specify the location of a WSDL file for this service. Multiple entries may exist pointing to the same file hosted in multiple locations, or to variations on the content within the WSDL files.

/system/wsdlMap/wsdl/@wsdlLocation (anyURI minOccurs=0 maxOccurs=1)

    This attribute is a URI that specifies the location of the WSDL file.

/system/wsdlMap/wsdl/*{any}* (minOccurs=0 maxOccurs=unbounded)

/system/wsdlMap/disco (minOccurs=0 maxOccurs=unbounded)

    This element is used to specify the location of a DISCO file for this service. Multiple entries may exist pointing to the same file hosted in multiple locations, or to variations on the content within the DISCO files.

/system/wsdlMap/disco/@discoLocation (anyURI minOccurs=0 maxOccurs=1)

    This attribute is a URI that specifies the location of the DISCO file.

/system/wsdlMap/disco/*{any}* (minOccurs=0 maxOccurs=unbounded)

/system/*{any}* (minOccurs=0 maxOccurs=unbounded)

The .NET Application Settings Service/Methods

The .NET application settings service supports the following standard methods:

- query
- insert
- replace
- delete
- update

The standard methods operate on this service using the same message format and method-interchange techniques described in the hsdl section of this document. The only service-specific information to note is the schema that is in effect for each of the methods. These schemas, and how they relate to the standard methods and roles are described in the roles section of this document.

CHAPTER 11

.NET calendar service/Introduction

This service is designed to store and manage organizational calendaring tasks typically used for the scheduling of personal and work-related events, appointments, and tasks that are associated with an identity. The .NET calendar service supplies scheduling information on demand to .NET-based services, applications, and devices. The .NET calendar service can be used for regular scheduling or group collaboration.

The .NET calendar service integrates with the .NET notifications service to perform meeting requests and reminder alerts, and with the .NET inbox service to retrieve event attachments.

We anticipate that .NET calendar service will eventually support calendar publishing, a feature that allows users to open their calendars to other users such as friends and family members. The .NET calendar service uses .NET My Services-based services to supports a rich sharing model based upon the access control list, role map, and identity header.

The .NET calendar service schema format builds upon the work of Microsoft Exchange, Microsoft Outlook, and Microsoft MSN Calendar to define a compatible, full-featured calendar schema that can host any of these properties.

The .NET calendar service/Roles

The .NET calendar service controls access by using the following roleTemplates:

- rt0
- rt1
- rt2
- rt3
- rt99

The .NET calendar service uses the following scopes:

- **scope id 1**

```
<hs:scope id=1>

    <hs:shape base=t>

    </hs:shape>

</hs:scope>
```

- **scope id 2**

```
<hs:scope id=2>

    <hs:shape base=nil>

        <hs:include select=//*[@creator='$callerId']/>

    </hs:shape>

</hs:scope>
```

- **scope id 3**

```
<hs:scope id=3>

    <hs:shape base=nil>

        <hs:include select=//subscription[@creator='$callerId']/>

    </hs:shape>

</hs:scope>
```

- **scope id 4**

```
<hs:scope id=4>

    <hs:shape base=nil>

        <hs:include select=//*[cat/@ref='hs:public']/>

        <hs:include select=//subscription[@creator='$callerId']/>

    </hs:shape>

</hs:scope>
```

The .NET calendar service roleTemplate rt0

The purpose of this role is to give complete read/write access to all information within the content document of the service being protected through this roleTemplate.

The following table illustrates the available methods and the scope in effect when accessing the .NET calendar service through that method while mapped to this roleTemplate.

method	scopeRef
query	scopeRef=1
insert	scopeRef=1
replace	scopeRef=1
delete	scopeRef=1
update	scopeRef=1
getCalendarDays	scopeRef=1
getFreeBusyDays	scopeRef=1
getQuickView	scopeRef=1
setCalendarAttachment	scopeRef=1
getCalendarAttachment	scopeRef=1
meetingUpdate	scopeRef=1
respond	scopeRef=1
updateReminder	scopeRef=1

.NET calendar roleTemplate rt1

The purpose of this role is to give complete read access to all information within the content document of the service being protected through this roleTemplate. Applications mapping to this role also have a limited ability to write to information in the content document. They may create nodes in any location, but may only change/replace or delete nodes that they created.

The following table illustrates the available methods and the scope in effect when accessing the .NET calendar service through that method while mapped to this roleTemplate.

method	scopeRef
query	scopeRef=1
insert	scopeRef=2
replace	scopeRef=2
delete	scopeRef=2
getCalendarDays	scopeRef=1
getFreeBusyDays	scopeRef=1
getQuickView	scopeRef=1
setCalendarAttachment	scopeRef=2
getCalendarAttachment	scopeRef=1
meetingUpdate	scopeRef=2
respond	scopeRef=2
updateReminder	scopeRef=2

.NET calendar roleTemplate rt2

The purpose of this role is to give complete read access to all information within the content document of the service being protected through this roleTemplate. Applications mapping to this role have very limited write access and are only able to create and manipulate their own subscription nodes.

The following table illustrates the available methods and the scope in effect when accessing the .NET calendar service through that method while mapped to this roleTemplate.

method	scopeRef
query	scopeRef=1
insert	scopeRef=3
replace	scopeRef=3
delete	scopeRef=3
getCalendarDays	scopeRef=1
getFreeBusyDays	scopeRef=1
getQuickView	scopeRef=1
getCalendarAttachment	scopeRef=1

.NET calendar roleTemplate rt3

The purpose of this role is to give limited read access within the content document to information that is categorized as "public."

The following table illustrates the available methods and the scope in effect when accessing the .NET calendar service through that method while mapped to this roleTemplate.

method	scopeRef
query	scopeRef=4
getCalendarDays	scopeRef=4
getFreeBusyDays	scopeRef=4
getQuickView	scopeRef=4
getCalendarAttachment	scopeRef=4

.NET calendar roleTemplate rt99

The purpose of this role is to block all access to the content document. Note that lack of a role in the roleList has the same effect as assigning someone to rt99.

.NET calendar service/content

The content document is an identity-centric document. Its content and meaning is a function of the PUID used to address the service. Accessing the document is controlled by the associated roleList document.

This schema outline illustrates the layout and meaning of the information found in the content document for the .NET calendar service.

```
<m:myCalendar changeNumber="..." instanceId="..."
    xmlns:m="http://schemas.microsoft.com/hs/2001/10/myCalendar"
    xmlns:hs="http://schemas.microsoft.com/hs/2001/10/core">₁..₁
    <m:event calendarType="..." advanceHijriValue="..." changeNumber="..."
id="..." creator="...">₀..unbounded
        <m:body changeNumber="...">₁..₁
            <m:cat ref="...">₀..unbounded</m:cat>
            <m:title xml:lang="...">₁..₁</m:title>
            <m:fullDescription xml:lang="...">₀..₁</m:fullDescription>
            <m:location xml:lang="...">₀..₁</m:location>
            <m:recurrenceId>₀..₁</m:recurrenceId>
            <m:lastUpdateTime>₀..₁</m:lastUpdateTime>
            <m:startTime>₁..₁</m:startTime>
            <m:endTime>₁..₁</m:endTime>
            <m:allDay>₀..₁</m:allDay>
            <m:floating>₀..₁</m:floating>
            <m:travelTimeTo>₀..₁</m:travelTimeTo>
            <m:travelTimeFrom>₀..₁</m:travelTimeFrom>
            <m:freeBusyStatus>₀..₁</m:freeBusyStatus>
            <m:cuid>₀..₁</m:cuid>
            <m:organizer>₀..₁
                <hs:name xml:lang="...">₀..₁</hs:name>
                <hs:puid>₀..₁</hs:puid>
                <hs:email>₀..₁</hs:email>
            </m:organizer>
            {any}
        </m:body>
        <m:attendeeEventExtra changeNumber="...">₀..₁
            <m:intendedFreeBusy>₀..₁</m:intendedFreeBusy>
            <m:delegateResponder>₀..₁
                <hs:name xml:lang="...">₀..₁</hs:name>
                <hs:puid>₀..₁</hs:puid>
                <hs:email>₀..₁</hs:email>
            </m:delegateResponder>
            <m:responseTime>₁..₁</m:responseTime>
            <m:responseType>₁..₁</m:responseType>
            <m:counterProposeStartTime>₀..₁</m:counterProposeStartTime>
```

(continued)

(continued)

```
        <m:counterProposeEndTime>₀..₁</m:counterProposeEndTime>
        <m:counterProposeLocation>₀..₁</m:counterProposeLocation>
        {any}
    </m:attendeeEventExtra>
    <m:attachment changeNumber="..." id="..." creator="...">₀..unbounded
        <m:name xml:lang="...">₁..₁</m:name>
        <m:contentType>₁..₁</m:contentType>
        <m:contentTransferEncoding>₁..₁</m:contentTransferEncoding>
        <m:size>₁..₁</m:size>
    </m:attachment>
    <m:reminder changeNumber="..." id="..." creator="...">₀..₁
        <m:set>₁..₁</m:set>
        <m:to xml:lang="...">₁..₁</m:to>
        <m:offset>₁..₁</m:offset>
        <m:interruptability>₀..₁</m:interruptability>
        <m:lastSentTime>₁..₁</m:lastSentTime>
        <m:nextTriggerTime>₁..₁</m:nextTriggerTime>
    </m:reminder>
    <m:attendee changeNumber="..." id="..." creator="...">₀..unbounded
        <hs:name xml:lang="...">₀..₁</hs:name>
        <hs:puid>₀..₁</hs:puid>
        <hs:email>₀..₁</hs:email>
        <m:inviteType>₁..₁</m:inviteType>
        <m:invitationStatus>₁..₁</m:invitationStatus>
        <m:body xml:lang="...">₀..₁</m:body>
        <m:responseTime>₁..₁</m:responseTime>
        <m:responseType>₁..₁</m:responseType>
        <m:counterProposeStartTime>₀..₁</m:counterProposeStartTime>
        <m:counterProposeEndTime>₀..₁</m:counterProposeEndTime>
        <m:counterProposeLocation>₀..₁</m:counterProposeLocation>
        {any}
    </m:attendee>
    <m:recurrence changeNumber="...">₀..₁
        <m:rule changeNumber="...">₁..₁
            <m:firstDayOfWeek>₁..₁</m:firstDayOfWeek>
            <m:tzid>₀..₁</m:tzid>
            <m:repeat>₁..₁
                <m:daily dayFrequency="...">₀..₁</m:daily>
                <m:weekly su="..." mo="..." tu="..." we="..." th="..."
fr="..." sa="..." weekFrequency="...">₀..₁</m:weekly>
                <m:monthlyByDay su="..." mo="..." tu="..." we="..." th="..."
fr="..." sa="..." monthFrequency="..." weekOfMonth="...">₀..₁</m:monthlyByDay>
                <m:monthly monthFrequency="..." day="...">₀..₁</m:monthly>
```

```
                <m:yearlyByDay su="..." mo="..." tu="..." we="..." th="..."
fr="..." sa="..." yearFrequency="..." weekOfMonth="..."
month="...">₀..₁</m:yearlyByDay>
                <m:yearly yearFrequency="..." month="..."
day="...">₀..₁</m:yearly>
            </m:repeat>
            <m:windowStart isLeapYear="..."
leapMonthValue="...">₁..₁</m:windowStart>
            <m:windowEnd>₀..₁</m:windowEnd>
            <m:repeatForever>₀..₁</m:repeatForever>
            <m:repeatInstances>₀..₁</m:repeatInstances>
            <m:deletedExceptionDate>₀..unbounded</m:deletedExceptionDate>
            {any}
        </m:rule>
        <m:exception changeNumber="..." id="..." creator="...">₀..unbounded
            <m:recurrenceId>₁..₁</m:recurrenceId>
            <m:body>₀..₁
                <m:title xml:lang="...">₀..₁</m:title>
                <m:fullDescription xml:lang="...">₀..₁</m:fullDescription>
                <m:location xml:lang="...">₀..₁</m:location>
                <m:startTime>₀..₁</m:startTime>
                <m:endTime>₀..₁</m:endTime>
                <m:allDay>₀..₁</m:allDay>
                <m:travelTimeTo>₀..₁</m:travelTimeTo>
                <m:travelTimeFrom>₀..₁</m:travelTimeFrom>
                <m:freeBusyStatus>₀..₁</m:freeBusyStatus>
                <m:organizer>₀..₁
                    <hs:name xml:lang="...">₀..₁</hs:name>
                    <hs:puid>₀..₁</hs:puid>
                    <hs:email>₀..₁</hs:email>
                </m:organizer>
            </m:body>
            <m:deletedAttendee>₀..unbounded</m:deletedAttendee>
            <m:deletedAttachment>₀..unbounded</m:deletedAttachment>
            <m:attachment>₀..unbounded
                <m:name xml:lang="...">₁..₁</m:name>
                <m:contentType>₁..₁</m:contentType>
                <m:contentTransferEncoding>₁..₁</m:contentTransferEncoding>
                <m:size>₁..₁</m:size>
            </m:attachment>
            <m:attendee>₀..unbounded
                <hs:name xml:lang="...">₀..₁</hs:name>
                <hs:puid>₀..₁</hs:puid>
                <hs:email>₀..₁</hs:email>
                <m:inviteType>₁..₁</m:inviteType>
```

(continued)

(continued)

```
                    <m:invitationStatus>₁.₁</m:invitationStatus>
                    <m:body xml:lang="...">₀.₁</m:body>
                    <m:responseTime>₁.₁</m:responseTime>
                    <m:responseType>₁.₁</m:responseType>
                    <m:counterProposeStartTime>₀.₁</m:counterProposeStartTime>
                    <m:counterProposeEndTime>₀.₁</m:counterProposeEndTime>
                    <m:counterProposeLocation>₀.₁</m:counterProposeLocation>
                    {any}
                </m:attendee>
                <m:reminder>₀.₁
                    <m:set>₀.₁</m:set>
                    <m:offset>₀.₁</m:offset>
                    <m:interruptability>₀.₁</m:interruptability>
                </m:reminder>
                {any}
            </m:exception>
            {any}
        </m:recurrence>
    </m:event>
    <m:subscription changeNumber="..." id="..." creator="...">₀.unbounded
        <hs:trigger select="..." mode="..."
baseChangeNumber="...">₁.₁</hs:trigger>
        <hs:expiresAt>₀.₁</hs:expiresAt>
        <hs:context uri="...">₁.₁ {any}</hs:context>
        <hs:to>₁.₁</hs:to>
    </m:subscription>
    {any}
</m:myCalendar>
```

The meaning of the attributes and elements shown in the preceding sample document fragment are listed in the following section.

/myCalendar (minOccurs=1 maxOccurs=1)

This element encapsulates the content document for this service. This element establishes a global cache scope for the service and contains other root-level system attributes for this instance of the service.

/myCalendar/@changeNumber (minOccurs=0 maxOccurs=1)

The changeNumber attribute is designed to facilitate caching of the element and its descendants. This attribute is assigned to this element by the .NET My Services system. The attribute is read-only to applications. Attempts to write this attribute are silently ignored.

/myCalendar/@instanceId (string minOccurs=0 maxOccurs=1)

This attribute is a unique identifier typically assigned to the root element of a service. It is a read-only element and assigned by the .NET My Services system when a user is provisioned for a particular service.

/myCalendar/event (minOccurs=0 maxOccurs=unbounded)

The event is the .NET calendar service root object for calendar events, appointments, and meetings.

/myCalendar/event/@calendarType (string minOccurs=0 maxOccurs=1)

This field identifies an enumeration that determines the kind of calendar event this is. .NET My Services version 1 will only support CAL_GREGORIAN_US. http://msdn.microsoft.com/library/psdk/winbase/nls_9bg8.htm plus several others:

Value	Enumeration Constant	Description
−1	HSCAL_ALL_CALENDARS	Unknown Calendar; system default (HSCAL_GREGORIAN_US)
1	HSCAL_GREGORIAN	Gregorian (localized) calendar
2	HSCAL_GREGORIAN_US	Gregorian (U.S.) calendar
3	HSCAL_JAPAN	Japanese Emperor Era calendar
4	HSCAL_TAIWAN	Taiwan Era calendar
5	HSCAL_KOREA	Korean Tangun Era calendar
6	HSCAL_HIJRI	Hijri (Arabic Lunar) calendar
7	HSCAL_THAI	Thai calendar
8	HSCAL_HEBREW	Hebrew (Lunar) calendar
9	HSCAL_GREGORIAN_ME_FRENCH	Gregorian Middle East French calendar
10	HSCAL_GREGORIAN_ARABIC	Gregorian Arabic calendar
11	HSCAL_GREGORIAN_XLIT_ENGLISH	Gregorian Transliterated English calendar
12	HSCAL_GREGORIAN_XLIT_FRENCH	Gregorian Transliterated French calendar
13	HSCAL_KOREA_LUNAR	Default Korea Lunar calendar (implementation identical to 14)
14	HSCAL_JAPAN_LUNAR	Default Japanese Lunar calendar (implementation identical to 13)
15	HSCAL_CHINESE_LUNAR	Chinese Lunar calendar
16	HSCAL_SAKA	Indian Saka calendar
17	HSCAL_LUNAR_ETO_CHN	Chinese Zodiac calendar
18	HSCAL_LUNAR_ETO_KOR	Korean Zodiac calendar
19	HSCAL_LUNAR_ROKUYOU	Japanese Lucky days calendar

/myCalendar/event/@advanceHijriValue (int minOccurs=0 maxOccurs=1)

Required for Hijri calendar support with an optional attribute.

/myCalendar/event/@changeNumber (minOccurs=0 maxOccurs=1)

The changeNumber attribute is designed to facilitate caching of the element and its descendants. This attribute is assigned to this element by the .NET My Services system. The attribute is read-only to applications. Attempts to write this attribute are silently ignored.

/myCalendar/event/@id (minOccurs=0 maxOccurs=1)

This attribute is a globally unique ID assigned to this element by .NET My Services. Normally, .NET My Services will generate and assign this ID during an insertRequest operation, or possibly during a replaceRequest. Application software can override this ID generation by specifying the useClientIds attribute in the request message. Once an ID is assigned, the attribute is read-only and attempts to write it are silently ignored.

/myCalendar/event/@creator (string minOccurs=0 maxOccurs=1)

This attribute identifies the creator in terms of userId, appId, and platformId of the node.

/myCalendar/event/body (minOccurs=1 maxOccurs=1)

/myCalendar/event/body/@changeNumber (minOccurs=0 maxOccurs=1)

The changeNumber attribute is designed to facilitate caching of the element and its descendants. This attribute is assigned to this element by the .NET My Services system. The attribute is read-only to applications. Attempts to write this attribute are silently ignored.

/myCalendar/event/body/cat (minOccurs=0 maxOccurs=unbounded)

This element is used to categorize the element that contains it by referencing a global category definition in either the myCategories service system document or an external resource containing category definitions, or by referencing an identity-centric category definition in the content document of the myCategories service for a particular PUID.

/myCalendar/event/body/cat/@ref (anyURI minOccurs=0 maxOccurs=1)

This attribute references a category definition (<catDef/>) element using the rules outlined in the myCategories section of the *XMI Manual.*

/myCalendar/event/body/title (string minOccurs=1 maxOccurs=1)

/myCalendar/event/body/title/@xml:lang (minOccurs=1 maxOccurs=1)

This required attribute is used to specify an ISO 639 language code or an ISO 3166 country code as described in RFC 1766. The value of this attribute indicates the language type of the content within this element.

/myCalendar/event/body/fullDescription (string minOccurs=0 maxOccurs=1)

This element contains an xhtml-compliant, free-form, full description of the event.

/myCalendar/event/body/fullDescription/@xml:lang (minOccurs=1 maxOccurs=1)

This required attribute is used to specify an ISO 639 language code or an ISO 3166 country code as described in RFC 1766. The value of this attribute indicates the language type of the content within this element.

/myCalendar/event/body/location (string minOccurs=0 maxOccurs=1)

This optional element contains the event's location.

/myCalendar/event/body/location/@xml:lang (minOccurs=1 maxOccurs=1)
This required attribute is used to specify an ISO 639 language code or an ISO 3166 country code as described in RFC 1766. The value of this attribute indicates the language type of the content within this element.

/myCalendar/event/body/recurrenceId (dateTime minOccurs=0 maxOccurs=1)
The recurrence id indicates the original start time of an occurrence of a recurring master appointment. It is required to identify what instance an orphan exception is modifying, since users are allowed to change the start time on the orphan. The recurrenceId method is stored in UTC. It does not appear in the master schema, except in the specific case that an attendee is invited to an instance of a recurring event. Otherwise, <recurrenceId> is usually only a part of getCalendarDays.

Outlook Equivalent: Part of GlobalObjectID. **ICAL Equivalent**: RECURRENCEID

/myCalendar/event/body/lastUpdateTime (dateTime minOccurs=0 maxOccurs=1)
This is updated by the organizer whenever he or she creates and sends a new meeting request. This helps the attendee to identify which meeting request is the most recent one. It is stored in UTC. This property is not modifiable by clients and is assigned by the server on modification and by the updateMeetingRequest.

Outlook Equivalent: OwnerCriticalChange. **ICAL Equivalent**: DTSTAMP.

/myCalendar/event/body/startTime (dateTime minOccurs=1 maxOccurs=1)
The startTime method defines the start time of the event. An all-day event will by convention starts at 12:00:00 a.m. of the day of the event. This is stored in UTC. Maximum range is January 1, 1753 to December 31, 9999 to an accuracy of 3.33 milliseconds.

/myCalendar/event/body/endTime (dateTime minOccurs=1 maxOccurs=1)
The endTime method defines the end time of the event. An all-day event will by convention end at 11:59:59 p.m. of the ending day. Duration is inferred from the start and end times of the event. This is stored in UTC. Maximum range is January 1, 1753 to December 31, 9999 to an accuracy of 3.33 milliseconds.

/myCalendar/event/body/allDay (boolean minOccurs=0 maxOccurs=1)
False or absence of this element indicates a regular event. Otherwise, this attribute indicates that the event is an all-day event. All day events may span multiple days. By convention, all day events start at 12:00:00 am of the day of startTime, regardless of what time it actually is, and it will end at 11:59:59 pm of the endTime date. In other words, if the allDay element is present and has value=true, the .NET calendar service will ignore the actual times of the events and consider only the date part of the field. The allDay tag is meant to operate as a hint to UI renders to display specialized icons indicating an all-day event. allDay events are distinguishable between 24-hr events starting at 12am. In the case of a meeting request, an allDay event will not appear in the local user's time zone, but rather in the organizer's time zone.

/myCalendar/event/body/floating (boolean minOccurs=0 maxOccurs=1)
The floating attribute indicates that this event is to occur in the current local time zone no matter what time zone the system is currently in (that is, it floats). For example, holidays are floating events. Floating values are stored as-is: no time-zone translations are needed to convert them to UTC or any local time zone.

/myCalendar/event/body/travelTimeTo (int minOccurs=0 maxOccurs=1)
> This is the amount of time (in minutes) that it takes to travel to the meeting location.
>
> This optional element shows in free/busy calculations.

/myCalendar/event/body/travelTimeFrom (int minOccurs=0 maxOccurs=1)
> This is the amount of time (in minutes) that it takes to return from the meeting location.
>
> This optional element shows in free/busy calculations.

/myCalendar/event/body/freeBusyStatus (string minOccurs=0 maxOccurs=1)
> This optional element annotates the freeBusy behavior of this event. All events by default appear as "busy". The user may explicitly define this event to be annotated by setting the .NET calendar service values to free, tentative, busy, or away.

/myCalendar/event/body/cuid (string minOccurs=0 maxOccurs=1)
> The cuid (CorrelationUID) links an organizer's event to an attendee's event. It identifies which response from an attendee is for which request from an organizer, and which meeting request update from the organizer is for which previously accepted meeting by the attendee. The "cuid" is the same on both the attendee's and the organizer's copy of the appointment. It is also identical on the orphan exception and the recurring master. This value is assigned by the .NET calendar services server and is non-modifiable.
>
> **Outlook Equivalent**: Part of GlobalObjectId. **ICAL Equivalent**: UID.

/.NET calendar /event/body/organizer (minOccurs=0 maxOccurs=1)
> This is the e-mail address of the event organizer for non-.NET My Services organizers.
>
> **Outlook Equivalent**: PR_SENT_REPRESENTING. **ICAL Equivalent**: ORGANIZER.

/myCalendar/event/body/organizer/name (string minOccurs=0 maxOccurs=1)
> This optional element specifies the name for the enclosing element.

/myCalendar/event/body/organizer/name/@xml:lang (minOccurs=1 maxOccurs=1)
> This required attribute is used to specify an ISO 639 language code or an ISO 3166 country code as described in RFC 1766. The value of this attribute indicates the language type of the content within this element.

/myCalendar/event/body/organizer/puid (string minOccurs=0 maxOccurs=1)
> This optional element specifies the name for the enclosing element.

/myCalendar/event/body/organizer/email (string minOccurs=0 maxOccurs=1)
> This optional name specifies an e-mail address for the enclosing element.

/myCalendar/event/body/*{any}* (minOccurs=0 maxOccurs=unbounded)
> Additional body elements.

/myCalendar/event/attendeeEventExtra (minOccurs=0 maxOccurs=1)
> Additional information about an event, found only in an event invitee's schema

/myCalendar/event/attendeeEventExtra/@changeNumber (minOccurs=0 maxOccurs=1)

The changeNumber attribute is designed to facilitate caching of the element and its descendants. This attribute is assigned to this element by the .NET My Services system. The attribute is read-only to applications. Attempts to write this attribute are silently ignored.

/myCalendar/event/attendeeEventExtra/intendedFreeBusy (string minOccurs=0 maxOccurs=1)

The intendedFreeBusy element is the event organizer's freeBusy information and is thus equal to event/freeBusyStatus. Invitees may overwrite event/freeBusyStatus with a new value, and intendedFreeBusy is intended to store the organizer's original freeBusyStatus.

/myCalendar/event/attendeeEventExtra/delegateResponder (minOccurs=0 maxOccurs=1)

A delegate who responds on behalf of an invitee will have their information stored here.

/myCalendar/event/attendeeEventExtra/delegateResponder/name (string minOccurs=0 maxOccurs=1)

This optional element specifies the name for the enclosing element.

/myCalendar/event/attendeeEventExtra/delegateResponder/name/@xml:lang (minOccurs=1 maxOccurs=1)

This required attribute is used to specify an ISO 639 language code or an ISO 3166 country code as described in RFC 1766. The value of this attribute indicates the language type of the content within this element.

/myCalendar/event/attendeeEventExtra/delegateResponder/puid (string minOccurs=0 maxOccurs=1)

This optional element specifies the name for the enclosing element.

/myCalendar/event/attendeeEventExtra/delegateResponder/email (string minOccurs=0 maxOccurs=1)

This optional name specifies an e-mail address for the enclosing element.

/myCalendar/event/attendeeEventExtra/responseTime (dateTime minOccurs=1 maxOccurs=1)

The reply time on each attendee is set to "Now" when the organizer creates and sends a meeting. When the attendees respond, they always update their replyTime. When the organizer receives responses, he or she honors only those that have a higher replyTime than what is maintained in his/her own copy of the event for each attendee. While processing the response, the organizer will update the replyTime. This guarantees that the organizer honors only the most recent response from the attendee. This is stored in UTC.

Outlook Equivalent: RECIPIENT_TRACKSTATUSTIME. **ICAL Equivalent**: reply time on message.

/myCalendar/event/attendeeEventExtra/responseType (string minOccurs=1 maxOccurs=1)

> The accept status indicates the valid types of responses that an attendee can reply with {accept, decline, tentative, counterpropose}.

/myCalendar/event/attendeeEventExtra/counterProposeStartTime (dateTime minOccurs=0 maxOccurs=1)

> If responseType=[counterPropose], the {startTime, endTime}, or location, or both can be present. This is the invitee's counterProposal for a new start time for the meeting. This is stored in UTC.

/myCalendar/event/attendeeEventExtra/counterProposeEndTime (dateTime minOccurs=0 maxOccurs=1)

> If responseType=[counterPropose], the {startTime, endTime}, or location, or both can be present. This is the invitee's counterProposal for a new end time for the meeting. This is stored in UTC.

/myCalendar/event/attendeeEventExtra/counterProposeLocation (string minOccurs=0 maxOccurs=1)

> If responseType=[counterPropose], the {startTime, endTime}, or location, or both can be present. This is the invitee's counterProposal for a location for the meeting.

/myCalendar/event/attendeeEventExtra/*{any}* (minOccurs=0 maxOccurs=unbounded)

> Additional attendee properties.

/myCalendar/event/attachment (minOccurs=0 maxOccurs=unbounded)

> This element contains attachment metadata, name, content-type and IDs, and may also contain the attachmentBody.

/myCalendar/event/attachment/@changeNumber (minOccurs=0 maxOccurs=1)

> The changeNumber attribute is designed to facilitate caching of the element and its descendants. This attribute is assigned to this element by the .NET My Services system. The attribute is read-only to applications. Attempts to write this attribute are silently ignored.

/myCalendar/event/attachment/@id (minOccurs=0 maxOccurs=1)

> This attribute is a globally unique ID assigned to this element by .NET My Services. Normally, .NET My Services will generate and assign this ID during an insertRequest operation, or possibly during a replaceRequest. Application software can override this ID generation by specifying the useClientIds attribute in the request message. Once an ID is assigned, the attribute is read-only and attempts to write it are silently ignored.

/myCalendar/event/attachment/@creator (string minOccurs=0 maxOccurs=1)

> This attribute identifies the creator in terms of userId, appId, and platformId of the node.

/myCalendar/event/attachment/name (string minOccurs=1 maxOccurs=1)

> This element contains information about an individual attachment in an e-mail message.

/myCalendar/event/attachment/name/@xml:lang (minOccurs=1 maxOccurs=1)

This required attribute is used to specify an ISO 639 language code or an ISO 3166 country code as described in RFC 1766. The value of this attribute indicates the language type of the content within this element.

/myCalendar/event/attachment/contentType (string minOccurs=1 maxOccurs=1)

This element contains the content type of the attachment.

/myCalendar/event/attachment/contentTransferEncoding (string minOccurs=1 maxOccurs=1)

This element contains the encoding of the attachment. This information is necessary for decoding the attachment.

/myCalendar/event/attachment/size (unsignedLong minOccurs=1 maxOccurs=1)

This element contains the size of the attachment in bytes.

/myCalendar/event/reminder (minOccurs=0 maxOccurs=1)

A user may optionally define a reminder for this appointment. Reminders for recurring appointments will be sent periodically before the appointment according to the rules defined in the reminder subschema. A non-recurring event may have the following:

- Define no reminders
- Define a reminder with <set> = "true"
- Define a reminder with <set> = "false"

A recurring meeting may have any of the following:

- Define no reminders
- Define a recurring reminder with all instances receiving reminders
- To define no reminders by default, but to define reminders for particular meeting instances in the exception body, create a reminder <set> = "false", and turn it on or modify it for particular instances.
- To define a recurring reminder, but turn it off for particular meeting instances, create a reminder <set> = "true", and turn it off for particular instances.
  If the event's reminder subschema is nonexistent but the exception body has a reminder blob, the exception reminder is ignored. The alternative is to require 1..1.

/myCalendar/event/reminder/@changeNumber (minOccurs=0 maxOccurs=1)

The changeNumber attribute is designed to facilitate caching of the element and its descendants. This attribute is assigned to this element by the .NET My Services system. The attribute is read-only to applications. Attempts to write this attribute are silently ignored.

/myCalendar/event/reminder/@id (minOccurs=0 maxOccurs=1)

This attribute is a globally unique ID assigned to this element by .NET My Services. Normally, .NET My Services will generate and assign this ID during an insertRequest operation, or possibly during a replaceRequest. Application software can override this ID generation by specifying the useClientIds attribute in the request message. Once an ID is assigned, the attribute is read-only and attempts to write it are silently ignored.

/myCalendar/event/reminder/@creator (string minOccurs=0 maxOccurs=1)
This attribute identifies the creator in terms of userId, appId, and platformId of the node.

/myCalendar/event/reminder/set (boolean minOccurs=1 maxOccurs=1)
Boolean flag that indicates whether the reminder is active for this event. In most cases, this will be true, but in the case of a recurring appointment, this flag may default to true with specific instances not to be reminded, or default to false with specific instances to be reminded.

/myCalendar/event/reminder/to (string minOccurs=1 maxOccurs=1)
/myCalendar/event/reminder/to/@xml:lang (minOccurs=1 maxOccurs=1)
This required attribute is used to specify an ISO 639 language code or an ISO 3166 country code as described in RFC 1766. The value of this attribute indicates the language type of the content within this element.

/myCalendar/event/reminder/offset (int minOccurs=1 maxOccurs=1)
Specifies, in minutes, the amount of time before the event the user should be reminded. Following are the recommended values:

Value	Description
5, 10, 20, 30, 45	5, 10, 20, 30, 45 minutes before the event
60, 120, 180,	1, 2, 3 hours before the event
startTime - startDay	The day of the event (reminder sent at 12:00am)
startTime - (startDay - (1440 * x))	x days before the event (reminder sent at 12:00am x days before)

/myCalendar/event/reminder/interruptability (int minOccurs=0 maxOccurs=1)
This optional element defines how interruptible this event is. This element is used by notification routing software to make decisions about the relay and deferral of notifications that might occur while this meeting is active. The value contained in this element is a numeric value between 1 and 10. Low values represent a high cost of disruption; high values represent a low cost of disruption.

/myCalendar/event/reminder/lastSentTime (dateTime minOccurs=1 maxOccurs=1)
Required by reminder engine.

/myCalendar/event/reminder/nextTriggerTime (dateTime minOccurs=1 maxOccurs=1)
Determines the next time to trigger reminder.

/myCalendar/event/attendee (minOccurs=0 maxOccurs=unbounded)
The attendeeType contains the full information about an attendee: the display, e-mail, PUID, and the attendee's response.

/myCalendar/event/attendee/@changeNumber (minOccurs=0 maxOccurs=1)
The changeNumber attribute is designed to facilitate caching of the element and its descendants. This attribute is assigned to this element by the .NET My Services system. The attribute is read-only to applications. Attempts to write this attribute are silently ignored.

/myCalendar/event/attendee/@id (minOccurs=0 maxOccurs=1)

This attribute is a globally unique ID assigned to this element by .NET My Services. Normally, .NET My Services will generate and assign this ID during an insertRequest operation, or possibly during a replaceRequest. Application software can override this ID generation by specifying the useClientIds attribute in the request message. Once an ID is assigned, the attribute is read-only and attempts to write it are silently ignored.

/myCalendar/event/attendee/@creator (string minOccurs=0 maxOccurs=1)

This attribute identifies the creator in terms of userId, appId, and platformId of the node.

/myCalendar/event/attendee/name (string minOccurs=0 maxOccurs=1)

This optional element specifies the name for the enclosing element.

/myCalendar/event/attendee/name/@xml:lang (minOccurs=1 maxOccurs=1)

This required attribute is used to specify an ISO 639 language code or an ISO 3166 country code as described in RFC 1766. The value of this attribute indicates the language type of the content within this element.

/myCalendar/event/attendee/puid (string minOccurs=0 maxOccurs=1)

This optional element specifies the name for the enclosing element.

/myCalendar/event/attendee/email (string minOccurs=0 maxOccurs=1)

This optional name specifies an e-mail address for the enclosing element.

/myCalendar/event/attendee/inviteType (string minOccurs=1 maxOccurs=1)

The meeting organizer uses this to define the kind of invitee {required, optional, resource}.

/myCalendar/event/attendee/invitationStatus (string minOccurs=1 maxOccurs=1)

Tracks the status of invitations {not-sent, sent, cancelled}.

/myCalendar/event/attendee/body (string minOccurs=0 maxOccurs=1)

Optional message from the invitees back to the meeting organizer.

/myCalendar/event/attendee/body/@xml:lang (minOccurs=1 maxOccurs=1)

This required attribute is used to specify an ISO 639 language code or an ISO 3166 country code as described in RFC 1766. The value of this attribute indicates the language type of the content within this element.

/myCalendar/event/attendee/responseTime (dateTime minOccurs=1 maxOccurs=1)

The reply time on each attendee is set to "Now" when the organizer creates and sends a meeting. When the attendees respond, they always update their replyTime. When the organizer receives responses, he or she honors only those that have a higher replyTime than what is maintained in his/her own copy of the event for each attendee. While processing the response, the organizer updates the replyTime. This guarantees that the organizer honors only the most recent response from the attendee. This is stored in UTC.

Outlook Equivalent: RECIPIENT_TRACKSTATUSTIME. **ICAL Equivalent**: reply time on message.

/myCalendar/event/attendee/responseType (string minOccurs=1 maxOccurs=1)
> The accept status indicates the valid types of responses that an attendee can reply with {accept, decline, tentative, counterpropose}.

/myCalendar/event/attendee/counterProposeStartTime (dateTime minOccurs=0 maxOccurs=1)
> If responseType=[counterPropose], the {startTime, endTime}, or location, or both can be present. This is the invitee's counterProposal for a new start time for the meeting. This is stored in UTC.

/myCalendar/event/attendee/counterProposeEndTime (dateTime minOccurs=0 maxOccurs=1)
> If responseType=[counterPropose], the {startTime, endTime}, or location, or both can be present. This is the invitee's counterProposal for a new end time for the meeting. This is stored in UTC.

/myCalendar/event/attendee/counterProposeLocation (string minOccurs=0 maxOccurs=1)
> If responseType=[counterPropose], the {startTime, endTime}, or location, or both can be present. This is the invitee's counterProposal for a location for the meeting.

/myCalendar/event/attendee/*{any}* (minOccurs=0 maxOccurs=unbounded)
/myCalendar/event/recurrence (minOccurs=0 maxOccurs=1)
/myCalendar/event/recurrence/@changeNumber (minOccurs=0 maxOccurs=1)
> The changeNumber attribute is designed to facilitate caching of the element and its descendants. This attribute is assigned to this element by the .NET My Services system. The attribute is read-only to applications. Attempts to write this attribute are silently ignored.

/myCalendar/event/recurrence/rule (minOccurs=1 maxOccurs=1)
/myCalendar/event/recurrence/rule/@changeNumber (minOccurs=0 maxOccurs=1)
> The changeNumber attribute is designed to facilitate caching of the element and its descendants. This attribute is assigned to this element by the .NET My Services system. The attribute is read-only to applications. Attempts to write this attribute are silently ignored.

/myCalendar/event/recurrence/rule/firstDayOfWeek (string minOccurs=1 maxOccurs=1)
> This stores what the first day of the week is for this user. Typical values are (su) Sunday or (mo) Monday.

> Recurrence rule's specified FirstDOW for calculating the recurrence expansion. Allows recurring meetings to be expanded in the organizer's FirstDOW instead of the invitee's FirstDOW.

> **Outlook and ICAL Equivalents**: FirstDOW

/myCalendar/event/recurrence/rule/tzid (int minOccurs=0 maxOccurs=1)

Identifies the time zone for this recurring event. **All dateTime information in this event is stored in UTC** (converted from the local time zone defined by the time zone sub-schema). If this field is absent, the recurring event is assumed to be recurring in UTC time. However, it is only a **floating recurring event** if the <floating> attribute is set. **@afterDay is used as a placeholder for version 1. @afterDay will not be used in .NET My Services version 1.**

```
<timeZone floating="..." id="...">1..1
    <standardBias>1..1
    </standardBias>
    <additionalDaylightBias>0..1
    </additionalDaylightBias>
    <standardDate>0..1
        <transitionRule weekOfMonth="..." day="..." dayOfMonth="..."
month="..." afterDay="...">1..1
        </transitionRule>
        <transitionTime>1..1
        </transitionTime>
    </standardDate>
    <daylightDate>0..1
        <transitionRule weekOfMonth="..." day="..." dayOfMonth="..."
month="..." afterDay="...">1..1
        </transitionRule>
        <transitionTime>1..1
        </transitionTime>
    </daylightDate>
</timeZone>
```

/myCalendar/event/recurrence/rule/repeat (minOccurs=1 maxOccurs=1)
/myCalendar/event/recurrence/rule/repeat/daily (minOccurs=0 maxOccurs=1)

Repeat every [...] days.

/myCalendar/event/recurrence/rule/repeat/daily/@dayFrequency (int minOccurs=0 maxOccurs=1)

The period of days over which repetition occurs; for example, repeat every 3 days.

/myCalendar/event/recurrence/rule/repeat/weekly (minOccurs=0 maxOccurs=1)

Repeat every [...] week(s) on {su,mo,tu,we,th,fr,sa}.

The presence of a weekday attribute means to repeat on this particular day. Any combination of the seven days is valid.

/myCalendar/event/recurrence/rule/repeat/weekly/@su (boolean minOccurs=0 maxOccurs=1)
/myCalendar/event/recurrence/rule/repeat/weekly/@mo (boolean minOccurs=0 maxOccurs=1)
/myCalendar/event/recurrence/rule/repeat/weekly/@tu (boolean minOccurs=0 maxOccurs=1)

/myCalendar/event/recurrence/rule/repeat/weekly/@we (boolean minOccurs=0 maxOccurs=1)

/myCalendar/event/recurrence/rule/repeat/weekly/@th (boolean minOccurs=0 maxOccurs=1)

/myCalendar/event/recurrence/rule/repeat/weekly/@fr (boolean minOccurs=0 maxOccurs=1)

/myCalendar/event/recurrence/rule/repeat/weekly/@sa (boolean minOccurs=0 maxOccurs=1)

/myCalendar/event/recurrence/rule/repeat/weekly/@weekFrequency (int minOccurs=0 maxOccurs=1)

The repeatWeekly recurrence occurs every period of weeks. If this attribute is not present, the default is 1 (every week).

/myCalendar/event/recurrence/rule/repeat/monthlyByDay (minOccurs=0 maxOccurs=1)

Repeat on the [First, Second, Third, Fourth, Last] {su, mo, tu, we, th, fr, sa} of every [...] month(s).

Any combination of the {weekday} attributes is valid, including user-defined combinations for weekdays and weekend days.

/myCalendar/event/recurrence/rule/repeat/monthlyByDay/@su (boolean minOccurs=0 maxOccurs=1)

/myCalendar/event/recurrence/rule/repeat/monthlyByDay/@mo (boolean minOccurs=0 maxOccurs=1)

/myCalendar/event/recurrence/rule/repeat/monthlyByDay/@tu (boolean minOccurs=0 maxOccurs=1)

/myCalendar/event/recurrence/rule/repeat/monthlyByDay/@we (boolean minOccurs=0 maxOccurs=1)

/myCalendar/event/recurrence/rule/repeat/monthlyByDay/@th (boolean minOccurs=0 maxOccurs=1)

/myCalendar/event/recurrence/rule/repeat/monthlyByDay/@fr (boolean minOccurs=0 maxOccurs=1)

/myCalendar/event/recurrence/rule/repeat/monthlyByDay/@sa (boolean minOccurs=0 maxOccurs=1)

/myCalendar/event/recurrence/rule/repeat/monthlyByDay/@monthFrequency (int minOccurs=0 maxOccurs=1)

Specifies the period of months to recur on. If this attribute is not present, the default is 1 (every month).

/myCalendar/event/recurrence/rule/repeat/monthlyByDay/@weekOfMonth (string minOccurs=0 maxOccurs=1)

Specifies which week in a month [first, second, third, fourth, last].

/myCalendar/event/recurrence/rule/repeat/monthly (minOccurs=0 maxOccurs=1)
Repeats the occurrence every month on a particular day. The first occurrence is created from the parent event's startTime and endTime, but the recurrence occurs as follows:

- Repeat every month on [day] of [month].
- Repeat every [monthFrequency] month(s) on [day] of [month]. Typically, the first occurrence is also an instance of the recurrence, but this need not be the case.

/myCalendar/event/recurrence/rule/repeat/monthly/@monthFrequency (int minOccurs=0 maxOccurs=1)
This optional attribute indicates the month periodicity. By default, it is 1 (periodic every month). The start of the periodicity is determined from windowStart.

/myCalendar/event/recurrence/rule/repeat/monthly/@day (int minOccurs=0 maxOccurs=1)
Specifies the day of the month to recur on. Value is between 1 and 31. An invalid starting [month ,day] combination (such as [6, 31]) is ignored and is not included as an instance of the recurrence. myCalendar follows ICAL behavior.

- day=31 will only pick up months that have 31 days.
- day=30 will pick up all months except February.
- day=29 will pick up all months except February, except on leap years. February 29 is included on leap years. The proper recurrence pattern for repeating on the last day of the month is to use repeatMonthlyByDay ("Repeat on the [last] [day, weekday, weekend day] of ...").

/myCalendar/event/recurrence/rule/repeat/yearlyByDay (minOccurs=0 maxOccurs=1)
Repeat on the [First, Second, Third, Fourth, Last] {su, mo, tu, we, th, fr, sa} of [Jan, Feb, Mar, Apr, May, Jun, Jul, Aug, Sep, Oct, Nov, Dec] every [yearFrequency] years.

Any combination of the {weekday} attributes is valid, including user-defined combinations denoting weekdays and weekend days. This element's attributes indicate whether a given day is or is not considered by the user as part of the work week. If this element has no attributes, it is assumed that the user has a Monday-to-Friday work week.

/myCalendar/event/recurrence/rule/repeat/yearlyByDay/@su (boolean minOccurs=0 maxOccurs=1)
/myCalendar/event/recurrence/rule/repeat/yearlyByDay/@mo (boolean minOccurs=0 maxOccurs=1)
/myCalendar/event/recurrence/rule/repeat/yearlyByDay/@tu (boolean minOccurs=0 maxOccurs=1)
/myCalendar/event/recurrence/rule/repeat/yearlyByDay/@we (boolean minOccurs=0 maxOccurs=1)
/myCalendar/event/recurrence/rule/repeat/yearlyByDay/@th (boolean minOccurs=0 maxOccurs=1)
/myCalendar/event/recurrence/rule/repeat/yearlyByDay/@fr (boolean minOccurs=0 maxOccurs=1)

/myCalendar/event/recurrence/rule/repeat/yearlyByDay/@sa (boolean minOccurs=0 maxOccurs=1)

/myCalendar/event/recurrence/rule/repeat/yearlyByDay/@yearFrequency (int minOccurs=0 maxOccurs=1)

> This optional attribute indicates the year periodicity. The default is 1 (repeat every year).

/myCalendar/event/recurrence/rule/repeat/yearlyByDay/@weekOfMonth (string minOccurs=0 maxOccurs=1)

> Specifies which week in a month [first, second, third, fourth, last].

/myCalendar/event/recurrence/rule/repeat/yearlyByDay/@month (int minOccurs=0 maxOccurs=1)

> Restrict to values between 1 and 13. (Some calendars have 13 months.)

/myCalendar/event/recurrence/rule/repeat/yearly (minOccurs=0 maxOccurs=1)

> Repeat every year on a particular date. The first occurrence is created from the parent event's startTime and endTime, but the recurrence occurs as follows:

> - Repeat yearly on [day] of [month].
> - Repeat every [yearFrequency] years on [day] of [month]. Typically, the first occurrence is also an instance of the recurrence, but this need not be the case.

/myCalendar/event/recurrence/rule/repeat/yearly/@yearFrequency (int minOccurs=0 maxOccurs=1)

> This optional attribute indicates the year periodicity. By default, it is 1 (repeat every year).

/myCalendar/event/recurrence/rule/repeat/yearly/@month (int minOccurs=0 maxOccurs=1)

> Specifies the month to recur on.

/myCalendar/event/recurrence/rule/repeat/yearly/@day (int minOccurs=0 maxOccurs=1)

> Specifies the day of the month to recur on. Value is between 1 and 31. An invalid starting [month, day] combination (such as [6, 31]) is ignored and is not included as an instance of the recurrence. The .NET calendar service follows ICAL behavior. Recurring on the 29th of every month will pick up [2,29] on leap years.

/myCalendar/event/recurrence/rule/windowStart (dateTime minOccurs=1 maxOccurs=1)

> The windowStart is the beginning of the timeSpan over which the recurrence occurs. This is typically set to equal the startTime of a recurring event upon its creation. However, there are no provisions that this must be the case. This is stored in UTC. Maximum range is January 1, 1753 to December 31, 9999 to an accuracy of 3.33 milliseconds.

/myCalendar/event/recurrence/rule/windowStart/@isLeapYear (boolean minOccurs=0 maxOccurs=1)

> International calendar support is used to save some information about the year in which the recurrence was created.

/myCalendar/event/recurrence/rule/windowStart/@leapMonthValue (int minOccurs=0 maxOccurs=1)

International calendar support is used to save some information about the year in which the recurrence was created.

/myCalendar/event/recurrence/rule/windowEnd (dateTime minOccurs=0 maxOccurs=1)

This dateTime indicates the end of the window over which the recurrence occurs. This is stored in UTC. Maximum range is January 1, 1753 to December 31, 9999 to an accuracy of 3.33 milliseconds.

/myCalendar/event/recurrence/rule/repeatForever (boolean minOccurs=0 maxOccurs=1)

Overrides the windowEnd date and specifies that this recurrence repeats forever. Client implementations cannot depend on date values repeating forever, as with 23:59:59pm Dec 31, 9999 or 23:59 Aug 31, 4500.

/myCalendar/event/recurrence/rule/repeatInstances (int minOccurs=0 maxOccurs=1)

Overrides the windowEnd date and specifies that this recurrence repeats for the specified number of instances. repeatInstances and repeatForever are mutually exclusive, but repeatInstances will override repeatForever for errant schemas.

/myCalendar/event/recurrence/rule/deletedExceptionDate (dateTime minOccurs=0 maxOccurs=unbounded)

Exceptions to a recurrence rule are added as an element list of dates. The service logic ignores the hh:mm:ss of the dateTime and merely blocks out the particular day. Any days can be added to an exception rule, including days where no occurrences of a recurrence rule would fall in the first place (ICAL EXDATE). This is stored in UTC.

/myCalendar/event/recurrence/rule/*{any}* (minOccurs=0 maxOccurs=unbounded)

Additional recurrence rule logic that cannot be expressed in the .NET calendar service logic.

/The .NET calendar service/event/recurrence/exception (minOccurs=0 maxOccurs=unbounded)

Contains a list of modified event properties for this particular orphan event. The properties that are not modified are inherited from the original event upon recurrence expansion (client-side). recurrenceId is always present. It is used to determine which instance of the original rule this modifiedException applies to.

/myCalendar/event/recurrence/exception/@changeNumber (minOccurs=0 maxOccurs=1)

The changeNumber attribute is designed to facilitate caching of the element and its descendants. This attribute is assigned to this element by the .NET My Services system. The attribute is read-only to applications. Attempts to write this attribute are silently ignored.

/myCalendar/event/recurrence/exception/@id (minOccurs=0 maxOccurs=1)

This attribute is a globally unique ID assigned to this element by .NET My Services. Normally, .NET My Services will generate and assign this ID during an insertRequest operation, or possibly during a replaceRequest. Application software can override this ID generation by specifying the useClientIds attribute in the request message. Once an ID is assigned, the attribute is read-only and attempts to write it are silently ignored.

/myCalendar/event/recurrence/exception/@creator (string minOccurs=0 maxOccurs=1)
This attribute identifies the creator in terms of userId, appId, and platformId of the node.

/myCalendar/event/recurrence/exception/recurrenceId (dateTime minOccurs=1 maxOccurs=1)
This is the original start time (recurrenceId) of the occurrence that is being modified by this exception. ModifiedExceptions with recurrenceIds that do not match the recurrenceId of any occurrence are ignored. This is stored in UTC. modifiedException does not expose the id attribute. recurrenceId should be used to predicate instead; it functions as the id of modifiedException.

/myCalendar/event/recurrence/exception/body (minOccurs=0 maxOccurs=1)
This contains only the modifiable properties of the eventBody.

/myCalendar/event/recurrence/exception/body/title (string minOccurs=0 maxOccurs=1)
Suppose the title changes.

/myCalendar/event/recurrence/exception/body/title/@xml:lang (minOccurs=1 maxOccurs=1)
This required attribute is used to specify an ISO 639 language code or an ISO 3166 country code as described in RFC 1766. The value of this attribute indicates the language type of the content within this element.

/myCalendar/event/recurrence/exception/body/fullDescription (string minOccurs=0 maxOccurs=1)
Suppose this particular instance has a revised description.

/myCalendar/event/recurrence/exception/body/fullDescription/@xml:lang (minOccurs=1 maxOccurs=1)
This required attribute is used to specify an ISO 639 language code or an ISO 3166 country code as described in RFC 1766. The value of this attribute indicates the language type of the content within this element.

/myCalendar/event/recurrence/exception/body/location (string minOccurs=0 maxOccurs=1)
Switch meeting location for this instance only.

/myCalendar/event/recurrence/exception/body/location/@xml:lang (minOccurs=1 maxOccurs=1)
This required attribute is used to specify an ISO 639 language code or an ISO 3166 country code as described in RFC 1766. The value of this attribute indicates the language type of the content within this element.

/myCalendar/event/recurrence/exception/body/startTime (dateTime minOccurs=0 maxOccurs=1)
Switch the start time for this instance only.

/myCalendar/event/recurrence/exception/body/endTime (dateTime minOccurs=0 maxOccurs=1)
Switch the end time for this instance only.

/myCalendar/event/recurrence/exception/body/allDay (boolean minOccurs=0 maxOccurs=1)

This particular instance is allDay.

/myCalendar/event/recurrence/exception/body/travelTimeTo (int minOccurs=0 maxOccurs=1)

Suppose traffic is really bad for this instance.

/myCalendar/event/recurrence/exception/body/travelTimeFrom (int minOccurs=0 maxOccurs=1)

Suppose traffic is really bad for this instance.

/myCalendar/event/recurrence/exception/body/freeBusyStatus (string minOccurs=0 maxOccurs=1)

Priority is changed for this meeting.

/myCalendar/event/recurrence/exception/body/organizer (minOccurs=0 maxOccurs=1)

Suppose the original organizer is replaced by another organizer.

/myCalendar/event/recurrence/exception/body/organizer/name (string minOccurs=0 maxOccurs=1)

This optional element specifies the name for the enclosing element.

/myCalendar/event/recurrence/exception/body/organizer/name/@xml:lang (minOccurs=1 maxOccurs=1)

This required attribute is used to specify an ISO 639 language code or an ISO 3166 country code as described in RFC 1766. The value of this attribute indicates the language type of the content within this element.

/myCalendar/event/recurrence/exception/body/organizer/puid (string minOccurs=0 maxOccurs=1)

This optional element specifies the name for the enclosing element.

/myCalendar/event/recurrence/exception/body/organizer/email (string minOccurs=0 maxOccurs=1)

This optional name specifies an e-mail address for the enclosing element.

/myCalendar/event/recurrence/exception/deletedAttendee (minOccurs=0 maxOccurs=unbounded)

The meeting organizer of a recurring meeting may wish to exclude a particular attendee for an instance of the meeting. This hs:idType (PUID) indicates which attendees (from the list of attendees at the event level) are not invited to this particular meeting instance.

/myCalendar/event/recurrence/exception/deletedAttachment (string minOccurs=0 maxOccurs=unbounded)

The meeting organizer of a recurring meeting may wish to exclude a particular attachment for an instance of the meeting.

/myCalendar/event/recurrence/exception/attachment (minOccurs=0 maxOccurs=unbounded)

The scheme in which the message contents were encoded. Examples of this are '7bit', '8bit' and 'base64'.

/myCalendar/event/recurrence/exception/attachment/name (string minOccurs=1 maxOccurs=1)

> This element contains information about an individual attachment in an e-mail message.

/myCalendar/event/recurrence/exception/attachment/name/@xml:lang (minOccurs=1 maxOccurs=1)

> This required attribute is used to specify an ISO 639 language code or an ISO 3166 country code as described in RFC 1766. The value of this attribute indicates the language type of the content within this element.

/myCalendar/event/recurrence/exception/attachment/contentType (string minOccurs=1 maxOccurs=1)

> This element contains the content type of the attachment.

/myCalendar/event/recurrence/exception/attachment/contentTransferEncoding (string minOccurs=1 maxOccurs=1)

> This element contains the encoding of the attachment. This information is necessary for decoding the attachment.

/myCalendar/event/recurrence/exception/attachment/size (unsignedLong minOccurs=1 maxOccurs=1)

> This element indicates the size, in bytes, of the attachment.

/myCalendar/event/recurrence/exception/attendee (minOccurs=0 maxOccurs=unbounded)

> The attendeeType contains the full information about an attendee: the display, e-mail, PUID, and the attendee's response.

/myCalendar/event/recurrence/exception/attendee/name (string minOccurs=0 maxOccurs=1)

> This optional element specifies the name for the enclosing element.

/myCalendar/event/recurrence/exception/attendee/name/@xml:lang (minOccurs=1 maxOccurs=1)

> This required attribute is used to specify an ISO 639 language code or an ISO 3166 country code as described in RFC 1766. The value of this attribute indicates the language type of the content within this element.

/myCalendar/event/recurrence/exception/attendee/puid (string minOccurs=0 maxOccurs=1)

> This optional element specifies the name for the enclosing element.

/myCalendar/event/recurrence/exception/attendee/email (string minOccurs=0 maxOccurs=1)

> This optional name specifies an e-mail address for the enclosing element.

/myCalendar/event/recurrence/exception/attendee/inviteType (string minOccurs=1 maxOccurs=1)

> The meeting organizer uses this to define the kind of invitee {required, optional, resource}.

/myCalendar/event/recurrence/exception/attendee/invitationStatus (string minOccurs=1 maxOccurs=1)

Tracks the status of invitations {not-sent, sent, cancelled}.

/myCalendar/event/recurrence/exception/attendee/body (string minOccurs=0 maxOccurs=1)

Optional message from the invitees back to the meeting organizer.

/myCalendar/event/recurrence/exception/attendee/body/@xml:lang (minOccurs=1 maxOccurs=1)

This required attribute is used to specify an ISO 639 language code or an ISO 3166 country code as described in RFC 1766. The value of this attribute indicates the language type of the content within this element.

/myCalendar/event/recurrence/exception/attendee/responseTime (dateTime minOccurs=1 maxOccurs=1)

The reply time on each attendee is set to "Now" when the organizer creates and sends a meeting. When the attendees respond, they always update their replyTime. When the organizer receives responses, he or she honors only those that have a higher replyTime than what is maintained in his/her own copy of the event for each attendee. While processing the response, the organizer will update their replyTime. This guarantees that the organizer honors only the most recent response from the attendee. This is stored in UTC.

Outlook Equivalent: RECIPIENT_TRACKSTATUSTIME. **ICAL Equivalent**: reply time on message.

/myCalendar/event/recurrence/exception/attendee/responseType (string minOccurs=1 maxOccurs=1)

The accept status indicates the valid types of responses that an attendee can reply with {accept, decline, tentative, counterpropose}.

/myCalendar/event/recurrence/exception/attendee/counterProposeStartTime (dateTime minOccurs=0 maxOccurs=1)

If responseType=[counterPropose], the {startTime, endTime}, or location, or both can be present. This is the invitee's counterProposal for a new start time for the meeting. This is stored in UTC.

/myCalendar/event/recurrence/exception/attendee/counterProposeEndTime (dateTime minOccurs=0 maxOccurs=1)

If responseType=[counterPropose], the {startTime, endTime}, or location, or both can be present. This is the invitee's counterProposal for a new end time for the meeting. This is stored in UTC.

/myCalendar/event/recurrence/exception/attendee/counterProposeLocation (string minOccurs=0 maxOccurs=1)

If responseType=[counterPropose], the {startTime, endTime}, or location, or both can be present. This is the invitee's counterProposal for a location for the meeting.

/myCalendar/event/recurrence/exception/attendee/*{any}* (minOccurs=0 maxOccurs=unbounded)

/myCalendar/event/recurrence/exception/reminder (minOccurs=0 maxOccurs=1)
>   These are the properties of the reminder that can be modified. If there is no reminder subschema in the event body, exception reminders are ignored.

/myCalendar/event/recurrence/exception/reminder/set (boolean minOccurs=0 maxOccurs=1)
/myCalendar/event/recurrence/exception/reminder/offset (int minOccurs=0 maxOccurs=1)
/myCalendar/event/recurrence/exception/reminder/interruptability (int minOccurs=0 maxOccurs=1)

/myCalendar/event/recurrence/exception/*{any}* (minOccurs=0 maxOccurs=unbounded)
>   Additional properties of the *myCalendar/BaseEventType* schema. Only certain event properties can exist here.

/myCalendar/event/recurrence/*{any}* (minOccurs=0 maxOccurs=unbounded)
>   Additional recurrence rule elements.

/myCalendar/subscription (minOccurs=0 maxOccurs=unbounded)
>   This element defines a subscription node that is designed to be an xdb:blue node that, when placed in a content document, causes a subscription to be registered. A subscription contains a trigger element that selects a scope of coverage. When items under this scope change, a subscriptionResponse message is generated and sent to the specified destination address.

/myCalendar/subscription/@changeNumber (minOccurs=0 maxOccurs=1)
>   The changeNumber attribute is designed to facilitate caching of the element and its descendants. This attribute is assigned to this element by the .NET My Services system. The attribute is read-only to applications. Attempts to write this attribute are silently ignored.

/myCalendar/subscription/@id (minOccurs=0 maxOccurs=1)
>   This attribute is a globally unique ID assigned to this element by .NET My Services. Normally, .NET My Services will generate and assign this ID during an insertRequest operation, or possibly during a replaceRequest. Application software can override this ID generation by specifying the useClientIds attribute in the request message. Once an ID is assigned, the attribute is read-only and attempts to write it are silently ignored.

/myCalendar/subscription/@creator (string minOccurs=0 maxOccurs=1)
>   This attribute identifies the creator in terms of userId, appId, and platformId of the node.

/myCalendar/subscription/trigger (minOccurs=1 maxOccurs=1)
/myCalendar/subscription/trigger/@select (string minOccurs=0 maxOccurs=1)
>   This item specifies an XPath expression that specifies the nodes that are to be selected and watched for changes. The selection can only select xdb:blue nodes. As changes in this node set occur, they trigger the generation of a subscription message. These messages are then sent to the SOAP receiver listed in the "to" element.

/myCalendar/subscription/trigger/@mode (string minOccurs=0 maxOccurs=1)
This attribute specifies whether or not the content of the changes that triggered the subscription are delivered in the subscription message, or if the message simply indicates that something changed under the trigger. The attribute can be:

includeData
The data that changed, causing the subscription to trigger, is included in the subscription message. Note that deleted nodes are specified by their ID, not by value.

excludeData
The data that changed, causing the subscription to trigger, is NOT included in the subscription message.

/myCalendar/subscription/trigger/@baseChangeNumber (minOccurs=0 maxOccurs=1)
This attribute specifies the changeNumber value to which the trigger relates. All changes between the specified change number and the current state of the document relative to the selection are transmitted as subscription messages. This allows a client application to establish a subscription relative to some baseline. As with changeQuery, if the baseChangeNumber is substantially out of date relative to the current state of the document, and the service cannot supply the changes in the subscription message, the subscription insert is rejected. A value of 0 means that the current values of the selected nodes are transmitted in the subscription message.

/myCalendar/subscription/expiresAt (dateTime minOccurs=0 maxOccurs=1)
This optional element specifies an absolute time after which the subscription is no longer active. The subscription node is automatically removed when the subscription expires. If this element is missing, the subscription does not expire.

/myCalendar/subscription/context (minOccurs=1 maxOccurs=1)
This element returns the context element from the original subscription. Applications should use this element and only this element to correlate the subscription response with one of their subscriptions.

/myCalendar/subscription/context/@uri (anyURI minOccurs=0 maxOccurs=1)
This attribute specifies the URI value chosen by the subscriber that is associated with this subscription.

/myCalendar/subscription/context/*{any}* (minOccurs=0 maxOccurs=unbounded)
/myCalendar/subscription/to (anyURI minOccurs=1 maxOccurs=1)
This attribute specifies the location that is to receive the subscription message. The value of this element can be one of the following forms:

- *hs:myNotifications*—This URI indicates that generated subscription messages are to be delivered inside the body of a notification and delivered to the default myNotifications service of the creator.

- *protocol://service*—This URI indicates that generated subscription messages are delivered to the specified service at the domain of the creator's platformId. For instance, a platformId indicating microsoft.com and a value in this element of "http://subscriptionResponse" would cause delivery of the subscription message to http://subscriptionResponse.microsoft.com.

If this value is not specified, the subscription message is delivered as a notification to the "creator's" .NET notifications service.

/myCalendar/{any} (minOccurs=0 maxOccurs=unbounded)

The .NET calendar service/system

The system document is a global document for the service. Its content and meaning are independent of the PUID used to address the service, and the document is read-only to all users. The system document contains a set of base items common to all .NET My Services services, and is optionally extended by each service to include service-specific global information.

This schema outline illustrates the layout and meaning of the information found in the system document for the .NET calendar service.

```
<sys:system changeNumber="..." instanceId="..."
    xmlns:hs="http://schemas.microsoft.com/hs/2001/10/core"
    xmlns:sys="http://schemas.microsoft.com/hs/2001/10/myCalendar/system">1..1
    <hs:roleMap changeNumber="..." id="..." creator="...">1..1
        <hs:scope id="...">0..unbounded
            <hs:shape base="...">1..1
                <hs:include select="...">1..unbounded</hs:include>
                <hs:exclude select="...">0..unbounded</hs:exclude>
            </hs:shape>
        </hs:scope>
        <hs:roleTemplate name="..." priority="...">0..unbounded
            <hs:fullDescription xml:lang="...">0..1</hs:fullDescription>
            <hs:method name="..." scopeRef="...">0..unbounded</hs:method>
        </hs:roleTemplate>
    </hs:roleMap>
    <hs:methodMap changeNumber="..." id="..." creator="...">1..1
        <hs:method name="...">0..unbounded {any}</hs:method>
    </hs:methodMap>
    <hs:schemaMap changeNumber="..." id="..." creator="...">1..1
        <hs:schema namespace="..." schemaLocation="..." alias="...">0..unbounded
{any}</hs:schema>
    </hs:schemaMap>
    <hs:wsdlMap changeNumber="..." id="..." creator="...">1..1
        <hs:wsdl wsdlLocation="...">0..unbounded {any}</hs:wsdl>
        <hs:disco discoLocation="...">0..unbounded {any}</hs:disco>
    </hs:wsdlMap>
    {any}
</sys:system>
```

The meaning of the attributes and elements shown in the preceding sample document fragment are listed in the following section.

/system (minOccurs=1 maxOccurs=1)

This element encapsulates the system document for the .NET calendar service.

/system/@changeNumber (minOccurs=0 maxOccurs=1)

The changeNumber attribute is designed to facilitate caching of the element and its descendants. This attribute is assigned to this element by the .NET My Services system. The attribute is read-only to applications. Attempts to write this attribute are silently ignored.

/system/@instanceId (string minOccurs=0 maxOccurs=1)

This attribute is a unique identifier typically assigned to the root element of a service. It is a read-only element and assigned by the .NET My Services system when a user is provisioned for a particular service.

/system/roleMap (minOccurs=1 maxOccurs=1)

This element encapsulates all the elements that make up a roleMap, which include document class relative roleTemplate, priority, name, method, and per-method scope. An individual roleTemplate defines the maximum scope of information, and the allowable methods used to access that information for each request mapped into the template.

/system/roleMap/@changeNumber (minOccurs=0 maxOccurs=1)

The changeNumber attribute is designed to facilitate caching of the element and its descendants. This attribute is assigned to this element by the .NET My Services system. The attribute is read-only to applications. Attempts to write this attribute are silently ignored.

/system/roleMap/@id (minOccurs=0 maxOccurs=1)

This attribute is a globally unique ID assigned to this element by .NET My Services. Normally, .NET My Services will generate and assign this ID during an insertRequest operation, or possibly during a replaceRequest. Application software can override this ID generation by specifying the useClientIds attribute in the request message. Once an ID is assigned, the attribute is read-only and attempts to write it are silently ignored.

/system/roleMap/@creator (string minOccurs=0 maxOccurs=1)

This attribute identifies the creator in terms of userId, appId, and platformId of the node.

/system/roleMap/scope (minOccurs=0 maxOccurs=unbounded)

This element defines a scope that may be referred to by roles within this roleMap to indicate what portions of the document are visible to this role for the specified method.

/system/roleMap/scope/@id (minOccurs=0 maxOccurs=1)

This attribute is a globally unique ID assigned to this element by .NET My Services. Normally, .NET My Services will generate and assign this ID during an insertRequest operation, or possibly during a replaceRequest. Application software can override this ID generation by specifying the useClientIds attribute in the request message. Once an ID is assigned, the attribute is read-only and attempts to write it are silently ignored.

/system/roleMap/scope/shape (minOccurs=1 maxOccurs=1)

A shape defines the node set visible through the document when operating through this shape element.

/system/roleMap/scope/shape/@base (string minOccurs=0 maxOccurs=1)

This attribute specifies the initial set of nodes visible through the shape.

A value of **t** indicates that the shape is initialized to include all possible nodes relative to the shape that is currently in effect. For instance, each role defines a scope containing a shape. When defining a shape for a role, the value **t** indicates all possible nodes available in the specified document for this role. When defining a shape in an ACL entry, a value of **t** means all of the nodes visible in the shape for the computed role. When using a shape in an HSDL operation, a value of **t** indicates all of the possible nodes selected by the HSDL operation (relative to the ACL shape, which itself is relative to the role's shape).

The value **nil** indicates the opposite of **t**, which is the empty node set. Nodes from this set may then be included into the shape.

/system/roleMap/scope/shape/include (minOccurs=1 maxOccurs=unbounded)

This element specifies the set of nodes that should be included into the shape relative to the possible set of nodes indicated by the base attribute.

/system/roleMap/scope/shape/include/@select (string minOccurs=0 maxOccurs=1)

This item specifies an XPath expression that selects a set of nodes relative to the externally established context. The expression can never travel outside the node-set established by this externally established current context. The expression may match zero or more nodes, and the operation manipulates all selected nodes. The minOccurs and maxOccurs attributes are optional and place restrictions and limitations on the number of nodes selected.

/system/roleMap/scope/shape/exclude (minOccurs=0 maxOccurs=unbounded)

This element specifies the set of nodes that should be excluded from the shape relative to the possible set of nodes indicated by the base attribute.

/system/roleMap/scope/shape/exclude/@select (string minOccurs=0 maxOccurs=1)

This item specifies an XPath expression that selects a set of nodes relative to the externally established context. The expression can never travel outside the node-set established by this externally established current context. The expression may match zero or more nodes, and the operation manipulates all selected nodes. The minOccurs and maxOccurs attributes are optional and place restrictions and limitations on the number of nodes selected.

/system/roleMap/roleTemplate (minOccurs=0 maxOccurs=unbounded)
This element encapsulates the definition of a role. The attribute set for this element includes the document class that this roleTemplate refers to, the name of the roleTemplate, and the priority of the roleTemplate.

/system/roleMap/roleTemplate/@name (string minOccurs=0 maxOccurs=1)
This element specifies the name of the role.

/system/roleMap/roleTemplate/@priority (int minOccurs=0 maxOccurs=1)
This element specifies the priority of the roleTemplate, which is used to select that actual roleTemplate when the role evaluation determines that the subject maps to multiple roleTemplates.

/system/roleMap/roleTemplate/fullDescription (string minOccurs=0 maxOccurs=1)
This element contains a description of this role template which specifies the capabilities a caller will have when accessing information through this role.

/system/roleMap/roleTemplate/fullDescription/@xml:lang (minOccurs=1 maxOccurs=1)
This required attribute is used to specify an ISO 639 language code or an ISO 3166 country code as described in RFC 1766. The value of this attribute indicates the language type of the content within this element.

/system/roleMap/roleTemplate/method (minOccurs=0 maxOccurs=unbounded)
This element specifies the methods available within this roleTemplate by name and by scope. When a subject maps to a roleTemplate, the method in the request must match one of these elements for the message to continue to flow. If the method exists, the data available to the method is a function of the scope referenced by this method combined with an optional scope referenced by the role defined in the roleList.

/system/roleMap/roleTemplate/method/@name (string minOccurs=0 maxOccurs=1)
This element specifies the name of the method.

/system/roleMap/roleTemplate/method/@scopeRef (string minOccurs=0 maxOccurs=1)
This attribute specifies the scope within this document that is in effect for this method.

/system/methodMap (minOccurs=1 maxOccurs=1)
This element defines the methodMap. While in most cases the roleMap section contains a definitive list of methods, these methods are likely to be scattered about the roleMap in various templates. This section contains the definitive list of methods available within the service.

/system/methodMap/@changeNumber (minOccurs=0 maxOccurs=1)
The changeNumber attribute is designed to facilitate caching of the element and its descendants. This attribute is assigned to this element by the .NET My Services system. The attribute is read-only to applications. Attempts to write this attribute are silently ignored.

/system/methodMap/@id (minOccurs=0 maxOccurs=1)
> This attribute is a globally unique ID assigned to this element by .NET My Services. Normally, .NET My Services will generate and assign this ID during an insertRequest operation, or possibly during a replaceRequest. Application software can override this ID generation by specifying the useClientIds attribute in the request message. Once an ID is assigned, the attribute is read-only and attempts to write it are silently ignored.

/system/methodMap/@creator (string minOccurs=0 maxOccurs=1)
> This attribute identifies the creator in terms of userId, appId, and platformId of the node.

/system/methodMap/method (minOccurs=0 maxOccurs=unbounded)
> This element defines a method that is available within this service.

/system/methodMap/method/@name (string minOccurs=0 maxOccurs=1)
> This attribute specifies the name of a method available within the service.

/system/methodMap/method/**{any}** (minOccurs=0 maxOccurs=unbounded)

/system/schemaMap (minOccurs=1 maxOccurs=1)
> This element defines the various schema's that define the data structures and shape of information managed by this service. Each schema is defined by its namespace URI, its location, and a preferred namespace alias.

/system/schemaMap/@changeNumber (minOccurs=0 maxOccurs=1)
> The changeNumber attribute is designed to facilitate caching of the element and its descendants. This attribute is assigned to this element by the .NET My Services system. The attribute is read-only to applications. Attempts to write this attribute are silently ignored.

/system/schemaMap/@id (minOccurs=0 maxOccurs=1)
> This attribute is a globally unique ID assigned to this element by .NET My Services. Normally, .NET My Services will generate and assign this ID during an insertRequest operation, or possibly during a replaceRequest. Application software can override this ID generation by specifying the useClientIds attribute in the request message. Once an ID is assigned, the attribute is read-only and attempts to write it are silently ignored.

/system/schemaMap/@creator (string minOccurs=0 maxOccurs=1)
> This attribute identifies the creator in terms of userId, appId, and platformId of the node.

/system/schemaMap/schema (minOccurs=0 maxOccurs=unbounded)
> This element defines a schema which defines data structures and the shape of information managed by this service. Multiple schema elements exist for each service, once for each logical grouping of information exposed by the service.

/system/schemaMap/schema/@namespace (anyURI minOccurs=0 maxOccurs=1)
> This attribute specifies the namespace URI of this schema.

/system/schemaMap/schema/@schemaLocation (anyURI minOccurs=0 maxOccurs=1)
This attribute specifies the location (in the form of a URI) of the resource containing schema. When a schema is reachable through a variety of URIs, one schema element will exist for each location.

/system/schemaMap/schema/@alias (string minOccurs=0 maxOccurs=1)
This attribute specifies the preferred alias that should be used if possible when manipulating information covered by this schema in the context of this service.

/system/schemaMap/schema/*{any}* (minOccurs=0 maxOccurs=unbounded)
/system/wsdlMap (minOccurs=1 maxOccurs=1)
This element defines the wsdlMap for this service. This map includes the location of WSDL documents, DISCO documents, and WISL documents for this Web service. These documents are used by applications to understand the format of messages that may be sent to the various services.

/system/wsdlMap/@changeNumber (minOccurs=0 maxOccurs=1)
The changeNumber attribute is designed to facilitate caching of the element and its descendants. This attribute is assigned to this element by the .NET My Services system. The attribute is read-only to applications. Attempts to write this attribute are silently ignored.

/system/wsdlMap/@id (minOccurs=0 maxOccurs=1)
This attribute is a globally unique ID assigned to this element by .NET My Services. Normally, .NET My Services will generate and assign this ID during an insertRequest operation, or possibly during a replaceRequest. Application software can override this ID generation by specifying the useClientIds attribute in the request message. Once an ID is assigned, the attribute is read-only and attempts to write it are silently ignored.

/system/wsdlMap/@creator (string minOccurs=0 maxOccurs=1)
This attribute identifies the creator in terms of userId, appId, and platformId of the node.

/system/wsdlMap/wsdl (minOccurs=0 maxOccurs=unbounded)
This element is used to specify the location of a WSDL file for this service. Multiple entries may exist pointing to the same file hosted in multiple locations, or to variations on the content within the WSDL files.

/system/wsdlMap/wsdl/@wsdlLocation (anyURI minOccurs=0 maxOccurs=1)
This attribute is a URI that specifies the location of the WSDL file.

/system/wsdlMap/wsdl/*{any}* (minOccurs=0 maxOccurs=unbounded)
/system/wsdlMap/disco (minOccurs=0 maxOccurs=unbounded)
This element is used to specify the location of a DISCO file for this service. Multiple entries may exist pointing to the same file hosted in multiple locations, or to variations on the content within the DISCO files.

/system/wsdlMap/disco/@discoLocation (anyURI minOccurs=0 maxOccurs=1)
This attribute is a URI that specifies the location of the DISCO file.

/system/wsdlMap/disco/*{any}* (minOccurs=0 maxOccurs=unbounded)
/system/*{any}* (minOccurs=0 maxOccurs=unbounded)

The .NET calendar service/Methods

The .NET calendar service supports the following standard and domain-specific methods:

- query
- insert
- replace
- delete
- update
- getCalendarDays
- getFreeBusyDays
- getQuickView
- setCalendarAttachment
- getCalendarAttachment
- meetingUpdate
- respond
- updateReminder

The standard methods operate on this service using the same message format and method-interchange techniques described in the HSDL section of this document. The only service-specific information to note is the schema that is in effect for each of the methods. These schemas, and how they relate to the standard methods and roles, are described in the roles section of this document.

The domain-specific methods operate as described in the .NET calendar service/Domain Specific Methods section of this document, and are governed by the various schemas outlined in the section The .NET calendar service/Roles for this service.

The .NET calendar service/Domain Specific Methods

The .NET calendar service has several domain-specific messages.

The .NET calendar service/getCalendarDays Method

Calendar date range event generator.

The .NET calendar service/getCalendarDaysRequest

This method is accessed using a request message, and in response may generate a response message or a SOAP Fault message. The following sample document fragments illustrate the structure and meaning of the elements and attributes in the request and response messages.

The following section describes the request message for this method.

This is the request message XML fragment for getCalendarDays. It takes a startDate and an endDate to define the duration over which calendar events are returned.

```
<m:getCalendarDaysRequest
    xmlns:m="http://schemas.microsoft.com/hs/2001/10/myCalendar"
    xmlns:hs="http://schemas.microsoft.com/hs/2001/10/core">1..1
    <m:calendarType>0..1</m:calendarType>
    <m:startTime>1..1</m:startTime>
    <m:endTime>1..1</m:endTime>
    <m:removeRecurrence>0..1</m:removeRecurrence>
</m:getCalendarDaysRequest>
```

The meaning of the attributes and elements shown in the preceding sample document fragment are listed in the following section.

/getCalendarDaysRequest (minOccurs=1 maxOccurs=1)
This function returns an XML stream of calendar appointments and/or events between two dates. Recurrence rules are expanded to create individual calendar items. Holidays are represented as all-day events, and these are returned as well. getCalendarDays is a query-retrieval of data, but the behavior expands recurrence rules into individual (aliased) events, adds in holidays, and adds regular events and sorts the entire list based on start time. No merging of event blocks occurs. Any object that overlaps the method parameters {startTime, endTime} will be returned. For example, if an event crosses midnight and the startTime is 12 a.m., that event will be returned. In cases where the startDate and endDate are one day, the events are sorted in the following order: holidays, all-day events, and regular events (based on startTime).

The {startTime, endTime] time window can define any interval: 24-hour period, week, month, or any other user-defined period.

getCalendarDays returns the calendaring info of any PUID that is specified for which the caller has sufficient privileges. The user's own PUID must be specified to retrieve their own information.

/getCalendarDaysRequest/calendarType (string minOccurs=0 maxOccurs=1)
Optional calendar type to return. Defaults to Gregorian.

/getCalendarDaysRequest/startTime (dateTime minOccurs=1 maxOccurs=1)
The starting time window of calendar objects to retrieve. This dateTime also contains the timeZone in which to retrieve the calendar information.

/getCalendarDaysRequest/endTime (dateTime minOccurs=1 maxOccurs=1)
> The ending time window to retrieve calendar objects. This dateTime also contains the timeZone in which to retrieve the calendar information. It must be the same timeZone as startTime.

/getCalendarDaysRequest/removeRecurrence (boolean minOccurs=0 maxOccurs=1)
> Normally, the recurrence sub-schema (minus modifiedException and minus deletedExceptionDate components) is returned with each instance of a recurring event, like "recurring-instance" and "recurring-exception". This allows clients to render the recurrence pattern properly without having to query the recurring-master explicitly. However, because it is heavy on bandwidth, the .NET calendar service includes the option to not return this data.

The .NET calendar service/getCalendarDaysResponse

Upon successful completion of this method, a response message is generated. The format of the response message is described below.

Calendar events are returned with their recurrence rules expanded into first-class events. These events have aliased PUIDs, logically as part of the same event. Recurrence information is stripped from the original event.

```
<m:getCalendarDaysResponse
    xmlns:m="http://schemas.microsoft.com/hs/2001/10/myCalendar"
    xmlns:hs="http://schemas.microsoft.com/hs/2001/10/core">1..1
    <m:event instanceType="..." calendarType="..." advanceHijriValue="..."
changeNumber="..." id="..." creator="...">0..unbounded
        <m:body changeNumber="...">1..1
            <m:cat ref="...">0..unbounded</m:cat>
            <m:title xml:lang="...">1..1</m:title>
            <m:fullDescription xml:lang="...">0..1</m:fullDescription>
            <m:location xml:lang="...">0..1</m:location>
            <m:recurrenceId>0..1</m:recurrenceId>
            <m:lastUpdateTime>0..1</m:lastUpdateTime>
            <m:startTime>1..1</m:startTime>
            <m:endTime>1..1</m:endTime>
            <m:allDay>0..1</m:allDay>
            <m:floating>0..1</m:floating>
            <m:travelTimeTo>0..1</m:travelTimeTo>
            <m:travelTimeFrom>0..1</m:travelTimeFrom>
            <m:freeBusyStatus>0..1</m:freeBusyStatus>
            <m:cuid>0..1</m:cuid>
            <m:organizer>0..1
                <hs:name xml:lang="...">0..1</hs:name>
                <hs:puid>0..1</hs:puid>
                <hs:email>0..1</hs:email>
```

```
          </m:organizer>
          {any}
      </m:body>
      <m:attachment>₀..unbounded → <m:attachment>$_{0..unbounded}$
          <m:name xml:lang="...">$_{1..1}$</m:name>
          <m:contentType>$_{1..1}$</m:contentType>
          <m:contentTransferEncoding>$_{1..1}$</m:contentTransferEncoding>
          <m:size>$_{1..1}$</m:size>
      </m:attachment>
      <m:reminder>$_{0..1}$
          <m:set>$_{1..1}$</m:set>
          <m:to xml:lang="...">$_{1..1}$</m:to>
          <m:offset>$_{1..1}$</m:offset>
          <m:interruptability>$_{0..1}$</m:interruptability>
          <m:lastSentTime>$_{1..1}$</m:lastSentTime>
          <m:nextTriggerTime>$_{1..1}$</m:nextTriggerTime>
      </m:reminder>
      <m:attendee>$_{0..unbounded}$
          <hs:name xml:lang="...">$_{0..1}$</hs:name>
          <hs:puid>$_{0..1}$</hs:puid>
          <hs:email>$_{0..1}$</hs:email>
          <m:inviteType>$_{1..1}$</m:inviteType>
          <m:invitationStatus>$_{1..1}$</m:invitationStatus>
          <m:body xml:lang="...">$_{0..1}$</m:body>
          <m:responseTime>$_{1..1}$</m:responseTime>
          <m:responseType>$_{1..1}$</m:responseType>
          <m:counterProposeStartTime>$_{0..1}$</m:counterProposeStartTime>
          <m:counterProposeEndTime>$_{0..1}$</m:counterProposeEndTime>
          <m:counterProposeLocation>$_{0..1}$</m:counterProposeLocation>
          {any}
      </m:attendee>
      <m:recurrence>$_{0..1}$
          <m:rule>$_{1..1}$
              <m:firstDayOfWeek>$_{1..1}$</m:firstDayOfWeek>
              <m:tzid>$_{0..1}$</m:tzid>
              <m:repeat>$_{1..1}$
                  <m:daily dayFrequency="...">$_{0..1}$</m:daily>
                  <m:weekly su="..." mo="..." tu="..." we="..." th="..."
fr="..." sa="..." weekFrequency="...">$_{0..1}$</m:weekly>
                  <m:monthlyByDay su="..." mo="..." tu="..." we="..." th="..."
fr="..." sa="..." monthFrequency="..." weekOfMonth="...">$_{0..1}$</m:monthlyByDay>
                  <m:monthly monthFrequency="..." day="...">$_{0..1}$</m:monthly>
                  <m:yearlyByDay su="..." mo="..." tu="..." we="..." th="..."
fr="..." sa="..." yearFrequency="..." weekOfMonth="..."
month="...">$_{0..1}$</m:yearlyByDay>
```

(continued)

(continued)

```
                    <m:yearly yearFrequency="..." month="..."
day="...">₀..₁</m:yearly>
                </m:repeat>
                <m:windowStart isLeapYear="..."
leapMonthValue="...">₁..₁</m:windowStart>
                <m:windowEnd>₀..₁</m:windowEnd>
                <m:repeatForever>₀..₁</m:repeatForever>
                <m:repeatInstances>₀..₁</m:repeatInstances>
            </m:rule>
        </m:recurrence>
    </m:event>
</m:getCalendarDaysResponse>
```

The meaning of the attributes and elements shown in the preceding sample document fragment are listed in the following section.

/getCalendarDaysResponse (minOccurs=1 maxOccurs=1)
> Response XML blob format; consists of the base event type minus recurrence.

/getCalendarDaysResponse/event (minOccurs=0 maxOccurs=unbounded)

/getCalendarDaysResponse/event/@instanceType (string minOccurs=0 maxOccurs=1)
> Distinguishes between a single instance of an event or an instance of a recurring event. The recurring instance is a modified exception if eventBody/recurrenceId is present: single, recurring-master, recurring-instance, recurring-exception.

/getCalendarDaysResponse/event/@calendarType (string minOccurs=0 maxOccurs=1)
> This field identifies an enumeration that determines the kind of calendar event this is. **.NET My Services version 1 will only support CAL_GREGORIAN_US.**
> http://msdn.microsoft.com/library/psdk/winbase/nls_9bg8.htm plus several others:

Value	Enumeration Constant	Description
−1	HSCAL_ALL_CALENDARS	Unknown Calendar; system default (HSCAL_GREGORIAN_US)
1	HSCAL_GREGORIAN	Gregorian (localized) calendar
2	HSCAL_GREGORIAN_US	Gregorian (U.S.) calendar
3	HSCAL_JAPAN	Japanese Emperor Era calendar
4	HSCAL_TAIWAN	Taiwan Era calendar
5	HSCAL_KOREA	Korean Tangun Era calendar
6	HSCAL_HIJRI	Hijri (Arabic Lunar) calendar
7	HSCAL_THAI	Thai calendar
8	HSCAL_HEBREW	Hebrew (Lunar) calendar
9	HSCAL_GREGORIAN_ME_FRENCH	Gregorian Middle East French calendar

Value	Enumeration Constant	Description
10	HSCAL_GREGORIAN_ ARABIC	Gregorian Arabic calendar
11	HSCAL_GREGORIAN_ XLIT_ENGLISH	Gregorian Transliterated English calendar
12	HSCAL_GREGORIAN_ XLIT_FRENCH	Gregorian Transliterated French calendar
13	HSCAL_KOREA_LUNAR	Default Korea Lunar calendar (implementation identical to 14)
14	HSCAL_JAPAN_LUNAR	Default Japanese Lunar calendar (implementation identical to 13)
15	HSCAL_CHINESE_LUNAR	Chinese Lunar calendar
16	HSCAL_SAKA	Indian Saka calendar
17	HSCAL_LUNAR_ETO_CHN	Chinese Zodiac calendar
18	HSCAL_LUNAR_ETO_KOR	Korean Zodiac calendar
19	HSCAL_LUNAR_ROKUYOU	Japanese Lucky days calendar

/getCalendarDaysResponse/event/@advanceHijriValue (int minOccurs=0 maxOccurs=1)
/getCalendarDaysResponse/event/@changeNumber (minOccurs=0 maxOccurs=1)
The changeNumber attribute is designed to facilitate caching of the element and its descendants. This attribute is assigned to this element by the .NET My Services system. The attribute is read-only to applications. Attempts to write this attribute are silently ignored.

/getCalendarDaysResponse/event/@id (minOccurs=0 maxOccurs=1)
This attribute is a globally unique ID assigned to this element by .NET My Services. Normally, .NET My Services will generate and assign this ID during an insertRequest operation, or possibly during a replaceRequest. Application software can override this ID generation by specifying the useClientIds attribute in the request message. Once an ID is assigned, the attribute is read-only and attempts to write it are silently ignored.

/getCalendarDaysResponse/event/@creator (string minOccurs=0 maxOccurs=1)
This attribute identifies the creator in terms of userId, appId, and platformId of the node.

/getCalendarDaysResponse/event/body (minOccurs=1 maxOccurs=1)
/getCalendarDaysResponse/event/body/@changeNumber (minOccurs=0 maxOccurs=1)
The changeNumber attribute is designed to facilitate caching of the element and its descendants. This attribute is assigned to this element by the .NET My Services system. The attribute is read-only to applications. Attempts to write this attribute are silently ignored.

/getCalendarDaysResponse/event/body/cat (minOccurs=0 maxOccurs=unbounded)
This element is used to categorize the element that contains it by referencing a global category definition in either the myCategories service system document or an external resource containing category definitions, or by referencing an identity-centric category definition in the content document of the myCategories service for a particular PUID.

/getCalendarDaysResponse/event/body/cat/@ref (anyURI minOccurs=0 maxOccurs=1)
This attribute references a category definition (<catDef/>) element using the rules outlined in the myCategories portion of the *XMI Manual*.

/getCalendarDaysResponse/event/body/title (string minOccurs=1 maxOccurs=1)
/getCalendarDaysResponse/event/body/title/@xml:lang (minOccurs=1 maxOccurs=1)
This required attribute is used to specify an ISO 639 language code or an ISO 3166 country code as described in RFC 1766. The value of this attribute indicates the language type of the content within this element.

/getCalendarDaysResponse/event/body/fullDescription (string minOccurs=0 maxOccurs=1)
This element contains an xhtml-compliant, free-form, full description of the event.

/getCalendarDaysResponse/event/body/fullDescription/@xml:lang (minOccurs=1 maxOccurs=1)
This required attribute is used to specify an ISO 639 language code or an ISO 3166 country code as described in RFC 1766. The value of this attribute indicates the language type of the content within this element.

/getCalendarDaysResponse/event/body/location (string minOccurs=0 maxOccurs=1)
This optional element contains the event's location.

/getCalendarDaysResponse/event/body/location/@xml:lang (minOccurs=1 maxOccurs=1)
This required attribute is used to specify an ISO 639 language code or an ISO 3166 country code as described in RFC 1766. The value of this attribute indicates the language type of the content within this element.

/getCalendarDaysResponse/event/body/recurrenceId (dateTime minOccurs=0 maxOccurs=1)
The recurrence id indicates the original start time of an occurrence of a recurring master appointment. It is required to identify what instance an orphan exception is modifying, because users are allowed to change the start time on the orphan. The recurrenceId method is stored in UTC. It does not appear in the master schema, except in the specific case that an attendee is invited to an instance of a recurring event. Otherwise, <recurrenceId> is usually only a part of getCalendarDays.

Outlook Equivalent: Part of GlobalObjectID. **ICAL Equivalent**: RECURRENCEID

/getCalendarDaysResponse/event/body/lastUpdateTime (dateTime minOccurs=0 maxOccurs=1)

This is updated by the organizer whenever he or she creates and sends a new meeting request. This helps the attendee to identify which meeting request is the most recent one. It is stored in UTC. This property is not modifiable by clients and is assigned by the server on modification and by the updateMeetingRequest.

Outlook Equivalent: OwnerCriticalChange. **ICAL Equivalent**: DTSTAMP.

/getCalendarDaysResponse/event/body/startTime (dateTime minOccurs=1 maxOccurs=1)

The startTime method defines the start time of the event. An all-day event, by convention, starts at 12:00:00 a.m. of the day of the event. This is stored in UTC. Maximum range is January 1, 1753 to December 31, 9999 to an accuracy of 3.33 milliseconds.

/getCalendarDaysResponse/event/body/endTime (dateTime minOccurs=1 maxOccurs=1)

The endTime method defines the end time of the event. An all-day event, by convention, ends at 11:59:59 p.m. of the ending day. Duration is inferred from the start and end times of the event. This is stored in UTC. Maximum range is January 1, 1753 to December 31, 9999 to an accuracy of 3.33 milliseconds.

/getCalendarDaysResponse/event/body/allDay (boolean minOccurs=0 maxOccurs=1)

If this element is false or absent, it indicates a regular event. Otherwise, this attribute indicates that the event is an all-day event. All-day events may span multiple days. By convention, all day events start at 12:00:00 a.m. of the day of startTime, regardless of what time it actually is, and end at 11:59:59 p.m. of the endTime date. In other words, if the allDay element is present and has value=true, myCalendar will ignore the actual times of the events and consider only the date part of the field.

The allDay tag is meant to operate as a hint to UI renders to display specialized icons indicating an all-day event. allDay events are distinguishable between 24-hour events starting at 12 a.m. In the case of a meeting request, an allDay event will not appear in the local user's time zone, but rather in the organizer's time zone.

/getCalendarDaysResponse/event/body/floating (boolean minOccurs=0 maxOccurs=1)

The floating attribute indicates that this event is to occur in the current local time zone no matter what time zone the system is currently in (that is, it floats). For example, holidays are floating events. Floating values are stored as-is: no time-zone translations are needed to convert them to UTC or any local time zone.

/getCalendarDaysResponse/event/body/travelTimeTo (int minOccurs=0 maxOccurs=1)

This is the amount of time (in minutes) that it takes to travel to the meeting location.

This optional element shows in free/busy calculations.

/getCalendarDaysResponse/event/body/travelTimeFrom (int minOccurs=0 maxOccurs=1)

This is the amount of time (in minutes) that it takes to return from the meeting location.

This optional element shows in free/busy calculations.

/getCalendarDaysResponse/event/body/freeBusyStatus (string minOccurs=0 maxOccurs=1)

This optional element annotates the freeBusy behavior of this event. All events by default appear as "busy". The user may explicitly define this event to be annotated by setting .NET calendar service values to free, tentative, busy, or away.

/getCalendarDaysResponse/event/body/cuid (string minOccurs=0 maxOccurs=1)

The cuid (CorrelationUID) links an organizer's event to an attendee's event. It identifies which response from an attendee is for which request from an organizer, and which meeting request update from the organizer is for which previously accepted meeting by the attendee. The "cuid" is the same on both the attendee's and the organizer's copy of the appointment. It is also identical on the orphan exception and the recurring master. This value is assigned by the .NET calendar service server and is non-modifiable.

Outlook Equivalent: Part of GlobalObjectId. **ICAL Equivalent**: UID.

/getCalendarDaysResponse/event/body/organizer (minOccurs=0 maxOccurs=1)

This is the e-mail address of the event organizer for non-.NET My Services organizers.

Outlook Equivalent: PR_SENT_REPRESENTING. **ICAL Equivalent**: ORGANIZER.

/getCalendarDaysResponse/event/body/organizer/name (string minOccurs=0 maxOccurs=1)

This optional element specifies the name for the enclosing element.

/getCalendarDaysResponse/event/body/organizer/name/@xml:lang (minOccurs=1 maxOccurs=1)

This required attribute is used to specify an ISO 639 language code or an ISO 3166 country code as described in RFC 1766. The value of this attribute indicates the language type of the content within this element.

/getCalendarDaysResponse/event/body/organizer/puid (string minOccurs=0 maxOccurs=1)

This optional element specifies the name for the enclosing element.

/getCalendarDaysResponse/event/body/organizer/email (string minOccurs=0 maxOccurs=1)

This optional name specifies an e-mail address for the enclosing element.

/getCalendarDaysResponse/event/body/*{any}* (minOccurs=0 maxOccurs=unbounded)

Additional body elements.

/getCalendarDaysResponse/event/attachment (minOccurs=0 maxOccurs=unbounded)

The scheme the message contents were encoded in. Examples of this are "7bit", "8bit", and "base64".

/getCalendarDaysResponse/event/attachment/name (string minOccurs=1 maxOccurs=1)

This element contains information about an individual attachment in an e-mail message.

/getCalendarDaysResponse/event/attachment/name/@xml:lang (minOccurs=1 maxOccurs=1)

This required attribute is used to specify an ISO 639 language code or an ISO 3166 country code as described in RFC 1766. The value of this attribute indicates the language type of the content within this element.

/getCalendarDaysResponse/event/attachment/contentType (string minOccurs=1 maxOccurs=1)

This element contains the content type of the attachment.

/getCalendarDaysResponse/event/attachment/contentTransferEncoding (string minOccurs=1 maxOccurs=1)

This element contains the encoding of the attachment. This information is necessary for decoding the attachment.

/getCalendarDaysResponse/event/attachment/size (unsignedLong minOccurs=1 maxOccurs=1)

This element specifies the size, in bytes, of the attachment.

/getCalendarDaysResponse/event/reminder (minOccurs=0 maxOccurs=1)
/getCalendarDaysResponse/event/reminder/set (boolean minOccurs=1 maxOccurs=1)

Boolean flag that indicates whether the reminder is active for this event. In most cases, this will be true. In the case of a recurring appointment, however, this flag may default to true with specific instances not to be reminded, or default to false with specific instances to be reminded.

/getCalendarDaysResponse/event/reminder/to (string minOccurs=1 maxOccurs=1)
/getCalendarDaysResponse/event/reminder/to/@xml:lang (minOccurs=1 maxOccurs=1)

This required attribute is used to specify an ISO 639 language code or an ISO 3166 country code as described in RFC 1766. The value of this attribute indicates the language type of the content within this element.

/getCalendarDaysResponse/event/reminder/offset (int minOccurs=1 maxOccurs=1)

Specifies how long, in minutes, before the event the user should be reminded. Recommended values are the following:

Value	Description
5, 10, 20, 30, 45	5, 10, 20, 30, 45 minutes before the event
60, 120, 180,	1, 2, 3 hours before the event
startTime - startDay	The day of the event (reminder sent at 12:00am)
startTime - (startDay - (1440 * x))	"x" days before the event (reminder sent at 12:00am "x" days before)

/getCalendarDaysResponse/event/reminder/interruptability (int minOccurs=0 maxOccurs=1)

This optional element defines how interruptible this event is and it is used by notification routing software to make decisions about the relay and deferral of notifications that might occur while this meeting is active. The value contained in this element is a numeric value between 1 and 10. Low values represent a high cost of disruption, high values represent a low cost of disruption.

/getCalendarDaysResponse/event/reminder/lastSentTime (dateTime minOccurs=1 maxOccurs=1)

Required by reminder engine.

/getCalendarDaysResponse/event/reminder/nextTriggerTime (dateTime minOccurs=1 maxOccurs=1)

Determines the next time to trigger reminder.

/getCalendarDaysResponse/event/attendee (minOccurs=0 maxOccurs=unbounded)

The attendeeType contains the full information about an attendee. The display, e-mail, PUID, and the attendee's response.

/getCalendarDaysResponse/event/attendee/name (string minOccurs=0 maxOccurs=1)

This optional element specifies the name for the enclosing element.

/getCalendarDaysResponse/event/attendee/name/@xml:lang (minOccurs=1 maxOccurs=1)

This required attribute is used to specify an ISO 639 language code or an ISO 3166 country code as described in RFC 1766. The value of this attribute indicates the language type of the content within this element.

/getCalendarDaysResponse/event/attendee/puid (string minOccurs=0 maxOccurs=1)

This optional element specifies the name for the enclosing element.

/getCalendarDaysResponse/event/attendee/email (string minOccurs=0 maxOccurs=1)

This optional name specifies an e-mail address for the enclosing element.

/getCalendarDaysResponse/event/attendee/inviteType (string minOccurs=1 maxOccurs=1)

The meeting organizer uses this to define the kind of invitee {required, optional, resource}.

/getCalendarDaysResponse/event/attendee/invitationStatus (string minOccurs=1 maxOccurs=1)

Tracks the status of invitations {not-sent, sent, cancelled}.

/getCalendarDaysResponse/event/attendee/body (string minOccurs=0 maxOccurs=1)

Optional message from the invitees back to the meeting organizer.

/getCalendarDaysResponse/event/attendee/body/@xml:lang (minOccurs=1 maxOccurs=1)

This required attribute is used to specify an ISO 639 language code or an ISO 3166 country code as described in RFC 1766. The value of this attribute indicates the language type of the content within this element.

/getCalendarDaysResponse/event/attendee/responseTime (dateTime minOccurs=1 maxOccurs=1)

The reply time on each attendee is set to "Now" when the organizer creates and sends a meeting. When the attendee responds, they always update their replyTime. When the organizer receives responses, they will honor only those that have a higher replyTime than what he or she maintains in his/her own copy of the event for each attendee. While processing the response, the organizer will update their replyTime. This guarantees that the organizer honors only the most recent response from the attendee. This is stored in UTC.

Outlook Equivalent: RECIPIENT_TRACKSTATUSTIME. **ICAL Equivalent**: reply time on message.

/getCalendarDaysResponse/event/attendee/responseType (string minOccurs=1 maxOccurs=1)

The accept status indicates the valid types of responses that an attendee can reply with {accept, decline, tentative, counterpropose}.

/getCalendarDaysResponse/event/attendee/counterProposeStartTime (dateTime minOccurs=0 maxOccurs=1)

If responseType=[counterPropose], the {startTime, endTime}, or location, or both can be present. This is the invitee's counterProposal for a new start time for the meeting. This is stored in UTC.

/getCalendarDaysResponse/event/attendee/counterProposeEndTime (dateTime minOccurs=0 maxOccurs=1)

If responseType=[counterPropose], the {startTime, endTime}, or location, or both can be present. This is the invitee's counterProposal for a new end time for the meeting. This is stored in UTC.

/getCalendarDaysResponse/event/attendee/counterProposeLocation (string minOccurs=0 maxOccurs=1)

If responseType=[counterPropose], the {startTime, endTime}, or location, or both can be present. This is the invitee's counterProposal for a location for the meeting.

/getCalendarDaysResponse/event/attendee/*{any}* (minOccurs=0 maxOccurs=unbounded)

/getCalendarDaysResponse/event/recurrence (minOccurs=0 maxOccurs=1)

Depending on if <removeRecurrence> parameter is passed into getCalendarDays

/getCalendarDaysResponse/event/recurrence/rule (minOccurs=1 maxOccurs=1)
/getCalendarDaysResponse/event/recurrence/rule/firstDayOfWeek (string minOccurs=1 maxOccurs=1)

This specifies the first day of the week for this user. Typical values are (su) Sunday or (mo) Monday.

Recurrence rules specified FirstDOW for calculating the recurrence expansion. Allows recurring meetings to be expanded in the organizer's FirstDOW instead of the invitee's FirstDOW.

Outlook and ICAL Equivalents: FirstDOW

/getCalendarDaysResponse/event/recurrence/rule/tzid (int minOccurs=0 maxOccurs=1)
Identifies the time zone for this recurring event. **All dateTime information in this event is stored in UTC** (converted from the local time zone defined by the time-zone subschema). If this field is absent, the recurring event is assumed to be recurring in UTC time. However, it is only a **floating recurring event** if the <floating> attribute is set. **@afterDay is used as a placeholder for version 1. @afterDay will not be used for .NET My Services version 1.**

```
        <timeZone floating="..."

id

="...">
1..1

            <standardBias>
1..1
</standardBias>
            <additionalDaylightBias>
0..1
</additionalDaylightBias>
            <standardDate>
0..1

                <transitionRule weekOfMonth="..." day="..." dayOfMonth="..."
month="..." afterDay="...">
1..1
</transitionRule>
                <transitionTime>
1..1
</transitionTime>
            </standardDate>
            <daylightDate>
0..1

                <transitionRule weekOfMonth="..." day="..." dayOfMonth="..."
month="..." afterDay="...">
1..1
</transitionRule>
                <transitionTime>
1..1
</transitionTime>
            </daylightDate>
        </timeZone>
```

/getCalendarDaysResponse/event/recurrence/rule/repeat (minOccurs=1 maxOccurs=1)

/getCalendarDaysResponse/event/recurrence/rule/repeat/daily (minOccurs=0 maxOccurs=1)

Repeat every [...] days.

/getCalendarDaysResponse/event/recurrence/rule/repeat/daily/@dayFrequency (int minOccurs=0 maxOccurs=1)

The periodicity of days over which repetition occurs; for example, repeat every 3 days.

/getCalendarDaysResponse/event/recurrence/rule/repeat/weekly (minOccurs=0 maxOccurs=1)

Repeat every [...] week(s) on {su,mo,tu,we,th,fr,sa}.

The presence of a weekday attribute means to repeat on this particular day. Any combination of the seven days is valid.

/getCalendarDaysResponse/event/recurrence/rule/repeat/weekly/@su (boolean minOccurs=0 maxOccurs=1)
/getCalendarDaysResponse/event/recurrence/rule/repeat/weekly/@mo (boolean minOccurs=0 maxOccurs=1)
/getCalendarDaysResponse/event/recurrence/rule/repeat/weekly/@tu (boolean minOccurs=0 maxOccurs=1)
/getCalendarDaysResponse/event/recurrence/rule/repeat/weekly/@we (boolean minOccurs=0 maxOccurs=1)
/getCalendarDaysResponse/event/recurrence/rule/repeat/weekly/@th (boolean minOccurs=0 maxOccurs=1)
/getCalendarDaysResponse/event/recurrence/rule/repeat/weekly/@fr (boolean minOccurs=0 maxOccurs=1)
/getCalendarDaysResponse/event/recurrence/rule/repeat/weekly/@sa (boolean minOccurs=0 maxOccurs=1)
/getCalendarDaysResponse/event/recurrence/rule/repeat/weekly/@weekFrequency (int minOccurs=0 maxOccurs=1)

The repeatWeekly recurrence occurs every period of weeks. If the attribute is not present, it defaults to 1 (every week).

/getCalendarDaysResponse/event/recurrence/rule/repeat/monthlyByDay (minOccurs=0 maxOccurs=1)

Repeat on the [First, Second, Third, Fourth, Last] {su, mo, tu, we, th, fr, sa} of every [...] month(s).

Any combination of the {weekday} attributes is valid, including user-defined combinations for weekdays and weekend days.

/getCalendarDaysResponse/event/recurrence/rule/repeat/monthlyByDay/@su (boolean minOccurs=0 maxOccurs=1)
/getCalendarDaysResponse/event/recurrence/rule/repeat/monthlyByDay/@mo (boolean minOccurs=0 maxOccurs=1)
/getCalendarDaysResponse/event/recurrence/rule/repeat/monthlyByDay/@tu (boolean minOccurs=0 maxOccurs=1)
/getCalendarDaysResponse/event/recurrence/rule/repeat/monthlyByDay/@we (boolean minOccurs=0 maxOccurs=1)

/getCalendarDaysResponse/event/recurrence/rule/repeat/monthlyByDay/@th (boolean minOccurs=0 maxOccurs=1)
/getCalendarDaysResponse/event/recurrence/rule/repeat/monthlyByDay/@fr (boolean minOccurs=0 maxOccurs=1)
/getCalendarDaysResponse/event/recurrence/rule/repeat/monthlyByDay/@sa (boolean minOccurs=0 maxOccurs=1)
/getCalendarDaysResponse/event/recurrence/rule/repeat/monthlyByDay/@monthFrequ ency (int minOccurs=0 maxOccurs=1)

> Specifies the month periodicity to recur on. If this attribute is not present, the default is 1 (every month).

/getCalendarDaysResponse/event/recurrence/rule/repeat/monthlyByDay/@weekOfMont h (string minOccurs=0 maxOccurs=1)

> Specifies which week in a month [first, second, third, fourth, last].

/getCalendarDaysResponse/event/recurrence/rule/repeat/monthly (minOccurs=0 maxOccurs=1)

> Repeats the occurrence every month on a particular day. The first occurrence is created from the parent event's startTime and endTime, but the recurrence occurs as follows:
>
> * Repeat every month on [day] of [month].
> * Repeat every [monthFrequency] month(s) on [day] of [month]. Typically, the first occurrence is also an instance of the recurrence, but this need not be the case.

/getCalendarDaysResponse/event/recurrence/rule/repeat/monthly/@monthFrequency (int minOccurs=0 maxOccurs=1)

> This optional attribute indicates the month periodicity. The default is 1, periodic every month. The start of the periodicity is determined from windowStart.

/getCalendarDaysResponse/event/recurrence/rule/repeat/monthly/@day (int minOccurs=0 maxOccurs=1)

> Specifies the day of the month to recur on. Value is between 1 and 31. An invalid starting [month ,day] combination (such as [6, 31]) is ignored and is not included as an instance of the recurrence. The .NET calendar service follows ICAL behavior.
>
> * day=31 will only pick up months that have 31 days.
> * day=30 will pick up all months except February.
> * day=29 will pick up all months except February, except on leap years. February 29 is included on leap years. The proper recurrence pattern for repeating on the last day of the month is to use repeatMonthlyByDay. "Repeat on the [last] [day, weekday, weekend day] of ..."

/getCalendarDaysResponse/event/recurrence/rule/repeat/yearlyByDay (minOccurs=0 maxOccurs=1)

> Repeat on the [First, Second, Third, Fourth, Last] {su, mo, tu, we, th, fr, sa} of [Jan, Feb, Mar, Apr, May, Jun, Jul, Aug, Sep, Oct, Nov, Dec] every [yearFrequency] years.
>
> Any combination of the {weekday} attributes is valid, including user-defined combinations denoting weekdays and weekend days. This element's attributes contain whether a given day is or is not considered by the user as part of the work week. If this element has no attributes, it is assumed that the user has a Monday-to-Friday work week.

/getCalendarDaysResponse/event/recurrence/rule/repeat/yearlyByDay/@su (boolean minOccurs=0 maxOccurs=1)

/getCalendarDaysResponse/event/recurrence/rule/repeat/yearlyByDay/@mo (boolean minOccurs=0 maxOccurs=1)

/getCalendarDaysResponse/event/recurrence/rule/repeat/yearlyByDay/@tu (boolean minOccurs=0 maxOccurs=1)

/getCalendarDaysResponse/event/recurrence/rule/repeat/yearlyByDay/@we (boolean minOccurs=0 maxOccurs=1)

/getCalendarDaysResponse/event/recurrence/rule/repeat/yearlyByDay/@th (boolean minOccurs=0 maxOccurs=1)

/getCalendarDaysResponse/event/recurrence/rule/repeat/yearlyByDay/@fr (boolean minOccurs=0 maxOccurs=1)

/getCalendarDaysResponse/event/recurrence/rule/repeat/yearlyByDay/@sa (boolean minOccurs=0 maxOccurs=1)

/getCalendarDaysResponse/event/recurrence/rule/repeat/yearlyByDay/@yearFrequency (int minOccurs=0 maxOccurs=1)

> This optional attribute indicates the year periodicity. The default is 1 (repeat every year).

/getCalendarDaysResponse/event/recurrence/rule/repeat/yearlyByDay/@weekOfMonth (string minOccurs=0 maxOccurs=1)

> Specifies which week in a month [first, second, third, fourth, last].

/getCalendarDaysResponse/event/recurrence/rule/repeat/yearlyByDay/@month (int minOccurs=0 maxOccurs=1)

> Restrict to 1 through 13. Some calendars have 13 months.

/getCalendarDaysResponse/event/recurrence/rule/repeat/yearly (minOccurs=0 maxOccurs=1)

> Repeat every year on a particular date. The very first occurrence is created from the parent event's startTime and endTime, but the recurrence occurs as follows:
>
> • Repeat yearly on [day] of [month].
>
> • Repeat every [yearFrequency] years on [day] of [month]. Typically, the first occurrence is also an instance of the recurrence, but this need not be the case.

/getCalendarDaysResponse/event/recurrence/rule/repeat/yearly/@yearFrequency (int minOccurs=0 maxOccurs=1)

> This optional attribute indicates the year periodicity. By default, it is 1 (repeat every year).

/getCalendarDaysResponse/event/recurrence/rule/repeat/yearly/@month (int minOccurs=0 maxOccurs=1)

Specifies the month to recur on.

/getCalendarDaysResponse/event/recurrence/rule/repeat/yearly/@day (int minOccurs=0 maxOccurs=1)

Specifies the day of the month to recur on. Value is between 1 and 31. An invalid starting [month, day] combination (such as [6, 31]) is ignored and is not included as an instance of the recurrence. The .NET calendar service follows ICAL behavior. Recurring on the 29th of every month will pick up [2,29] on leap years.

/getCalendarDaysResponse/event/recurrence/rule/windowStart (dateTime minOccurs=1 maxOccurs=1)

The windowStart is the beginning of the timeSpan over which the recurrence occurs. This is typically set to equal the startTime of a recurring event upon its creation. However, there are no provisions that this must be the case. This is stored in UTC. Maximum range is January 1, 1753 to December 31, 9999 to an accuracy of 3.33 milliseconds.

/getCalendarDaysResponse/event/recurrence/rule/windowStart/@isLeapYear (boolean minOccurs=0 maxOccurs=1)

International calendar support is used to save some information about the year in which the recurrence was created.

/getCalendarDaysResponse/event/recurrence/rule/windowStart/@leapMonthValue (int minOccurs=0 maxOccurs=1)

International calendar support is used to save some information about the year in which the recurrence was created.

/getCalendarDaysResponse/event/recurrence/rule/windowEnd (dateTime minOccurs=0 maxOccurs=1)

This dateTime indicates the end of the window over which the recurrence occurs. This is stored in UTC. Maximum range is January 1, 1753 to December 31, 9999 to an accuracy of 3.33 milliseconds.

/getCalendarDaysResponse/event/recurrence/rule/repeatForever (boolean minOccurs=0 maxOccurs=1)

Overrides the windowEnd date and specifies that this recurrence repeats forever. Client implementations cannot depend on date values repeating forever, as with 23:59:59pm Dec 31, 9999 or 23:59 Aug 31, 4500.

/getCalendarDaysResponse/event/recurrence/rule/repeatInstances (int minOccurs=0 maxOccurs=1)

Overrides the windowEnd date and specifies that this recurrence repeats for the specified number of instances. repeatInstances and repeatForever are mutually exclusive, but repeatInstances will override repeatForever for errant schemas.

The .NET calendar service/Error Cases

If the method causes a failure response to be generated, the failure is noted by generating a SOAP Fault message. Failures can include a failure to understand a header marked as "s:mustUnderstand", a .NET My Services standard error, security violation, load-balance redirect, or any service-specific, severe error condition.

The .NET calendar service/getFreeBusyDays Method

FreeBusy service function.

The .NET calendar service/getFreeBusyDaysRequest

This method is accessed using a request message, and in response may generate a response message or a SOAP Fault message. The following sample document fragments illustrate the structure and meaning of the elements and attributes in the request and response messages.

The following section describes the request message for this method.

This is the request message XML fragment for getFreeBusyDays.

```
<m:getFreeBusyDaysRequest
    xmlns:m="http://schemas.microsoft.com/hs/2001/10/myCalendar"
    xmlns:hs="http://schemas.microsoft.com/hs/2001/10/core">_{1..1}
    <m:calendarType>_{0..1}</m:calendarType>
    <m:startTime>_{1..1}</m:startTime>
    <m:endTime>_{1..1}</m:endTime>
    <m:getFreeBlocks>_{0..1}</m:getFreeBlocks>
    <m:returnIndividualBlocks>_{0..1}</m:returnIndividualBlocks>
</m:getFreeBusyDaysRequest>
```

The meaning of the attributes and elements shown in the preceding sample document fragment are listed in the following section.

/getFreeBusyDaysRequest (minOccurs=1 maxOccurs=1)

This function returns a stream of XML fragments defining the user's freeBusy information between two dates. Single events and recurring events within the time window are translated into blocks of free/busy time.

getFreeBusyDays returns only the blocks and their associated type. There is no explicit method to return unmerged freeBusy info; that kind of behavior is fully contained within getCalendarDays.

This method follows the precedence order:

- Away(OOF), Busy, Tentative, Free
- Overlapping blocks of the same freeOrBusyStatus kind are coalesced to form larger blocks.
- Overlapping blocks of different freeOrBusyStatus are overlaid. The events with higher precedence overlay on top (**not** by starting time).

For example:

- Busy from 8 to 9
- Tentative from 8:30 to 10
- OOF from 9:30 to 11
- Free from 10:30 to 12
  Merged as:
- Busy from 8 to 9
- Tentative from 9 to 9:30
- OOF from 9:30 to 11
- Free from 11 to 12

  Multiple users' freeBusy information is retrieved by specifying a PUID for each user in question. The caller of this function must also specify their own PUID; no implicit assumptions are made.

  The calling method takes a startDate and an endDate to define the duration over which freebusy information is returned. A third parameter determines if free blocks are explicitly returned. Free blocks are intervals where no calendar object exists.

/getFreeBusyDaysRequest/calendarType (string minOccurs=0 maxOccurs=1)
Optional calendar type to return. Defaults to Gregorian.

/getFreeBusyDaysRequest/startTime (dateTime minOccurs=1 maxOccurs=1)
The starting time window of calendar objects to retrieve. This dateTime also contains the timeZone to retrieve the calendar information in.

/getFreeBusyDaysRequest/endTime (dateTime minOccurs=1 maxOccurs=1)
The ending time window to retrieve calendar objects. This dateTime also contains the timeZone to retrieve the calendar information in. It must be the same timeZone as startTime.

/getFreeBusyDaysRequest/getFreeBlocks (boolean minOccurs=0 maxOccurs=1)
This Boolean causes the .NET calendar service to explicitly return free time as freeBusy blocks. By default, free blocks are not returned.

/getFreeBusyDaysRequest/returnIndividualBlocks (boolean minOccurs=0 maxOccurs=1)
This Boolean causes the .NET calendar service not to coalesce/merge freeBusy information. By default, freeBusy information is merged.

The .NET calendar service/getFreeBusyDaysResponse

Upon successful completion of this method, a response message is generated. The format of the response message is described below.

FreeBusy information is returned as XML fragments.

```
<m:getFreeBusyDaysResponse
    xmlns:m="http://schemas.microsoft.com/hs/2001/10/myCalendar"
    xmlns:hs="http://schemas.microsoft.com/hs/2001/10/core">1..1
    <m:freeOrBusyEvent>0..unbounded
        <m:startTime>1..1</m:startTime>
        <m:endTime>1..1</m:endTime>
        <m:type>1..1</m:type>
    </m:freeOrBusyEvent>
</m:getFreeBusyDaysResponse>
```

The meaning of the attributes and elements shown in the preceding sample document fragment are listed in the following section.

/getFreeBusyDaysResponse (minOccurs=1 maxOccurs=1)
    Response XML blob format, consists of freebusy XML fragments.

/getFreeBusyDaysResponse/freeOrBusyEvent (minOccurs=0 maxOccurs=unbounded)
/getFreeBusyDaysResponse/freeOrBusyEvent/startTime (dateTime minOccurs=1 maxOccurs=1)
/getFreeBusyDaysResponse/freeOrBusyEvent/endTime (dateTime minOccurs=1 maxOccurs=1)
/getFreeBusyDaysResponse/freeOrBusyEvent/type (string minOccurs=1 maxOccurs=1)
    The type belongs to the following enumeration {free, tentative, busy, away}.

The .NET calendar service/Error Cases

If the method causes a failure response to be generated, the failure is noted by generating a SOAP Fault message. Failures can include a failure to understand a header marked as "s:mustUnderstand", a .NET My Services standard error, security violation, load balance redirect, or any service-specific severe error condition.

The .NET calendar service/getQuickView Method

QuickView/DatePicker service function.

The .NET calendar service/getQuickViewRequest

This method is accessed using a request message, and in response may generate a response message or a SOAP Fault message. The following sample document fragments illustrate the structure and meaning of the elements and attributes in the request and response messages.

The following section describes the request message for this method.

This is the request message XML fragment for getQuickView.

```
<m:getQuickViewRequest
    xmlns:m="http://schemas.microsoft.com/hs/2001/10/myCalendar"
    xmlns:hs="http://schemas.microsoft.com/hs/2001/10/core">1..1
    <m:startDay>1..1</m:startDay>
    <m:endDay>1..1</m:endDay>
    <m:getFreeBlocks>1..1</m:getFreeBlocks>
    <m:calendarType>0..1</m:calendarType>
</m:getQuickViewRequest>
```

The meaning of the attributes and elements shown in the preceding sample document fragment are listed in the following section.

/getQuickViewRequest (minOccurs=1 maxOccurs=1)
> This function provides an efficient, lightweight means to query a date range to indicate days that have 1 or more appointments (1) and days without appointments (0). Outlook and OWA use this for their datepicker functionality.

> The date range takes timeZone-specific start and end times, using just the year, month, and day. The time zone can be a simple bias, since this is merely a request for data. startTime and endTime are required to have the same time-zone bias. In effect, the method "overlays" the incoming time zone onto the user's calendar to define the dayblocks for which the QuickView returns data.

/getQuickViewRequest/startDay (dateTime minOccurs=1 maxOccurs=1)
> The starting day for the quickView. hour, minute, and seconds are ignored.

/getQuickViewRequest/endDay (dateTime minOccurs=1 maxOccurs=1)
> The ending day for the quickView. hour, minute, and seconds are ignored.

/getQuickViewRequest/getFreeBlocks (boolean minOccurs=1 maxOccurs=1)
> This Boolean causes the .NET calendar service to consider events explicitly tagged as free to appear in the quickView request. If this is false, a day which has an event marked as 'free' will not appear.

/getQuickViewRequest/calendarType (string minOccurs=0 maxOccurs=1)
> Optional calendar type to return. Defaults to Gregorian.

The .NET calendar service/getQuickViewResponse

Upon successful completion of this method, a response message is generated. The format of the response message is described below.

QuickView information is returned as XML fragments.

```
<m:getQuickViewResponse
    xmlns:m="http://schemas.microsoft.com/hs/2001/10/The .NET calendar service"
    xmlns:hs="http://schemas.microsoft.com/hs/2001/10/core">_{1..1}
    <m:month m="..." year="...">_{1..unbounded}
        <m:day d="...">_{1..31}</m:day>
    </m:month>
</m:getQuickViewResponse>
```

The meaning of the attributes and elements shown in the preceding sample document fragment are listed in the following section.

/getQuickViewResponse (minOccurs=1 maxOccurs=1)
   The return value of getQuickView is a list of calendar days grouped into months.

/getQuickViewResponse/month (minOccurs=1 maxOccurs=unbounded)
   Specifies the month block for the grouping of calendar days.

/getQuickViewResponse/month/@m (int minOccurs=0 maxOccurs=1)
   Restrict to 1–13. Some calendars have 13 months.

/getQuickViewResponse/month/@year (int minOccurs=0 maxOccurs=1)
/getQuickViewResponse/month/day (boolean minOccurs=1 maxOccurs=31)
   Specifies whether this day is free (0) or has at least one event on it or overlapping (1).

/getQuickViewResponse/month/day/@d (int minOccurs=0 maxOccurs=1)
   Specifies day in this month.

The .NET calendar service/Error Cases

If the method causes a failure response to be generated, the failure is noted by generating a SOAP Fault message. Failures can include a failure to understand a header marked as "s:mustUnderstand", a .NET My Services standard error, security violation, load balance redirect or any service-specific severe error condition.

The .NET calendar service/setCalendarAttachment Method

Attaches a calendar MIME attachment to the .NET calendar service.

The .NET calendar service/setCalendarAttachmentRequest

This method is accessed using a request message, and in response may generate a response message or a SOAP Fault message. The following sample document fragments illustrate the structure and meaning of the elements and attributes in the request and response messages.

The following section describes the request message for this method.

This is the request message XML fragment for setCalendarAttachment.

```
<m:setCalendarAttachmentRequest
    xmlns:m="http://schemas.microsoft.com/hs/2001/10/myCalendar"
    xmlns:hs="http://schemas.microsoft.com/hs/2001/10/core">1..1
    <m:calendarAttachment>0..unbounded
        <m:name xml:lang="...">1..1</m:name>
        <m:contentType>1..1</m:contentType>
        <m:contentTransferEncoding>1..1</m:contentTransferEncoding>
        <m:size>1..1</m:size>
        <m:attachmentBody>1..1</m:attachmentBody>
    </m:calendarAttachment>
</m:setCalendarAttachmentRequest>
```

The meaning of the attributes and elements shown in the preceding sample document fragment are listed in the following section.

/setCalendarAttachmentRequest (minOccurs=1 maxOccurs=1)

The purpose of this method is to store a calendar attachment to the .NET calendar service. This method takes a location element that contains an XPATH expression indicating which event to set the attachment for. It also takes one or more calendarAttachment fragments that contain the attachment to set.

AttachmentId's are issued by the server. If @attachmentId is specified, the .NET calendar service will attempt to replace an existing attachment with the new attachment information. If @attachmentId is not specified, The .NET calendar service will add the attachment to the event.

/setCalendarAttachmentRequest/calendarAttachment (minOccurs=0 maxOccurs=unbounded)

This XML fragment contains the complete MIME body of the attachment.

/setCalendarAttachmentRequest/calendarAttachment/name (string minOccurs=1 maxOccurs=1)

This element contains information about an individual attachment in an e-mail message.

/setCalendarAttachmentRequest/calendarAttachment/name/@xml:lang (minOccurs=1 maxOccurs=1)

> This required attribute is used to specify an ISO 639 language code or an ISO 3166 country code as described in RFC 1766. The value of this attribute indicates the language type of the content within this element.

/setCalendarAttachmentRequest/calendarAttachment/contentType (string minOccurs=1 maxOccurs=1)

> This element contains the content type of the attachment.

/setCalendarAttachmentRequest/calendarAttachment/contentTransferEncoding (string minOccurs=1 maxOccurs=1)

> This element contains the encoding of the attachment. This information is necessary for decoding the attachment.

/setCalendarAttachmentRequest/calendarAttachment/size (unsignedLong minOccurs=1 maxOccurs=1)

> This element contains the size of the attachment in bytes.

/setCalendarAttachmentRequest/calendarAttachment/attachmentBody (string minOccurs=1 maxOccurs=1)

> Contains the attachment body.

The .NET calendar service/setCalendarAttachmentResponse

Upon successful completion of this method, a response message is generated. The format of the response message is described below.

Returns the attachmentId that was assigned, plus the metadata information or "echoback".

```
<m:setCalendarAttachmentResponse
    xmlns:m="http://schemas.microsoft.com/hs/2001/10/myCalendar"
    xmlns:hs="http://schemas.microsoft.com/hs/2001/10/core">₁..₁
    <m:calendarAttachment>₀..unbounded
        <m:name xml:lang="...">₁..₁</m:name>
        <m:contentType>₁..₁</m:contentType>
        <m:contentTransferEncoding>₁..₁</m:contentTransferEncoding>
        <m:size>₁..₁</m:size>
        <m:error>₁..₁</m:error>
    </m:calendarAttachment>
</m:setCalendarAttachmentResponse>
```

The meaning of the attributes and elements shown in the preceding sample document fragment are listed in the following section.

/setCalendarAttachmentResponse (minOccurs=1 maxOccurs=1)

> Echoback message.

/setCalendarAttachmentResponse/calendarAttachment (minOccurs=0 maxOccurs=unbounded)

   This XML fragment contains the echoback metadata.

/setCalendarAttachmentResponse/calendarAttachment/name (string minOccurs=1 maxOccurs=1)

   This element contains information about an individual attachment in an e-mail message.

/setCalendarAttachmentResponse/calendarAttachment/name/@xml:lang (minOccurs=1 maxOccurs=1)

   This required attribute is used to specify an ISO 639 language code or an ISO 3166 country code as described in RFC 1766. The value of this attribute indicates the language type of the content within this element.

/setCalendarAttachmentResponse/calendarAttachment/contentType (string minOccurs=1 maxOccurs=1)

   This element contains the content type of the attachment.

/setCalendarAttachmentResponse/calendarAttachment/contentTransferEncoding (string minOccurs=1 maxOccurs=1)

   This element contains the encoding of the attachment. This information is necessary for decoding the attachment.

/setCalendarAttachmentResponse/calendarAttachment/size (unsignedLong minOccurs=1 maxOccurs=1)

   This element contains the size of the attachment in bytes.

/setCalendarAttachmentResponse/calendarAttachment/error (string minOccurs=1 maxOccurs=1)

   Returns error information (i.e., not found).

The .NET calendar service/Error Cases

   If the method causes a failure response to be generated, the failure is noted by generating a SOAP Fault message. Failures can include a failure to understand a header marked as "s:mustUnderstand", a .NET My Services standard error, security violation, load balance redirect or any service-specific severe error condition.

The .NET calendar service/getCalendarAttachment Method

   Retrieves a calendar MIME attachment from the .NET calendar service.

The .NET calendar service/getCalendarAttachmentRequest

This method is accessed using a request message, and in response may generate a response message or a SOAP Fault message. The following sample document fragments illustrate the structure and meaning of the elements and attributes in the request and response messages.

The following section describes the request message for this method.

This is the request message XML fragment for getCalendarAttachment.

```
<m:getCalendarAttachmentRequest select="..."
    xmlns:m="http://schemas.microsoft.com/hs/2001/10/myCalendar"
    xmlns:hs="http://schemas.microsoft.com/hs/2001/10/core">1..1
    <m:attachmentId>1..unbounded</m:attachmentId>
</m:getCalendarAttachmentRequest>
```

The meaning of the attributes and elements shown in the preceding sample document fragment are listed in the following section.

/getCalendarAttachmentRequest (minOccurs=1 maxOccurs=1)
   The purpose of this method is to retrieve a calendar attachment from the .NET calendar service. This method takes a location element that contains an XPATH expression indicating which event to retrieve the attachment for. It also takes one or more attachmentId elements that contain the id of the attachment to retrieve.

/getCalendarAttachmentRequest/@select (string minOccurs=0 maxOccurs=1)
   The location of appointment to get the attachment for. Ex: /myCalendar/event[@id="00000001"]

/getCalendarAttachmentRequest/attachmentId (string minOccurs=1 maxOccurs=unbounded)
   This required element contains the id of the attachment to retrieve. One or more elements are required in the request meeting.

The .NET calendar service/getCalendarAttachmentResponse

Upon successful completion of this method, a response message is generated. The format of the response message is described below.

Returns the MIME attachment.

```
<m:getCalendarAttachmentResponse
    xmlns:m="http://schemas.microsoft.com/hs/2001/10/myCalendar"
    xmlns:hs="http://schemas.microsoft.com/hs/2001/10/core">1..1
    <m:calendarAttachment>0..unbounded
        <m:name xml:lang="...">1..1</m:name>
        <m:contentType>1..1</m:contentType>
        <m:contentTransferEncoding>1..1</m:contentTransferEncoding>
        <m:size>1..1</m:size>
        <m:attachmentBody>1..1</m:attachmentBody>
        <m:error>1..1</m:error>
    </m:calendarAttachment>
</m:getCalendarAttachmentResponse>
```

The meaning of the attributes and elements shown in the preceding sample document fragment are listed in the following section.

/getCalendarAttachmentResponse (minOccurs=1 maxOccurs=1)
Contains the calendar attachments that were requested.

/getCalendarAttachmentResponse/calendarAttachment (minOccurs=0 maxOccurs=unbounded)
This XML fragment contains the complete MIME body of the attachment.

/getCalendarAttachmentResponse/calendarAttachment/name (string minOccurs=1 maxOccurs=1)
This element contains information about an individual attachment in an e-mail message.

/getCalendarAttachmentResponse/calendarAttachment/name/@xml:lang (minOccurs=1 maxOccurs=1)
This required attribute is used to specify an ISO 639 language code or an ISO 3166 country code as described in RFC 1766. The value of this attribute indicates the language type of the content within this element.

/getCalendarAttachmentResponse/calendarAttachment/contentType (string minOccurs=1 maxOccurs=1)
This element contains the content type of the attachment.

/getCalendarAttachmentResponse/calendarAttachment/contentTransferEncoding (string minOccurs=1 maxOccurs=1)
This element contains the encoding of the attachment. This information is necessary for decoding the attachment.

/getCalendarAttachmentResponse/calendarAttachment/size (unsignedLong minOccurs=1 maxOccurs=1)

   This element contains the size of the attachment in bytes.

/getCalendarAttachmentResponse/calendarAttachment/attachmentBody (string minOccurs=1 maxOccurs=1)

   Contains the attachment body.

/getCalendarAttachmentResponse/calendarAttachment/error (string minOccurs=1 maxOccurs=1)

   Returns error information (i.e., not found).

The .NET calendar service/Error Cases

If the method causes a failure response to be generated, the failure is noted by generating a SOAP Fault message. Failures can include a failure to understand a header marked as "s:mustUnderstand", a .NET My Services standard error, security violation, load balance redirect, or any service-specific severe error condition.

The .NET calendar service/meetingUpdate Method

Organizer meeting request domain method.

The .NET calendar service/meetingUpdateRequest

This method is accessed using a request message, and in response may generate a response message or a SOAP Fault message. The following sample document fragments illustrate the structure and meaning of the elements and attributes in the request and response messages.

The following section describes the request message for this method.

This is the request message XML fragment for invite.

```
<m:meetingUpdateRequest
    xmlns:m="http://schemas.microsoft.com/hs/2001/10/myCalendar"
    xmlns:hs="http://schemas.microsoft.com/hs/2001/10/core">1..1
    <m:uninvite>1..1
        <m:attendeeId>0..unbounded</m:attendeeId>
        <m:attendee>0..unbounded
            <hs:name xml:lang="...">0..1</hs:name>
            <hs:puid>0..1</hs:puid>
            <hs:email>0..1</hs:email>
            <m:inviteType>1..1</m:inviteType>
            <m:invitationStatus>1..1</m:invitationStatus>
        </m:attendee>
    </m:uninvite>
```

(continued)

(continued)

```
    <m:eventId>₁..₁</m:eventId>
    <m:invite>₁..₁
        <m:attendee>₀..unbounded
            <hs:name xml:lang="...">₀..₁</hs:name>
            <hs:puid>₀..₁</hs:puid>
            <hs:email>₀..₁</hs:email>
            <m:inviteType>₁..₁</m:inviteType>
            <m:invitationStatus>₁..₁</m:invitationStatus>
        </m:attendee>
    </m:invite>
</m:meetingUpdateRequest>
```

The meaning of the attributes and elements shown in the preceding sample document fragment are listed in the following section.

/meetingUpdateRequest (minOccurs=1 maxOccurs=1)

The purpose of this method is for a meeting organizer to invite and uninvite (cancel) attendees to this event. meetingUpdate also sends updated invitations to existing invitees. Inviting a user to a single instance of a recurring event will cause only that instance to be sent. However, future updates to that event will overwrite the existing instance, including the case where an update is the full recurring event.

PRELIMINARY meeting requests will be sent out as ICAL attachments from an SMTP server unknown at this point in the design. Integration with the .NET notifications service ongoing TBD.

/meetingUpdateRequest/uninvite (minOccurs=1 maxOccurs=1)

/meetingUpdateRequest/uninvite/attendeeId (minOccurs=0 maxOccurs=unbounded)

Contains the blue-node attendee id to uninvite. If found, the <invitationStatus> field will be set to {cancelled}.

/meetingUpdateRequest/uninvite/attendee (minOccurs=0 maxOccurs=unbounded)

Contains information about a particular attendee to be uninvited.

/meetingUpdateRequest/uninvite/attendee/name (string minOccurs=0 maxOccurs=1)

This optional element specifies the name for the enclosing element.

/meetingUpdateRequest/uninvite/attendee/name/@xml:lang (minOccurs=1 maxOccurs=1)

This required attribute is used to specify an ISO 639 language code or an ISO 3166 country code as described in RFC 1766. The value of this attribute indicates the language type of the content within this element.

/meetingUpdateRequest/uninvite/attendee/puid (string minOccurs=0 maxOccurs=1)

This optional element specifies the name for the enclosing element.

/meetingUpdateRequest/uninvite/attendee/email (string minOccurs=0 maxOccurs=1)

This optional name specifies an e-mail address for the enclosing element.

/meetingUpdateRequest/uninvite/attendee/inviteType (string minOccurs=1 maxOccurs=1)
> The meeting organizer uses this to define the kind of invitee {required, optional, resource}.

/meetingUpdateRequest/uninvite/attendee/invitationStatus (string minOccurs=1 maxOccurs=1)
> Tracks the status of invitations {not-sent, sent, cancelled}.

/meetingUpdateRequest/eventId (minOccurs=1 maxOccurs=1)
> The eventId for the meeting.

/meetingUpdateRequest/invite (minOccurs=1 maxOccurs=1)

/meetingUpdateRequest/invite/attendee (minOccurs=0 maxOccurs=unbounded)
> Contains information about this attendee to be invited.

/meetingUpdateRequest/invite/attendee/name (string minOccurs=0 maxOccurs=1)
> This optional element specifies the name for the enclosing element.

/meetingUpdateRequest/invite/attendee/name/@xml:lang (minOccurs=1 maxOccurs=1)
> This required attribute is used to specify an ISO 639 language code or an ISO 3166 country code as described in RFC 1766. The value of this attribute indicates the language type of the content within this element.

/meetingUpdateRequest/invite/attendee/puid (string minOccurs=0 maxOccurs=1)
> This optional element specifies the name for the enclosing element.

/meetingUpdateRequest/invite/attendee/email (string minOccurs=0 maxOccurs=1)
> This optional name specifies an e-mail address for the enclosing element.

/meetingUpdateRequest/invite/attendee/inviteType (string minOccurs=1 maxOccurs=1)
> The meeting organizer uses this to define the kind of invitee {required, optional, resource}.

/meetingUpdateRequest/invite/attendee/invitationStatus (string minOccurs=1 maxOccurs=1)
> Tracks the status of invitations {not-sent, sent, cancelled}.

The .NET calendar service/meetingUpdateResponse

Upon successful completion of this method, a response message is generated. The format of the response message is described below.

The .NET calendar service/Error Cases

If the method causes a failure response to be generated, the failure is noted by generating a SOAP Fault message. Failures can include a failure to understand a header marked as "s:mustUnderstand", a .NET My Services standard error, security violation, load balance redirect, or any service-specific severe error condition.

The .NET calendar service/respond Method

Method for invitees to respond to an invite.

The .NET calendar service/respondRequest

This method is accessed using a request message, and in response may generate a response message or a SOAP Fault message. The following sample document fragments illustrate the structure and meaning of the elements and attributes in the request and response messages.

The following section describes the request message for this method.

This is the request message XML fragment for respond.

```
<m:respondRequest
    xmlns:m="http://schemas.microsoft.com/hs/2001/10/myCalendar"
    xmlns:hs="http://schemas.microsoft.com/hs/2001/10/core">1..1
    <m:responseTime>1..1</m:responseTime>
    <m:responseType>1..1</m:responseType>
    <m:counterProposeStartTime>0..1</m:counterProposeStartTime>
    <m:counterProposeEndTime>0..1</m:counterProposeEndTime>
    <m:counterProposeLocation>0..1</m:counterProposeLocation>
    <m:eventId>1..1</m:eventId>
    <m:puid>1..1</m:puid>
</m:respondRequest>
```

The meaning of the attributes and elements shown in the preceding sample document fragment are listed in the following section.

/respondRequest (minOccurs=1 maxOccurs=1)
  The purpose of this method is for a meeting invitee to respond to an invitation. Invitees may accept, decline, accept tentatively, or counterpropose in some circumstances. Currently, .NET My Services allows counterproposal of time and location, but future additions may be considered.

/respondRequest/responseTime (dateTime minOccurs=1 maxOccurs=1)
  The reply time on each attendee is set to "Now" when the organizer creates and sends a meeting. When the attendee responds, they always update their replyTime. When the organizer receives responses, they will honor only those that have a higher replyTime than what he or she maintains in his/her own copy of the event for each attendee. While processing the response, the organizer will update their replyTime. This guarantees that the organizer honors only the most recent response from the attendee. This is stored in UTC.

  Outlook Equivalent: RECIPIENT_TRACKSTATUSTIME. **ICAL Equivalent**: reply time on message.

/respondRequest/responseType (string minOccurs=1 maxOccurs=1)
> The accept status indicates the valid types of responses that an attendee can reply with {accept, decline, tentative, counterpropose}.

/respondRequest/counterProposeStartTime (dateTime minOccurs=0 maxOccurs=1)
> If responseType=[counterPropose], the {startTime, endTime}, or location, or both can be present. This is the invitee's counterProposal for a new start time for the meeting. This is stored in UTC.

/respondRequest/counterProposeEndTime (dateTime minOccurs=0 maxOccurs=1)
> If responseType=[counterPropose], the {startTime, endTime}, or location, or both can be present. This is the invitee's counterProposal for a new end time for the meeting. This is stored in UTC.

/respondRequest/counterProposeLocation (string minOccurs=0 maxOccurs=1)
> If responseType=[counterPropose], the {startTime, endTime}, or location, or both can be present. This is the invitee's counterProposal for a location for the meeting.

/respondRequest/eventId (minOccurs=1 maxOccurs=1)
> The eventId for the meeting.

/respondRequest/puid (string minOccurs=1 maxOccurs=1)
> The invitee.

The .NET calendar service/respondResponse

Upon successful completion of this method, a response message is generated. The format of the response message is described below.

The .NET calendar service/Error Cases

If the method causes a failure response to be generated, the failure is noted by generating a SOAP Fault message. Failures can include a failure to understand a header marked as "s:mustUnderstand", a .NET My Services standard error, security violation, load balance redirect or any service-specific severe error condition.

The .NET calendar service/updateReminder Method

Delegate function to the .NET notifications service for creating or modifying calendar meeting reminders.

The .NET calendar service/updateReminderRequest

This method is accessed using a request message, and in response may generate a response message or a SOAP Fault message. The following sample document fragments illustrate the structure and meaning of the elements and attributes in the request and response messages.

The following section describes the request message for this method.

This is the request message XML fragment for setReminder.

```
<m:updateReminderRequest
    xmlns:m="http://schemas.microsoft.com/hs/2001/10/myCalendar"
    xmlns:hs="http://schemas.microsoft.com/hs/2001/10/core">1..1
    <m:reminder>1..1
        <m:set>1..1</m:set>
        <m:to xml:lang="...">1..1</m:to>
        <m:offset>1..1</m:offset>
        <m:interruptability>0..1</m:interruptability>
        <m:lastSentTime>1..1</m:lastSentTime>
        <m:nextTriggerTime>1..1</m:nextTriggerTime>
    </m:reminder>
    <m:id>1..1</m:id>
</m:updateReminderRequest>
```

The meaning of the attributes and elements shown in the preceding sample document fragment are listed in the following section.

/updateReminderRequest (minOccurs=1 maxOccurs=1)
This function is used to update the status of a reminder once the user has received the notification. We may expose this as an HTTP API so that non-.NET My Services clients have a means to dismiss, snooze, or be reminded again at a different time. (WIP)

/updateReminderRequest/reminder (minOccurs=1 maxOccurs=1)

/updateReminderRequest/reminder/set (boolean minOccurs=1 maxOccurs=1)
Boolean flag that indicates whether the reminder is active for this event. In most cases, this will be true, but in the case of a recurring appointment, this flag may default to true with specific instances not to be reminded, or default to false, with specific instances to be reminded.

/updateReminderRequest/reminder/to (string minOccurs=1 maxOccurs=1)

/updateReminderRequest/reminder/to/@xml:lang (minOccurs=1 maxOccurs=1)
This required attribute is used to specify an ISO 639 language code or an ISO 3166 country code as described in RFC 1766. The value of this attribute indicates the language type of the content within this element.

/updateReminderRequest/reminder/offset (int minOccurs=1 maxOccurs=1)
Specifies the offset, in minutes, of how long before the event the user should be reminded. Recommended values are the following:

Value	Description
5, 10, 20, 30, 45	5, 10, 20, 30, 45 minutes before the event
60, 120, 180,	1, 2, 3 hours before the event
startTime - startDay	The day of the event (reminder sent at 12:00am)
startTime - (startDay - (1440 * x))	"x" days before the event (reminder sent at 12:00am "x" days before)

/updateReminderRequest/reminder/interruptability (int minOccurs=0 maxOccurs=1)
This optional element defines how interruptible this event is and it is used by notification routing software to make decisions about the relay and deferral of notifications that might occur while this meeting is active. The value contained in this element is a numeric value between 1 and 10. Low values represent a high cost of disruption, high values represent a low cost of disruption.

/updateReminderRequest/reminder/lastSentTime (dateTime minOccurs=1 maxOccurs=1)
Required by reminder engine.

/updateReminderRequest/reminder/nextTriggerTime (dateTime minOccurs=1 maxOccurs=1)
Determines the next time to trigger reminder.

/updateReminderRequest/id (minOccurs=1 maxOccurs=1)
This attribute is a globally unique ID assigned to this element by .NET My Services. Normally, .NET My Services will generate and assign this ID during an insertRequest operation, or possibly during a replaceRequest. Application software can override this ID generation by specifying the useClientIds attribute in the request message. Once an ID is assigned, the attribute is read-only and attempts to write it are silently ignored.

The .NET calendar service/updateReminderResponse

Upon successful completion of this method, a response message is generated. The format of the response message is described below.

Standard HS response message.

The .NET calendar service/Error Cases

If the method causes a failure response to be generated, the failure is noted by generating a SOAP Fault message. Failures can include a failure to understand a header marked as "s:mustUnderstand", a .NET My Services standard error, security violation, load balance redirect, or any service-specific severe error condition.

CHAPTER 12

The .NET Categories Service/Introduction

The .NET categories service is designed to support a classification model for data within the Microsoft .NET My Services universe. The classification model is generic and makes very few assumptions about application usage. As a result, the design is minimal and open. This model of categorization will be used by a wide spectrum of applications, without burdening the developer of the service.

The .NET categories service manages a list of category definitions. Examples of category definitions include child, anniversary, employee, etc. Each category definition has a human readable name and a description which contains hints about the meaning of that category. A given category implies a more general category, while friends implies acquaintances. A category may be classified by using other categories. For example, anniversary and birthday are categorized as specialDate.

Like all .NET My Services services, the .NET categories service exposes a global system document, and an identity-centric content document. The global system document is an extension of the standard system document which contains global category definitions available to all .NET My Services applications. The identity-centric content document contains category definitions local to the identity.

Within other .NET My Services services, category references are used to mark an XML element as belonging to the group represented by the category definition. The schema of each service defines which nodes (if any) can be categorized. For example, .NET contacts/contacts/address can be categorized, but .NET calendar/event/event body cannot. The roleList and system schemas also define nodes that can be categorized. For example, roleList/role can be categorized.

Categories use a declarative syntax for encoding relationships that an application deems important. .NET My Services neither provides nor requires any consistency checks or enforcements implied by the semantics of these relationships.

There are two primary elements used to define and reference categories—the catDef element and the cat element. The catDef element is used to define a category, and the cat element is used to refer to a category. .NET My Services allows the catDef element to appear in the following locations:

- the system document of the .NET categories service
- the content document of the .NET categories service
- an arbitrary XML file located by URI

The cat element refers to a category definition by absolute or relative URI. The linkage between the two is through the catDef/@catId attribute and the cat/@ref attribute. The catDef/@catId attribute specifies the local ID for the category definition, and the cat/@ref attribute is the value of that reference.

The value of the cat/@ref attribute may take the following forms:

system#*name-of-category*
> The category definition being referenced is located in the system document of the .NET categories service, and its catDef/@catId attribute is "name-of-category". For example, the category reference of <cat ref="system#public"/> is a reference to the category definition whose catDef/@catId value is "public", and this category definition is located in the system document of the .NET categories service, i.e., <catDef id="public"/>.

content#*name-of-category*[?puid=puid-value]
> The category definition being referenced is located in the content document of the .NET categories service, and its catDef/@catId attribute is "name-of-category". The instance of the .NET categories service (i.e., the Microsoft Passport Unique ID (PUID) of the service) is implied by the context of the reference. This may be made explicit by appending ?puid=puid-value to the URI, and when this is done, it means the content document of the .NET categories service whose PUID is "puid-value" holds the category definition. For example, the category reference of <cat ref="content#LaQuintaHouse"/> is a reference to the category definition whose catDef/@catId value is "LaQuintaHouse", and that this category definition is located in the content document of the .NET categories service for the current PUID, i.e., <catDef id="LaQuintaHouse"/>.

any-uri#*name-of-category*
> The category definition being referenced is located in an external (to .NET My Services) resource. The "any-uri" portion of the reference refers to a resource containing the catDef element whose @catId attribute matches the "name-of-category". The mapping between the "any-uri" portion of the reference and an XML document containing the catDef elements is a function of the "any-uri". By convention, this URI is the name of an XML document containing those elements. The purpose of this reference form is to allow and support a free form set of extended categorizations that are global and available to all. For example, the category reference of <cat ref="http://schemas.someDomain.com/im/globalCategories.xml#imBuddy"/> is a reference to the category definition whose catDef/@catId value is "imBuddy", and that this category definition is located in an external resource located at "http://schemas.someDomain.com/im/globalCategories.xml". Note that our expectation is that category definitions will exist in the appropriate locations, but there is no requirement or enforcement of this.

In all cases, the mapping between a category reference and the category definition is very simple:

1. Locate the document containing the category definition by taking the name prior to the "#".

2. If the document is "system", then the document containing the category definition is the system document of the .NET categories service and is addressed using request/@service="*myCategories*" and request/@document="system".

3. If the document is "content", then the document containing the category definition is the content document of the .NET categories service and is addressed using request/@service="*myCategories*" and request/@document="content". If the ?puid=puid-value argument is present, the request is further qualified by request/key/@puid="puid-value". Otherwise, this attribute contains the PUID of the document containing the reference.

4. For any other document, the value is the URI of the XML document containing the category definition.

5. Locate the category ID which is the portion of the reference after the "#" and before an optional "?". This is the "category-id".

6. With the document in hand, the xpath expression //catDef[@catId='category-id'] selects the category definition.

The .NET Categories Service/Roles

The .NET categories service controls access by using the following roleTemplates:

- rt0
- rt1
- rt2
- rt3
- rt99

The .NET categories service uses the following scopes:

- **scope id 1**

```
<hs:scope id=1>

    <hs:shape base=t>

    </hs:shape>

</hs:scope>
```

- scope id 2

```
<hs:scope id=2>

    <hs:shape base=nil>

        <hs:include select=//*[@creator='$callerId']/>

    </hs:shape>

</hs:scope>
```

- scope id 3

```
<hs:scope id=3>

    <hs:shape base=nil>

        <hs:include select=//subscription[@creator='$callerId']/>

    </hs:shape>

</hs:scope>
```

- scope id 4

```
<hs:scope id=4>

    <hs:shape base=nil>

        <hs:include select=//*[cat/@ref='hs:public']/>

        <hs:include select=//subscription[@creator='$callerId']/>

    </hs:shape>

</hs:scope>
```

The .NET categories service roleTemplate rt0

The purpose of this role is to give complete read/write access to all information within the content document of the service being protected through this roleTemplate.

The following table illustrates the available methods and the scope in effect when accessing the .NET categories service through that method while mapped to this roleTemplate.

method	scopeRef
query	scopeRef=1
insert	scopeRef=1
replace	scopeRef=1
delete	scopeRef=1
update	scopeRef=1

The .NET categories service roleTemplate rt1

The purpose of this role is to give complete read access to all information within the content document of the service being protected through this roleTemplate. Applications mapping to this role also have a limited ability to write to information in the content document. They may create nodes in any location, but may only change/replace, or delete nodes that they created.

The following table illustrates the available methods and the scope in effect when accessing the .NET categories service through that method while mapped to this roleTemplate.

method	scopeRef
query	scopeRef=1
insert	scopeRef=2
replace	scopeRef=2
delete	scopeRef=2

The .NET categories service roleTemplate rt2

The purpose of this role is to give complete read access to all information within the content document of the service being protected through this roleTemplate. Applications mapping to this role have very limited write access and are only able to create and manipulate their own subscription nodes.

The following table illustrates the available methods and the scope in effect when accessing the .NET categories service through that method while mapped to this roleTemplate.

method	scopeRef
query	scopeRef=1
insert	scopeRef=3
replace	scopeRef=3
delete	scopeRef=3

The .NET categories service roleTemplate rt3

The purpose of this role is to give limited read access to information within the content document that is categorized as "public".

The following table illustrates the available methods and the scope in effect when accessing the .NET categories service through that method while mapped to this roleTemplate.

method	scopeRef
query	scopeRef=4

The .NET categories service roleTemplate rt99

The purpose of this role is to block all access to the content document. Note that lack of a role in the roleList has the same effect as assigning someone to rt99.

The .NET Categories Service/Content

The content document is an identity-centric document. Its content and meaning are a function of the PUID used to address the service. Accessing the document is made possible by controlling the associated roleList document.

This schema outline illustrates the layout and meaning of the information found in the content document for the .NET categories service.

```
<m:myCategories changeNumber="..." instanceId="..."
    xmlns:m="http://schemas.microsoft.com/hs/2001/10/myCategories"
    xmlns:hs="http://schemas.microsoft.com/hs/2001/10/core">1..1
    <m:catDef catId="..." changeNumber="..." id="..." creator="...">0..unbounded
        <hs:name xml:lang="...">0..unbounded</hs:name>
        <hs:description xml:lang="...">0..1</hs:description>
        <hs:implies ref="...">0..unbounded</hs:implies>
        <hs:cat ref="...">0..unbounded</hs:cat>
        {any}
    </m:catDef>
    <m:subscription changeNumber="..." id="..." creator="...">0..unbounded
        <hs:trigger select="..." mode="..."
baseChangeNumber="...">1..1</hs:trigger>
        <hs:expiresAt>0..1</hs:expiresAt>
        <hs:context uri="...">1..1 {any}</hs:context>
        <hs:to>1..1</hs:to>
    </m:subscription>
    {any}
</m:myCategories>
```

The meaning of the attributes and elements shown in the preceding sample document fragment are listed in the following section.

/myCategories (minOccurs=1 maxOccurs=1)

This element encapsulates the content document for the *myCategories* service. The service is designed to store identity-centric category definitions that may be refered to using the **content**#*name-of-category[?puid=puid-value]* relative URI scheme.

/myCategories/@changeNumber (minOccurs=0 maxOccurs=1)

The changeNumber attribute is designed to facilitate caching of the element and its descendants. This attribute is assigned to this element by the .NET My Services system. The attribute is read-only to applications. Attempts to write this attribute are silently ignored.

/myCategories/@instanceId (string minOccurs=0 maxOccurs=1)

This attribute is a unique identifier typically assigned to the root element of a service. It is a read-only element and assigned by the .NET My Services system when a user is provisioned for a particular service.

/myCategories/catDef (minOccurs=0 maxOccurs=unbounded)

This element encapsulates the definition of a category. It may appear in the system or content document of the *myCategories* service, or may appear in an external resource.

/myCategories/catDef/@catId (string minOccurs=0 maxOccurs=1)

This attribute specifies the unique ID of the category in the form of the category name.

/myCategories/catDef/@changeNumber (minOccurs=0 maxOccurs=1)

The changeNumber attribute is designed to facilitate caching of the element and its descendants. This attribute is assigned to this element by the .NET My Services system. The attribute is read-only to applications. Attempts to write this attribute are silently ignored.

/myCategories/catDef/@id (minOccurs=0 maxOccurs=1)

This attribute is a globally unique ID assigned to this element by .NET My Services. Normally, .NET My Services will generate and assign this ID during an insertRequest operation, or possibly during a replaceRequest. Application software can override this ID generation by specifying the useClientIds attribute in the request message. Once an ID is assigned, the attribute is read-only and attempts to write it are silently ignored.

/myCategories/catDef/@creator (string minOccurs=0 maxOccurs=1)

This attribute identifies the creator in terms of userId, appId, and platformId of the node.

/myCategories/catDef/name (string minOccurs=0 maxOccurs=unbounded)

This element specifies the localized name of the category.

/myCategories/catDef/name/@xml:lang (minOccurs=1 maxOccurs=1)

This required attribute is used to specify an ISO 639 language code or an ISO 3166 country code as described in RFC 1766. The value of this attribute indicates the language type of the content within this element.

/myCategories/catDef/description (string minOccurs=0 maxOccurs=1)
This element specifies a full description of the category definition.

/myCategories/catDef/description/@xml:lang (minOccurs=1 maxOccurs=1)
This required attribute is used to specify an ISO 639 language code or an ISO 3166 country code as described in RFC 1766. The value of this attribute indicates the language type of the content within this element.

/myCategories/catDef/implies (minOccurs=0 maxOccurs=unbounded)
This element specifies that this category definition also implies that another category (designated by the ref attribute) also applies.

/myCategories/catDef/implies/@ref (anyURI minOccurs=0 maxOccurs=1)
This attribute references a category definition (<catDef/>) element.

/myCategories/catDef/cat (minOccurs=0 maxOccurs=unbounded)
This element is used to categorize the element that contains it by referencing a global category definition in either the .NET categories service system document or an external resource containing category definitions, or by referencing an identity-centric category definition in the content document of the .NET categories service for a particular PUID.

/myCategories/catDef/cat/@ref (anyURI minOccurs=0 maxOccurs=1)
This attribute references a category definition (<catDef/>) element.

/myCategories/catDef/*{any}* (minOccurs=0 maxOccurs=unbounded)

/myCategories/subscription (minOccurs=0 maxOccurs=unbounded)
This element defines a subscription node that is designed to be an xdb:blue node which when placed in a content document causes a subscription to be registered. A subscription contains a trigger element which selects a scope of coverage. When items change that are under this scope of coverage, a subscriptionResponse message is generated and sent to the specified destination address.

/myCategories/subscription/@changeNumber (minOccurs=0 maxOccurs=1)
The changeNumber attribute is designed to facilitate caching of the element and its descendants. This attribute is assigned to this element by the .NET My Services system. The attribute is read-only to applications. Attempts to write this attribute are silently ignored.

/myCategories/subscription/@id (minOccurs=0 maxOccurs=1)
This attribute is a globally unique ID assigned to this element by .NET My Services. Normally, .NET My Services will generate and assign this ID during an insertRequest operation, or possibly during a replaceRequest. Application software can override this ID generation by specifying the useClientIds attribute in the request message. Once an ID is assigned, the attribute is read-only and attempts to write it are silently ignored.

/myCategories/subscription/@creator (string minOccurs=0 maxOccurs=1)
This attribute identifies the creator in terms of userId, appId, and platformId of the node.

/myCategories/subscription/trigger (minOccurs=1 maxOccurs=1)

/myCategories/subscription/trigger/@select (string minOccurs=0 maxOccurs=1)

> This item specifies an XPATH expression that specifies the nodes that are to be selected and watched for changes. The selection may only select xdb:blue nodes. As changes in this node set occur, they trigger the generation of a subscription message. The message is then sent to the SOAP receiver listed in the "to" element.

/myCategories/subscription/trigger/@mode (string minOccurs=0 maxOccurs=1)

> This attribute specifies whether or not the content of the changes that triggered the subscription are delivered in the subscription message, or if the message simply indicates that something changed under the trigger. The attribute may be:

> includeData

>> The data that changed, causing the subscription to trigger is included in the subscription message. Note that deleted nodes are specified by their ID, not by value.

> excludeData

>> The data that changed, causing the subscription to trigger is NOT included in the subscription message.

/myCategories/subscription/trigger/@baseChangeNumber (minOccurs=0 maxOccurs=1)

> This attribute specifies the changeNumber value that the trigger is relative to. All changes between the specified change number, and the current state of the document relative to the selection are transmitted as subscription messages. This allows a client application to establish a subscription relative to some baseline. As in changeQuery, if the baseChangeNumber is way out of date relative to the current state of the document, and the service cannot supply the changes in the subscription message, the subscription insert is rejected. A value of 0 means that the current values of the selected nodes are transmitted in the subscription message.

/myCategories/subscription/expiresAt (dateTime minOccurs=0 maxOccurs=1)

> This optional element specifies an absolute time after which the subscription is no longer active. The subscription node is automatically removed when the subscription expires. If this element is missing, the subscription does not expire.

/myCategories/subscription/context (minOccurs=1 maxOccurs=1)

> This element returns the context element from the original subscription. Applications should use this element, and only this element, to correlate the subscription response with one of their subscriptions.

/myCategories/subscription/context/@uri (anyURI minOccurs=0 maxOccurs=1)

> This attribute specifies the URI value chosen by the subscriber that is associated with this subscription.

/myCategories/subscription/context/*{any}* (minOccurs=0 maxOccurs=unbounded)

/myCategories/subscription/to (anyURI minOccurs=1 maxOccurs=1)

This attribute specifies the location that is to receive the subscription message. The value of this element may be one of the following forms:

- *hs:myNotifications*—This URI indicates that generated subscription messages are to be delivered inside the body of a notification and delivered to the default .NET notifications service of the creator.

- *protocol://service*—This URI indicates that generated subscription messages are delivered to the specified service at the domain of the creator's platformId. For instance, a platformId indicating microsoft.com, and a value in this element of http://subscriptionResponse would cause delivery of the subscription message to http://subscriptionResponse.microsoft.com.

If this value is not specified, then the subscription message is delivered as a notification to the "creator's" .NET notifications service.

/myCategories/{any} (minOccurs=0 maxOccurs=unbounded)

The .NET Categories Service/System

The system document is a global document for the service. Its content and meaning are independent of the PUID used to address the service, and the document is read-only to all users. The system document contains a set of base items common to all .NET My Services services, and is optionally extended by each service to include service-specific global information.

This schema outline illustrates the layout and meaning of the information found in the system document for the .NET categories service.

The system document for the .NET categories service contains the global category definition elements for global categories defined by .NET My Services. As described in the introduction to this chapter, these category definitions may be referenced by using the **system**#*name-of-category* notation in the cat/@ref attribute.

```
<sys:system changeNumber="..." instanceId="..."
    xmlns:hs="http://schemas.microsoft.com/hs/2001/10/core"
    xmlns:sys="http://schemas.microsoft.com/hs/2001/10/myCategories/system">1..1
    <hs:roleMap changeNumber="..." id="..." creator="...">1..1
        <hs:scope id="...">0..unbounded
            <hs:shape base="...">1..1
                <hs:include select="...">1..unbounded</hs:include>
                <hs:exclude select="...">0..unbounded</hs:exclude>
            </hs:shape>
        </hs:scope>
        <hs:roleTemplate name="..." priority="...">0..unbounded
            <hs:fullDescription xml:lang="...">0..1</hs:fullDescription>
            <hs:method name="..." scopeRef="...">0..unbounded</hs:method>
        </hs:roleTemplate>
    </hs:roleMap>
```

```
    <hs:methodMap changeNumber="..." id="..." creator="...">₁.₁
        <hs:method name="...">₀..unbounded {any}</hs:method>
    </hs:methodMap>
    <hs:schemaMap changeNumber="..." id="..." creator="...">₁.₁
        <hs:schema namespace="..." schemaLocation="..." alias="...">₀..unbounded
{any}</hs:schema>
    </hs:schemaMap>
    <hs:wsdlMap changeNumber="..." id="..." creator="...">₁.₁
        <hs:wsdl wsdlLocation="...">₀..unbounded {any}</hs:wsdl>
        <hs:disco discoLocation="...">₀..unbounded {any}</hs:disco>
    </hs:wsdlMap>
    <sys:catDef catId="..." changeNumber="..." id="..." creator="...">₀..unbounded
        <hs:name xml:lang="...">₀..unbounded</hs:name>
        <hs:description xml:lang="...">₀..₁</hs:description>
        <hs:implies ref="...">₀..unbounded</hs:implies>
        <hs:cat ref="...">₀..unbounded</hs:cat>
        {any}
    </sys:catDef>
    {any}
</sys:system>
```

The meaning of the attributes and elements shown in the preceding sample document fragment are listed in the following section.

/system (minOccurs=1 maxOccurs=1)

This element encapsulates the system document for the .NET categories service. This document extends the basic system document with the addition of global category definitions that may be referred to using the **system**#*name-of-category* relative URI scheme.

/system/@changeNumber (minOccurs=0 maxOccurs=1)

The changeNumber attribute is designed to facilitate caching of the element and its descendants. This attribute is assigned to this element by the .NET My Services system. The attribute is read-only to applications. Attempts to write this attribute are silently ignored.

/system/@instanceId (string minOccurs=0 maxOccurs=1)

This attribute is a unique identifier typically assigned to the root element of a service. It is a read-only element and assigned by the .NET My Services system when a user is provisioned for a particular service.

/system/roleMap (minOccurs=1 maxOccurs=1)

This element encapsulates all the elements that make up a roleMap, which includes a document class relative to a roleTemplate, priority, name, method, and per-method scope. An individual roleTemplate defines the maximum scope of information, and the allowable methods used to access that information for each request mapped into the template.

/system/roleMap/@changeNumber (minOccurs=0 maxOccurs=1)

The changeNumber attribute is designed to facilitate caching of the element and its descendants. This attribute is assigned to this element by the .NET My Services system. The attribute is read-only to applications. Attempts to write this attribute are silently ignored.

/system/roleMap/@id (minOccurs=0 maxOccurs=1)

This attribute is a globally unique ID assigned to this element by .NET My Services. Normally, .NET My Services will generate and assign this ID during an insertRequest operation, or possibly during a replaceRequest. Application software can override this ID generation by specifying the useClientIds attribute in the request message. Once an ID is assigned, the attribute is read-only and attempts to write it are silently ignored.

/system/roleMap/@creator (string minOccurs=0 maxOccurs=1)

This attribute identifies the creator in terms of userId, appId, and platformId of the node.

/system/roleMap/scope (minOccurs=0 maxOccurs=unbounded)

This element defines a scope which may be referred to by roles within this roleMap to indicate what portions of the document are visible to this role for the specified method.

/system/roleMap/scope/@id (minOccurs=0 maxOccurs=1)

This attribute is a globally unique ID assigned to this element by .NET My Services. Normally, .NET My Services will generate and assign this ID during an insertRequest operation, or possibly during a replaceRequest. Application software can override this ID generation by specifying the useClientIds attribute in the request message. Once an ID is assigned, the attribute is read-only and attempts to write it are silently ignored.

/system/roleMap/scope/shape (minOccurs=1 maxOccurs=1)

A shape defines the node set visible through the document when operating through this shape element.

/system/roleMap/scope/shape/@base (string minOccurs=0 maxOccurs=1)

This attribute specifies the initial set of nodes visible through the shape.

A value of t indicates that the shape is initialized to include all possible nodes relative to the shape that is currently in effect. For instance, each role defines a scope containing a shape. When defining a shape for a role, the value t indicates all possible nodes available in the specified document for this role. When defining a shape in an ACL entry, a value of t means all of the nodes visible in the shape for the computed role. When using a shape in an hsdl operation, a value of t indicates all of the possible nodes selected by the hsdl operation (relative to the ACL shape which itself is relative to the role's shape).

The value nil indicates the opposite of t, which is the empty node set. Nodes from this set may then be included into the shape.

/system/roleMap/scope/shape/include (minOccurs=1 maxOccurs=unbounded)

This element specifies the set of nodes that should be included into the shape relative to the possible set of nodes indicated by the base attribute.

/system/roleMap/scope/shape/include/@select (string minOccurs=0 maxOccurs=1)
This item specifies an XPATH expression that selects a set of nodes relative to the externally established context. The expression can never travel outside the node-set established by this externally established current context. The expression may match 0 or more nodes, and the operation manipulates all selected nodes. The minOccurs and maxOccurs attributes are optional and place restrictions and limitations on the number of nodes selected.

/system/roleMap/scope/shape/exclude (minOccurs=0 maxOccurs=unbounded)
This element specifies the set of nodes that should be excluded from the shape relative to the possible set of nodes indicated by the base attribute.

/system/roleMap/scope/shape/exclude/@select (string minOccurs=0 maxOccurs=1)
This item specifies an XPATH expression that selects a set of nodes relative to the externally established context. The expression can never travel outside the node-set established by this externally established current context. The expression may match 0 or more nodes, and the operation manipulates all selected nodes. The minOccurs and maxOccurs attributes are optional and place restrictions and limitations on the number of nodes selected.

/system/roleMap/roleTemplate (minOccurs=0 maxOccurs=unbounded)
This element encapsulates the definition of a role. The attribute set for this element includes the document class that this roleTemplate refers to, the name of the roleTemplate, and the priority of the roleTemplate.

/system/roleMap/roleTemplate/@name (string minOccurs=0 maxOccurs=1)
This element specifies the name of the role.

/system/roleMap/roleTemplate/@priority (int minOccurs=0 maxOccurs=1)
This element specifies the priority of the roleTemplate which is used to select that actual roleTemplate when the role evaluation determines that the subject maps to multiple roleTemplates.

/system/roleMap/roleTemplate/fullDescription (string minOccurs=0 maxOccurs=1)
This element contains a description of this role template which specifies the capabilities a caller will have when accessing information through this role.

/system/roleMap/roleTemplate/fullDescription/@xml:lang (minOccurs=1 maxOccurs=1)
This required attribute is used to specify an ISO 639 language code or an ISO 3166 country code as described in RFC 1766. The value of this attribute indicates the language type of the content within this element.

/system/roleMap/roleTemplate/method (minOccurs=0 maxOccurs=unbounded)
This element specifies the methods available within this roleTemplate by name, and by scope. When a subject maps to a roleTemplate, the method in the request must match one of these elements for the message to continue to flow. If the method exists, the data available to the method is a function of the scope referenced by this method combined with an optional scope referenced by the role defined in the roleList.

/system/roleMap/roleTemplate/method/@name (string minOccurs=0 maxOccurs=1)
This element specifies the name of the method.

/system/roleMap/roleTemplate/method/@scopeRef (string minOccurs=0 maxOccurs=1)
This attribute specifies the scope within this document that is in effect for this method.

/system/methodMap (minOccurs=1 maxOccurs=1)
This element defines the methodMap. While it is true that in most cases, the roleMap section contains a definitive list of methods, these methods are likely to be scattered about the roleMap in various templates. This section contains the definitive non-duplicated list of methods available within the service.

/system/methodMap/@changeNumber (minOccurs=0 maxOccurs=1)
The changeNumber attribute is designed to facilitate caching of the element and its descendants. This attribute is assigned to this element by the .NET My Services system. The attribute is read-only to applications. Attempts to write this attribute are silently ignored.

/system/methodMap/@id (minOccurs=0 maxOccurs=1)
This attribute is a globally unique ID assigned to this element by .NET My Services. Normally, .NET My Services will generate and assign this ID during an insertRequest operation, or possibly during a replaceRequest. Application software can override this ID generation by specifying the useClientIds attribute in the request message. Once an ID is assigned, the attribute is read-only and attempts to write it are silently ignored.

/system/methodMap/@creator (string minOccurs=0 maxOccurs=1)
This attribute identifies the creator in terms of userId, appId, and platformId of the node.

/system/methodMap/method (minOccurs=0 maxOccurs=unbounded)
This element defines a method that is available within this service.

/system/methodMap/method/@name (string minOccurs=0 maxOccurs=1)
This attribute specifies the name of a method available within this service.

/system/methodMap/method/**{any}** (minOccurs=0 maxOccurs=unbounded)
/system/schemaMap (minOccurs=1 maxOccurs=1)
This element defines the various schemas that define the data structures and shape of information managed by this service. Each schema is defined by its namespace URI, its location, and a preferred namespace alias.

/system/schemaMap/@changeNumber (minOccurs=0 maxOccurs=1)
The changeNumber attribute is designed to facilitate caching of the element and its descendants. This attribute is assigned to this element by the .NET My Services system. The attribute is read-only to applications. Attempts to write this attribute are silently ignored.

/system/schemaMap/@id (minOccurs=0 maxOccurs=1)
This attribute is a globally unique ID assigned to this element by .NET My Services. Normally, .NET My Services will generate and assign this ID during an insertRequest operation, or possibly during a replaceRequest. Application software can override this ID generation by specifying the useClientIds attribute in the request message. Once an ID is assigned, the attribute is read-only and attempts to write it are silently ignored.

/system/schemaMap/@creator (string minOccurs=0 maxOccurs=1)
> This attribute identifies the creator in terms of userId, appId, and platformId of the node.

/system/schemaMap/schema (minOccurs=0 maxOccurs=unbounded)
> This element defines a schema which defines data structures and the shape of information managed by this service. Multiple schema elements exist for each service, one for each logical grouping of information exposed by the service.

/system/schemaMap/schema/@namespace (anyURI minOccurs=0 maxOccurs=1)
> This attribute specifies the namespace URI of this schema.

/system/schemaMap/schema/@schemaLocation (anyURI minOccurs=0 maxOccurs=1)
> This attribute specifies the location (in the form of a URI) of the resource containing schema. When a schema is reachable through a variety of URIs, one schema element will exist for each location.

/system/schemaMap/schema/@alias (string minOccurs=0 maxOccurs=1)
> This attribute specifies the preferred alias that should be used if possible when manipulating information covered by this schema in the context of this service.

/system/schemaMap/schema/*{any}* (minOccurs=0 maxOccurs=unbounded)
/system/wsdlMap (minOccurs=1 maxOccurs=1)
> This element defines the wsdlMap for this service. This map includes the location of WSDL documents, DISCO documents, and WISL documents for this Web service. These documents are used by applications to understand the format of messages that may be sent to the various services.

/system/wsdlMap/@changeNumber (minOccurs=0 maxOccurs=1)
> The changeNumber attribute is designed to facilitate caching of the element and its descendants. This attribute is assigned to this element by the .NET My Services system. The attribute is read-only to applications. Attempts to write this attribute are silently ignored.

/system/wsdlMap/@id (minOccurs=0 maxOccurs=1)
> This attribute is a globally unique ID assigned to this element by .NET My Services. Normally, .NET My Services will generate and assign this ID during an insertRequest operation, or possibly during a replaceRequest. Application software can override this ID generation by specifying the useClientIds attribute in the request message. Once an ID is assigned, the attribute is read-only and attempts to write it are silently ignored.

/system/wsdlMap/@creator (string minOccurs=0 maxOccurs=1)
> This attribute identifies the creator in terms of userId, appId, and platformId of the node.

/system/wsdlMap/wsdl (minOccurs=0 maxOccurs=unbounded)
> This element is used to specify the location of a WSDL file for this service. Multiple entries may exist pointing to the same file hosted in multiple locations, or to variations on the content within the WSDL files.

/system/wsdlMap/wsdl/@wsdlLocation (anyURI minOccurs=0 maxOccurs=1)
> This attribute is a URI that specifies the location of the WSDL file.

/system/wsdlMap/wsdl/*{any}* (minOccurs=0 maxOccurs=unbounded)
/system/wsdlMap/disco (minOccurs=0 maxOccurs=unbounded)
> This element is used to specify the location of a DISCO file for this service. Multiple entries may exist pointing to the same file hosted in multiple locations, or to variations on the content within the DISCO files.

/system/wsdlMap/disco/@discoLocation (anyURI minOccurs=0 maxOccurs=1)
> This attribute is a URI that specifies the location of the DISCO file.

/system/wsdlMap/disco/*{any}* (minOccurs=0 maxOccurs=unbounded)
/system/catDef (minOccurs=0 maxOccurs=unbounded)
> This element encapsulates category definitions global and accessible to all .NET My Services applications. Category references of the form **system**#*name-of-category* may be used to refer to these category definitions.

/system/catDef/@catId (string minOccurs=0 maxOccurs=1)
> This attribute specifies the unique ID of the category in the form of the category name.

/system/catDef/@changeNumber (minOccurs=0 maxOccurs=1)
> The changeNumber attribute is designed to facilitate caching of the element and its descendants. This attribute is assigned to this element by the .NET My Services system. The attribute is read-only to applications. Attempts to write this attribute are silently ignored.

/system/catDef/@id (minOccurs=0 maxOccurs=1)
> This attribute is a globally unique ID assigned to this element by .NET My Services. Normally, .NET My Services will generate and assign this ID during an insertRequest operation, or possibly during a replaceRequest. Application software can override this ID generation by specifying the useClientIds attribute in the request message. Once an ID is assigned, the attribute is read-only and attempts to write it are silently ignored.

/system/catDef/@creator (string minOccurs=0 maxOccurs=1)
> This attribute identifies the creator in terms of userId, appId, and platformId of the node.

/system/catDef/name (string minOccurs=0 maxOccurs=unbounded)
> This element specifies the localized name of the category.

/system/catDef/name/@xml:lang (minOccurs=1 maxOccurs=1)
> This required attribute is used to specify an ISO 639 language code or an ISO 3166 country code as described in RFC 1766. The value of this attribute indicates the language type of the content within this element.

/system/catDef/description (string minOccurs=0 maxOccurs=1)
> This element specifies a full description of the category definition.

/system/catDef/description/@xml:lang (minOccurs=1 maxOccurs=1)
> This required attribute is used to specify an ISO 639 language code or an ISO 3166 country code as described in RFC 1766. The value of this attribute indicates the language type of the content within this element.

/system/catDef/implies (minOccurs=0 maxOccurs=unbounded)
> This element specifies that this category definition also implies that another category (designated by the ref attribute) also applies.

/system/catDef/implies/@ref (anyURI minOccurs=0 maxOccurs=1)
> This attribute references a category definition (<catDef/>) element.

/system/catDef/cat (minOccurs=0 maxOccurs=unbounded)
> This element is used to categorize the element that contains it by referencing a global category definition in either the .NET categories service system document or an external resource containing category definitions, or by referencing an identity-centric category definition in the content document of the .NET categories service for a particular PUID.

/system/catDef/cat/@ref (anyURI minOccurs=0 maxOccurs=1)
> This attribute references a category definition (<catDef/>) element.

/system/catDef/*{any}* (minOccurs=0 maxOccurs=unbounded)
/system/*{any}* (minOccurs=0 maxOccurs=unbounded)

The .NET Categories Service/Methods

The .NET categories service supports the following standard and domain-specific methods:

- query
- insert
- replace
- delete
- update

The standard methods operate on this service using the same message format and method-interchange techniques described in the hsdl section of this document. The only service-specific information to note is the schema that is in effect for each of the methods. These schemas and how they relate to the standard methods and roles are described in the roles section of this document.

The domain-specific methods operate as described in the domain-specific methods section of this document, and are governed by the various schemas outlined in the .NET Categories Service/Roles section for this service.

CHAPTER 13

The .NET my contacts service/Introduction

The .NET my contacts service forms the foundation for an electronic address book, or a set of electronic relationships. This service contains a list of contacts, organized by category. A contact is a simple schema element containing an ID for the contact in the Microsoft .NET My Services ID space, a local name for that contact, a set of categories that the contact belongs to (dl's, groups, classifications, etc.), an address as defined by the .NET address service schema, and a set of profile information as defined by the .NET profile service schema.

Contact information stored within the .NET my contacts service can be derived from the owner's .NET address service and .NET profile service. For example, if Shaun wishes to add Mark as a contact in Shaun's .NET my contacts service, the information used to populate this contact can be queried from Mark's .NET address service and .NET profile service. Mark's access control mechanisms determine how much information from his .NET address service and .NET profile service are allowed to be seen. This ability to query the source of the information at the .NET address service and the .NET profile service is possible only if the user is a .NET My Services customer with a compliant Passport Unique Id (PUID).

The .NET my contacts service is designed to support live contacts. In this mode of operation, the queries described above that are used to populate a contact happen automatically each time a change occurs in a contact's address or profile. This synchronization can be enabled or suppressed on a contact-by-contact basis.

the .NET my contacts service/Roles

The .NET my contacts service controls access by using the following roleTemplates:

- rt0
- rt1
- rt2
- rt3
- rt99

The .NET my contacts service uses the following scopes:

- **scope id 1**

```
<hs:scope id=1>

    <hs:shape base=t>

    </hs:shape>

</hs:scope>
```

- **scope id 2**

```
<hs:scope id=2>

    <hs:shape base=nil>

        <hs:include select=//*[@creator='$callerId']/>

    </hs:shape>

</hs:scope>
```

- **scope id 3**

```
<hs:scope id=3>

    <hs:shape base=nil>

        <hs:include select=//subscription[@creator='$callerId']/>

    </hs:shape>

</hs:scope>
```

- **scope id 4**

```
<hs:scope id=4>

    <hs:shape base=nil>

        <hs:include select=//*[cat/@ref='hs:public']/>

        <hs:include select=//subscription[@creator='$callerId']/>

    </hs:shape>

</hs:scope>
```

The .NET my contacts service roleTemplate rt0

The purpose of this role is to give complete read/write access to all information within the content document of the service being protected through this roleTemplate.

The following table illustrates the available methods and the scope in effect when accessing the .NET my contacts service through that method while mapped to this roleTemplate.

method	scopeRef
query	scopeRef=1
insert	scopeRef=1
replace	scopeRef=1
delete	scopeRef=1
update	scopeRef=1

The .NET my contacts service roleTemplate rt1

The purpose of this role is to give complete read access to all information within the content document of the service being protected through this roleTemplate. Applications mapping to this role also have a limited ability to write to information in the content document. They may create nodes in any location, but may only change/replace or delete nodes that they created.

The following table illustrates the available methods and the scope in effect when accessing the .NET my contacts service through that method while mapped to this roleTemplate.

method	scopeRef
query	scopeRef=1
insert	scopeRef=2
replace	scopeRef=2
delete	scopeRef=2

The .NET my contacts service roleTemplate rt2

The purpose of this role is to give complete read access to all information within the content document of the service being protected through this roleTemplate. Applications mapping to this role have very limited write access and are only able to create and manipulate their own subscription nodes.

The following table illustrates the available methods and the scope in effect when accessing the .NET my contacts service through that method while mapped to this roleTemplate.

method	scopeRef
query	scopeRef=1
insert	scopeRef=3
replace	scopeRef=3
delete	scopeRef=3

The .NET my contacts service roleTemplate rt3

The purpose of this role is to give limited read access to information within the content document that is categorized as "public".

The following table illustrates the available methods and the scope in effect when accessing the .NET my contacts service through that method while mapped to this roleTemplate.

method	scopeRef
query	scopeRef=4

The .NET my contacts service roleTemplate rt99

The purpose of this role is to block all access to the content document. Note that the lack of a role in the roleList has the same effect as assigning someone to rt99.

The .NET my contacts service/content

The content document is an identity-centric document. Its content and meaning is a function of the PUID used to address the service. Access to the document is controlled by the associated roleList document.

This schema outline illustrates the layout and meaning of the information found in the content document for the .NET my contacts service.

```
<m:myContacts changeNumber="..." instanceId="..."
    xmlns:m="http://schemas.microsoft.com/hs/2001/10/myContacts"
    xmlns:mp="http://schemas.microsoft.com/hs/2001/10/myProfile"
    xmlns:mc="http://schemas.microsoft.com/hs/2001/10/myCalendar"
    xmlns:hs="http://schemas.microsoft.com/hs/2001/10/core">1..1
    <m:contact synchronize="..." changeNumber="..." id="..." creator="...">0..unbounded
        <m:cat ref="...">0..unbounded</m:cat>
        <m:name changeNumber="..." id="..." creator="...">0..unbounded
            <mp:cat ref="...">0..unbounded</mp:cat>
            <mp:title xml:lang="...">0..unbounded</mp:title>
```

```
        <mp:givenName xml:lang="...">_{0..unbounded}</mp:givenName>
        <mp:middleName xml:lang="...">_{0..unbounded}</mp:middleName>
        <mp:surName xml:lang="...">_{0..unbounded}</mp:surName>
        <mp:suffix xml:lang="...">_{0..unbounded}</mp:suffix>
        <mp:fileAsName xml:lang="...">_{0..unbounded}</mp:fileAsName>
        {any}
    </m:name>
    <m:puid>_{0..1}</m:puid>
    <m:specialDate calendarType="...">_{0..unbounded}
        <mp:cat ref="...">_{0..unbounded}</mp:cat>
        <mp:date>_{1..1}</mp:date>
        {any}
    </m:specialDate>
    <m:picture>_{0..unbounded}
        <mp:cat ref="...">_{0..unbounded}</mp:cat>
        <mp:url>_{1..1}</mp:url>
        {any}
    </m:picture>
    <m:gender>_{0..1}</m:gender>
    <m:notes xml:lang="...">_{0..1}</m:notes>
    <m:address changeNumber="..." id="..." creator="...">_{0..unbounded}
        <mp:cat ref="...">_{0..unbounded}</mp:cat>
        <mp:officialAddressLine xml:lang="...">_{0..1}</mp:officialAddressLine>
        <mp:internalAddressLine xml:lang="...">_{0..1}</mp:internalAddressLine>
        <mp:primaryCity xml:lang="...">_{0..1}</mp:primaryCity>
        <mp:secondaryCity xml:lang="...">_{0..1}</mp:secondaryCity>
        <mp:subdivision xml:lang="...">_{0..1}</mp:subdivision>
        <mp:postalCode>_{0..1}</mp:postalCode>
        <mp:countryCode>_{0..1}</mp:countryCode>
        <mp:geoLocation>_{0..1}
            <mp:reportingDevice>_{0..1}
                <mp:deviceId>_{0..1}</mp:deviceId>
                <mp:deviceName>_{0..1}</mp:deviceName>
                {any}
            </mp:reportingDevice>
            <mp:latitude>_{0..1}</mp:latitude>
            <mp:longitude>_{0..1}</mp:longitude>
            <mp:elevation>_{0..1}</mp:elevation>
            <mp:confidence>_{0..1}</mp:confidence>
            <mp:precision>_{0..1}</mp:precision>
            {any}
        </mp:geoLocation>
        {any}
    </m:address>
```

(continued)

(continued)

```
    <m:emailAddress changeNumber="..." id="..." creator="...">0..unbounded
        <mp:cat ref="...">0..unbounded</mp:cat>
        <mp:email>1..1</mp:email>
        <mp:name xml:lang="...">0..1</mp:name>
        {any}
    </m:emailAddress>
    <m:webSite changeNumber="..." id="..." creator="...">0..unbounded
        <mp:cat ref="...">0..unbounded</mp:cat>
        <mp:url>1..1</mp:url>
        {any}
    </m:webSite>
    <m:screenName>0..unbounded
        <mp:cat ref="...">0..unbounded</mp:cat>
        <mp:name xml:lang="...">1..1</mp:name>
        {any}
    </m:screenName>
    <m:telephoneNumber changeNumber="..." id="..." creator="...">0..unbounded
        <hs:cat ref="...">0..unbounded</hs:cat>
        <hs:countryCode>0..1</hs:countryCode>
        <hs:nationalCode>1..1</hs:nationalCode>
        <hs:number>1..1</hs:number>
        <hs:numberExtension>0..1</hs:numberExtension>
        <hs:pin>0..1</hs:pin>
        {any}
    </m:telephoneNumber>
    <m:identificationNumber>0..unbounded
        <mp:cat ref="...">0..unbounded</mp:cat>
        <mp:number>1..1</mp:number>
        {any}
    </m:identificationNumber>
    <m:workInformation changeNumber="..." id="..." creator="...">0..unbounded
        <mp:cat ref="...">0..unbounded</mp:cat>
        <mp:profession xml:lang="...">0..1</mp:profession>
        <mp:company>0..unbounded
            <hs:name xml:lang="...">0..1</hs:name>
            <hs:puid>0..1</hs:puid>
            <hs:email>0..1</hs:email>
            <hs:cat ref="...">1..1</hs:cat>
        </mp:company>
```

```
            <mp:department>$_{0..unbounded}$
                <hs:name xml:lang="...">$_{0..1}$</hs:name>
                <hs:puid>$_{0..1}$</hs:puid>
                <hs:email>$_{0..1}$</hs:email>
                <hs:cat ref="...">$_{1..1}$</hs:cat>
            </mp:department>
            <mp:jobTitle xml:lang="...">$_{0..unbounded}$</mp:jobTitle>
            <mp:officeLocation xml:lang="...">$_{0..1}$</mp:officeLocation>
            <mp:manager>$_{0..unbounded}$
                <hs:name xml:lang="...">$_{0..1}$</hs:name>
                <hs:puid>$_{0..1}$</hs:puid>
                <hs:email>$_{0..1}$</hs:email>
                <hs:cat ref="...">$_{1..1}$</hs:cat>
            </mp:manager>
            <mp:assistant>$_{0..unbounded}$
                <hs:name xml:lang="...">$_{0..1}$</hs:name>
                <hs:puid>$_{0..1}$</hs:puid>
                <hs:email>$_{0..1}$</hs:email>
                <hs:cat ref="...">$_{1..1}$</hs:cat>
            </mp:assistant>
            {any}
        </m:workInformation>
        <m:userReference>$_{0..unbounded}$
                <hs:name xml:lang="...">$_{0..1}$</hs:name>
                <hs:puid>$_{0..1}$</hs:puid>
                <hs:email>$_{0..1}$</hs:email>
                <hs:cat ref="...">$_{1..1}$</hs:cat>
        </m:userReference>
        <m:securityCertificate>$_{0..unbounded}$
                <mp:cat ref="...">$_{0..unbounded}$</mp:cat>
                <mp:certificate>$_{1..1}$</mp:certificate>
        </m:securityCertificate>
        {any}
    </m:contact>
    <m:subscription changeNumber="..." id="..." creator="...">$_{0..unbounded}$
        <hs:trigger select="..." mode="..."
baseChangeNumber="...">$_{1..1}$</hs:trigger>
        <hs:expiresAt>$_{0..1}$</hs:expiresAt>
        <hs:context uri="...">$_{1..1}$ {any}</hs:context>
        <hs:to>$_{1..1}$</hs:to>
    </m:subscription>
    {any}
</m:myContacts>
```

The meaning of the attributes and elements shown in the preceding sample document fragment are listed in the following section.

/myContacts (minOccurs=1 maxOccurs=1)

This element encapsulates the content document for this service. This element establishes a global cache scope for the service and contains other root-level system attributes for this instance of the service.

/myContacts/@changeNumber (minOccurs=0 maxOccurs=1)

The changeNumber attribute is designed to facilitate caching of the element and its descendants. This attribute is assigned to this element by the .NET My Services system. The attribute is read-only to applications. Attempts to write this attribute are silently ignored.

/myContacts/@instanceId (string minOccurs=0 maxOccurs=1)

This attribute is a unique identifier typically assigned to the root element of a service. It is a read-only element and assigned by the .NET My Services system when a user is provisioned for a particular service.

/myContacts/contact (minOccurs=0 maxOccurs=unbounded)

This element represents a contact.

/myContacts/contact/@synchronize (string minOccurs=0 maxOccurs=1)

This attribute controls/enables synchronization of this contact node. When this attribute is enabled (set to a value of "yes"), .NET My Services will attempt to keep the contact nodes in sync with the reference data stored in the referenced PUID's myProfile default store. This is subject to permission, of course. A value of "no" indicates that the system should not attempt to keep this contact node in sync.

/myContacts/contact/@changeNumber (minOccurs=0 maxOccurs=1)

The changeNumber attribute is designed to facilitate caching of the element and its descendants. This attribute is assigned to this element by the .NET My Services system. The attribute is read-only to applications. Attempts to write this attribute are silently ignored.

/myContacts/contact/@id (minOccurs=0 maxOccurs=1)

This attribute is a globally unique ID assigned to this element by .NET My Services. Normally, .NET My Services will generate and assign this ID during an insertRequest operation, or possibly during a replaceRequest. Application software can override this ID generation by specifying the useClientIds attribute in the request message. Once an ID is assigned, the attribute is read-only and attempts to write it are silently ignored.

/myContacts/contact/@creator (string minOccurs=0 maxOccurs=1)

This attribute identifies the creator in terms of userId, appId, and platformId of the node.

/myContacts/contact/cat (minOccurs=0 maxOccurs=unbounded)

This element is used to categorize the element that contains it by referencing a global category definition in either the myCategories service system document or an external resource containing category definitions, or by referencing an identity-centric category definition in the content document of the myCategories service for a particular PUID.

/myContacts/contact/cat/@ref (anyURI minOccurs=0 maxOccurs=1)

This attribute references a category definition (<catDef/>) element using the rules outlined in the myCategories XMI manual.

/myContacts/contact/name (minOccurs=0 maxOccurs=unbounded)

This element encapsulates a name associated with the identity. An identity can have multiple names associated with it. These name nodes are not intended to be used for storing screen names or other electronic names, but rather to store a commonly used name for the entity. Names contain five parts and are meant to be combined in proper order, with spaces separating the parts and empty content parts excluded.

/myContacts/contact/name/@changeNumber (minOccurs=0 maxOccurs=1)

The changeNumber attribute is designed to facilitate caching of the element and its descendants. This attribute is assigned to this element by the .NET My Services system. The attribute is read-only to applications. Attempts to write this attribute are silently ignored.

/myContacts/contact/name/@id (minOccurs=0 maxOccurs=1)

This attribute is a globally unique ID assigned to this element by .NET My Services. Normally, .NET My Services will generate and assign this ID during an insertRequest operation, or possibly during a replaceRequest. Application software can override this ID generation by specifying the useClientIds attribute in the request message. Once an ID is assigned, the attribute is read-only and attempts to write it are silently ignored.

/myContacts/contact/name/@creator (string minOccurs=0 maxOccurs=1)

This attribute identifies the creator in terms of userId, appId, and platformId of the node.

/myContacts/contact/name/cat (minOccurs=0 maxOccurs=unbounded)

This element is used to categorize the element that contains it by referencing a global category definition in either the myCategories service system document or an external resource containing category definitions, or by referencing an identity-centric category definition in the content document of the myCategories service for a particular PUID.

/myContacts/contact/name/cat/@ref (anyURI minOccurs=0 maxOccurs=1)

This attribute references a category definition (<catDef/>) element using the rules outlined in the myCategories XMI manual

/myContacts/contact/name/title (string minOccurs=0 maxOccurs=unbounded)

This optional element is designed to store a title or prefix associated with the name. Examples are 'Mr.', 'Mrs.', 'Dr.', or any other commonly used names, titles, or prefixes.

/myContacts/contact/name/title/@xml:lang (minOccurs=1 maxOccurs=1)

This required attribute is used to specify an ISO 639 language code or an ISO 3166 country code as described in RFC 1766. The value of this attribute indicates the language type of the content within this element.

/myContacts/contact/name/givenName (string minOccurs=0 maxOccurs=unbounded)

This optional element is meant to store the first portion of a name.

/myContacts/contact/name/givenName/@xml:lang (minOccurs=1 maxOccurs=1)
This required attribute is used to specify an ISO 639 language code or an ISO 3166 country code as described in RFC 1766. The value of this attribute indicates the language type of the content within this element.

/myContacts/contact/name/middleName (string minOccurs=0 maxOccurs=unbounded)
This optional element is meant to store the middle portion or initial of a name.

/myContacts/contact/name/middleName/@xml:lang (minOccurs=1 maxOccurs=1)
This required attribute is used to specify an ISO 639 language code or an ISO 3166 country code as described in RFC 1766. The value of this attribute indicates the language type of the content within this element.

/myContacts/contact/name/surName (string minOccurs=0 maxOccurs=unbounded)
This optional element is meant to store the last portion of a name.

/myContacts/contact/name/surName/@xml:lang (minOccurs=1 maxOccurs=1)
This required attribute is used to specify an ISO 639 language code or an ISO 3166 country code as described in RFC 1766. The value of this attribute indicates the language type of the content within this element.

/myContacts/contact/name/suffix (string minOccurs=0 maxOccurs=unbounded)
This optional element is designed to store a suffix associated with the name. Examples include 'Jr.', 'Sr.', 'III', or any other commonly used name suffix.

/myContacts/contact/name/suffix/@xml:lang (minOccurs=1 maxOccurs=1)
This required attribute is used to specify an ISO 639 language code or an ISO 3166 country code as described in RFC 1766. The value of this attribute indicates the language type of the content within this element.

/myContacts/contact/name/fileAsName (string minOccurs=0 maxOccurs=unbounded)
A complete name is usually the combination of title, givenName, middleName, surName, and suffix. This optional element is present to indicate that a different order should be used or that the identity prefers to have the name filed differently.

/myContacts/contact/name/fileAsName/@xml:lang (minOccurs=1 maxOccurs=1)
This required attribute is used to specify an ISO 639 language code or an ISO 3166 country code as described in RFC 1766. The value of this attribute indicates the language type of the content within this element.

/myContacts/contact/name/*{any}* (minOccurs=0 maxOccurs=unbounded)
/myContacts/contact/puid (string minOccurs=0 maxOccurs=1)
This element is used to specify a Passport Unique ID (PUID). The ID itself is in raw form, it is not encrypted in any way.

/myContacts/contact/specialDate (minOccurs=0 maxOccurs=unbounded)
This element encapsulates a special date that is important to this entity. Multiple special date nodes may exist. This is not a substitute for dates stored on an entity's myCalendar service. The main purpose is to provide a convenient place to store a birth date or an anniversary date, because these dates are frequently imported into a contact record.

/myContacts/contact/specialDate/@calendarType (string minOccurs=0 maxOccurs=1)
This field identifies an enumeration which determines the kind of calendar event this is. *.NET My Services v1 will only support CAL_GREGORIAN_US.*

Value	Enumeration Constant	Description
−1	HSCAL_ALL_CALENDARS	Unknown Calendar; system default (HSCAL_GREGORIAN_US)
1	HSCAL_GREGORIAN	Gregorian (localized) calendar
2	HSCAL_GREGORIAN_US	Gregorian (U.S.) calendar
3	HSCAL_JAPAN	Japanese Emperor Era calendar
4	HSCAL_TAIWAN	Taiwan Era calendar
5	HSCAL_KOREA	Korean Tangun Era calendar
6	HSCAL_HIJRI	Hijri (Arabic Lunar) calendar
7	HSCAL_THAI	Thai calendar
8	HSCAL_HEBREW	Hebrew (Lunar) calendar
9	HSCAL_GREGORIAN_ME_FRENCH	Gregorian Middle East French calendar
10	HSCAL_GREGORIAN_ARABIC	Gregorian Arabic calendar
11	HSCAL_GREGORIAN_XLIT_ENGLISH	Gregorian Transliterated English calendar
12	HSCAL_GREGORIAN_XLIT_FRENCH	Gregorian Transliterated French calendar
13	HSCAL_KOREA_LUNAR	Default Korea Lunar calendar (implementation identical to 14)
14	HSCAL_JAPAN_LUNAR	Default Japanese Lunar calendar (implementation identical to 13)
15	HSCAL_CHINESE_LUNAR	Chinese Lunar calendar
16	HSCAL_SAKA	Indian Saka calendar
17	HSCAL_LUNAR_ETO_CHN	Chinese Zodiac calendar
18	HSCAL_LUNAR_ETO_KOR	Korean Zodiac calendar
19	HSCAL_LUNAR_ROKUYOU	Japanese Lucky days calendar

/myContacts/contact/specialDate/cat (minOccurs=0 maxOccurs=unbounded)
This element is used to categorize the element that contains it by referencing a global category definition in either the .NET categories service system document or an external resource containing category definitions, or by referencing an identity-centric category definition in the content document of the .NET categories service for a particular PUID.

/myContacts/contact/specialDate/cat/@ref (anyURI minOccurs=0 maxOccurs=1)
    This attribute references a category definition (<catDef/>) element using the rules
    outlined in the .NET categories service XMI manual.

/myContacts/contact/specialDate/date (dateTime minOccurs=1 maxOccurs=1)
    The special date. hour, minute, and seconds are ignored.

/myContacts/contact/specialDate/*{any}* (minOccurs=0 maxOccurs=unbounded)
/myContacts/contact/picture (minOccurs=0 maxOccurs=unbounded)
    This optional element encapsulates a URL that points to a picture of the identity.

/myContacts/contact/picture/cat (minOccurs=0 maxOccurs=unbounded)
    This element is used to categorize the element that contains it by referencing a global
    category definition in either the myCategories service system document or an external
    resource containing category definitions, or by referencing an identity-centric category
    definition in the content document of the myCategories service for a particular PUID.

/myContacts/contact/picture/cat/@ref (anyURI minOccurs=0 maxOccurs=1)
    This attribute references a category definition (<catDef/>) element using the rules
    outlined in the .NET categories service XMI manual

/myContacts/contact/picture/url (string minOccurs=1 maxOccurs=1)
    This element contains the URL that points to the actual picture.

/myContacts/contact/picture/*{any}* (minOccurs=0 maxOccurs=unbounded)
/myContacts/contact/gender (string minOccurs=0 maxOccurs=1)
    This element specifies the gender for this entity. There can only be a single gender
    associated with an entity. The format of this element is a single, 7-bit ASCII character
    with one of two possible values: 'm' for male, and 'f' for female.

/myContacts/contact/notes (string minOccurs=0 maxOccurs=1)
    This element contains free-form notes related to this contact.

/myContacts/contact/notes/@xml:lang (minOccurs=1 maxOccurs=1)
    This required attribute is used to specify an ISO 639 language code or an ISO 3166
    country code as described in RFC 1766. The value of this attribute indicates the
    language type of the content within this element.

/myContacts/contact/address (minOccurs=0 maxOccurs=unbounded)
    This element encapsulates a geographic address. The contained nodes describe the
    geographic address in detail. This element may be repeated any number of times.
    Typical use is one address element for each geographical address for this identity.
    For instance, a user with a primary home and a vacation home might have two
    address elements in this service.

/myContacts/contact/address/@changeNumber (minOccurs=0 maxOccurs=1)
    The changeNumber attribute is designed to facilitate caching of the element and its
    descendants. This attribute is assigned to this element by the .NET My Services
    system. The attribute is read-only to applications. Attempts to write this attribute are
    silently ignored.

/myContacts/contact/address/@id (minOccurs=0 maxOccurs=1)

This attribute is a globally unique ID assigned to this element by .NET My Services. Normally, .NET My Services will generate and assign this ID during an insertRequest operation, or possibly during a replaceRequest. Application software can override this ID generation by specifying the useClientIds attribute in the request message. Once an ID is assigned, the attribute is read-only and attempts to write it are silently ignored.

/myContacts/contact/address/@creator (string minOccurs=0 maxOccurs=1)

This attribute identifies the creator in terms of userId, appId, and platformId of the node.

/myContacts/contact/address/cat (minOccurs=0 maxOccurs=unbounded)

This element is used to categorize the element that contains it by referencing a global category definition in either the myCategories service system document or an external resource containing category definitions, or by referencing an identity-centric category definition in the content document of the myCategories service for a particular PUID.

/myContacts/contact/address/cat/@ref (anyURI minOccurs=0 maxOccurs=1)

This attribute references a category definition (<catDef/>) element using the rules outlined in the .NET categories service XMI manual

/myContacts/contact/address/officialAddressLine (string minOccurs=0 maxOccurs=1)

This element contains the most precise, official line for the address relative to the postal agency servicing the area specified by the city(s)/postalCode. When parsing an address for official postal usage, this element contains the official, parsable address line that the regional postal system cares about. Typical usage of this element would be to enclose a street address, post office box address, private bag, or any other similar official address. Internal routing information like department name, suite number within a building, internal mailstop number, or similar properties should be placed within the internalAddressLine element.

/myContacts/contact/address/officialAddressLine/@xml:lang (minOccurs=1 maxOccurs=1)

This required attribute is used to specify an ISO 639 language code or an ISO 3166 country code as described in RFC 1766. The value of this attribute indicates the language type of the content within this element.

/myContacts/contact/address/internalAddressLine (string minOccurs=0 maxOccurs=1)

This element contains internal routing information relative to the address specified by the officialAddressLine. Items like department name, suite number within a building, internal mailstop number, or similar properties should be placed within this element.

/myContacts/contact/address/internalAddressLine/@xml:lang (minOccurs=1 maxOccurs=1)

This required attribute is used to specify an ISO 639 language code or an ISO 3166 country code as described in RFC 1766. The value of this attribute indicates the language type of the content within this element.

/myContacts/contact/address/primaryCity (string minOccurs=0 maxOccurs=1)

This element defines the primary city for this address.

/myContacts/contact/address/primaryCity/@xml:lang (minOccurs=1 maxOccurs=1)
This required attribute is used to specify an ISO 639 language code or an ISO 3166 country code as described in RFC 1766. The value of this attribute indicates the language type of the content within this element.

/myContacts/contact/address/secondaryCity (string minOccurs=0 maxOccurs=1)
This optional element defines the secondary city for this address. Example types for this element include city district, city wards, postal towns, etc.

/myContacts/contact/address/secondaryCity/@xml:lang (minOccurs=1 maxOccurs=1)
This required attribute is used to specify an ISO 639 language code or an ISO 3166 country code as described in RFC 1766. The value of this attribute indicates the language type of the content within this element.

/myContacts/contact/address/subdivision (string minOccurs=0 maxOccurs=1)
This element contains the official subdivision name within the country or region for this address. In the United States, this element would contain the two letter abbreviation for the name of the state. This element is also commonly treated as the "first order admin subdivision" and will typically contain subdivision names referring to:

- administrative division
- Bundesstaat
- canton
- federal district
- province
- region
- state
- territory

/myContacts/contact/address/subdivision/@xml:lang (minOccurs=1 maxOccurs=1)
This required attribute is used to specify an ISO 639 language code or an ISO 3166 country code as described in RFC 1766. The value of this attribute indicates the language type of the content within this element.

/myContacts/contact/address/postalCode (string minOccurs=0 maxOccurs=1)
This element contains the official postal code for this address.

/myContacts/contact/address/countryCode (string minOccurs=0 maxOccurs=1)
This element contains the 2 letter ISO-3166 ID of the country, dependency, or functionally equivalent region for this address.

/myContacts/contact/address/geoLocation (minOccurs=0 maxOccurs=1)
This element encapsulates a geographic, or earth, position corresponding to the enclosing address.

/myContacts/contact/address/geoLocation/reportingDevice (minOccurs=0 maxOccurs=1)
This element contains the UUID and name for this specific device. The UUID for a specific device is the same as the "Universal Device Number" as exposed by the Universal Plug and Play infrastructure.

/myContacts/contact/address/geoLocation/reportingDevice/deviceId (minOccurs=0 maxOccurs=1)
> This element specifies UUID or Universal Device Number for this device.

/myContacts/contact/address/geoLocation/reportingDevice/deviceName (string minOccurs=0 maxOccurs=1)
> This element specifies a friendly name for this device.

/myContacts/contact/address/geoLocation/reportingDevice/*{any}* (minOccurs=0 maxOccurs=unbounded)

/myContacts/contact/address/geoLocation/latitude (string minOccurs=0 maxOccurs=1)
> This element specifies the latitude value for this geoLocation in units of decimal degrees. Geodetic datum WGS84 is required.

/myContacts/contact/address/geoLocation/longitude (string minOccurs=0 maxOccurs=1)
> This element specifies the longitude value for this geoLocation in units of decimal degrees. Geodetic datum WGS84 is required.

/myContacts/contact/address/geoLocation/elevation (string minOccurs=0 maxOccurs=1)
> This element specifies the elevation above sea level with respect to WGS84 geodetic datum. The unit for this value is the meter.

/myContacts/contact/address/geoLocation/confidence (string minOccurs=0 maxOccurs=1)
> This element specifies a percentage value that indicates the confidence value that this location is accurate within the specified precision.

/myContacts/contact/address/geoLocation/precision (string minOccurs=0 maxOccurs=1)
> This element specifies the precision in meters of this location. The value defines a spherical zone that the location falls within.

/myContacts/contact/address/geoLocation/*{any}* (minOccurs=0 maxOccurs=unbounded)
/myContacts/contact/address/*{any}* (minOccurs=0 maxOccurs=unbounded)

/myContacts/contact/emailAddress (minOccurs=0 maxOccurs=unbounded)
> This element encapsulates an electronic address for this entity, specifically, it contains an email address associated with this identity. This element may be repeated any number of times. Typical use is one emailAddress element for each email address associated with this identity.

/myContacts/contact/emailAddress/@changeNumber (minOccurs=0 maxOccurs=1)
> The changeNumber attribute is designed to facilitate caching of the element and its descendants. This attribute is assigned to this element by the .NET My Services system. The attribute is read-only to applications. Attempts to write this attribute are silently ignored.

/myContacts/contact/emailAddress/@id (minOccurs=0 maxOccurs=1)
> This attribute is a globally unique ID assigned to this element by .NET My Services. Normally, .NET My Services will generate and assign this ID during an insertRequest operation, or possibly during a replaceRequest. Application software can override this ID generation by specifying the useClientIds attribute in the request message. Once an ID is assigned, the attribute is read-only and attempts to write it are silently ignored.

/myContacts/contact/emailAddress/@creator (string minOccurs=0 maxOccurs=1)
This attribute identifies the creator in terms of userId, appId, and platformId of the node.

/myContacts/contact/emailAddress/cat (minOccurs=0 maxOccurs=unbounded)
This element is used to categorize the element that contains it by referencing a global category definition in either the myCategories service system document or an external resource containing category definitions, or by referencing an identity-centric category definition in the content document of the myCategories service for a particular PUID.

/myContacts/contact/emailAddress/cat/@ref (anyURI minOccurs=0 maxOccurs=1)
This attribute references a category definition (<catDef/>) element using the rules outlined in the .NET categories service XMI manual.

/myContacts/contact/emailAddress/email (string minOccurs=1 maxOccurs=1)
This element contains the actual value of the email address (e.g. someone@microsoft.com).

/myContacts/contact/emailAddress/name (string minOccurs=0 maxOccurs=1)
This element contains the friendly name, or display name, associated with this email address.

/myContacts/contact/emailAddress/name/@xml:lang (minOccurs=1 maxOccurs=1)
This required attribute is used to specify an ISO 639 language code or an ISO 3166 country code as described in RFC 1766. The value of this attribute indicates the language type of the content within this element.

/myContacts/contact/emailAddress/{any} (minOccurs=0 maxOccurs=unbounded)
/myContacts/contact/webSite (minOccurs=0 maxOccurs=unbounded)
This element encapsulates an electronic address for this entity, specifically, it contains a Web site or URL associated with this identity. This element may be repeated any number of times. Typical use is one Web site element for each Web site associated with this identity.

/myContacts/contact/webSite/@changeNumber (minOccurs=0 maxOccurs=1)
The changeNumber attribute is designed to facilitate caching of the element and its descendants. This attribute is assigned to this element by the .NET My Services system. The attribute is read-only to applications. Attempts to write this attribute are silently ignored.

/myContacts/contact/webSite/@id (minOccurs=0 maxOccurs=1)
This attribute is a globally unique ID assigned to this element by .NET My Services. Normally, .NET My Services will generate and assign this ID during an insertRequest operation, or possibly during a replaceRequest. Application software can override this ID generation by specifying the useClientIds attribute in the request message. Once an ID is assigned, the attribute is read-only and attempts to write it are silently ignored.

/myContacts/contact/webSite/@creator (string minOccurs=0 maxOccurs=1)
This attribute identifies the creator in terms of userId, appId, and platformId of the node.

/myContacts/contact/webSite/cat (minOccurs=0 maxOccurs=unbounded)
> This element is used to categorize the element that contains it by referencing a global category definition in either the myCategories service system document or an external resource containing category definitions, or by referencing an identity-centric category definition in the content document of the myCategories service for a particular PUID.

/myContacts/contact/webSite/cat/@ref (anyURI minOccurs=0 maxOccurs=1)
> This attribute references a category definition (<catDef/>) element using the rules outlined in the .NET categories service XMI manual.

/myContacts/contact/webSite/url (string minOccurs=1 maxOccurs=1)
> This element contains the URL for this Web site. If the site is accessible through multiple URLs, this element may be repeated an appropriate number of times.

/myContacts/contact/webSite/*{any}* (minOccurs=0 maxOccurs=unbounded)

/myContacts/contact/screenName (minOccurs=0 maxOccurs=unbounded)
> This element encapsulates an electronic address for this entity, specifically, it contains a screen name commonly used in real time communications applications like instant messaging applications, chat rooms, etc. This element may be repeated any number of times, and the type attribute may be used for simple classifications on the screenName.

/myContacts/contact/screenName/cat (minOccurs=0 maxOccurs=unbounded)
> This element is used to categorize the element that contains it by referencing a global category definition in either the myCategories service system document or an external resource containing category definitions, or by referencing an identity-centric category definition in the content document of the .NET categories service for a particular PUID.

/myContacts/contact/screenName/cat/@ref (anyURI minOccurs=0 maxOccurs=1)
> This attribute references a category definition (<catDef/>) element using the rules outlined in the .NET categories service XMI manual.

/myContacts/contact/screenName/name (string minOccurs=1 maxOccurs=1)
> This element contains the value of the screen name.

/myContacts/contact/screenName/name/@xml:lang (minOccurs=1 maxOccurs=1)
> This required attribute is used to specify an ISO 639 language code or an ISO 3166 country code as described in RFC 1766. The value of this attribute indicates the language type of the content within this element.

/myContacts/contact/screenName/*{any}* (minOccurs=0 maxOccurs=unbounded)

/myContacts/contact/telephoneNumber (minOccurs=0 maxOccurs=unbounded)
> This element encapsulates an electronic address for this entity, specifically, it contains a telephone number. This element may be repeated any number of times. Typical use is one telephoneNumber element for each phone number associated with this identity.
>
> A telephone number consists of an optional country code, a required nationalCode (US area code), a number, an optional extension, and a optional PIN.

/myContacts/contact/telephoneNumber/@changeNumber (minOccurs=0 maxOccurs=1)
The changeNumber attribute is designed to facilitate caching of the element and its descendants. This attribute is assigned to this element by the .NET My Services system. The attribute is read-only to applications. Attempts to write this attribute are silently ignored.

/myContacts/contact/telephoneNumber/@id (minOccurs=0 maxOccurs=1)
This attribute is a globally unique ID assigned to this element by .NET My Services. Normally, .NET My Services will generate and assign this ID during an insertRequest operation, or possibly during a replaceRequest. Application software can override this ID generation by specifying the useClientIds attribute in the request message. Once an ID is assigned, the attribute is read-only and attempts to write it are silently ignored.

/myContacts/contact/telephoneNumber/@creator (string minOccurs=0 maxOccurs=1)
This attribute identifies the creator in terms of userId, appId, and platformId of the node.

/myContacts/contact/telephoneNumber/cat (minOccurs=0 maxOccurs=unbounded)
This element is used to categorize the element that contains it by referencing a global category definition in either the .NET categories service system document or an external resource containing category definitions, or by referencing an identity-centric category definition in the content document of the .NET categories service for a particular PUID.

/myContacts/contact/telephoneNumber/cat/@ref (anyURI minOccurs=0 maxOccurs=1)
This attribute references a category definition (<catDef/>) element using the rules outlined in the .NET categories service XMI manual.

/myContacts/contact/telephoneNumber/countryCode (string minOccurs=0 maxOccurs=1)
This optional element specifies the country code for this telephone number.

/myContacts/contact/telephoneNumber/nationalCode (string minOccurs=1 maxOccurs=1)
This element specifies the national code for this phone number. For US telephone numbers, this is equivalent to the area code.

/myContacts/contact/telephoneNumber/number (string minOccurs=1 maxOccurs=1)
This element specifies the actual telephone number within the country and national code number scheme.

/myContacts/contact/telephoneNumber/numberExtension (string minOccurs=0 maxOccurs=1)
This optional element specifies an extension used to reach this identity and this number.

/myContacts/contact/telephoneNumber/pin (string minOccurs=0 maxOccurs=1)
This optional element specifies a PIN number used on this phone number. A PIN is similar to an extension, but PINs are commonly used to address pagers while extensions are typically used to address phones relative to a local pbx.

/myContacts/contact/telephoneNumber/*{any}* (minOccurs=0 maxOccurs=unbounded)

/myContacts/contact/identificationNumber (minOccurs=0 maxOccurs=unbounded)
This optional element encapsulates an identification number for the entity. Things like an employee ID number, social security number, national ID number, driver's license number, and so on, may be stored within this element.

/myContacts/contact/identificationNumber/cat (minOccurs=0 maxOccurs=unbounded)
This element is used to categorize the element that contains it by referencing a global category definition in either the .NET categories service system document or an external resource containing category definitions, or by referencing an identity-centric category definition in the content document of the .NET categories service for a particular PUID.

/myContacts/contact/identificationNumber/cat/@ref (anyURI minOccurs=0 maxOccurs=1)
This attribute references a category definition (<catDef/>) element using the rules outlined in the .NET categories service XMI manual.

/myContacts/contact/identificationNumber/number (string minOccurs=1 maxOccurs=1)
This element contains the actual identification number value.

/myContacts/contact/identificationNumber/*{any}* (minOccurs=0 maxOccurs=unbounded)
/myContacts/contact/workInformation (minOccurs=0 maxOccurs=unbounded)
This element encapsulates work or occupation-related information for this entity.

/myContacts/contact/workInformation/@changeNumber (minOccurs=0 maxOccurs=1)
The changeNumber attribute is designed to facilitate caching of the element and its descendants. This attribute is assigned to this element by the .NET My Services system. The attribute is read-only to applications. Attempts to write this attribute are silently ignored.

/myContacts/contact/workInformation/@id (minOccurs=0 maxOccurs=1)
This attribute is a globally unique ID assigned to this element by .NET My Services. Normally, .NET My Services will generate and assign this ID during an insertRequest operation, or possibly during a replaceRequest. Application software can override this ID generation by specifying the useClientIds attribute in the request message. Once an ID is assigned, the attribute is read-only and attempts to write it are silently ignored.

/myContacts/contact/workInformation/@creator (string minOccurs=0 maxOccurs=1)
This attribute identifies the creator in terms of userId, appId, and platformId of the node.

/myContacts/contact/workInformation/cat (minOccurs=0 maxOccurs=unbounded)
This element is used to categorize the element that contains it by referencing a global category definition in either the .NET categories service system document or an external resource containing category definitions, or by referencing an identity-centric category definition in the content document of the .NET categories service for a particular PUID.

/myContacts/contact/workInformation/cat/@ref (anyURI minOccurs=0 maxOccurs=1)
This attribute references a category definition (<catDef/>) element using the rules outlined in the .NET categories service XMI manual.

/myContacts/contact/workInformation/profession (string minOccurs=0 maxOccurs=1)
This optional element specifies the entity's profession within this particular workInformation element.

/myContacts/contact/workInformation/profession/@xml:lang (minOccurs=1 maxOccurs=1)
This required attribute is used to specify an ISO 639 language code or an ISO 3166 country code as described in RFC 1766. The value of this attribute indicates the language type of the content within this element.

/myContacts/contact/workInformation/company (minOccurs=0 maxOccurs=unbounded)
This element encapsulates the company information for this entity, including its name and its PUID. Using this anchor information, additional details may be obtained.

/myContacts/contact/workInformation/company/name (string minOccurs=0 maxOccurs=1)
This optional element specifies the name for the enclosing element.

/myContacts/contact/workInformation/company/name/@xml:lang (minOccurs=1 maxOccurs=1)
This required attribute is used to specify an ISO 639 language code or an ISO 3166 country code as described in RFC 1766. The value of this attribute indicates the language type of the content within this element.

/myContacts/contact/workInformation/company/puid (string minOccurs=0 maxOccurs=1)
This optional element specifies the name for the enclosing element.

/myContacts/contact/workInformation/company/email (string minOccurs=0 maxOccurs=1)
This optional name specifies an email address for the enclosing element.

/myContacts/contact/workInformation/company/cat (minOccurs=1 maxOccurs=1)
This element is used to categorize the element that contains it by referencing a global category definition in either the .NET categories service system document or an external resource containing category definitions, or by referencing an identity-centric category definition in the content document of the .NET categories service for a particular PUID.

/myContacts/contact/workInformation/company/cat/@ref (anyURI minOccurs=0 maxOccurs=1)
This attribute references a category definition (<catDef/>) element using the rules outlined in the .NET categories service XMI manual.

/myContacts/contact/workInformation/department (minOccurs=0 maxOccurs=unbounded)
This element encapsulates the department information for this entity including its name, and its PUID. Using this anchor information, additional details may be obtained.

/myContacts/contact/workInformation/department/name (string minOccurs=0 maxOccurs=1)
This optional element specifies the name for the enclosing element.

/myContacts/contact/workInformation/department/name/@xml:lang (minOccurs=1 maxOccurs=1)

> This required attribute is used to specify an ISO 639 language code or an ISO 3166 country code as described in RFC 1766. The value of this attribute indicates the language type of the content within this element.

/myContacts/contact/workInformation/department/puid (string minOccurs=0 maxOccurs=1)

> This optional element specifies the name for the enclosing element.

/myContacts/contact/workInformation/department/email (string minOccurs=0 maxOccurs=1)

> This optional name specifies an email address for the enclosing element.

/myContacts/contact/workInformation/department/cat (minOccurs=1 maxOccurs=1)

> This element is used to categorize the element that contains it by referencing a global category definition in either the .NET categories service system document or an external resource containing category definitions, or by referencing an identity-centric category definition in the content document of the .NET categories service for a particular PUID.

/myContacts/contact/workInformation/department/cat/@ref (anyURI minOccurs=0 maxOccurs=1)

> This attribute references a category definition (<catDef/>) element using the rules outlined in the .NET categories service XMI manual.

/myContacts/contact/workInformation/jobTitle (string minOccurs=0 maxOccurs=unbounded)

> This element specifies the job title for this piece of work information.

/myContacts/contact/workInformation/jobTitle/@xml:lang (minOccurs=1 maxOccurs=1)

> This required attribute is used to specify an ISO 639 language code or an ISO 3166 country code as described in RFC 1766. The value of this attribute indicates the language type of the content within this element.

/myContacts/contact/workInformation/officeLocation (string minOccurs=0 maxOccurs=1)

> This element specifies the office location for this piece of work information.

/myContacts/contact/workInformation/officeLocation/@xml:lang (minOccurs=1 maxOccurs=1)

> This required attribute is used to specify an ISO 639 language code or an ISO 3166 country code as described in RFC 1766. The value of this attribute indicates the language type of the content within this element.

/myContacts/contact/workInformation/manager (minOccurs=0 maxOccurs=unbounded)

> This element encapsulates the manager information for this entity, including its name and its PUID. Using this anchor information, additional details may be obtained.

/myContacts/contact/workInformation/manager/name (string minOccurs=0 maxOccurs=1)

> This optional element specifies the name for the enclosing element.

/myContacts/contact/workInformation/manager/name/@xml:lang (minOccurs=1 maxOccurs=1)

This required attribute is used to specify an ISO 639 language code or an ISO 3166 country code as described in RFC 1766. The value of this attribute indicates the language type of the content within this element.

/myContacts/contact/workInformation/manager/puid (string minOccurs=0 maxOccurs=1)

This optional element specifies the name for the enclosing element.

/myContacts/contact/workInformation/manager/email (string minOccurs=0 maxOccurs=1)

This optional name specifies an email address for the enclosing element.

/myContacts/contact/workInformation/manager/cat (minOccurs=1 maxOccurs=1)

This element is used to categorize the element that contains it by referencing a global category definition in either the .NET categories service system document or an external resource containing category definitions, or by referencing an identity-centric category definition in the content document of the .NET categories service for a particular PUID.

/myContacts/contact/workInformation/manager/cat/@ref (anyURI minOccurs=0 maxOccurs=1)

This attribute references a category definition (<catDef/>) element using the rules outlined in the .NET categories service XMI manual.

/myContacts/contact/workInformation/assistant (minOccurs=0 maxOccurs=unbounded)

This element encapsulates the assistant information for this entity, including its name and its PUID. Using this anchor information, additional details may be obtained.

/myContacts/contact/workInformation/assistant/name (string minOccurs=0 maxOccurs=1)

This optional element specifies the name for the enclosing element.

/myContacts/contact/workInformation/assistant/name/@xml:lang (minOccurs=1 maxOccurs=1)

This required attribute is used to specify an ISO 639 language code or an ISO 3166 country code as described in RFC 1766. The value of this attribute indicates the language type of the content within this element.

/myContacts/contact/workInformation/assistant/puid (string minOccurs=0 maxOccurs=1)

This optional element specifies the name for the enclosing element.

/myContacts/contact/workInformation/assistant/email (string minOccurs=0 maxOccurs=1)

This optional name specifies an email address for the enclosing element.

/myContacts/contact/workInformation/assistant/cat (minOccurs=1 maxOccurs=1)

This element is used to categorize the element that contains it by referencing a global category definition in either the .NET categories service system document or an external resource containing category definitions, or by referencing an identity-centric category definition in the content document of the .NET categories service for a particular PUID.

/myContacts/contact/workInformation/assistant/cat/@ref (anyURI minOccurs=0 maxOccurs=1)
> This attribute references a category definition (<catDef/>) element using the rules outlined in the .NET categories service XMI manual.

/myContacts/contact/workInformation/*{any}* (minOccurs=0 maxOccurs=unbounded)
/myContacts/contact/userReference (minOccurs=0 maxOccurs=unbounded)
/myContacts/contact/userReference/name (string minOccurs=0 maxOccurs=1)
> This optional element specifies the name for the enclosing element.

/myContacts/contact/userReference/name/@xml:lang (minOccurs=1 maxOccurs=1)
> This required attribute is used to specify an ISO 639 language code or an ISO 3166 country code as described in RFC 1766. The value of this attribute indicates the language type of the content within this element.

/myContacts/contact/userReference/puid (string minOccurs=0 maxOccurs=1)
> This optional element specifies the name for the enclosing element.

/myContacts/contact/userReference/email (string minOccurs=0 maxOccurs=1)
> This optional name specifies an email address for the enclosing element.

/myContacts/contact/userReference/cat (minOccurs=1 maxOccurs=1)
> This element is used to categorize the element that contains it by referencing a global category definition in either the .NET categories service system document or an external resource containing category definitions, or by referencing an identity-centric category definition in the content document of the .NET categories service for a particular PUID.

/myContacts/contact/userReference/cat/@ref (anyURI minOccurs=0 maxOccurs=1)
> This attribute references a category definition (<catDef/>) element using the rules outlined in the .NET categories service XMI manual.

/myContacts/contact/securityCertificate (minOccurs=0 maxOccurs=unbounded)
/myContacts/contact/securityCertificate/cat (minOccurs=0 maxOccurs=unbounded)
> This element is used to categorize the element that contains it by referencing a global category definition in either the .NET categories service system document or an external resource containing category definitions, or by referencing an identity-centric category definition in the content document of the .NET categories service for a particular PUID.

/myContacts/contact/securityCertificate/cat/@ref (anyURI minOccurs=0 maxOccurs=1)
> This attribute references a category definition (<catDef/>) element using the rules outlined in the .NET categories service XMI manual.

/myContacts/contact/securityCertificate/certificate (hexBinary minOccurs=1 maxOccurs=1)
/myContacts/contact/*{any}* (minOccurs=0 maxOccurs=unbounded)

/myContacts/subscription (minOccurs=0 maxOccurs=unbounded)

This element defines a subscription node that is an xdb:blue node and when placed in a content document causes a subscription to be registered. A subscription contains a trigger element that selects a scope of coverage. When items change that are under this scope of coverage, a subscriptionResponse message is generated and sent to the specified destination address.

/myContacts/subscription/@changeNumber (minOccurs=0 maxOccurs=1)

The changeNumber attribute is designed to facilitate caching of the element and its descendants. This attribute is assigned to this element by the .NET My Services system. The attribute is read-only to applications. Attempts to write this attribute are silently ignored.

/myContacts/subscription/@id (minOccurs=0 maxOccurs=1)

This attribute is a globally unique ID assigned to this element by .NET My Services. Normally, .NET My Services will generate and assign this ID during an insertRequest operation, or possibly during a replaceRequest. Application software can override this ID generation by specifying the useClientIds attribute in the request message. Once an ID is assigned, the attribute is read-only and attempts to write it are silently ignored.

/myContacts/subscription/@creator (string minOccurs=0 maxOccurs=1)

This attribute identifies the creator in terms of userId, appId, and platformId of the node.

/myContacts/subscription/trigger (minOccurs=1 maxOccurs=1)
/myContacts/subscription/trigger/@select (string minOccurs=0 maxOccurs=1)

This item specifies an XPATH expression that specifies the nodes that are to be selected and watched for changes. The selection may only select xdb:blue nodes. As changes in this node set occur, they trigger the generation of a subscription message. These messages are then sent to the SOAP receiver listed in the "to" element.

/myContacts/subscription/trigger/@mode (string minOccurs=0 maxOccurs=1)

This attribute specifies whether or not the content of the changes that triggered the subscription are delivered in the subscription message, or if the message simply indicates that something changed under the trigger. The value of the attribute may be:

includeData

The data that changed, triggering the subscription, is included in the subscription message. Note that deleted nodes are specified by id, not by value.

excludeData

The data that changed, triggering the subscription, is NOT included in the subscription message.

/myContacts/subscription/trigger/@baseChangeNumber (minOccurs=0 maxOccurs=1)
This attribute specifies the changeNumber value that the trigger is relative to. All changes between the specified change number and the current state of the document relative to the selection are transmitted as subscription messages. This allows a client application to establish a subscription relative to some baseline. As in changeQuery, if the baseChangeNumber is way out of date relative to the current state of the document, and the service can not supply the changes in the subscription message, the subscription insert is rejected. A value of 0 means that the current values of the selected nodes are transmitted in the subscription message.

/myContacts/subscription/expiresAt (dateTime minOccurs=0 maxOccurs=1)
This optional element specifies an absolute time after which the subscription is no longer active. The subscription node is automatically removed when the subscription expires. If this element is missing, the subscription does not expire.

/myContacts/subscription/context (minOccurs=1 maxOccurs=1)
This element returns the context element from the original subscription. Applications should use this element, and only this element, to correlate the subscription response with one of their subscriptions.

/myContacts/subscription/context/@uri (anyURI minOccurs=0 maxOccurs=1)
This attribute specifies the URI value chosen by the subscriber that is associated with this subscription.

/myContacts/subscription/context/*{any}* (minOccurs=0 maxOccurs=unbounded)
/myContacts/subscription/to (anyURI minOccurs=1 maxOccurs=1)
This attribute specifies the location that is to receive the subscription message. The value of this element may be one of the following forms:

- *hs:myNotifications*—this URI indicates that generated subscription messages are to be delivered inside the body of a notification and delivered to the default .NET notifications service of the creator.

- *protocol://service*—this URI indicates that generated subscription messages are delivered to the specified service at the domain of the creator's platformId. For instance, a platformId indicating microsoft.com, and a value in this element of http://subscriptionResponse would cause delivery of the subscription message to http://subscriptionResponse.microsoft.com.

If this value is not specified, the subscription message is delivered as a notification to the "creator's" .NET notifications service.

/myContacts/*{any}* (minOccurs=0 maxOccurs=unbounded)

The .NET my contacts service/system

The system document is a global document for the service. It is read-only to all users and its content and meaning are independent of the PUID used to address the service. The system document contains a set of base items common to all .NET My Services services, and is optionally extended by each service to include service-specific global information.

This schema outline illustrates the layout and meaning of the information found in the system document for the .NET my contacts service.

```
<sys:system changeNumber="..." instanceId="..."
    xmlns:hs="http://schemas.microsoft.com/hs/2001/10/core"
    xmlns:sys="http://schemas.microsoft.com/hs/2001/10/myContacts/system">1..1
    <hs:roleMap changeNumber="..." id="..." creator="...">1..1
        <hs:scope id="...">0..unbounded
            <hs:shape base="...">1..1
                <hs:include select="...">1..unbounded</hs:include>
                <hs:exclude select="...">0..unbounded</hs:exclude>
            </hs:shape>
        </hs:scope>
        <hs:roleTemplate name="..." priority="...">0..unbounded
            <hs:fullDescription xml:lang="...">0..1</hs:fullDescription>
            <hs:method name="..." scopeRef="...">0..unbounded</hs:method>
        </hs:roleTemplate>
    </hs:roleMap>
    <hs:methodMap changeNumber="..." id="..." creator="...">1..1
        <hs:method name="...">0..unbounded {any}</hs:method>
    </hs:methodMap>
    <hs:schemaMap changeNumber="..." id="..." creator="...">1..1
        <hs:schema namespace="..." schemaLocation="..." alias="...">0..unbounded
{any}</hs:schema>
    </hs:schemaMap>
    <hs:wsdlMap changeNumber="..." id="..." creator="...">1..1
        <hs:wsdl wsdlLocation="...">0..unbounded {any}</hs:wsdl>
        <hs:disco discoLocation="...">0..unbounded {any}</hs:disco>
    </hs:wsdlMap>
    {any}
</sys:system>
```

The meaning of the attributes and elements shown in the preceding sample document fragment are listed in the following section.

/system (minOccurs=1 maxOccurs=1)

This element encapsulates the system document for the .NET my contacts service.

/system/@changeNumber (minOccurs=0 maxOccurs=1)

The changeNumber attribute is designed to facilitate caching of the element and its descendants. This attribute is assigned to this element by the .NET My Services system. The attribute is read-only to applications. Attempts to write this attribute are silently ignored.

/system/@instanceId (string minOccurs=0 maxOccurs=1)

This attribute is a unique identifier typically assigned to the root element of a service. It is a read-only element and assigned by the .NET My Services system when a user is provisioned for a particular service.

/system/roleMap (minOccurs=1 maxOccurs=1)

This element encapsulates all the elements that make up a roleMap, which include document class relative to roleTemplate, priority, name, method, and per-method scope. An individual roleTemplate defines the maximum scope of information, and the allowable methods used to access that information for each request mapped into the template.

/system/roleMap/@changeNumber (minOccurs=0 maxOccurs=1)

The changeNumber attribute is designed to facilitate caching of the element and its descendants. This attribute is assigned to this element by the .NET My Services system. The attribute is read-only to applications. Attempts to write this attribute are silently ignored.

/system/roleMap/@id (minOccurs=0 maxOccurs=1)

This attribute is a globally unique ID assigned to this element by .NET My Services. Normally, .NET My Services will generate and assign this ID during an insertRequest operation, or possibly during a replaceRequest. Application software can override this ID generation by specifying the useClientIds attribute in the request message. Once an ID is assigned, the attribute is read-only and attempts to write it are silently ignored.

/system/roleMap/@creator (string minOccurs=0 maxOccurs=1)

This attribute identifies the creator in terms of userId, appId, and platformId of the node.

/system/roleMap/scope (minOccurs=0 maxOccurs=unbounded)

This element defines a scope which may be referred to by roles within this roleMap to indicate what portions of the document are visible to this role for the specified method.

/system/roleMap/scope/@id (minOccurs=0 maxOccurs=1)

This attribute is a globally unique ID assigned to this element by .NET My Services. Normally, .NET My Services will generate and assign this ID during an insertRequest operation, or possibly during a replaceRequest. Application software can override this ID generation by specifying the useClientlds attribute in the request message. Once an ID is assigned, the attribute is read-only and attempts to write it are silently ignored.

/system/roleMap/scope/shape (minOccurs=1 maxOccurs=1)

A shape defines the node set visible through the document when operating through this shape element.

/system/roleMap/scope/shape/@base (string minOccurs=0 maxOccurs=1)

This attribute specifies the initial set of nodes visible through the shape.

A value of t indicates that the shape is initialized to include all possible nodes relative to the shape that is currently in effect. For example, each role defines a scope containing a shape. When defining a shape for a role, the value t indicates all possible nodes available in the specified document for this role. When defining a shape in an ACL entry, a value of t denotes all of the nodes visible in the shape for the computed role. When using a shape in an hsdl operation, a value of t indicates all of the possible nodes selected by the hsdl operation (relative to the ACL shape, which itself is relative to the role's shape).

The value nil indicates the opposite of t, which is the empty node set. Nodes from this set may then be included in the shape.

/system/roleMap/scope/shape/include (minOccurs=1 maxOccurs=unbounded)

This element specifies the set of nodes that should be included in the shape relative to the possible set of nodes indicated by the base attribute.

/system/roleMap/scope/shape/include/@select (string minOccurs=0 maxOccurs=1)

This item specifies an XPATH expression that selects a set of nodes relative to the externally established context. The expression can never travel outside the node-set established by this externally established current context. The expression may match 0 or more nodes, and the operation manipulates all selected nodes. The minOccurs and maxOccurs attributes are optional and place restrictions and limitations on the number of nodes selected.

/system/roleMap/scope/shape/exclude (minOccurs=0 maxOccurs=unbounded)

This element specifies the set of nodes that should be excluded from the shape relative to the possible set of nodes indicated by the base attribute.

/system/roleMap/scope/shape/exclude/@select (string minOccurs=0 maxOccurs=1)

This item specifies an XPATH expression that selects a set of nodes relative to the externally established context. The expression can never travel outside the node-set established by this externally established current context. The expression may match 0 or more nodes, and the operation manipulates all selected nodes. The minOccurs and maxOccurs attributes are optional and place restrictions and limitations on the number of nodes selected.

/system/roleMap/roleTemplate (minOccurs=0 maxOccurs=unbounded)
This element encapsulates the definition of a role. The attribute set for this element includes the document class to which this roleTemplate refers, the name of the roleTemplate, and the priority of the roleTemplate.

/system/roleMap/roleTemplate/@name (string minOccurs=0 maxOccurs=1)
This element specifies the name of the role.

/system/roleMap/roleTemplate/@priority (int minOccurs=0 maxOccurs=1)
This element specifies the priority of the roleTemplate that is used to select that actual roleTemplate when the role evaluation determines that the subject maps to multiple roleTemplates.

/system/roleMap/roleTemplate/fullDescription (string minOccurs=0 maxOccurs=1)
This element contains a description of this role template which specifies the capabilities a caller will have when accessing information through this role.

/system/roleMap/roleTemplate/fullDescription/@xml:lang (minOccurs=1 maxOccurs=1)
This required attribute is used to specify an ISO 639 language code or an ISO 3166 country code as described in RFC 1766. The value of this attribute indicates the language type of the content within this element.

/system/roleMap/roleTemplate/method (minOccurs=0 maxOccurs=unbounded)
This element specifies the methods available within this roleTemplate by name, and by scope. When a subject maps to a roleTemplate, the method in the request must match one of these elements for the message to continue to flow. If the method exists, the data available to the method is a function of the scope referenced by this method combined with an optional scope referenced by the role defined in the roleList.

/system/roleMap/roleTemplate/method/@name (string minOccurs=0 maxOccurs=1)
This element specifies the name of the method.

/system/roleMap/roleTemplate/method/@scopeRef (string minOccurs=0 maxOccurs=1)
This attribute specifies the scope within this document that is in effect for this method.

/system/methodMap (minOccurs=1 maxOccurs=1)
This element defines the methodMap. While it is true that in most cases the roleMap section contains a definitive list of methods, these methods are likely to be scattered about the roleMap in various templates. This section contains the definitive non-duplicated list of methods available within the service.

/system/methodMap/@changeNumber (minOccurs=0 maxOccurs=1)
The changeNumber attribute is designed to facilitate caching of the element and its descendants. This attribute is assigned to this element by the .NET My Services system. The attribute is read-only to applications. Attempts to write this attribute are silently ignored.

/system/methodMap/@id (minOccurs=0 maxOccurs=1)
> This attribute is a globally unique ID assigned to this element by .NET My Services. Normally, .NET My Services will generate and assign this ID during an insertRequest operation, or possibly during a replaceRequest. Application software can override this ID generation by specifying the useClientIds attribute in the request message. Once an ID is assigned, the attribute is read-only and attempts to write it are silently ignored.

/system/methodMap/@creator (string minOccurs=0 maxOccurs=1)
> This attribute identifies the creator in terms of userId, appId, and platformId of the node.

/system/methodMap/method (minOccurs=0 maxOccurs=unbounded)
> This element defines a method that is available within this service.

/system/methodMap/method/@name (string minOccurs=0 maxOccurs=1)
> This attribute specifies the name of a method available within the service.

/system/methodMap/method/*{any}* (minOccurs=0 maxOccurs=unbounded)

/system/schemaMap (minOccurs=1 maxOccurs=1)
> This element defines the various schema's that define the data structures and shape of information managed by this service. Each schema is defined by its namespace URI, its location, and a preferred namespace alias.

/system/schemaMap/@changeNumber (minOccurs=0 maxOccurs=1)
> The changeNumber attribute is designed to facilitate caching of the element and its descendants. This attribute is assigned to this element by the .NET My Services system. The attribute is read-only to applications. Attempts to write this attribute are silently ignored.

/system/schemaMap/@id (minOccurs=0 maxOccurs=1)
> This attribute is a globally unique ID assigned to this element by .NET My Services. Normally, .NET My Services will generate and assign this ID during an insertRequest operation, or possibly during a replaceRequest. Application software can override this ID generation by specifying the useClientIds attribute in the request message. Once an ID is assigned, the attribute is read-only and attempts to write it are silently ignored.

/system/schemaMap/@creator (string minOccurs=0 maxOccurs=1)
> This attribute identifies the creator in terms of userId, appId, and platformId of the node.

/system/schemaMap/schema (minOccurs=0 maxOccurs=unbounded)
> This element defines a schema which defines data-structures and the shape of information managed by this service. Multiple schema elements exist for each service, one for each logical grouping of information exposed by the service.

/system/schemaMap/schema/@namespace (anyURI minOccurs=0 maxOccurs=1)
> This attribute specifies the namespace URI of this schema.

/system/schemaMap/schema/@schemaLocation (anyURI minOccurs=0 maxOccurs=1)
> This attribute specifies the location (in the form of a URI) of the resource containing schema. When a schema is reachable through a variety of URIs, one schema element will exist for each location.

/system/schemaMap/schema/@alias (string minOccurs=0 maxOccurs=1)
> This attribute specifies the preferred alias that should be used if possible when manipulating information covered by this schema in the context of this service.

/system/schemaMap/schema/*{any}* (minOccurs=0 maxOccurs=unbounded)
/system/wsdlMap (minOccurs=1 maxOccurs=1)
> This element defines the wsdlMap for this service. This map includes the location of WSDL documents, DISCO documents, and WISL documents for this web service. These documents are used by applications to understand the format of messages that may be sent to the various services.

/system/wsdlMap/@changeNumber (minOccurs=0 maxOccurs=1)
> The changeNumber attribute is designed to facilitate caching of the element and its descendants. This attribute is assigned to this element by the .NET My Services system. The attribute is read-only to applications. Attempts to write this attribute are silently ignored.

/system/wsdlMap/@id (minOccurs=0 maxOccurs=1)
> This attribute is a globally unique ID assigned to this element by .NET My Services. Normally, .NET My Services will generate and assign this ID during an insertRequest operation, or possibly during a replaceRequest. Application software can override this ID generation by specifying the useClientIds attribute in the request message. Once an ID is assigned, the attribute is read-only and attempts to write it are silently ignored.

/system/wsdlMap/@creator (string minOccurs=0 maxOccurs=1)
> This attribute identifies the creator in terms of userId, appId, and platformId of the node.

/system/wsdlMap/wsdl (minOccurs=0 maxOccurs=unbounded)
> This element is used to specify the location of a WSDL file for this service. Multiple entries may exist pointing to the same file hosted in multiple locations, or to variations on the content within the WSDL files.

/system/wsdlMap/wsdl/@wsdlLocation (anyURI minOccurs=0 maxOccurs=1)
> This attribute is a URI that specifies the location of the WSDL file.

/system/wsdlMap/wsdl/*{any}* (minOccurs=0 maxOccurs=unbounded)
/system/wsdlMap/disco (minOccurs=0 maxOccurs=unbounded)
> This element is used to specify the location of a DISCO file for this service. Multiple entries may exist pointing to the same file hosted in multiple locations, or to variations on the content within the DISCO files.

/system/wsdlMap/disco/@discoLocation (anyURI minOccurs=0 maxOccurs=1)
> This attribute is a URI that specifies the location of the DISCO file.

/system/wsdlMap/disco/*{any}* (minOccurs=0 maxOccurs=unbounded)
/system/*{any}* (minOccurs=0 maxOccurs=unbounded)

the .NET my contacts service/Methods

The .NET my contacts service supports the following standard and domain-specific methods:

- query
- insert
- replace
- delete
- update

The standard methods operate on this service using the same message format and method-interchange techniques described in the hsdl section of this document. The only service-specific information to note is the schema that is in effect for each of the methods. These schemas, and how they relate to the standard methods and roles are described in the roles section of this document.

The domain specific methods operate as described in the domain specific methods section of this document, and are governed by the various schemas outlined in the the .NET my contacts service/Roles section for this service.

CHAPTER 14

The .NET Documents Service/Introduction

This is the .NET documents service. This service allows storage of users' documents. Users can access those documents through any application they have authorized to handle them.

The .NET Documents Service/Roles

The .NET documents service controls access by using the following roleTemplates:

- rt0
- rt1
- rt2
- rt3
- rt99

The .NET documents service uses the following scopes:

- **scope id 1**

```
<hs:scope id=1>

    <hs:shape base=t>

    </hs:shape>

</hs:scope>
```

- **scope id 2**

```
<hs:scope id=2>

    <hs:shape base=nil>

        <hs:include select=//*[@creator='$callerId']/>

    </hs:shape>

</hs:scope>
```

- **scope id 3**

```
<hs:scope id=3>

    <hs:shape base=nil>

        <hs:include select=//subscription[@creator='$callerId']/>

    </hs:shape>

</hs:scope>
```

- **scope id 4**

```
<hs:scope id=4>

    <hs:shape base=nil>

        <hs:include select=//*[cat/@ref='hs:public']/>

        <hs:include select=//subscription[@creator='$callerId']/>

    </hs:shape>

</hs:scope>
```

The .NET documents service roleTemplate rt0

The purpose of this role is to give complete read/write access to all information within the content document of the service being protected through this roleTemplate.

The following table illustrates the available methods and the scope in effect when accessing the .NET documents service through that method while mapped to this roleTemplate.

method	scopeRef
query	scopeRef=1
insert	scopeRef=1
replace	scopeRef=1
delete	scopeRef=1
update	scopeRef=1

The .NET documents service roleTemplate rt1

The purpose of this role is to give complete read access to all information within the content document of the service being protected through this roleTemplate. Applications mapping to this role also have a limited ability to write to information in the content document. They may create nodes in any location, but may only change/replace, or delete nodes that they created.

The following table illustrates the available methods and the scope in effect when accessing the .NET documents service through that method while mapped to this roleTemplate.

method	scopeRef
query	scopeRef=1
insert	scopeRef=2
replace	scopeRef=2
delete	scopeRef=2

The .NET documents service roleTemplate rt2

The purpose of this role is to give complete read access to all information within the content document of the service being protected through this roleTemplate. Applications mapping to this role have very limited write access and are only able to create and manipulate their own subscription nodes.

The following table illustrates the available methods and the scope in effect when accessing the .NET documents service through that method while mapped to this roleTemplate.

method	scopeRef
query	scopeRef=1
insert	scopeRef=3
replace	scopeRef=3
delete	scopeRef=3

The .NET documents service roleTemplate rt3

The purpose of this role is to give limited read access to information within the content document that is categorized as "public".

The following table illustrates the available methods and the scope in effect when accessing the .NET documents service through that method while mapped to this roleTemplate.

method	scopeRef
query	scopeRef=4

The .NET documents service roleTemplate rt99

The purpose of this role is to block all access to the content document. Note that lack of a role in the roleList has the same effect as assigning someone to rt99.

The .NET Documents Service/Content

The content document is an identity-centric document. Its content and meaning is a function of the PUID used to address the service. Accessing the document is controlled by the associated roleList document.

This schema outline illustrates the layout and meaning of the information found in the content document for the .NET documents service.

```
<m:myDocuments changeNumber="..." instanceId="..."
    xmlns:m="http://schemas.microsoft.com/hs/2001/10/myDocuments"
    xmlns:hs="http://schemas.microsoft.com/hs/2001/10/core">1..1
    <m:document changeNumber="..." id="..." creator="...">0..unbounded
        <m:cat ref="...">0..unbounded</m:cat>
        <m:name xml:lang="...">1..unbounded</m:name>
        <m:attributes>0..1
            <m:hidden>1..1</m:hidden>
            <m:system>1..1</m:system>
            <m:readOnly>1..1</m:readOnly>
        </m:attributes>
        <m:lastAccessDate>0..1</m:lastAccessDate>
        <m:creationDate>0..1</m:creationDate>
        <m:ref folderId="..." name="...">0..unbounded</m:ref>
        <m:blob>0..1</m:blob>
        {any}
    </m:document>
    <m:folder parent="..." path="..." changeNumber="..." id="..."
creator="...">0..unbounded
        <m:name xml:lang="...">1..unbounded</m:name>
        <m:attributes>1..1
            <m:hidden>1..1</m:hidden>
            <m:system>1..1</m:system>
            <m:readOnly>1..1</m:readOnly>
        </m:attributes>
    </m:folder>
```

```
    <m:subscription changeNumber="..." id="..." creator="...">0..unbounded
        <hs:trigger select="..." mode="..."
baseChangeNumber="...">1..1</hs:trigger>
        <hs:expiresAt>0..1</hs:expiresAt>
        <hs:context uri="...">1..1 {any}</hs:context>
        <hs:to>1..1</hs:to>
    </m:subscription>
    {any}
</m:myDocuments>
```

The meaning of the attributes and elements shown in the preceding sample document fragment are listed in the following section.

/myDocuments (minOccurs=1 maxOccurs=1)

This element encapsulates the content document for the service. The cache scope for this document is the entire content document; that is, there is a single changeNumber attribute, and it occurs at the root element. Any change to the document changes this attribute.

/myDocuments/@changeNumber (minOccurs=0 maxOccurs=1)

The changeNumber attribute is designed to facilitate caching of the element and its descendants. This attribute is assigned to this element by the Microsoft .NET My Services system. The attribute is read-only to applications. Attempts to write this attribute are silently ignored.

/myDocuments/@instanceId (string minOccurs=0 maxOccurs=1)

This attribute is a unique identifier typically assigned to the root element of a service. It is a read-only element and assigned by the Microsoft .NET My Services system when a user is provisioned for a particular service.

/myDocuments/document (minOccurs=0 maxOccurs=unbounded)

This element defines the basic document type.

/myDocuments/document/@changeNumber (minOccurs=0 maxOccurs=1)

The changeNumber attribute is designed to facilitate caching of the element and its descendants. This attribute is assigned to this element by the .NET My Services system. The attribute is read-only to applications. Attempts to write this attribute are silently ignored.

/myDocuments/document/@id (minOccurs=0 maxOccurs=1)

This attribute is a globally unique ID assigned to this element by .NET My Services. Normally, .NET My Services will generate and assign this ID during an insertRequest operation, or possibly during a replaceRequest. Application software can override this ID generation by specifying the useClientIds attribute in the request message. Once an ID is assigned, the attribute is read-only and attempts to write it are silently ignored.

/myDocuments/document/@creator (string minOccurs=0 maxOccurs=1)

This attribute identifies the creator in terms of userId, appId, and platformId of the node.

/myDocuments/document/cat (minOccurs=0 maxOccurs=unbounded)
> This element is used to categorize the element that contains it by referencing a global category definition in either the .NET categories service system document or an external resource containing category definitions, or by referencing an identity centric category definition in the content document of the .NET categories service for a particular PUID.

/myDocuments/document/cat/@ref (anyURI minOccurs=0 maxOccurs=1)
> This attribute references a category definition (<catDef/>) element using the rules outlined in the .NET Categories Service XMI manual.

/myDocuments/document/name (string minOccurs=1 maxOccurs=unbounded)
> The name of the document.

/myDocuments/document/name/@xml:lang (minOccurs=1 maxOccurs=1)
> This required attribute is used to specify an ISO 639 language code or an ISO 3166 country code as described in RFC 1766. The value of this attribute indicates the language type of the content within this element.

/myDocuments/document/attributes (minOccurs=0 maxOccurs=1)
> File attribute definitions.

/myDocuments/document/attributes/hidden (int minOccurs=1 maxOccurs=1)
> hidden file attribute.

/myDocuments/document/attributes/system (int minOccurs=1 maxOccurs=1)
> system file attribute.

/myDocuments/document/attributes/readOnly (int minOccurs=1 maxOccurs=1)
> readOnly file attribute.

/myDocuments/document/lastAccessDate (dateTime minOccurs=0 maxOccurs=1)
/myDocuments/document/creationDate (dateTime minOccurs=0 maxOccurs=1)
/myDocuments/document/ref (minOccurs=0 maxOccurs=unbounded)
> This element defines the basic reference type.

/myDocuments/document/ref/@folderId (string minOccurs=0 maxOccurs=1)
> The folder being referred to.

/myDocuments/document/ref/@name (string minOccurs=1 maxOccurs=1)
> Name of the document under this reference.

/myDocuments/document/blob (string minOccurs=0 maxOccurs=1)
/myDocuments/document/*{any}* (minOccurs=0 maxOccurs=unbounded)
/myDocuments/folder (minOccurs=0 maxOccurs=unbounded)
> This element defines the basic folder type.

/myDocuments/folder/@parent (string minOccurs=0 maxOccurs=1)
> Parent folder ID.

/myDocuments/folder/@path (string minOccurs=0 maxOccurs=1)
> Fully qualified path to this folder.

/myDocuments/folder/@changeNumber (minOccurs=0 maxOccurs=1)

The changeNumber attribute is designed to facilitate caching of the element and its descendants. This attribute is assigned to this element by the .NET My Services system. The attribute is read-only to applications. Attempts to write this attribute are silently ignored.

/myDocuments/folder/@id (minOccurs=0 maxOccurs=1)

This attribute is a globally unique ID assigned to this element by .NET My Services. Normally, .NET My Services will generate and assign this ID during an insertRequest operation, or possibly during a replaceRequest. Application software can override this ID generation by specifying the useClientIds attribute in the request message. Once an ID is assigned, the attribute is read-only and attempts to write it are silently ignored.

/myDocuments/folder/@creator (string minOccurs=0 maxOccurs=1)

This attribute identifies the creator in terms of userId, appId, and platformId of the node.

/myDocuments/folder/name (string minOccurs=1 maxOccurs=unbounded)

The default name of the folder.

/myDocuments/folder/name/@xml:lang (minOccurs=1 maxOccurs=1)

This required attribute is used to specify an ISO 639 language code or an ISO 3166 country code as described in RFC 1766. The value of this attribute indicates the language type of the content within this element.

/myDocuments/folder/attributes (minOccurs=1 maxOccurs=1)

File attribute definitions.

/myDocuments/folder/attributes/hidden (int minOccurs=1 maxOccurs=1)

hidden file attribute.

/myDocuments/folder/attributes/system (int minOccurs=1 maxOccurs=1)

system file attribute.

/myDocuments/folder/attributes/readOnly (int minOccurs=1 maxOccurs=1)

readOnly file attribute.

/myDocuments/subscription (minOccurs=0 maxOccurs=unbounded)

This element defines a subscription node that is designed to be an xdb:blue node which when placed in a content document causes a subscription to be registered. A subscription contains a trigger element which selects a scope of coverage. When items change that are under this scope of coverage, and subscriptionResponse message is generated and sent to the specified destination address.

/myDocuments/subscription/@changeNumber (minOccurs=0 maxOccurs=1)

The changeNumber attribute is designed to facilitate caching of the element and its descendants. This attribute is assigned to this element by the .NET My Services system. The attribute is read-only to applications. Attempts to write this attribute are silently ignored.

/myDocuments/subscription/@id (minOccurs=0 maxOccurs=1)

This attribute is a globally unique ID assigned to this element by .NET My Services. Normally, .NET My Services will generate and assign this ID during an insertRequest operation, or possibly during a replaceRequest. Application software can override this ID generation by specifying the useClientIds attribute in the request message. Once an ID is assigned, the attribute is read-only and attempts to write it are silently ignored.

/myDocuments/subscription/@creator (string minOccurs=0 maxOccurs=1)

This attribute identifies the creator in terms of userId, appId, and platformId of the node.

/myDocuments/subscription/trigger (minOccurs=1 maxOccurs=1)

/myDocuments/subscription/trigger/@select (string minOccurs=0 maxOccurs=1)

This item specifies an XPATH expression that specifies the nodes that are to be selected and watched for changes. The selection may only select xdb:blue nodes. As changes in this node set occur, they trigger the generation of a subscription message. These messages are then sent to the SOAP receiver listed in the "to" element.

/myDocuments/subscription/trigger/@mode (string minOccurs=0 maxOccurs=1)

This attribute specifies whether or not the content of the changes that triggered the subscription is delivered in the subscription message, or whether the message simply indicates that something changed under the trigger. The attribute may be:

includeData

The data that changed, causing the subscription to trigger, is included in the subscription message. Note that deleted nodes are specified by their ID, not by value.

excludeData

The data that changed, causing the subscription to trigger, is NOT included in the subscription message.

/myDocuments/subscription/trigger/@baseChangeNumber (minOccurs=0 maxOccurs=1)

This attribute specifies the changeNumber value that the trigger is relative to. All changes between the specified change number, and the current state of the document relative to the selection are transmitted as subscription messages. This allows a client application to establish a subscription relative to some baseline. As in changeQuery, if the baseChangeNumber is way out of date relative to the current state of the document, and the service can not supply the changes in the subscription message, the subscription insert is rejected. A value of 0 means that the current values of the selected nodes are transmitted in the subscription message.

/myDocuments/subscription/expiresAt (dateTime minOccurs=0 maxOccurs=1)

This optional element specifies an absolute time after which the subscription is no longer active. The subscription node is automatically removed when the subscription expires. If this element is missing, the subscription does not expire.

/myDocuments/subscription/context (minOccurs=1 maxOccurs=1)

This element returns the context element from the original subscription. Applications should use this element, and only this element, to correlate the subscription response with one of their subscriptions.

/myDocuments/subscription/context/@uri (anyURI minOccurs=0 maxOccurs=1)

This attribute specifies the URI value chosen by the subscriber that is associated with this subscription.

/myDocuments/subscription/context/*{any}* (minOccurs=0 maxOccurs=unbounded)
/myDocuments/subscription/to (anyURI minOccurs=1 maxOccurs=1)

This attribute specifies the location that is to receive the subscription message. The value of this element may be one of the following forms:

- *hs:myNotifications*—this URI indicates that generated subscription messages are to be delivered inside the body of a notification and delivered to the default .NET notifications service of the creator.

- *protocol://service*—this URI indicates that generated subscription messages are delivered to the specified service at the domain of the creator's platformId. For instance, a platformId indicating msn.com, and a value in this element of http://subscriptionResponse would cause delivery of the subscription message to http://subscriptionResponse.msn.com.

If this value is not specified, then the subscription message is delivered as a notification to the "creator's" .NET notifications service.

/myDocuments/*{any}* (minOccurs=0 maxOccurs=unbounded)

The .NET Documents Service/System

The system document is a global document for the service. Its content and meaning is independent of the PUID used to address the service, and the document is read only to all users. The system document contains a set of base items common to all .NET My Services services, and is optionally extended by each service to include service-specific global information.

This schema outline illustrates the layout and meaning of the information found in the system document for the .NET documents service.

```
<sys:system changeNumber="..." instanceId="..."
    xmlns:hs="http://schemas.microsoft.com/hs/2001/10/core"
    xmlns:sys="http://schemas.microsoft.com/hs/2001/10/myDocuments/system">1..1
    <hs:roleMap changeNumber="..." id="..." creator="...">1..1
        <hs:scope id="...">0..unbounded
            <hs:shape base="...">1..1
                <hs:include select="...">1..unbounded</hs:include>
                <hs:exclude select="...">0..unbounded</hs:exclude>
            </hs:shape>
        </hs:scope>
        <hs:roleTemplate name="..." priority="...">0..unbounded
            <hs:fullDescription xml:lang="...">0..1</hs:fullDescription>
            <hs:method name="..." scopeRef="...">0..unbounded</hs:method>
        </hs:roleTemplate>
    </hs:roleMap>
```

(continued)

(continued)

```
    <hs:methodMap changeNumber="..." id="..." creator="...">1..1
        <hs:method name="...">0..unbounded {any}</hs:method>
    </hs:methodMap>
    <hs:schemaMap changeNumber="..." id="..." creator="...">1..1
        <hs:schema namespace="..." schemaLocation="..." alias="...">0..unbounded
{any}</hs:schema>
    </hs:schemaMap>
    <hs:wsdlMap changeNumber="..." id="..." creator="...">1..1
        <hs:wsdl wsdlLocation="...">0..unbounded {any}</hs:wsdl>
        <hs:disco discoLocation="...">0..unbounded {any}</hs:disco>
    </hs:wsdlMap>
    {any}
</sys:system>
```

The meaning of the attributes and elements shown in the preceding sample document fragment are listed in the following section.

/system (minOccurs=1 maxOccurs=1)

This element encapsulates the system document for the .NET documents service.

/system/@changeNumber (minOccurs=0 maxOccurs=1)

The changeNumber attribute is designed to facilitate caching of the element and its descendants. This attribute is assigned to this element by the .NET My Services system. The attribute is read-only to applications. Attempts to write this attribute are silently ignored.

/system/@instanceId (string minOccurs=0 maxOccurs=1)

This attribute is a unique identifier typically assigned to the root element of a service. It is a read-only element and assigned by the .NET My Services system when a user is provisioned for a particular service.

/system/roleMap (minOccurs=1 maxOccurs=1)

This element encapsulates all the elements that make up a roleMap, which include document class relative roleTemplate, priority, name, method, and per-method scope. An individual roleTemplate defines the maximum scope of information, and the allowable methods used to access that information for each request mapped into the template.

/system/roleMap/@changeNumber (minOccurs=0 maxOccurs=1)

The changeNumber attribute is designed to facilitate caching of the element and its descendants. This attribute is assigned to this element by the .NET My Services system. The attribute is read-only to applications. Attempts to write this attribute are silently ignored.

/system/roleMap/@id (minOccurs=0 maxOccurs=1)

This attribute is a globally unique ID assigned to this element by .NET My Services. Normally, .NET My Services will generate and assign this ID during an insertRequest operation, or possibly during a replaceRequest. Application software can override this ID generation by specifying the useClientIds attribute in the request message. Once an ID is assigned, the attribute is read-only and attempts to write it are silently ignored.

/system/roleMap/@creator (string minOccurs=0 maxOccurs=1)

This attribute identifies the creator in terms of userId, appId, and platformId of the node.

/system/roleMap/scope (minOccurs=0 maxOccurs=unbounded)

This element defines a scope which may be referred to by roles within this roleMap to indicate what portions of the document are visible to this role for the specified method.

/system/roleMap/scope/@id (minOccurs=0 maxOccurs=1)

This attribute is a globally unique ID assigned to this element by .NET My Services. Normally, .NET My Services will generate and assign this ID during an insertRequest operation, or possibly during a replaceRequest. Application software can override this ID generation by specifying the useClientIds attribute in the request message. Once an ID is assigned, the attribute is read-only and attempts to write it are silently ignored.

/system/roleMap/scope/shape (minOccurs=1 maxOccurs=1)

A shape defines the node set visible through the document when operating through this shape element.

/system/roleMap/scope/shape/@base (string minOccurs=0 maxOccurs=1)

This attribute specifies the initial set of nodes visible through the shape.

A value of t indicates that the shape is initialized to include all possible nodes relative to the shape that is currently in effect. For instance, each role defines a scope containing a shape. When defining a shape for a role, the value t indicates all possible nodes available in the specified document for this role. When defining a shape in an ACL entry, a value of t means all of the nodes visible in the shape for the computed role. When using a shape in an hsdl operation, a value of t indicates all of the possible nodes selected by the hsdl operation (relative to the ACL shape which itself is relative to the role's shape).

The value nil indicates the opposite of t, which is the empty node set. Nodes from this set may then be included into the shape.

/system/roleMap/scope/shape/include (minOccurs=1 maxOccurs=unbounded)

This element specifies the set of nodes that should be included into the shape relative to the possible set of nodes indicated by the base attribute.

/system/roleMap/scope/shape/include/@select (string minOccurs=0 maxOccurs=1)
   This item specifies an XPATH expression that selects a set of nodes relative to the
   externally established context. The expression can never travel outside the node-set
   established by this externally established current context. The expression may match
   0 or more nodes, and the operation manipulates all selected nodes. The minOccurs
   and maxOccurs attributes are optional and place restrictions and limitations on the
   number of nodes selected.

/system/roleMap/scope/shape/exclude (minOccurs=0 maxOccurs=unbounded)
   This element specifies the set of nodes that should be excluded from the shape
   relative to the possible set of nodes indicated by the base attribute.

/system/roleMap/scope/shape/exclude/@select (string minOccurs=0 maxOccurs=1)
   This item specifies an XPATH expression that selects a set of nodes relative to the
   externally established context. The expression can never travel outside the node-set
   established by this externally established current context. The expression may match
   0 or more nodes, and the operation manipulates all selected nodes. The minOccurs
   and maxOccurs attributes are optional and place restrictions and limitations on the
   number of nodes selected.

/system/roleMap/roleTemplate (minOccurs=0 maxOccurs=unbounded)
   This element encapsulates the definition of a role. The attribute set for this element
   includes the document class that this roleTemplate refers to, the name of the
   roleTemplate, and the priority of the roleTemplate.

/system/roleMap/roleTemplate/@name (string minOccurs=0 maxOccurs=1)
   This element specifies the name of the role.

/system/roleMap/roleTemplate/@priority (int minOccurs=0 maxOccurs=1)
   This element specifies the priority of the roleTemplate which is used to select that
   actual roleTemplate when the role evaluation determines that the subject maps to
   multiple roleTemplates.

/system/roleMap/roleTemplate/fullDescription (string minOccurs=0 maxOccurs=1)
   This element contains a description of this role template which specifies the
   capabilities a caller will have when accessing information through this role.

/system/roleMap/roleTemplate/fullDescription/@xml:lang (minOccurs=1 maxOccurs=1)
   This required attribute is used to specify an ISO 639 language code or an ISO 3166
   country code as described in RFC 1766. The value of this attribute indicates the
   language type of the content within this element.

/system/roleMap/roleTemplate/method (minOccurs=0 maxOccurs=unbounded)
   This element specifies the methods available within this roleTemplate by name, and
   by scope. When a subject maps to a roleTemplate, the method in the request must
   match one of these elements for the message to continue to flow. If the method
   exists, the data available to the method is a function of the scope referenced by this
   method combined with an optional scope referenced by the role defined in the
   roleList.

/system/roleMap/roleTemplate/method/@name (string minOccurs=0 maxOccurs=1)
   This element specifies the name of the method.

/system/roleMap/roleTemplate/method/@scopeRef (string minOccurs=0 maxOccurs=1)
This attribute specifies the scope within this document that is in effect for this method.

/system/methodMap (minOccurs=1 maxOccurs=1)
This element defines the methodMap. While it is true that in most cases, the roleMap section contains a definitive list of methods, these methods are likely to be scattered about the roleMap in various templates. This section contains the definitive non-duplicated list of methods available within the service.

/system/methodMap/@changeNumber (minOccurs=0 maxOccurs=1)
The changeNumber attribute is designed to facilitate caching of the element and its descendants. This attribute is assigned to this element by the .NET My Services system. The attribute is read-only to applications. Attempts to write this attribute are silently ignored.

/system/methodMap/@id (minOccurs=0 maxOccurs=1)
This attribute is a globally unique ID assigned to this element by .NET My Services. Normally, .NET My Services will generate and assign this ID during an insertRequest operation, or possibly during a replaceRequest. Application software can override this ID generation by specifying the useClientIds attribute in the request message. Once an ID is assigned, the attribute is read-only and attempts to write it are silently ignored.

/system/methodMap/@creator (string minOccurs=0 maxOccurs=1)
This attribute identifies the creator in terms of userId, appId, and platformId of the node.

/system/methodMap/method (minOccurs=0 maxOccurs=unbounded)
This element defines a method that is available within this service.

/system/methodMap/method/@name (string minOccurs=0 maxOccurs=1)
This attribute specifies the name of a method available within the service.

/system/methodMap/method/*{any}* (minOccurs=0 maxOccurs=unbounded)
/system/schemaMap (minOccurs=1 maxOccurs=1)
This element defines the various schema's that define the data structures and shape of information managed by this service. Each schema is defined by its namespace URI, its location, and a preferred namespace alias.

/system/schemaMap/@changeNumber (minOccurs=0 maxOccurs=1)
The changeNumber attribute is designed to facilitate caching of the element and its descendants. This attribute is assigned to this element by the .NET My Services system. The attribute is read-only to applications. Attempts to write this attribute are silently ignored.

/system/schemaMap/@id (minOccurs=0 maxOccurs=1)
This attribute is a globally unique ID assigned to this element by .NET My Services. Normally, .NET My Services will generate and assign this ID during an insertRequest operation, or possibly during a replaceRequest. Application software can override this ID generation by specifying the useClientIds attribute in the request message. Once an ID is assigned, the attribute is read-only and attempts to write it are silently ignored.

/system/schemaMap/@creator (string minOccurs=0 maxOccurs=1)
> This attribute identifies the creator in terms of userId, appId, and platformId of the node.

/system/schemaMap/schema (minOccurs=0 maxOccurs=unbounded)
> This element defines a schema which defines data-structures and the shape of information managed by this service. Multiple schema elements exist for each service, once for each logical grouping of information exposed by the service.

/system/schemaMap/schema/@namespace (anyURI minOccurs=0 maxOccurs=1)
> This attribute specifies the namespace URI of this schema.

/system/schemaMap/schema/@schemaLocation (anyURI minOccurs=0 maxOccurs=1)
> This attribute specifies the location (in the form of a URI) of the resource containing schema. When a schema is reachable through a variety of URIs, one schema element will exist for each location.

/system/schemaMap/schema/@alias (string minOccurs=0 maxOccurs=1)
> This attribute specifies the preferred alias that should be used if possible when manipulating information covered by this schema in the context of this service.

/system/schemaMap/schema/*{any}* (minOccurs=0 maxOccurs=unbounded)

/system/wsdlMap (minOccurs=1 maxOccurs=1)
> This element defines the wsdlMap for this service. This map includes the location of WSDL documents, DISCO documents, and WISL documents for this Web service. These documents are used by applications to understand the format of messages that may be sent to the various services.

/system/wsdlMap/@changeNumber (minOccurs=0 maxOccurs=1)
> The changeNumber attribute is designed to facilitate caching of the element and its descendants. This attribute is assigned to this element by the .NET My Services system. The attribute is read-only to applications. Attempts to write this attribute are silently ignored.

/system/wsdlMap/@id (minOccurs=0 maxOccurs=1)
> This attribute is a globally unique ID assigned to this element by .NET My Services. Normally, .NET My Services will generate and assign this ID during an insertRequest operation, or possibly during a replaceRequest. Application software can override this ID generation by specifying the useClientIds attribute in the request message. Once an ID is assigned, the attribute is read-only and attempts to write it are silently ignored.

/system/wsdlMap/@creator (string minOccurs=0 maxOccurs=1)
> This attribute identifies the creator in terms of userId, appId, and platformId of the node.

/system/wsdlMap/wsdl (minOccurs=0 maxOccurs=unbounded)
> This element is used to specify the location of a WSDL file for this service. Multiple entries may exist pointing to the same file hosted in multiple locations, or to variations on the content within the WSDL files.

/system/wsdlMap/wsdl/@wsdlLocation (anyURI minOccurs=0 maxOccurs=1)
> This attribute is a URI that specifies the location of the WSDL file.

/system/wsdlMap/wsdl/**{any}** (minOccurs=0 maxOccurs=unbounded)
/system/wsdlMap/disco (minOccurs=0 maxOccurs=unbounded)
> This element is used to specify the location of a DISCO file for this service. Multiple entries may exist pointing to the same file hosted in multiple locations, or to variations on the content within the DISCO files.

/system/wsdlMap/disco/@discoLocation (anyURI minOccurs=0 maxOccurs=1)
> This attribute is a URI that specifies the location of the DISCO file.

/system/wsdlMap/disco/**{any}** (minOccurs=0 maxOccurs=unbounded)
/system/{any} (minOccurs=0 maxOccurs=unbounded)

The .NET Documents Service/Methods

The .NET documents service supports the following standard and domain-specific methods:

- query
- insert
- replace
- delete
- update

The standard methods operate on this service using the same message format and method-interchange techniques described in the hsdl section of this document. The only service-specific information to note is the schema that is in effect for each of the methods. These schemas, and how they relate to the standard methods and roles, are described in the roles section of this document.

The domain specific methods operate as described in the domain specific methods section of this document, and are governed by the various schemas outlined in the .NET Documents Service/Roles section for this service.

CHAPTER 15

The .NET favorite web sites service/Introduction

This service is designed to store and manage the addresses and information of the favorite Web sites for an end user. In many ways, it is similar to the **Favorites** menu item in Internet Explorer or the **Favorites** button in MSN Explorer. Both of these applications maintain the user's favorite Web sites, and track usage. Microsoft .NET My Services provides this service so that the end user's favorite Web sites can be accessed anytime, anywhere and can be used in multiple applications.

The .NET favorite web sites service/Roles

The .NET favorite web sites service controls access by using the following roleTemplates:

- rt0
- rt1
- rt2
- rt3
- rt99

The .NET favorite web sites service uses the following scopes:

- **scope id 1**

```
<hs:scope id=1>

    <hs:shape base=t>

    </hs:shape>

</hs:scope>
```

- **scope id 2**

```
<hs:scope id=2>

    <hs:shape base=nil>

        <hs:include select=//*[@creator='$callerId']/>

    </hs:shape>

</hs:scope>
```

- **scope id 3**

```
<hs:scope id=3>

    <hs:shape base=nil>

        <hs:include select=//subscription[@creator='$callerId']/>

    </hs:shape>

</hs:scope>
```

- **scope id 4**

```
<hs:scope id=4>

    <hs:shape base=nil>

        <hs:include select=//*[cat/@ref='hs:public']/>

        <hs:include select=//subscription[@creator='$callerId']/>

    </hs:shape>

</hs:scope>
```

The .NET favorite web sites service roleTemplate rt0

The purpose of this role is to give complete read/write access to all information within the content document of the service being protected through this roleTemplate.

The following table illustrates the available methods and the scope in effect when accessing the .NET favorite web sites service through that method while mapped to this roleTemplate.

method	scopeRef
query	scopeRef=1
insert	scopeRef=1
replace	scopeRef=1
delete	scopeRef=1
update	scopeRef=1

The .NET favorite web sites service roleTemplate rt1

The purpose of this role is to give complete read access to all information within the content document of the service being protected through this roleTemplate. Applications mapping to this role also have a limited ability to write to information in the content document. They may create nodes in any location, but may only change/replace, or delete nodes that they created.

The following table illustrates the available methods and the scope in effect when accessing the .NET favorite web sites service through that method while mapped to this roleTemplate.

method	scopeRef
query	scopeRef=1
insert	scopeRef=2
replace	scopeRef=2
delete	scopeRef=2

The .NET favorite web sites service roleTemplate rt2

The purpose of this role is to give complete read access to all information within the content document of the service being protected through this roleTemplate. Applications mapping to this role have very limited write access and are only able to create and manipulate their own subscription nodes.

The following table illustrates the available methods and the scope in effect when accessing the .NET favorite web sites service through that method while mapped to this roleTemplate.

method	scopeRef
query	scopeRef=1
insert	scopeRef=3
replace	scopeRef=3
delete	scopeRef=3

The .NET favorite web sites service roleTemplate rt3

The purpose of this role is to give limited read access to information within the content document that is categorized as "public".

The following table illustrates the available methods and the scope in effect when accessing the .NET favorite web sites service through that method while mapped to this roleTemplate.

method	scopeRef
query	scopeRef=4

The .NET favorite web sites service roleTemplate rt99

The purpose of this role is to block all access to the content document. Note that lack of a role in the roleList has the same effect as assigning someone to rt99.

The .NET favorite web sites service/content

The content document is an identity-centric document. Its content and meaning is a function of the PUID used to address the service. Accessing the document is controlled by the associated roleList document.

This schema outline illustrates the layout and meaning of the information found in the content document for the .NET favorite web sites service.

```
<m:myFavoriteWebSites changeNumber="..." instanceId="..."
    xmlns:m="http://schemas.microsoft.com/hs/2001/10/myFavoriteWebSites"
    xmlns:hs="http://schemas.microsoft.com/hs/2001/10/core">1..1
    <m:favoriteWebSite changeNumber="..." id="..." creator="...">0..unbounded
        <m:cat ref="...">0..unbounded</m:cat>
        <m:title xml:lang="...">0..unbounded</m:title>
        <m:url>1..1</m:url>
        {any}
    </m:favoriteWebSite>
    <m:subscription changeNumber="..." id="..." creator="...">0..unbounded
        <hs:trigger select="..." mode="..."
baseChangeNumber="...">1..1</hs:trigger>
        <hs:expiresAt>0..1</hs:expiresAt>
        <hs:context uri="...">1..1 {any}</hs:context>
        <hs:to>1..1</hs:to>
    </m:subscription>
    {any}
</m:myFavoriteWebSites>
```

The meaning of the attributes and elements shown in the preceding sample document fragment are listed in the following section.

/myFavoriteWebSites (minOccurs=1 maxOccurs=1)
This element encapsulates the content document for the service. The cache scope for this document is the entire content document—that is, there is a single changeNumber attribute, and it occurs at the root element. Any change to the document changes this attribute.

/myFavoriteWebSites/@changeNumber (minOccurs=0 maxOccurs=1)
The changeNumber attribute is designed to facilitate caching of the element and its descendants. This attribute is assigned to this element by the .NET My Services system. The attribute is read-only to applications. Attempts to write this attribute are silently ignored.

/myFavoriteWebSites/@instanceId (string minOccurs=0 maxOccurs=1)
This attribute is a unique identifier typically assigned to the root element of a service. It is a read-only element and assigned by the .NET My Services system when a user is provisioned for a particular service.

/myFavoriteWebSites/favoriteWebSite (minOccurs=0 maxOccurs=unbounded)
This element describes a complete favorite Web site, including the title, URL, and free-form extensions. This element may contain 0 or more category elements that are used to organize favorite Web sites.

/myFavoriteWebSites/favoriteWebSite/@changeNumber (minOccurs=0 maxOccurs=1)
The changeNumber attribute is designed to facilitate caching of the element and its descendants. This attribute is assigned to this element by the .NET My Services system. The attribute is read-only to applications. Attempts to write this attribute are silently ignored.

/myFavoriteWebSites/favoriteWebSite/@id (minOccurs=0 maxOccurs=1)
This attribute is a globally unique ID assigned to this element by .NET My Services. Normally, .NET My Services will generate and assign this ID during an insertRequest operation, or possibly during a replaceRequest. Application software can override this ID generation by specifying the useClientIds attribute in the request message. Once an ID is assigned, the attribute is read-only and attempts to write it are silently ignored.

/myFavoriteWebSites/favoriteWebSite/@creator (string minOccurs=0 maxOccurs=1)
This attribute identifies the creator in terms of userId, appId, and platformId of the node.

/myFavoriteWebSites/favoriteWebSite/cat (minOccurs=0 maxOccurs=unbounded)
This element is used to categorize the element that contains it by referencing a global category definition in either the .NET categories service system document or an external resource containing category definitions, or by referencing an identity centric category definition in the content document of the .NET categories service for a particular PUID.

/myFavoriteWebSites/favoriteWebSite/cat/@ref (anyURI minOccurs=0 maxOccurs=1)
This attribute references a category definition (<catDef/>) element using the rules outlined in the .NET categories XMI manual.

/myFavoriteWebSites/favoriteWebSite/title (string minOccurs=0 maxOccurs=unbounded)
This element specifies the title of the favorite Web site. Its typical use is to fill this element from the HTML <title> element in the Web site referred to by this entry.

/myFavoriteWebSites/favoriteWebSite/title/@xml:lang (minOccurs=1 maxOccurs=1)
This required attribute is used to specify an ISO 639 language code or an ISO 3166 country code as described in RFC 1766. The value of this attribute indicates the language type of the content within this element.

/myFavoriteWebSites/favoriteWebSite/url (anyURI minOccurs=1 maxOccurs=1)
This required element specifies the URL used to navigate to the Web site referred to by this entry. Its content should be URL-encoded.

/myFavoriteWebSites/favoriteWebSite/*{any}* (minOccurs=0 maxOccurs=unbounded)

/myFavoriteWebSites/subscription (minOccurs=0 maxOccurs=unbounded)
This element defines a subscription node that is designed to be an xdb:blue node which when placed in a content document causes a subscription to be registered. A subscription contains a trigger element which selects a scope of coverage. When items change that are under this scope of coverage, a subscriptionResponse message is generated and sent to the specified destination address.

/myFavoriteWebSites/subscription/@changeNumber (minOccurs=0 maxOccurs=1)
The changeNumber attribute is designed to facilitate caching of the element and its descendants. This attribute is assigned to this element by the .NET My Services system. The attribute is read-only to applications. Attempts to write this attribute are silently ignored.

/myFavoriteWebSites/subscription/@id (minOccurs=0 maxOccurs=1)
This attribute is a globally unique ID assigned to this element by .NET My Services. Normally, .NET My Services will generate and assign this ID during an insertRequest operation, or possibly during a replaceRequest. Application software can override this ID generation by specifying the useClientIds attribute in the request message. Once an ID is assigned, the attribute is read-only and attempts to write it are silently ignored.

/myFavoriteWebSites/subscription/@creator (string minOccurs=0 maxOccurs=1)
This attribute identifies the creator in terms of userId, appId, and platformId of the node.

/myFavoriteWebSites/subscription/trigger (minOccurs=1 maxOccurs=1)

/myFavoriteWebSites/subscription/trigger/@select (string minOccurs=0 maxOccurs=1)
This item specifies an XPATH expression that specifies the nodes that are to be selected and watched for changes. The selection may only select xdb:blue nodes. As changes in this node set occur, they trigger the generation of a subscription message. These messages are then sent to the SOAP receiver listed in the "to" element.

/myFavoriteWebSites/subscription/trigger/@mode (string minOccurs=0 maxOccurs=1)
This attribute specifies whether or not the content of the changes that triggered the subscription is delivered in the subscription message, or whether the message simply indicates that something changed under the trigger. The attribute may be:

includeData
The data that changed, causing the subscription to trigger, is included in the subscription message. Note that deleted nodes are specified by their id, not by value.

excludeData
The data that changed, causing the subscription to trigger, is NOT included in the subscription message.

/myFavoriteWebSites/subscription/trigger/@baseChangeNumber (minOccurs=0 maxOccurs=1)
This attribute specifies the changeNumber value that the trigger is relative to. All changes between the specified change number, and the current state of the document relative to the selection are transmitted as subscription messages. This allows a client application to establish a subscription relative to some baseline. As in changeQuery, if the baseChangeNumber is way out of date relative to the current state of the document, and the service can not supply the changes in the subscription message, the subscription insert is rejected. A value of 0 means that the current values of the selected nodes are transmitted in the subscription message.

/myFavoriteWebSites/subscription/expiresAt (dateTime minOccurs=0 maxOccurs=1)
This optional element specifies an absolute time after which the subscription is no longer active. The subscription node is automatically removed when the subscription expires. If this element is missing, the subscription does not expire.

/myFavoriteWebSites/subscription/context (minOccurs=1 maxOccurs=1)
This element returns the context element from the original subscription. Applications should use this element, and only this element, to correlate the subscription response with one of their subscriptions.

/myFavoriteWebSites/subscription/context/@uri (anyURI minOccurs=0 maxOccurs=1)
This attribute specifies the URI value chosen by the subscriber that is associated with this subscription.

/myFavoriteWebSites/subscription/context/*{any}* (minOccurs=0 maxOccurs=unbounded)

/myFavoriteWebSites/subscription/to (anyURI minOccurs=1 maxOccurs=1)
> This attribute specifies the location that is to receive the subscription message. The value of this element may be one of the following forms:
>
> - *hs:myNotifications*—This URI indicates that generated subscription messages are to be delivered inside the body of a notification and delivered to the default .NET notifications service of the creator.
> - *protocol://service*—This URI indicates that generated subscription messages are delivered to the specified service at the domain of the creator's platformId. For instance, a platformId indicating msn.com, and a value in this element of http://subscriptionResponse would cause delivery of the subscription message to http://subscriptionResponse.msn.com.
>
> If this value is not specified, then the subscription message is delivered as a notification to the "creator's" .NET notifications service.

/myFavoriteWebSites/{any} (minOccurs=0 maxOccurs=unbounded)

The .NET favorite web sites service/system

The system document is a global document for the service. Its content and meaning is independent of the PUID used to address the service, and the document is read only to all users. The system document contains a set of base items common to all .NET My Services services, and is optionally extended by each service to include service-specific global information.

This schema outline illustrates the layout and meaning of the information found in the system document for the .NET favorite web sites service.

```
<sys:system changeNumber="..." instanceId="..."
    xmlns:hs="http://schemas.microsoft.com/hs/2001/10/core"

xmlns:sys="http://schemas.microsoft.com/hs/2001/10/myFavoriteWebSites/system">1..1
    <hs:roleMap changeNumber="..." id="..." creator="...">1..1
        <hs:scope id="...">0..unbounded
            <hs:shape base="...">1..1
                <hs:include select="...">1..unbounded</hs:include>
                <hs:exclude select="...">0..unbounded</hs:exclude>
            </hs:shape>
        </hs:scope>
        <hs:roleTemplate name="..." priority="...">0..unbounded
            <hs:fullDescription xml:lang="...">0..1</hs:fullDescription>
            <hs:method name="..." scopeRef="...">0..unbounded</hs:method>
        </hs:roleTemplate>
    </hs:roleMap>
    <hs:methodMap changeNumber="..." id="..." creator="...">1..1
        <hs:method name="...">0..unbounded {any}</hs:method>
    </hs:methodMap>
```

```
    <hs:schemaMap changeNumber="..." id="..." creator="...">₁..₁
        <hs:schema namespace="..." schemaLocation="..." alias="...">₀..unbounded
{any}</hs:schema>
    </hs:schemaMap>
    <hs:wsdlMap changeNumber="..." id="..." creator="...">₁..₁
        <hs:wsdl wsdlLocation="...">₀..unbounded {any}</hs:wsdl>
        <hs:disco discoLocation="...">₀..unbounded {any}</hs:disco>
    </hs:wsdlMap>
    {any}
</sys:system>
```

The meaning of the attributes and elements shown in the preceding sample document fragment are listed in the following section.

/system (minOccurs=1 maxOccurs=1)

This element encapsulates the system document for the .NET favorite web sites service.

/system/@changeNumber (minOccurs=0 maxOccurs=1)

The changeNumber attribute is designed to facilitate caching of the element and its descendants. This attribute is assigned to this element by the .NET My Services system. The attribute is read-only to applications. Attempts to write this attribute are silently ignored.

/system/@instanceId (string minOccurs=0 maxOccurs=1)

This attribute is a unique identifier typically assigned to the root element of a service. It is a read-only element and assigned by the .NET My Services system when a user is provisioned for a particular service.

/system/roleMap (minOccurs=1 maxOccurs=1)

This element encapsulates all the elements that make up a roleMap, which include document class relative roleTemplate, priority, name, method, and per-method scope. An individual roleTemplate defines the maximum scope of information, and the allowable methods used to access that information for each request mapped into the template.

/system/roleMap/@changeNumber (minOccurs=0 maxOccurs=1)

The changeNumber attribute is designed to facilitate caching of the element and its descendants. This attribute is assigned to this element by the .NET My Services system. The attribute is read-only to applications. Attempts to write this attribute are silently ignored.

/system/roleMap/@id (minOccurs=0 maxOccurs=1)

This attribute is a globally unique ID assigned to this element by .NET My Services. Normally, .NET My Services will generate and assign this ID during an insertRequest operation, or possibly during a replaceRequest. Application software can override this ID generation by specifying the useClientIds attribute in the request message. Once an ID is assigned, the attribute is read-only and attempts to write it are silently ignored.

/system/roleMap/@creator (string minOccurs=0 maxOccurs=1)
>   This attribute identifies the creator in terms of userId, appId, and platformId of the node.

/system/roleMap/scope (minOccurs=0 maxOccurs=unbounded)
>   This element defines a scope which may be referred to by roles within this roleMap to indicate what portions of the document are visible to this role for the specified method.

/system/roleMap/scope/@id (minOccurs=0 maxOccurs=1)
>   This attribute is a globally unique ID assigned to this element by .NET My Services. Normally, .NET My Services will generate and assign this ID during an insertRequest operation, or possibly during a replaceRequest. Application software can override this ID generation by specifying the useClientIds attribute in the request message. Once an ID is assigned, the attribute is read-only and attempts to write it are silently ignored.

/system/roleMap/scope/shape (minOccurs=1 maxOccurs=1)
>   A shape defines the node set visible through the document when operating through this shape element.

/system/roleMap/scope/shape/@base (string minOccurs=0 maxOccurs=1)
>   This attribute specifies the initial set of nodes visible through the shape.
>
>   A value of t indicates that the shape is initialized to include all possible nodes relative to the shape that is currently in effect. For instance, each role defines a scope containing a shape. When defining a shape for a role, the value t indicates all possible nodes available in the specified document for this role. When defining a shape in an ACL entry, a value of t means all of the nodes visible in the shape for the computed role. When using a shape in an hsdl operation, a value of t indicates all of the possible nodes selected by the hsdl operation (relative to the ACL shape which itself is relative to the role's shape).
>
>   The value nil indicates the opposite of t, which is the empty node set. Nodes from this set may then be included into the shape.

/system/roleMap/scope/shape/include (minOccurs=1 maxOccurs=unbounded)
>   This element specifies the set of nodes that should be included into the shape relative to the possible set of nodes indicated by the base attribute.

/system/roleMap/scope/shape/include/@select (string minOccurs=0 maxOccurs=1)
>   This item specifies an XPATH expression that selects a set of nodes relative to the externally established context. The expression can never travel outside the node-set established by this externally established current context. The expression may match 0 or more nodes, and the operation manipulates all selected nodes. The minOccurs and maxOccurs attributes are optional and place restrictions and limitations on the number of nodes selected.

/system/roleMap/scope/shape/exclude (minOccurs=0 maxOccurs=unbounded)
>   This element specifies the set of nodes that should be excluded from the shape relative to the possible set of nodes indicated by the base attribute.

/system/roleMap/scope/shape/exclude/@select (string minOccurs=0 maxOccurs=1)
This item specifies an XPATH expression that selects a set of nodes relative to the externally established context. The expression can never travel outside the node-set established by this externally established current context. The expression may match 0 or more nodes, and the operation manipulates all selected nodes. The minOccurs and maxOccurs attributes are optional and place restrictions and limitations on the number of nodes selected.

/system/roleMap/roleTemplate (minOccurs=0 maxOccurs=unbounded)
This element encapsulates the definition of a role. The attribute set for this element includes the document class that this roleTemplate refers to, the name of the roleTemplate, and the priority of the roleTemplate.

/system/roleMap/roleTemplate/@name (string minOccurs=0 maxOccurs=1)
This element specifies the name of the role.

/system/roleMap/roleTemplate/@priority (int minOccurs=0 maxOccurs=1)
This element specifies the priority of the roleTemplate which is used to select that actual roleTemplate when the role evaluation determines that the subject maps to multiple roleTemplates.

/system/roleMap/roleTemplate/fullDescription (string minOccurs=0 maxOccurs=1)
This element contains a description of this role template which specifies the capabilities a caller will have when accessing information through this role.

/system/roleMap/roleTemplate/fullDescription/@xml:lang (minOccurs=1 maxOccurs=1)
This required attribute is used to specify an ISO 639 language code or an ISO 3166 country code as described in RFC 1766. The value of this attribute indicates the language type of the content within this element.

/system/roleMap/roleTemplate/method (minOccurs=0 maxOccurs=unbounded)
This element specifies the methods available within this roleTemplate by name, and by scope. When a subject maps to a roleTemplate, the method in the request must match one of these elements for the message to continue to flow. If the method exists, the data available to the method is a function of the scope referenced by this method combined with an optional scope referenced by the role defined in the roleList.

/system/roleMap/roleTemplate/method/@name (string minOccurs=0 maxOccurs=1)
This element specifies the name of the method.

/system/roleMap/roleTemplate/method/@scopeRef (string minOccurs=0 maxOccurs=1)
This attribute specifies the scope within this document that is in effect for this method.

/system/methodMap (minOccurs=1 maxOccurs=1)
This element defines the methodMap. While it is true that in most cases, the roleMap section contains a definitive list of methods, these methods are likely to be scattered about the roleMap in various templates. This section contains the definitive non-duplicated list of methods available within the service.

/system/methodMap/@changeNumber (minOccurs=0 maxOccurs=1)
  The changeNumber attribute is designed to facilitate caching of the element and its
  descendants. This attribute is assigned to this element by the .NET My Services
  system. The attribute is read-only to applications. Attempts to write this attribute are
  silently ignored.

/system/methodMap/@id (minOccurs=0 maxOccurs=1)
  This attribute is a globally unique ID assigned to this element by .NET My Services.
  Normally, .NET My Services will generate and assign this ID during an insertRequest
  operation, or possibly during a replaceRequest. Application software can override this
  ID generation by specifying the useClientIds attribute in the request message. Once
  an ID is assigned, the attribute is read-only and attempts to write it are silently
  ignored.

/system/methodMap/@creator (string minOccurs=0 maxOccurs=1)
  This attribute identifies the creator in terms of userId, appId, and platformId of the
  node.

/system/methodMap/method (minOccurs=0 maxOccurs=unbounded)
  This element defines a method that is available within this service.

/system/methodMap/method/@name (string minOccurs=0 maxOccurs=1)
  This attribute specifies the name of a method available within the service.

/system/methodMap/method/*{any}* (minOccurs=0 maxOccurs=unbounded)
/system/schemaMap (minOccurs=1 maxOccurs=1)
  This element defines the various schemas that define the data structures and shape
  of information managed by this service. Each schema is defined by its namespace
  URI, its location, and a preferred namespace alias.

/system/schemaMap/@changeNumber (minOccurs=0 maxOccurs=1)
  The changeNumber attribute is designed to facilitate caching of the element and its
  descendants. This attribute is assigned to this element by the .NET My Services
  system. The attribute is read-only to applications. Attempts to write this attribute are
  silently ignored.

/system/schemaMap/@id (minOccurs=0 maxOccurs=1)
  This attribute is a globally unique ID assigned to this element by .NET My Services.
  Normally, .NET My Services will generate and assign this ID during an insertRequest
  operation, or possibly during a replaceRequest. Application software can override this
  ID generation by specifying the useClientIds attribute in the request message. Once
  an ID is assigned, the attribute is read-only and attempts to write it are silently
  ignored.

/system/schemaMap/@creator (string minOccurs=0 maxOccurs=1)
  This attribute identifies the creator in terms of userId, appId, and platformId of the
  node.

/system/schemaMap/schema (minOccurs=0 maxOccurs=unbounded)
  This element defines a schema which defines data-structures and the shape of
  information managed by this service. Multiple schema elements exist for each service,
  once for each logical grouping of information exposed by the service.

/system/schemaMap/schema/@namespace (anyURI minOccurs=0 maxOccurs=1)
This attribute specifies the namespace URI of this schema.

/system/schemaMap/schema/@schemaLocation (anyURI minOccurs=0 maxOccurs=1)
This attribute specifies the location (in the form of a URI) of the resource containing schema. When a schema is reachable through a variety of URIs, one schema element will exist for each location.

/system/schemaMap/schema/@alias (string minOccurs=0 maxOccurs=1)
This attribute specifies the preferred alias that should be used if possible when manipulating information covered by this schema in the context of this service.

/system/schemaMap/schema/*{any}* (minOccurs=0 maxOccurs=unbounded)
/system/wsdlMap (minOccurs=1 maxOccurs=1)
This element defines the wsdlMap for this service. This map includes the location of WSDL documents, DISCO documents, and WISL documents for this web service. These documents are used by applications to understand the format of messages that may be sent to the various services.

/system/wsdlMap/@changeNumber (minOccurs=0 maxOccurs=1)
The changeNumber attribute is designed to facilitate caching of the element and its descendants. This attribute is assigned to this element by the .NET My Services system. The attribute is read-only to applications. Attempts to write this attribute are silently ignored.

/system/wsdlMap/@id (minOccurs=0 maxOccurs=1)
This attribute is a globally unique ID assigned to this element by .NET My Services. Normally, .NET My Services will generate and assign this ID during an insertRequest operation, or possibly during a replaceRequest. Application software can override this ID generation by specifying the useClientIds attribute in the request message. Once an ID is assigned, the attribute is read-only and attempts to write it are silently ignored.

/system/wsdlMap/@creator (string minOccurs=0 maxOccurs=1)
This attribute identifies the creator in terms of userId, appId, and platformId of the node.

/system/wsdlMap/wsdl (minOccurs=0 maxOccurs=unbounded)
This element is used to specify the location of a WSDL file for this service. Multiple entries may exist pointing to the same file hosted in multiple locations, or to variations on the content within the WSDL files.

/system/wsdlMap/wsdl/@wsdlLocation (anyURI minOccurs=0 maxOccurs=1)
This attribute is a URI that specifies the location of the WSDL file.

/system/wsdlMap/wsdl/*{any}* (minOccurs=0 maxOccurs=unbounded)
/system/wsdlMap/disco (minOccurs=0 maxOccurs=unbounded)
This element is used to specify the location of a DISCO file for this service. Multiple entries may exist pointing to the same file hosted in multiple locations, or to variations on the content within the DISCO files.

/system/wsdlMap/disco/@discoLocation (anyURI minOccurs=0 maxOccurs=1)
    This attribute is a URI that specifies the location of the DISCO file.

/system/wsdlMap/disco/*{any}* (minOccurs=0 maxOccurs=unbounded)
/system/*{any}* (minOccurs=0 maxOccurs=unbounded)

The .NET favorite web sites service/Methods

The .NET favorite web sites service supports the following standard and domain-specific methods:

- query
- insert
- replace
- delete
- update

The standard methods operate on this service using the same message format and method-interchange techniques described in the hsdl section of this document. The only service-specific information to note is the schema that is in effect for each of the methods. These schemas, and how they relate to the standard methods and roles are described in the roles section of this document.

The domain specific methods operate as described in the domain specific methods section of this document, and are governed by the various schemas outlined in the .NET favorite web sites/Roles section for this service.

C H A P T E R   1 6

The .NET inbox service/Introduction

This service is designed to store and manage e-mail for the associated end user. Its primary purpose is to supply this information, on demand, to applications operating on the user's behalf. Using this service, the end user can manage e-mail from a variety of devices, and even manage multiple accounts from the same application.

Our expectation is that this service will eventually support some form of subscription or pending query, so that applications or services can reliably cache information contained within the service. An example of this caching might be an e-mail application or service. For each folder and message in the store, a subscription is issued against this service for that item. If the item changes, the application can refresh itself.

The .NET inbox service/Roles

The .NET inbox service controls access by using the following roleTemplates:

- rt0
- rt2
- rt99

The .NET inbox service uses the following scopes:

- **scope id 1**

```
<hs:scope id=1>

    <hs:shape base=t>

    </hs:shape>

</hs:scope>
```

- **scope id 2**

```
<hs:scope id=2>

    <hs:shape base=nil>

        <hs:include select=//*[@creator='$callerId']/>

    </hs:shape>

</hs:scope>
```

- **scope id 3**

```
<hs:scope id=3>

    <hs:shape base=nil>

        <hs:include select=//subscription[@creator='$callerId']/>

    </hs:shape>

</hs:scope>
```

- **scope id 4**

```
<hs:scope id=4>

    <hs:shape base=nil>

        <hs:include select=//*[cat/@ref='hs:public']/>

        <hs:include select=//subscription[@creator='$callerId']/>

    </hs:shape>

</hs:scope>
```

.NET inbox service roleTemplate rt0

The purpose of this role is to give complete read/write access to all information within the content document of the service being protected through this roleTemplate.

The following table illustrates the available methods and the scope in effect when accessing the .NET inbox service through that method while mapped to this roleTemplate.

method	scopeRef
query	scopeRef=1
insert	scopeRef=1
replace	scopeRef=1
delete	scopeRef=1
update	scopeRef=1
sendMessage	scopeRef=1
saveMessage	scopeRef=1
copyMessage	scopeRef=1

.NET inbox service roleTemplate rt2

The purpose of this role is to give complete read access to all information within the content document of the service being protected through this roleTemplate. Applications mapping to this role have very limited write access and are only able to create and manipulate their own subscription nodes.

The following table illustrates the available methods and the scope in effect when accessing the .NET inbox service through that method while mapped to this roleTemplate.

method	scopeRef
query	scopeRef=1
insert	scopeRef=3
replace	scopeRef=3
delete	scopeRef=3
sendMessage	scopeRef=1
saveMessage	scopeRef=1

.NET inbox service roleTemplate rt99

The purpose of this role is to block all access to the content document. Note that lack of a role in the roleList has the same effect as assigning someone to rt99.

.NET inbox service/content

The content document is an identity-centric document. Its content and meaning is a function of the PUID used to address the service. Accessing the document is controlled by the associated roleList document.

This schema outline illustrates the layout and meaning of the information found in the content document for the .NET inbox service.

```
<m:myInbox changeNumber="..." instanceId="..."
    xmlns:m="http://schemas.microsoft.com/hs/2001/10/myInbox"
    xmlns:hs="http://schemas.microsoft.com/hs/2001/10/core">1..1
    <m:account changeNumber="..." id="..." creator="...">1..unbounded
        <m:name xml:lang="...">1..1</m:name>
        <m:email>1..1</m:email>
        <m:cat ref="...">0..unbounded</m:cat>
        <m:pop3Settings>0..1
            <m:server>1..1</m:server>
            <m:userName>1..1</m:userName>
            <m:password>1..1</m:password>
        </m:pop3Settings>
        {any}
    </m:account>
    <m:folder changeNumber="..." id="..." creator="...">0..unbounded
        <m:name xml:lang="...">1..1</m:name>
        <m:type>1..1</m:type>
        <m:unread>1..1</m:unread>
        <m:parentFolder ref="...">1..1</m:parentFolder>
        <m:childFolderCount>1..1</m:childFolderCount>
        {any}
    </m:folder>
    <m:message changeNumber="..." id="..." creator="...">0..unbounded
        <m:messageStatus changeNumber="...">1..1
            <m:readState>1..1</m:readState>
            <m:folder ref="...">1..1</m:folder>
            <m:flag>0..1
                <m:state>1..1</m:state>
                <m:title xml:lang="...">1..1</m:title>
                <m:reminderDate>0..1</m:reminderDate>
                {any}
            </m:flag>
            <m:state>1..1</m:state>
            {any}
        </m:messageStatus>
```

```
<m:messageContent changeNumber="...">$_{1..1}$
    <m:cat ref="...">$_{0..unbounded}$</m:cat>
    <m:account ref="...">$_{1..1}$</m:account>
    <m:messageType>$_{1..1}$
        <m:type>$_{1..1}$</m:type>
        <m:contentType>$_{0..1}$</m:contentType>
        {any}
    </m:messageType>
    <m:size>$_{1..1}$</m:size>
    <m:importance>$_{1..1}$</m:importance>
    <m:sensitivity>$_{1..1}$</m:sensitivity>
    <m:hasAttachments>$_{1..1}$</m:hasAttachments>
    <m:conversationId>$_{0..1}$</m:conversationId>
    <m:conversationIndex>$_{0..1}$</m:conversationIndex>
    <m:dateReceived>$_{1..1}$</m:dateReceived>
    <m:dateSent>$_{1..1}$</m:dateSent>
    <m:subject xml:lang="...">$_{1..1}$
        <m:prefix>$_{1..1}$</m:prefix>
        <m:text>$_{1..1}$</m:text>
    </m:subject>
    <m:from>$_{1..1}$
        <m:name xml:lang="...">$_{1..1}$</m:name>
        <m:email>$_{1..1}$</m:email>
    </m:from>
    <m:recipient type="...">$_{0..unbounded}$
        <m:name xml:lang="...">$_{1..1}$</m:name>
        <m:email>$_{1..1}$</m:email>
    </m:recipient>
    <m:messagePart id="...">$_{0..unbounded}$
        <m:parentPart ref="...">$_{1..1}$</m:parentPart>
        <m:order>$_{1..1}$</m:order>
        <m:contentType>$_{1..1}$</m:contentType>
        <m:size>$_{1..1}$</m:size>
        <m:contentDisposition>$_{0..1}$</m:contentDisposition>
        <m:contentId>$_{0..1}$</m:contentId>
        <m:contentLocation>$_{0..1}$</m:contentLocation>
        <m:contentTransferEncoding>$_{0..1}$</m:contentTransferEncoding>
        <m:partContent>$_{0..1}$</m:partContent>
    </m:messagePart>
    <m:preview xml:lang="...">$_{0..1}$</m:preview>
    <m:single2822Header>$_{0..unbounded}$</m:single2822Header>
    <m:raw2822Content>$_{0..1}$</m:raw2822Content>
    <m:raw2822Headers>$_{0..1}$</m:raw2822Headers>
    {any}
</m:messageContent>
```

(continued)

(continued)

```
        {any}
    </m:message>
    <m:draft changeNumber="..." id="..." creator="...">₀..unbounded
        <m:messageStatus changeNumber="...">₁..₁
            <m:readState>₁..₁</m:readState>
            <m:folder ref="...">₁..₁</m:folder>
            <m:flag>₀..₁
                <m:state>₁..₁</m:state>
                <m:title xml:lang="...">₁..₁</m:title>
                <m:reminderDate>₀..₁</m:reminderDate>
                {any}
            </m:flag>
            <m:state>₁..₁</m:state>
            {any}
        </m:messageStatus>
        <m:messageContent changeNumber="...">₁..₁
            <m:cat ref="...">₀..unbounded</m:cat>
            <m:account ref="...">₁..₁</m:account>
            <m:messageType>₁..₁
                <m:type>₁..₁</m:type>
                <m:contentType>₀..₁</m:contentType>
                {any}
            </m:messageType>
            <m:size>₁..₁</m:size>
            <m:importance>₁..₁</m:importance>
            <m:sensitivity>₁..₁</m:sensitivity>
            <m:hasAttachments>₁..₁</m:hasAttachments>
            <m:conversationId>₀..₁</m:conversationId>
            <m:conversationIndex>₀..₁</m:conversationIndex>
            <m:subject xml:lang="...">₁..₁
                <m:prefix>₁..₁</m:prefix>
                <m:text>₁..₁</m:text>
            </m:subject>
            <m:from>₁..₁
                <m:name xml:lang="...">₁..₁</m:name>
                <m:email>₁..₁</m:email>
            </m:from>
            <m:recipient type="...">₀..unbounded
                <m:name xml:lang="...">₁..₁</m:name>
                <m:email>₁..₁</m:email>
            </m:recipient>
```

```
        <m:messagePart changeNumber="...">0..unbounded
            <m:parentPart ref="...">1..1</m:parentPart>
            <m:order>1..1</m:order>
            <m:contentType>1..1</m:contentType>
            <m:size>1..1</m:size>
            <m:contentDisposition>0..1</m:contentDisposition>
            <m:contentId>0..1</m:contentId>
            <m:contentLocation>0..1</m:contentLocation>
            <m:contentTransferEncoding>0..1</m:contentTransferEncoding>
            <m:partContent>0..1</m:partContent>
            {any}
        </m:messagePart>
        <m:preview xml:lang="...">0..1</m:preview>
        <m:single2822Header>0..unbounded</m:single2822Header>
        <m:raw2822Content>0..1</m:raw2822Content>
        <m:raw2822Headers>0..1</m:raw2822Headers>
        {any}
    </m:messageContent>
    {any}
</m:draft>
<m:rule sequence="..." changeNumber="..." id="..." creator="...">0..unbounded
    <m:name xml:lang="...">1..1</m:name>
    <m:enabled>1..1</m:enabled>
    <m:runat>1..1</m:runat>
    <m:runwhen>1..1</m:runwhen>
    <m:type>1..1</m:type>
    <m:provider xml:lang="...">1..1</m:provider>
    <m:condition select="...">1..1</m:condition>
    <m:action sequence="...">1..unbounded
        <m:copyMessage>0..1
            <m:targetFolder select="...">1..1</m:targetFolder>

<m:stopProcessingRulesOfThisType>0..1</m:stopProcessingRulesOfThisType>
        </m:copyMessage>
        <m:moveMessage>0..1
            <m:targetFolder select="...">1..1</m:targetFolder>

<m:stopProcessingRulesOfThisType>0..1</m:stopProcessingRulesOfThisType>
        </m:moveMessage>
        <m:deleteMessage>0..1

<m:stopProcessingRulesOfThisType>0..1</m:stopProcessingRulesOfThisType>
        </m:deleteMessage>
```

(continued)

(continued)

```
        <m:assignCategory>₀...₁
            <m:cat ref="...">₀...unbounded</m:cat>

<m:stopProcessingRulesOfThisType>₀...₁</m:stopProcessingRulesOfThisType>
        </m:assignCategory>
        <m:forwardMessage>₀...₁
            <m:recipient type="...">₀...unbounded
                <m:name xml:lang="...">₁...₁</m:name>
                <m:email>₁...₁</m:email>
            </m:recipient>

<m:stopProcessingRulesOfThisType>₀...₁</m:stopProcessingRulesOfThisType>
        </m:forwardMessage>
        <m:forwardAsAttachment>₀...₁
            <m:recipient type="...">₀...unbounded
                <m:name xml:lang="...">₁...₁</m:name>
                <m:email>₁...₁</m:email>
            </m:recipient>

<m:stopProcessingRulesOfThisType>₀...₁</m:stopProcessingRulesOfThisType>
        </m:forwardAsAttachment>
        <m:serverReply>₀...₁
            <m:subject xml:lang="...">₁...₁
                <m:prefix>₁...₁</m:prefix>
                <m:text>₁...₁</m:text>
            </m:subject>
            <m:simpleBody xml:lang="...">₁...₁</m:simpleBody>

<m:stopProcessingRulesOfThisType>₀...₁</m:stopProcessingRulesOfThisType>
        </m:serverReply>
        <m:redirectMessage>₀...₁
            <m:recipient type="...">₀...unbounded
                <m:name xml:lang="...">₁...₁</m:name>
                <m:email>₁...₁</m:email>
            </m:recipient>

<m:stopProcessingRulesOfThisType>₀...₁</m:stopProcessingRulesOfThisType>
        </m:redirectMessage>
        <m:flagMessage>₀...₁
            <m:flag>₁...₁
                <m:state>₁...₁</m:state>
                <m:title xml:lang="...">₁...₁</m:title>
                <m:reminderDate>₀...₁</m:reminderDate>
```

```
                        {any}
                    </m:flag>

<m:stopProcessingRulesOfThisType>₀..₁</m:stopProcessingRulesOfThisType>
            </m:flagMessage>
            <m:markAsRead>₀..₁

<m:stopProcessingRulesOfThisType>₀..₁</m:stopProcessingRulesOfThisType>
            </m:markAsRead>
        </m:action>
        {any}
    </m:rule>
    <m:subscription changeNumber="..." id="..." creator="...">₀..unbounded
        <hs:trigger select="..." mode="..."
baseChangeNumber="...">₁..₁</hs:trigger>
        <hs:expiresAt>₀..₁</hs:expiresAt>
        <hs:context uri="...">₁..₁ {any}</hs:context>
        <hs:to>₁..₁</hs:to>
    </m:subscription>
    {any}
</m:myInbox>
```

The meaning of the attributes and elements shown in the preceding sample document fragment are listed in the following section.

/myInbox (minOccurs=1 maxOccurs=1)

This represents the root element of *myInbox*.

/myInbox/@changeNumber (minOccurs=0 maxOccurs=1)

The changeNumber attribute is designed to facilitate caching of the element and its descendants. This attribute is assigned to this element by the Microsoft .NET My Services system. The attribute is read-only to applications. Attempts to write this attribute are silently ignored.

/myInbox/@instanceId (string minOccurs=0 maxOccurs=1)

This attribute is a unique identifier typically assigned to the root element of a service. It is a read-only element and assigned by the .NET My Services system when a user is provisioned for a particular service.

/myInbox/account (minOccurs=1 maxOccurs=unbounded)

This represents an email account that this service abstracts.

/myInbox/account/@changeNumber (minOccurs=0 maxOccurs=1)

The changeNumber attribute is designed to facilitate caching of the element and its descendants. This attribute is assigned to this element by the .NET My Services system. The attribute is read-only to applications. Attempts to write this attribute are silently ignored.

/myInbox/account/@id (minOccurs=0 maxOccurs=1)

This attribute is a globally unique ID assigned to this element by .NET My Services. Normally, .NET My Services will generate and assign this ID during an insertRequest operation, or possibly during a replaceRequest. Application software can override this ID generation by specifying the useClientIds attribute in the request message. Once an ID is assigned, the attribute is read-only and attempts to write it are silently ignored.

/myInbox/account/@creator (string minOccurs=0 maxOccurs=1)

This attribute identifies the creator in terms of userId, appId, and platformId of the node.

/myInbox/account/name (string minOccurs=1 maxOccurs=1)

This displays the name of the account.

/myInbox/account/name/@xml:lang (minOccurs=1 maxOccurs=1)

This required attribute is used to specify an ISO 639 language code or an ISO 3166 country code as described in RFC 1766. The value of this attribute indicates the language type of the content within this element.

/myInbox/account/email (string minOccurs=1 maxOccurs=1)

This displays the name of the email account.

/myInbox/account/cat (minOccurs=0 maxOccurs=unbounded)

This element is used to categorize this account as a primary or non-primary account.

/myInbox/account/cat/@ref (anyURI minOccurs=0 maxOccurs=1)

This attribute references a category definition (<catDef/>) element using the rules outlined in the .NET categories service XMI manual.

/myInbox/account/pop3Settings (minOccurs=0 maxOccurs=1)

If this account is a pop3 account, this defines pop3 settings.

/myInbox/account/pop3Settings/server (string minOccurs=1 maxOccurs=1)

If this account is a pop3 account, this defines pop3 server settings.

/myInbox/account/pop3Settings/userName (string minOccurs=1 maxOccurs=1)

If this account is a pop3 account, this defines pop3 user settings.

/myInbox/account/pop3Settings/password (string minOccurs=1 maxOccurs=1)

If this account is a pop3 account, this defines pop3 password settings.

/myInbox/account/{any} (minOccurs=0 maxOccurs=unbounded)

/myInbox/folder (minOccurs=0 maxOccurs=unbounded)

Folder elements in .NET inbox service are containers for messages, although not directly. Messages are related to folders via the */myInbox/message/messageStatus/folder ref=""* attribute. Folders can be organized hierarchically, although again not directly. Instead, folder containment is modeled using the */myInbox/folder/parentFolder ref=""* attribute. If a folder is deleted, all associated messages, folders, and their messages are deleted. It is recommended that instead of deleting a folder directly, you move it to the type="deleted" folder first. There are four built-in types of folders and these can be identified by four special type element values: */folder/type = 'inbox'* is the Inbox folder. */folder/type = 'sent'* is the Sent Items folder. */folder/type = 'drafts'* is the Drafts folder. */folder/type = 'deleted'* is the Deleted Items folder. These four special folders will always exist in a provisioned .NET inbox service account. They can never be deleted or modified. To create user-defined folders, you can use the standard .NET My Services insert method and set the type to 'custom'. Custom folders can be deleted or modified.

/myInbox/folder/@changeNumber (minOccurs=0 maxOccurs=1)

The changeNumber attribute is designed to facilitate caching of the element and its descendants. This attribute is assigned to this element by the .NET My Services system. The attribute is read-only to applications. Attempts to write this attribute are silently ignored.

/myInbox/folder/@id (minOccurs=0 maxOccurs=1)

This attribute is a globally unique ID assigned to this element by .NET My Services. Normally, .NET My Services will generate and assign this ID during an insertRequest operation, or possibly during a replaceRequest. Application software can override this ID generation by specifying the useClientIds attribute in the request message. Once an ID is assigned, the attribute is read-only and attempts to write it are silently ignored.

/myInbox/folder/@creator (string minOccurs=0 maxOccurs=1)

This attribute identifies the creator in terms of userId, appId, and platformId of the node.

/myInbox/folder/name (string minOccurs=1 maxOccurs=1)

This element contains the name of the e-mail folder. For the four special folders, this element is read-only. For custom folders, this element can be edited.

/myInbox/folder/name/@xml:lang (minOccurs=1 maxOccurs=1)

This required attribute is used to specify an ISO 639 language code or an ISO 3166 country code as described in RFC 1766. The value of this attribute indicates the language type of the content within this element.

/myInbox/folder/type (string minOccurs=1 maxOccurs=1)

This element contains a type identifier for this folder and will contain the value '*inbox*, '*sent*', '*drafts*', or '*delete*' for the four special folders. For all other folders, this value will be '*custom*'.

/myInbox/folder/unread (unsignedLong minOccurs=1 maxOccurs=1)

The calculated count of the unread messages associated with this folder. This element is read-only.

/myInbox/folder/parentFolder (minOccurs=1 maxOccurs=1)

This element contains a ref attribute that specifies the ID of the parent folder. For top-level folders, this attribute = "". This attribute cannot be set on the four special folders as they must always remain top-level folders.

/myInbox/folder/parentFolder/@ref (minOccurs=0 maxOccurs=1)

The uuidType is used to specify a UUID. Note that the base type below is probably wrong and needs to be fixed to match a correct definition for a UUID.

/myInbox/folder/childFolderCount (unsignedLong minOccurs=1 maxOccurs=1)

This calculated attribute indicates how many sub-folders that folder contains. See also '*parentFolder*'.

/myInbox/folder/{*any*} (minOccurs=0 maxOccurs=unbounded)

/myInbox/message (minOccurs=0 maxOccurs=unbounded)

This element defines a single message in the .NET inbox service in the base schema. A message represents an email and is divided into two sub-groups: '*messageStatus*' and '*messageContent*'.

/myInbox/message/@changeNumber (minOccurs=0 maxOccurs=1)

The changeNumber attribute is designed to facilitate caching of the element and its descendants. This attribute is assigned to this element by the .NET My Services system. The attribute is read-only to applications. Attempts to write this attribute are silently ignored.

/myInbox/message/@id (minOccurs=0 maxOccurs=1)

This attribute is a globally unique ID assigned to this element by .NET My Services. Normally, .NET My Services will generate and assign this ID during an insertRequest operation, or possibly during a replaceRequest. Application software can override this ID generation by specifying the useClientIds attribute in the request message. Once an ID is assigned, the attribute is read-only and attempts to write it are silently ignored.

/myInbox/message/@creator (string minOccurs=0 maxOccurs=1)

This attribute identifies the creator in terms of userId, appId, and platformId of the node.

/myInbox/message/messageStatus (minOccurs=1 maxOccurs=1)

This element defines the status of the email and frequently changes. Caching clients should take advantage of this when deciding which part of the message to change

/myInbox/message/messageStatus/@changeNumber (minOccurs=0 maxOccurs=1)

The changeNumber attribute is designed to facilitate caching of the element and its descendants. This attribute is assigned to this element by the .NET My Services system. The attribute is read-only to applications. Attempts to write this attribute are silently ignored.

/myInbox/message/messageStatus/readState (boolean minOccurs=1 maxOccurs=1)

This element defines the read/unread state of the message and can be modified.

/myInbox/message/messageStatus/folder (minOccurs=1 maxOccurs=1)

This element defines the single folder that this message logically belongs to.

/myInbox/message/messageStatus/folder/@ref (minOccurs=0 maxOccurs=1)
> The *uuidType* is used to specify a UUID. Note that the base type below is probably wrong and needs to be fixed to match a correct definition for a UUID.

/myInbox/message/messageStatus/flag (minOccurs=0 maxOccurs=1)
> This optional element defines the flag state of the message. It includes an {any} element that can be used for extensible flags.

/myInbox/message/messageStatus/flag/state (string minOccurs=1 maxOccurs=1)
> The state of a message flag.

/myInbox/message/messageStatus/flag/title (string minOccurs=1 maxOccurs=1)
> The client defined text of the flag.

/myInbox/message/messageStatus/flag/title/@xml:lang (minOccurs=1 maxOccurs=1)
> This required attribute is used to specify an ISO 639 language code or an ISO 3166 country code as described in RFC 1766. The value of this attribute indicates the language type of the content within this element.

/myInbox/message/messageStatus/flag/reminderDate (dateTime minOccurs=0 maxOccurs=1)
> The client-defined reminder date of the flag.

/myInbox/message/messageStatus/flag/*{any}* (minOccurs=0 maxOccurs=unbounded)
/myInbox/message/messageStatus/state (string minOccurs=1 maxOccurs=1)
> This element defines the sent/draft/received state of the message. This element is read-only, which means that it can be queried for, but not updated.

/myInbox/message/messageStatus/*{any}* (minOccurs=0 maxOccurs=unbounded)
/myInbox/message/messageContent (minOccurs=1 maxOccurs=1)
> This element defines the content of the message. This data changes rarely in a normal application.

/myInbox/message/messageContent/@changeNumber (minOccurs=0 maxOccurs=1)
> The changeNumber attribute is designed to facilitate caching of the element and its descendants. This attribute is assigned to this element by the .NET My Services system. The attribute is read-only to applications. Attempts to write this attribute are silently ignored.

/myInbox/message/messageContent/cat (minOccurs=0 maxOccurs=unbounded)
> This element is used to categorize the element that contains it by referencing a global category definition in either the .NET categories service system document or an external resource containing category definitions, or by referencing an identity centric category definition in the content document of the .NET categories service for a particular PUID.

/myInbox/message/messageContent/cat/@ref (anyURI minOccurs=0 maxOccurs=1)
> This attribute references a category definition (<catDef/>) element using the rules outlined in the .NET categories service XMI manual.

/myInbox/message/messageContent/account (minOccurs=1 maxOccurs=1)
> This element contains a reference to the */myInbox/account* element that this message was sent to.

/myInbox/message/messageContent/account/@ref (minOccurs=0 maxOccurs=1)
> The *uuidType* is used to specify a UUID. Note that the base type below is probably wrong and needs to be fixed to match a correct definition for a UUID.

/myInbox/message/messageContent/messageType (minOccurs=1 maxOccurs=1)
> The subelements of this element describe the contents of the message.

/myInbox/message/messageContent/messageType/type (string minOccurs=1 maxOccurs=1)
> This element contains a value that provides the client with enough information to render an 'Inbox' view of the messages. Valid values are *'voice'*, *'subscription'*, *'fax'*, *'dsn'*, *'readReceipt'*, *'meetingResponse'*, *'meetingRequest'*, *'email'* or *'liveEmail'*.

/myInbox/message/messageContent/messageType/contentType (string minOccurs=0 maxOccurs=1)
> The *contentType* of the message (in accordance with RFC 2045). Examples of this are: 'text/plain' and 'multipart/mime'.

/myInbox/message/messageContent/messageType/***{any}*** (minOccurs=0 maxOccurs=unbounded)

/myInbox/message/messageContent/size (unsignedLong minOccurs=1 maxOccurs=1)
> This element contains the size, in bytes, of the entire RFC2822 message in the store.

/myInbox/message/messageContent/importance (string minOccurs=1 maxOccurs=1)
> This element indicates the importance of this message. The value can be '*low*', '*normal*', or '*high*'. The default is '*normal*'.

/myInbox/message/messageContent/sensitivity (string minOccurs=1 maxOccurs=1)
> This element indicates the sensitivity of the message. The value can be *'normal'*, *'personal'*, *'private'*, or *'confidential'*.

/myInbox/message/messageContent/hasAttachments (boolean minOccurs=1 maxOccurs=1)
> This element indicates whether a message has one or more attachments. The value will either be 0 (to indicate that the message has no attachments) or 1 (to indicate that the message has one or more attachments).

/myInbox/message/messageContent/conversationId (string minOccurs=0 maxOccurs=1)
> This optional element identifies the conversation, or e-mail thread, of which this message is a part.

/myInbox/message/messageContent/conversationIndex (string minOccurs=0 maxOccurs=1)
> This optional element identifies the conversation, or e-mail thread of which this message is a part.

/myInbox/message/messageContent/dateReceived (dateTime minOccurs=1 maxOccurs=1)
> This read-only element contains the UTC date/time the message was received, and appears in all messages except ones that were sent by the user.

/myInbox/message/messageContent/dateSent (dateTime minOccurs=1 maxOccurs=1)
This read-only element contains the UTC date/time the message was sent. For */message/messageStatus/state="sent"* messages, this element represents the time the message was sent. For */messssage/messageStatus/state="received",* this element represents the time the sender sent the message.

/myInbox/message/messageContent/subject (minOccurs=1 maxOccurs=1)
The subject of the message. This element contains both a prefix and text subelements to allow clients to sort on the non-prefix part of the subject (so RE: RE: doesn't get sorted).

/myInbox/message/messageContent/subject/@xml:lang (minOccurs=1 maxOccurs=1)
This required attribute is used to specify an ISO 639 language code or an ISO 3166 country code as described in RFC 1766. The value of this attribute indicates the language type of the content within this element.

/myInbox/message/messageContent/subject/prefix (string minOccurs=1 maxOccurs=1)
The prefix of a message subject (example: 'FW: ').

/myInbox/message/messageContent/subject/text (string minOccurs=1 maxOccurs=1)
The subject of a message minus the prefix (example: 'hello there').

/myInbox/message/messageContent/from (minOccurs=1 maxOccurs=1)
This read-only element describes who this message is from.

/myInbox/message/messageContent/from/name (string minOccurs=1 maxOccurs=1)
The display name of an e-mail address.

/myInbox/message/messageContent/from/name/@xml:lang (minOccurs=1 maxOccurs=1)
This required attribute is used to specify an ISO 639 language code or an ISO 3166 country code as described in RFC 1766. The value of this attribute indicates the language type of the content within this element.

/myInbox/message/messageContent/from/email (string minOccurs=1 maxOccurs=1)
An e-mail address (for example, someone@microsoft.com).

/myInbox/message/messageContent/recipient (minOccurs=0 maxOccurs=unbounded)
Specifies the recipient of this message and where they appear. A collection of recipient elements is returned only if the query option 'expandRecipients' is specified.

/myInbox/message/messageContent/recipient/@type (string minOccurs=0 maxOccurs=1)
Specifies whether the recipient is in the 'to' or 'cc' list.

/myInbox/message/messageContent/recipient/name (string minOccurs=1 maxOccurs=1)
The display name of an e-mail address.

/myInbox/message/messageContent/recipient/name/@xml:lang (minOccurs=1 maxOccurs=1)
This required attribute is used to specify an ISO 639 language code or an ISO 3166 country code as described in RFC 1766. The value of this attribute indicates the language type of the content within this element.

/myInbox/message/messageContent/recipient/email (string minOccurs=1 maxOccurs=1)
> An e-mail address (for example, someone@microsoft.com).

/myInbox/message/messageContent/messagePart (minOccurs=0 maxOccurs=unbounded)
> The element and its children define the message structure (including the mime body) This element is returned by passing the '*includeMessagePartStructure*' element in query options.

/myInbox/message/messageContent/messagePart/@id (minOccurs=0 maxOccurs=1)

/myInbox/message/messageContent/messagePart/parentPart (minOccurs=1 maxOccurs=1)
> This element points to the parent part of this part.

/myInbox/message/messageContent/messagePart/parentPart/@ref (minOccurs=0 maxOccurs=1)
> The *uuidType* is used to specify a UUID. Note that the base type below is probably wrong and needs to be fixed to match a correct definition for a UUID.

/myInbox/message/messageContent/messagePart/order (unsignedLong minOccurs=1 maxOccurs=1)
> This element defines the order of this part relative to its siblings.

/myInbox/message/messageContent/messagePart/contentType (string minOccurs=1 maxOccurs=1)
> This element defines the contentType of the part (example: message/rfc or text/plain.a).

/myInbox/message/messageContent/messagePart/size (unsignedLong minOccurs=1 maxOccurs=1)
> The size in bytes of the message part (including mime headers).

/myInbox/message/messageContent/messagePart/contentDisposition (string minOccurs=0 maxOccurs=1)
> The element defines the content-disposition of the part (example: attachment; filename="txt1.txt").

/myInbox/message/messageContent/messagePart/contentId (string minOccurs=0 maxOccurs=1)
> The element defines the content-id of the part.

/myInbox/message/messageContent/messagePart/contentLocation (string minOccurs=0 maxOccurs=1)
> The element defines the content-location of the part.

/myInbox/message/messageContent/messagePart/contentTransferEncoding (string minOccurs=0 maxOccurs=1)
> The element defines the content-transfer-encoding of this part.

/myInbox/message/messageContent/messagePart/partContent (base64Binary minOccurs=0 maxOccurs=1)
> This element contains the content of this message part.

/myInbox/message/messageContent/preview (string minOccurs=0 maxOccurs=1)
> The first 256 characters of the message body. This element is returned only if the query option 'includePreview' is specified.

/myInbox/message/messageContent/preview/@xml:lang (minOccurs=1 maxOccurs=1)
> This required attribute is used to specify an ISO 639 language code or an ISO 3166 country code as described in RFC 1766. The value of this attribute indicates the language type of the content within this element.

/myInbox/message/messageContent/single2822Header (string minOccurs=0 maxOccurs=unbounded)
> The rfc2822 headers not included in the base schema (example: x-apparently-to). This element is returned by passing the 'includeSingle2822Headers' element in query options .

/myInbox/message/messageContent/raw2822Content (base64Binary minOccurs=0 maxOccurs=1)
> The raw 2822 message (including headers and body). This element is returned by passing the includeRaw2822Contentelement in query options.

/myInbox/message/messageContent/raw2822Headers (base64Binary minOccurs=0 maxOccurs=1)
> The raw rfc2822 headers not included in the base schema (example: x-apparently-to). This element is returned by passing the 'includeRaw2822Headers' element in query options.

/myInbox/message/messageContent/*{any}* (minOccurs=0 maxOccurs=unbounded)
/myInbox/message/*{any}* (minOccurs=0 maxOccurs=unbounded)
/myInbox/draft (minOccurs=0 maxOccurs=unbounded)
> This element defines a single draft in the .NET inbox service in the base schema. A draft represents an unsent email and is divided into two sub-groups: '*messageStatus*' and '*messageContent*'.

/myInbox/draft/@changeNumber (minOccurs=0 maxOccurs=1)
> The changeNumber attribute is designed to facilitate caching of the element and its descendants. This attribute is assigned to this element by the .NET My Services system. The attribute is read-only to applications. Attempts to write this attribute are silently ignored.

/myInbox/draft/@id (minOccurs=0 maxOccurs=1)
> This attribute is a globally unique ID assigned to this element by .NET My Services. Normally, .NET My Services will generate and assign this ID during an insertRequest operation, or possibly during a replaceRequest. Application software can override this ID generation by specifying the useClientIds attribute in the request message. Once an ID is assigned, the attribute is read-only and attempts to write it are silently ignored.

/myInbox/draft/@creator (string minOccurs=0 maxOccurs=1)
> This attribute identifies the creator in terms of userId, appId, and platformId of the node.

/myInbox/draft/messageStatus (minOccurs=1 maxOccurs=1)

/myInbox/draft/messageStatus/@changeNumber (minOccurs=0 maxOccurs=1)
> The changeNumber attribute is designed to facilitate caching of the element and its descendants. This attribute is assigned to this element by the .NET My Services system. The attribute is read-only to applications. Attempts to write this attribute are silently ignored.

/myInbox/draft/messageStatus/readState (boolean minOccurs=1 maxOccurs=1)
> This element defines the read/unread state of the message and can be modified.

/myInbox/draft/messageStatus/folder (minOccurs=1 maxOccurs=1)
> This element defines the single folder that this message logically belongs to. For drafts this must always point to the drafts folder.

/myInbox/draft/messageStatus/folder/@ref (minOccurs=0 maxOccurs=1)
> The *uuidType* is used to specify a UUID. Note that the base type below is probably wrong and needs to be fixed to match a correct definition for a UUID.

/myInbox/draft/messageStatus/flag (minOccurs=0 maxOccurs=1)
> This optional element defines the flag state of the message. It includes an {any} element that can be used for extensible flags.

/myInbox/draft/messageStatus/flag/state (string minOccurs=1 maxOccurs=1)
> The state of a message flag.

/myInbox/draft/messageStatus/flag/title (string minOccurs=1 maxOccurs=1)
> The client-defined text of the flag.

/myInbox/draft/messageStatus/flag/title/@xml:lang (minOccurs=1 maxOccurs=1)
> This required attribute is used to specify an ISO 639 language code or an ISO 3166 country code as described in RFC 1766. The value of this attribute indicates the language type of the content within this element.

/myInbox/draft/messageStatus/flag/reminderDate (dateTime minOccurs=0 maxOccurs=1)
> The client-defined reminder date of the flag.

/myInbox/draft/messageStatus/flag/*{any}* (minOccurs=0 maxOccurs=unbounded)

/myInbox/draft/messageStatus/state (string minOccurs=1 maxOccurs=1)
> The value of this element will always be 'draft' and is provided for compatibility with messages.

/myInbox/draft/messageStatus/*{any}* (minOccurs=0 maxOccurs=unbounded)

/myInbox/draft/messageContent (minOccurs=1 maxOccurs=1)

/myInbox/draft/messageContent/@changeNumber (minOccurs=0 maxOccurs=1)
> The changeNumber attribute is designed to facilitate caching of the element and its descendants. This attribute is assigned to this element by the .NET My Services system. The attribute is read-only to applications. Attempts to write this attribute are silently ignored.

/myInbox/draft/messageContent/cat (minOccurs=0 maxOccurs=unbounded)
> This element is used to categorize the element that contains it by referencing a global category definition in either the .NET categories service system document or an external resource containing category definitions, or by referencing an identity centric category definition in the content document of the .NET categories service for a particular PUID.

/myInbox/draft/messageContent/cat/@ref (anyURI minOccurs=0 maxOccurs=1)
> This attribute references a category definition (<catDef/>) element using the rules outlined in the .NET categories service XMI manual.

/myInbox/draft/messageContent/account (minOccurs=1 maxOccurs=1)
> This element contains a reference to the */myInbox/account* element ref that this message should be sent from.

/myInbox/draft/messageContent/account/@ref (minOccurs=0 maxOccurs=1)
> The *uuidType* is used to specify a UUID. Note that the base type below is probably wrong and needs to be fixed to match a correct definition for a UUID.

/myInbox/draft/messageContent/messageType (minOccurs=1 maxOccurs=1)
> The subelements of this element describe the contents of the message.

/myInbox/draft/messageContent/messageType/type (string minOccurs=1 maxOccurs=1)
> This element contains a value that provides the client with enough information to render an 'Inbox' view of the messages. Valid values are '*voice*', '*subscription*', '*fax*', '*dsn*', '*readReceipt*', '*meetingResponse*', '*meetingRequest*', '*email*', or '*liveEmail*'.

/myInbox/draft/messageContent/messageType/contentType (string minOccurs=0 maxOccurs=1)
> The contentType of the message (in accordance with RFC 2045). Examples of this are: '*text/plain*' and '*multipart/mime*'.

/myInbox/draft/messageContent/messageType/*{any}* (minOccurs=0 maxOccurs=unbounded)

/myInbox/draft/messageContent/size (unsignedLong minOccurs=1 maxOccurs=1)
> This read-only element contains the size, in bytes, of the entire RFC2822 message in the store.

/myInbox/draft/messageContent/importance (string minOccurs=1 maxOccurs=1)
> This element indicates the importance of this message. The value can be '*low*', '*normal*', or '*high*'. The default is '*normal*'.

/myInbox/draft/messageContent/sensitivity (string minOccurs=1 maxOccurs=1)
> This element indicates the sensitivity of the message. The value can be '*normal*', '*personal*', '*private*', or '*confidential*'.

/myInbox/draft/messageContent/hasAttachments (boolean minOccurs=1 maxOccurs=1)
> This read-only element indicates whether a message has one or more attachments. The value will either be 0 (to indicate that the message has no attachments) or 1 (to indicate that the message has one or more attachments).

/myInbox/draft/messageContent/conversationId (string minOccurs=0 maxOccurs=1)
> This optional element identifies the conversation, or e-mail thread, of which this message is a part.

/myInbox/draft/messageContent/conversationIndex (string minOccurs=0 maxOccurs=1)
> This optional element identifies the conversation, or e-mail thread, of which this message is a part.

/myInbox/draft/messageContent/subject (minOccurs=1 maxOccurs=1)
> The subject of the message. This element contains both a prefix and text subelements to allow clients to sort on the non-prefix part of the subject (so RE: RE: doesn't get sorted).

/myInbox/draft/messageContent/subject/@xml:lang (minOccurs=1 maxOccurs=1)
> This required attribute is used to specify an ISO 639 language code or an ISO 3166 country code as described in RFC 1766. The value of this attribute indicates the language type of the content within this element.

/myInbox/draft/messageContent/subject/prefix (string minOccurs=1 maxOccurs=1)
> The prefix of a message subject (example: 'FW: ').

/myInbox/draft/messageContent/subject/text (string minOccurs=1 maxOccurs=1)
> The subject of a message minus the prefix (example: 'hello there').

/myInbox/draft/messageContent/from (minOccurs=1 maxOccurs=1)
> This read-only element describes who this message is from. To set this value, set the account element.

/myInbox/draft/messageContent/from/name (string minOccurs=1 maxOccurs=1)
> The display name of an e-mail address.

/myInbox/draft/messageContent/from/name/@xml:lang (minOccurs=1 maxOccurs=1)
> This required attribute is used to specify an ISO 639 language code or an ISO 3166 country code as described in RFC 1766. The value of this attribute indicates the language type of the content within this element.

/myInbox/draft/messageContent/from/email (string minOccurs=1 maxOccurs=1)
> An e-mail address (for example, someone@microsoft.com).

/myInbox/draft/messageContent/recipient (minOccurs=0 maxOccurs=unbounded)
> Specifies the recipient of this message and where they appear.

/myInbox/draft/messageContent/recipient/@type (string minOccurs=0 maxOccurs=1)
> Specifies whether the recipient is in the to, cc, or bcc list.

/myInbox/draft/messageContent/recipient/name (string minOccurs=1 maxOccurs=1)
> The display name of an e-mail address.

/myInbox/draft/messageContent/recipient/name/@xml:lang (minOccurs=1 maxOccurs=1)
> This required attribute is used to specify an ISO 639 language code or an ISO 3166 country code as described in RFC 1766. The value of this attribute indicates the language type of the content within this element.

/myInbox/draft/messageContent/recipient/email (string minOccurs=1 maxOccurs=1)
> An e-mail address (for example, someone@microsoft.com).

/myInbox/draft/messageContent/messagePart (minOccurs=0 maxOccurs=unbounded)
> The element and its children define the message structure (including the mime body).

/myInbox/draft/messageContent/messagePart/@changeNumber (minOccurs=0 maxOccurs=1)

The changeNumber attribute is designed to facilitate caching of the element and its descendants. This attribute is assigned to this element by the .NET My Services system. The attribute is read-only to applications. Attempts to write this attribute are silently ignored.

/myInbox/draft/messageContent/messagePart/parentPart (minOccurs=1 maxOccurs=1)

This element points to the parent part of this part.

/myInbox/draft/messageContent/messagePart/parentPart/@ref (minOccurs=0 maxOccurs=1)

The *uuidType* is used to specify a UUID. Note that the base type below is probably wrong and needs to be fixed to match a correct definition for a UUID.

/myInbox/draft/messageContent/messagePart/order (unsignedLong minOccurs=1 maxOccurs=1)

This element defines the order of this part relative to its siblings.

/myInbox/draft/messageContent/messagePart/contentType (string minOccurs=1 maxOccurs=1)

This element defines the contentType of the part (example: message/rfc or text/plain.a).

/myInbox/draft/messageContent/messagePart/size (unsignedLong minOccurs=1 maxOccurs=1)

The size in bytes of the message part (including mime headers).

/myInbox/draft/messageContent/messagePart/contentDisposition (string minOccurs=0 maxOccurs=1)

The element defines the content-disposition of the part (example: attachment; filename="txt1.txt").

/myInbox/draft/messageContent/messagePart/contentId (string minOccurs=0 maxOccurs=1)

The element defines the content-id of the part.

/myInbox/draft/messageContent/messagePart/contentLocation (string minOccurs=0 maxOccurs=1)

The element defines the content-location of the part.

/myInbox/draft/messageContent/messagePart/contentTransferEncoding (string minOccurs=0 maxOccurs=1)

The element defines the content-transfer-encoding of this part.

/myInbox/draft/messageContent/messagePart/partContent (base64Binary minOccurs=0 maxOccurs=1)

This elements contains the content of this message part.

/myInbox/draft/messageContent/messagePart/*{any}* (minOccurs=0 maxOccurs=unbounded)

/myInbox/draft/messageContent/preview (string minOccurs=0 maxOccurs=1)

The first 256 characters of the message body. This element is returned only if the query option '*includePreview*' is specified.

/myInbox/draft/messageContent/preview/@xml:lang (minOccurs=1 maxOccurs=1)
> This required attribute is used to specify an ISO 639 language code or an ISO 3166 country code as described in RFC 1766. The value of this attribute indicates the language type of the content within this element.

/myInbox/draft/messageContent/single2822Header (string minOccurs=0 maxOccurs=unbounded)
> The rfc2822 headers not included in the base schema (example: x-apparently-to). This element is returned by passing the '*includeSingle2822Headers*' element in query options.

/myInbox/draft/messageContent/raw2822Content (base64Binary minOccurs=0 maxOccurs=1)
> The raw 2822 message (including headers and body). This element is returned by passing the *includeRaw2822Content* element in query options.

/myInbox/draft/messageContent/raw2822Headers (base64Binary minOccurs=0 maxOccurs=1)
> The raw rfc2822 headers not included in the base schema (example: x-apparently-to). This element is returned by passing the '*includeRaw2822Headers*' element in query options.

/myInbox/draft/messageContent/*{any}* (minOccurs=0 maxOccurs=unbounded)

/myInbox/draft/*{any}* (minOccurs=0 maxOccurs=unbounded)

/myInbox/rule (minOccurs=0 maxOccurs=unbounded)
> Rules specify actions that should be performed on the active message during sending or delivery.

/myInbox/rule/@sequence (unsignedLong minOccurs=0 maxOccurs=1)
> This required attribute specifies the order that this action should be performed relative to all other actions for this rule.

/myInbox/rule/@changeNumber (minOccurs=0 maxOccurs=1)
> The changeNumber attribute is designed to facilitate caching of the element and its descendants. This attribute is assigned to this element by the .NET My Services system. The attribute is read-only to applications. Attempts to write this attribute are silently ignored.

/myInbox/rule/@id (minOccurs=0 maxOccurs=1)
> This attribute is a globally unique ID assigned to this element by .NET My Services. Normally, .NET My Services will generate and assign this ID during an insertRequest operation, or possibly during a replaceRequest. Application software can override this ID generation by specifying the useClientIds attribute in the request message. Once an ID is assigned, the attribute is read-only and attempts to write it are silently ignored.

/myInbox/rule/@creator (string minOccurs=0 maxOccurs=1)
> This attribute identifies the creator in terms of userId, appId, and platformId of the node.

/myInbox/rule/name (string minOccurs=1 maxOccurs=1)
> The application-defined, human-readable identifier of the rule.

/myInbox/rule/name/@xml:lang (minOccurs=1 maxOccurs=1)

This required attribute is used to specify an ISO 639 language code or an ISO 3166 country code as described in RFC 1766. The value of this attribute indicates the language type of the content within this element.

/myInbox/rule/enabled (boolean minOccurs=1 maxOccurs=1)

Indicates whether the rule is currently enabled.

/myInbox/rule/runat (string minOccurs=1 maxOccurs=1)

This required attribute specifies where the rule must run. The only allowable value to date is '*server*'.

/myInbox/rule/runwhen (string minOccurs=1 maxOccurs=1)

This required attribute specifies when the rule must run. The only allowable values are '*sending*' and '*receiving*'.

/myInbox/rule/type (string minOccurs=1 maxOccurs=1)

Specifies if this is of type 'oof' or 'normal'.

/myInbox/rule/provider (string minOccurs=1 maxOccurs=1)

The application-defined provider of the rule. This is provided so that multiple applications can (if they so desire) only alter their own rules.

/myInbox/rule/provider/@xml:lang (minOccurs=1 maxOccurs=1)

This required attribute is used to specify an ISO 639 language code or an ISO 3166 country code as described in RFC 1766. The value of this attribute indicates the language type of the content within this element.

/myInbox/rule/condition (minOccurs=1 maxOccurs=1)

This element's select attribute specifies the xpath expression used to evaluate if the this rule applies to the active message.

/myInbox/rule/condition/@select (string minOccurs=0 maxOccurs=1)

This attribute specifies an xpath expression used to determine if this rule applies to the active message. Because rules apply only to messages, this statement must be scoped to the message element. The following are legal examples: "./importance = 'high'" "./from/email = 'someone@microsoft.com' and contains(./subject/full, 'hello')". The following are illegal examples: "/myInbox/message[./importance = 'high']" "/myInbox/folder" "/myInbox/rule".

/myInbox/rule/action (minOccurs=1 maxOccurs=unbounded)

Specifies an individual action to perform if the select element matches minOccurs-maxOccurs messages.

/myInbox/rule/action/@sequence (unsignedLong minOccurs=0 maxOccurs=1)

This required attribute specifies the order that this action should be performed relative to all other actions for this rule.

/myInbox/rule/action/copyMessage (minOccurs=0 maxOccurs=1)

This action is used to copy the active message in rules processing to another folder specified by the '*targetFolder*' element.

/myInbox/rule/action/copyMessage/targetFolder (minOccurs=1 maxOccurs=1)

This element specifies the folder to save the message to. If omitted, the message is saved in the drafts folder.

/myInbox/rule/action/copyMessage/targetFolder/@select (string minOccurs=0 maxOccurs=1)

The location of the folder to which save the message. For example, /myInbox/folder[@id=""].

/myInbox/rule/action/copyMessage/stopProcessingRulesOfThisType (minOccurs=0 maxOccurs=1)

/myInbox/rule/action/moveMessage (minOccurs=0 maxOccurs=1)

/myInbox/rule/action/moveMessage/targetFolder (minOccurs=1 maxOccurs=1)

This element specifies the folder to save the message to. If omitted, the message is saved in the drafts folder.

/myInbox/rule/action/moveMessage/targetFolder/@select (string minOccurs=0 maxOccurs=1)

The location of the folder to which save the message. For example, /myInbox/folder[@id=""].

/myInbox/rule/action/moveMessage/stopProcessingRulesOfThisType (minOccurs=0 maxOccurs=1)

/myInbox/rule/action/deleteMessage (minOccurs=0 maxOccurs=1)

/myInbox/rule/action/deleteMessage/stopProcessingRulesOfThisType (minOccurs=0 maxOccurs=1)

/myInbox/rule/action/assignCategory (minOccurs=0 maxOccurs=1)

/myInbox/rule/action/assignCategory/cat (minOccurs=0 maxOccurs=unbounded)

This element is used to categorize the element that contains it by referencing a global category definition in either the .NET categories service system document or an external resource containing category definitions, or by referencing an identity centric category definition in the content document of the .NET categories service for a particular PUID.

/myInbox/rule/action/assignCategory/cat/@ref (anyURI minOccurs=0 maxOccurs=1)

This attribute references a category definition (<catDef/>) element using the rules outlined in the .NET categories XMI manual.

/myInbox/rule/action/assignCategory/stopProcessingRulesOfThisType (minOccurs=0 maxOccurs=1)

/myInbox/rule/action/forwardMessage (minOccurs=0 maxOccurs=1)

/myInbox/rule/action/forwardMessage/recipient (minOccurs=0 maxOccurs=unbounded)

Specifies an e-mail address and display name or the PUID that represents them.

/myInbox/rule/action/forwardMessage/recipient/@type (string minOccurs=0 maxOccurs=1)

Specifies whether the recipient is in the to, cc, or bcc list.

/myInbox/rule/action/forwardMessage/recipient/name (string minOccurs=1 maxOccurs=1)

The display name of an e-mail address.

/myInbox/rule/action/forwardMessage/recipient/name/@xml:lang (minOccurs=1
maxOccurs=1)

> This required attribute is used to specify an ISO 639 language code or an ISO 3166
> country code as described in RFC 1766. The value of this attribute indicates the
> language type of the content within this element.

/myInbox/rule/action/forwardMessage/recipient/email (string minOccurs=1
maxOccurs=1)

> An e-mail address (for example, someone@microsoft.com).

/myInbox/rule/action/forwardMessage/stopProcessingRulesOfThisType (minOccurs=0
maxOccurs=1)

/myInbox/rule/action/forwardAsAttachment (minOccurs=0 maxOccurs=1)

/myInbox/rule/action/forwardAsAttachment/recipient (minOccurs=0
maxOccurs=unbounded)

> Specifies an e-mail address and display name or the PUID that represents them.

/myInbox/rule/action/forwardAsAttachment/recipient/@type (string minOccurs=0
maxOccurs=1)

> Specifies whether the recipient is in the to, cc, or bcc list.

/myInbox/rule/action/forwardAsAttachment/recipient/name (string minOccurs=1
maxOccurs=1)

> The display name of an e-mail address.

/myInbox/rule/action/forwardAsAttachment/recipient/name/@xml:lang (minOccurs=1
maxOccurs=1)

> This required attribute is used to specify an ISO 639 language code or an ISO 3166
> country code as described in RFC 1766. The value of this attribute indicates the
> language type of the content within this element.

/myInbox/rule/action/forwardAsAttachment/recipient/email (string minOccurs=1
maxOccurs=1)

> An e-mail address (for example, someone@microsoft.com).

/myInbox/rule/action/forwardAsAttachment/stopProcessingRulesOfThisType
(minOccurs=0 maxOccurs=1)

/myInbox/rule/action/serverReply (minOccurs=0 maxOccurs=1)

/myInbox/rule/action/serverReply/subject (minOccurs=1 maxOccurs=1)

> The subject of the message.

/myInbox/rule/action/serverReply/subject/@xml:lang (minOccurs=1 maxOccurs=1)

> This required attribute is used to specify an ISO 639 language code or an ISO 3166
> country code as described in RFC 1766. The value of this attribute indicates the
> language type of the content within this element.

/myInbox/rule/action/serverReply/subject/prefix (string minOccurs=1 maxOccurs=1)

> The prefix of a message subject (example: 'FW: ').

/myInbox/rule/action/serverReply/subject/text (string minOccurs=1 maxOccurs=1)

> The subject of a message minus the prefix (example: 'hello there').

/myInbox/rule/action/serverReply/simpleBody (string minOccurs=1 maxOccurs=1)
> The simpleBody element can be used to save/send a simple mail body without requiring the sender to construct a MIME message structure. It can optionally appear twice, but if it does one part must be type="plain" and the other must be type="html". This is then used to construct a multipart/alternative MIME message.

/myInbox/rule/action/serverReply/simpleBody/@xml:lang (minOccurs=1 maxOccurs=1)
> This required attribute is used to specify an ISO 639 language code or an ISO 3166 country code as described in RFC 1766. The value of this attribute indicates the language type of the content within this element.

/myInbox/rule/action/serverReply/stopProcessingRulesOfThisType (minOccurs=0 maxOccurs=1)

/myInbox/rule/action/redirectMessage (minOccurs=0 maxOccurs=1)

/myInbox/rule/action/redirectMessage/recipient (minOccurs=0 maxOccurs=unbounded)
> Specifies an e-mail address and display name or the PUID that represents them.

/myInbox/rule/action/redirectMessage/recipient/@type (string minOccurs=0 maxOccurs=1)
> Specifies whether the recipient is in the to, cc or bcc list.

/myInbox/rule/action/redirectMessage/recipient/name (string minOccurs=1 maxOccurs=1)
> The display name of an e-mail address.

/myInbox/rule/action/redirectMessage/recipient/name/@xml:lang (minOccurs=1 maxOccurs=1)
> This required attribute is used to specify an ISO 639 language code or an ISO 3166 country code as described in RFC 1766. The value of this attribute indicates the language type of the content within this element.

/myInbox/rule/action/redirectMessage/recipient/email (string minOccurs=1 maxOccurs=1)
> An e-mail address (for example, someone@microsoft.com).

/myInbox/rule/action/redirectMessage/stopProcessingRulesOfThisType (minOccurs=0 maxOccurs=1)

/myInbox/rule/action/flagMessage (minOccurs=0 maxOccurs=1)

/myInbox/rule/action/flagMessage/flag (minOccurs=1 maxOccurs=1)
> This optional element defines the flag state of the message. It includes an {any} element that can be used for extensible flags.

/myInbox/rule/action/flagMessage/flag/state (string minOccurs=1 maxOccurs=1)
> The state of a message flag.

/myInbox/rule/action/flagMessage/flag/title (string minOccurs=1 maxOccurs=1)
> The client-defined text of the flag.

/myInbox/rule/action/flagMessage/flag/title/@xml:lang (minOccurs=1 maxOccurs=1)
> This required attribute is used to specify an ISO 639 language code or an ISO 3166 country code as described in RFC 1766. The value of this attribute indicates the language type of the content within this element.

/myInbox/rule/action/flagMessage/flag/reminderDate (dateTime minOccurs=0 maxOccurs=1)

The client-defined reminder date of the flag.

/myInbox/rule/action/flagMessage/flag/**{any}** (minOccurs=0 maxOccurs=unbounded)
/myInbox/rule/action/flagMessage/stopProcessingRulesOfThisType (minOccurs=0 maxOccurs=1)
/myInbox/rule/action/markAsRead (minOccurs=0 maxOccurs=1)
/myInbox/rule/action/markAsRead/stopProcessingRulesOfThisType (minOccurs=0 maxOccurs=1)
/myInbox/rule/**{any}** (minOccurs=0 maxOccurs=unbounded)
/myInbox/subscription (minOccurs=0 maxOccurs=unbounded)

This element defines a subscription node that is designed to be an xdb:blue node that, when placed in a content document, causes a subscription to be registered. A subscription contains a trigger element that selects a scope of coverage. When items change that are under this scope of coverage, a subscriptionResponse message is generated and sent to the specified destination address.

/myInbox/subscription/@changeNumber (minOccurs=0 maxOccurs=1)

The changeNumber attribute is designed to facilitate caching of the element and its descendants. This attribute is assigned to this element by the .NET My Services system. The attribute is read-only to applications. Attempts to write this attribute are silently ignored.

/myInbox/subscription/@id (minOccurs=0 maxOccurs=1)

This attribute is a globally unique ID assigned to this element by .NET My Services. Normally, .NET My Services will generate and assign this ID during an insertRequest operation, or possibly during a replaceRequest. Application software can override this ID generation by specifying the useClientIds attribute in the request message. Once an ID is assigned, the attribute is read-only and attempts to write it are silently ignored.

/myInbox/subscription/@creator (string minOccurs=0 maxOccurs=1)

This attribute identifies the creator in terms of userId, appId, and platformId of the node.

/myInbox/subscription/trigger (minOccurs=1 maxOccurs=1)
/myInbox/subscription/trigger/@select (string minOccurs=0 maxOccurs=1)

This item specifies an XPATH expression that specifies the nodes that are to be selected and watched for changes. The selection may only select xdb:blue nodes. As changes in this node set occur, they trigger the generation of a subscription message. These messages are then sent to the SOAP receiver listed in the "to" element.

/myInbox/subscription/trigger/@mode (string minOccurs=0 maxOccurs=1)

> This attribute specifies whether or not the content of the changes that triggered the subscription is delivered in the subscription message, or whether the message simply indicates that something changed under the trigger. The attribute may be:

> includeData

> > The data that changed, causing the subscription to trigger, is included in the subscription message. Note that deleted nodes are specified by their id, not by value.

> excludeData

> > The data that changed, causing the subscription to trigger, is NOT included in the subscription message.

/myInbox/subscription/trigger/@baseChangeNumber (minOccurs=0 maxOccurs=1)

> This attribute specifies the changeNumber value that the trigger is relative to. All changes between the specified change number, and the current state of the document relative to the selection are transmitted as subscription messages. This allows a client application to establish a subscription relative to some baseline. As in changeQuery, if the baseChangeNumber is way out of date relative to the current state of the document, and the service can not supply the changes in the subscription message, the subscription insert is rejected. A value of 0 means that the current values of the selected nodes are transmitted in the subscription message.

/myInbox/subscription/expiresAt (dateTime minOccurs=0 maxOccurs=1)

> This optional element specifies an absolute time after which the subscription is no longer active. The subscription node is automatically removed when the subscription expires. If this element is missing, the subscription does not expire.

/myInbox/subscription/context (minOccurs=1 maxOccurs=1)

> This element returns the context element from the original subscription. Applications should use this element, and only this element, to correlate the subscription response with one of their subscriptions.

/myInbox/subscription/context/@uri (anyURI minOccurs=0 maxOccurs=1)

> This attribute specifies the URI value chosen by the subscriber that is associated with this subscription.

/myInbox/subscription/context/*{any}* (minOccurs=0 maxOccurs=unbounded)

/myInbox/subscription/to (anyURI minOccurs=1 maxOccurs=1)

> This attribute specifies the location that is to receive the subscription message. The value of this element may be one of the following forms:

> - *hs:myNotifications*—This URI indicates that generated subscription messages are to be delivered inside the body of a notification and delivered to the default .NET notifications service of the creator.

> - *protocol://service*—This URI indicates that generated subscription messages are delivered to the specified service at the domain of the creator's platformId. For instance, a platformId indicating msn.com and a value in this element of http://subscriptionResponse would cause delivery of the subscription message to http://subscriptionResponse.msn.com.

If this value is not specified, the subscription message is delivered as a notification to the "creator's" .NET notifications service.

/myInbox/*{any}* (minOccurs=0 maxOccurs=unbounded)

The .NET inbox service/system

The system document is a global document for the service. Its content and meaning is independent of the PUID used to address the service, and the document is read-only to all users. The system document contains a set of base items common to all .NET My Services services, and is optionally extended by each service to include service-specific global information.

This schema outline illustrates the layout and meaning of the information found in the system document for the .NET inbox service.

```
<sys:system changeNumber="..." instanceId="..."
    xmlns:hs="http://schemas.microsoft.com/hs/2001/10/core"
    xmlns:sys="http://schemas.microsoft.com/hs/2001/10/myInbox/system">1..1
    <hs:roleMap changeNumber="..." id="..." creator="...">1..1
        <hs:scope id="...">0..unbounded
            <hs:shape base="...">1..1
                <hs:include select="...">1..unbounded</hs:include>
                <hs:exclude select="...">0..unbounded</hs:exclude>
            </hs:shape>
        </hs:scope>
        <hs:roleTemplate name="..." priority="...">0..unbounded
            <hs:fullDescription xml:lang="...">0..1</hs:fullDescription>
            <hs:method name="..." scopeRef="...">0..unbounded</hs:method>
        </hs:roleTemplate>
    </hs:roleMap>
    <hs:methodMap changeNumber="..." id="..." creator="...">1..1
        <hs:method name="...">0..unbounded {any}</hs:method>
    </hs:methodMap>
    <hs:schemaMap changeNumber="..." id="..." creator="...">1..1
        <hs:schema namespace="..." schemaLocation="..." alias="...">0..unbounded
{any}</hs:schema>
    </hs:schemaMap>
    <hs:wsdlMap changeNumber="..." id="..." creator="...">1..1
        <hs:wsdl wsdlLocation="...">0..unbounded {any}</hs:wsdl>
        <hs:disco discoLocation="...">0..unbounded {any}</hs:disco>
    </hs:wsdlMap>
    {any}
</sys:system>
```

The meaning of the attributes and elements shown in the preceding sample document fragment are listed in the following section.

/system (minOccurs=1 maxOccurs=1)
This element encapsulates the system document for the .NET inbox service.

/system/@changeNumber (minOccurs=0 maxOccurs=1)
The changeNumber attribute is designed to facilitate caching of the element and its descendants. This attribute is assigned to this element by the .NET My Services system. The attribute is read-only to applications. Attempts to write this attribute are silently ignored.

/system/@instanceId (string minOccurs=0 maxOccurs=1)
This attribute is a unique identifier typically assigned to the root element of a service. It is a read-only element and assigned by the .NET My Services system when a user is provisioned for a particular service.

/system/roleMap (minOccurs=1 maxOccurs=1)
This element encapsulates all the elements that make up a roleMap, which include document class relative roleTemplate, priority, name, method, and per-method scope. An individual roleTemplate defines the maximum scope of information, and the allowable methods used to access that information for each request mapped into the template.

/system/roleMap/@changeNumber (minOccurs=0 maxOccurs=1)
The changeNumber attribute is designed to facilitate caching of the element and its descendants. This attribute is assigned to this element by the .NET My Services system. The attribute is read-only to applications. Attempts to write this attribute are silently ignored.

/system/roleMap/@id (minOccurs=0 maxOccurs=1)
This attribute is a globally unique ID assigned to this element by .NET My Services. Normally, .NET My Services will generate and assign this ID during an insertRequest operation, or possibly during a replaceRequest. Application software can override this ID generation by specifying the useClientIds attribute in the request message. Once an ID is assigned, the attribute is read-only and attempts to write it are silently ignored.

/system/roleMap/@creator (string minOccurs=0 maxOccurs=1)
This attribute identifies the creator in terms of userId, appId, and platformId of the node.

/system/roleMap/scope (minOccurs=0 maxOccurs=unbounded)
This element defines a scope that may be referred to by roles within this roleMap to indicate what portions of the document are visible to this role for the specified method.

/system/roleMap/scope/@id (minOccurs=0 maxOccurs=1)

This attribute is a globally unique ID assigned to this element by .NET My Services. Normally, .NET My Services will generate and assign this ID during an insertRequest operation, or possibly during a replaceRequest. Application software can override this ID generation by specifying the useClientIds attribute in the request message. Once an ID is assigned, the attribute is read-only and attempts to write it are silently ignored.

/system/roleMap/scope/shape (minOccurs=1 maxOccurs=1)

A shape defines the node set visible through the document when operating through this shape element.

/system/roleMap/scope/shape/@base (string minOccurs=0 maxOccurs=1)

This attribute specifies the initial set of nodes visible through the shape.

A value of t indicates that the shape is initialized to include all possible nodes relative to the shape that is currently in effect. For instance, each role defines a scope containing a shape. When defining a shape for a role, the value t indicates all possible nodes available in the specified document for this role. When defining a shape in an ACL entry, a value of t means all of the nodes visible in the shape for the computed role. When using a shape in an hsdl operation, a value of t indicates all of the possible nodes selected by the hsdl operation (relative to the ACL shape which itself is relative to the role's shape).

The value nil indicates the opposite of t, which is the empty node set. Nodes from this set may then be included into the shape.

/system/roleMap/scope/shape/include (minOccurs=1 maxOccurs=unbounded)

This element specifies the set of nodes that should be included in the shape relative to the possible set of nodes indicated by the base attribute.

/system/roleMap/scope/shape/include/@select (string minOccurs=0 maxOccurs=1)

This item specifies an XPATH expression that selects a set of nodes relative to the externally established context. The expression can never travel outside the node-set established by this externally established current context. The expression may match 0 or more nodes, and the operation manipulates all selected nodes. The minOccurs and maxOccurs attributes are optional and place restrictions and limitations on the number of nodes selected.

/system/roleMap/scope/shape/exclude (minOccurs=0 maxOccurs=unbounded)

This element specifies the set of nodes that should be excluded from the shape relative to the possible set of nodes indicated by the base attribute.

/system/roleMap/scope/shape/exclude/@select (string minOccurs=0 maxOccurs=1)

This item specifies an XPATH expression that selects a set of nodes relative to the externally established context. The expression can never travel outside the node-set established by this externally established current context. The expression may match 0 or more nodes, and the operation manipulates all selected nodes. The minOccurs and maxOccurs attributes are optional and place restrictions and limitations on the number of nodes selected.

/system/roleMap/roleTemplate (minOccurs=0 maxOccurs=unbounded)
This element encapsulates the definition of a role. The attribute set for this element includes the document class that this roleTemplate refers to, the name of the roleTemplate, and the priority of the roleTemplate.

/system/roleMap/roleTemplate/@name (string minOccurs=0 maxOccurs=1)
This element specifies the name of the role.

/system/roleMap/roleTemplate/@priority (int minOccurs=0 maxOccurs=1)
This element specifies the priority of the roleTemplate, which is used to select that actual roleTemplate when the role evaluation determines that the subject maps to multiple roleTemplates.

/system/roleMap/roleTemplate/fullDescription (string minOccurs=0 maxOccurs=1)
This element contains a description of this role template, which specifies the capabilities a caller will have when accessing information through this role.

/system/roleMap/roleTemplate/fullDescription/@xml:lang (minOccurs=1 maxOccurs=1)
This required attribute is used to specify an ISO 639 language code or an ISO 3166 country code as described in RFC 1766. The value of this attribute indicates the language type of the content within this element.

/system/roleMap/roleTemplate/method (minOccurs=0 maxOccurs=unbounded)
This element specifies the methods available within this roleTemplate by name, and by scope. When a subject maps to a roleTemplate, the method in the request must match one of these elements for the message to continue to flow. If the method exists, the data available to the method is a function of the scope referenced by this method combined with an optional scope referenced by the role defined in the roleList.

/system/roleMap/roleTemplate/method/@name (string minOccurs=0 maxOccurs=1)
This element specifies the name of the method.

/system/roleMap/roleTemplate/method/@scopeRef (string minOccurs=0 maxOccurs=1)
This attribute specifies the scope within this document that is in effect for this method.

/system/methodMap (minOccurs=1 maxOccurs=1)
This element defines the methodMap. While it is true that in most cases, the roleMap section contains a definitive list of methods, these methods are likely to be scattered about the roleMap in various templates. This section contains the definitive non-duplicated list of methods available within the service.

/system/methodMap/@changeNumber (minOccurs=0 maxOccurs=1)
The changeNumber attribute is designed to facilitate caching of the element and its descendants. This attribute is assigned to this element by the .NET My Services system. The attribute is read-only to applications. Attempts to write this attribute are silently ignored.

/system/methodMap/@id (minOccurs=0 maxOccurs=1)

This attribute is a globally unique ID assigned to this element by .NET My Services. Normally, .NET My Services will generate and assign this ID during an insertRequest operation, or possibly during a replaceRequest. Application software can override this ID generation by specifying the useClientIds attribute in the request message. Once an ID is assigned, the attribute is read-only and attempts to write it are silently ignored.

/system/methodMap/@creator (string minOccurs=0 maxOccurs=1)

This attribute identifies the creator in terms of userId, appId, and platformId of the node.

/system/methodMap/method (minOccurs=0 maxOccurs=unbounded)

This element defines a method that is available within this service.

/system/methodMap/method/@name (string minOccurs=0 maxOccurs=1)

This attribute specifies the name of a method available within the service.

/system/methodMap/method/*{any}* (minOccurs=0 maxOccurs=unbounded)

/system/schemaMap (minOccurs=1 maxOccurs=1)

This element defines the various schemas that define the data structures and shape of information managed by this service. Each schema is defined by its namespace URI, its location, and a preferred namespace alias.

/system/schemaMap/@changeNumber (minOccurs=0 maxOccurs=1)

The changeNumber attribute is designed to facilitate caching of the element and its descendants. This attribute is assigned to this element by the .NET My Services system. The attribute is read-only to applications. Attempts to write this attribute are silently ignored.

/system/schemaMap/@id (minOccurs=0 maxOccurs=1)

This attribute is a globally unique ID assigned to this element by .NET My Services. Normally, .NET My Services will generate and assign this ID during an insertRequest operation, or possibly during a replaceRequest. Application software can override this ID generation by specifying the useClientIds attribute in the request message. Once an ID is assigned, the attribute is read-only and attempts to write it are silently ignored.

/system/schemaMap/@creator (string minOccurs=0 maxOccurs=1)

This attribute identifies the creator in terms of userId, appId, and platformId of the node.

/system/schemaMap/schema (minOccurs=0 maxOccurs=unbounded)

This element defines a schema which defines data-structures and the shape of information managed by this service. Multiple schema elements exist for each service, once for each logical grouping of information exposed by the service.

/system/schemaMap/schema/@namespace (anyURI minOccurs=0 maxOccurs=1)

This attribute specifies the namespace URI of this schema.

/system/schemaMap/schema/@schemaLocation (anyURI minOccurs=0 maxOccurs=1)
This attribute specifies the location (in the form of a URI) of the resource containing schema. When a schema is reachable through a variety of URIs, one schema element will exist for each location.

/system/schemaMap/schema/@alias (string minOccurs=0 maxOccurs=1)
This attribute specifies the preferred alias that should be used if possible when manipulating information covered by this schema in the context of this service.

/system/schemaMap/schema/{any} (minOccurs=0 maxOccurs=unbounded)
/system/wsdlMap (minOccurs=1 maxOccurs=1)
This element defines the wsdlMap for this service. This map includes the location of WSDL documents, DISCO documents, and WISL documents for this Web service. These documents are used by applications to understand the format of messages that may be sent to the various services.

/system/wsdlMap/@changeNumber (minOccurs=0 maxOccurs=1)
The changeNumber attribute is designed to facilitate caching of the element and its descendants. This attribute is assigned to this element by the .NET My Services system. The attribute is read-only to applications. Attempts to write this attribute are silently ignored.

/system/wsdlMap/@id (minOccurs=0 maxOccurs=1)
This attribute is a globally unique ID assigned to this element by .NET My Services. Normally, .NET My Services will generate and assign this ID during an insertRequest operation, or possibly during a replaceRequest. Application software can override this ID generation by specifying the useClientIds attribute in the request message. Once an ID is assigned, the attribute is read-only and attempts to write it are silently ignored.

/system/wsdlMap/@creator (string minOccurs=0 maxOccurs=1)
This attribute identifies the creator in terms of userId, appId, and platformId of the node.

/system/wsdlMap/wsdl (minOccurs=0 maxOccurs=unbounded)
This element is used to specify the location of a WSDL file for this service. Multiple entries may exist pointing to the same file hosted in multiple locations, or to variations on the content within the WSDL files.

/system/wsdlMap/wsdl/@wsdlLocation (anyURI minOccurs=0 maxOccurs=1)
This attribute is a URI that specifies the location of the WSDL file.

/system/wsdlMap/wsdl/{any} (minOccurs=0 maxOccurs=unbounded)
/system/wsdlMap/disco (minOccurs=0 maxOccurs=unbounded)
This element is used to specify the location of a DISCO file for this service. Multiple entries may exist pointing to the same file hosted in multiple locations, or to variations on the content within the DISCO files.

/system/wsdlMap/disco/@discoLocation (anyURI minOccurs=0 maxOccurs=1)
This attribute is a URI that specifies the location of the DISCO file.

/system/wsdlMap/disco/{any} (minOccurs=0 maxOccurs=unbounded)
/system/{any} (minOccurs=0 maxOccurs=unbounded)

The .NET inbox service/Methods

The .NET inbox service supports the following standard and domain-specific methods:

- query
- insert
- replace
- delete
- update
- sendMessage
- saveMessage
- copyMessage

The standard methods operate on this service using the same message format and method-interchange techniques described in the hsdl section of this document. The only service-specific information to note is the schema that is in effect for each of the methods. These schemas, and how they relate to the standard methods and roles, are described in the roles section of this document.

The domain-specific methods operate as described in the domain-specific methods section of this document, and are governed by the various schemas outlined in the section The .NET inbox service/Roles.

The .NET inbox service/Domain Specific Methods

The .NET inbox service has seven domain-specific messages.

The .NET inbox service/sendMessage Method

The purpose of this method is to send a plain-text or fully MIME-encoded message from the user's account. If the optional, "saveSentMessage" is included, a copy of the sent message will be saved in the Sent Messages folder and the responseBody will include a header element with the new system-defined ID attribute.

The .NET inbox service/sendMessageRequest

This method is accessed using a request message, and in response may generate a response message or a SOAP Fault message. The following sample document fragments illustrate the structure and meaning of the elements and attributes in the request and response messages.

The following section describes the request message for this method.

This is the request message.

```
<m:sendMessageRequest
    xmlns:m="http://schemas.microsoft.com/hs/2001/10/myInbox"
    xmlns:hs="http://schemas.microsoft.com/hs/2001/10/core">_{1..1}
    <m:draftMessage select="...">_{0..1}
        <m:saveInFolder ref="...">_{0..1}</m:saveInFolder>
    </m:draftMessage>
    <m:rawMessage>_{0..1}
        <m:messageStatus>_{0..1}
            <m:saveInFolder ref="...">_{0..1}</m:saveInFolder>
            <m:flag>_{0..1}
                <m:state>_{1..1}</m:state>
                <m:title xml:lang="...">_{1..1}</m:title>
                <m:reminderDate>_{0..1}</m:reminderDate>
                {any}
            </m:flag>
            {any}
        </m:messageStatus>
        <m:messageContent>_{0..1}
            <m:cat ref="...">_{0..unbounded}</m:cat>
            <m:raw2822Content>_{1..1}</m:raw2822Content>
            {any}
        </m:messageContent>
    </m:rawMessage>
</m:sendMessageRequest>
```

The meaning of the attributes and elements shown in the preceding sample document fragment are listed in the following section.

/sendMessageRequest (minOccurs=1 maxOccurs=1)
> This method is accessed using a request message, and in response may generate a domain-specific response message or may generate a SOAP fault message. The types used in these messages are fully specified in the services base schema document referenced above. The following sample document fragments illustrate the structure and meaning of the elements and attributes in the request and response messages.

/sendMessageRequest/draftMessage (minOccurs=0 maxOccurs=1)
/sendMessageRequest/draftMessage/@select (string minOccurs=0 maxOccurs=1)
> This item specifies an XPATH expression that selects a set of nodes relative to the externally established context. The expression can never travel outside the node-set established by this externally established current context. The expression may match 0 or more nodes, and the operation manipulates all selected nodes. The minOccurs and maxOccurs attributes are optional and place restrictions and limitations on the number of nodes selected.

/sendMessageRequest/draftMessage/saveInFolder (minOccurs=0 maxOccurs=1)
> This element defines the folder that a copy of this message should be saved in.

/sendMessageRequest/draftMessage/saveInFolder/@ref (minOccurs=0 maxOccurs=1)
> The uuidType is used to specify a UUID. Note that the base type below is probably wrong and needs to be fixed to match a correct definition for a UUID.

/sendMessageRequest/rawMessage (minOccurs=0 maxOccurs=1)
/sendMessageRequest/rawMessage/messageStatus (minOccurs=0 maxOccurs=1)
/sendMessageRequest/rawMessage/messageStatus/saveInFolder (minOccurs=0 maxOccurs=1)
> This element defines the folder that a copy of this message should be saved in.

/sendMessageRequest/rawMessage/messageStatus/saveInFolder/@ref (minOccurs=0 maxOccurs=1)
> The uuidType is used to specify a UUID. Note that the base type below is probably wrong and needs to be fixed to match a correct definition for a UUID.

/sendMessageRequest/rawMessage/messageStatus/flag (minOccurs=0 maxOccurs=1)
> This optional element defines the flag state of the message. It includes an {any} element that can be used for extensible flags.

/sendMessageRequest/rawMessage/messageStatus/flag/state (string minOccurs=1 maxOccurs=1)
> The state of a message flag.

/sendMessageRequest/rawMessage/messageStatus/flag/title (string minOccurs=1 maxOccurs=1)
> The client-defined text of the flag.

/sendMessageRequest/rawMessage/messageStatus/flag/title/@xml:lang (minOccurs=1 maxOccurs=1)
> This required attribute is used to specify an ISO 639 language code or an ISO 3166 country code as described in RFC 1766. The value of this attribute indicates the language type of the content within this element.

/sendMessageRequest/rawMessage/messageStatus/flag/reminderDate (dateTime minOccurs=0 maxOccurs=1)
> The client-defined reminder date of the flag.

/sendMessageRequest/rawMessage/messageStatus/flag/*{any}* (minOccurs=0 maxOccurs=unbounded)
/sendMessageRequest/rawMessage/messageStatus/*{any}* (minOccurs=0 maxOccurs=unbounded)
/sendMessageRequest/rawMessage/messageContent (minOccurs=0 maxOccurs=1)
/sendMessageRequest/rawMessage/messageContent/cat (minOccurs=0 maxOccurs=unbounded)
> This element is used to categorize the element that contains it by referencing a global category definition in either the .NET categories service system document or an external resource containing category definitions, or by referencing an identity-centric category definition in the content document of the .NET categories service for a particular PUID.

/sendMessageRequest/rawMessage/messageContent/cat/@ref (anyURI minOccurs=0 maxOccurs=1)

>   This attribute references a category definition (<catDef/>) element using the rules outlined in the .NET categories service XMI manual.

/sendMessageRequest/rawMessage/messageContent/raw2822Content (base64Binary minOccurs=1 maxOccurs=1)

/sendMessageRequest/rawMessage/messageContent/*{any}* (minOccurs=0 maxOccurs=unbounded)

The .NET inbox service/sendMessageResponse

Upon successful completion of this method, a response message is generated. The format of the response message is described below.

This is the response.

```
<m:sendMessageResponse
    xmlns:m="http://schemas.microsoft.com/hs/2001/10/myInbox"
    xmlns:hs="http://schemas.microsoft.com/hs/2001/10/core">1..1
    <m:newBlueId id="...">1..1</m:newBlueId>
</m:sendMessageResponse>
```

The meaning of the attributes and elements shown in the preceding sample document fragment are listed in the following section.

/sendMessageResponse (minOccurs=1 maxOccurs=1)
/sendMessageResponse/newBlueId (minOccurs=1 maxOccurs=1)
/sendMessageResponse/newBlueId/@id (minOccurs=0 maxOccurs=1)

>   This attribute specifies the id of the deleted item.

The .NET inbox service/Error Cases

If the method causes a failure response to be generated, the failure is noted by generating a SOAP Fault message. Failures can include a failure to understand a header marked as "s:mustUnderstand", a .NET My Services standard error, security violation, load balance redirect, or any service-specific severe error condition.

The following method-specific errors (including the .NET My Services standard errors and any argument-type-specific errors) can occur during the processing of this message.

The .NET inbox service/saveMessage Method

This method allows a client to add either a complete rfc822 local message to .NET inbox or to save a draft message.

The .NET inbox service/saveMessageRequest

This method is accessed using a request message, and in response may generate a response message or a SOAP Fault message. The following sample document fragments illustrate the structure and meaning of the elements and attributes in the request and response messages.

The following section describes the request message for this method.

This is the request message.

```
<m:saveMessageRequest
    xmlns:m="http://schemas.microsoft.com/hs/2001/10/myInbox"
    xmlns:hs="http://schemas.microsoft.com/hs/2001/10/core">₁..₁
    <m:completeLocalMessage>₀..₁
        <m:messageStatus>₀..₁
            <m:readState>₁..₁</m:readState>
            <m:folder ref="...">₁..₁</m:folder>
            <m:flag>₀..₁
                <m:state>₁..₁</m:state>
                <m:title xml:lang="...">₁..₁</m:title>
                <m:reminderDate>₀..₁</m:reminderDate>
                {any}
            </m:flag>
            <m:state>₁..₁</m:state>
            {any}
        </m:messageStatus>
        <m:messageContent>₀..₁
            <m:cat ref="...">₀..unbounded</m:cat>
            <m:raw2822Content>₁..₁</m:raw2822Content>
            {any}
        </m:messageContent>
    </m:completeLocalMessage>
</m:saveMessageRequest>
```

The meaning of the attributes and elements shown in the preceding sample document fragment are listed in the following section.

/saveMessageRequest (minOccurs=1 maxOccurs=1)
   This method is accessed using a request message, and in response may generate a domain-specific response message, or may generate a SOAP fault message. The types used in these messages are fully specified in the services base schema document referenced above. The following sample document fragments illustrate the structure and meaning of the elements and attributes in the request and response messages.

/saveMessageRequest/completeLocalMessage (minOccurs=0 maxOccurs=1)
/saveMessageRequest/completeLocalMessage/messageStatus (minOccurs=0 maxOccurs=1)

/saveMessageRequest/completeLocalMessage/messageStatus/readState (boolean minOccurs=1 maxOccurs=1)

This element defines the read/unread state of the message and can be modified.

/saveMessageRequest/completeLocalMessage/messageStatus/folder (minOccurs=1 maxOccurs=1)

This element defines the single folder that this message logically belongs to.

/saveMessageRequest/completeLocalMessage/messageStatus/folder/@ref (minOccurs=0 maxOccurs=1)

The uuidType is used to specify a UUID. Note that the base type below is probably wrong and needs to be fixed to match a correct definition for a UUID.

/saveMessageRequest/completeLocalMessage/messageStatus/flag (minOccurs=0 maxOccurs=1)

This optional element defines the flag state of the message. It includes an {any} element that can be used for extensible flags.

/saveMessageRequest/completeLocalMessage/messageStatus/flag/state (string minOccurs=1 maxOccurs=1)

The state of a message flag.

/saveMessageRequest/completeLocalMessage/messageStatus/flag/title (string minOccurs=1 maxOccurs=1)

The client-defined text of the flag.

/saveMessageRequest/completeLocalMessage/messageStatus/flag/title/@xml:lang (minOccurs=1 maxOccurs=1)

This required attribute is used to specify an ISO 639 language code or an ISO 3166 country code as described in RFC 1766. The value of this attribute indicates the language type of the content within this element.

/saveMessageRequest/completeLocalMessage/messageStatus/flag/reminderDate (dateTime minOccurs=0 maxOccurs=1)

The client-defined reminder date of the flag.

/saveMessageRequest/completeLocalMessage/messageStatus/flag/*{any}* (minOccurs=0 maxOccurs=unbounded)

/saveMessageRequest/completeLocalMessage/messageStatus/state (string minOccurs=1 maxOccurs=1)

This element defines the sent/received state of the message.

/saveMessageRequest/completeLocalMessage/messageStatus/*{any}* (minOccurs=0 maxOccurs=unbounded)

/saveMessageRequest/completeLocalMessage/messageContent (minOccurs=0 maxOccurs=1)

/saveMessageRequest/completeLocalMessage/messageContent/cat (minOccurs=0 maxOccurs=unbounded)

This element is used to categorize the element that contains it by referencing a global category definition in either the .NET categories service system document or an external resource containing category definitions, or by referencing an identity centric category definition in the content document of the .NET categories service for a particular PUID.

/saveMessageRequest/completeLocalMessage/messageContent/cat/@ref (anyURI minOccurs=0 maxOccurs=1)

This attribute references a category definition (<catDef/>) element using the rules outlined in the .NET categories service XMI manual.

/saveMessageRequest/completeLocalMessage/messageContent/raw2822Content (base64Binary minOccurs=1 maxOccurs=1)

/saveMessageRequest/completeLocalMessage/messageContent/*{any}* (minOccurs=0 maxOccurs=unbounded)

The .NET inbox service/saveMessageResponse

Upon successful completion of this method, a response message is generated. The format of the response message is described below.

This is the response.

```
<m:saveMessageResponse
    xmlns:m="http://schemas.microsoft.com/hs/2001/10/myInbox"
    xmlns:hs="http://schemas.microsoft.com/hs/2001/10/core">₁..₁
    <m:newBlueId id="...">₁..₁</m:newBlueId>
</m:saveMessageResponse>
```

The meaning of the attributes and elements shown in the preceding sample document fragment are listed in the following section.

/saveMessageResponse (minOccurs=1 maxOccurs=1)

The saveMessage response contains a newBlueId for each message that was successfully saved.

/saveMessageResponse/newBlueId (minOccurs=1 maxOccurs=1)

This elements represents the new or saved message.

/saveMessageResponse/newBlueId/@id (minOccurs=0 maxOccurs=1)

This attribute specifies the id of the deleted item.

The .NET inbox service/Error Cases

If the method causes a failure response to be generated, the failure is noted by generating a SOAP Fault message. Failures can include a failure to understand a header marked as "s:mustUnderstand", a .NET My Services standard error, security violation, load balance redirect, or any service-specific severe error condition.

The following method-specific errors (including the .NET My Services standard errors and any argument-type-specific errors) can occur during the processing of this message.

The .NET inbox service/copyMessage Method

This method allows clients to copy one or more messages into a folder. The message data (including attachments) is copied and new message headers are returned with unique header ID values.

The .NET inbox service/copyMessageRequest

This method is accessed using a request message, and in response may generate a response message or a SOAP Fault message. The following sample document fragments illustrate the structure and meaning of the elements and attributes in the request and response messages.

The following section describes the request message for this method.

This is the request message.

```
<m:copyMessageRequest
    xmlns:m="http://schemas.microsoft.com/hs/2001/10/myInbox"
    xmlns:hs="http://schemas.microsoft.com/hs/2001/10/core">1..1
    <m:message select="..." copyAsDraft="..."
useClientId="...">1..unbounded</m:message>
    <m:targetFolder select="...">1..1</m:targetFolder>
</m:copyMessageRequest>
```

The meaning of the attributes and elements shown in the preceding sample document fragment are listed in the following section.

/copyMessageRequest (minOccurs=1 maxOccurs=1)
> This message allows clients to copy one or more messages to a folder. The message data (including attachments) is copied and new message messages are returned with unique message ID values. This element encapsulates the arguments to the copyMessage method. It must contain a message element and a targetFolder element.

/copyMessageRequest/message (minOccurs=1 maxOccurs=unbounded)
> This element contains a select statement that contains an XPATH expression indicating a message message for which to copy the associated message.

/copyMessageRequest/message/@select (string minOccurs=0 maxOccurs=1)
> The location of the message (which is associated with the message) to copy. For example, /myInbox/message[@id=""].

/copyMessageRequest/message/@copyAsDraft (boolean minOccurs=0 maxOccurs=1)
> If this value is present and set to true, the message is copied as a draft into the target folder.

/copyMessageRequest/message/@useClientId (minOccurs=0 maxOccurs=1)
> If this optional attribute is present, the new message id will be set to the client id.

/copyMessageRequest/targetFolder (minOccurs=1 maxOccurs=1)
> This element contains a select statement that contains an XPATH expression to the folder to which to copy the selected messages.

/copyMessageRequest/targetFolder/@select (string minOccurs=0 maxOccurs=1)
> The location of the folder to which to save the message. For example, /myInbox/folder[@id=""].

The .NET inbox service/copyMessageResponse

Upon successful completion of this method, a response message is generated. The format of the response message is described below.

This is the response.

```
<m:copyMessageResponse
    xmlns:m="http://schemas.microsoft.com/hs/2001/10/myInbox"
    xmlns:hs="http://schemas.microsoft.com/hs/2001/10/core">_{1..1}
    <m:newBlueId id="...">_{1..1}</m:newBlueId>
</m:copyMessageResponse>
```

The meaning of the attributes and elements shown in the preceding sample document fragment are listed in the following section.

/copyMessageResponse (minOccurs=1 maxOccurs=1)
> The response from copyMessage includes a newBlueId element for each successfully copied message.

/copyMessageResponse/newBlueId (minOccurs=1 maxOccurs=1)
> This element is typically found in the body of an insertResponse, updateResponse, or replaceResponse to indicate that a new id value was generated by the corresponding request operation. Applications must, in response, walk through their changes in order and apply the returned id to any cached value of the node they just inserted. Only new id generation triggers this. So in the case of id-preserving replaceRequest, the root of the replacement will never generate one of these, but an inner xdb:blue will.

/copyMessageResponse/newBlueId/@id (minOccurs=0 maxOccurs=1)
> This attribute specifies the id of the deleted item.

The .NET inbox service/Error Cases

If the method causes a failure response to be generated, the failure is noted by generating a SOAP Fault message. Failures can include a failure to understand a header marked as "s:mustUnderstand", a .NET My Services standard error, security violation, load balance redirect, or any service-specific severe error condition.

CHAPTER 17

The .NET lists services/Introduction

The .NET lists service is a general purpose service designed to manage very simple lists with minimal structure. It defines what a list is, and what an item is within a list. Like all Microsoft .NET My Services services, the lists service allows free-form, name-space qualified extensions to be added to a list, or an item within a list. This mechanism is useful to add semi-structured information to the service. However, the service is unable to schema-validate these extensions.

The .NET lists service breaks down a list into two major components. The list is defined by the list element, and an item defined by the item attribute. A list element defines a list which includes a title and description, a unique id, and categories which define the type of list. Items contain a title and description as well as optional categories, an optional due date, status, and priority. One interesting aspect of an item is that an item can be part of multiple lists. This allows applications to build and manage real-world lists. Suppose for instance that you have a list of things to buy at the mall, and a list of things to do for an upcoming trip. It is very reasonable to have an item like "buy new shoes" appear on both of these lists.

Like several other .NET My Services services, the .NET lists service makes heavy use of categorization in order to classify, categorize, and type lists and items contained within a list. For instance, to specify that a list is a "todo" list, the cat element with a ref attribute of "todo" is specified.

The .NET lists services/Roles

The .NET lists service controls access by using the following roleTemplates:

- rt0
- rt1
- rt2
- rt3
- rt99

The .NET lists service uses the following scopes:

- **scope id 1**

```
<hs:scope id=1>

    <hs:shape base=t>

    </hs:shape>

</hs:scope>
```

- **scope id 2**

```
<hs:scope id=2>

    <hs:shape base=nil>

        <hs:include, select=//*[@creator='$callerId']/>

    </hs:shape>

</hs:scope>
```

- **scope id 3**

```
<hs:scope id=3>

    <hs:shape base=nil>

        <hs:include select=//subscription[@creator='$callerId']/>

    </hs:shape>

</hs:scope>
```

- **scope id 4**

```
<hs:scope id=4>

    <hs:shape base=nil>

        <hs:include select=//*[cat/@ref='hs:public']/>

        <hs:include select=//subscription[@creator='$callerId']/>

    </hs:shape>

</hs:scope>
```

.NET lists services roleTemplate rt0

The purpose of this role is to give complete read/write access to all information within the content document of the service being protected through this roleTemplate.

The following table illustrates the available methods and the scope in effect when accessing the .NET lists service through that method while mapped to this roleTemplate.

method	scopeRef
query	scopeRef=1
insert	scopeRef=1
replace	scopeRef=1
delete	scopeRef=1
update	scopeRef=1

.NET lists services roleTemplate rt1

The purpose of this role is to give complete read access to all information within the content document of the service being protected through this roleTemplate. Applications mapping to this role also have a limited ability to write to information in the content document. They may create nodes in any location, but may only change/replace, or delete nodes that they created.

The following table illustrates the available methods and the scope in effect when accessing the .NET lists service through that method while mapped to this roleTemplate.

method	scopeRef
query	scopeRef=1
insert	scopeRef=2
replace	scopeRef=2
delete	scopeRef=2

.NET lists services roleTemplate rt2

The purpose of this role is to give complete read access to all information within the content document of the service being protected through this roleTemplate. Applications mapping to this role have very limited write access and are only able to create and manipulate their own subscription nodes.

The following table illustrates the available methods and the scope in effect when accessing the .NET lists service through that method while mapped to this roleTemplate.

method	scopeRef
query	scopeRef=1
insert	scopeRef=3
replace	scopeRef=3
delete	scopeRef=3

.NET lists services roleTemplate rt3

The purpose of this role is to give limited read access to information within the content document that is categorized as "public".

The following table illustrates the available methods and the scope in effect when accessing the .NET lists service through that method while mapped to this roleTemplate.

method	scopeRef
query	scopeRef=4

.NET lists services roleTemplate rt99

The purpose of this role is to block all access to the content document. Note that lack of a role in the roleList has the same effect as assigning someone to rt99.

The .NET lists services/Content

The content document is an identity-centric document. Its content and meaning is a function of the PUID used to address the service. Access to the document is controlled by the associated roleList document.

This schema outline illustrates the layout and meaning of the information found in the content document for the .NET lists service.

```
<m:myLists changeNumber="..." instanceId="..."
    xmlns:m="http://schemas.microsoft.com/hs/2001/10/myLists"
    xmlns:hs="http://schemas.microsoft.com/hs/2001/10/core">1..1
    <m:list changeNumber="..." id="..." creator="...">0..unbounded
        <m:cat ref="...">0..unbounded</m:cat>
        <m:title xml:lang="...">0..unbounded</m:title>
        <m:description xml:lang="...">0..unbounded</m:description>
        {any}
    </m:list>
    <m:item changeNumber="..." id="..." creator="...">0..unbounded
        <m:cat ref="...">0..unbounded</m:cat>
        <m:title xml:lang="...">0..unbounded</m:title>
        <m:description xml:lang="...">0..unbounded</m:description>
        <m:url>0..unbounded</m:url>
        <m:listRef ref="...">0..unbounded</m:listRef>
        <m:dueDate>0..1</m:dueDate>
        <m:status>0..1</m:status>
        <m:priority>0..1</m:priority>
        <m:assignedTo>0..unbounded
            <hs:name xml:lang="...">0..1</hs:name>
            <hs:puid>0..1</hs:puid>
            <hs:email>0..1</hs:email>
        </m:assignedTo>
        {any}
    </m:item>
    <m:subscription changeNumber="..." id="..." creator="...">0..unbounded
        <hs:trigger select="..." mode="..."
baseChangeNumber="...">1..1</hs:trigger>
        <hs:expiresAt>0..1</hs:expiresAt>
        <hs:context uri="...">1..1 {any}</hs:context>
        <hs:to>1..1</hs:to>
    </m:subscription>
    {any}
</m:myLists>
```

The meaning of the attributes and elements shown in the preceding sample document fragment are listed in the following section.

/myLists (minOccurs=1 maxOccurs=1)

This element encapsulates the content document for the .NET lists service.

/myLists/@changeNumber (minOccurs=0 maxOccurs=1)

The changeNumber attribute is designed to facilitate caching of the element and its descendants. This attribute is assigned to this element by the .NET My Services system. The attribute is read-only to applications. Attempts to write this attribute are silently ignored.

/myLists/@instanceId (string minOccurs=0 maxOccurs=1)

This attribute is a unique identifier typically assigned to the root element of a service. It is a read-only element and assigned by the .NET My Services system when a user is provisioned for a particular service.

/myLists/list (minOccurs=0 maxOccurs=unbounded)

This element defines a list which includes categorization of the list, a localized name for the list, and a brief description of the list.

/myLists/list/@changeNumber (minOccurs=0 maxOccurs=1)

The changeNumber attribute is designed to facilitate caching of the element and its descendants. This attribute is assigned to this element by the .NET My Services system. The attribute is read-only to applications. Attempts to write this attribute are silently ignored.

/myLists/list/@id (minOccurs=0 maxOccurs=1)

This attribute is a globally unique ID assigned to this element by .NET My Services. Normally, .NET My Services will generate and assign this ID during an insertRequest operation, or possibly during a replaceRequest. Application software can override this ID generation by specifying the useClientIds attribute in the request message. Once an ID is assigned, the attribute is read-only and attempts to write it are silently ignored.

/myLists/list/@creator (string minOccurs=0 maxOccurs=1)

This attribute identifies the creator in terms of userId, appId, and platformId of the node.

/myLists/list/cat (minOccurs=0 maxOccurs=unbounded)

This element is used to categorize the element that contains it, by referencing a global category definition in either the .NET categories service system document or an external resource containing category definitions, or by referencing an identity centric category definition in the content document of the .NET categories service for a particular PUID.

/myLists/list/cat/@ref (anyURI minOccurs=0 maxOccurs=1)

This attribute references a category definition (<catDef/>) element using the rules outlined in the .NET categories XMI manual.

/myLists/list/title (string minOccurs=0 maxOccurs=unbounded)

This element specifies the title of the list.

/myLists/list/title/@xml:lang (minOccurs=1 maxOccurs=1)
>   This required attribute is used to specify an ISO 639 language code or an ISO 3166
>   country code as described in RFC 1766. The value of this attribute indicates the
>   language type of the content within this element.

/myLists/list/description (string minOccurs=0 maxOccurs=unbounded)
>   This element specifies a more detailed description of the list.

/myLists/list/description/@xml:lang (minOccurs=1 maxOccurs=1)
>   This required attribute is used to specify an ISO 639 language code or an ISO 3166
>   country code as described in RFC 1766. The value of this attribute indicates the
>   language type of the content within this element.

/myLists/list/*{any}* (minOccurs=0 maxOccurs=unbounded)

/myLists/item (minOccurs=0 maxOccurs=unbounded)
>   This element defines a list item, something that is considered as part of a list. An item
>   may be part of multiple lists, or can simply be a free form item that is not part of any
>   list.

/myLists/item/@changeNumber (minOccurs=0 maxOccurs=1)
>   The changeNumber attribute is designed to facilitate caching of the element and its
>   descendants. This attribute is assigned to this element by the .NET My Services
>   system. The attribute is read-only to applications. Attempts to write this attribute are
>   silently ignored.

/myLists/item/@id (minOccurs=0 maxOccurs=1)
>   This attribute is a globally unique ID assigned to this element by .NET My Services.
>   Normally, .NET My Services will generate and assign this ID during an insertRequest
>   operation, or possibly during a replaceRequest. Application software can override this
>   ID generation by specifying the useClientIds attribute in the request message. Once
>   an ID is assigned, the attribute is read-only and attempts to write it are silently
>   ignored.

/myLists/item/@creator (string minOccurs=0 maxOccurs=1)
>   This attribute identifies the creator in terms of userId, appId, and platformId of the
>   node.

/myLists/item/cat (minOccurs=0 maxOccurs=unbounded)
>   This element is used to categorize the element that contains it by referencing a global
>   category definition in either the .NET categories service system document or an
>   external resource containing category definitions, or by referencing an identity centric
>   category definition in the content document of the .NET categories service for a
>   particular PUID.

/myLists/item/cat/@ref (anyURI minOccurs=0 maxOccurs=1)
>   This attribute references a category definition (<catDef/>) element using the rules
>   outlined in the .NET categories XMI manual

/myLists/item/title (string minOccurs=0 maxOccurs=unbounded)
>   This element specifies the title of the list item.

/myLists/item/title/@xml:lang (minOccurs=1 maxOccurs=1)
> This required attribute is used to specify an ISO 639 language code or an ISO 3166 country code as described in RFC 1766. The value of this attribute indicates the language type of the content within this element.

/myLists/item/description (string minOccurs=0 maxOccurs=unbounded)
> This element specifies a more detailed description of the list item.

/myLists/item/description/@xml:lang (minOccurs=1 maxOccurs=1)
> This required attribute is used to specify an ISO 639 language code or an ISO 3166 country code as described in RFC 1766. The value of this attribute indicates the language type of the content within this element.

/myLists/item/url (anyURI minOccurs=0 maxOccurs=unbounded)
> This optional element specifies a a URL associated with this list item.

/myLists/item/listRef (minOccurs=0 maxOccurs=unbounded)
> This element specifies the lists that this item is considered to be contained within. Note that it is perfectly valid to have a free-form list item that is not considered to be in part of any list which is why this element is minOccurs=0.

/myLists/item/listRef/@ref (string minOccurs=0 maxOccurs=1)
> This attribute contains the ID of a list element and is treated as a reference to that element.

/myLists/item/dueDate (dateTime minOccurs=0 maxOccurs=1)
> This optional element specifies a date/time when this item is considered "due". No special action occurs when an item is "due", it's just a typed note.

/myLists/item/status (string minOccurs=0 maxOccurs=1)
> The status type may accept the following values to indicate the status of an item in a list:

- notStarted
- inProgress
- completed

/myLists/item/priority (string minOccurs=0 maxOccurs=1)
> The priority may indicate the relative priority of this item in a list. Valid values include:

- low
- normal
- high

/myLists/item/assignedTo (minOccurs=0 maxOccurs=unbounded)
> This optional element may be repeated and specifies who the item is "assigned" to. It is most useful when sharing a list in *myLists*.

/myLists/item/assignedTo/name (string minOccurs=0 maxOccurs=1)
> This optional element specifies the name for the enclosing element.

/myLists/item/assignedTo/name/@xml:lang (minOccurs=1 maxOccurs=1)
  This required attribute is used to specify an ISO 639 language code or an ISO 3166 country code as described in RFC 1766. The value of this attribute indicates the language type of the content within this element.

/myLists/item/assignedTo/puid (string minOccurs=0 maxOccurs=1)
  This optional element specifies the name for the enclosing element.

/myLists/item/assignedTo/email (string minOccurs=0 maxOccurs=1)
  This optional name specifies an email address for the enclosing element.

/myLists/item/*{any}* (minOccurs=0 maxOccurs=unbounded)
/myLists/subscription (minOccurs=0 maxOccurs=unbounded)
  This element defines a subscription node that is designed to be an xdb:blue node which when placed in a content document causes a subscription to be registered. A subscription contains a trigger element which selects a scope of coverage. When items change that are under this scope of coverage, a subscriptionResponse message is generated and sent to the specified destination address.

/myLists/subscription/@changeNumber (minOccurs=0 maxOccurs=1)
  The changeNumber attribute is designed to facilitate caching of the element and its descendants. This attribute is assigned to this element by the .NET My Services system. The attribute is read-only to applications. Attempts to write this attribute are silently ignored.

/myLists/subscription/@id (minOccurs=0 maxOccurs=1)
  This attribute is a globally unique ID assigned to this element by .NET My Services. Normally, .NET My Services will generate and assign this ID during an insertRequest operation, or possibly during a replaceRequest. Application software can override this ID generation by specifying the useClientIds attribute in the request message. Once an ID is assigned, the attribute is read-only and attempts to write it are silently ignored.

/myLists/subscription/@creator (string minOccurs=0 maxOccurs=1)
  This attribute identifies the creator in terms of userId, appId, and platformId of the node.

/myLists/subscription/trigger (minOccurs=1 maxOccurs=1)
/myLists/subscription/trigger/@select (string minOccurs=0 maxOccurs=1)
  This item specifies an XPATH expression that specifies the nodes that are to be selected and watched for changes. The selection may only select xdb:blue nodes. As changes in this node set occur, they trigger the generation of a subscription message. These messages are then sent to the SOAP receiver listed in the, "to" element.

/myLists/subscription/trigger/@.mode (string minOccurs=0 maxOccurs=1)

This attribute specifies whether or not the content of the changes that triggered the subscription are delivered in the subscription message, or if the message simply indicates that something changed under the trigger. The attribute may be:

includeData

The data that changed, causing the subscription to trigger is included in the subscription message. Note that deleted nodes are specified by their ID, not by value.

excludeData

The data that changed, causing the subscription to trigger is NOT included in the subscription message.

/myLists/subscription/trigger/@baseChangeNumber (minOccurs=0 maxOccurs=1)

This attribute specifies the changeNumber value that the trigger is relative to. All changes between the specified change number, and the current state of the document relative to the selection are transmitted as subscription messages. This allows a client application to establish a subscription relative to some baseline. As in changeQuery, if the baseChangeNumber is way out of date relative to the current state of the document, and the service can not supply the changes in the subscription message, the subscription insert is rejected. A value of 0 means that the current values of the selected nodes are transmitted in the subscription message.

/myLists/subscription/expiresAt (dateTime minOccurs=0 maxOccurs=1)

This optional element specifies an absolute time after which the subscription is no longer active. The subscription node is automatically removed when the subscription expires. If this element is missing, the subscription does not expire.

/myLists/subscription/context (minOccurs=1 maxOccurs=1)

This element returns the context element from the original subscription. Applications should use this element, AND ONLY this element to correlate the subscription response with one of their subscriptions.

/myLists/subscription/context/@uri (anyURI minOccurs=0 maxOccurs=1)

This attribute specifies the URI value chosen by the subscriber that is associated with this subscription.

/myLists/subscription/context/*{any}* (minOccurs=0 maxOccurs=unbounded)

/myLists/subscription/to (anyURI minOccurs=1 maxOccurs=1)

> This attribute specifies the location that is to receive the subscription message. The value of this element may be one of the following forms:

- *hs:myNotifications*—This URI indicates that generated subscription messages are to be delivered inside the body of a notification and delivered to the default myNotifications service of the creator.

- *protocol://service*—This URI indicates that generated subscription messages are delivered to the specified service at the domain of the creator's platformId. For instance, a platformId indicating msdn.com, and a value in this element of http://subscriptionResponse would cause delivery of the subscription message to http://subscriptionResponse.msdn.com.

> If this value is not specified, then the subscription message is delivered as a notification to the "creator's" myNotifications service.

/myLists/{any} (minOccurs=0 maxOccurs=unbounded)

The .NET lists services/Example/simple todo list

The following fragment illustrates the structure and contents of a simple "todo" list. Note that changeNumbers, creator attributes, and other bookkeeping items are not included in this example. These omissions are intended so that we can focus on the list related content rather than the .NET My Services infrastructure content.

```
<myLists>

    <list id="1">
        <cat ref="toDo"/>
    </list>

    <item id="2">
        <title xml:lang="EN">Make Dental Appointment</title>
        <listRef ref="1"/>
        <status>notStarted</status>
    </item>

    <item id="3">
        <title xml:lang="EN">Pick up Suit</title>
        <listRef ref="1"/>
        <status>notStarted</status>
    </item>

    <item id="3">
        <title xml:lang="EN">Work on Resume</title>
        <listRef ref="1"/>
        <status>inProgress</status>
    </item>

</myLists>
```

With this information, a simple list display might present this list as:

To Do List:
___

Not Started	Make Dental Appointment
Not Started	Pick up Suit
In Progress	*Work on Resume*

The .NET lists services/Example/todo and mall list

The following fragment illustrates the structure and contents of a simple "todo" list and a shopping list for things to purchase or pick up at the mall. Note that some elements appear in both lists. Note that changeNumbers, creator attributes, and other bookkeeping items are not included in this example. These omissions are intended so that we can focus on the list related content rather than the .NET My Services infrastructure content.

```xml
<myLists>

    <list id="1">
        <cat ref="toDo"/>
    </list>

    <list id="10">
        <cat ref="shopping"/>
        <title xml:lang="EN">Bellvue Square</title>
    </list>

    <item id="2">
        <title xml:lang="EN">Make Dental Appointment</title>
        <listRef ref="1"/>
        <status>notStarted</status>
    </item>

    <item id="3">
        <title xml:lang="EN">Pick up Suit</title>
        <listRef ref="1"/>
        <listRef ref="10"/>
        <status>notStarted</status>
    </item>

    <item id="3">
        <title xml:lang="EN">Work on Resume</title>
        <listRef ref="1"/>
        <status>inProgress</status>
    </item>
```

(continued)

(continued)

```
      <item id="4">
          <title xml:lang="EN">Tennis Shoes</title>
          <listRef ref="10"/>
          <status>notStarted</status>
      </item>

      <item id="5">
          <title xml:lang="EN">N'Sync CD</title>
          <listRef ref="10"/>
          <status>notStarted</status>
      </item>

  </myLists>
```

With this information, a simple list display might present these lists as:

To Do List:

Not Started	Make Dental Appointment
Not Started	Pick up Suit
In Progress	*Work on Resume*

To Do List: Bellevue Square

Not Started	Pick up Suit
Not Started	Tennis Shoes
Done	N'Sync CD

The .NET lists services/System

The system document is a global document for the service. Its content and meaning is independent of the PUID used to address the service, and the document is read only to all users. The system document contains a set of base items common to all .NET My Services services, and is optionally extended by each service to include service-specific global information.

This schema outline illustrates the layout and meaning of the information found in the system document for the .NET lists service.

```
<sys:system changeNumber="..." instanceId="..."
    xmlns:hs="http://schemas.microsoft.com/hs/2001/10/core"
    xmlns:sys="http://schemas.microsoft.com/hs/2001/10/myLists/system">1..1
    <hs:roleMap changeNumber="..." id="..." creator="...">1..1
        <hs:scope id="...">0..unbounded
            <hs:shape base="...">1..1
```

```
                    <hs:include select="...">1..unbounded</hs:include>
                    <hs:exclude select="...">0..unbounded</hs:exclude>
            </hs:shape>
        </hs:scope>
        <hs:roleTemplate name="..." priority="...">0..unbounded
            <hs:fullDescription xml:lang="...">0..1</hs:fullDescription>
            <hs:method name="..." scopeRef="...">0..unbounded</hs:method>
        </hs:roleTemplate>
    </hs:roleMap>
    <hs:methodMap changeNumber="..." id="..." creator="...">1..1
        <hs:method name="...">0..unbounded {any}</hs:method>
    </hs:methodMap>
    <hs:schemaMap changeNumber="..." id="..." creator="...">1..1
        <hs:schema namespace="..." schemaLocation="..." alias="...">0..unbounded
{any}</hs:schema>
    </hs:schemaMap>
    <hs:wsdlMap changeNumber="..." id="..." creator="...">1..1
        <hs:wsdl wsdlLocation="...">0..unbounded {any}</hs:wsdl>
        <hs:disco discoLocation="...">0..unbounded {any}</hs:disco>
    </hs:wsdlMap>
    {any}
</sys:system>
```

The meaning of the attributes and elements shown in the preceding sample document fragment are listed in the following section.

/system (minOccurs=1 maxOccurs=1)

This element encapsulates the system document for the .NET lists service.

/system/@changeNumber (minOccurs=0 maxOccurs=1)

The changeNumber attribute is designed to facilitate caching of the element and its descendants. This attribute is assigned to this element by the .NET My Services system. The attribute is read-only to applications. Attempts to write this attribute are silently ignored.

/system/@instanceId (string minOccurs=0 maxOccurs=1)

This attribute is a unique identifier typically assigned to the root element of a service. It is a read-only element and assigned by the .NET My Services system when a user is provisioned for a particular service.

/system/roleMap (minOccurs=1 maxOccurs=1)

This element encapsulates all the elements that make up a roleMap, which include document class relative roleTemplate, priority, name, method, and per-method scope. An individual roleTemplate defines the maximum scope of information, and the allowable methods used to access that information for each request mapped into the template.

/system/roleMap/@changeNumber (minOccurs=0 maxOccurs=1)

The changeNumber attribute is designed to facilitate caching of the element and its descendants. This attribute is assigned to this element by the .NET My Services system. The attribute is read-only to applications. Attempts to write this attribute are silently ignored.

/system/roleMap/@id (minOccurs=0 maxOccurs=1)

This attribute is a globally unique ID assigned to this element by .NET My Services. Normally, .NET My Services will generate and assign this ID during an insertRequest operation, or possibly during a replaceRequest. Application software can override this ID generation by specifying the useClientIds attribute in the request message. Once an ID is assigned, the attribute is read-only and attempts to write it are silently ignored.

/system/roleMap/@creator (string minOccurs=0 maxOccurs=1)

This attribute identifies the creator in terms of userId, appId, and platformId of the node.

/system/roleMap/scope (minOccurs=0 maxOccurs=unbounded)

This element defines a scope which may be referred to by roles within this roleMap to indicate what portions of the document are visible to this role for the specified method.

/system/roleMap/scope/@id (minOccurs=0 maxOccurs=1)

This attribute is a globally unique ID assigned to this element by .NET My Services. Normally, .NET My Services will generate and assign this ID during an insertRequest operation, or possibly during a replaceRequest. Application software can override this ID generation by specifying the useClientIds attribute in the request message. Once an ID is assigned, the attribute is read-only and attempts to write it are silently ignored.

/system/roleMap/scope/shape (minOccurs=1 maxOccurs=1)

A shape defines the node set visible through the document when operating through this shape element.

/system/roleMap/scope/shape/@base (string minOccurs=0 maxOccurs=1)

This attribute specifies the initial set of nodes visible through the shape.

A value of t indicates that the shape is initialized to include all possible nodes relative to the shape that is currently in effect. For instance, each role defines a scope containing a shape. When defining a shape for a role, the value t indicates all possible nodes available in the specified document for this role. When defining a shape in an ACL entry, a value of t means all of the nodes visible in the shape for the computed role. When using a shape in an hsdl operation, a value of t indicates all of the possible nodes selected by the hsdl operation (relative to the ACL shape which itself is relative to the role's shape).

The value nil indicates the opposite of t, which is the empty node set. Nodes from this set may then be included into the shape.

/system/roleMap/scope/shape/include (minOccurs=1 maxOccurs=unbounded)

This element specifies the set of nodes that should be included into the shape relative to the possible set of nodes indicated by the base attribute.

/system/roleMap/scope/shape/include/@select (string minOccurs=0 maxOccurs=1)
>   This item specifies an XPATH expression that selects a set of nodes relative to the externally established context. The expression can never travel outside the node-set established by this externally established current context. The expression may match 0 or more nodes, and the operation manipulates all selected nodes. The minOccurs and maxOccurs attributes are optional and place restrictions and limitations on the number of nodes selected.

/system/roleMap/scope/shape/exclude (minOccurs=0 maxOccurs=unbounded)
>   This element specifies the set of nodes that should be excluded from the shape relative to the possible set of nodes indicated by the base attribute.

/system/roleMap/scope/shape/exclude/@select (string minOccurs=0 maxOccurs=1)
>   This item specifies an XPATH expression that selects a set of nodes relative to the externally established context. The expression can never travel outside the node-set established by this externally established current context. The expression may match 0 or more nodes, and the operation manipulates all selected nodes. The minOccurs and maxOccurs attributes are optional and place restrictions and limitations on the number of nodes selected.

/system/roleMap/roleTemplate (minOccurs=0 maxOccurs=unbounded)
>   This element encapsulates the definition of a role. The attribute set for this element includes the document class that this roleTemplate refers to, the name of the roleTemplate, and the priority of the roleTemplate.

/system/roleMap/roleTemplate/@name (string minOccurs=0 maxOccurs=1)
>   This element specifies the name of the role.

/system/roleMap/roleTemplate/@priority (int minOccurs=0 maxOccurs=1)
>   This element specifies the priority of the roleTemplate which is used to select that actual roleTemplate when the role evaluation determines that the subject maps to multiple roleTemplates.

/system/roleMap/roleTemplate/fullDescription (string minOccurs=0 maxOccurs=1)
>   This element contains a description of this role template which specifies the capabilities a caller will have when accessing information through this role.

/system/roleMap/roleTemplate/fullDescription/@xml:lang (minOccurs=1 maxOccurs=1)
>   This required attribute is used to specify an ISO 639 language code or an ISO 3166 country code as described in RFC 1766. The value of this attribute indicates the language type of the content within this element.

/system/roleMap/roleTemplate/method (minOccurs=0 maxOccurs=unbounded)
>   This element specifies the methods available within this roleTemplate by name, and by scope. When a subject maps to a roleTemplate, the method in the request must match one of these elements for the message to continue to flow. If the method exists, the data available to the method is a function of the scope referenced by this method combined with an optional scope referenced by the role defined in the roleList.

/system/roleMap/roleTemplate/method/@name (string minOccurs=0 maxOccurs=1)
>   This element specifies the name of the method.

/system/roleMap/roleTemplate/method/@scopeRef (string minOccurs=0 maxOccurs=1)
This attribute specifies the scope within this document that is in effect for this method.

/system/methodMap (minOccurs=1 maxOccurs=1)
This element defines the methodMap. While it is true that in most cases, the roleMap section contains a definitive list of methods, these methods are likely to be scattered about the roleMap in various templates. This section contains the definitive non-duplicated list of methods available within the service.

/system/methodMap/@changeNumber (minOccurs=0 maxOccurs=1)
The changeNumber attribute is designed to facilitate caching of the element and its descendants. This attribute is assigned to this element by the .NET My Services system. The attribute is read-only to applications. Attempts to write this attribute are silently ignored.

/system/methodMap/@id (minOccurs=0 maxOccurs=1)
This attribute is a globally unique ID assigned to this element by .NET My Services. Normally, .NET My Services will generate and assign this ID during an insertRequest operation, or possibly during a replaceRequest. Application software can override this ID generation by specifying the useClientIds attribute in the request message. Once an ID is assigned, the attribute is read-only and attempts to write it are silently ignored.

/system/methodMap/@creator (string minOccurs=0 maxOccurs=1)
This attribute identifies the creator in terms of userId, appId, and platformId of the node.

/system/methodMap/method (minOccurs=0 maxOccurs=unbounded)
This element defines a method that is available within this service.

/system/methodMap/method/@name (string minOccurs=0 maxOccurs=1)
This attribute specifies the name of a method available within the service.

/system/methodMap/method/*{any}* (minOccurs=0 maxOccurs=unbounded)

/system/schemaMap (minOccurs=1 maxOccurs=1)
This element defines the various schemas that define the data structures and shape of information managed by this service. Each schema is defined by its namespace URI, its location, and a preferred namespace alias.

/system/schemaMap/@changeNumber (minOccurs=0 maxOccurs=1)
The changeNumber attribute is designed to facilitate caching of the element and its descendants. This attribute is assigned to this element by the .NET My Services system. The attribute is read-only to applications. Attempts to write this attribute are silently ignored.

/system/schemaMap/@id (minOccurs=0 maxOccurs=1)
This attribute is a globally unique ID assigned to this element by .NET My Services. Normally, .NET My Services will generate and assign this ID during an insertRequest operation, or possibly during a replaceRequest. Application software can override this ID generation by specifying the useClientIds attribute in the request message. Once an ID is assigned, the attribute is read-only and attempts to write it are silently ignored.

/system/schemaMap/@creator (string minOccurs=0 maxOccurs=1)
> This attribute identifies the creator in terms of userId, appId, and platformId of the node.

/system/schemaMap/schema (minOccurs=0 maxOccurs=unbounded)
> This element defines a schema which defines data-structures and the shape of information managed by this service. Multiple schema elements exist for each service, once for each logical grouping of information exposed by the service.

/system/schemaMap/schema/@namespace (anyURI minOccurs=0 maxOccurs=1)
> This attribute specifies the namespace URI of this schema.

/system/schemaMap/schema/@schemaLocation (anyURI minOccurs=0 maxOccurs=1)
> This attribute specifies the location (in the form of a URI) of the resource containing schema. When a schema is reachable through a variety of URIs, one schema element will exist for each location.

/system/schemaMap/schema/@alias (string minOccurs=0 maxOccurs=1)
> This attribute specifies the preferred alias that should be used if possible when manipulating information covered by this schema in the context of this service.

/system/schemaMap/schema/*{any}* (minOccurs=0 maxOccurs=unbounded)
/system/wsdlMap (minOccurs=1 maxOccurs=1)
> This element defines the wsdlMap for this service. This map includes the location of WSDL documents, DISCO documents, and WISL documents for this web service. These documents are used by applications to understand the format of messages that may be sent to the various services.

/system/wsdlMap/@changeNumber (minOccurs=0 maxOccurs=1)
> The changeNumber attribute is designed to facilitate caching of the element and its descendants. This attribute is assigned to this element by the .NET My Services system. The attribute is read-only to applications. Attempts to write this attribute are silently ignored.

/system/wsdlMap/@id (minOccurs=0 maxOccurs=1)
> This attribute is a globally unique ID assigned to this element by .NET My Services. Normally, .NET My Services will generate and assign this ID during an insertRequest operation, or possibly during a replaceRequest. Application software can override this ID generation by specifying the useClientIds attribute in the request message. Once an ID is assigned, the attribute is read-only and attempts to write it are silently ignored.

/system/wsdlMap/@creator (string minOccurs=0 maxOccurs=1)
> This attribute identifies the creator in terms of userId, appId, and platformId of the node.

/system/wsdlMap/wsdl (minOccurs=0 maxOccurs=unbounded)
> This element is used to specify the location of a WSDL file for this service. Multiple entries may exist pointing to the same file hosted in multiple locations, or to variations on the content within the WSDL files.

/system/wsdlMap/wsdl/@wsdlLocation (anyURI minOccurs=0 maxOccurs=1)
> This attribute is a URI that specifies the location of the WSDL file.

/system/wsdlMap/wsdl/*{any}* (minOccurs=0 maxOccurs=unbounded)
/system/wsdlMap/disco (minOccurs=0 maxOccurs=unbounded)
> This element is used to specify the location of a DISCO file for this service. Multiple entries may exist pointing to the same file hosted in multiple locations, or to variations on the content within the DISCO files.

/system/wsdlMap/disco/@discoLocation (anyURI minOccurs=0 maxOccurs=1)
> This attribute is a URI that specifies the location of the DISCO file.

/system/wsdlMap/disco/*{any}* (minOccurs=0 maxOccurs=unbounded)
/system/*{any}* (minOccurs=0 maxOccurs=unbounded)

.NET lists services/Methods

The .NET lists service supports the following standard and domain-specific methods:

- query
- insert
- replace
- delete
- update

The standard methods operate on this service using the same message format and method-interchange techniques described in the hsdl section of this document. The only service-specific information to note is the schema that is in effect for each of the methods. These schemas, and how they relate to the standard methods and roles are described in the roles section of this document.

The domain specific methods operate as described in the domain specific methods section of this document, and are governed by the various schemas outlined in the .NET lists/Roles section for this service.

C H A P T E R   1 8

The .NET Notifications Service/Introduction

This chapter describes the .NET notifications service.

The .NET Notifications Service/Roles

The .NET notifications service controls access by using the following roleTemplates:

- rt0
- rt3
- rt99

The .NET notifications service uses the following scopes:

- **scope id 1**

```
<hs:scope id=1>

    <hs:shape base=t>

    </hs:shape>

</hs:scope>
```

- **scope id 2**

```
<hs:scope id=2>

    <hs:shape base=nil>

        <hs:include select=//*[@creator='$callerId']/>

    </hs:shape>

</hs:scope>
```

- **scope id 3**

```
<hs:scope id=3>

    <hs:shape base=nil>

        <hs:include select=//subscription[@creator='$callerId']/>

    </hs:shape>

</hs:scope>
```

- **scope id 4**

```
<hs:scope id=4>

    <hs:shape base=nil>

        <hs:include select=//*[cat/@ref='hs:public']/>

        <hs:include select=//subscription[@creator='$callerId']/>

    </hs:shape>

</hs:scope>
```

The .NET notifications service roleTemplate rt0

The purpose of this role is to give complete read/write access to all information within the content document of the service being protected through this roleTemplate.

The following table illustrates the available methods and the scope in effect when accessing the .NET notifications service through that method while mapped to this roleTemplate.

method	scopeRef
query	scopeRef=1
insert	scopeRef=1
replace	scopeRef=1
delete	scopeRef=1
update	scopeRef=1
notify	scopeRef=1
route	scopeRef=1
do	scopeRef=1

The .NET notifications service roleTemplate rt3

The purpose of this role is to give limited read access to information within the content document that is categorized as "public".

The following table illustrates the available methods and the scope in effect when accessing the .NET notifications service through that method while mapped to this roleTemplate.

method	scopeRef
query	scopeRef=4
notify	scopeRef=1
do	scopeRef=1

The .NET notifications service roleTemplate rt99

The purpose of this role is to block all access to the content document. Note that lack of a role in the roleList has the same effect as assigning someone to rt99.

The .NET Notifications Service/Content

The content document is an identity centric document. Its content and meaning is a function of the Microsoft Passport Unique ID (PUID) used to address the service. Accessing the document is controlled by the associated roleList document.

This schema outline illustrates the layout and meaning of the information found in the content document for the .NET notifications service.

```
<m:myNotifications changeNumber="..." instanceId="..."
    xmlns:m="http://schemas.microsoft.com/hs/2001/10/myNotifications"
    xmlns:hs="http://schemas.microsoft.com/hs/2001/10/core">_{1..1}
    <m:stream changeNumber="..." id="..." creator="...">_{1..unbounded}
        <m:class>_{1..1}</m:class>
        <m:expiration>_{0..1}</m:expiration>
        <m:position>_{1..1}</m:position>
        <m:xpQuery>_{0..1}</m:xpQuery>
        <m:argot argotURI="...">_{0..unbounded} {any}</m:argot>
    </m:stream>
    <m:connection changeNumber="..." id="..." creator="...">_{0..unbounded}
        <m:class>_{1..1}</m:class>
        <m:status>_{1..1}</m:status>
        <m:characteristics>_{1..1}</m:characteristics>
        <m:expiration>_{1..1}</m:expiration>
        <m:xpQuery>_{1..1}</m:xpQuery>
```

(continued)

(continued)

```
        <m:argot argotURI="...">₀..unbounded {any}</m:argot>
    </m:connection>
    <m:subscription changeNumber="..." id="..." creator="...">₀..unbounded
        <hs:trigger select="..." mode="..."
baseChangeNumber="...">₁..₁</hs:trigger>
        <hs:expiresAt>₀..₁</hs:expiresAt>
        <hs:context uri="...">₁..₁ {any}</hs:context>
        <hs:to>₁..₁</hs:to>
    </m:subscription>
</m:myNotifications>
```

The meaning of the attributes and elements shown in the preceding sample document fragment are listed in the following section.

/myNotifications (minOccurs=1 maxOccurs=1)

myNotifications is the user content document for notification routing. It contains streams, connections, and preferences (general provisioning). The document doesn't contain a list of notifications—notifications are transitory. Use the notifyRequest, route, and PollRequest verbs to send and receive notifications.

/myNotifications/@changeNumber (minOccurs=0 maxOccurs=1)

The changeNumber attribute is designed to facilitate caching of the element and its descendants. This attribute is assigned to this element by the Microsoft .NET My Services system. The attribute is read-only to applications. Attempts to write this attribute are silently ignored.

/myNotifications/@instanceId (string minOccurs=0 maxOccurs=1)

This attribute is a unique identifier typically assigned to the root element of a service. It is a read-only element and assigned by the .NET My Services system when a user is provisioned for a particular service.

/myNotifications/stream (minOccurs=1 maxOccurs=unbounded)

A stream is an internal object that processes notifications before they are routed to connections. Streams can do things like buffering and rerouting.

/myNotifications/stream/@changeNumber (minOccurs=0 maxOccurs=1)

The changeNumber attribute is designed to facilitate caching of the element and its descendants. This attribute is assigned to this element by the .NET My Services system. The attribute is read-only to applications. Attempts to write this attribute are silently ignored.

/myNotifications/stream/@id (minOccurs=0 maxOccurs=1)

This attribute is a globally unique ID assigned to this element by .NET My Services. Normally, .NET My Services will generate and assign this ID during an insertRequest operation, or possibly during a replaceRequest. Application software can override this ID generation by specifying the useClientIds attribute in the request message. Once an ID is assigned, the attribute is read-only and attempts to write it are silently ignored.

<u>/myNotifications/stream/@creator</u> (string minOccurs=0 maxOccurs=1)
> This attribute identifies the creator in terms of userId, appId, and platformId of the node.

/myNotifications/stream/class (string minOccurs=1 maxOccurs=1)
> Defines what kind of stream.

/myNotifications/stream/expiration (string minOccurs=0 maxOccurs=1)
> Lifetime of a connection in absolute time (GMT). This can be used to clean up the content document.

/myNotifications/stream/position (string minOccurs=1 maxOccurs=1)
> Defines where the stream fits into the streamFork processing.

/myNotifications/stream/xpQuery (string minOccurs=0 maxOccurs=1)
> The query against incoming notifications. This is optional because the stream may do its own selection set based on the streamClass argots. If not present, the query is "*".

/myNotifications/stream/argot (minOccurs=0 maxOccurs=unbounded)
> An argot is a domain-specific blob of data, qualified by a name and ID. The contents are free. Argots are opaque to .NET My Services.

/myNotifications/stream/argot/@argotURI (anyURI minOccurs=0 maxOccurs=1)
> This URI points to a location containing the XSD for this argot, as well as uniquely identifying the type of argot.

/myNotifications/stream/argot/*{any}* (minOccurs=0 maxOccurs=unbounded)

/myNotifications/connection (minOccurs=0 maxOccurs=unbounded)
> Abbreviations: CXN (Connection): The Connection exists inside of the .NET notifications service. UA (UserAgent): The User Agent exists outside of the .NET notifications service. There are mainly two types of connections: Push, Notifications are pushed by CXN to UA. Pull, Notifications are downloaded by the UA by issuing a request to CXN. The response contains the Notifications. A CXN is created (added to the .NET notifications service content document) by either: 1) a UA directly adds the CXN to the content document 2) Some entity acts on behalf of a UA. In order to transfer the Notifications, a session is established between CXN and UA. The session can be persistent or transient. The CXN persists in the case where sessions are transient. Establishment of a session can be initiated by either CXN or UA, either when the CXN is created or based on, say, a timer or some signaling mechanism between CXN and UA. The session may be closed after a period of time (including 0) by either entity. Based on these types we can have different models of UA-CXN interaction. A few examples are listed below: 1) UA establishes a session with a CXN, and pulls Notifications from CXN. 2) UA establishes a session with a CXN, and the CXN pushes Notifications to the UA. 3) CXN establishes a session with a UA, and the UA pulls Notifications. 4) CXN establishes a session with a UA and pushes Notifications to UA. 5) UA polls the CXN, periodically on a timer, and UA will initiate process #1 or #2 above. 6) CXN polls the UA when Notifications arrive or periodically on a timer when there are pending Notifications in the queue, and UA will initiate process #1 or #2 above.

/myNotifications/connection/@changeNumber (minOccurs=0 maxOccurs=1)
> The changeNumber attribute is designed to facilitate caching of the element and its descendants. This attribute is assigned to this element by the .NET My Services system. The attribute is read-only to applications. Attempts to write this attribute are silently ignored.

/myNotifications/connection/@id (minOccurs=0 maxOccurs=1)
> This attribute is a globally unique ID assigned to this element by .NET My Services. Normally, .NET My Services will generate and assign this ID during an insertRequest operation, or possibly during a replaceRequest. Application software can override this ID generation by specifying the useClientIds attribute in the request message. Once an ID is assigned, the attribute is read-only and attempts to write it are silently ignored.

/myNotifications/connection/@creator (string minOccurs=0 maxOccurs=1)
> This attribute identifies the creator in terms of userId, appId, and platformId of the node.

/myNotifications/connection/class (string minOccurs=1 maxOccurs=1)
> This element specifies the class of a connection. Push over Soap-RP, Pull over Soap-RP etc.

/myNotifications/connection/status (string minOccurs=1 maxOccurs=1)
> Flags indicating the current status of the connection. Flags can be used by the Stream modules to manage traffic, buffer, and generate Non Delivery Reports and Delayed Delivery Reports for the Sender.

/myNotifications/connection/characteristics (string minOccurs=1 maxOccurs=1)
> Information about the nature of the connection, used mainly by the Stream modules. Reliable could mean it supports Acks; Unreliable means fire-and-forget. Type of polling used (Connection vs. UserAgent).

/myNotifications/connection/expiration (string minOccurs=1 maxOccurs=1)
> Lifetime of a connection in absolute time (GMT). This can be used to clean up the content document.

/myNotifications/connection/xpQuery (string minOccurs=1 maxOccurs=1)
> A connection can request only those notifications that satisfy this query/filter from Stream modules.

/myNotifications/connection/argot (minOccurs=0 maxOccurs=unbounded)
> An argot is a domain-specific blob of data, qualified by a name and ID. The contents are free. Argots are opaque to .NET My Services.

/myNotifications/connection/argot/@argotURI (anyURI minOccurs=0 maxOccurs=1)
> This URI points to a location containing the XSD for this argot, as well as uniquely identifying the type of argot.

/myNotifications/connection/argot/*{any}* (minOccurs=0 maxOccurs=unbounded)

/myNotifications/subscription (minOccurs=0 maxOccurs=unbounded)

> This element defines a subscription node that is designed to be an xdb:blue node, which when placed in a content document, causes a subscription to be registered. A subscription contains a trigger element which selects a scope of coverage. When items change that are under this scope of coverage, a subscriptionResponse message is generated and sent to the specified destination address.

/myNotifications/subscription/@changeNumber (minOccurs=0 maxOccurs=1)

> The changeNumber attribute is designed to facilitate caching of the element and its descendants. This attribute is assigned to this element by the .NET My Services system. The attribute is read-only to applications. Attempts to write this attribute are silently ignored.

/myNotifications/subscription/@id (minOccurs=0 maxOccurs=1)

> This attribute is a globally unique ID assigned to this element by .NET My Services. Normally, .NET My Services will generate and assign this ID during an insertRequest operation, or possibly during a replaceRequest. Application software can override this ID generation by specifying the useClientIds attribute in the request message. Once an ID is assigned, the attribute is read-only and attempts to write it are silently ignored.

/myNotifications/subscription/@creator (string minOccurs=0 maxOccurs=1)

> This attribute identifies the creator in terms of userId, appId, and platformId of the node.

/myNotifications/subscription/trigger (minOccurs=1 maxOccurs=1)

/myNotifications/subscription/trigger/@select (string minOccurs=0 maxOccurs=1)

> This item specifies an XPATH expression that specifies the nodes that are to be selected and watched for changes. The selection may only select xdb:blue nodes. As changes in this node set occur, they trigger the generation of a subscription message. A message is then sent to the SOAP receiver listed in the "to" element.

/myNotifications/subscription/trigger/@mode (string minOccurs=0 maxOccurs=1)

> This attribute specifies whether or not the content of the changes that triggered the subscription is delivered in the subscription message, or whether the message simply indicates that something changed under the trigger. The attribute may be:
>
> includeData
>
>> The data that changed, causing the subscription to trigger, is included in the subscription message. Note that deleted nodes are specified by their ID, not by value.
>
> excludeData
>
>> The data that changed, causing the subscription to trigger, is not included in the subscription message.

/myNotifications/subscription/trigger/@baseChangeNumber (minOccurs=0 maxOccurs=1)

This attribute specifies the changeNumber value that the trigger is relative to. All changes between the specified change number, and the current state of the document relative to the selection are transmitted as subscription messages. This allows a client application to establish a subscription relative to some baseline. As in changeQuery, if the baseChangeNumber is way out of date relative to the current state of the document, and the service cannot supply the changes in the subscription message, the subscription insert is rejected. A value of 0 means that the current values of the selected nodes are transmitted in the subscription message.

/myNotifications/subscription/expiresAt (dateTime minOccurs=0 maxOccurs=1)

This optional element specifies an absolute time after which the subscription is no longer active. The subscription node is automatically removed when the subscription expires. If this element is missing, the subscription does not expire.

/myNotifications/subscription/context (minOccurs=1 maxOccurs=1)

This element returns the context element from the original subscription. Applications should use this element, and only this element, to correlate the subscription response with one of their subscriptions.

/myNotifications/subscription/context/@uri (anyURI minOccurs=0 maxOccurs=1)

This attribute specifies the URI value chosen by the subscriber that is associated with this subscription.

/myNotifications/subscription/context/*{any}* (minOccurs=0 maxOccurs=unbounded)

/myNotifications/subscription/to (anyURI minOccurs=1 maxOccurs=1)

This attribute specifies the location that is to receive the subscription message. The value of this element may be one of the following forms:

- *hs:myNotifications*—This URI indicates that generated subscription messages are to be delivered inside the body of a notification and delivered to the default .NET notifications service of the creator.

- *protocol://service*—This URI indicates that generated subscription messages are delivered to the specified service at the domain of the creator's platformId. For instance, a platformId indicating msn.com, and a value in this element of http://subscriptionResponse would cause delivery of the subscription message to http://subscriptionResponse.msn.com.

If this value is not specified, then the subscription message is delivered as a notification to the "creator's" .NET notification service.

The .NET Notifications Service/System

The system document is a global document for the service. Its content and meaning is independent of the PUID used to address the service, and the document is read-only to all users. The system document contains a set of base items common to all .NET My Services services, and is optionally extended by each service to include service-specific global information.

This schema outline illustrates the layout and meaning of the information found in the system document for the .NET notifications service.

```
<sys:system changeNumber="..." instanceId="..."
    xmlns:hs="http://schemas.microsoft.com/hs/2001/10/core"
    xmlns:sys="http://schemas.microsoft.com/hs/2001/10/myNotifications/system">1..1
    <hs:roleMap changeNumber="..." id="..." creator="...">1..1
        <hs:scope id="...">0..unbounded
            <hs:shape base="...">1..1
                <hs:include select="...">1..unbounded</hs:include>
                <hs:exclude select="...">0..unbounded</hs:exclude>
            </hs:shape>
        </hs:scope>
        <hs:roleTemplate name="..." priority="...">0..unbounded
            <hs:fullDescription xml:lang="...">0..1</hs:fullDescription>
            <hs:method name="..." scopeRef="...">0..unbounded</hs:method>
        </hs:roleTemplate>
    </hs:roleMap>
    <hs:methodMap changeNumber="..." id="..." creator="...">1..1
        <hs:method name="...">0..unbounded {any}</hs:method>
    </hs:methodMap>
    <hs:schemaMap changeNumber="..." id="..." creator="...">1..1
        <hs:schema namespace="..." schemaLocation="..." alias="...">0..unbounded
{any}</hs:schema>
    </hs:schemaMap>
    <hs:wsdlMap changeNumber="..." id="..." creator="...">1..1
        <hs:wsdl wsdlLocation="...">0..unbounded {any}</hs:wsdl>
        <hs:disco discoLocation="...">0..unbounded {any}</hs:disco>
    </hs:wsdlMap>
    {any}
</sys:system>
```

The meaning of the attributes and elements shown in the preceding sample document fragment are listed in the following section.

/system (minOccurs=1 maxOccurs=1)

This element encapsulates the system document for the .NET notifications service.

/system/@changeNumber (minOccurs=0 maxOccurs=1)

The changeNumber attribute is designed to facilitate caching of the element and its descendants. This attribute is assigned to this element by the .NET My Services system. The attribute is read-only to applications. Attempts to write this attribute are silently ignored.

/system/@instanceId (string minOccurs=0 maxOccurs=1)

This attribute is a unique identifier typically assigned to the root element of a service. It is a read-only element and assigned by the .NET My Services system when a user is provisioned for a particular service.

/system/roleMap (minOccurs=1 maxOccurs=1)

This element encapsulates all the elements that make up a roleMap, which includes a document class relative to a roleTemplate, priority, name, method, and per-method scope. An individual roleTemplate defines the maximum scope of information, and the allowable methods used to access that information for each request mapped into the template.

/system/roleMap/@changeNumber (minOccurs=0 maxOccurs=1)

The changeNumber attribute is designed to facilitate caching of the element and its descendants. This attribute is assigned to this element by the .NET My Services system. The attribute is read-only to applications. Attempts to write this attribute are silently ignored.

/system/roleMap/@id (minOccurs=0 maxOccurs=1)

This attribute is a globally unique ID assigned to this element by .NET My Services. Normally, .NET My Services will generate and assign this ID during an insertRequest operation, or possibly during a replaceRequest. Application software can override this ID generation by specifying the useClientIds attribute in the request message. Once an ID is assigned, the attribute is read-only and attempts to write it are silently ignored.

/system/roleMap/@creator (string minOccurs=0 maxOccurs=1)

This attribute identifies the creator in terms of userId, appId, and platformId of the node.

/system/roleMap/scope (minOccurs=0 maxOccurs=unbounded)

This element defines a scope which may be referred to by roles within this roleMap to indicate what portions of the document are visible to this role for the specified method.

/system/roleMap/scope/@id (minOccurs=0 maxOccurs=1)

This attribute is a globally unique ID assigned to this element by .NET My Services. Normally, .NET My Services will generate and assign this ID during an insertRequest operation, or possibly during a replaceRequest. Application software can override this ID generation by specifying the useClientIds attribute in the request message. Once an ID is assigned, the attribute is read-only and attempts to write it are silently ignored.

/system/roleMap/scope/shape (minOccurs=1 maxOccurs=1)
A shape defines the node set visible through the document when operating through this shape element.

/system/roleMap/scope/shape/@base (string minOccurs=0 maxOccurs=1)
This attribute specifies the initial set of nodes visible through the shape.

A value of t indicates that the shape is initialized to include all possible nodes relative to the shape that is currently in effect. For instance, each role defines a scope containing a shape. When defining a shape for a role, the value t indicates all possible nodes available in the specified document for this role. When defining a shape in an ACL entry, a value of t means all of the nodes are visible in the shape for the computed role. When using a shape in an hsdl operation, a value of t indicates all of the possible nodes selected by the hsdl operation (relative to the ACL shape which itself is relative to the role's shape).

The value nil indicates the opposite of t, which is the empty node set. Nodes from this set may then be included into the shape.

/system/roleMap/scope/shape/include (minOccurs=1 maxOccurs=unbounded)
This element specifies the set of nodes that should be included into the shape relative to the possible set of nodes indicated by the base attribute.

/system/roleMap/scope/shape/include/@select (string minOccurs=0 maxOccurs=1)
This item specifies an XPATH expression that selects a set of nodes relative to the externally established context. The expression can never travel outside the node-set established by this externally established current context. The expression may match 0 or more nodes, and the operation manipulates all selected nodes. The minOccurs and maxOccurs attributes are optional and place restrictions and limitations on the number of nodes selected.

/system/roleMap/scope/shape/exclude (minOccurs=0 maxOccurs=unbounded)
This element specifies the set of nodes that should be excluded from the shape relative to the possible set of nodes indicated by the base attribute.

/system/roleMap/scope/shape/exclude/@select (string minOccurs=0 maxOccurs=1)
This item specifies an XPATH expression that selects a set of nodes relative to the externally established context. The expression can never travel outside the node-set established by this externally established current context. The expression may match 0 or more nodes, and the operation manipulates all selected nodes. The minOccurs and maxOccurs attributes are optional and place restrictions and limitations on the number of nodes selected.

/system/roleMap/roleTemplate (minOccurs=0 maxOccurs=unbounded)
This element encapsulates the definition of a role. The attribute set for this element includes the document class that this roleTemplate refers to, the name of the roleTemplate, and the priority of the roleTemplate.

/system/roleMap/roleTemplate/@name (string minOccurs=0 maxOccurs=1)
This element specifies the name of the role.

/system/roleMap/roleTemplate/@priority (int minOccurs=0 maxOccurs=1)
This element specifies the priority of the roleTemplate which is used to select that actual roleTemplate when the role evaluation determines that the subject maps to multiple roleTemplates.

/system/roleMap/roleTemplate/fullDescription (string minOccurs=0 maxOccurs=1)
This element contains a description of this role template which specifies the capabilities a caller will have when accessing information through this role.

/system/roleMap/roleTemplate/fullDescription/@xml:lang (minOccurs=1 maxOccurs=1)
This required attribute is used to specify an ISO 639 language code or an ISO 3166 country code as described in RFC 1766. The value of this attribute indicates the language type of the content within this element.

/system/roleMap/roleTemplate/method (minOccurs=0 maxOccurs=unbounded)
This element specifies the methods available within this roleTemplate by name, and by scope. When a subject maps to a roleTemplate, the method in the request must match one of these elements for the message to continue to flow. If the method exists, the data available to the method is a function of the scope referenced by this method combined with an optional scope referenced by the role defined in the roleList.

/system/roleMap/roleTemplate/method/@name (string minOccurs=0 maxOccurs=1)
This element specifies the name of the method.

/system/roleMap/roleTemplate/method/@scopeRef (string minOccurs=0 maxOccurs=1)
This attribute specifies the scope within this document that is in effect for this method.

/system/methodMap (minOccurs=1 maxOccurs=1)
This element defines the methodMap. While it is true that in most cases the roleMap section contains a definitive list of methods, these methods are likely to be scattered about the roleMap in various templates. This section contains the definitive non-duplicated list of methods available within the service.

/system/methodMap/@changeNumber (minOccurs=0 maxOccurs=1)
The changeNumber attribute is designed to facilitate caching of the element and its descendants. This attribute is assigned to this element by the .NET My Services system. The attribute is read-only to applications. Attempts to write this attribute are silently ignored.

/system/methodMap/@id (minOccurs=0 maxOccurs=1)
This attribute is a globally unique ID assigned to this element by .NET My Services. Normally, .NET My Services will generate and assign this ID during an insertRequest operation, or possibly during a replaceRequest. Application software can override this ID generation by specifying the useClientIds attribute in the request message. Once an ID is assigned, the attribute is read-only and attempts to write it are silently ignored.

/system/methodMap/@creator (string minOccurs=0 maxOccurs=1)
This attribute identifies the creator in terms of userId, appId, and platformId of the node.

/system/methodMap/method (minOccurs=0 maxOccurs=unbounded)
This element defines a method that is available within this service.

/system/methodMap/method/@name (string minOccurs=0 maxOccurs=1)
This attribute specifies the name of a method available within this service.

/system/methodMap/method/*{any}* (minOccurs=0 maxOccurs=unbounded)
/system/schemaMap (minOccurs=1 maxOccurs=1)
This element defines the various schemas that define the data structures and shape of information managed by this service. Each schema is defined by its namespace URI, its location, and a preferred namespace alias.

/system/schemaMap/@changeNumber (minOccurs=0 maxOccurs=1)
The changeNumber attribute is designed to facilitate caching of the element and its descendants. This attribute is assigned to this element by the .NET My Services system. The attribute is read-only to applications. Attempts to write this attribute are silently ignored.

/system/schemaMap/@id (minOccurs=0 maxOccurs=1)
This attribute is a globally unique ID assigned to this element by .NET My Services. Normally, .NET My Services will generate and assign this ID during an insertRequest operation, or possibly during a replaceRequest. Application software can override this ID generation by specifying the useClientIds attribute in the request message. Once an ID is assigned, the attribute is read-only and attempts to write it are silently ignored.

/system/schemaMap/@creator (string minOccurs=0 maxOccurs=1)
This attribute identifies the creator in terms of userId, appId, and platformId of the node.

/system/schemaMap/schema (minOccurs=0 maxOccurs=unbounded)
This element defines a schema which defines data structures and the shape of information managed by this service. Multiple schema elements exist for each service, once for each logical grouping of information exposed by the service.

/system/schemaMap/schema/@namespace (anyURI minOccurs=0 maxOccurs=1)
This attribute specifies the namespace URI of this schema.

/system/schemaMap/schema/@schemaLocation (anyURI minOccurs=0 maxOccurs=1)
This attribute specifies the location (in the form of a URI) of the resource containing schema. When a schema is reachable through a variety of URIs, one schema element will exist for each location.

/system/schemaMap/schema/@alias (string minOccurs=0 maxOccurs=1)
This attribute specifies the preferred alias that should be used if possible when manipulating information covered by this schema in the context of this service.

/system/schemaMap/schema/*{any}* (minOccurs=0 maxOccurs=unbounded)

/system/wsdlMap (minOccurs=1 maxOccurs=1)

This element defines the wsdlMap for this service. This map includes the location of WSDL documents, DISCO documents, and WISL documents for this Web service. These documents are used by applications to understand the format of messages that may be sent to the various services.

/system/wsdlMap/@changeNumber (minOccurs=0 maxOccurs=1)

The changeNumber attribute is designed to facilitate caching of the element and its descendants. This attribute is assigned to this element by the .NET My Services system. The attribute is read-only to applications. Attempts to write this attribute are silently ignored.

/system/wsdlMap/@id (minOccurs=0 maxOccurs=1)

This attribute is a globally unique ID assigned to this element by .NET My Services. Normally, .NET My Services will generate and assign this ID during an insertRequest operation, or possibly during a replaceRequest. Application software can override this ID generation by specifying the useClientIds attribute in the request message. Once an ID is assigned, the attribute is read-only and attempts to write it are silently ignored.

/system/wsdlMap/@creator (string minOccurs=0 maxOccurs=1)

This attribute identifies the creator in terms of userId, appId, and platformId of the node.

/system/wsdlMap/wsdl (minOccurs=0 maxOccurs=unbounded)

This element is used to specify the location of a WSDL file for this service. Multiple entries may exist pointing to the same file hosted in multiple locations, or to variations of the content within the WSDL files.

/system/wsdlMap/wsdl/@wsdlLocation (anyURI minOccurs=0 maxOccurs=1)

This attribute is a URI that specifies the location of the WSDL file.

/system/wsdlMap/wsdl/*{any}* (minOccurs=0 maxOccurs=unbounded)

/system/wsdlMap/disco (minOccurs=0 maxOccurs=unbounded)

This element is used to specify the location of a DISCO file for this service. Multiple entries may exist pointing to the same file hosted in multiple locations, or to variations of the content within the DISCO files.

/system/wsdlMap/disco/@discoLocation (anyURI minOccurs=0 maxOccurs=1)

This attribute is a URI that specifies the location of the DISCO file.

/system/wsdlMap/disco/*{any}* (minOccurs=0 maxOccurs=unbounded)

/system/*{any}* (minOccurs=0 maxOccurs=unbounded)

The .NET Notifications Service/Methods

The .NET notifications service supports the following standard and domain-specific methods:

- query
- insert
- replace
- delete
- update
- notify
- route
- do

The standard methods operate on this service using the same message format and method-interchange techniques described in the hsdl section of this document. The only service-specific information to note is the schema that is in effect for each of the methods. These schemas, and how they relate to the standard methods and roles are described in the roles section of this document.

The domain specific methods operate as described in the domain-specific methods section of this document, and are governed by the various schemas outlined in the .NET Notifications Service/Roles section for this service.

The .NET Notifications Service/Domain Specific Methods

The .NET notifications service has three domain specific messages.

The .NET Notifications Service/Notify Method

Sends one or more notifications to the targeted receiver. If the receiver is the .NET notifications service, the notification(s) will be delivered to the appropriate set of UserAgents connected.

The .NET Notifications Service/Notify Request

This method is accessed using a request message, and in response may generate a response message or a SOAP Fault message. The following sample document fragment illustrates the structure and meaning of the elements and attributes in the request and response messages.

The following section describes the request message for this method.

This is the request message XML fragment.

```
<m:notifyRequest
    xmlns:m="http://schemas.microsoft.com/hs/2001/10/myNotifications"
    xmlns:hs="http://schemas.microsoft.com/hs/2001/10/core">1..1
    <m:notification uuid="...">0..unbounded
        <m:from>1..1
            <m:identityHeader type="...">1..1
                <m:onBehalfOfUser>1..1</m:onBehalfOfUser>
                <m:licenseHolder>1..1</m:licenseHolder>
                <m:platformId>1..1</m:platformId>
            </m:identityHeader>
            <m:expires ttl="..." onDate="..." replace="...">1..1</m:expires>
            <m:acknowledge>0..1</m:acknowledge>
        </m:from>
        <m:to>0..1
            <m:originalUser>0..1</m:originalUser>
        </m:to>
        <m:contents>1..1
            <m:argot argotURI="..." name="..." id="...">0..unbounded {any}</m:argot>
        </m:contents>
        <m:routing>1..1
            <m:timestamp>0..1</m:timestamp>
            <m:hops>0..1</m:hops>
        </m:routing>
    </m:notification>
</m:notifyRequest>
```

The meaning of the attributes and elements shown in the preceding sample document fragment are listed in the following section.

/notifyRequest (minOccurs=1 maxOccurs=1)

This method attempts to send the enclosed notifications to the user using standard routing by the .NET notifications service. There can be one or more notification elements specified. If none is specified, the notify request should be interpreted as a query of whether the receiver is willing to accept notifications from this sender.

/notifyRequest/notification (minOccurs=0 maxOccurs=unbounded)
> A notification to be delivered.

/notifyRequest/notification/@uuid (minOccurs=0 maxOccurs=1)
> The uuidType is used to specify a UUID.

/notifyRequest/notification/from (minOccurs=1 maxOccurs=1)
> This tag contains all data from the sender, including sender authentication as well as preferences and requests from the sender.

/notifyRequest/notification/from/identityHeader (minOccurs=1 maxOccurs=1)
/notifyRequest/notification/from/identityHeader/@type (string minOccurs=0 maxOccurs=1)
/notifyRequest/notification/from/identityHeader/onBehalfOfUser (minOccurs=1 maxOccurs=1)
> The uuidType is used to specify a UUID.

/notifyRequest/notification/from/identityHeader/licenseHolder (minOccurs=1 maxOccurs=1)
> The uuidType is used to specify a UUID.

/notifyRequest/notification/from/identityHeader/platformId (minOccurs=1 maxOccurs=1)
> The uuidType is used to specify a UUID.

/notifyRequest/notification/from/expires (string minOccurs=1 maxOccurs=1)
/notifyRequest/notification/from/expires/@ttl (string minOccurs=0 maxOccurs=1)
/notifyRequest/notification/from/expires/@onDate (string minOccurs=0 maxOccurs=1)
/notifyRequest/notification/from/expires/@replace (string minOccurs=0 maxOccurs=1)
/notifyRequest/notification/from/acknowledge (string minOccurs=0 maxOccurs=1)
/notifyRequest/notification/to (minOccurs=0 maxOccurs=1)
> This tag contains all data pertaining to the receiver. This data may be set by the sender or by any processing/routing agent between the sender and the receiver.

/notifyRequest/notification/to/originalUser (minOccurs=0 maxOccurs=1)
> This element defines who the original receiver of the notification was. A routing agent may change (forward or fan-out) a notification to new/different receivers. If so, it should add this element to the notification.

/notifyRequest/notification/contents (minOccurs=1 maxOccurs=1)
> This tag is an argot list conveying the application domain-specific data of the notification.

/notifyRequest/notification/contents/argot (minOccurs=0 maxOccurs=unbounded)
> An argot is a domain-specific blob of data, qualified by a name and ID. The contents are free. Argots are opaque to .NET My Services.

/notifyRequest/notification/contents/argot/@argotURI (anyURI minOccurs=0 maxOccurs=1)
> This URI points to a location containing the XSD for this argot, as well as uniquely identifying the type of argot.

/notifyRequest/notification/contents/argot/@name (string minOccurs=0 maxOccurs=1)

/notifyRequest/notification/contents/argot/@id (minOccurs=0 maxOccurs=1)

This attribute is a globally unique ID assigned to this element by .NET My Services. Normally, .NET My Services will generate and assign this ID during an insertRequest operation, or possibly during a replaceRequest. Application software can override this ID generation by specifying the useClientIds attribute in the request message. Once an ID is assigned, the attribute is read-only and attempts to write it are silently ignored.

/notifyRequest/notification/contents/argot/*{any}* (minOccurs=0 maxOccurs=unbounded)

/notifyRequest/notification/routing (minOccurs=1 maxOccurs=1)

This tag contains any routing data inserted by the .NET notifications service notification routing process.

/notifyRequest/notification/routing/timestamp (string minOccurs=0 maxOccurs=1)

This element defines who the original receiver of the notification was. A routing agent may change (forward or fan-out) a notification to new/different receivers. If so, it should add this element to the notification.

/notifyRequest/notification/routing/hops (string minOccurs=0 maxOccurs=1)

This element defines the actors that have processed the notification to date. The .NET notifications service may use this data to recognize and stop infinite loops.

The .NET Notifications Service/Notify Response

Upon successful completion of this method, a response message is generated. The format of the response message is described below.

Standard (no) response.

The .NET Notifications Service/Error Cases

If the method causes a failure response to be generated, the failure is noted by generating a SOAP Fault message. Failures can include a failure to understand a header marked as "s:mustUnderstand", a .NET My Services standard error, security violation, load balance redirect or any service-specific severe error condition.

The .NET Notifications Service/Route Method

Sends one or more notifications to the .NET notifications service, specifying how the notifications should be routed internally within the .NET notifications service.

The .NET Notifications Service/Route Request

This method is accessed using a request message, and in response may generate a response message or a SOAP Fault message. The following sample document fragment illustrates the structure and meaning of the elements and attributes in the request and response messages.

The following section describes the request message for this method.

This is the request message XML fragment.

```
<m:routeRequest
    xmlns:m="http://schemas.microsoft.com/hs/2001/10/myNotifications"
    xmlns:hs="http://schemas.microsoft.com/hs/2001/10/core">1..1
    <m:routing>1..1
        <m:streamFork atStreamID="..." afterStreamID="...">0..1</m:streamFork>
        <m:connectionFork>0..1
            <m:connectionID>0..unbounded</m:connectionID>
        </m:connectionFork>
    </m:routing>
    <m:notification uuid="...">0..unbounded
        <m:from>1..1
            <m:identityHeader type="...">1..1
                <m:onBehalfOfUser>1..1</m:onBehalfOfUser>
                <m:licenseHolder>1..1</m:licenseHolder>
                <m:platformId>1..1</m:platformId>
            </m:identityHeader>
            <m:expires ttl="..." onDate="..." replace="...">1..1</m:expires>
            <m:acknowledge>0..1</m:acknowledge>
        </m:from>
        <m:to>0..1
            <m:originalUser>0..1</m:originalUser>
        </m:to>
        <m:contents>1..1
            <m:argot argotURI="..." name="..." id="...">0..unbounded {any}</m:argot>
        </m:contents>
        <m:routing>1..1
            <m:timestamp>0..1</m:timestamp>
            <m:hops>0..1</m:hops>
        </m:routing>
    </m:notification>
</m:routeRequest>
```

The meaning of the attributes and elements shown in the preceding sample document fragment are listed in the following section.

/routeRequest (minOccurs=1 maxOccurs=1)

This method is similar to notifyRequest but allows the caller to specify control of the .NET notifications service internal routing for the notification.

/routeRequest/routing (minOccurs=1 maxOccurs=1)

The routing dictates how to process the notifications within the .NET notifications service routing. You may specify either the streamFork or connectionFork directions or both.

/routeRequest/routing/streamFork (string minOccurs=0 maxOccurs=1)

The streamFork directive indicates the notification should be processed by streams. If the streamFork tag is not present, no streams will process the notification; routing will begin directly at the connectionFork point. If one of the streamID attributes are not included, streamFork processing begins at the first stream defined for the user.

/routeRequest/routing/streamFork/@atStreamID (minOccurs=0 maxOccurs=1)

This attribute is a globally unique ID assigned to this element by .NET My Services. Normally, .NET My Services will generate and assign this ID during an insertRequest operation, or possibly during a replaceRequest. Application software can override this ID generation by specifying the useClientIds attribute in the request message. Once an ID is assigned, the attribute is read-only and attempts to write it are silently ignored.

/routeRequest/routing/streamFork/@afterStreamID (minOccurs=0 maxOccurs=1)

This attribute is a globally unique ID assigned to this element by .NET My Services. Normally, .NET My Services will generate and assign this ID during an insertRequest operation, or possibly during a replaceRequest. Application software can override this ID generation by specifying the useClientIds attribute in the request message. Once an ID is assigned, the attribute is read-only and attempts to write it are silently ignored.

/routeRequest/routing/connectionFork (minOccurs=0 maxOccurs=1)

The connectionFork directive indicates which connection(s) the notification may be routed through. If not included, all connections may potentially deliver the notification. A connection may not deliver the notification even if specified in the list of connectionIDs; the notification must always match the connection's query to be delivered through the connection.

/routeRequest/routing/connectionFork/connectionID (minOccurs=0 maxOccurs=unbounded)

The connectionFork directive indicates which connection(s) the notification may be routed through. If not included, all connections may potentially deliver the notification. A connection may not deliver the notification even if specified in the list of connectionIDs; the notification must always match the connection's query to be delivered through the connection.

/routeRequest/notification (minOccurs=0 maxOccurs=unbounded)
  A notification to be routed through a specific stream/connection.

/routeRequest/notification/@uuid (minOccurs=0 maxOccurs=1)
  The uuidType is used to specify a UUID.

/routeRequest/notification/from (minOccurs=1 maxOccurs=1)
  This tag contains all data from the sender, including sender authentication as well as preferences and requests from the sender.

/routeRequest/notification/from/identityHeader (minOccurs=1 maxOccurs=1)
/routeRequest/notification/from/identityHeader/@type (string minOccurs=0 maxOccurs=1)
/routeRequest/notification/from/identityHeader/onBehalfOfUser (minOccurs=1 maxOccurs=1)
  The uuidType is used to specify a UUID.

/routeRequest/notification/from/identityHeader/licenseHolder (minOccurs=1 maxOccurs=1)
  The uuidType is used to specify a UUID.

/routeRequest/notification/from/identityHeader/platformId (minOccurs=1 maxOccurs=1)
  The uuidType is used to specify a UUID.

/routeRequest/notification/from/expires (string minOccurs=1 maxOccurs=1)
/routeRequest/notification/from/expires/@ttl (string minOccurs=0 maxOccurs=1)
/routeRequest/notification/from/expires/@onDate (string minOccurs=0 maxOccurs=1)
/routeRequest/notification/from/expires/@replace (string minOccurs=0 maxOccurs=1)
/routeRequest/notification/from/acknowledge (string minOccurs=0 maxOccurs=1)
/routeRequest/notification/to (minOccurs=0 maxOccurs=1)
  This tag contains all data pertaining to the receiver. This data may be set by the sender or by any processing/routing agent between the sender and the receiver.

/routeRequest/notification/to/originalUser (minOccurs=0 maxOccurs=1)
  This element defines who the original receiver of the notification was. A routing agent may change (forward or fan-out) a notification to new/different receivers. If so, it should add this element to the notification.

/routeRequest/notification/contents (minOccurs=1 maxOccurs=1)
  This tag is an argot list conveying the application domain-specific data of the notification.

/routeRequest/notification/contents/argot (minOccurs=0 maxOccurs=unbounded)
  An argot is a domain-specific blob of data, qualified by a name and ID. The contents are free. Argots are opaque to .NET My Services.

/routeRequest/notification/contents/argot/@argotURI (anyURI minOccurs=0 maxOccurs=1)
  This URI points to a location containing the XSD for this argot, as well as uniquely identifying the type of argot.

/routeRequest/notification/contents/argot/@name (string minOccurs=0 maxOccurs=1)
/routeRequest/notification/contents/argot/@id (minOccurs=0 maxOccurs=1)
> This attribute is a globally unique ID assigned to this element by .NET My Services. Normally, .NET My Services will generate and assign this ID during an insertRequest operation, or possibly during a replaceRequest. Application software can override this ID generation by specifying the useClientIds attribute in the request message. Once an ID is assigned, the attribute is read-only and attempts to write it are silently ignored.

/routeRequest/notification/contents/argot/*{any}* (minOccurs=0 maxOccurs=unbounded)
/routeRequest/notification/routing (minOccurs=1 maxOccurs=1)
> This tag contains any routing data inserted by the .NET notifications service notification routing process.

/routeRequest/notification/routing/timestamp (string minOccurs=0 maxOccurs=1)
> This element defines who the original receiver of the notification was. A routing agent may change (forward or fan-out) a notification to new/different receivers. If so, it should add this element to the notification.

/routeRequest/notification/routing/hops (string minOccurs=0 maxOccurs=1)
> This element defines the actors that have processed the notification to date. The .NET notifications service may use this data to recognize and stop infinite loops.

The .NET Notifications Service/Route Response

Upon successful completion of this method, a response message is generated. The format of the response message is described below.

No response.

The .NET Notifications Service/Error Cases

If the method causes a failure response to be generated, the failure is noted by generating a SOAP Fault message. Failures can include a failure to understand a header marked as "s:mustUnderstand", a .NET My Services standard error, security violation, load balance redirect or any service-specific severe error condition.

The following method-specific errors, (including the .NET My Services standard errors and any argument-type-specific errors) can occur during the processing of this message.

The .NET Notifications Service/Do Method

Issues a nested method to the specified stream(s) or connection(s) within the .NET notifications service. This method makes it possible to perform methods directly on an object within the .NET notifications service. For example, a UserAgent would execute this method specifying "poll" as the methodName to poll a connection for notifications.

The .NET Notifications Service/Do Request

This method is accessed using a request message, and in response may generate a response message or a SOAP Fault message. The following sample document fragment illustrates the structure and meaning of the elements and attributes in the request and response messages.

The following section describes the request message for this method.

This is the request message XML fragment for the request.

```
<m:doRequest
    xmlns:m="http://schemas.microsoft.com/hs/2001/10/myNotifications"
    xmlns:hs="http://schemas.microsoft.com/hs/2001/10/core">₁..₁
    <m:objects>₁..₁
        <m:streamID id="...">₀..unbounded</m:streamID>
        <m:connectionID id="...">₀..unbounded</m:connectionID>
    </m:objects>
    <m:methodName>₁..₁</m:methodName>
    <m:argot argotURI="...">₀..unbounded {any}</m:argot>
</m:doRequest>
```

The meaning of the attributes and elements shown in the preceding sample document fragment are listed in the following section.

/doRequest (minOccurs=1 maxOccurs=1)

This method issues a request to the specified streams or connections within the .NET notifications service schema to execute an object-specific method. Parameters are passed in and out through argot lists. The actual object method is specified by the methodName tag.

/doRequest/objects (minOccurs=1 maxOccurs=1)

List of one or more streams or connections to perform the requested object method.

/doRequest/objects/streamID (minOccurs=0 maxOccurs=unbounded)
/doRequest/objects/streamID/@id (minOccurs=0 maxOccurs=1)

This attribute is a globally unique ID assigned to this element by .NET My Services. Normally, .NET My Services will generate and assign this ID during an insertRequest operation, or possibly during a replaceRequest. Application software can override this ID generation by specifying the useClientIds attribute in the request message. Once an ID is assigned, the attribute is read-only and attempts to write it are silently ignored.

/doRequest/objects/connectionID (minOccurs=0 maxOccurs=unbounded)

/doRequest/objects/connectionID/@id (minOccurs=0 maxOccurs=1)

This attribute is a globally unique ID assigned to this element by .NET My Services. Normally, .NET My Services will generate and assign this ID during an insertRequest operation, or possibly during a replaceRequest. Application software can override this ID generation by specifying the useClientIds attribute in the request message. Once an ID is assigned, the attribute is read-only and attempts to write it are silently ignored.

/doRequest/methodName (string minOccurs=1 maxOccurs=1)

This specifies the method that the selected object(s) should execute.

/doRequest/argot (minOccurs=0 maxOccurs=unbounded)

This list contains data passed to the connection. The data is passed as a list of argots that the connection class will understand.

/doRequest/argot/@argotURI (anyURI minOccurs=0 maxOccurs=1)

This URI points to a location containing the XSD for this argot, as well as uniquely identifying the type of argot.

/doRequest/argot/*{any}* (minOccurs=0 maxOccurs=unbounded)

The .NET Notifications Service/Do Response

Upon successful completion of this method, a response message is generated. The format of the response message is described below.

This is the response message XML fragment for the do request. This response will return zero or more notifications.

```
<m:doResponse
    xmlns:m="http://schemas.microsoft.com/hs/2001/10/myNotifications"
    xmlns:hs="http://schemas.microsoft.com/hs/2001/10/core">1..1
    <m:argot argotURI="...">0..unbounded    {any}</m:argot>
    <m:notification uuid="...">0..unbounded
        <m:from>1..1
            <m:identityHeader type="...">1..1
                <m:onBehalfOfUser>1..1</m:onBehalfOfUser>
                <m:licenseHolder>1..1</m:licenseHolder>
                <m:platformId>1..1</m:platformId>
            </m:identityHeader>
            <m:expires ttl="..." onDate="..." replace="...">1..1</m:expires>
            <m:acknowledge>0..1</m:acknowledge>
        </m:from>
        <m:to>0..1
            <m:originalUser>0..1</m:originalUser>
        </m:to>
```

```
        <m:contents>₁..₁
            <m:argot argotURI="..." name="..." id="...">₀..unbounded {any}</m:argot>
        </m:contents>
        <m:routing>₁..₁
            <m:timestamp>₀..₁</m:timestamp>
            <m:hops>₀..₁</m:hops>
        </m:routing>
    </m:notification>
</m:doResponse>
```

The meaning of the attributes and elements shown in the preceding sample document fragment are listed in the following section.

/doResponse (minOccurs=1 maxOccurs=1)
   This is the response to doRequest.

/doResponse/argot (minOccurs=0 maxOccurs=unbounded)
   This contains data other than notifications that is returned by the connection. The data is passed as a list of argots that the connection class generates.

/doResponse/argot/@argotURI (anyURI minOccurs=0 maxOccurs=1)
   This URI points to a location containing the XSD for this argot, as well as uniquely identifying the type of argot.

/doResponse/argot/{any} (minOccurs=0 maxOccurs=unbounded)
/doResponse/notification (minOccurs=0 maxOccurs=unbounded)
   An optional returned notification.

/doResponse/notification/@uuid (minOccurs=0 maxOccurs=1)
   The uuidType is used to specify a UUID. Note that the base type below is probably wrong and needs to be fixed to match a correct definition for a UUID.

/doResponse/notification/from (minOccurs=1 maxOccurs=1)
   This tag contains all data from the sender, including sender authentication as well as preferences and requests from the sender.

/doResponse/notification/from/identityHeader (minOccurs=1 maxOccurs=1)
/doResponse/notification/from/identityHeader/@type (string minOccurs=0 maxOccurs=1)
/doResponse/notification/from/identityHeader/onBehalfOfUser (minOccurs=1 maxOccurs=1)
   The uuidType is used to specify a UUID.

/doResponse/notification/from/identityHeader/licenseHolder (minOccurs=1 maxOccurs=1)
   The uuidType is used to specify a UUID.

/doResponse/notification/from/identityHeader/platformId (minOccurs=1 maxOccurs=1)
   The uuidType is used to specify a UUID.

/doResponse/notification/from/expires (string minOccurs=1 maxOccurs=1)
/doResponse/notification/from/expires/@ttl (string minOccurs=0 maxOccurs=1)
/doResponse/notification/from/expires/@onDate (string minOccurs=0 maxOccurs=1)
/doResponse/notification/from/expires/@replace (string minOccurs=0 maxOccurs=1)
/doResponse/notification/from/acknowledge (string minOccurs=0 maxOccurs=1)
/doResponse/notification/to (minOccurs=0 maxOccurs=1)

> This tag contains all data pertaining to the receiver. This data may be set by the sender or by any processing/routing agent between the sender and the receiver.

/doResponse/notification/to/originalUser (minOccurs=0 maxOccurs=1)

> This element defines who the original receiver of the notification was. A routing agent may change (forward or fan-out) a notification to new/different receivers. If so, it should add this element to the notification.

/doResponse/notification/contents (minOccurs=1 maxOccurs=1)

> This tag is an argot list conveying the application domain-specific data of the notification.

/doResponse/notification/contents/argot (minOccurs=0 maxOccurs=unbounded)

> An argot is a domain-specific blob of data, qualified by a name and ID. The contents are free. Argots are opaque to .NET My Services.

/doResponse/notification/contents/argot/@argotURI (anyURI minOccurs=0 maxOccurs=1)

> This URI points to a location containing the XSD for this argot, as well as uniquely identifying the type of argot.

/doResponse/notification/contents/argot/@name (string minOccurs=0 maxOccurs=1)
/doResponse/notification/contents/argot/@id (minOccurs=0 maxOccurs=1)

> This attribute is a globally unique ID assigned to this element by .NET My Services. Normally, .NET My Services will generate and assign this ID during an insertRequest operation, or possibly during a replaceRequest. Application software can override this ID generation by specifying the useClientIds attribute in the request message. Once an ID is assigned, the attribute is read-only and attempts to write it are silently ignored.

/doResponse/notification/contents/argot/*{any}* (minOccurs=0 maxOccurs=unbounded)
/doResponse/notification/routing (minOccurs=1 maxOccurs=1)

> This tag contains any routing data inserted by the .NET notifications service notification routing process.

/doResponse/notification/routing/timestamp (string minOccurs=0 maxOccurs=1)

> This element defines who the original receiver of the notification was. A routing agent may change (forward or fan-out) a notification to new/different receivers. If so, it should add this element to the notification.

/doResponse/notification/routing/hops (string minOccurs=0 maxOccurs=1)

> This element defines the actors that have processed the notification to date. The .NET notifications service may use this data to recognize and stop infinite loops.

The .NET Notifications Service/Error Cases

If the method causes a failure response to be generated, the failure is noted by generating a SOAP Fault message. Failures can include a failure to understand a header marked as "s:mustUnderstand", a .NET My Services standard error, security violation, load balance redirect or any service-specific severe error condition.

CHAPTER 19

The .NET presence service/Introduction

This is a specification of the .NET presence service. The .NET presence service contains the electronic presence information for users, who control access to this information themselves.

The .NET presence service/Roles

The .NET presence service controls access by using the following roleTemplates:

- rt0
- rt1
- rt2
- rt3
- rt99

The .NET presence service uses the following scopes:

- **scope id 1**

```
<hs:scope id=1>

    <hs:shape base=t>

    </hs:shape>

</hs:scope>
```

- **scope id 2**

```
<hs:scope id=2>

    <hs:shape base=nil>

        <hs:include select=//*[@creator='$callerId']/>

    </hs:shape>

</hs:scope>
```

- **scope id 3**

```
<hs:scope id=3>

    <hs:shape base=nil>

        <hs:include select=//subscription[@creator='$callerId']/>

    </hs:shape>

</hs:scope>
```

- **scope id 4**

```
<hs:scope id=4>

    <hs:shape base=nil>

        <hs:include select=//*[cat/@ref='hs:public']/>

        <hs:include select=//subscription[@creator='$callerId']/>

    </hs:shape>

</hs:scope>
```

The .NET presence service roleTemplate rt0

The purpose of this role is to give complete read/write access to all information within the content document of the service being protected through this roleTemplate.

The following table illustrates the available methods and the scope in effect when accessing the .NET presence service through that method while mapped to this roleTemplate.

method	scopeRef
query	scopeRef=1
insert	scopeRef=1
replace	scopeRef=1
delete	scopeRef=1
update	scopeRef=1

The .NET presence service roleTemplate rt1

The purpose of this role is to give complete read access to all information within the content document of the service being protected through this roleTemplate. Applications mapping to this role also have a limited ability to write to information in the content document. They may create nodes in any location, but may only change/replace, or delete nodes that they created.

The following table illustrates the available methods and the scope in effect when accessing the .NET presence service through that method while mapped to this roleTemplate.

method	scopeRef
query	scopeRef=1
insert	scopeRef=2
replace	scopeRef=2
delete	scopeRef=2

The .NET presence service roleTemplate rt2

The purpose of this role is to give complete read access to all information within the content document of the service being protected through this roleTemplate. Applications mapping to this role have very limited write access and are only able to create and manipulate their own subscription nodes.

The following table illustrates the available methods and the scope in effect when accessing the .NET presence service through that method while mapped to this roleTemplate.

method	scopeRef
query	scopeRef=1
insert	scopeRef=3
replace	scopeRef=3
delete	scopeRef=3

The .NET presence service roleTemplate rt3

The purpose of this role is to give limited read access to information within the content document that is categorized as "public".

The following table illustrates the available methods and the scope in effect when accessing the .NET presence service through that method while mapped to this roleTemplate.

method	scopeRef
query	scopeRef=4

.NET Presence roleTemplate rt99

The purpose of this role is to block all access to the content document. Note that lack of a role in the roleList has the same effect as assigning someone to rt99.

The .NET presence service/content

The content document is an identity centric document. Its content and meaning is a function of the Passport Unique ID (PUID) used to address the service. Accessing the document is controlled by the associated roleList document.

This schema outline illustrates the layout and meaning of the information found in the content document for the .NET presence service.

```
<m:myPresence changeNumber="..." instanceId="..."
    xmlns:m="http://schemas.microsoft.com/hs/2001/10/myPresence"
    xmlns:mn="http://schemas.microsoft.com/hs/2001/10/myNotifications"
    xmlns:hs="http://schemas.microsoft.com/hs/2001/10/core">1..1
    <m:endpoint name="..." changeNumber="..." id="..." creator="...">0..unbounded
        <m:deviceUuid>0..1</m:deviceUuid>
        <m:expiresAt>0..1</m:expiresAt>
        <m:argot argotURI="..." name="..." changeNumber="..." id="..."
creator="...">0..unbounded {any}</m:argot>
    </m:endpoint>
    <m:subscription changeNumber="..." id="..." creator="...">0..unbounded
        <hs:trigger select="..." mode="..."
baseChangeNumber="...">1..1</hs:trigger>
        <hs:expiresAt>0..1</hs:expiresAt>
        <hs:context uri="...">1..1 {any}</hs:context>
        <hs:to>1..1</hs:to>
    </m:subscription>
</m:myPresence>
```

The meaning of the attributes and elements shown in the preceding sample document fragment are listed in the following section.

/myPresence (minOccurs=1 maxOccurs=1)

This element defines the basic .NET presence service types.

/myPresence/@changeNumber (minOccurs=0 maxOccurs=1)

The changeNumber attribute is designed to facilitate caching of the element and its descendants. This attribute is assigned to this element by the Microsoft .NET My Services system. The attribute is read-only to applications. Attempts to write this attribute are silently ignored.

/myPresence/@instanceId (string minOccurs=0 maxOccurs=1)

This attribute is a unique identifier typically assigned to the root element of a service. It is a read-only element and assigned by the .NET My Services system when a user is provisioned for a particular service.

/myPresence/endpoint (minOccurs=0 maxOccurs=unbounded)

Collection of endpoints for this user's *myPresence*.

/myPresence/endpoint/@name (string minOccurs=0 maxOccurs=1)
/myPresence/endpoint/@changeNumber (minOccurs=0 maxOccurs=1)

The changeNumber attribute is designed to facilitate caching of the element and its descendants. This attribute is assigned to this element by the .NET My Services system. The attribute is read-only to applications. Attempts to write this attribute are silently ignored.

/myPresence/endpoint/@id (minOccurs=0 maxOccurs=1)

This attribute is a globally unique ID assigned to this element by .NET My Services. Normally, .NET My Services will generate and assign this ID during an insertRequest operation, or possibly during a replaceRequest. Application software can override this ID generation by specifying the useClientIds attribute in the request message. Once an ID is assigned, the attribute is read-only and attempts to write it are silently ignored.

/myPresence/endpoint/@creator (string minOccurs=0 maxOccurs=1)

This attribute identifies the creator in terms of userId, appId, and platformId of the node.

/myPresence/endpoint/deviceUuid (minOccurs=0 maxOccurs=1)

The uuidType is used to specify a UUID.

/myPresence/endpoint/expiresAt (dateTime minOccurs=0 maxOccurs=1)
/myPresence/endpoint/argot (minOccurs=0 maxOccurs=unbounded)

Collection of argots for this endpoint.

/myPresence/endpoint/argot/@argotURI (anyURI minOccurs=0 maxOccurs=1)

This URI points to a location containing the XSD for this argot, as well as uniquely identifying the type of argot.

/myPresence/endpoint/argot/@name (string minOccurs=0 maxOccurs=1)
/myPresence/endpoint/argot/@changeNumber (minOccurs=0 maxOccurs=1)

The changeNumber attribute is designed to facilitate caching of the element and its descendants. This attribute is assigned to this element by the .NET My Services system. The attribute is read-only to applications. Attempts to write this attribute are silently ignored.

/myPresence/endpoint/argot/@id (minOccurs=0 maxOccurs=1)
> This attribute is a globally unique ID assigned to this element by .NET My Services. Normally, .NET My Services will generate and assign this ID during an insertRequest operation, or possibly during a replaceRequest. Application software can override this ID generation by specifying the useClientIds attribute in the request message. Once an ID is assigned, the attribute is read-only and attempts to write it are silently ignored.

/myPresence/endpoint/argot/@creator (string minOccurs=0 maxOccurs=1)
> This attribute identifies the creator in terms of userId, appId, and platformId of the node.

/myPresence/endpoint/argot/*{any}* (minOccurs=0 maxOccurs=unbounded)

/myPresence/subscription (minOccurs=0 maxOccurs=unbounded)
> This element defines a subscription node that is designed to be an xdb:blue node which when placed in a content document causes a subscription to be registered. A subscription contains a trigger element which selects a scope of coverage. When items change that are under this scope of coverage, and subscriptionResponse message is generated and sent to the specified destination address.

/myPresence/subscription/@changeNumber (minOccurs=0 maxOccurs=1)
> The changeNumber attribute is designed to facilitate caching of the element and its descendants. This attribute is assigned to this element by the .NET My Services system. The attribute is read-only to applications. Attempts to write this attribute are silently ignored.

/myPresence/subscription/@id (minOccurs=0 maxOccurs=1)
> This attribute is a globally unique ID assigned to this element by .NET My Services. Normally, .NET My Services will generate and assign this ID during an insertRequest operation, or possibly during a replaceRequest. Application software can override this ID generation by specifying the useClientIds attribute in the request message. Once an ID is assigned, the attribute is read-only and attempts to write it are silently ignored.

/myPresence/subscription/@creator (string minOccurs=0 maxOccurs=1)
> This attribute identifies the creator in terms of userId, appId, and platformId of the node.

/myPresence/subscription/trigger (minOccurs=1 maxOccurs=1)

/myPresence/subscription/trigger/@select (string minOccurs=0 maxOccurs=1)
> This item specifies an XPATH expression that specifies the nodes that are to be selected and watched for changes. The selection may only select xdb:blue nodes. As changes in this node set occur, they trigger the generation of a subscription message. The message is then sent to the SOAP receiver listed in the "to" element.

/myPresence/subscription/trigger/@mode (string minOccurs=0 maxOccurs=1)
> This attribute specifies whether or not the content of the changes that triggered the subscription are delivered in the subscription message, or if the message simply indicates that something changed under the trigger. The attribute may be:

includeData

> The data that changed, causing the subscription to trigger, is included in the subscription message. Note that deleted nodes are specified by their ID, not by value.

excludeData

> The data that changed, causing the subscription to trigger is NOT included in the subscription message.

/myPresence/subscription/trigger/@baseChangeNumber (minOccurs=0 maxOccurs=1)

> This attribute specifies the changeNumber value that the trigger is relative to. All changes between the specified change number, and the current state of the document relative to the selection are transmitted as subscription messages. This allows a client application to establish a subscription relative to some baseline. As in changeQuery, if the baseChangeNumber is way out of date relative to the current state of the document, and the service cannot supply the changes in the subscription message, the subscription insert is rejected. A value of 0 means that the current values of the selected nodes are transmitted in the subscription message.

/myPresence/subscription/expiresAt (dateTime minOccurs=0 maxOccurs=1)

> This optional element specifies an absolute time after which the subscription is no longer active. The subscription node is automatically removed when the subscription expires. If this element is missing, the subscription does not expire.

/myPresence/subscription/context (minOccurs=1 maxOccurs=1)

> This element returns the context element from the original subscription. Applications should use this element, and only this element, to correlate the subscription response with one of their subscriptions.

/myPresence/subscription/context/@uri (anyURI minOccurs=0 maxOccurs=1)

> This attribute specifies the URI value chosen by the subscriber that is associated with this subscription.

/myPresence/subscription/context/*{any}* (minOccurs=0 maxOccurs=unbounded)

/myPresence/subscription/to (anyURI minOccurs=1 maxOccurs=1)

> This attribute specifies the location that is to receive the subscription message. The value of this element may be one of the following forms:

- *hs:myNotifications*—This URI indicates that generated subscription messages are to be delivered inside the body of a notification and delivered to the default .NET notifications service of the creator.

- *protocol://service*—This URI indicates that generated subscription messages are delivered to the specified service at the domain of the creator's platformId. For instance, a platformId indicating microsoft.com, and a value in this element of http://subscriptionResponse would cause delivery of the subscription message to http://subscriptionResponse.microsoft.com.

> If this value is not specified, then the subscription message is delivered as a notification to the "creator's" .NET notifications service.

The .NET presence service/system

The system document is a global document for the service. Its content and meaning is independent of the PUID used to address the service, and the document is read-only to all users. The system document contains a set of base items common to all .NET My Services services, and is optionally extended by each service to include service-specific global information.

This schema outline illustrates the layout and meaning of the information found in the system document for the .NET presence service.

```
<sys:system changeNumber="..." instanceId="..."
    xmlns:hs="http://schemas.microsoft.com/hs/2001/10/core"
    xmlns:sys="http://schemas.microsoft.com/hs/2001/10/myPresence/system">1..1
    <hs:roleMap changeNumber="..." id="..." creator="...">1..1
        <hs:scope id="...">0..unbounded
            <hs:shape base="...">1..1
                <hs:include select="...">1..unbounded</hs:include>
                <hs:exclude select="...">0..unbounded</hs:exclude>
            </hs:shape>
        </hs:scope>
        <hs:roleTemplate name="..." priority="...">0..unbounded
            <hs:fullDescription xml:lang="...">0..1</hs:fullDescription>
            <hs:method name="..." scopeRef="...">0..unbounded</hs:method>
        </hs:roleTemplate>
    </hs:roleMap>
    <hs:methodMap changeNumber="..." id="..." creator="...">1..1
        <hs:method name="...">0..unbounded {any}</hs:method>
    </hs:methodMap>
    <hs:schemaMap changeNumber="..." id="..." creator="...">1..1
        <hs:schema namespace="..." schemaLocation="..." alias="...">0..unbounded
{any}</hs:schema>
    </hs:schemaMap>
    <hs:wsdlMap changeNumber="..." id="..." creator="...">1..1
        <hs:wsdl wsdlLocation="...">0..unbounded {any}</hs:wsdl>
        <hs:disco discoLocation="...">0..unbounded {any}</hs:disco>
    </hs:wsdlMap>
    {any}
</sys:system>
```

The meaning of the attributes and elements shown in the preceding sample document fragment are listed in the following section.

/system (minOccurs=1 maxOccurs=1)

This element encapsulates the system document for the .NET presence service.

/system/@changeNumber (minOccurs=0 maxOccurs=1)

The changeNumber attribute is designed to facilitate caching of the element and its descendants. This attribute is assigned to this element by the .NET My Services system. The attribute is read-only to applications. Attempts to write this attribute are silently ignored.

/system/@instanceId (string minOccurs=0 maxOccurs=1)

This attribute is a unique identifier typically assigned to the root element of a service. It is a read-only element and assigned by the .NET My Services system when a user is provisioned for a particular service.

/system/roleMap (minOccurs=1 maxOccurs=1)

This element encapsulates all the elements that make up a roleMap, which includes a document class relative to a roleTemplate, priority, name, method, and per-method scope. An individual roleTemplate defines the maximum scope of information, and the allowable methods used to access that information for each request mapped into the template.

/system/roleMap/@changeNumber (minOccurs=0 maxOccurs=1)

The changeNumber attribute is designed to facilitate caching of the element and its descendants. This attribute is assigned to this element by the .NET My Services system. The attribute is read-only to applications. Attempts to write this attribute are silently ignored.

/system/roleMap/@id (minOccurs=0 maxOccurs=1)

This attribute is a globally unique ID assigned to this element by .NET My Services. Normally, .NET My Services will generate and assign this ID during an insertRequest operation, or possibly during a replaceRequest. Application software can override this ID generation by specifying the useClientIds attribute in the request message. Once an ID is assigned, the attribute is read-only and attempts to write it are silently ignored.

/system/roleMap/@creator (string minOccurs=0 maxOccurs=1)

This attribute identifies the creator in terms of userId, appId, and platformId of the node.

/system/roleMap/scope (minOccurs=0 maxOccurs=unbounded)

This element defines a scope which may be referred to by roles within this roleMap to indicate what portions of the document are visible to this role for the specified method.

/system/roleMap/scope/@id (minOccurs=0 maxOccurs=1)

This attribute is a globally unique ID assigned to this element by .NET My Services. Normally, .NET My Services will generate and assign this ID during an insertRequest operation, or possibly during a replaceRequest. Application software can override this ID generation by specifying the useClientIds attribute in the request message. Once an ID is assigned, the attribute is read-only and attempts to write it are silently ignored.

/system/roleMap/scope/shape (minOccurs=1 maxOccurs=1)
> A shape defines the node set visible through the document when operating through this shape element.

/system/roleMap/scope/shape/@base (string minOccurs=0 maxOccurs=1)
> This attribute specifies the initial set of nodes visible through the shape.
>
> A value of t indicates that the shape is initialized to include all possible nodes relative to the shape that is currently in effect. For instance, each role defines a scope containing a shape. When defining a shape for a role, the value t indicates all possible nodes available in the specified document for this role. When defining a shape in an ACL entry, a value of t means all of the nodes visible in the shape for the computed role. When using a shape in an hsdl operation, a value of t indicates all of the possible nodes selected by the hsdl operation (relative to the ACL shape which itself is relative to the role's shape).
>
> The value nil indicates the opposite of t, which is the empty node set. Nodes from this set may then be included into the shape.

/system/roleMap/scope/shape/include (minOccurs=1 maxOccurs=unbounded)
> This element specifies the set of nodes that should be included into the shape relative to the possible set of nodes indicated by the base attribute.

/system/roleMap/scope/shape/include/@select (string minOccurs=0 maxOccurs=1)
> This item specifies an XPATH expression that selects a set of nodes relative to the externally established context. The expression can never travel outside the node-set established by this externally established current context. The expression may match 0 or more nodes, and the operation manipulates all selected nodes. The minOccurs and maxOccurs attributes are optional and place restrictions and limitations on the number of nodes selected.

/system/roleMap/scope/shape/exclude (minOccurs=0 maxOccurs=unbounded)
> This element specifies the set of nodes that should be excluded from the shape relative to the possible set of nodes indicated by the base attribute.

/system/roleMap/scope/shape/exclude/@select (string minOccurs=0 maxOccurs=1)
> This item specifies an XPATH expression that selects a set of nodes relative to the externally established context. The expression can never travel outside the node-set established by this externally established current context. The expression may match 0 or more nodes, and the operation manipulates all selected nodes. The minOccurs and maxOccurs attributes are optional and place restrictions and limitations on the number of nodes selected.

/system/roleMap/roleTemplate (minOccurs=0 maxOccurs=unbounded)
> This element encapsulates the definition of a role. The attribute set for this element includes the document class that this roleTemplate refers to, the name of the roleTemplate, and the priority of the roleTemplate.

/system/roleMap/roleTemplate/@name (string minOccurs=0 maxOccurs=1)
> This element specifies the name of the role.

/system/roleMap/roleTemplate/@priority (int minOccurs=0 maxOccurs=1)
> This element specifies the priority of the roleTemplate which is used to select that actual roleTemplate when the role evaluation determines that the subject maps to multiple roleTemplates.

/system/roleMap/roleTemplate/fullDescription (string minOccurs=0 maxOccurs=1)
> This element contains a description of this role template which specifies the capabilities a caller will have when accessing information through this role.

/system/roleMap/roleTemplate/fullDescription/@xml:lang (minOccurs=1 maxOccurs=1)
> This required attribute is used to specify an ISO 639 language code or an ISO 3166 country code as described in RFC 1766. The value of this attribute indicates the language type of the content within this element.

/system/roleMap/roleTemplate/method (minOccurs=0 maxOccurs=unbounded)
> This element specifies the methods available within this roleTemplate by name, and by scope. When a subject maps to a roleTemplate, the method in the request must match one of these elements for the message to continue to flow. If the method exists, the data available to the method is a function of the scope referenced by this method combined with an optional scope referenced by the role defined in the roleList.

/system/roleMap/roleTemplate/method/@name (string minOccurs=0 maxOccurs=1)
> This element specifies the name of the method.

/system/roleMap/roleTemplate/method/@scopeRef (string minOccurs=0 maxOccurs=1)
> This attribute specifies the scope within this document that is in effect for this method.

/system/methodMap (minOccurs=1 maxOccurs=1)
> This element defines the methodMap. While it is true that in most cases, the roleMap section contains a definitive list of methods, these methods are likely to be scattered about the roleMap in various templates. This section contains the definitive non-duplicated list of methods available within the service.

/system/methodMap/@changeNumber (minOccurs=0 maxOccurs=1)
> The changeNumber attribute is designed to facilitate caching of the element and its descendants. This attribute is assigned to this element by the .NET My Services system. The attribute is read-only to applications. Attempts to write this attribute are silently ignored.

/system/methodMap/@id (minOccurs=0 maxOccurs=1)
> This attribute is a globally unique ID assigned to this element by .NET My Services. Normally, .NET My Services will generate and assign this ID during an insertRequest operation, or possibly during a replaceRequest. Application software can override this ID generation by specifying the useClientIds attribute in the request message. Once an ID is assigned, the attribute is read-only and attempts to write it are silently ignored.

/system/methodMap/@creator (string minOccurs=0 maxOccurs=1)
> This attribute identifies the creator in terms of userId, appId, and platformId of the node.

/system/methodMap/method (minOccurs=0 maxOccurs=unbounded)
   This element defines a method that is available within this service.

/system/methodMap/method/@name (string minOccurs=0 maxOccurs=1)
   This attribute specifies the name of a method available within this service.

/system/methodMap/method/*{any}* (minOccurs=0 maxOccurs=unbounded)
/system/schemaMap (minOccurs=1 maxOccurs=1)
   This element defines the various schemas that define the data structures and shape
   of information managed by this service. Each schema is defined by its namespace
   URI, its location, and a preferred namespace alias.

/system/schemaMap/@changeNumber (minOccurs=0 maxOccurs=1)
   The changeNumber attribute is designed to facilitate caching of the element and its
   descendants. This attribute is assigned to this element by the .NET My Services
   system. The attribute is read-only to applications. Attempts to write this attribute are
   silently ignored.

/system/schemaMap/@id (minOccurs=0 maxOccurs=1)
   This attribute is a globally unique ID assigned to this element by .NET My Services.
   Normally, .NET My Services will generate and assign this ID during an insertRequest
   operation, or possibly during a replaceRequest. Application software can override this
   ID generation by specifying the useClientIds attribute in the request message. Once
   an ID is assigned, the attribute is read-only and attempts to write it are silently
   ignored.

/system/schemaMap/@creator (string minOccurs=0 maxOccurs=1)
   This attribute identifies the creator in terms of userId, appId, and platformId of the
   node.

/system/schemaMap/schema (minOccurs=0 maxOccurs=unbounded)
   This element defines a schema which defines data structures and the shape of
   information managed by this service. Multiple schema elements exist for each service,
   one for each logical grouping of information exposed by the service.

/system/schemaMap/schema/@namespace (anyURI minOccurs=0 maxOccurs=1)
   This attribute specifies the namespace URI of this schema.

/system/schemaMap/schema/@schemaLocation (anyURI minOccurs=0 maxOccurs=1)
   This attribute specifies the location (in the form of a URI) of the resource containing
   schema. When a schema is reachable through a variety of URIs, one schema
   element will exist for each location.

/system/schemaMap/schema/@alias (string minOccurs=0 maxOccurs=1)
   This attribute specifies the preferred alias that should be used if possible when
   manipulating information covered by this schema in the context of this service.

/system/schemaMap/schema/*{any}* (minOccurs=0 maxOccurs=unbounded)

/system/wsdlMap (minOccurs=1 maxOccurs=1)

This element defines the wsdlMap for this service. This map includes the location of WSDL documents, DISCO documents, and WISL documents for this Web service. These documents are used by applications to understand the format of messages that may be sent to the various services.

/system/wsdlMap/@changeNumber (minOccurs=0 maxOccurs=1)

The changeNumber attribute is designed to facilitate caching of the element and its descendants. This attribute is assigned to this element by the .NET My Services system. The attribute is read-only to applications. Attempts to write this attribute are silently ignored.

/system/wsdlMap/@id (minOccurs=0 maxOccurs=1)

This attribute is a globally unique ID assigned to this element by .NET My Services. Normally, .NET My Services will generate and assign this ID during an insertRequest operation, or possibly during a replaceRequest. Application software can override this ID generation by specifying the useClientIds attribute in the request message. Once an ID is assigned, the attribute is read-only and attempts to write it are silently ignored.

/system/wsdlMap/@creator (string minOccurs=0 maxOccurs=1)

This attribute identifies the creator in terms of userId, appId, and platformId of the node.

/system/wsdlMap/wsdl (minOccurs=0 maxOccurs=unbounded)

This element is used to specify the location of a WSDL file for this service. Multiple entries may exist pointing to the same file hosted in multiple locations, or to variations of the content within the WSDL files.

/system/wsdlMap/wsdl/@wsdlLocation (anyURI minOccurs=0 maxOccurs=1)

This attribute is a URI that specifies the location of the WSDL file.

/system/wsdlMap/wsdl/*{any}* (minOccurs=0 maxOccurs=unbounded)

/system/wsdlMap/disco (minOccurs=0 maxOccurs=unbounded)

This element is used to specify the location of a DISCO file for this service. Multiple entries may exist pointing to the same file hosted in multiple locations, or to variations of the content within the DISCO files.

/system/wsdlMap/disco/@discoLocation (anyURI minOccurs=0 maxOccurs=1)

This attribute is a URI that specifies the location of the DISCO file.

/system/wsdlMap/disco/*{any}* (minOccurs=0 maxOccurs=unbounded)

/system/*{any}* (minOccurs=0 maxOccurs=unbounded)

The .NET presence service/Methods

The .NET presence service supports the following standard and domain-specific methods:

- query
- insert
- replace
- delete
- update

The standard methods operate on this service using the same message format and method-interchange techniques described in the hsdl section of this document. The only service-specific information to note is the schema that is in effect for each of the methods. These schemas, and how they relate to the standard methods and roles are described in the roles section of this document.

The domain specific methods operate as described in the domain-specific methods section of this document, and are governed by the various schemas outlined in the .NET Presence/Roles section for this service.

The .NET presence service/Domain Specific Methods

The .NET presence service has one domain specific message.

The .NET presence service/notifyEndpoint Method

Sends a notification to a specified endpoint.

The .NET presence service/notifyEndpointRequest

This method is accessed using a request message, and in response may generate a response message or a SOAP Fault message. The following sample document fragment illustrates the structure and meaning of the elements and attributes in the request and response messages.

The following section describes the request message for this method.

This is the request message XML fragment for notifyEndpoint.

```
<m:notifyEndpointRequest
    xmlns:m="http://schemas.microsoft.com/hs/2001/10/myPresence"
    xmlns:mn="http://schemas.microsoft.com/hs/2001/10/myNotifications"
    xmlns:hs="http://schemas.microsoft.com/hs/2001/10/core">₁..₁
    <m:endpointId>₁..₁</m:endpointId>
    <m:notification uuid="...">₁..₁
        <mn:from>₁..₁
            <mn:identityHeader type="...">₁..₁
                <mn:onBehalfOfUser>₁..₁</mn:onBehalfOfUser>
                <mn:licenseHolder>₁..₁</mn:licenseHolder>
                <mn:platformId>₁..₁</mn:platformId>
            </mn:identityHeader>
            <mn:expires ttl="..." onDate="..." replace="...">₁..₁</mn:expires>
            <mn:acknowledge>₀..₁</mn:acknowledge>
        </mn:from>
        <mn:to>₀..₁
            <mn:originalUser>₀..₁</mn:originalUser>
        </mn:to>
        <mn:contents>₁..₁
            <mn:argot argotURI="..." name="..." id="...">₀..unbounded {any}</mn:argot>
        </mn:contents>
        <mn:routing>₁..₁
            <mn:timestamp>₀..₁</mn:timestamp>
            <mn:hops>₀..₁</mn:hops>
        </mn:routing>
    </m:notification>
</m:notifyEndpointRequest>
```

The meaning of the attributes and elements shown in the preceding sample document fragment are listed in the following section.

/notifyEndpointRequest (minOccurs=1 maxOccurs=1)

This method takes an endpoint and sends a specified notification to it by means of the endpoint's owner's .NET notifications. The endpoint must expose the "notifiableEndpoint" argot, so that the .NET presence service knows which connection to target in *myNotifications*. This method serves two purposes: first, as an abstraction layer over individual connections, so that users may target groups of connections classified as endpoints. And second, as a privacy measure, so that a specific connection associated with an endpoint may be targeted without that connection being exposed to the user invoking the method.

/notifyEndpointRequest/endpointId (minOccurs=1 maxOccurs=1)

This attribute is a globally unique ID assigned to this element by .NET My Services. Normally, .NET My Services will generate and assign this ID during an insertRequest operation, or possibly during a replaceRequest. Application software can override this ID generation by specifying the useClientIds attribute in the request message. Once an ID is assigned, the attribute is read-only and attempts to write it are silently ignored.

/notifyEndpointRequest/notification (minOccurs=1 maxOccurs=1)

A notification has contents, "from" (sender) data, optional "to" (receiver) data, and optional "routing" data. The contents are a set of argots (domain-specific blobs). The sender and receiver must agree on and both understand the argots that are transmitted in the notification. In the .NET notifications service, both streams and connections usually choose which notifications they process based on the argots contained within the notifications.

/notifyEndpointRequest/notification/@uuid (minOccurs=0 maxOccurs=1)

The uuidType is used to specify a UUID.

/notifyEndpointRequest/notification/from (minOccurs=1 maxOccurs=1)

This tag contains all data from the sender, including sender authentication as well as preferences and requests from the sender.

/notifyEndpointRequest/notification/from/identityHeader (minOccurs=1 maxOccurs=1)
/notifyEndpointRequest/notification/from/identityHeader/@type (string minOccurs=0 maxOccurs=1)
/notifyEndpointRequest/notification/from/identityHeader/onBehalfOfUser (minOccurs=1 maxOccurs=1)

The uuidType is used to specify a UUID.

/notifyEndpointRequest/notification/from/identityHeader/licenseHolder (minOccurs=1 maxOccurs=1)

The uuidType is used to specify a UUID.

/notifyEndpointRequest/notification/from/identityHeader/platformId (minOccurs=1 maxOccurs=1)

The uuidType is used to specify a UUID.

/notifyEndpointRequest/notification/from/expires (string minOccurs=1 maxOccurs=1)
/notifyEndpointRequest/notification/from/expires/@ttl (string minOccurs=0 maxOccurs=1)
/notifyEndpointRequest/notification/from/expires/@onDate (string minOccurs=0 maxOccurs=1)
/notifyEndpointRequest/notification/from/expires/@replace (string minOccurs=0 maxOccurs=1)
/notifyEndpointRequest/notification/from/acknowledge (string minOccurs=0 maxOccurs=1)

/notifyEndpointRequest/notification/to (minOccurs=0 maxOccurs=1)
> This tag contains all data pertaining to the receiver. This data may be set by the sender or by any processing/routing agent between the sender and the receiver.

/notifyEndpointRequest/notification/to/originalUser (minOccurs=0 maxOccurs=1)
> This element defines who the original receiver of the notification was. A routing agent may change (forward or fan-out) a notification to new/different receivers. If so, it should add this element to the notification.

/notifyEndpointRequest/notification/contents (minOccurs=1 maxOccurs=1)
> This tag is an argot list conveying the application domain-specific data of the notification.

/notifyEndpointRequest/notification/contents/argot (minOccurs=0 maxOccurs=unbounded)
> An argot is a domain-specific blob of data, qualified by a name and ID. The contents are free. Argots are opaque to .NET My Services.

/notifyEndpointRequest/notification/contents/argot/@argotURI (anyURI minOccurs=0 maxOccurs=1)
> This URI points to a location containing the XSD for this argot, as well as uniquely identifying the type of argot.

/notifyEndpointRequest/notification/contents/argot/@name (string minOccurs=0 maxOccurs=1)

/notifyEndpointRequest/notification/contents/argot/@id (minOccurs=0 maxOccurs=1)
> This attribute is a globally unique ID assigned to this element by .NET My Services. Normally, .NET My Services will generate and assign this ID during an insertRequest operation, or possibly during a replaceRequest. Application software can override this ID generation by specifying the useClientIds attribute in the request message. Once an ID is assigned, the attribute is read-only and attempts to write it are silently ignored.

/notifyEndpointRequest/notification/contents/argot/*{any}* (minOccurs=0 maxOccurs=unbounded)

/notifyEndpointRequest/notification/routing (minOccurs=1 maxOccurs=1)
> This tag contains any routing data inserted by the *myNotifications* notification routing process.

/notifyEndpointRequest/notification/routing/timestamp (string minOccurs=0 maxOccurs=1)
> This element defines who the original receiver of the notification was. A routing agent may change (forward or fan-out) a notification to new/different receivers. If so, it should add this element to the notification.

/notifyEndpointRequest/notification/routing/hops (string minOccurs=0 maxOccurs=1)
> This element defines the actors that have processed the notification to date. The .NET notifications service may use this data to recognize and stop infinite loops.

The .NET presence service/notifyEndpointResponse

Upon successful completion of this method, a response message is generated. The format of the response message is described below.

No response.

.NET Presence/Error Cases

If the method causes a failure response to be generated, the failure is noted by generating a SOAP Fault message. Failures can include a failure to understand a header marked as "s:mustUnderstand", a .NET My Services standard error, security violation, load balance redirect or any service-specific severe error condition.

The .NET presence service/.

This schema fragment illustrates a sample argot, for a basic instant messaging presence application.

```
<m:MessengerArgot status="..."
    xmlns:m="http://schemas.microsoft.com/hs/2001/10/myPresence"
    xmlns:mn="http://schemas.microsoft.com/hs/2001/10/myNotifications"
    xmlns:hs="http://schemas.microsoft.com/hs/2001/10/core">1..1
    <m:statusMessage>0..1</m:statusMessage>
</m:MessengerArgot>
```

The meaning of the attributes and elements shown in the preceding sample document fragment are listed in the following section.

/MessengerArgot (minOccurs=1 maxOccurs=1)
    This argot is used to represent an instant messaging client's presence.

/MessengerArgot/@status (string minOccurs=0 maxOccurs=1)
    The presence state of the Messenger client.

/MessengerArgot/statusMessage (string minOccurs=0 maxOccurs=1)
    An unrestricted status message reflecting presence.

CHAPTER 20

The .NET profile service/Introduction

This service is designed to store and manage personal profile information like name, identification numbers, picture pointers, address, etc. for an entity.

The .NET profile service exposes the changeNotify method to be used on the <profile> element only. When such an operation occurs on profile with a pending changeNotify request, a notification will be sent to the subscriber via the .NET notifications service. This is used to inform interested parties when the profile information changes. In this way applications or services may reliably cache information contained within this service. An example of this caching might be an address book application or service where for each entry in the address book, a changeNotify request is issued against this service for that entry so that if profile information changes, the address book is notified and may refresh itself. This way, the address book may present, high-speed access to a large set of contacts, and is able to present accurate information by value even though it is based on a by-reference model.

The .NET profile service/Roles

The .NET profile service controls access by using the following roleTemplates:

- rt0
- rt1
- rt2
- rt3
- rt99

The .NET profile service uses the following scopes:

- **scope id 1**

```
<hs:scope id=1>

    <hs:shape base=t>

    </hs:shape>

</hs:scope>
```

- **scope id 2**

```
<hs:scope id=2>

    <hs:shape base=nil>

        <hs:include select=//*[@creator='$callerId']/>

    </hs:shape>

</hs:scope>
```

- **scope id 3**

```
<hs:scope id=3>

    <hs:shape base=nil>

        <hs:include select=//subscription[@creator='$callerId']/>

    </hs:shape>

</hs:scope>
```

- **scope id 4**

```
<hs:scope id=4>

    <hs:shape base=nil>

        <hs:include select=//*[cat/@ref='hs:public']/>

        <hs:include select=//subscription[@creator='$callerId']/>

    </hs:shape>

</hs:scope>
```

The .NET profile service roleTemplate rt0

The purpose of this role is to give complete read/write access to all information within the content document of the service being protected through this roleTemplate.

The following table illustrates the available methods and the scope in effect when accessing the .NET profile service through that method while mapped to this roleTemplate.

method	scopeRef
query	scopeRef=1
insert	scopeRef=1
replace	scopeRef=1
delete	scopeRef=1
update	scopeRef=1

The .NET profile service roleTemplate rt1

The purpose of this role is to give complete read access to all information within the content document of the service being protected through this roleTemplate. Applications mapping to this role also have a limited ability to write to information in the content document. They may create nodes in any location, but may only change/replace, or delete nodes that they created.

The following table illustrates the available methods and the scope in effect when accessing the .NET profile service through that method while mapped to this roleTemplate.

method	scopeRef
query	scopeRef=1
insert	scopeRef=2
replace	scopeRef=2
delete	scopeRef=2

The .NET profile service roleTemplate rt2

The purpose of this role is to give complete read access to all information within the content document of the service being protected through this roleTemplate. Applications mapping to this role have very limited write access and are only able to create and manipulate their own subscription nodes.

The following table illustrates the available methods and the scope in effect when accessing the .NET profile service through that method while mapped to this roleTemplate.

method	scopeRef
query	scopeRef=1
insert	scopeRef=3
replace	scopeRef=3
delete	scopeRef=3

The .NET profile service roleTemplate rt3

The purpose of this role is to give limited read access to information within the content document that is categorized as "public".

The following table illustrates the available methods and the scope in effect when accessing the .NET profile service through that method while mapped to this roleTemplate.

method	scopeRef
query	scopeRef=4

The .NET profile service roleTemplate rt99

The purpose of this role is to block all access to the content document. Note that lack of a role in the roleList has the same effect as assigning someone to rt99.

The .NET profile service/content

The content document is an identity-centric document. Its content and meaning is a function of the Passport Unique ID (PUID) used to address the service. Accessing the document is controlled by the associated roleList document.

This schema outline illustrates the layout and meaning of the information found in the content document for the .NET profile service.

```
<m:myProfile changeNumber="..." instanceId="..."
    xmlns:m="http://schemas.microsoft.com/hs/2001/10/myProfile"
    xmlns:mc="http://schemas.microsoft.com/hs/2001/10/myCalendar"
    xmlns:hs="http://schemas.microsoft.com/hs/2001/10/core">1..1
    <m:name changeNumber="..." id="..." creator="...">0..unbounded
        <m:cat ref="...">0..unbounded</m:cat>
        <m:title xml:lang="...">0..unbounded</m:title>
        <m:givenName xml:lang="...">0..unbounded</m:givenName>
        <m:middleName xml:lang="...">0..unbounded</m:middleName>
        <m:surName xml:lang="...">0..unbounded</m:surName>
        <m:suffix xml:lang="...">0..unbounded</m:suffix>
        <m:fileAsName xml:lang="...">0..unbounded</m:fileAsName>
        {any}
    </m:name>
    <m:memberInformation changeNumber="..." id="..." creator="...">0..unbounded
        <m:memberNamePortion xml:lang="...">1..1</m:memberNamePortion>
        <m:domainNamePortion>1..1</m:domainNamePortion>
    </m:memberInformation>
    <m:languagePreference level="..." changeNumber="..." id="..."
creator="...">0..unbounded</m:languagePreference>
    <m:timeZonePreference changeNumber="..." id="..." creator="...">0..unbounded
```

```
        <m:cat ref="...">$_{0..unbounded}$</m:cat>
        <m:timeZone>$_{1..1}$</m:timeZone>
    </m:timeZonePreference>
    <m:specialDate calendarType="..." changeNumber="..." id="..."
creator="...">$_{0..unbounded}$
        <m:cat ref="...">$_{0..unbounded}$</m:cat>
        <m:date>$_{1..1}$</m:date>
        {any}
    </m:specialDate>
    <m:userReference changeNumber="..." id="..." creator="...">$_{0..unbounded}$
        <hs:name xml:lang="...">$_{0..1}$</hs:name>
        <hs:puid>$_{0..1}$</hs:puid>
        <hs:email>$_{0..1}$</hs:email>
        <hs:cat ref="...">$_{1..1}$</hs:cat>
        {any}
    </m:userReference>
    <m:picture changeNumber="..." id="..." creator="...">$_{0..unbounded}$
        <m:cat ref="...">$_{0..unbounded}$</m:cat>
        <m:url>$_{1..1}$</m:url>
        {any}
    </m:picture>
    <m:gender changeNumber="..." id="..." creator="...">$_{0..1}$</m:gender>
    <m:identificationNumber changeNumber="..." id="..." creator="...">$_{0..unbounded}$
        <m:cat ref="...">$_{0..unbounded}$</m:cat>
        <m:number>$_{1..1}$</m:number>
        {any}
    </m:identificationNumber>
    <m:workInformation changeNumber="..." id="..." creator="...">$_{0..unbounded}$
        <m:cat ref="...">$_{0..unbounded}$</m:cat>
        <m:profession xml:lang="...">$_{0..1}$</m:profession>
        <m:company>$_{0..unbounded}$
            <hs:name xml:lang="...">$_{0..1}$</hs:name>
            <hs:puid>$_{0..1}$</hs:puid>
            <hs:email>$_{0..1}$</hs:email>
            <hs:cat ref="...">$_{1..1}$</hs:cat>
        </m:company>
        <m:department>$_{0..unbounded}$
            <hs:name xml:lang="...">$_{0..1}$</hs:name>
            <hs:puid>$_{0..1}$</hs:puid>
            <hs:email>$_{0..1}$</hs:email>
            <hs:cat ref="...">$_{1..1}$</hs:cat>
        </m:department>
        <m:jobTitle xml:lang="...">$_{0..unbounded}$</m:jobTitle>
        <m:officeLocation xml:lang="...">$_{0..1}$</m:officeLocation>
```

(continued)

(continued)

```
    <m:manager>₀..unbounded
        <hs:name xml:lang="...">₀..₁</hs:name>
        <hs:puid>₀..₁</hs:puid>
        <hs:email>₀..₁</hs:email>
        <hs:cat ref="...">₁..₁</hs:cat>
    </m:manager>
    <m:assistant>₀..unbounded
        <hs:name xml:lang="...">₀..₁</hs:name>
        <hs:puid>₀..₁</hs:puid>
        <hs:email>₀..₁</hs:email>
        <hs:cat ref="...">₁..₁</hs:cat>
    </m:assistant>
    {any}
</m:workInformation>
<m:address changeNumber="..." id="..." creator="...">₀..unbounded
    <m:cat ref="...">₀..unbounded</m:cat>
    <m:officialAddressLine xml:lang="...">₀..₁</m:officialAddressLine>
    <m:internalAddressLine xml:lang="...">₀..₁</m:internalAddressLine>
    <m:primaryCity xml:lang="...">₀..₁</m:primaryCity>
    <m:secondaryCity xml:lang="...">₀..₁</m:secondaryCity>
    <m:subdivision xml:lang="...">₀..₁</m:subdivision>
    <m:postalCode>₀..₁</m:postalCode>
    <m:countryCode>₀..₁</m:countryCode>
    <m:geoLocation>₀..₁
        <m:reportingDevice>₀..₁
            <m:deviceId>₀..₁</m:deviceId>
            <m:deviceName>₀..₁</m:deviceName>
            {any}
        </m:reportingDevice>
        <m:latitude>₀..₁</m:latitude>
        <m:longitude>₀..₁</m:longitude>
        <m:elevation>₀..₁</m:elevation>
        <m:confidence>₀..₁</m:confidence>
        <m:precision>₀..₁</m:precision>
        {any}
    </m:geoLocation>
    {any}
</m:address>
<m:webSite changeNumber="..." id="..." creator="...">₀..unbounded
    <m:cat ref="...">₀..unbounded</m:cat>
    <m:url>₁..₁</m:url>
    {any}
</m:webSite>
```

```
        <m:emailAddress changeNumber="..." id="..." creator="...">0..unbounded
            <m:cat ref="...">0..unbounded</m:cat>
            <m:email>1..1</m:email>
            <m:name xml:lang="...">0..1</m:name>
            {any}
        </m:emailAddress>
        <m:screenName changeNumber="..." id="..." creator="...">0..unbounded
            <m:cat ref="...">0..unbounded</m:cat>
            <m:name xml:lang="...">1..1</m:name>
            {any}
        </m:screenName>
        <m:telephoneNumber changeNumber="..." id="..." creator="...">0..unbounded
            <hs:cat ref="...">0..unbounded</hs:cat>
            <hs:countryCode>0..1</hs:countryCode>
            <hs:nationalCode>1..1</hs:nationalCode>
            <hs:number>1..1</hs:number>
            <hs:numberExtension>0..1</hs:numberExtension>
            <hs:pin>0..1</hs:pin>
            {any}
        </m:telephoneNumber>
        <m:subscription changeNumber="..." id="..." creator="...">0..unbounded
            <hs:trigger select="..." mode="..."
baseChangeNumber="...">1..1</hs:trigger>
            <hs:expiresAt>0..1</hs:expiresAt>
            <hs:context uri="...">1..1 {any}</hs:context>
            <hs:to>1..1</hs:to>
        </m:subscription>
        <m:securityCertificate changeNumber="..." id="..." creator="...">0..unbounded
            <m:cat ref="...">0..unbounded</m:cat>
            <m:certificate>1..1</m:certificate>
        </m:securityCertificate>
        {any}
</m:myProfile>
```

The meaning of the attributes and elements shown in the preceding sample document fragment are listed in the following section.

/myProfile (minOccurs=1 maxOccurs=1)

This element encapsulates the content document for this service. This element establishes a global cache scope for the service and contains other root-level system attributes for this instance of the service.

/myProfile/@changeNumber (minOccurs=0 maxOccurs=1)

The changeNumber attribute is designed to facilitate caching of the element and its descendants. This attribute is assigned to this element by the Microsoft .NET My Services system. The attribute is read-only to applications. Attempts to write this attribute are silently ignored.

/myProfile/@instanceId (string minOccurs=0 maxOccurs=1)
This attribute is a unique identifier typically assigned to the root element of a service. It is a read-only element and assigned by the .NET My Services system when a user is provisioned for a particular service.

/myProfile/name (minOccurs=0 maxOccurs=unbounded)
This element encapsulates a name associated with the identity. An identity can have multiple names associated with it. These name nodes are not intended to be used for storing screen names or other electronic names, but rather to store a commonly used name for the entity. Names contain five parts and are meant to be combined in proper order, with spaces separating the parts and empty content parts excluded.

/myProfile/name/@changeNumber (minOccurs=0 maxOccurs=1)
The changeNumber attribute is designed to facilitate caching of the element and its descendants. This attribute is assigned to this element by the .NET My Services system. The attribute is read-only to applications. Attempts to write this attribute are silently ignored.

/myProfile/name/@id (minOccurs=0 maxOccurs=1)
This attribute is a globally unique ID assigned to this element by .NET My Services. Normally, .NET My Services will generate and assign this ID during an insertRequest operation, or possibly during a replaceRequest. Application software can override this ID generation by specifying the useClientIds attribute in the request message. Once an ID is assigned, the attribute is read-only and attempts to write it are silently ignored.

/myProfile/name/@creator (string minOccurs=0 maxOccurs=1)
This attribute identifies the creator in terms of userId, appId, and platformId of the node.

/myProfile/name/cat (minOccurs=0 maxOccurs=unbounded)
This element is used to categorize the element that contains it by referencing a global category definition in either the .NET categories service system document or an external resource containing category definitions, or by referencing an identity-centric category definition in the content document of the .NET categories service for a particular PUID.

/myProfile/name/cat/@ref (anyURI minOccurs=0 maxOccurs=1)
This attribute references a category definition (<catDef/>) element using the rules outlined in the .NET categories service.

/myProfile/name/title (string minOccurs=0 maxOccurs=unbounded)
This optional element is designed to store a title or prefix associated with the name. Examples are 'Mr.', 'Mrs.', 'Dr.', or any other commonly used name title or prefix.

/myProfile/name/title/@xml:lang (minOccurs=1 maxOccurs=1)
This required attribute is used to specify an ISO 639 language code or an ISO 3166 country code as described in RFC 1766. The value of this attribute indicates the language type of the content within this element.

/myProfile/name/givenName (string minOccurs=0 maxOccurs=unbounded)
This optional element is meant to store the first portion of a name.

/myProfile/name/givenName/@xml:lang (minOccurs=1 maxOccurs=1)
> This required attribute is used to specify an ISO 639 language code or an ISO 3166 country code as described in RFC 1766. The value of this attribute indicates the language type of the content within this element.

/myProfile/name/middleName (string minOccurs=0 maxOccurs=unbounded)
> This optional element is meant to store the middle portion or initial of a name.

/myProfile/name/middleName/@xml:lang (minOccurs=1 maxOccurs=1)
> This required attribute is used to specify an ISO 639 language code or an ISO 3166 country code as described in RFC 1766. The value of this attribute indicates the language type of the content within this element.

/myProfile/name/surName (string minOccurs=0 maxOccurs=unbounded)
> This optional element is meant to store the last portion of a name.

/myProfile/name/surName/@xml:lang (minOccurs=1 maxOccurs=1)
> This required attribute is used to specify an ISO 639 language code or an ISO 3166 country code as described in RFC 1766. The value of this attribute indicates the language type of the content within this element.

/myProfile/name/suffix (string minOccurs=0 maxOccurs=unbounded)
> This optional element is designed to store a suffix associated with the name. Examples include 'Jr.', 'Sr.', 'III', or any other commonly used name suffix.

/myProfile/name/suffix/@xml:lang (minOccurs=1 maxOccurs=1)
> This required attribute is used to specify an ISO 639 language code or an ISO 3166 country code as described in RFC 1766. The value of this attribute indicates the language type of the content within this element.

/myProfile/name/fileAsName (string minOccurs=0 maxOccurs=unbounded)
> A complete name is usually the combination of title, givenName, middleName, surName, and suffix. This optional element is present to indicate that a different order should be used or that the identity prefers to have the name filed differently.

/myProfile/name/fileAsName/@xml:lang (minOccurs=1 maxOccurs=1)
> This required attribute is used to specify an ISO 639 language code or an ISO 3166 country code as described in RFC 1766. The value of this attribute indicates the language type of the content within this element.

/myProfile/name/*{any}* (minOccurs=0 maxOccurs=unbounded)

/myProfile/memberInformation (minOccurs=0 maxOccurs=unbounded)
> This node wraps member-specific public information for this entity. The information is not changeable, which is reflected in the schemas that modify the content document.

/myProfile/memberInformation/@changeNumber (minOccurs=0 maxOccurs=1)
> The changeNumber attribute is designed to facilitate caching of the element and its descendants. This attribute is assigned to this element by the .NET My Services system. The attribute is read-only to applications. Attempts to write this attribute are silently ignored.

/myProfile/memberInformation/@id (minOccurs=0 maxOccurs=1)
This attribute is a globally unique ID assigned to this element by .NET My Services. Normally, .NET My Services will generate and assign this ID during an insertRequest operation, or possibly during a replaceRequest. Application software can override this ID generation by specifying the useClientIds attribute in the request message. Once an ID is assigned, the attribute is read-only and attempts to write it are silently ignored.

/myProfile/memberInformation/@creator (string minOccurs=0 maxOccurs=1)
This attribute identifies the creator in terms of userId, appId, and platformId of the node.

/myProfile/memberInformation/memberNamePortion (string minOccurs=1 maxOccurs=1)
A member name is a combination of a user name portion, and a domain name portion. These names are separated with an '@' character to form a fully qualified member name. This element contains the user name portion of the name. For a fully qualified member name of someone@microsoft.com, this element contains the value 'someone'.

/myProfile/memberInformation/memberNamePortion/@xml:lang (minOccurs=1 maxOccurs=1)
This required attribute is used to specify an ISO 639 language code or an ISO 3166 country code as described in RFC 1766. The value of this attribute indicates the language type of the content within this element.

/myProfile/memberInformation/domainNamePortion (string minOccurs=1 maxOccurs=1)
This is the other part of the fully qualified member name described above. This element contains the domain name portion. For a fully qualified member name of someone@microsoft.com, this element contains the value 'microsoft.com'.

/myProfile/languagePreference (string minOccurs=0 maxOccurs=unbounded)
This element specifies the preferred language code of the identity encoded using ISO 639 language codes or ISO 3166 country codes as defined by RFC 1766. The purpose of this value in this service is to help guide applications regarding the languages understood by this identity. When manipulating localizable content, they should choose from an appropriate language preference. When encountering localized content not falling within this set, the software should translate into a language understood by this set.

/myProfile/languagePreference/@level (string minOccurs=0 maxOccurs=1)
This attribute indicates how well this language is understood by this identity. Valid values include:

- native
- fluent
- intermediate
- beginner

/myProfile/languagePreference/@changeNumber (minOccurs=0 maxOccurs=1)
> The changeNumber attribute is designed to facilitate caching of the element and its descendants. This attribute is assigned to this element by the .NET My Services system. The attribute is read-only to applications. Attempts to write this attribute are silently ignored.

/myProfile/languagePreference/@id (minOccurs=0 maxOccurs=1)
> This attribute is a globally unique ID assigned to this element by .NET My Services. Normally, .NET My Services will generate and assign this ID during an insertRequest operation, or possibly during a replaceRequest. Application software can override this ID generation by specifying the useClientIds attribute in the request message. Once an ID is assigned, the attribute is read-only and attempts to write it are silently ignored.

/myProfile/languagePreference/@creator (string minOccurs=0 maxOccurs=1)
> This attribute identifies the creator in terms of userId, appId, and platformId of the node.

/myProfile/timeZonePreference (minOccurs=0 maxOccurs=unbounded)
> This element supplies the base time-zone preference for this entity.

/myProfile/timeZonePreference/@changeNumber (minOccurs=0 maxOccurs=1)
> The changeNumber attribute is designed to facilitate caching of the element and its descendants. This attribute is assigned to this element by the .NET My Services system. The attribute is read-only to applications. Attempts to write this attribute are silently ignored.

/myProfile/timeZonePreference/@id (minOccurs=0 maxOccurs=1)
> This attribute is a globally unique ID assigned to this element by .NET My Services. Normally, .NET My Services will generate and assign this ID during an insertRequest operation, or possibly during a replaceRequest. Application software can override this ID generation by specifying the useClientIds attribute in the request message. Once an ID is assigned, the attribute is read-only and attempts to write it are silently ignored.

/myProfile/timeZonePreference/@creator (string minOccurs=0 maxOccurs=1)
> This attribute identifies the creator in terms of userId, appId, and platformId of the node.

/myProfile/timeZonePreference/cat (minOccurs=0 maxOccurs=unbounded)
> This element is used to categorize the element that contains it by referencing a global category definition in either the .NET categories service system document or an external resource containing category definitions, or by referencing an identity-centric category definition in the content document of the .NET categories service for a particular PUID.

/myProfile/timeZonePreference/cat/@ref (anyURI minOccurs=0 maxOccurs=1)
> This attribute references a category definition (<catDef/>) element using the rules outlined in the >NET categories service.

/myProfile/timeZonePreference/timeZone (string minOccurs=1 maxOccurs=1)

/myProfile/specialDate (minOccurs=0 maxOccurs=unbounded)

This element encapsulates a special date that is important to this entity. Multiple special date nodes may exist. This is not a substitute for dates stored on an entity's .NET calendar service. The main purpose is to provide a convenient place to store a birth date or an anniversary date, because these dates are frequently imported into a contact record.

/myProfile/specialDate/@calendarType (string minOccurs=0 maxOccurs=1)

This field identifies an enumeration which determines the kind of calendar event used.

.NET My Services v1 will only support CAL_GREGORIAN_US.

http://msdn.microsoft.com/library/psdk/winbase/nls_9bg8.htm plus several others:

Value	Enumeration Constant	Description
−1	HSCAL_ALL_CALENDARS	Unknown Calendar; system default (HSCAL_GREGORIAN_US)
1	HSCAL_GREGORIAN	Gregorian (localized) calendar
2	HSCAL_GREGORIAN_US	Gregorian (U.S.) calendar
3	HSCAL_JAPAN	Japanese Emperor Era calendar
4	HSCAL_TAIWAN	Taiwan Era calendar
5	HSCAL_KOREA	Korean Tangun Era calendar
6	HSCAL_HIJRI	Hijri (Arabic Lunar) calendar
7	HSCAL_THAI	Thai calendar
8	HSCAL_HEBREW	Hebrew (Lunar) calendar
9	HSCAL_GREGORIAN_ME_FRENCH	Gregorian Middle East French calendar
10	HSCAL_GREGORIAN_ARABIC	Gregorian Arabic calendar
11	HSCAL_GREGORIAN_XLIT_ENGLISH	Gregorian Transliterated English calendar
12	HSCAL_GREGORIAN_XLIT_FRENCH	Gregorian Transliterated French calendar
13	HSCAL_KOREA_LUNAR	Default Korea Lunar calendar (implementation identical to 14)
14	HSCAL_JAPAN_LUNAR	Default Japanese Lunar calendar (implementation identical to 13)
15	HSCAL_CHINESE_LUNAR	Chinese Lunar calendar
16	HSCAL_SAKA	Indian Saka calendar
17	HSCAL_LUNAR_ETO_CHN	Chinese Zodiac calendar
18	HSCAL_LUNAR_ETO_KOR	Korean Zodiac calendar
19	HSCAL_LUNAR_ROKUYOU	Japanese Lucky days calendar

/myProfile/specialDate/@changeNumber (minOccurs=0 maxOccurs=1)

The changeNumber attribute is designed to facilitate caching of the element and its descendants. This attribute is assigned to this element by the .NET My Services system. The attribute is read-only to applications. Attempts to write this attribute are silently ignored.

/myProfile/specialDate/@id (minOccurs=0 maxOccurs=1)

This attribute is a globally unique ID assigned to this element by .NET My Services. Normally, .NET My Services will generate and assign this ID during an insertRequest operation, or possibly during a replaceRequest. Application software can override this ID generation by specifying the useClientIds attribute in the request message. Once an ID is assigned, the attribute is read-only and attempts to write it are silently ignored.

/myProfile/specialDate/@creator (string minOccurs=0 maxOccurs=1)

This attribute identifies the creator in terms of userId, appId, and platformId of the node.

/myProfile/specialDate/cat (minOccurs=0 maxOccurs=unbounded)

This element is used to categorize the element that contains it by referencing a global category definition in either the .NET categories service system document or an external resource containing category definitions, or by referencing an identity-centric category definition in the content document of the .NET categories service for a particular PUID.

/myProfile/specialDate/cat/@ref (anyURI minOccurs=0 maxOccurs=1)

This attribute references a category definition (<catDef/>) element using the rules outlined in the .NET categories service.

/myProfile/specialDate/date (dateTime minOccurs=1 maxOccurs=1)

The special date. Hour, minute, and seconds are ignored.

/myProfile/specialDate/*{any}* (minOccurs=0 maxOccurs=unbounded)
/myProfile/userReference (minOccurs=0 maxOccurs=unbounded)
/myProfile/userReference/@changeNumber (minOccurs=0 maxOccurs=1)

The changeNumber attribute is designed to facilitate caching of the element and its descendants. This attribute is assigned to this element by the .NET My Services system. The attribute is read-only to applications. Attempts to write this attribute are silently ignored.

/myProfile/userReference/@id (minOccurs=0 maxOccurs=1)

This attribute is a globally unique ID assigned to this element by .NET My Services. Normally, .NET My Services will generate and assign this ID during an insertRequest operation, or possibly during a replaceRequest. Application software can override this ID generation by specifying the useClientIds attribute in the request message. Once an ID is assigned, the attribute is read-only and attempts to write it are silently ignored.

/myProfile/userReference/@creator (string minOccurs=0 maxOccurs=1)

This attribute identifies the creator in terms of userId, appId, and platformId of the node.

/myProfile/userReference/name (string minOccurs=0 maxOccurs=1)
This optional element specifies the name for the enclosing element.

/myProfile/userReference/name/@xml:lang (minOccurs=1 maxOccurs=1)
This required attribute is used to specify an ISO 639 language code or an ISO 3166 country code as described in RFC 1766. The value of this attribute indicates the language type of the content within this element.

/myProfile/userReference/puid (string minOccurs=0 maxOccurs=1)
This optional element specifies the name for the enclosing element.

/myProfile/userReference/email (string minOccurs=0 maxOccurs=1)
This optional name specifies an e-mail address for the enclosing element.

/myProfile/userReference/cat (minOccurs=1 maxOccurs=1)
This element is used to categorize the element that contains it by referencing a global category definition in either the .NET categories service system document or an external resource containing category definitions, or by referencing an identity-centric category definition in the content document of the NET categories service for a particular PUID.

/myProfile/userReference/cat/@ref (anyURI minOccurs=0 maxOccurs=1)
This attribute references a category definition (<catDef/>) element using the rules outlined in the .NET categories service.

/myProfile/userReference/*{any}* (minOccurs=0 maxOccurs=unbounded)
/myProfile/picture (minOccurs=0 maxOccurs=unbounded)
This optional element encapsulates a URL that points to a picture of the identity.

/myProfile/picture/@changeNumber (minOccurs=0 maxOccurs=1)
The changeNumber attribute is designed to facilitate caching of the element and its descendants. This attribute is assigned to this element by the .NET My Services system. The attribute is read-only to applications. Attempts to write this attribute are silently ignored.

/myProfile/picture/@id (minOccurs=0 maxOccurs=1)
This attribute is a globally unique ID assigned to this element by .NET My Services. Normally, .NET My Services will generate and assign this ID during an insertRequest operation, or possibly during a replaceRequest. Application software can override this ID generation by specifying the useClientIds attribute in the request message. Once an ID is assigned, the attribute is read-only and attempts to write it are silently ignored.

/myProfile/picture/@creator (string minOccurs=0 maxOccurs=1)
This attribute identifies the creator in terms of userId, appId, and platformId of the node.

/myProfile/picture/cat (minOccurs=0 maxOccurs=unbounded)
This element is used to categorize the element that contains it by referencing a global category definition in either the .NET categories service system document or an external resource containing category definitions, or by referencing an identity-centric category definition in the content document of the .NET categories service for a particular PUID.

/myProfile/picture/cat/@ref (anyURI minOccurs=0 maxOccurs=1)
> This attribute references a category definition (<catDef/>) element using the rules outlined in the .NET categories service.

/myProfile/picture/url (string minOccurs=1 maxOccurs=1)
> This element contains the URL that points to the actual picture.

/myProfile/picture/**{any}** (minOccurs=0 maxOccurs=unbounded)

/myProfile/gender (string minOccurs=0 maxOccurs=1)
> This element specifies the gender for this entity. There can only be a single gender associated with an entity. The format of this element is a single, 7-bit ASCII character with one of two possible values: 'm' for male, and 'f' for female.

/myProfile/gender/@changeNumber (minOccurs=0 maxOccurs=1)
> The changeNumber attribute is designed to facilitate caching of the element and its descendants. This attribute is assigned to this element by the .NET My Services system. The attribute is read-only to applications. Attempts to write this attribute are silently ignored.

/myProfile/gender/@id (minOccurs=0 maxOccurs=1)
> This attribute is a globally unique ID assigned to this element by .NET My Services. Normally, .NET My Services will generate and assign this ID during an insertRequest operation, or possibly during a replaceRequest. Application software can override this ID generation by specifying the useClientIds attribute in the request message. Once an ID is assigned, the attribute is read-only and attempts to write it are silently ignored.

/myProfile/gender/@creator (string minOccurs=0 maxOccurs=1)
> This attribute identifies the creator in terms of userId, appId, and platformId of the node.

/myProfile/identificationNumber (minOccurs=0 maxOccurs=unbounded)
> This optional element encapsulates an identification number for the entity. Things like an employee ID number, social security number, national ID number, driver's license number, and so on, may be stored within this element.

/myProfile/identificationNumber/@changeNumber (minOccurs=0 maxOccurs=1)
> The changeNumber attribute is designed to facilitate caching of the element and its descendants. This attribute is assigned to this element by the .NET My Services system. The attribute is read-only to applications. Attempts to write this attribute are silently ignored.

/myProfile/identificationNumber/@id (minOccurs=0 maxOccurs=1)
> This attribute is a globally unique ID assigned to this element by .NET My Services. Normally, .NET My Services will generate and assign this ID during an insertRequest operation, or possibly during a replaceRequest. Application software can override this ID generation by specifying the useClientIds attribute in the request message. Once an ID is assigned, the attribute is read-only and attempts to write it are silently ignored.

/myProfile/identificationNumber/@creator (string minOccurs=0 maxOccurs=1)
   This attribute identifies the creator in terms of userId, appId, and platformId of the node.

/myProfile/identificationNumber/cat (minOccurs=0 maxOccurs=unbounded)
   This element is used to categorize the element that contains it by referencing a global category definition in either the .NET categories service system document or an external resource containing category definitions, or by referencing an identity-centric category definition in the content document of the .NET categories service for a particular PUID.

/myProfile/identificationNumber/cat/@ref (anyURI minOccurs=0 maxOccurs=1)
   This attribute references a category definition (<catDef/>) element using the rules outlined in the .NET categories service.

/myProfile/identificationNumber/number (string minOccurs=1 maxOccurs=1)
   This element contains the actual identification number value.

/myProfile/identificationNumber/*{any}* (minOccurs=0 maxOccurs=unbounded)
/myProfile/workInformation (minOccurs=0 maxOccurs=unbounded)
   This element encapsulates work- or occupation-related information for this entity.

/myProfile/workInformation/@changeNumber (minOccurs=0 maxOccurs=1)
   The changeNumber attribute is designed to facilitate caching of the element and its descendants. This attribute is assigned to this element by the .NET My Services system. The attribute is read-only to applications. Attempts to write this attribute are silently ignored.

/myProfile/workInformation/@id (minOccurs=0 maxOccurs=1)
   This attribute is a globally unique ID assigned to this element by .NET My Services. Normally, .NET My Services will generate and assign this ID during an insertRequest operation, or possibly during a replaceRequest. Application software can override this ID generation by specifying the useClientIds attribute in the request message. Once an ID is assigned, the attribute is read-only and attempts to write it are silently ignored.

/myProfile/workInformation/@creator (string minOccurs=0 maxOccurs=1)
   This attribute identifies the creator in terms of userId, appId, and platformId of the node.

/myProfile/workInformation/cat (minOccurs=0 maxOccurs=unbounded)
   This element is used to categorize the element that contains it by referencing a global category definition in either the .NET categories service system document or an external resource containing category definitions, or by referencing an identity-centric category definition in the content document of the .NET categories service for a particular PUID.

/myProfile/workInformation/cat/@ref (anyURI minOccurs=0 maxOccurs=1)
   This attribute references a category definition (<catDef/>) element using the rules outlined in the .NET categories service.

/myProfile/workInformation/profession (string minOccurs=0 maxOccurs=1)
   This optional element specifies the entity's profession within this particular
   workInformation element.

/myProfile/workInformation/profession/@xml:lang (minOccurs=1 maxOccurs=1)
   This required attribute is used to specify an ISO 639 language code or an ISO 3166
   country code as described in RFC 1766. The value of this attribute indicates the
   language type of the content within this element.

/myProfile/workInformation/company (minOccurs=0 maxOccurs=unbounded)
   This element encapsulates the company information for this entity, including its name
   and its PUID. Using this anchor information, additional details may be obtained.

/myProfile/workInformation/company/name (string minOccurs=0 maxOccurs=1)
   This optional element specifies the name for the enclosing element.

/myProfile/workInformation/company/name/@xml:lang (minOccurs=1 maxOccurs=1)
   This required attribute is used to specify an ISO 639 language code or an ISO 3166
   country code as described in RFC 1766. The value of this attribute indicates the
   language type of the content within this element.

/myProfile/workInformation/company/puid (string minOccurs=0 maxOccurs=1)
   This optional element specifies the name for the enclosing element.

/myProfile/workInformation/company/email (string minOccurs=0 maxOccurs=1)
   This optional name specifies an e-mail address for the enclosing element.

/myProfile/workInformation/company/cat (minOccurs=1 maxOccurs=1)
   This element is used to categorize the element that contains it by referencing a global
   category definition in either the .NET categories service system document or an
   external resource containing category definitions, or by referencing an identity-centric
   category definition in the content document of the .NET categories service for a
   particular PUID.

/myProfile/workInformation/company/cat/@ref (anyURI minOccurs=0 maxOccurs=1)
   This attribute references a category definition (<catDef/>) element using the rules
   outlined in the .NET categories service.

/myProfile/workInformation/department (minOccurs=0 maxOccurs=unbounded)
   This element encapsulates the department information for this entity including its
   name and its PUID. Using this anchor information, additional details may be obtained.

/myProfile/workInformation/department/name (string minOccurs=0 maxOccurs=1)
   This optional element specifies the name for the enclosing element.

/myProfile/workInformation/department/name/@xml:lang (minOccurs=1 maxOccurs=1)
   This required attribute is used to specify an ISO 639 language code or an ISO 3166
   country code as described in RFC 1766. The value of this attribute indicates the
   language type of the content within this element.

/myProfile/workInformation/department/puid (string minOccurs=0 maxOccurs=1)
   This optional element specifies the name for the enclosing element.

/myProfile/workInformation/department/email (string minOccurs=0 maxOccurs=1)
   This optional name specifies an e-mail address for the enclosing element.

/myProfile/workInformation/department/cat (minOccurs=1 maxOccurs=1)
This element is used to categorize the element that contains it by referencing a global category definition in either the .NET categories service system document or an external resource containing category definitions, or by referencing an identity-centric category definition in the content document of the .NET categories service for a particular PUID.

/myProfile/workInformation/department/cat/@ref (anyURI minOccurs=0 maxOccurs=1)
This attribute references a category definition (<catDef/>) element using the rules outlined in the .NET categories service.

/myProfile/workInformation/jobTitle (string minOccurs=0 maxOccurs=unbounded)
This element specifies the job title for this piece of work information.

/myProfile/workInformation/jobTitle/@xml:lang (minOccurs=1 maxOccurs=1)
This required attribute is used to specify an ISO 639 language code or an ISO 3166 country code as described in RFC 1766. The value of this attribute indicates the language type of the content within this element.

/myProfile/workInformation/officeLocation (string minOccurs=0 maxOccurs=1)
This element specifies the office location for this piece of work information.

/myProfile/workInformation/officeLocation/@xml:lang (minOccurs=1 maxOccurs=1)
This required attribute is used to specify an ISO 639 language code or an ISO 3166 country code as described in RFC 1766. The value of this attribute indicates the language type of the content within this element.

/myProfile/workInformation/manager (minOccurs=0 maxOccurs=unbounded)
This element encapsulates the manager information for this entity, including its name, and its PUID. Using this anchor information, additional details may be obtained.

/myProfile/workInformation/manager/name (string minOccurs=0 maxOccurs=1)
This optional element specifies the name for the enclosing element.

/myProfile/workInformation/manager/name/@xml:lang (minOccurs=1 maxOccurs=1)
This required attribute is used to specify an ISO 639 language code or an ISO 3166 country code as described in RFC 1766. The value of this attribute indicates the language type of the content within this element.

/myProfile/workInformation/manager/puid (string minOccurs=0 maxOccurs=1)
This optional element specifies the name for the enclosing element.

/myProfile/workInformation/manager/email (string minOccurs=0 maxOccurs=1)
This optional name specifies an e-mail address for the enclosing element.

/myProfile/workInformation/manager/cat (minOccurs=1 maxOccurs=1)
This element is used to categorize the element that contains it by referencing a global category definition in either the .NET categories service system document or an external resource containing category definitions, or by referencing an identity-centric category definition in the content document of the .NET categories service for a particular PUID.

/myProfile/workInformation/manager/cat/@ref (anyURI minOccurs=0 maxOccurs=1)
This attribute references a category definition (<catDef/>) element using the rules outlined in the .NET categories service.

/myProfile/workInformation/assistant (minOccurs=0 maxOccurs=unbounded)
> This element encapsulates the assistant information for this entity, including its name and its PUID. Using this anchor information, additional details may be obtained.

/myProfile/workInformation/assistant/name (string minOccurs=0 maxOccurs=1)
> This optional element specifies the name for the enclosing element.

/myProfile/workInformation/assistant/name/@xml:lang (minOccurs=1 maxOccurs=1)
> This required attribute is used to specify an ISO 639 language code or an ISO 3166 country code as described in RFC 1766. The value of this attribute indicates the language type of the content within this element.

/myProfile/workInformation/assistant/puid (string minOccurs=0 maxOccurs=1)
> This optional element specifies the name for the enclosing element.

/myProfile/workInformation/assistant/email (string minOccurs=0 maxOccurs=1)
> This optional name specifies an e-mail address for the enclosing element.

/myProfile/workInformation/assistant/cat (minOccurs=1 maxOccurs=1)
> This element is used to categorize the element that contains it by referencing a global category definition in either the .NET categories service system document or an external resource containing category definitions, or by referencing an identity-centric category definition in the content document of the .NET categories service for a particular PUID.

/myProfile/workInformation/assistant/cat/@ref (anyURI minOccurs=0 maxOccurs=1)
> This attribute references a category definition (<catDef/>) element using the rules outlined in the .NET categories service.

/myProfile/workInformation/*{any}* (minOccurs=0 maxOccurs=unbounded)

/myProfile/address (minOccurs=0 maxOccurs=unbounded)
> This element encapsulates a geographic address. The contained nodes describe the geographic address in detail. This element may be repeated any number of times. Typical use is one address element for each geographical address for this identity. For instance, a user with a primary home and a vacation home might have two address elements in this service.

/myProfile/address/@changeNumber (minOccurs=0 maxOccurs=1)
> The changeNumber attribute is designed to facilitate caching of the element and its descendants. This attribute is assigned to this element by the .NET My Services system. The attribute is read-only to applications. Attempts to write this attribute are silently ignored.

/myProfile/address/@id (minOccurs=0 maxOccurs=1)
> This attribute is a globally unique ID assigned to this element by .NET My Services. Normally, .NET My Services will generate and assign this ID during an insertRequest operation, or possibly during a replaceRequest. Application software can override this ID generation by specifying the useClientIds attribute in the request message. Once an ID is assigned, the attribute is read-only and attempts to write it are silently ignored.

/myProfile/address/@creator (string minOccurs=0 maxOccurs=1)
> This attribute identifies the creator in terms of userId, appId, and platformId of the node.

/myProfile/address/cat (minOccurs=0 maxOccurs=unbounded)
> This element is used to categorize the element that contains it by referencing a global category definition in either the .NET categories service system document or an external resource containing category definitions, or by referencing an identity-centric category definition in the content document of the .NET categories service for a particular PUID.

/myProfile/address/cat/@ref (anyURI minOccurs=0 maxOccurs=1)
> This attribute references a category definition (<catDef/>) element using the rules outlined in the .NET categories service.

/myProfile/address/officialAddressLine (string minOccurs=0 maxOccurs=1)
> This element contains the most precise, official line for the address relative to the postal agency servicing the area specified by the city/postalCode. When parsing an address for official postal usage, this element contains the official, parsable address line that the regional postal system cares about. Typical usage of this element would be to enclose a street address, post office box address, private bag, or any other similar official address. Internal routing information like department name, suite number within a building, internal mailstop number, or similar properties should be placed witin the internalAddressLine element.

/myProfile/address/officialAddressLine/@xml:lang (minOccurs=1 maxOccurs=1)
> This required attribute is used to specify an ISO 639 language code or an ISO 3166 country code as described in RFC 1766. The value of this attribute indicates the language type of the content within this element.

/myProfile/address/internalAddressLine (string minOccurs=0 maxOccurs=1)
> This element contains internal routing information relative to the address specified by the officialAddressLine. Items like department name, suite number within a building, internal mailstop number, or similar properties should be placed within this element.

/myProfile/address/internalAddressLine/@xml:lang (minOccurs=1 maxOccurs=1)
> This required attribute is used to specify an ISO 639 language code or an ISO 3166 country code as described in RFC 1766. The value of this attribute indicates the language type of the content within this element.

/myProfile/address/primaryCity (string minOccurs=0 maxOccurs=1)
> This element defines the primary city for this address.

/myProfile/address/primaryCity/@xml:lang (minOccurs=1 maxOccurs=1)
> This required attribute is used to specify an ISO 639 language code or an ISO 3166 country code as described in RFC 1766. The value of this attribute indicates the language type of the content within this element.

/myProfile/address/secondaryCity (string minOccurs=0 maxOccurs=1)
> This optional element defines the secondary city for this address. Example types for this element include city district, city wards, postal towns, etc.

/myProfile/address/secondaryCity/@xml:lang (minOccurs=1 maxOccurs=1)

This required attribute is used to specify an ISO 639 language code or an ISO 3166 country code as described in RFC 1766. The value of this attribute indicates the language type of the content within this element.

/myProfile/address/subdivision (string minOccurs=0 maxOccurs=1)

This element contains the official subdivision name within the country or region for this address. In the United States, this element would contain the two letter abbreviation for the name of the state. This element is also commonly treated as the "first order admin subdivision" and will typically contain subdivision names referring to:

- administrative division
- Bundesstaat
- canton
- federal district
- province
- region
- state
- territory

/myProfile/address/subdivision/@xml:lang (minOccurs=1 maxOccurs=1)

This required attribute is used to specify an ISO 639 language code or an ISO 3166 country code as described in RFC 1766. The value of this attribute indicates the language type of the content within this element.

/myProfile/address/postalCode (string minOccurs=0 maxOccurs=1)

This element contains the official postal code for this address.

/myProfile/address/countryCode (string minOccurs=0 maxOccurs=1)

This element contains the 2 letter ISO-3166 ID of the country, dependency, or functionally equivalent region for this address.

/myProfile/address/geoLocation (minOccurs=0 maxOccurs=1)

This element encapsulates a geographic or earth position corresponding to the enclosing address.

/myProfile/address/geoLocation/reportingDevice (minOccurs=0 maxOccurs=1)

This element contains the UUID and name for this specific device. The UUID for a specific device is the same as the "Universal Device Number" as exposed by the Universal Plug and Play infrastructure.

/myProfile/address/geoLocation/reportingDevice/deviceId (minOccurs=0 maxOccurs=1)

This element specifies UUID or Universal Device Number for this device.

/myProfile/address/geoLocation/reportingDevice/deviceName (string minOccurs=0 maxOccurs=1)

This element specifies a friendly name for this device.

/myProfile/address/geoLocation/reportingDevice/*{any}* (minOccurs=0 maxOccurs=unbounded)

/myProfile/address/geoLocation/latitude (string minOccurs=0 maxOccurs=1)
This element specifies the latitude value for this geoLocation in units of decimal degrees. Geodetic datum WGS84 is required.

/myProfile/address/geoLocation/longitude (string minOccurs=0 maxOccurs=1)
This element specifies the longitude value for this geoLocation in units of decimal degrees. Geodetic datum WGS84 is required.

/myProfile/address/geoLocation/elevation (string minOccurs=0 maxOccurs=1)
This element specifies the elevation above sea level with respect to WGS84 geodetic datum. The unit for this value is the meter.

/myProfile/address/geoLocation/confidence (string minOccurs=0 maxOccurs=1)
This element specifies a percentage value that indicates the confidence value that this location is accurate within the specified precision.

/myProfile/address/geoLocation/precision (string minOccurs=0 maxOccurs=1)
This element specifies the precision in meters of this location. The value defines a spherical zone that the location falls within.

/myProfile/address/geoLocation/*{any}* (minOccurs=0 maxOccurs=unbounded)
/myProfile/address/*{any}* (minOccurs=0 maxOccurs=unbounded)
/myProfile/webSite (minOccurs=0 maxOccurs=unbounded)
This element encapsulates an electronic address for this entity, specifically, it contains a Web site or URL associated with this identity. This element may be repeated any number of times. Typical use is one webSite element for each Web site associated with this identity.

/myProfile/webSite/@changeNumber (minOccurs=0 maxOccurs=1)
The changeNumber attribute is designed to facilitate caching of the element and its descendants. This attribute is assigned to this element by the .NET My Services system. The attribute is read-only to applications. Attempts to write this attribute are silently ignored.

/myProfile/webSite/@id (minOccurs=0 maxOccurs=1)
This attribute is a globally unique ID assigned to this element by .NET My Services. Normally, .NET My Services will generate and assign this ID during an insertRequest operation, or possibly during a replaceRequest. Application software can override this ID generation by specifying the useClientIds attribute in the request message. Once an ID is assigned, the attribute is read-only and attempts to write it are silently ignored.

/myProfile/webSite/@creator (string minOccurs=0 maxOccurs=1)
This attribute identifies the creator in terms of userId, appId, and platformId of the node.

/myProfile/webSite/cat (minOccurs=0 maxOccurs=unbounded)
This element is used to categorize the element that contains it by referencing a global category definition in either the .NET categories service system document or an external resource containing category definitions, or by referencing an identity-centric category definition in the content document of the .NET categories service for a particular PUID.

/myProfile/webSite/cat/@ref (anyURI minOccurs=0 maxOccurs=1)

This attribute references a category definition (<catDef/>) element using the rules outlined in the .NET categories service.

/myProfile/webSite/url (string minOccurs=1 maxOccurs=1)

This element contains the URL for this Web site. If the site is accessible through multiple URLs, this element may be repeated an appropriate number of times.

/myProfile/webSite/*{any}* (minOccurs=0 maxOccurs=unbounded)

/myProfile/emailAddress (minOccurs=0 maxOccurs=unbounded)

This element encapsulates an electronic address for this entity, specifically, it contains an e-mail address associated with this identity. This element may be repeated any number of times. Typical use is one emailAddress element for each e-mail address associated with this identity.

/myProfile/emailAddress/@changeNumber (minOccurs=0 maxOccurs=1)

The changeNumber attribute is designed to facilitate caching of the element and its descendants. This attribute is assigned to this element by the .NET My Services system. The attribute is read-only to applications. Attempts to write this attribute are silently ignored.

/myProfile/emailAddress/@id (minOccurs=0 maxOccurs=1)

This attribute is a globally unique ID assigned to this element by .NET My Services. Normally, .NET My Services will generate and assign this ID during an insertRequest operation, or possibly during a replaceRequest. Application software can override this ID generation by specifying the useClientIds attribute in the request message. Once an ID is assigned, the attribute is read-only and attempts to write it are silently ignored.

/myProfile/emailAddress/@creator (string minOccurs=0 maxOccurs=1)

This attribute identifies the creator in terms of userId, appId, and platformId of the node.

/myProfile/emailAddress/cat (minOccurs=0 maxOccurs=unbounded)

This element is used to categorize the element that contains it by referencing a global category definition in either the .NET categories service system document or an external resource containing category definitions, or by referencing an identity-centric category definition in the content document of the .NET categories service for a particular PUID.

/myProfile/emailAddress/cat/@ref (anyURI minOccurs=0 maxOccurs=1)

This attribute references a category definition (<catDef/>) element using the rules outlined in the .NET categories service.

/myProfile/emailAddress/email (string minOccurs=1 maxOccurs=1)

This element contains the actual value of the e-mail address (e.g., fred1232@hotmail.com).

/myProfile/emailAddress/name (string minOccurs=0 maxOccurs=1)

This element contains the friendly or display name associated with this e-mail address.

/myProfile/emailAddress/name/@xml:lang (minOccurs=1 maxOccurs=1)
> This required attribute is used to specify an ISO 639 language code or an ISO 3166 country code as described in RFC 1766. The value of this attribute indicates the language type of the content within this element.

/myProfile/emailAddress/*{any}* (minOccurs=0 maxOccurs=unbounded)

/myProfile/screenName (minOccurs=0 maxOccurs=unbounded)
> This element encapsulates an electronic address for this entity. Specifically, it contains a screen name commonly used in real time communications applications like instant messaging applications, chat rooms, etc. This element may be repeated any number of times, and the type attribute may be used for simple classifications on the screenName.

/myProfile/screenName/@changeNumber (minOccurs=0 maxOccurs=1)
> The changeNumber attribute is designed to facilitate caching of the element and its descendants. This attribute is assigned to this element by the .NET My Services system. The attribute is read-only to applications. Attempts to write this attribute are silently ignored.

/myProfile/screenName/@id (minOccurs=0 maxOccurs=1)
> This attribute is a globally unique ID assigned to this element by .NET My Services. Normally, .NET My Services will generate and assign this ID during an insertRequest operation, or possibly during a replaceRequest. Application software can override this ID generation by specifying the useClientIds attribute in the request message. Once an ID is assigned, the attribute is read-only and attempts to write it are silently ignored.

/myProfile/screenName/@creator (string minOccurs=0 maxOccurs=1)
> This attribute identifies the creator in terms of userId, appId, and platformId of the node.

/myProfile/screenName/cat (minOccurs=0 maxOccurs=unbounded)
> This element is used to categorize the element that contains it by referencing a global category definition in either the .NET categories service system document or an external resource containing category definitions, or by referencing an identity-centric category definition in the content document of the .NET categories service for a particular PUID.

/myProfile/screenName/cat/@ref (anyURI minOccurs=0 maxOccurs=1)
> This attribute references a category definition (<catDef/>) element using the rules outlined in the .NET categories service.

/myProfile/screenName/name (string minOccurs=1 maxOccurs=1)
> This element contains the value of the screen name.

/myProfile/screenName/name/@xml:lang (minOccurs=1 maxOccurs=1)
> This required attribute is used to specify an ISO 639 language code or an ISO 3166 country code as described in RFC 1766. The value of this attribute indicates the language type of the content within this element.

/myProfile/screenName/*{any}* (minOccurs=0 maxOccurs=unbounded)

/myProfile/telephoneNumber (minOccurs=0 maxOccurs=unbounded)
> This element encapsulates an electronic address for this entity. Specifically, it contains a telephone number. This element may be repeated any number of times. Typical use is one telephoneNumber element for each phone number associated with this identity.
>
> A telephone number is an optional country code, a required nationalCode (U.S. area code), a number, an optional extension, and a optional PIN.

/myProfile/telephoneNumber/@changeNumber (minOccurs=0 maxOccurs=1)
> The changeNumber attribute is designed to facilitate caching of the element and its descendants. This attribute is assigned to this element by the .NET My Services system. The attribute is read-only to applications. Attempts to write this attribute are silently ignored.

/myProfile/telephoneNumber/@id (minOccurs=0 maxOccurs=1)
> This attribute is a globally unique ID assigned to this element by .NET My Services. Normally, .NET My Services will generate and assign this ID during an insertRequest operation, or possibly during a replaceRequest. Application software can override this ID generation by specifying the useClientIds attribute in the request message. Once an ID is assigned, the attribute is read-only and attempts to write it are silently ignored.

/myProfile/telephoneNumber/@creator (string minOccurs=0 maxOccurs=1)
> This attribute identifies the creator in terms of userId, appId, and platformId of the node.

/myProfile/telephoneNumber/cat (minOccurs=0 maxOccurs=unbounded)
> This element is used to categorize the element that contains it by referencing a global category definition in either the .NET categories service system document or an external resource containing category definitions, or by referencing an identity-centric category definition in the content document of the .NET categories service for a particular PUID.

/myProfile/telephoneNumber/cat/@ref (anyURI minOccurs=0 maxOccurs=1)
> This attribute references a category definition (<catDef/>) element using the rules outlined in the .NET categories service.

/myProfile/telephoneNumber/countryCode (string minOccurs=0 maxOccurs=1)
> This optional element specifies the country code for this telephone number.

/myProfile/telephoneNumber/nationalCode (string minOccurs=1 maxOccurs=1)
> This element specifies the national code for this phone number. For U.S. telephone numbers, this is equivalent to the area code.

/myProfile/telephoneNumber/number (string minOccurs=1 maxOccurs=1)
> This element specifies the actual telephone number within the country and national code number scheme.

/myProfile/telephoneNumber/numberExtension (string minOccurs=0 maxOccurs=1)
> This optional element specifies an extension used to reach this identity and this number.

/myProfile/telephoneNumber/pin (string minOccurs=0 maxOccurs=1)

This optional element specifies a PIN number used on this phone number. A PIN is similar to an extension, but PINs are commonly used to address pagers while extensions are typically used to address phones relative to a local pbx.

/myProfile/telephoneNumber/*{any}* (minOccurs=0 maxOccurs=unbounded)

/myProfile/subscription (minOccurs=0 maxOccurs=unbounded)

This element defines a subscription node that is designed to be an xdb:blue node which when placed in a content document causes a subscription to be registered. A subscription contains a trigger element which selects a scope of coverage. When items change that are under this scope of coverage, and subscriptionResponse message is generated and sent to the specified destination address.

/myProfile/subscription/@changeNumber (minOccurs=0 maxOccurs=1)

The changeNumber attribute is designed to facilitate caching of the element and its descendants. This attribute is assigned to this element by the .NET My Services system. The attribute is read-only to applications. Attempts to write this attribute are silently ignored.

/myProfile/subscription/@id (minOccurs=0 maxOccurs=1)

This attribute is a globally unique ID assigned to this element by .NET My Services. Normally, .NET My Services will generate and assign this ID during an insertRequest operation, or possibly during a replaceRequest. Application software can override this ID generation by specifying the useClientIds attribute in the request message. Once an ID is assigned, the attribute is read-only and attempts to write it are silently ignored.

/myProfile/subscription/@creator (string minOccurs=0 maxOccurs=1)

This attribute identifies the creator in terms of userId, appId, and platformId of the node.

/myProfile/subscription/trigger (minOccurs=1 maxOccurs=1)

/myProfile/subscription/trigger/@select (string minOccurs=0 maxOccurs=1)

This item specifies an XPATH expression that specifies the nodes that are to be selected and watched for changes. The selection may only select xdb:blue nodes. As changes in this node set occur, they trigger the generation of a subscription message. The message is then sent to the SOAP receiver listed in the "to" element.

/myProfile/subscription/trigger/@mode (string minOccurs=0 maxOccurs=1)

This attribute specifies whether or not the content of the changes that triggered the subscription are delivered in the subscription message, or if the message simply indicates that something changed under the trigger. The attribute may be:

includeData

The data that changed, causing the subscription to trigger is included in the subscription message. Note that deleted nodes are specified by their ID, not by value.

excludeData

The data that changed, causing the subscription to trigger is NOT included in the subscription message.

/myProfile/subscription/trigger/@baseChangeNumber (minOccurs=0 maxOccurs=1)
This attribute specifies the changeNumber value that the trigger is relative to. All changes between the specified change number, and the current state of the document relative to the selection are transmitted as subscription messages. This allows a client application to establish a subscription relative to some baseline. As in changeQuery, if the baseChangeNumber is way out of date relative to the current state of the document, and the service cannot supply the changes in the subscription message, the subscription insert is rejected. A value of 0 means that the current values of the selected nodes are transmitted in the subscription message.

/myProfile/subscription/expiresAt (dateTime minOccurs=0 maxOccurs=1)
This optional element specifies an absolute time after which the subscription is no longer active. The subscription node is automatically removed when the subscription expires. If this element is missing, the subscription does not expire.

/myProfile/subscription/context (minOccurs=1 maxOccurs=1)
This element returns the context element from the original subscription. Applications should use this element, AND ONLY this element to correlate the subscription response with one of their subscriptions.

/myProfile/subscription/context/@uri (anyURI minOccurs=0 maxOccurs=1)
This attribute specifies the URI value chosen by the subscriber that is associated with this subscription.

/myProfile/subscription/context/{any} (minOccurs=0 maxOccurs=unbounded)
/myProfile/subscription/to (anyURI minOccurs=1 maxOccurs=1)
This attribute specifies the location that is to receive the subscription message. The value of this element may be one of the following forms:

- *hs:myNotifications*—This URI indicates that generated subscription messages are to be delivered inside the body of a notification and delivered to the default .NET notifications service of the creator.

- *protocol://service*—This URI indicates that generated subscription messages are delivered to the specified service at the domain of the creator's platformId. For instance, a platformId indicating microsoft.com, and a value in this element of http://subscriptionResponse would cause delivery of the subscription message to http://subscriptionResponse.microsoft.com.

If this value is not specified, then the subscription message is delivered as a notification to the "creator's" .NET notifications service.

/myProfile/securityCertificate (minOccurs=0 maxOccurs=unbounded)
/myProfile/securityCertificate/@changeNumber (minOccurs=0 maxOccurs=1)
The changeNumber attribute is designed to facilitate caching of the element and its descendants. This attribute is assigned to this element by the .NET My Services system. The attribute is read-only to applications. Attempts to write this attribute are silently ignored.

/myProfile/securityCertificate/@id (minOccurs=0 maxOccurs=1)

This attribute is a globally unique ID assigned to this element by .NET My Services. Normally, .NET My Services will generate and assign this ID during an insertRequest operation, or possibly during a replaceRequest. Application software can override this ID generation by specifying the useClientIds attribute in the request message. Once an ID is assigned, the attribute is read-only and attempts to write it are silently ignored.

/myProfile/securityCertificate/@creator (string minOccurs=0 maxOccurs=1)

This attribute identifies the creator in terms of userId, appId, and platformId of the node.

/myProfile/securityCertificate/cat (minOccurs=0 maxOccurs=unbounded)

This element is used to categorize the element that contains it by referencing a global category definition in either the .NET categories service system document or an external resource containing category definitions, or by referencing an identity-centric category definition in the content document of the .NET categories service for a particular PUID.

/myProfile/securityCertificate/cat/@ref (anyURI minOccurs=0 maxOccurs=1)

This attribute references a category definition (<catDef/>) element using the rules outlined in the .NET categories service.

/myProfile/securityCertificate/certificate (hexBinary minOccurs=1 maxOccurs=1)
/myProfile/{any} (minOccurs=0 maxOccurs=unbounded)

The .NET profile service/system

The system document is a global document for the service. Its content and meaning is independent of the PUID used to address the service, and the document is read-only to all users. The system document contains a set of base items common to all .NET My Services services, and is optionally extended by each service to include service-specific global information.

This schema outline illustrates the layout and meaning of the information found in the system document for the .NET profile service.

```
<sys:system changeNumber="..." instanceId="..."
    xmlns:hs="http://schemas.microsoft.com/hs/2001/10/core"
    xmlns:sys="http://schemas.microsoft.com/hs/2001/10/myProfile/system">1..1
    <hs:roleMap changeNumber="..." id="..." creator="...">1..1
        <hs:scope id="...">0..unbounded
            <hs:shape base="...">1..1
                <hs:include select="...">1..unbounded</hs:include>
                <hs:exclude select="...">0..unbounded</hs:exclude>
            </hs:shape>
        </hs:scope>
```

```
        <hs:roleTemplate name="..." priority="...">0..unbounded
            <hs:fullDescription xml:lang="...">0..1</hs:fullDescription>
            <hs:method name="..." scopeRef="...">0..unbounded</hs:method>
        </hs:roleTemplate>
    </hs:roleMap>
    <hs:methodMap changeNumber="..." id="..." creator="...">1..1
        <hs:method name="...">0..unbounded {any}</hs:method>
    </hs:methodMap>
    <hs:schemaMap changeNumber="..." id="..." creator="...">1..1
        <hs:schema namespace="..." schemaLocation="..." alias="...">0..unbounded
{any}</hs:schema>
    </hs:schemaMap>
    <hs:wsdlMap changeNumber="..." id="..." creator="...">1..1
        <hs:wsdl wsdlLocation="...">0..unbounded {any}</hs:wsdl>
        <hs:disco discoLocation="...">0..unbounded {any}</hs:disco>
    </hs:wsdlMap>
    {any}
</sys:system>
```

The meaning of the attributes and elements shown in the preceding sample document fragment are listed in the following section.

/system (minOccurs=1 maxOccurs=1)

This element encapsulates the system document for the .NET profile service.

/system/@changeNumber (minOccurs=0 maxOccurs=1)

The changeNumber attribute is designed to facilitate caching of the element and its descendants. This attribute is assigned to this element by the .NET My Services system. The attribute is read-only to applications. Attempts to write this attribute are silently ignored.

/system/@instanceId (string minOccurs=0 maxOccurs=1)

This attribute is a unique identifier typically assigned to the root element of a service. It is a read-only element and assigned by the .NET My Services system when a user is provisioned for a particular service.

/system/roleMap (minOccurs=1 maxOccurs=1)

This element encapsulates all the elements that make up a roleMap, which includes a document class relative to a roleTemplate, priority, name, method, and per-method scope. An individual roleTemplate defines the maximum scope of information, and the allowable methods used to access that information for each request mapped into the template.

/system/roleMap/@changeNumber (minOccurs=0 maxOccurs=1)

The changeNumber attribute is designed to facilitate caching of the element and its descendants. This attribute is assigned to this element by the .NET My Services system. The attribute is read-only to applications. Attempts to write this attribute are silently ignored.

/system/roleMap/@id (minOccurs=0 maxOccurs=1)

This attribute is a globally unique ID assigned to this element by .NET My Services. Normally, .NET My Services will generate and assign this ID during an insertRequest operation, or possibly during a replaceRequest. Application software can override this ID generation by specifying the useClientIds attribute in the request message. Once an ID is assigned, the attribute is read-only and attempts to write it are silently ignored.

/system/roleMap/@creator (string minOccurs=0 maxOccurs=1)

This attribute identifies the creator in terms of userId, appId, and platformId of the node.

/system/roleMap/scope (minOccurs=0 maxOccurs=unbounded)

This element defines a scope which may be referred to by roles within this roleMap to indicate what portions of the document are visible to this role for the specified method.

/system/roleMap/scope/@id (minOccurs=0 maxOccurs=1)

This attribute is a globally unique ID assigned to this element by .NET My Services. Normally, .NET My Services will generate and assign this ID during an insertRequest operation, or possibly during a replaceRequest. Application software can override this ID generation by specifying the useClientIds attribute in the request message. Once an ID is assigned, the attribute is read-only and attempts to write it are silently ignored.

/system/roleMap/scope/shape (minOccurs=1 maxOccurs=1)

A shape defines the node set visible through the document when operating through this shape element.

/system/roleMap/scope/shape/@base (string minOccurs=0 maxOccurs=1)

This attribute specifies the initial set of nodes visible through the shape.

A value of t indicates that the shape is initialized to include all possible nodes relative to the shape that is currently in effect. For instance, each role defines a scope containing a shape. When defining a shape for a role, the value t indicates all possible nodes available in the specified document for this role. When defining a shape in an ACL entry, a value of t means all of the nodes visible in the shape for the computed role. When using a shape in an hsdl operation, a value of t indicates all of the possible nodes selected by the hsdl operation (relative to the ACL shape which itself is relative to the role's shape).

The value nil indicates the opposite of t, which is the empty node set. Nodes from this set may then be included into the shape.

/system/roleMap/scope/shape/include (minOccurs=1 maxOccurs=unbounded)

This element specifies the set of nodes that should be included into the shape relative to the possible set of nodes indicated by the base attribute.

/system/roleMap/scope/shape/include/@select (string minOccurs=0 maxOccurs=1)
This item specifies an XPATH expression that selects a set of nodes relative to the externally established context. The expression can never travel outside the node-set established by this externally established current context. The expression may match 0 or more nodes, and the operation manipulates all selected nodes. The minOccurs and maxOccurs attributes are optional and place restrictions and limitations on the number of nodes selected.

/system/roleMap/scope/shape/exclude (minOccurs=0 maxOccurs=unbounded)
This element specifies the set of nodes that should be excluded from the shape relative to the possible set of nodes indicated by the base attribute.

/system/roleMap/scope/shape/exclude/@select (string minOccurs=0 maxOccurs=1)
This item specifies an XPATH expression that selects a set of nodes relative to the externally established context. The expression can never travel outside the node-set established by this externally established current context. The expression may match 0 or more nodes, and the operation manipulates all selected nodes. The minOccurs and maxOccurs attributes are optional and place restrictions and limitations on the number of nodes selected.

/system/roleMap/roleTemplate (minOccurs=0 maxOccurs=unbounded)
This element encapsulates the definition of a role. The attribute set for this element includes the document class that this roleTemplate refers to, the name of the roleTemplate, and the priority of the roleTemplate.

/system/roleMap/roleTemplate/@name (string minOccurs=0 maxOccurs=1)
This element specifies the name of the role.

/system/roleMap/roleTemplate/@priority (int minOccurs=0 maxOccurs=1)
This element specifies the priority of the roleTemplate which is used to select that actual roleTemplate when the role evaluation determines that the subject maps to multiple roleTemplates.

/system/roleMap/roleTemplate/fullDescription (string minOccurs=0 maxOccurs=1)
This element contains a description of this role template which specifies the capabilities a caller will have when accessing information through this role.

/system/roleMap/roleTemplate/fullDescription/@xml:lang (minOccurs=1 maxOccurs=1)
This required attribute is used to specify an ISO 639 language code or an ISO 3166 country code as described in RFC 1766. The value of this attribute indicates the language type of the content within this element.

/system/roleMap/roleTemplate/method (minOccurs=0 maxOccurs=unbounded)
This element specifies the methods available within this roleTemplate by name, and by scope. When a subject maps to a roleTemplate, the method in the request must match one of these elements for the message to continue to flow. If the method exists, the data available to the method is a function of the scope referenced by this method combined with an optional scope referenced by the role defined in the roleList.

/system/roleMap/roleTemplate/method/@name (string minOccurs=0 maxOccurs=1)
This element specifies the name of the method.

/system/roleMap/roleTemplate/method/@scopeRef (string minOccurs=0 maxOccurs=1)
This attribute specifies the scope within this document that is in effect for this method.

/system/methodMap (minOccurs=1 maxOccurs=1)
This element defines the methodMap. While it is true that in most cases, the roleMap section contains a definitive list of methods, these methods are likely to be scattered about the roleMap in various templates. This section contains the definitive non-duplicated list of methods available within the service.

/system/methodMap/@changeNumber (minOccurs=0 maxOccurs=1)
The changeNumber attribute is designed to facilitate caching of the element and its descendants. This attribute is assigned to this element by the .NET My Services system. The attribute is read-only to applications. Attempts to write this attribute are silently ignored.

/system/methodMap/@id (minOccurs=0 maxOccurs=1)
This attribute is a globally unique ID assigned to this element by .NET My Services. Normally, .NET My Services will generate and assign this ID during an insertRequest operation, or possibly during a replaceRequest. Application software can override this ID generation by specifying the useClientIds attribute in the request message. Once an ID is assigned, the attribute is read-only and attempts to write it are silently ignored.

/system/methodMap/@creator (string minOccurs=0 maxOccurs=1)
This attribute identifies the creator in terms of userId, appId, and platformId of the node.

/system/methodMap/method (minOccurs=0 maxOccurs=unbounded)
This element defines a method that is available within this service.

/system/methodMap/method/@name (string minOccurs=0 maxOccurs=1)
This attribute specifies the name of a method available within the service.

/system/methodMap/method/*{any}* (minOccurs=0 maxOccurs=unbounded)
/system/schemaMap (minOccurs=1 maxOccurs=1)
This element defines the various schemas that define the data structures and shape of information managed by this service. Each schema is defined by its namespace URI, its location, and a preferred namespace alias.

/system/schemaMap/@changeNumber (minOccurs=0 maxOccurs=1)
The changeNumber attribute is designed to facilitate caching of the element and its descendants. This attribute is assigned to this element by the .NET My Services system. The attribute is read-only to applications. Attempts to write this attribute are silently ignored.

/system/schemaMap/@id (minOccurs=0 maxOccurs=1)
This attribute is a globally unique ID assigned to this element by .NET My Services. Normally, .NET My Services will generate and assign this ID during an insertRequest operation, or possibly during a replaceRequest. Application software can override this ID generation by specifying the useClientIds attribute in the request message. Once an ID is assigned, the attribute is read-only and attempts to write it are silently ignored.

<u>/system/schemaMap/@creator</u> (string minOccurs=0 maxOccurs=1)
> This attribute identifies the creator in terms of userId, appId, and platformId of the node.

/system/schemaMap/schema (minOccurs=0 maxOccurs=unbounded)
> This element defines a schema which defines data-structures and the shape of information managed by this service. Multiple schema elements exist for each service, one for each logical grouping of information exposed by the service.

/system/schemaMap/schema/@namespace (anyURI minOccurs=0 maxOccurs=1)
> This attribute specifies the namespace URI of this schema.

/system/schemaMap/schema/@schemaLocation (anyURI minOccurs=0 maxOccurs=1)
> This attribute specifies the location (in the form of a URI) of the resource containing schema. When a schema is reachable through a variety of URIs, one schema element will exist for each location.

/system/schemaMap/schema/@alias (string minOccurs=0 maxOccurs=1)
> This attribute specifies the preferred alias that should be used if possible when manipulating information covered by this schema in the context of this service.

/system/schemaMap/schema/**{any}** (minOccurs=0 maxOccurs=unbounded)
/system/wsdlMap (minOccurs=1 maxOccurs=1)
> This element defines the wsdlMap for this service. This map includes the location of WSDL documents, DISCO documents, and WISL documents for this Web service. These documents are used by applications to understand the format of messages that may be sent to the various services.

<u>/system/wsdlMap/@changeNumber</u> (minOccurs=0 maxOccurs=1)
> The changeNumber attribute is designed to facilitate caching of the element and its descendants. This attribute is assigned to this element by the .NET My Services system. The attribute is read-only to applications. Attempts to write this attribute are silently ignored.

<u>/system/wsdlMap/@id</u> (minOccurs=0 maxOccurs=1)
> This attribute is a globally unique ID assigned to this element by .NET My Services. Normally, .NET My Services will generate and assign this ID during an insertRequest operation, or possibly during a replaceRequest. Application software can override this ID generation by specifying the useClientIds attribute in the request message. Once an ID is assigned, the attribute is read-only and attempts to write it are silently ignored.

<u>/system/wsdlMap/@creator</u> (string minOccurs=0 maxOccurs=1)
> This attribute identifies the creator in terms of userId, appId, and platformId of the node.

/system/wsdlMap/wsdl (minOccurs=0 maxOccurs=unbounded)
> This element is used to specify the location of a WSDL file for this service. Multiple entries may exist pointing to the same file hosted in multiple locations, or to variations on the content within the WSDL files.

/system/wsdlMap/wsdl/@wsdlLocation (anyURI minOccurs=0 maxOccurs=1)
> This attribute is a URI that specifies the location of the WSDL file.

/system/wsdlMap/wsdl/*{any}* (minOccurs=0 maxOccurs=unbounded)

/system/wsdlMap/disco (minOccurs=0 maxOccurs=unbounded)

> This element is used to specify the location of a DISCO file for this service. Multiple entries may exist pointing to the same file hosted in multiple locations, or to variations of the content within the DISCO files.

/system/wsdlMap/disco/@discoLocation (anyURI minOccurs=0 maxOccurs=1)

> This attribute is a URI that specifies the location of the DISCO file.

/system/wsdlMap/disco/*{any}* (minOccurs=0 maxOccurs=unbounded)

/system/*{any}* (minOccurs=0 maxOccurs=unbounded)

The .NET profile service/Methods

The .NET profile service supports the following standard and domain-specific methods:

- query
- insert
- replace
- delete
- update

The standard methods operate on this service using the same message format and method-interchange techniques described in the hsdl section of this document. The only service-specific information to note is the schema that is in effect for each of the methods. These schemas, and how they relate to the standard methods and roles are described in the roles section of this document.

The domain-specific methods operate as described in the domain-specific methods section of this document, and are governed by the various schemas outlined in the .NET Profile/Roles section for this service.

CHAPTER 21

The .NET services service/Introduction

This chapter describes the Microsoft .NET my services service. The .NET my services service keeps track of the services that an entity has subscribed to.

.NET services service/Roles

The .NET services service controls access by using the following roleTemplates:

- rt0
- rt1
- rt2
- rt3
- rt99

The .NET services service uses the following scopes:

- **scope id 1**

```
<hs:scope id=1>

    <hs:shape base=t>

    </hs:shape>

</hs:scope>
```

- **scope id 2**

```
<hs:scope id=2>

    <hs:shape base=nil>

        <hs:include select=//*[@creator='$callerId']/>

    </hs:shape>

</hs:scope>
```

- **scope id 3**

```
<hs:scope id=3>

    <hs:shape base=nil>

        <hs:include select=//subscription[@creator='$callerId']/>

    </hs:shape>

</hs:scope>
```

- **scope id 4**

```
<hs:scope id=4>

    <hs:shape base=nil>

        <hs:include select=//*[cat/@ref='hs:public']/>

        <hs:include select=//subscription[@creator='$callerId']/>

    </hs:shape>

</hs:scope>
```

The .NET services roleTemplate rt0

The purpose of this role is to give complete read/write access to all information within the content document of the service being protected through this roleTemplate.

The following table illustrates the available methods and the scope in effect when accessing the .NET services service through that method while mapped to this roleTemplate.

method	scopeRef
query	scopeRef=1
insert	scopeRef=1
replace	scopeRef=1
delete	scopeRef=1
update	scopeRef=1

The .NET services roleTemplate rt1

The purpose of this role is to give complete read access to all information within the content document of the service being protected through this roleTemplate. Applications mapping to this role also have a limited ability to write to information in the content document. They may create nodes in any location, but may only change/replace or delete nodes that they created.

The following table illustrates the available methods and the scope in effect when accessing the .NET services service through that method while mapped to this roleTemplate.

method	scopeRef
query	scopeRef=1
insert	scopeRef=2
replace	scopeRef=2
delete	scopeRef=2

The .NET services roleTemplate rt2

The purpose of this role is to give complete read access to all information within the content document of the service being protected through this roleTemplate. Applications mapping to this role have very limited write access and are only able to create and manipulate their own subscription nodes.

The following table illustrates the available methods and the scope in effect when accessing the .NET services service through that method while mapped to this roleTemplate.

method	scopeRef
query	scopeRef=1
insert	scopeRef=3
replace	scopeRef=3
delete	scopeRef=3

The .NET services roleTemplate rt3

The purpose of this role is to give limited read access to information within the content document that is categorized as "public".

The following table illustrates the available methods and the scope in effect when accessing the .NET services service through that method while mapped to this roleTemplate.

method	scopeRef
query	scopeRef=4

The .NET services roleTemplate rt99

The purpose of this role is to block all access to the content document. Note that lack of a role in the roleList has the same effect as assigning someone to rt99.

The .NET services service/content

The content document is an identity-centric document. Its content and meaning is a function of the Microsoft Passport Unique ID (PUID) used to address the service. Accessing the document is controlled by the associated roleList document.

This schema outline illustrates the layout and meaning of the information found in the content document for the .NET services service.

```
<m:myServices changeNumber="..." instanceId="..."
    xmlns:m="http://schemas.microsoft.com/hs/2001/10/myServices"
    xmlns:hs="http://schemas.microsoft.com/hs/2001/10/core">₁..₁
    <m:service name="..." changeNumber="..." id="..." creator="...">₀..unbounded
        <m:cat ref="...">₀..unbounded</m:cat>
        <m:key puid="..." instance="..." cluster="...">₀..₁</m:key>
        <m:refer>₀..₁</m:refer>
        <m:to>₁..₁</m:to>
        <m:spn>₁..₁</m:spn>
        <m:realm>₁..₁</m:realm>
        {any}
    </m:service>
    {any}
</m:myServices>
```

The meaning of the attributes and elements shown in the preceding sample document fragment are listed in the following section.

/myServices (minOccurs=1 maxOccurs=1)
This element encapsulates the content document for the service.

/myServices/@changeNumber (minOccurs=0 maxOccurs=1)
The changeNumber attribute is designed to facilitate caching of the element and its descendants. This attribute is assigned to this element by the .NET My Services system. The attribute is read-only to applications. Attempts to write this attribute are silently ignored.

/myServices/@instanceId (string minOccurs=0 maxOccurs=1)
This attribute is a unique identifier typically assigned to the root element of a service. It is a read-only element and assigned by the .NET My Services system when a user is provisioned for a particular service.

/myServices/service (minOccurs=0 maxOccurs=unbounded)
/myServices/service/@name (string minOccurs=0 maxOccurs=1)
This element contains the name of the service being accessed by this request message.

/myServices/service/@changeNumber (minOccurs=0 maxOccurs=1)
: The changeNumber attribute is designed to facilitate caching of the element and its descendants. This attribute is assigned to this element by the .NET My Services system. The attribute is read-only to applications. Attempts to write this attribute are silently ignored.

/myServices/service/@id (minOccurs=0 maxOccurs=1)
: This attribute is a globally unique ID assigned to this element by .NET My Services. Normally, .NET My Services will generate and assign this ID during an insertRequest operation, or possibly during a replaceRequest. Application software can override this ID generation by specifying the useClientIds attribute in the request message. Once an ID is assigned, the attribute is read-only and attempts to write it are silently ignored.

/myServices/service/@creator (string minOccurs=0 maxOccurs=1)
: This attribute identifies the creator in terms of userId, appId, and platformId of the node.

/myServices/service/cat (minOccurs=0 maxOccurs=unbounded)
: This element is used to categorize the element that contains it by referencing a global category definition in either the .NET categories service system document or an external resource containing category definitions, or by referencing an identity-centric category definition in the content document of the .NET categories service for a particular PUID.

/myServices/service/cat/@ref (anyURI minOccurs=0 maxOccurs=1)
: This attribute references a category definition (<catDef/>) element using the rules outlined in the .NET categories service.

/myServices/service/key (minOccurs=0 maxOccurs=1)
: This element specifies key information used to zoom in on the document being manipulated. This information includes the PUID that owns the document, the instance ID of the document, and the cluster or partition key used to locate the machine resources that hold the document.

  In certain situations, a client will want to send the same message to a number of instances of a particular service. In order to do this, the client may repeat this element multiple times. The cluster attributes in all elements must match each other, but the PUID and instance attributes may differ. A unique response message is generated for each key specified.

  The entire contents of this element come from the .NET services service.

/myServices/service/key/@puid (string minOccurs=0 maxOccurs=1)
: This element specifies the PUID of the entity that "owns" the service being accessed. In the case of a "myPresence" service, this element is equivalent to the "my".

/myServices/service/key/@instance (string minOccurs=0 maxOccurs=1)
: This element specifies the particular instance of the service for this ID being accessed. For example, if a given ID is provisioned with multiple .NET calendar service documents on the same cluster and in the same data center, the documents would differ only by this value.

/myServices/service/key/@cluster (string minOccurs=0 maxOccurs=1)
This element specifies information used by the .NET My Services system to locate the document on a particular back-end server or database. It is used as the virtual partition key for the document being addressed. This technique is preferable to computing this partition key based on some hash of the PUID/instance.

/myServices/service/refer (string minOccurs=0 maxOccurs=1)
This element specifies that the fields below are for a referral.

/myServices/service/to (string minOccurs=1 maxOccurs=1)
This element specifies the "to" destination URL.

/myServices/service/spn (string minOccurs=1 maxOccurs=1)
This element specifies the spn in question.

/myServices/service/realm (string minOccurs=1 maxOccurs=1)
This element specifies the authentication realm for the spn in question.

/myServices/service/*{any}* (minOccurs=0 maxOccurs=unbounded)
/myServices/*{any}* (minOccurs=0 maxOccurs=unbounded)

The .NET services service/system

The system document is a global document for the service. Its content and meaning are independent of the PUID used to address the service, and the document is read-only to all users. The system document contains a set of base items common to all .NET My Services services, and is optionally extended by each service to include service-specific global information.

This schema outline illustrates the layout and meaning of the information found in the system document for the .NET services service.

```
<sys:system changeNumber="..." instanceId="..."
    xmlns:hs="http://schemas.microsoft.com/hs/2001/10/core"
    xmlns:sys="http://schemas.microsoft.com/hs/2001/10/myServices/system">1..1
    <hs:roleMap changeNumber="..." id="..." creator="...">1..1
        <hs:scope id="...">0..unbounded
            <hs:shape base="...">1..1
                <hs:include select="...">1..unbounded</hs:include>
                <hs:exclude select="...">0..unbounded</hs:exclude>
            </hs:shape>
        </hs:scope>
        <hs:roleTemplate name="..." priority="...">0..unbounded
            <hs:fullDescription xml:lang="...">0..1</hs:fullDescription>
            <hs:method name="..." scopeRef="...">0..unbounded</hs:method>
        </hs:roleTemplate>
    </hs:roleMap>
```

```
    <hs:methodMap changeNumber="..." id="..." creator="...">₁..₁
        <hs:method name="...">₀..unbounded {any}</hs:method>
    </hs:methodMap>
    <hs:schemaMap changeNumber="..." id="..." creator="...">₁..₁
        <hs:schema namespace="..." schemaLocation="..." alias="...">₀..unbounded
{any}</hs:schema>
    </hs:schemaMap>
    <hs:wsdlMap changeNumber="..." id="..." creator="...">₁..₁
        <hs:wsdl wsdlLocation="...">₀..unbounded {any}</hs:wsdl>
        <hs:disco discoLocation="...">₀..unbounded {any}</hs:disco>
    </hs:wsdlMap>
    {any}
</sys:system>
```

The meaning of the attributes and elements shown in the preceding sample document fragment are listed in the following section.

/system (minOccurs=1 maxOccurs=1)

This element encapsulates the system document for the .NET services service.

/system/@changeNumber (minOccurs=0 maxOccurs=1)

The changeNumber attribute is designed to facilitate caching of the element and its descendants. This attribute is assigned to this element by the .NET My Services system. The attribute is read-only to applications. Attempts to write this attribute are silently ignored.

/system/@instanceId (string minOccurs=0 maxOccurs=1)

This attribute is a unique identifier typically assigned to the root element of a service. It is a read-only element and assigned by the .NET My Services system when a user is provisioned for a particular service.

/system/roleMap (minOccurs=1 maxOccurs=1)

This element encapsulates all the elements that make up a roleMap, which includes a document class relative to a roleTemplate, priority, name, method, and per-method scope. An individual roleTemplate defines the maximum scope of information and the allowable methods used to access that information for each request mapped into the template.

/system/roleMap/@changeNumber (minOccurs=0 maxOccurs=1)

The changeNumber attribute is designed to facilitate caching of the element and its descendants. This attribute is assigned to this element by the .NET My Services system. The attribute is read-only to applications. Attempts to write this attribute are silently ignored.

/system/roleMap/@id (minOccurs=0 maxOccurs=1)

This attribute is a globally unique ID assigned to this element by .NET My Services. Normally, .NET My Services will generate and assign this ID during an insertRequest operation, or possibly during a replaceRequest. Application software can override this ID generation by specifying the useClientIds attribute in the request message. Once an ID is assigned, the attribute is read-only and attempts to write it are silently ignored.

/system/roleMap/@creator (string minOccurs=0 maxOccurs=1)

This attribute identifies the creator in terms of userId, appId, and platformId of the node.

/system/roleMap/scope (minOccurs=0 maxOccurs=unbounded)

This element defines a scope that may be referred to by roles within this roleMap to indicate what portions of the document are visible to this role for the specified method.

/system/roleMap/scope/@id (minOccurs=0 maxOccurs=1)

This attribute is a globally unique ID assigned to this element by .NET My Services. Normally, .NET My Services will generate and assign this ID during an insertRequest operation, or possibly during a replaceRequest. Application software can override this ID generation by specifying the useClientIds attribute in the request message. Once an ID is assigned, the attribute is read-only and attempts to write it are silently ignored.

/system/roleMap/scope/shape (minOccurs=1 maxOccurs=1)

A shape defines the node set visible through the document when operating through this shape element.

/system/roleMap/scope/shape/@base (string minOccurs=0 maxOccurs=1)

This attribute specifies the initial set of nodes visible through the shape.

A value of t indicates that the shape is initialized to include all possible nodes relative to the shape that is currently in effect. For instance, each role defines a scope containing a shape. When defining a shape for a role, the value t indicates all possible nodes available in the specified document for this role. When defining a shape in an ACL entry, a value of t means all of the nodes visible in the shape for the computed role. When using a shape in an hsdl operation, a value of t indicates all of the possible nodes selected by the hsdl operation (relative to the ACL shape which itself is relative to the role's shape).

The value nil indicates the opposite of t, which is the empty node set. Nodes from this set may then be included in the shape.

/system/roleMap/scope/shape/include (minOccurs=1 maxOccurs=unbounded)

This element specifies the set of nodes that should be included in the shape relative to the possible set of nodes indicated by the base attribute.

/system/roleMap/scope/shape/include/@select (string minOccurs=0 maxOccurs=1)
This item specifies an XPATH expression that selects a set of nodes relative to the externally established context. The expression can never travel outside the node-set established by this externally established current context. The expression may match 0 or more nodes, and the operation manipulates all selected nodes. The minOccurs and maxOccurs attributes are optional and place restrictions and limitations on the number of nodes selected.

/system/roleMap/scope/shape/exclude (minOccurs=0 maxOccurs=unbounded)
This element specifies the set of nodes that should be excluded from the shape relative to the possible set of nodes indicated by the base attribute.

/system/roleMap/scope/shape/exclude/@select (string minOccurs=0 maxOccurs=1)
This item specifies an XPATH expression that selects a set of nodes relative to the externally established context. The expression can never travel outside the node-set established by this externally established current context. The expression may match 0 or more nodes, and the operation manipulates all selected nodes. The minOccurs and maxOccurs attributes are optional and place restrictions and limitations on the number of nodes selected.

/system/roleMap/roleTemplate (minOccurs=0 maxOccurs=unbounded)
This element encapsulates the definition of a role. The attribute set for this element includes the document class that this roleTemplate refers to, the name of the roleTemplate, and the priority of the roleTemplate.

/system/roleMap/roleTemplate/@name (string minOccurs=0 maxOccurs=1)
This element specifies the name of the role.

/system/roleMap/roleTemplate/@priority (int minOccurs=0 maxOccurs=1)
This element specifies the priority of the roleTemplate that is used to select that actual roleTemplate when the role evaluation determines that the subject maps to multiple roleTemplates.

/system/roleMap/roleTemplate/fullDescription (string minOccurs=0 maxOccurs=1)
This element contains a description of this role template which specifies the capabilities a caller will have when accessing information through this role.

/system/roleMap/roleTemplate/fullDescription/@xml:lang (minOccurs=1 maxOccurs=1)
This required attribute is used to specify an ISO 639 language code or an ISO 3166 country code as described in RFC 1766. The value of this attribute indicates the language type of the content within this element.

/system/roleMap/roleTemplate/method (minOccurs=0 maxOccurs=unbounded)
This element specifies the methods available within this roleTemplate by name, and by scope. When a subject maps to a roleTemplate, the method in the request must match one of these elements for the message to continue to flow. If the method exists, the data available to the method is a function of the scope referenced by this method combined with an optional scope referenced by the role defined in the roleList.

/system/roleMap/roleTemplate/method/@name (string minOccurs=0 maxOccurs=1)
This element specifies the name of the method.

/system/roleMap/roleTemplate/method/@scopeRef (string minOccurs=0 maxOccurs=1)
This attribute specifies the scope within this document that is in effect for this method.

/system/methodMap (minOccurs=1 maxOccurs=1)
This element defines the methodMap. While it is true that in most cases the roleMap section contains a definitive list of methods, these methods are likely to be scattered about the roleMap in various templates. This section contains the definitive non-duplicated list of methods available within the service.

/system/methodMap/@changeNumber (minOccurs=0 maxOccurs=1)
The changeNumber attribute is designed to facilitate caching of the element and its descendants. This attribute is assigned to this element by the .NET My Services system. The attribute is read-only to applications. Attempts to write this attribute are silently ignored.

/system/methodMap/@id (minOccurs=0 maxOccurs=1)
This attribute is a globally unique ID assigned to this element by .NET My Services. Normally, .NET My Services will generate and assign this ID during an insertRequest operation, or possibly during a replaceRequest. Application software can override this ID generation by specifying the useClientIds attribute in the request message. Once an ID is assigned, the attribute is read-only and attempts to write it are silently ignored.

/system/methodMap/@creator (string minOccurs=0 maxOccurs=1)
This attribute identifies the creator in terms of userId, appId, and platformId of the node.

/system/methodMap/method (minOccurs=0 maxOccurs=unbounded)
This element defines a method that is available within this service.

/system/methodMap/method/@name (string minOccurs=0 maxOccurs=1)
This attribute specifies the name of a method available within this service.

/system/methodMap/method/*{any}* (minOccurs=0 maxOccurs=unbounded)
/system/schemaMap (minOccurs=1 maxOccurs=1)
This element defines the various schemas that define the data structures and shape of information managed by this service. Each schema is defined by its namespace URI, its location, and a preferred namespace alias.

/system/schemaMap/@changeNumber (minOccurs=0 maxOccurs=1)
The changeNumber attribute is designed to facilitate caching of the element and its descendants. This attribute is assigned to this element by the .NET My Services system. The attribute is read-only to applications. Attempts to write this attribute are silently ignored.

/system/schemaMap/@id (minOccurs=0 maxOccurs=1)

This attribute is a globally unique ID assigned to this element by .NET My Services. Normally, .NET My Services will generate and assign this ID during an insertRequest operation, or possibly during a replaceRequest. Application software can override this ID generation by specifying the useClientIds attribute in the request message. Once an ID is assigned, the attribute is read-only and attempts to write it are silently ignored.

/system/schemaMap/@creator (string minOccurs=0 maxOccurs=1)

This attribute identifies the creator in terms of userId, appId, and platformId of the node.

/system/schemaMap/schema (minOccurs=0 maxOccurs=unbounded)

This element defines a schema that defines data structures and the shape of information managed by this service. Multiple schema elements exist for each service, one for each logical grouping of information exposed by the service.

/system/schemaMap/schema/@namespace (anyURI minOccurs=0 maxOccurs=1)

This attribute specifies the namespace URI of this schema.

/system/schemaMap/schema/@schemaLocation (anyURI minOccurs=0 maxOccurs=1)

This attribute specifies the location (in the form of a URI) of the resource containing schema. When a schema is reachable through a variety of URIs, one schema element will exist for each location.

/system/schemaMap/schema/@alias (string minOccurs=0 maxOccurs=1)

This attribute specifies the preferred alias that should be used if possible when manipulating information covered by this schema in the context of this service.

/system/schemaMap/schema/*{any}* (minOccurs=0 maxOccurs=unbounded)

/system/wsdlMap (minOccurs=1 maxOccurs=1)

This element defines the wsdlMap for this service. This map includes the location of WSDL documents, DISCO documents, and WISL documents for this Web service. These documents are used by applications to understand the format of messages that may be sent to the various services.

/system/wsdlMap/@changeNumber (minOccurs=0 maxOccurs=1)

The changeNumber attribute is designed to facilitate caching of the element and its descendants. This attribute is assigned to this element by the .NET My Services system. The attribute is read-only to applications. Attempts to write this attribute are silently ignored.

/system/wsdlMap/@id (minOccurs=0 maxOccurs=1)

This attribute is a globally unique ID assigned to this element by .NET My Services. Normally, .NET My Services will generate and assign this ID during an insertRequest operation, or possibly during a replaceRequest. Application software can override this ID generation by specifying the useClientIds attribute in the request message. Once an ID is assigned, the attribute is read-only and attempts to write it are silently ignored.

/system/wsdlMap/@creator (string minOccurs=0 maxOccurs=1)
> This attribute identifies the creator in terms of userId, appId, and platformId of the node.

/system/wsdlMap/wsdl (minOccurs=0 maxOccurs=unbounded)
> This element is used to specify the location of a WSDL file for this service. Multiple entries may exist pointing to the same file hosted in multiple locations, or to variations on the content within the WSDL files.

/system/wsdlMap/wsdl/@wsdlLocation (anyURI minOccurs=0 maxOccurs=1)
> This attribute is a URI that specifies the location of the WSDL file.

/system/wsdlMap/wsdl/*{any}* (minOccurs=0 maxOccurs=unbounded)
/system/wsdlMap/disco (minOccurs=0 maxOccurs=unbounded)
> This element is used to specify the location of a DISCO file for this service. Multiple entries may exist pointing to the same file hosted in multiple locations, or to variations on the content within the DISCO files.

/system/wsdlMap/disco/@discoLocation (anyURI minOccurs=0 maxOccurs=1)
> This attribute is a URI that specifies the location of the DISCO file.

/system/wsdlMap/disco/*{any}* (minOccurs=0 maxOccurs=unbounded)
/system/*{any}* (minOccurs=0 maxOccurs=unbounded)

The .NET services service/Methods

The .NET services service supports the following standard and domain-specific methods:

- query
- insert
- replace
- delete
- update

The standard methods operate on this service using the same message format and method-interchange techniques described in the hsdl section of this document. The only service-specific information to note is the schema that is in effect for each of the methods. These schemas and how they relate to the standard methods and roles are described in the roles section of this document.

The domain-specific methods operate as described in the domain-specific methods section of this document, and are governed by the various schemas outlined in the .NET services service/Roles section for this service.

CHAPTER 22

The .NET Wallet Service/Introduction

The .NET wallet service is designed to store and manage the following information for the associated identity:

- Payment Instruments information. A payment instrument is a payment method that the identity will use to pay. The .NET wallet service stores the following types of payment instruments.
- Card-based payment instruments like credit card, debit card, etc.
- Account-based payment instruments like traditional checking account and saving account or non-traditional account that allow a user to accumulate charges and be billed on a regular basis.

The .NET wallet service supplies the above information on demand to .Net-based services, applications, and devices. .NET wallet service uses Microsoft .NET My Services base services to support a rich sharing model based upon the access control list, role map, and identity header.

The .NET wallet service exposes the changeNotify method to be used on the .NET wallet element only. When such an operation occurs on .NET wallet with a pending changeNotify request, a notification will be sent to the subscriber via the .NET Notifications Service.

The .NET Wallet Service/Roles

The .NET wallet service controls access by using the following roleTemplates:

- rt0
- rt1
- rt2
- rt3
- rt99

The .NET wallet service uses the following scopes:

- **scope id 1**

```
<hs:scope id=1>

    <hs:shape base=t>

    </hs:shape>

</hs:scope>
```

- **scope id 2**

```
<hs:scope id=2>

    <hs:shape base=nil>

        <hs:include select=//*[@creator='$callerId']/>

    </hs:shape>

</hs:scope>
```

- **scope id 3**

```
<hs:scope id=3>

    <hs:shape base=nil>

        <hs:include select=//subscription[@creator='$callerId']/>

    </hs:shape>

</hs:scope>
```

- **scope id 4**

```
<hs:scope id=4>

    <hs:shape base=nil>

        <hs:include select=//*[cat/@ref='hs:public']/>

        <hs:include select=//subscription[@creator='$callerId']/>

    </hs:shape>

</hs:scope>
```

The .NET wallet service roleTemplate rt0

The purpose of this role is to give complete read/write access to all information within the content document of the service being protected through this roleTemplate.

The following table illustrates the available methods and the scope in effect when accessing the .NET wallet service through that method while mapped to this roleTemplate.

method	scopeRef
query	scopeRef=1
insert	scopeRef=1
replace	scopeRef=1
delete	scopeRef=1
update	scopeRef=1

The .NET wallet service roleTemplate rt1

The purpose of this role is to give complete read access to all information within the content document of the service being protected through this roleTemplate. Applications mapping to this role also have a limited ability to write to information in the content document. They may create nodes in any location, but may only change/replace, or delete nodes that they created.

The following table illustrates the available methods and the scope in effect when accessing the .NET wallet service through that method while mapped to this roleTemplate.

method	scopeRef
query	scopeRef=1
insert	scopeRef=2
replace	scopeRef=2
delete	scopeRef=2

The .NET wallet service roleTemplate rt2

The purpose of this role is to give complete read access to all information within the content document of the service being protected through this roleTemplate. Applications mapping to this role have very limited write access and are only able to create and manipulate their own subscription nodes.

The following table illustrates the available methods and the scope in effect when accessing the .NET wallet service through that method while mapped to this roleTemplate.

method	scopeRef
query	scopeRef=1
insert	scopeRef=3
replace	scopeRef=3
delete	scopeRef=3

The .NET wallet service roleTemplate rt3

The purpose of this role is to give limited read access to information within the content document that is categorized as "public".

The following table illustrates the available methods and the scope in effect when accessing the .NET wallet service through that method while mapped to this roleTemplate.

method	scopeRef
query	scopeRef=4

The .NET wallet service roleTemplate rt99

The purpose of this role is to block all access to the content document. Note that the lack of a role in the roleList has the same effect as assigning someone to rt99.

The .NET Wallet Service/Content

The content document is an identity-centric document. Its content and meaning is a function of the Microsoft Passport Unique ID (PUID) used to address the service. Access to the document is controlled by the associated roleList document.

This schema outline illustrates the layout and meaning of the information found in the content document for the .NET wallet service.

```
<m:myWallet changeNumber="..." instanceId="..."
    xmlns:m="http://schemas.microsoft.com/hs/2001/10/myWallet"
    xmlns:hs="http://schemas.microsoft.com/hs/2001/10/core">1..1
    <m:card changeNumber="..." id="..." creator="...">0..unbounded
        <m:cat ref="...">0..unbounded</m:cat>
        <m:typeOfCard>1..1</m:typeOfCard>
        <m:networkBrand>1..1</m:networkBrand>
        <m:affiliateBrand ref="...">0..1</m:affiliateBrand>
        <m:cardNumber>1..1</m:cardNumber>
        <m:displayNumber>1..1</m:displayNumber>
        <m:nameOnCard xml:lang="...">1..1</m:nameOnCard>
```

```
<m:description xml:lang="...">₁..₁</m:description>
<m:expirationDate>₀..₁</m:expirationDate>
<m:issueDate>₀..₁</m:issueDate>
<m:validFromDate>₀..₁</m:validFromDate>
<m:issueNumber>₀..₁</m:issueNumber>
<m:currency>₁..₁
    <m:currencyCode>₁..₁</m:currencyCode>
</m:currency>
<m:billingAddress>₁..₁
    <m:cat ref="...">₀..unbounded</m:cat>
    <m:officialAddressLine xml:lang="...">₀..₁</m:officialAddressLine>
    <m:internalAddressLine xml:lang="...">₀..₁</m:internalAddressLine>
    <m:primaryCity xml:lang="...">₀..₁</m:primaryCity>
    <m:secondaryCity xml:lang="...">₀..₁</m:secondaryCity>
    <m:subdivision xml:lang="...">₀..₁</m:subdivision>
    <m:postalCode>₀..₁</m:postalCode>
    <m:countryOrRegion xml:lang="...">₀..₁</m:countryOrRegion>
    <m:geoLocation>₀..₁
        <m:reportingDevice>₀..₁
            <m:deviceId>₀..₁</m:deviceId>
            <m:deviceName>₀..₁</m:deviceName>
            {any}
        </m:reportingDevice>
        <m:latitude>₀..₁</m:latitude>
        <m:longitude>₀..₁</m:longitude>
        <m:elevation>₀..₁</m:elevation>
        <m:confidence>₀..₁</m:confidence>
        <m:precision>₀..₁</m:precision>
        {any}
    </m:geoLocation>
    {any}
</m:billingAddress>
<m:paymentInstrumentsIssuer>₀..₁
    <m:typeOfIssuer>₁..₁</m:typeOfIssuer>
    <m:issuerPuid>₀..₁</m:issuerPuid>
    <m:issuerName xml:lang="...">₁..₁</m:issuerName>
    <m:issuerUrl>₀..₁</m:issuerUrl>
    <m:serviceUrl>₀..₁</m:serviceUrl>
    <m:address>₀..₁
        <m:cat ref="...">₀..unbounded</m:cat>
        <m:officialAddressLine xml:lang="...">₀..₁</m:officialAddressLine>
        <m:internalAddressLine xml:lang="...">₀..₁</m:internalAddressLine>
        <m:primaryCity xml:lang="...">₀..₁</m:primaryCity>
        <m:secondaryCity xml:lang="...">₀..₁</m:secondaryCity>
        <m:subdivision xml:lang="...">₀..₁</m:subdivision>
```

(continued)

(continued)

```
                <m:postalCode>₀․․₁</m:postalCode>
                <m:countryOrRegion xml:lang="...">₀․․₁</m:countryOrRegion>
                <m:geoLocation>₀․․₁
                    <m:reportingDevice>₀․․₁
                        <m:deviceId>₀․․₁</m:deviceId>
                        <m:deviceName>₀․․₁</m:deviceName>
                        {any}
                    </m:reportingDevice>
                    <m:latitude>₀․․₁</m:latitude>
                    <m:longitude>₀․․₁</m:longitude>
                    <m:elevation>₀․․₁</m:elevation>
                    <m:confidence>₀․․₁</m:confidence>
                    <m:precision>₀․․₁</m:precision>
                    {any}
                </m:geoLocation>
                {any}
            </m:address>
            <m:contactPhone>₀․․₁
                <hs:cat ref="...">₀․․unbounded</hs:cat>
                <hs:countryCode>₀․․₁</hs:countryCode>
                <hs:nationalCode>₁․․₁</hs:nationalCode>
                <hs:number>₁․․₁</hs:number>
                <hs:numberExtension>₀․․₁</hs:numberExtension>
                <hs:pin>₀․․₁</hs:pin>
                {any}
            </m:contactPhone>
            <m:contactEmail>₀․․₁</m:contactEmail>
            <m:swiftCode>₀․․₁</m:swiftCode>
        </m:paymentInstrumentsIssuer>
        {any}
    </m:card>
    <m:account changeNumber="..." id="..." creator="...">₀․․unbounded
        <m:cat ref="...">₀․․unbounded</m:cat>
        <m:typeOfAccount>₁․․₁</m:typeOfAccount>
        <m:accountRoutingNumber>₀․․₁</m:accountRoutingNumber>
        <m:accountNumber xml:lang="...">₁․․₁</m:accountNumber>
        <m:displayNumber>₁․․₁</m:displayNumber>
        <m:nameOnAccount xml:lang="...">₁․․₁</m:nameOnAccount>
        <m:description xml:lang="...">₁․․₁</m:description>
        <m:currency>₁․․₁
            <m:currencyCode>₁․․₁</m:currencyCode>
        </m:currency>
```

```
<m:accountAddress>₁..₁
    <m:cat ref="...">₀..unbounded</m:cat>
    <m:officialAddressLine xml:lang="...">₀..₁</m:officialAddressLine>
    <m:internalAddressLine xml:lang="...">₀..₁</m:internalAddressLine>
    <m:primaryCity xml:lang="...">₀..₁</m:primaryCity>
    <m:secondaryCity xml:lang="...">₀..₁</m:secondaryCity>
    <m:subdivision xml:lang="...">₀..₁</m:subdivision>
    <m:postalCode>₀..₁</m:postalCode>
    <m:countryOrRegion xml:lang="...">₀..₁</m:countryOrRegion>
    <m:geoLocation>₀..₁
        <m:reportingDevice>₀..₁
            <m:deviceId>₀..₁</m:deviceId>
            <m:deviceName>₀..₁</m:deviceName>
            {any}
        </m:reportingDevice>
        <m:latitude>₀..₁</m:latitude>
        <m:longitude>₀..₁</m:longitude>
        <m:elevation>₀..₁</m:elevation>
        <m:confidence>₀..₁</m:confidence>
        <m:precision>₀..₁</m:precision>
        {any}
    </m:geoLocation>
    {any}
</m:accountAddress>
<m:paymentInstrumentsIssuer>₀..₁
    <m:typeOfIssuer>₁..₁</m:typeOfIssuer>
    <m:issuerPuid>₀..₁</m:issuerPuid>
    <m:issuerName xml:lang="...">₁..₁</m:issuerName>
    <m:issuerUrl>₀..₁</m:issuerUrl>
    <m:serviceUrl>₀..₁</m:serviceUrl>
    <m:address>₀..₁
        <m:cat ref="...">₀..unbounded</m:cat>
        <m:officialAddressLine xml:lang="...">₀..₁</m:officialAddressLine>
        <m:internalAddressLine xml:lang="...">₀..₁</m:internalAddressLine>
        <m:primaryCity xml:lang="...">₀..₁</m:primaryCity>
        <m:secondaryCity xml:lang="...">₀..₁</m:secondaryCity>
        <m:subdivision xml:lang="...">₀..₁</m:subdivision>
        <m:postalCode>₀..₁</m:postalCode>
        <m:countryOrRegion xml:lang="...">₀..₁</m:countryOrRegion>
        <m:geoLocation>₀..₁
            <m:reportingDevice>₀..₁
                <m:deviceId>₀..₁</m:deviceId>
                <m:deviceName>₀..₁</m:deviceName>
                {any}
            </m:reportingDevice>
```

(continued)

(continued)

```
                    <m:latitude>₀..₁</m:latitude>
                    <m:longitude>₀..₁</m:longitude>
                    <m:elevation>₀..₁</m:elevation>
                    <m:confidence>₀..₁</m:confidence>
                    <m:precision>₀..₁</m:precision>
                    {any}
                </m:geoLocation>
                {any}
            </m:address>
            <m:contactPhone>₀..₁
                <hs:cat ref="...">₀..unbounded</hs:cat>
                <hs:countryCode>₀..₁</hs:countryCode>
                <hs:nationalCode>₁..₁</hs:nationalCode>
                <hs:number>₁..₁</hs:number>
                <hs:numberExtension>₀..₁</hs:numberExtension>
                <hs:pin>₀..₁</hs:pin>
                {any}
            </m:contactPhone>
            <m:contactEmail>₀..₁</m:contactEmail>
            <m:swiftCode>₀..₁</m:swiftCode>
        </m:paymentInstrumentsIssuer>
        {any}
    </m:account>
    <m:subscription changeNumber="..." id="..." creator="...">₀..unbounded
        <hs:trigger select="..." mode="..."
baseChangeNumber="...">₁..₁</hs:trigger>
        <hs:expiresAt>₀..₁</hs:expiresAt>
        <hs:context uri="...">₁..₁ {any}</hs:context>
        <hs:to>₁..₁</hs:to>
    </m:subscription>
</m:myWallet>
```

The meaning of the attributes and elements shown in the preceding sample document fragment are listed in the following section.

/myWallet (minOccurs=1 maxOccurs=1)

/myWallet/@changeNumber (minOccurs=0 maxOccurs=1)

The changeNumber attribute is designed to facilitate caching of the element and its descendants. This attribute is assigned to this element by the .NET My Services system. The attribute is read-only to applications. Attempts to write this attribute are silently ignored.

/myWallet/@instanceId (string minOccurs=0 maxOccurs=1)

This attribute is a unique identifier typically assigned to the root element of a service. It is a read-only element and assigned by the .NET My Services system when a user is provisioned for a particular service.

/myWallet/card (minOccurs=0 maxOccurs=unbounded)

This element encapsulates information associated with the card-like payment instruments.

/myWallet/card/@changeNumber (minOccurs=0 maxOccurs=1)

The changeNumber attribute is designed to facilitate caching of the element and its descendants. This attribute is assigned to this element by the .NET My Services system. The attribute is read-only to applications. Attempts to write this attribute are silently ignored.

/myWallet/card/@id (minOccurs=0 maxOccurs=1)

This attribute is a globally unique ID assigned to this element by .NET My Services. Normally, .NET My Services will generate and assign this ID during an insertRequest operation, or possibly during a replaceRequest. Application software can override this ID generation by specifying the useClientIds attribute in the request message. Once an ID is assigned, the attribute is read-only and attempts to write it are silently ignored.

/myWallet/card/@creator (string minOccurs=0 maxOccurs=1)

This attribute identifies the creator in terms of userId, appId, and platformId of the node.

/myWallet/card/cat (minOccurs=0 maxOccurs=unbounded)

This element is used to categorize the element that contains it by referencing a global category definition in either the .NET categories service system document or an external resource containing category definitions, or by referencing an identity-centric category definition in the content document of the .NET categories service for a particular PUID.

/myWallet/card/cat/@ref (anyURI minOccurs=0 maxOccurs=1)

This attribute references a category definition (<catDef/>) element using the rules outlined in the .NET Categories Service.

/myWallet/card/typeOfCard (string minOccurs=1 maxOccurs=1)

This required element is designed to store the card type. Examples are credit card, debit card, etc. Valid values are defined in the enumeration list in the schema.

/myWallet/card/networkBrand (string minOccurs=1 maxOccurs=1)

This required element is designed to store the global or regional/national well recognized and accepted card brand, also known as card type. This is to ensure a naming convention among various applications and/or services so that data is usable across these applications and/or services. Examples are VISA, MasterCard, American Express, Discover, Diners Club, and so on. Valid values are defined in the enumeration list in the schema.

/myWallet/card/affiliateBrand (minOccurs=0 maxOccurs=1)

This optional element is designed to store the affiliated brand (i.e. sub-brand) or private brand for the card. Examples are Carte Bleue (a co-branded VISA debit card used in France), NHL Platinum credit card (a cobranded MasterCard issued by MBNA), Sears card, Starbucks card, and so on. The .NET wallet service will not restrict the list. It is up to the application to validate and define a list of supported cards.

/myWallet/card/affiliateBrand/@ref (anyURI minOccurs=0 maxOccurs=1)
> This attribute references a category definition (<catDef/>) element using the rules outlined in the .NET Categories Service.

/myWallet/card/cardNumber (string minOccurs=1 maxOccurs=1)
> The card number. Required. Here is the validation rules for listed networkBrand types:
> - VISA—prefix 4, card# length 16 or 13, Luhn mod 10 check sum
> - Mastercard—prefix 51-55, card# length 16, Luhn mod 10 check sum
> - American Express, prefix 34 or 37, card# length 15, Luhn mod 10 check sum
> - Discover, prefix 6011, card# length 16, Luhn mod 10 check sum
> - Diners Club, prefix 300-305 or 36 or 38, card# length 14, Luhn mod 10 check sum
> - JCB, prefix 3, card# length 16, Luhn mod 10 check sum

/myWallet/card/displayNumber (string minOccurs=1 maxOccurs=1)
> The last four digits of the card number. Required. This will be a read-only field derived from the card number by the system.

/myWallet/card/nameOnCard (string minOccurs=1 maxOccurs=1)
> The card holder's name. This element is mandatory.

/myWallet/card/nameOnCard/@xml:lang (minOccurs=1 maxOccurs=1)
> This required attribute is used to specify an ISO 639 language code or an ISO 3166 country code as described in RFC 1766. The value of this attribute indicates the language type of the content within this element.

/myWallet/card/description (string minOccurs=1 maxOccurs=1)
> A short description of the card for easy reference (i.e. my Bank X Visa, my corp Amex, etc.). Mandatory.

/myWallet/card/description/@xml:lang (minOccurs=1 maxOccurs=1)
> This required attribute is used to specify an ISO 639 language code or an ISO 3166 country code as described in RFC 1766. The value of this attribute indicates the language type of the content within this element.

/myWallet/card/expirationDate (dateTime minOccurs=0 maxOccurs=1)
> The expiration date of a card. Optional.

/myWallet/card/issueDate (dateTime minOccurs=0 maxOccurs=1)
> The date that this card is issued. Optional.

/myWallet/card/validFromDate (dateTime minOccurs=0 maxOccurs=1)
> The date from which the card is valid. Optional.

/myWallet/card/issueNumber (string minOccurs=0 maxOccurs=1)
> The issue number of the card. Used by some types of debit card, (i.e. Switch card). Optional.

/myWallet/card/currency (minOccurs=1 maxOccurs=1)
> The billing currency of this card. Optional.

/myWallet/card/currency/currencyCode (string minOccurs=1 maxOccurs=1)
> The three letter ISO 4217 currency code. Examples are USD (U.S. dollar), GBP (United Kingdom pound), etc.

/myWallet/card/billingAddress (minOccurs=1 maxOccurs=1)
> The billing address of the card. Mandatory.

/myWallet/card/billingAddress/cat (minOccurs=0 maxOccurs=unbounded)
> This element is used to categorize the element that contains it by referencing a global category definition in either the .NET categories service system document or an external resource containing category definitions, or by referencing an identity-centric category definition in the content document of the .NET categories service for a particular PUID.

/myWallet/card/billingAddress/cat/@ref (anyURI minOccurs=0 maxOccurs=1)
> This attribute references a category definition (<catDef/>) element using the rules outlined in the .NET Categories Service.

/myWallet/card/billingAddress/officialAddressLine (string minOccurs=0 maxOccurs=1)
> This element contains the most precise, official line for the address, relative to the postal agency servicing the area specified by the city/postalCode. When an address is parsed for official postal usage, this element contains the official, parsable address line that the regional postal system cares about. Typical use of this element would be to enclose a street address, post office box address, private bag, or any other similar official address. Internal routing information (such as department name, suite number within a building, or internal mailstop number) should be placed within the internalAddressLine element.

/myWallet/card/billingAddress/officialAddressLine/@xml:lang (minOccurs=1 maxOccurs=1)
> This required attribute is used to specify an ISO 639 language code or an ISO 3166 country code as described in RFC 1766. The value of this attribute indicates the language type of the content within this element.

/myWallet/card/billingAddress/internalAddressLine (string minOccurs=0 maxOccurs=1)
> This element contains internal routing information relative to the address specified by the officialAddressLine. Items such as department name, suite number within a building, or internal mailstop number should be placed within this element.

/myWallet/card/billingAddress/internalAddressLine/@xml:lang (minOccurs=1 maxOccurs=1)
> This required attribute is used to specify an ISO 639 language code or an ISO 3166 country code as described in RFC 1766. The value of this attribute indicates the language type of the content within this element.

/myWallet/card/billingAddress/primaryCity (string minOccurs=0 maxOccurs=1)
> This element defines the primary city for this address.

/myWallet/card/billingAddress/primaryCity/@xml:lang (minOccurs=1 maxOccurs=1)
> This required attribute is used to specify an ISO 639 language code or an ISO 3166 country code as described in RFC 1766. The value of this attribute indicates the language type of the content within this element.

/myWallet/card/billingAddress/secondaryCity (string minOccurs=0 maxOccurs=1)
> This optional element defines the secondary city for this address. Example types for this element include city district, city wards, postal towns, and so on.

/myWallet/card/billingAddress/secondaryCity/@xml:lang (minOccurs=1 maxOccurs=1)
This required attribute is used to specify an ISO 639 language code or an ISO 3166 country code as described in RFC 1766. The value of this attribute indicates the language type of the content within this element.

/myWallet/card/billingAddress/subdivision (string minOccurs=0 maxOccurs=1)
This element contains the official subdivision name within the country or region for this address. In the United States, this element would contain the two-letter abbreviation for the name of the state. This element is also commonly treated as the "first order admin subdivision" and will typically contain subdivision names referring to:

- administrative division
- Bundesstaat
- canton
- federal district
- province
- region
- state
- territory

/myWallet/card/billingAddress/subdivision/@xml:lang (minOccurs=1 maxOccurs=1)
This required attribute is used to specify an ISO 639 language code or an ISO 3166 country code as described in RFC 1766. The value of this attribute indicates the language type of the content within this element.

/myWallet/card/billingAddress/postalCode (string minOccurs=0 maxOccurs=1)
This element contains the official postal code for this address.

/myWallet/card/billingAddress/countryOrRegion (string minOccurs=0 maxOccurs=1)
This element contains the name of the country, dependency, or functionally equivalent region for this address.

/myWallet/card/billingAddress/countryOrRegion/@xml:lang (minOccurs=1 maxOccurs=1)
This required attribute is used to specify an ISO 639 language code or an ISO 3166 country code as described in RFC 1766. The value of this attribute indicates the language type of the content within this element.

/myWallet/card/billingAddress/geoLocation (minOccurs=0 maxOccurs=1)
This element encapsulates a geographic (or earth) position corresponding to the enclosing address.

/myWallet/card/billingAddress/geoLocation/reportingDevice (minOccurs=0 maxOccurs=1)
This element contains the UUID and name for this specific device. The UUID for a specific device is the same as its "Universal Device Number," as exposed by the Universal Plug and Play infrastructure.

/myWallet/card/billingAddress/geoLocation/reportingDevice/deviceId (minOccurs=0 maxOccurs=1)
This element specifies the UUID or Universal Device Number for this device.

/myWallet/card/billingAddress/geoLocation/reportingDevice/deviceName (string minOccurs=0 maxOccurs=1)

This element specifies a friendly name for this device.

/myWallet/card/billingAddress/geoLocation/reportingDevice/*{any}* (minOccurs=0 maxOccurs=unbounded)

/myWallet/card/billingAddress/geoLocation/latitude (string minOccurs=0 maxOccurs=1)

This element specifies the latitude value for this geoLocation in units of decimal degrees. Geodetic datum WGS84 is required.

/myWallet/card/billingAddress/geoLocation/longitude (string minOccurs=0 maxOccurs=1)

This element specifies the longitude value for this geoLocation in units of decimal degrees. Geodetic datum WGS84 is required.

/myWallet/card/billingAddress/geoLocation/elevation (string minOccurs=0 maxOccurs=1)

This element specifies the elevation above sea level with respect to WGS84 geodetic datum. The measurement unit for this value is the meter.

/myWallet/card/billingAddress/geoLocation/confidence (string minOccurs=0 maxOccurs=1)

This element specifies a percentage value that indicates the level of confidence that this location is accurate within the specified precision.

/myWallet/card/billingAddress/geoLocation/precision (string minOccurs=0 maxOccurs=1)

This element specifies the precision in meters of this location. The value defines a spherical zone within which the location falls.

/myWallet/card/billingAddress/geoLocation/*{any}* (minOccurs=0 maxOccurs=unbounded)

/myWallet/card/billingAddress/*{any}* (minOccurs=0 maxOccurs=unbounded)

/myWallet/card/paymentInstrumentsIssuer (minOccurs=0 maxOccurs=1)

This optional element is meant to store the issuer for this card. An issuer for a card is usually a financial institution.

/myWallet/card/paymentInstrumentsIssuer/typeOfIssuer (string minOccurs=1 maxOccurs=1)

Indicates whether a payment instrument issuer is a bank, a credit card issuer (e.g. Amex), a service provider for a stored value account, a phone carrier, an ISP for billToAccount, etc.

/myWallet/card/paymentInstrumentsIssuer/issuerPuid (string minOccurs=0 maxOccurs=1)

The Passport ID of the issuer. Only a .NET My Services enabled issuer will have Passport ID. Optional.

/myWallet/card/paymentInstrumentsIssuer/issuerName (string minOccurs=1 maxOccurs=1)

Name of the issuer. Mandatory.

/myWallet/card/paymentInstrumentsIssuer/issuerName/@xml:lang (minOccurs=1 maxOccurs=1)

This required attribute is used to specify an ISO 639 language code or an ISO 3166 country code as described in RFC 1766. The value of this attribute indicates the language type of the content within this element.

/myWallet/card/paymentInstrumentsIssuer/issuerUrl (string minOccurs=0 maxOccurs=1)

The URL for the issuer's Web site. Optional.

/myWallet/card/paymentInstrumentsIssuer/serviceUrl (string minOccurs=0 maxOccurs=1)

The base URL to get various services (i.e. credit card balance, credit limit, etc). Optional.

/myWallet/card/paymentInstrumentsIssuer/address (minOccurs=0 maxOccurs=1)

The address of the issuer. Optional.

/myWallet/card/paymentInstrumentsIssuer/address/cat (minOccurs=0 maxOccurs=unbounded)

This element is used to categorize the element that contains it by referencing a global category definition in either the .NET categories service system document or an external resource containing category definitions, or by referencing an identity-centric category definition in the content document of the .NET categories service for a particular PUID.

/myWallet/card/paymentInstrumentsIssuer/address/cat/@ref (anyURI minOccurs=0 maxOccurs=1)

This attribute references a category definition (<catDef/>) element using the rules outlined in the .NET Categories Service.

/myWallet/card/paymentInstrumentsIssuer/address/officialAddressLine (string minOccurs=0 maxOccurs=1)

This element contains the most precise, official line for the address, relative to the postal agency servicing the area specified by the city/postalCode. When an address is parsed for official postal usage, this element contains the official, parseable address line that the regional postal system cares about. Typical use of this element would be to enclose a street address, post office box address, private bag, or any other similar official address. Internal routing information (such as department name, suite number within a building, or internal mailstop number) should be placed within the internalAddressLine element.

/myWallet/card/paymentInstrumentsIssuer/address/officialAddressLine/@xml:lang (minOccurs=1 maxOccurs=1)

This required attribute is used to specify an ISO 639 language code or an ISO 3166 country code as described in RFC 1766. The value of this attribute indicates the language type of the content within this element.

/myWallet/card/paymentInstrumentsIssuer/address/internalAddressLine (string minOccurs=0 maxOccurs=1)

This element contains internal routing information relative to the address specified by the officialAddressLine. Items such as department name, suite number within a building, or internal mailstop number should be placed within this element.

/myWallet/card/paymentInstrumentsIssuer/address/internalAddressLine/@xml:lang (minOccurs=1 maxOccurs=1)

> This required attribute is used to specify an ISO 639 language code or an ISO 3166 country code as described in RFC 1766. The value of this attribute indicates the language type of the content within this element.

/myWallet/card/paymentInstrumentsIssuer/address/primaryCity (string minOccurs=0 maxOccurs=1)

> This element defines the primary city for this address.

/myWallet/card/paymentInstrumentsIssuer/address/primaryCity/@xml:lang (minOccurs=1 maxOccurs=1)

> This required attribute is used to specify an ISO 639 language code or an ISO 3166 country code as described in RFC 1766. The value of this attribute indicates the language type of the content within this element.

/myWallet/card/paymentInstrumentsIssuer/address/secondaryCity (string minOccurs=0 maxOccurs=1)

> This optional element defines the secondary city for this address. Example types for this element include city district, city wards, postal towns, and so on.

/myWallet/card/paymentInstrumentsIssuer/address/secondaryCity/@xml:lang (minOccurs=1 maxOccurs=1)

> This required attribute is used to specify an ISO 639 language code or an ISO 3166 country code as described in RFC 1766. The value of this attribute indicates the language type of the content within this element.

/myWallet/card/paymentInstrumentsIssuer/address/subdivision (string minOccurs=0 maxOccurs=1)

> This element contains the official subdivision name within the country or region for this address. In the United States, this element would contain the two-letter abbreviation for the name of the state. This element is also commonly treated as the "first order admin subdivision" and will typically contain subdivision names referring to:

- administrative division
- Bundesstaat
- canton
- federal district
- province
- region
- state
- territory

/myWallet/card/paymentInstrumentsIssuer/address/subdivision/@xml:lang (minOccurs=1 maxOccurs=1)

> This required attribute is used to specify an ISO 639 language code or an ISO 3166 country code as described in RFC 1766. The value of this attribute indicates the language type of the content within this element.

/myWallet/card/paymentInstrumentsIssuer/address/postalCode (string minOccurs=0 maxOccurs=1)

This element contains the official postal code for this address.

/myWallet/card/paymentInstrumentsIssuer/address/countryOrRegion (string minOccurs=0 maxOccurs=1)

This element contains the name of the country, dependency, or functionally equivalent region for this address.

/myWallet/card/paymentInstrumentsIssuer/address/countryOrRegion/@xml:lang (minOccurs=1 maxOccurs=1)

This required attribute is used to specify an ISO 639 language code or an ISO 3166 country code as described in RFC 1766. The value of this attribute indicates the language type of the content within this element.

/myWallet/card/paymentInstrumentsIssuer/address/geoLocation (minOccurs=0 maxOccurs=1)

This element encapsulates a geographic (or earth) position corresponding to the enclosing address.

/myWallet/card/paymentInstrumentsIssuer/address/geoLocation/reportingDevice (minOccurs=0 maxOccurs=1)

This element contains the UUID and name for this specific device. The UUID for a specific device is the same as its "Universal Device Number," as exposed by the Universal Plug and Play infrastructure.

/myWallet/card/paymentInstrumentsIssuer/address/geoLocation/reportingDevice/deviceId (minOccurs=0 maxOccurs=1)

This element specifies the UUID or Universal Device Number for this device.

/myWallet/card/paymentInstrumentsIssuer/address/geoLocation/reportingDevice/deviceName (string minOccurs=0 maxOccurs=1)

This element specifies a friendly name for this device.

/myWallet/card/paymentInstrumentsIssuer/address/geoLocation/reportingDevice/*{any}* (minOccurs=0 maxOccurs=unbounded)

/myWallet/card/paymentInstrumentsIssuer/address/geoLocation/latitude (string minOccurs=0 maxOccurs=1)

This element specifies the latitude value for this geoLocation in units of decimal degrees. Geodetic datum WGS84 is required.

/myWallet/card/paymentInstrumentsIssuer/address/geoLocation/longitude (string minOccurs=0 maxOccurs=1)

This element specifies the longitude value for this geoLocation in units of decimal degrees. Geodetic datum WGS84 is required.

/myWallet/card/paymentInstrumentsIssuer/address/geoLocation/elevation (string minOccurs=0 maxOccurs=1)

This element specifies the elevation above sea level with respect to WGS84 geodetic datum. The measurement unit for this value is the meter.

/myWallet/card/paymentInstrumentsIssuer/address/geoLocation/confidence (string minOccurs=0 maxOccurs=1)

This element specifies a percentage value that indicates the level of confidence that this location is accurate within the specified precision.

/myWallet/card/paymentInstrumentsIssuer/address/geoLocation/precision (string minOccurs=0 maxOccurs=1)

This element specifies the precision in meters of this location. The value defines a spherical zone within which the location falls.

/myWallet/card/paymentInstrumentsIssuer/address/geoLocation/*{any}* (minOccurs=0 maxOccurs=unbounded)

/myWallet/card/paymentInstrumentsIssuer/address/*{any}* (minOccurs=0 maxOccurs=unbounded)

/myWallet/card/paymentInstrumentsIssuer/contactPhone (minOccurs=0 maxOccurs=1)

The contact phone number. Optional.

/myWallet/card/paymentInstrumentsIssuer/contactPhone/cat (minOccurs=0 maxOccurs=unbounded)

This element is used to categorize the element that contains it by referencing a global category definition in either the .NET categories service system document or an external resource containing category definitions, or by referencing an identity-centric category definition in the content document of the .NET categories service for a particular PUID.

/myWallet/card/paymentInstrumentsIssuer/contactPhone/cat/@ref (anyURI minOccurs=0 maxOccurs=1)

This attribute references a category definition (<catDef/>) element using the rules outlined in the .NET Categories Service.

/myWallet/card/paymentInstrumentsIssuer/contactPhone/countryCode (string minOccurs=0 maxOccurs=1)

This optional element specifies the country code for this telephone number.

/myWallet/card/paymentInstrumentsIssuer/contactPhone/nationalCode (string minOccurs=1 maxOccurs=1)

This element specifies the national code for this phone number. For US telephone numbers, this is equivalent to the area code.

/myWallet/card/paymentInstrumentsIssuer/contactPhone/number (string minOccurs=1 maxOccurs=1)

This element specifies the actual telephone number within the country and national code number scheme.

/myWallet/card/paymentInstrumentsIssuer/contactPhone/numberExtension (string minOccurs=0 maxOccurs=1)

This optional element specifies an extension used to reach this identity and this number.

/myWallet/card/paymentInstrumentsIssuer/contactPhone/pin (string minOccurs=0 maxOccurs=1)

> This optional element specifies a PIN number used on this phone number. A PIN is similar to an extension, but PINs are commonly used to address pagers while extensions are typically used to address phones relative to a local pbx.

/myWallet/card/paymentInstrumentsIssuer/contactPhone/*{any}* (minOccurs=0 maxOccurs=unbounded)

/myWallet/card/paymentInstrumentsIssuer/contactEmail (string minOccurs=0 maxOccurs=1)

> The contact e-mail address. Optional.

/myWallet/card/paymentInstrumentsIssuer/swiftCode (string minOccurs=0 maxOccurs=1)

> A global unique number that identifies the issuer in the SWIFT system for funds transfer between different countries.

/myWallet/card/*{any}* (minOccurs=0 maxOccurs=unbounded)

/myWallet/account (minOccurs=0 maxOccurs=unbounded)

> This element encapsulates information associated with the account like payment instruments. It can be a traditional bank account or it can be an account with a service provider that charges to the account are accumulated and billed to the account holder on a regular basis (such as phone bills, ISP bills, etc.).

/myWallet/account/@changeNumber (minOccurs=0 maxOccurs=1)

> The changeNumber attribute is designed to facilitate caching of the element and its descendants. This attribute is assigned to this element by the .NET My Services system. The attribute is read-only to applications. Attempts to write this attribute are silently ignored.

/myWallet/account/@id (minOccurs=0 maxOccurs=1)

> This attribute is a globally unique ID assigned to this element by .NET My Services. Normally, .NET My Services will generate and assign this ID during an insertRequest operation, or possibly during a replaceRequest. Application software can override this ID generation by specifying the useClientIds attribute in the request message. Once an ID is assigned, the attribute is read-only and attempts to write it are silently ignored.

/myWallet/account/@creator (string minOccurs=0 maxOccurs=1)

> This attribute identifies the creator in terms of userId, appId, and platformId of the node.

/myWallet/account/cat (minOccurs=0 maxOccurs=unbounded)

> This element is used to categorize the element that contains it by referencing a global category definition in either the .NET categories service system document or an external resource containing category definitions, or by referencing an identity-centric category definition in the content document of the .NET categories service for a particular PUID.

/myWallet/account/cat/@ref (anyURI minOccurs=0 maxOccurs=1)

> This attribute references a category definition (<catDef/>) element using the rules outlined in the .NET Categories Service.

/myWallet/account/typeOfAccount (string minOccurs=1 maxOccurs=1)
> This required element is designed to store the account type. Examples are checking, savings, stored value account, and billToAccount. Valid values are defined in the enumeration list in the schema.

/myWallet/account/accountRoutingNumber (string minOccurs=0 maxOccurs=1)
> This is the number that identifies the issuer of this account in a particular banking system. In the United States, it is the ACH routing transit number. Optional, as it is only applicable to traditional banking.

/myWallet/account/accountNumber (string minOccurs=1 maxOccurs=1)
> The account number. Mandatory.

/myWallet/account/accountNumber/@xml:lang (minOccurs=1 maxOccurs=1)
> This required attribute is used to specify an ISO 639 language code or an ISO 3166 country code as described in RFC 1766. The value of this attribute indicates the language type of the content within this element.

/myWallet/account/displayNumber (string minOccurs=1 maxOccurs=1)
> The last four characters or digits of the account number. Required. This will be a read-only field derived from account number by the system.

/myWallet/account/nameOnAccount (string minOccurs=1 maxOccurs=1)
> The account holder name.

/myWallet/account/nameOnAccount/@xml:lang (minOccurs=1 maxOccurs=1)
> This required attribute is used to specify an ISO 639 language code or an ISO 3166 country code as described in RFC 1766. The value of this attribute indicates the language type of the content within this element.

/myWallet/account/description (string minOccurs=1 maxOccurs=1)
> A short description for the account for easy reference (eg. my Bank X checking). Mandatory.

/myWallet/account/description/@xml:lang (minOccurs=1 maxOccurs=1)
> This required attribute is used to specify an ISO 639 language code or an ISO 3166 country code as described in RFC 1766. The value of this attribute indicates the language type of the content within this element.

/myWallet/account/currency (minOccurs=1 maxOccurs=1)
> The currency of this account. Optional.

/myWallet/account/currency/currencyCode (string minOccurs=1 maxOccurs=1)
> The three letter ISO 4217 currency code. Examples are USD (US dollar), GBP (United Kingdom pound), etc.

/myWallet/account/accountAddress (minOccurs=1 maxOccurs=1)
> The account address.

/myWallet/account/accountAddress/cat (minOccurs=0 maxOccurs=unbounded)
> This element is used to categorize the element that contains it by referencing a global category definition in either the .NET categories service system document or an external resource containing category definitions, or by referencing an identity-centric category definition in the content document of the .NET categories service for a particular PUID.

/myWallet/account/accountAddress/cat/@ref (anyURI minOccurs=0 maxOccurs=1)
This attribute references a category definition (<catDef/>) element using the rules outlined in the .NET Categories Service XMI manual

/myWallet/account/accountAddress/officialAddressLine (string minOccurs=0 maxOccurs=1)
This element contains the most precise, official line for the address, relative to the postal agency servicing the area specified by the city/postalCode. When an address is parsed for official postal usage, this element contains the official, parseable address line that the regional postal system cares about. Typical use of this element would be to enclose a street address, post office box address, private bag, or any other similar official address. Internal routing information (such as department name, suite number within a building, or internal mailstop number) should be placed within the internalAddressLine element.

/myWallet/account/accountAddress/officialAddressLine/@xml:lang (minOccurs=1 maxOccurs=1)
This required attribute is used to specify an ISO 639 language code or an ISO 3166 country code as described in RFC 1766. The value of this attribute indicates the language type of the content within this element.

/myWallet/account/accountAddress/internalAddressLine (string minOccurs=0 maxOccurs=1)
This element contains internal routing information relative to the address specified by the officialAddressLine. Items such as department name, suite number within a building, or internal mailstop number should be placed within this element.

/myWallet/account/accountAddress/internalAddressLine/@xml:lang (minOccurs=1 maxOccurs=1)
This required attribute is used to specify an ISO 639 language code or an ISO 3166 country code as described in RFC 1766. The value of this attribute indicates the language type of the content within this element.

/myWallet/account/accountAddress/primaryCity (string minOccurs=0 maxOccurs=1)
This element defines the primary city for this address.

/myWallet/account/accountAddress/primaryCity/@xml:lang (minOccurs=1 maxOccurs=1)
This required attribute is used to specify an ISO 639 language code or an ISO 3166 country code as described in RFC 1766. The value of this attribute indicates the language type of the content within this element.

/myWallet/account/accountAddress/secondaryCity (string minOccurs=0 maxOccurs=1)
This optional element defines the secondary city for this address. Example types for this element include city district, city wards, postal towns, and so on.

/myWallet/account/accountAddress/secondaryCity/@xml:lang (minOccurs=1 maxOccurs=1)
This required attribute is used to specify an ISO 639 language code or an ISO 3166 country code as described in RFC 1766. The value of this attribute indicates the language type of the content within this element.

/myWallet/account/accountAddress/subdivision (string minOccurs=0 maxOccurs=1)
This element contains the official subdivision name within the country or region for this address. In the United States, this element would contain the two-letter abbreviation for the name of the state. This element is also commonly treated as the "first order admin subdivision" and will typically contain subdivision names referring to:

- administrative division
- Bundesstaat
- canton
- federal district
- province
- region
- state
- territory

/myWallet/account/accountAddress/subdivision/@xml:lang (minOccurs=1 maxOccurs=1)
This required attribute is used to specify an ISO 639 language code or an ISO 3166 country code as described in RFC 1766. The value of this attribute indicates the language type of the content within this element.

/myWallet/account/accountAddress/postalCode (string minOccurs=0 maxOccurs=1)
This element contains the official postal code for this address.

/myWallet/account/accountAddress/countryOrRegion (string minOccurs=0 maxOccurs=1)
This element contains the name of the country, dependency, or functionally equivalent region for this address.

/myWallet/account/accountAddress/countryOrRegion/@xml:lang (minOccurs=1 maxOccurs=1)
This required attribute is used to specify an ISO 639 language code or an ISO 3166 country code as described in RFC 1766. The value of this attribute indicates the language type of the content within this element.

/myWallet/account/accountAddress/geoLocation (minOccurs=0 maxOccurs=1)
This element encapsulates a geographic (or earth) position corresponding to the enclosing address.

/myWallet/account/accountAddress/geoLocation/reportingDevice (minOccurs=0 maxOccurs=1)
This element contains the UUID and name for this specific device. The UUID for a specific device is the same as its "Universal Device Number," as exposed by the Universal Plug and Play infrastructure.

/myWallet/account/accountAddress/geoLocation/reportingDevice/deviceId (minOccurs=0 maxOccurs=1)
This element specifies the UUID or Universal Device Number for this device.

/myWallet/account/accountAddress/geoLocation/reportingDevice/deviceName (string minOccurs=0 maxOccurs=1)
This element specifies a friendly name for this device.

/myWallet/account/accountAddress/geoLocation/reportingDevice/*{any}* (minOccurs=0 maxOccurs=unbounded)

/myWallet/account/accountAddress/geoLocation/latitude (string minOccurs=0 maxOccurs=1)

This element specifies the latitude value for this geoLocation in units of decimal degrees. Geodetic datum WGS84 is required.

/myWallet/account/accountAddress/geoLocation/longitude (string minOccurs=0 maxOccurs=1)

This element specifies the longitude value for this geoLocation in units of decimal degrees. Geodetic datum WGS84 is required.

/myWallet/account/accountAddress/geoLocation/elevation (string minOccurs=0 maxOccurs=1)

This element specifies the elevation above sea level with respect to WGS84 geodetic datum. The measurement unit for this value is the meter.

/myWallet/account/accountAddress/geoLocation/confidence (string minOccurs=0 maxOccurs=1)

This element specifies a percentage value that indicates the level of confidence that this location is accurate within the specified precision.

/myWallet/account/accountAddress/geoLocation/precision (string minOccurs=0 maxOccurs=1)

This element specifies the precision in meters of this location. The value defines a spherical zone within which the location falls.

/myWallet/account/accountAddress/geoLocation/*{any}* (minOccurs=0 maxOccurs=unbounded)

/myWallet/account/accountAddress/*{any}* (minOccurs=0 maxOccurs=unbounded)

/myWallet/account/paymentInstrumentsIssuer (minOccurs=0 maxOccurs=1)

This optional element is meant to store the issuer for this account. An issuer for an account can be a financial institution for traditional bank accounts. It can also be a service provider for stored value accounts.

/myWallet/account/paymentInstrumentsIssuer/typeOfIssuer (string minOccurs=1 maxOccurs=1)

Indicates whether a payment instrument issuer is a bank, a credit card issuer (e.g. Amex), a service provider for a stored value account, a phone carrier or ISP for billToAccount, etc.

/myWallet/account/paymentInstrumentsIssuer/issuerPuid (string minOccurs=0 maxOccurs=1)

The Passport ID of the issuer. Only a .NET My Services enabled issuer will have Passport ID. Optional.

/myWallet/account/paymentInstrumentsIssuer/issuerName (string minOccurs=1 maxOccurs=1)

Name of the issuer. Mandatory.

/myWallet/account/paymentInstrumentsIssuer/issuerName/@xml:lang (minOccurs=1 maxOccurs=1)

This required attribute is used to specify an ISO 639 language code or an ISO 3166 country code as described in RFC 1766. The value of this attribute indicates the language type of the content within this element.

/myWallet/account/paymentInstrumentsIssuer/issuerUrl (string minOccurs=0 maxOccurs=1)

The URL for the issuer's Web site. Optional.

/myWallet/account/paymentInstrumentsIssuer/serviceUrl (string minOccurs=0 maxOccurs=1)

The base URL to get various services (for example credit card balance, credit limit, etc). Optional.

/myWallet/account/paymentInstrumentsIssuer/address (minOccurs=0 maxOccurs=1)

The address of the issuer. Optional.

/myWallet/account/paymentInstrumentsIssuer/address/cat (minOccurs=0 maxOccurs=unbounded)

This element is used to categorize the element that contains it by referencing a global category definition in either the .NET categories service system document or an external resource containing category definitions, or by referencing an identity-centric category definition in the content document of the .NET categories service for a particular PUID.

/myWallet/account/paymentInstrumentsIssuer/address/cat/@ref (anyURI minOccurs=0 maxOccurs=1)

This attribute references a category definition (<catDef/>) element using the rules outlined in the .NET Categories Service XMI manual

/myWallet/account/paymentInstrumentsIssuer/address/officialAddressLine (string minOccurs=0 maxOccurs=1)

This element contains the most precise, official line for the address, relative to the postal agency servicing the area specified by the city/postalCode. When an address is parsed for official postal usage, this element contains the official, parseable address line that the regional postal system cares about. Typical use of this element would be to enclose a street address, post office box address, private bag, or any other similar official address. Internal routing information (such as department name, suite number within a building, or internal mailstop number) should be placed within the internalAddressLine element.

/myWallet/account/paymentInstrumentsIssuer/address/officialAddressLine/@xml:lang (minOccurs=1 maxOccurs=1)

This required attribute is used to specify an ISO 639 language code or an ISO 3166 country code as described in RFC 1766. The value of this attribute indicates the language type of the content within this element.

/myWallet/account/paymentInstrumentsIssuer/address/internalAddressLine (string minOccurs=0 maxOccurs=1)

This element contains internal routing information relative to the address specified by the officialAddressLine. Items such as department name, suite number within a building, or internal mailstop number should be placed within this element.

/myWallet/account/paymentInstrumentsIssuer/address/internalAddressLine/@xml:lang (minOccurs=1 maxOccurs=1)

This required attribute is used to specify an ISO 639 language code or an ISO 3166 country code as described in RFC 1766. The value of this attribute indicates the language type of the content within this element.

/myWallet/account/paymentInstrumentsIssuer/address/primaryCity (string minOccurs=0 maxOccurs=1)

This element defines the primary city for this address.

/myWallet/account/paymentInstrumentsIssuer/address/primaryCity/@xml:lang (minOccurs=1 maxOccurs=1)

This required attribute is used to specify an ISO 639 language code or an ISO 3166 country code as described in RFC 1766. The value of this attribute indicates the language type of the content within this element.

/myWallet/account/paymentInstrumentsIssuer/address/secondaryCity (string minOccurs=0 maxOccurs=1)

This optional element defines the secondary city for this address. Example types for this element include city district, city wards, postal towns, and so on.

/myWallet/account/paymentInstrumentsIssuer/address/secondaryCity/@xml:lang (minOccurs=1 maxOccurs=1)

This required attribute is used to specify an ISO 639 language code or an ISO 3166 country code as described in RFC 1766. The value of this attribute indicates the language type of the content within this element.

/myWallet/account/paymentInstrumentsIssuer/address/subdivision (string minOccurs=0 maxOccurs=1)

This element contains the official subdivision name within the country or region for this address. In the United States, this element would contain the two-letter abbreviation for the name of the state. This element is also commonly treated as the "first order admin subdivision" and will typically contain subdivision names referring to:

- administrative division
- Bundesstaat
- canton
- federal district
- province
- region
- state
- territory

/myWallet/account/paymentInstrumentsIssuer/address/subdivision/@xml:lang
(minOccurs=1 maxOccurs=1)

This required attribute is used to specify an ISO 639 language code or an ISO 3166
country code as described in RFC 1766. The value of this attribute indicates the
language type of the content within this element.

/myWallet/account/paymentInstrumentsIssuer/address/postalCode (string minOccurs=0
maxOccurs=1)

This element contains the official postal code for this address.

/myWallet/account/paymentInstrumentsIssuer/address/countryOrRegion (string
minOccurs=0 maxOccurs=1)

This element contains the name of the country, dependency, or functionally equivalent
region for this address.

/myWallet/account/paymentInstrumentsIssuer/address/countryOrRegion/@xml:lang
(minOccurs=1 maxOccurs=1)

This required attribute is used to specify an ISO 639 language code or an ISO 3166
country code as described in RFC 1766. The value of this attribute indicates the
language type of the content within this element.

/myWallet/account/paymentInstrumentsIssuer/address/geoLocation (minOccurs=0
maxOccurs=1)

This element encapsulates a geographic (or earth) position corresponding to the
enclosing address.

/myWallet/account/paymentInstrumentsIssuer/address/geoLocation/reportingDevice
(minOccurs=0 maxOccurs=1)

This element contains the UUID and name for this specific device. The UUID for a
specific device is the same as its "Universal Device Number," as exposed by the
Universal Plug and Play infrastructure.

/myWallet/account/paymentInstrumentsIssuer/address/geoLocation/reportingDevice/devi
ceId (minOccurs=0 maxOccurs=1)

This element specifies the UUID or Universal Device Number for this device.

/myWallet/account/paymentInstrumentsIssuer/address/geoLocation/reportingDevice/devi
ceName (string minOccurs=0 maxOccurs=1)

This element specifies a friendly name for this device.

/myWallet/account/paymentInstrumentsIssuer/address/geoLocation/reportingDevice/
{any} (minOccurs=0 maxOccurs=unbounded)
/myWallet/account/paymentInstrumentsIssuer/address/geoLocation/latitude (string
minOccurs=0 maxOccurs=1)

This element specifies the latitude value for this geoLocation in units of decimal
degrees. Geodetic datum WGS84 is required.

/myWallet/account/paymentInstrumentsIssuer/address/geoLocation/longitude (string
minOccurs=0 maxOccurs=1)

This element specifies the longitude value for this geoLocation in units of decimal
degrees. Geodetic datum WGS84 is required.

/myWallet/account/paymentInstrumentsIssuer/address/geoLocation/elevation (string minOccurs=0 maxOccurs=1)

> This element specifies the elevation above sea level with respect to WGS84 geodetic datum. The measurement unit for this value is the meter.

/myWallet/account/paymentInstrumentsIssuer/address/geoLocation/confidence (string minOccurs=0 maxOccurs=1)

> This element specifies a percentage value that indicates the level of confidence that this location is accurate within the specified precision.

/myWallet/account/paymentInstrumentsIssuer/address/geoLocation/precision (string minOccurs=0 maxOccurs=1)

> This element specifies the precision in meters of this location. The value defines a spherical zone within which the location falls.

/myWallet/account/paymentInstrumentsIssuer/address/geoLocation/*{any}* (minOccurs=0 maxOccurs=unbounded)

/myWallet/account/paymentInstrumentsIssuer/address/*{any}* (minOccurs=0 maxOccurs=unbounded)

/myWallet/account/paymentInstrumentsIssuer/contactPhone (minOccurs=0 maxOccurs=1)

> The contact phone number. Optional.

/myWallet/account/paymentInstrumentsIssuer/contactPhone/cat (minOccurs=0 maxOccurs=unbounded)

> This element is used to categorize the element that contains it by referencing a global category definition in either the .NET categories service system document or an external resource containing category definitions, or by referencing an identity-centric category definition in the content document of the .NET categories service for a particular PUID.

/myWallet/account/paymentInstrumentsIssuer/contactPhone/cat/@ref (anyURI minOccurs=0 maxOccurs=1)

> This attribute references a category definition (<catDef/>) element using the rules outlined in the .NET Categories Service.

/myWallet/account/paymentInstrumentsIssuer/contactPhone/countryCode (string minOccurs=0 maxOccurs=1)

> This optional element specifies the country code for this telephone number.

/myWallet/account/paymentInstrumentsIssuer/contactPhone/nationalCode (string minOccurs=1 maxOccurs=1)

> This element specifies the national code for this phone number. For US telephone numbers, this is equivalent to the area code.

/myWallet/account/paymentInstrumentsIssuer/contactPhone/number (string minOccurs=1 maxOccurs=1)

> This element specifies the actual telephone number within the country and national code number scheme.

/myWallet/account/paymentInstrumentsIssuer/contactPhone/numberExtension (string minOccurs=0 maxOccurs=1)

> This optional element specifies an extension used to reach this identity and this number.

/myWallet/account/paymentInstrumentsIssuer/contactPhone/pin (string minOccurs=0 maxOccurs=1)

> This optional element specifies a PIN number used on this phone number. A PIN is similar to an extension, but PIN's are commonly used to address pagers while extensions are typically used to address phones relative to a local pbx.

/myWallet/account/paymentInstrumentsIssuer/contactPhone/*{any}* (minOccurs=0 maxOccurs=unbounded)

/myWallet/account/paymentInstrumentsIssuer/contactEmail (string minOccurs=0 maxOccurs=1)

> The contact e-mail address. Optional.

/myWallet/account/paymentInstrumentsIssuer/swiftCode (string minOccurs=0 maxOccurs=1)

> A global unique number that identifies the issuer in the SWIFT system for funds transfer between different countries.

/myWallet/account/*{any}* (minOccurs=0 maxOccurs=unbounded)

/myWallet/subscription (minOccurs=0 maxOccurs=unbounded)

> This element defines a subscription node that is designed to be an xdb:blue node which when placed in a content document causes a subscription to be registered. A subscription contains a trigger element which selects a scope of coverage. When items change that are under this scope of coverage, and subscriptionResponse message is generated and sent to the specified destination address.

/myWallet/subscription/@changeNumber (minOccurs=0 maxOccurs=1)

> The changeNumber attribute is designed to facilitate caching of the element and its descendants. This attribute is assigned to this element by the .NET My Services system. The attribute is read-only to applications. Attempts to write this attribute are silently ignored.

/myWallet/subscription/@id (minOccurs=0 maxOccurs=1)

> This attribute is a globally unique ID assigned to this element by .NET My Services. Normally, .NET My Services will generate and assign this ID during an insertRequest operation, or possibly during a replaceRequest. Application software can override this ID generation by specifying the useClientIds attribute in the request message. Once an ID is assigned, the attribute is read-only and attempts to write it are silently ignored.

/myWallet/subscription/@creator (string minOccurs=0 maxOccurs=1)

> This attribute identifies the creator in terms of userId, appId, and platformId of the node.

/myWallet/subscription/trigger (minOccurs=1 maxOccurs=1)

/myWallet/subscription/trigger/@select (string minOccurs=0 maxOccurs=1)
> This item specifies an XPATH expression that specifies the nodes that are to be selected and watched for changes. The selection may only select xdb:blue nodes. As changes in this node set occur, they trigger the generation of a subscription message. These messages are then sent to the SOAP receiver listed in the "to" element.

/myWallet/subscription/trigger/@mode (string minOccurs=0 maxOccurs=1)
> This attribute specifies whether or not the content of the changes that triggered the subscription are delivered in the subscription message, or if the message simply indicates that something changed under the trigger. The attribute may be:

> includeData
>> The data that changed, triggering subscription is included in the subscription message. Note that deleted nodes are specified by their ID, not by value.

> excludeData
>> The data that changed, triggering the subscription is NOT included in the subscription message.

/myWallet/subscription/trigger/@baseChangeNumber (minOccurs=0 maxOccurs=1)
> This attribute specifies the changeNumber value to which the trigger is relative. All changes between the specified change number, and the current state of the document relative to the selection are transmitted as subscription messages. This allows a client application to establish a subscription relative to some baseline. As in changeQuery, if the baseChangeNumber is way out of date relative to the current state of the document, and the service can not supply the changes in the subscription message, the subscription insert is rejected. A value of 0 means that the current values of the selected nodes are transmitted in the subscription message.

/myWallet/subscription/expiresAt (dateTime minOccurs=0 maxOccurs=1)
> This optional element specifies an absolute time after which the subscription is no longer active. The subscription node is automatically removed when the subscription expires. If this element is missing, the subscription does not expire.

/myWallet/subscription/context (minOccurs=1 maxOccurs=1)
> This element returns the context element from the original subscription. Applications should use this element, and only this element, to correlate the subscription response with one of their subscriptions.

/myWallet/subscription/context/@uri (anyURI minOccurs=0 maxOccurs=1)
> This attribute specifies the URI value chosen by the subscriber that is associated with this subscription.

/myWallet/subscription/context/*{any}* (minOccurs=0 maxOccurs=unbounded)

/myWallet/subscription/to (anyURI minOccurs=1 maxOccurs=1)

This attribute specifies the location that is to receive the subscription message. The value of this element may be one of the following forms:

- *hs:myNotifications* - this URI indicates that generated subscription messages are to be delivered inside the body of a notification and delivered to the default .NET notifications service of the creator.

- *protocol://service* - this URI indicates that generated subscription messages are delivered to the specified service at the domain of the creator's platformId. For instance, a platformId indicating msn.com, and a value in this element of http://subscriptionResponse would cause delivery of the subscription message to http://subscriptionResponse.msn.com.

If this value is not specified, then the subscription message is delivered as a notification to the "creator's" .NET notifications service.

The .NET Wallet Service/System

The system document is a global document for the service. Its content and meaning is independent of the PUID used to address the service, and the document is read only to all users. The system document contains a set of base items common to all .NET My Services services, and is optionally extended by each service to include service-specific global information.

This schema outline illustrates the layout and meaning of the information found in the system document for the .NET wallet service.

```
<sys:system changeNumber="..." instanceId="..."
    xmlns:hs="http://schemas.microsoft.com/hs/2001/10/core"
    xmlns:sys="http://schemas.microsoft.com/hs/2001/10/myWallet/system">1..1
    <hs:roleMap changeNumber="..." id="..." creator="...">1..1
        <hs:scope id="...">0..unbounded
            <hs:shape base="...">1..1
                <hs:include select="...">1..unbounded</hs:include>
                <hs:exclude select="...">0..unbounded</hs:exclude>
            </hs:shape>
        </hs:scope>
        <hs:roleTemplate name="..." priority="...">0..unbounded
            <hs:fullDescription xml:lang="...">0..1</hs:fullDescription>
            <hs:method name="..." scopeRef="...">0..unbounded</hs:method>
        </hs:roleTemplate>
    </hs:roleMap>
    <hs:methodMap changeNumber="..." id="..." creator="...">1..1
        <hs:method name="...">0..unbounded  {any}</hs:method>
    </hs:methodMap>
```

(continued)

(continued)

```
    <hs:schemaMap changeNumber="..." id="..." creator="...">₁..₁
        <hs:schema namespace="..." schemaLocation="..." alias="...">₀..unbounded
{any}</hs:schema>
    </hs:schemaMap>
    <hs:wsdlMap changeNumber="..." id="..." creator="...">₁..₁
        <hs:wsdl wsdlLocation="...">₀..unbounded {any}</hs:wsdl>
        <hs:disco discoLocation="...">₀..unbounded {any}</hs:disco>
    </hs:wsdlMap>
    {any}
</sys:system>
```

The meaning of the attributes and elements shown in the preceding sample document fragment are listed in the following section.

/system (minOccurs=1 maxOccurs=1)
This element encapsulates the system document for the .NET wallet service.

/system/@changeNumber (minOccurs=0 maxOccurs=1)
The changeNumber attribute is designed to facilitate caching of the element and its descendants. This attribute is assigned to this element by the .NET My Services system. The attribute is read-only to applications. Attempts to write this attribute are silently ignored.

/system/@instanceId (string minOccurs=0 maxOccurs=1)
This attribute is a unique identifier typically assigned to the root element of a service. It is a read-only element and assigned by the .NET My Services system when a user is provisioned for a particular service.

/system/roleMap (minOccurs=1 maxOccurs=1)
This element encapsulates all the elements that make up a roleMap, which include document class relative roleTemplate, priority, name, method, and per-method scope. An individual roleTemplate defines the maximum scope of information, and the allowable methods used to access that information for each request mapped into the template.

/system/roleMap/@changeNumber (minOccurs=0 maxOccurs=1)
The changeNumber attribute is designed to facilitate caching of the element and its descendants. This attribute is assigned to this element by the .NET My Services system. The attribute is read-only to applications. Attempts to write this attribute are silently ignored.

/system/roleMap/@id (minOccurs=0 maxOccurs=1)
This attribute is a globally unique ID assigned to this element by .NET My Services. Normally, .NET My Services will generate and assign this ID during an insertRequest operation, or possibly during a replaceRequest. Application software can override this ID generation by specifying the useClientIds attribute in the request message. Once an ID is assigned, the attribute is read-only and attempts to write it are silently ignored.

/system/roleMap/@creator (string minOccurs=0 maxOccurs=1)

This attribute identifies the creator in terms of userId, appId, and platformId of the node.

/system/roleMap/scope (minOccurs=0 maxOccurs=unbounded)

This element defines a scope which may be referred to by roles within this roleMap to indicate what portions of the document are visible to this role for the specified method.

/system/roleMap/scope/@id (minOccurs=0 maxOccurs=1)

This attribute is a globally unique ID assigned to this element by .NET My Services. Normally, .NET My Services will generate and assign this ID during an insertRequest operation, or possibly during a replaceRequest. Application software can override this ID generation by specifying the useClientIds attribute in the request message. Once an ID is assigned, the attribute is read-only and attempts to write it are silently ignored.

/system/roleMap/scope/shape (minOccurs=1 maxOccurs=1)

A shape defines the node set visible through the document when operating through this shape element.

/system/roleMap/scope/shape/@base (string minOccurs=0 maxOccurs=1)

This attribute specifies the initial set of nodes visible through the shape.

A value of "t" indicates that the shape is initialized to include all possible nodes relative to the shape that is currently in effect. For instance, each role defines a scope containing a shape. When defining a shape for a role, the value "t" indicates all possible nodes available in the specified document for this role. When defining a shape in an ACL entry, a value of "t" denotes all of the nodes visible in the shape for the computed role. When using a shape in an hsdl operation, a value of "t" indicates all of the possible nodes selected by the hsdl operation (relative to the ACL shape which itself is relative to the role's shape).

The value nil indicates the opposite of "t", which is the empty node set. Nodes from this set may then be included into the shape.

/system/roleMap/scope/shape/include (minOccurs=1 maxOccurs=unbounded)

This element specifies the set of nodes that should be included into the shape relative to the possible set of nodes indicated by the base attribute.

/system/roleMap/scope/shape/include/@select (string minOccurs=0 maxOccurs=1)

This item specifies an XPATH expression that selects a set of nodes relative to the externally established context. The expression can never travel outside the node-set established by this externally established current context. The expression may match 0 or more nodes, and the operation manipulates all selected nodes. The minOccurs and maxOccurs attributes are optional and place restrictions and limitations on the number of nodes selected.

/system/roleMap/scope/shape/exclude (minOccurs=0 maxOccurs=unbounded)

This element specifies the set of nodes that should be excluded from the shape relative to the possible set of nodes indicated by the base attribute.

/system/roleMap/scope/shape/exclude/@select (string minOccurs=0 maxOccurs=1)
This item specifies an XPATH expression that selects a set of nodes relative to the externally established context. The expression can never travel outside the node-set established by this externally established current context. The expression may match 0 or more nodes, and the operation manipulates all selected nodes. The minOccurs and maxOccurs attributes are optional and place restrictions and limitations on the number of nodes selected.

/system/roleMap/roleTemplate (minOccurs=0 maxOccurs=unbounded)
This element encapsulates the definition of a role. The attribute set for this element includes the document class that this roleTemplate refers to, the name of the roleTemplate, and the priority of the roleTemplate.

/system/roleMap/roleTemplate/@name (string minOccurs=0 maxOccurs=1)
This element specifies the name of the role.

/system/roleMap/roleTemplate/@priority (int minOccurs=0 maxOccurs=1)
This element specifies the priority of the roleTemplate which is used to select that actual roleTemplate when the role evaluation determines that the subject maps to multiple roleTemplates.

/system/roleMap/roleTemplate/fullDescription (string minOccurs=0 maxOccurs=1)
This element contains a description of this role template which specifies the capabilities a caller will have when accessing information through this role.

/system/roleMap/roleTemplate/fullDescription/@xml:lang (minOccurs=1 maxOccurs=1)
This required attribute is used to specify an ISO 639 language code or an ISO 3166 country code as described in RFC 1766. The value of this attribute indicates the language type of the content within this element.

/system/roleMap/roleTemplate/method (minOccurs=0 maxOccurs=unbounded)
This element specifies the methods available within this roleTemplate by name, and by scope. When a subject maps to a roleTemplate, the method in the request must match one of these elements for the message to continue to flow. If the method exists, the data available to the method is a function of the scope referenced by this method combined with an optional scope referenced by the role defined in the roleList.

/system/roleMap/roleTemplate/method/@name (string minOccurs=0 maxOccurs=1)
This element specifies the name of the method.

/system/roleMap/roleTemplate/method/@scopeRef (string minOccurs=0 maxOccurs=1)
This attribute specifies the scope within this document that is in effect for this method.

/system/methodMap (minOccurs=1 maxOccurs=1)
This element defines the methodMap. While it is true that in most cases, the roleMap section contains a definitive list of methods, these methods are likely to be scattered about the roleMap in various templates. This section contains the definitive non-duplicated list of methods available within the service.

/system/methodMap/@changeNumber (minOccurs=0 maxOccurs=1)

The changeNumber attribute is designed to facilitate caching of the element and its descendants. This attribute is assigned to this element by the .NET My Services system. The attribute is read-only to applications. Attempts to write this attribute are silently ignored.

/system/methodMap/@id (minOccurs=0 maxOccurs=1)

This attribute is a globally unique ID assigned to this element by .NET My Services. Normally, .NET My Services will generate and assign this ID during an insertRequest operation, or possibly during a replaceRequest. Application software can override this ID generation by specifying the useClientIds attribute in the request message. Once an ID is assigned, the attribute is read-only and attempts to write it are silently ignored.

/system/methodMap/@creator (string minOccurs=0 maxOccurs=1)

This attribute identifies the creator in terms of userId, appId, and platformId of the node.

/system/methodMap/method (minOccurs=0 maxOccurs=unbounded)

This element defines a method that is available within this service.

/system/methodMap/method/@name (string minOccurs=0 maxOccurs=1)

This attribute specifies the name of a method available within the service.

/system/methodMap/method/*{any}* (minOccurs=0 maxOccurs=unbounded)

/system/schemaMap (minOccurs=1 maxOccurs=1)

This element defines the various schema's that define the data structures and shape of information managed by this service. Each schema is defined by its namespace uri, its location, and a preferred namespace alias.

/system/schemaMap/@changeNumber (minOccurs=0 maxOccurs=1)

The changeNumber attribute is designed to facilitate caching of the element and its descendants. This attribute is assigned to this element by the .NET My Services system. The attribute is read-only to applications. Attempts to write this attribute are silently ignored.

/system/schemaMap/@id (minOccurs=0 maxOccurs=1)

This attribute is a globally unique ID assigned to this element by .NET My Services. Normally, .NET My Services will generate and assign this ID during an insertRequest operation, or possibly during a replaceRequest. Application software can override this ID generation by specifying the useClientIds attribute in the request message. Once an ID is assigned, the attribute is read-only and attempts to write it are silently ignored.

/system/schemaMap/@creator (string minOccurs=0 maxOccurs=1)

This attribute identifies the creator in terms of userId, appId, and platformId of the node.

/system/schemaMap/schema (minOccurs=0 maxOccurs=unbounded)

This element defines a schema which defines data-structures and the shape of information managed by this service. Multiple schema elements exist for each service, one for each logical grouping of information exposed by the service.

/system/schemaMap/schema/@namespace (anyURI minOccurs=0 maxOccurs=1)
This attribute specifies the namespace URI of this schema.

/system/schemaMap/schema/@schemaLocation (anyURI minOccurs=0 maxOccurs=1)
This attribute specifies the location (in the form of a URI) of the resource containing schema. When a schema is reachable through a variety of URIs, one schema element will exist for each location.

/system/schemaMap/schema/@alias (string minOccurs=0 maxOccurs=1)
This attribute specifies the preferred alias that should be used if possible when manipulating information covered by this schema in the context of this service.

/system/schemaMap/schema/*{any}* (minOccurs=0 maxOccurs=unbounded)
/system/wsdlMap (minOccurs=1 maxOccurs=1)
This element defines the wsdlMap for this service. This map includes the location of WSDL documents, DISCO documents, and WISL documents for this Web service. These documents are used by applications to understand the format of messages that may be sent to the various services.

/system/wsdlMap/@changeNumber (minOccurs=0 maxOccurs=1)
The changeNumber attribute is designed to facilitate caching of the element and its descendants. This attribute is assigned to this element by the .NET My Services system. The attribute is read-only to applications. Attempts to write this attribute are silently ignored.

/system/wsdlMap/@id (minOccurs=0 maxOccurs=1)
This attribute is a globally unique ID assigned to this element by .NET My Services. Normally, .NET My Services will generate and assign this ID during an insertRequest operation, or possibly during a replaceRequest. Application software can override this ID generation by specifying the useClientIds attribute in the request message. Once an ID is assigned, the attribute is read-only and attempts to write it are silently ignored.

/system/wsdlMap/@creator (string minOccurs=0 maxOccurs=1)
This attribute identifies the creator in terms of userId, appId, and platformId of the node.

/system/wsdlMap/wsdl (minOccurs=0 maxOccurs=unbounded)
This element is used to specify the location of a WSDL file for this service. Multiple entries may exist pointing to the same file hosted in multiple locations, or to variations on the content within the WSDL files.

/system/wsdlMap/wsdl/@wsdlLocation (anyURI minOccurs=0 maxOccurs=1)
This attribute is a URI that specifies the location of the WSDL file.

/system/wsdlMap/wsdl/*{any}* (minOccurs=0 maxOccurs=unbounded)
/system/wsdlMap/disco (minOccurs=0 maxOccurs=unbounded)
This element is used to specify the location of a DISCO file for this service. Multiple entries may exist pointing to the same file hosted in multiple locations, or to variations on the content within the DISCO files.

/system/wsdlMap/disco/@discoLocation (anyURI minOccurs=0 maxOccurs=1)
   This attribute is a URI that specifies the location of the DISCO file.

/system/wsdlMap/disco/*{any}* (minOccurs=0 maxOccurs=unbounded)
/system/*{any}* (minOccurs=0 maxOccurs=unbounded)

The .NET Wallet Service/Methods

The .NET wallet service supports the following standard and domain-specific methods:

- query
- insert
- replace
- delete
- update

The standard methods operate on this service using the same message format and method-interchange techniques described in the hsdl section of this document. The only service-specific information to note is the schema that is in effect for each of the methods. These schemas, and how they relate to the standard methods and roles are described in the roles section of this document.

The domain specific methods operate as described in the domain specific methods section of this document, and are governed by the various schemas outlined in the .NET Wallet Service/Roles section for this service.

Get the real .NET story with this succinct yet entertaining overview!

U.S.A. $29.99
Canada $43.99
ISBN: 0-7356-1377-X

What problems does Microsoft® .NET solve? What architectural approaches does it take to solve them? How do you start using .NET—and how do you profit from it? Get the answers to these questions and more in this entertaining, no-nonsense book. David S. Platt covers a single topic in each chapter, introducing simpler, conceptual material first, and then progressing into greater technical detail, so you can choose how deep you want to go. He makes his points with a minimum of jargon, a maximum of wit, a multitude of detailed diagrams, and a wealth of meaningful analogies and clear explanations. The accompanying code samples are included on the book's Web site. By the end of this illuminating .NET walkthrough, you'll know enough about this exciting development platform to plan for the future of software as a service.

mspress.microsoft.com

Get a **Free**
e-mail newsletter, updates,
special offers, links to related books,
and more when you
register on line!

Register your Microsoft Press® title on our Web site and you'll get a FREE subscription to our e-mail newsletter, *Microsoft Press Book Connections.* You'll find out about newly released and upcoming books and learning tools, online events, software downloads, special offers and coupons for Microsoft Press customers, and information about major Microsoft® product releases. You can also read useful additional information about all the titles we publish, such as detailed book descriptions, tables of contents and indexes, sample chapters, links to related books and book series, author biographies, and reviews by other customers.

Registration is easy. Just visit this Web page and fill in your information:

http://www.microsoft.com/mspress/register

Microsoft

Proof of Purchase

Microsoft® .NET My Services Specification
0-7356-1556-X

CUSTOMER NAME

Microsoft Press, PO Box 97017, Redmond, WA 98073-9830